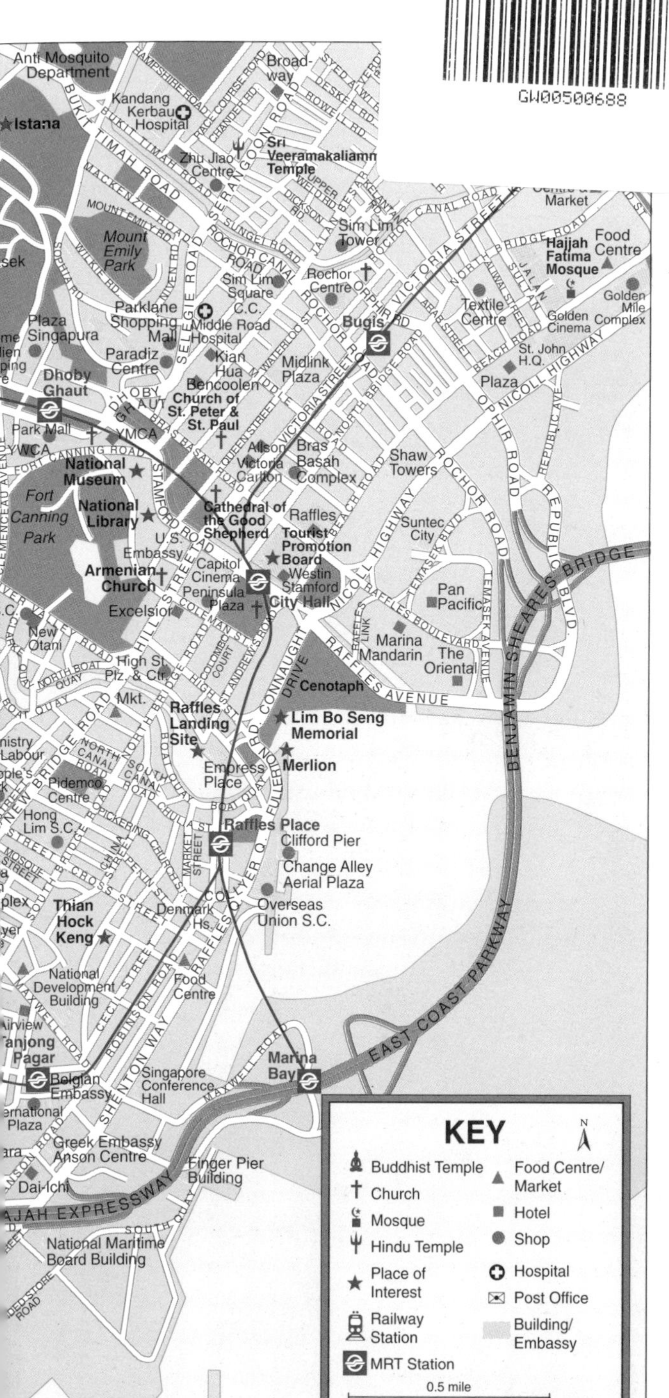
Anti Mosquito Department
Istana
Kandang Kerbau Hospital
Broadway
Hampshire Road
Race Course Road
Chander Rd.
Serangoon Road
Syed Alwi Rd.
Desker Rd.
Rowell Rd.
Bukit Timah Road
Zhu Jiao Centre
Sri Veeramakaliamn Temple
Upper Weld Rd.
Dickson Rd.
Mackenzie Road
Mount Emily Rd.
Mount Emily Park
Wilkie Rd.
Sophia Rd.
Niven Rd.
Selegie Road
Sungei Road
Rochor Canal Road
Jalan Besar
Sim Lim Tower
Sim Lim Square
Rochor Centre
Victoria Street
Ophir Rd.
Rochor Canal Road
Market
Bridge Road
Hajjah Fatima Mosque
Food Centre
Jalan Sultan
Textile Centre
Golden Mile Complex
Golden Cinema
Arab Street
Beach Road
St. John H.Q.
Plaza
Nicoll Highway
Plaza Singapura
Parklane Shopping Mall
C.C.
Middle Road Hospital
Paradiz Centre
Kian Hua
Bencoolen
Waterloo St.
Midlink Plaza
Bugis
Dhoby Ghaut
Church of St. Peter & St. Paul
Park Mall
YMCA
YWCA
Fort Canning Road
Clemenceau Avenue
Bras Basah Road
Queen Street
Allson
Victoria Carlton
Bras Basah Complex
Shaw Towers
Rochor Road
Ophir Road
Republic Ave.
National Museum
Fort Canning Park
National Library
Stamford Road
Cathedral of the Good Shepherd
Raffles
Tourist Promotion Board
Suntec City
Temasek Blvd.
U.S. Embassy
Capitol Cinema
Westin Stamford
Republic Blvd.
Benjamin Sheares Bridge
Armenian Church
Peninsula Plaza
City Hall
Nicoll Highway
Raffles Boulevard
Pan Pacific
Temasek Avenue
Excelsior
Hill Street
Coleman St.
Raffles Link
Marina Mandarin
The Oriental
New Otani
River Valley Road
High St. Plz. & Ctr.
Colombo Court
St. Andrew's Rd.
Connaught Drive
Cenotaph
Raffles Avenue
North Boat Quay
Boat Quay
Mkt.
Raffles Landing Site
Lim Bo Seng Memorial
Merlion
Empress Place
Fullerton Rd.
Ministry of Labour
New Bridge Road
North Canal Road
South Canal Road
Pidemco Centre
Hong Lim S.C.
Raffles Place
Clifford Pier
Market Street
Chulia St.
Pickering St.
Church St.
Change Alley Aerial Plaza
China Street
Mosque Street
South Bridge Road
Cross Street
Thian Hock Keng
Denmark Hs.
Collyer Q.
Overseas Union S.C.
Raffles Place
National Development Building
Maxwell Road
Cecil Street
Robinson Road
Food Centre
Tanjong Pagar
Belgian Embassy
Shenton Way
Singapore Conference Hall
Maxwell Road
Marina Bay
East Coast Parkway
Greek Embassy
Anson Centre
Finger Pier Building
Dai-Ichi
Rajah Expressway
South Quay
National Maritime Board Building
KEY
N
Buddhist Temple
Church
Mosque
Hindu Temple
Place of Interest
Railway Station
MRT Station
Food Centre/ Market
Hotel
Shop
Hospital
Post Office
Building/ Embassy
0.5 mile
1 km

Inset: A view of the busy Boat Quay on the Singapore River in the 1890's, looking across to Fort Canning.
Main picture: Gardens overlooking Telok Ayer Bay towards Collyer Quay, 1890's.

A public performance by the Prince of Wales Theatre Group, staged during the week of the 1897 Federal Conference at Kuala Kangsar.

Two Kayan men, Sarawak, taken c. 1900 by Charles Hose, the resident of Sarawak.
The interior of a Kayan house, also taken by Charles Hose, c. 1900.

EVERYMAN GUIDES
PUBLISHED BY DAVID CAMPBELL PUBLISHERS LTD, LONDON

SINGAPORE AND MALAYSIA – ISBN 1-85715-888-1



**NUMEROUS SPECIALISTS AND ACADEMICS HAVE CONTRIBUTED TO THIS GUIDE:**

**SINGAPORE AND MALAYSIA:**
**PICTURE RESEARCH:** John Falconer
**RESEARCH:** Coleen Beck, Heidi Munan
**NATURE:** Dr David Stone
**HISTORY:** Dr Ian Brown
**ARTS AND TRADITIONS:** Dr Khoo Joo Ee, Karpagam Karuna, Gilles Massot, Khoo Su Nin, Nelila Sathyalingam
**ARCHITECTURE:** Julian Davison (Thian Hock Keng, Peranakan House and Iban Textiles), Eddy Koh, Christopher Lee
**SINGAPORE AND MALAYSIA AS SEEN BY PAINTERS:** Julia Oh
**ITINERARIES:** David Brazil (West Malaysia), Wendy Moore, Khoo Su Nin and Mrs Eng-Lee Seok Chee (East Malaysia and Brunei Darussalam); Heidi Munan, Julian Davison, Peter Schoppert and Jeffrey Finestone

**PRACTICAL INFORMATION:**
David Brazil, Robert Basiuk, Wendy Moore

**ILLUSTRATIONS:**
**NATURE:** Anuar bin Abdul Rahim, Jeffery Mar Jansen
**ARCHITECTURE:** Anuar bin Abdul Rahim, Julian Davison, Timothy Freebairn, Lim Yew Cheong, Christopher Lee, Ruban Interarc
**ARTS AND TRADITIONS:** Anuar bin Abdul Rahim
**PRACTICAL INFORMATION:** Simon Ang, Lim Yew Cheong, Jimmy Ang Teck Beng

**PHOTOGRAPHY:**
Munshi Ahmed, Robert Basiuk, Tommyh Change, John Falconer, Jeffrey Finestone, Georg Gerster, Rio Helmi, Dinnis Lau Zen-sze, Lawrence Lim, Radin Mohd Noh Saleh, Gilles Massot, Guido Alberto Rossi, Tara Sosrowardoyo

**WE WOULD ALSO LIKE TO THANK:**
Singapore Tourist Promotion Board, Tourism Malaysia, Mass Rapid Transit Corporation (Singapore), National Museum (Singapore), Muzium Negara (Kuala Lumpur), Royal Selangor, Sarawak Museum, Botanic Gardens (Singapore), Jurong Birdpark (Singapore), Singapore Zoological Gardens, Marina Mahathir, Christopher Lee, John Falconer and Stephan Potter

EDITED AND TYPESET BY EDITIONS DIDIER MILLET PTE LTD.
PRINTED IN ITALY BY EDITORIALE LIBRARIA.



EVERYMAN GUIDES
79 Berwick Street
London W1V 3PF

# SINGAPORE AND MALAYSIA

EVERYMAN GUIDES

# CONTENTS
# KEYS TO UNDERSTANDING

## NATURE, *15*

## HISTORY, *31*



## ARTS AND TRADITIONS, *43*

## ARCHITECTURE, *71*

## SEEN BY PAINTERS, *91*



## SEEN BY WRITERS, *101*

# Contents
# Itineraries

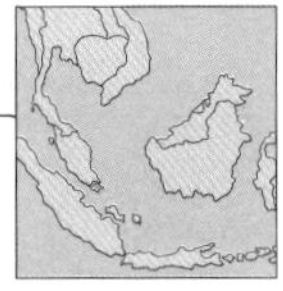

## Singapore, *125*

## West Malaysia, *181*

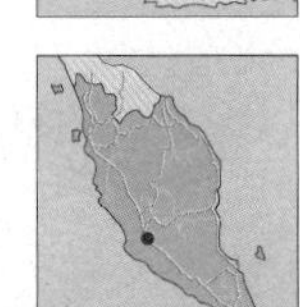

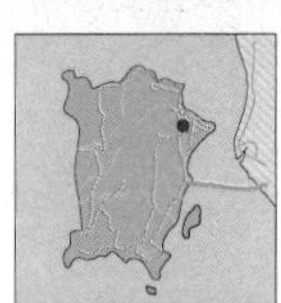

## East Malaysia, *269*

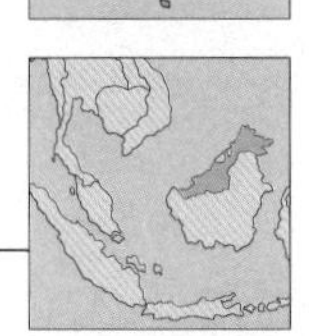



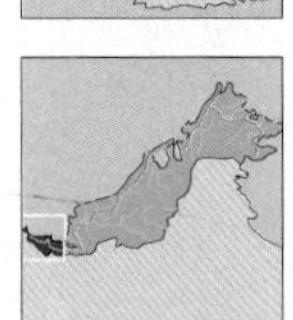

## Brunei Darussalam, *313*

# ▲ Singapore, Malaysia, and Brunei Darussalam

Vietnam
Ho Chi Minh City
Phnom Penh
Bangkok
Cambodia
Thailand
*Gulf of Thailand*
*South China Sea*
Pattani
Narathiwat
Langkawi
Kota Bharu
Mal
Penang
Butterworth
Taiping
Kuala Kangsar
Pangkor
Telok Intan
Klang
Medan
Bagansiapiapi
Melaka
*Straits of Malacca*
Dumai
Bengkalis
Sumatra
(Indonesia)

Mt Kinabalu
Kota Kinabalu
Sandakan
Lahad Datu
Tawau
Brunei Darussalam
Bandar Seri Begawan
Miri
Bario
Belaga
Sibu
Santubong
Kuching
Kalimantan (Indonesia)
Tioman
Mersing
Kota Tinggi
Johor Bahru
Singapore
Kukup
Sentosa
Bintan
Batam

# How to Use this Guide

*(Sample page shown from the guide to Venice)*

The symbols at the top of each page refer to the different parts of the guide.

- ■ Natural Environment
- ● Keys to Understanding
- ▲ Itineraries
- ◆ Practical Information

The itinerary map shows the main points of interest along the way and is intended to help you find your bearings.

The mini-map locates the particular itinerary within the wider area covered by the guide.

▲ Cannaregio

Church of Santa Maria degli Scalzi
Church of San Geremia
Palazzo Labia
Ghetto
Church of Santa Maria dei Servi
Palazzo Mastelli
Church of the Madonna dell'Orto
Palazzo Contarini dal Zaffo
Scuola Nuova della Misericordia
Church of Santa Maria della Misericordia
Church of Santa Sofia
Church of Santi Apostoli
Church of the Jesuits
Church of San Canciano
Cemetery of San Michele
Murano
Santa Lucia Station
Church of San Simeone Piccolo
Church of San Marcuola
Palazzo Vendramin-Calergi
Church of Santa Maria della Maddalena
Ca' d'Oro
Church of San Felice
Church of San Marziale
Church of Santa Fosca
Rialto Bridge
Fondaco dei Tedeschi
Teatro Malibran
Church of Santa Maria dei Miracoli
Church of Santi Giovanni e Paolo

Immediately outside the railway station lies Cannaregio, the first of the six sestieri of Venice. Situated at the north-west end of the city, this is the second largest sestiere after Castello ▲ 155, covering an area of 150 hectares. Nearly a third of the population of Venice is concentrated here, amounting to more than twenty thousand people. There are two theories about the origins of the name Cannaregio; according to one, it comes from *Canal regio* (the Royal Canal), meaning the broad waterway which once provided convenient access to the city from the mainland, by prolonging the lagoon canal of San Secondo (which runs parallel to the railway bridge). The other hypothesis is that the word derives from the reeds and canes which used to abound in this area. In any case, a system of straight, parallel canals, with long fondamenta abutting southwards and linked by calli, criss-cross this zone of workmen's houses interspersed with magnificent palaces. To the south, behind the palaces of the Grand Canal a wide street known as the Strada Nuova was built at the end of the last century. Now pedestrianized, this street runs from the station to the Campo Santi Apostoli, crossing the sestiere from one side to the other and adopting a number of different names as it goes. Few people lived in this sestiere until the 11th century, and it seems to have taken form only gradually, as the process of draining and consolidating the site progressed. From the 15th century onwards, Cannaregio was a definable quarter, though it was still peripheral to Venice proper. Before the railway bridge and the station were built, manufacturing was the principal industry in the district, despite attempts to create a new area of growth with the Fondamenta Nuove. A similar project in the 16th century, the draining of the Sacca della Misericordia, was also never realized.

"The gateway to Venice, after all, is neither the station nor the Piazzale, but the Grand Canal before us, churned by propellers, turbulent as a great river."
Fernand Braudel, *Venise*

Santa Lucia Station.

136

The Gateway to Venice ★

**Ponte della Libertà.** Built by the Austrians 50 years after the Treaty of Campo Formio in 1797 ● *34*, to link Venice with Milan. The bridge ended the thousand-year separation from the mainland and shook the city's economy to its roots as Venice, already in the throes of the industrial revolution, saw its dependence on the mainland grow out of all recognition. **Santa Lucia Station.** The present station dates from 1955, but still bears the name of the Renaissance church demolished in 1861 to make way for it. Opposite is the green dome of the Church of San Simeone Piccolo.

Half a day

**Bridges to Venice**
The Austrians conceived a project for a bridge between Mestre and Venice as early as 1814, but it was not until 1846 that construction of the Ponte della Libertà was finally begun. The span of this new viaduct was almost 11,500 feet, and it included 222 stone arches. On April 25, 1933, the Ponte delle Littorale was opened. Built in less than two years by the engineer Umberto Fantucci, this bridge was intended for use by motor cars.

136

● ▲ ■ ◆
The symbols alongside a title or within the text itself provide cross-references to a theme or place dealt with elsewhere in the guide.

★ The star symbol signifies that a particular site has been singled out by the publishers for its special beauty, atmosphere or cultural interest.

At the beginning of each itinerary, the suggested means of transport to be used and the time it will take to cover the area are indicated:

- By boat
- On foot
- By bicycle
- Duration


## The Gateway to Venice ★

**Ponte della Libertà.** Built by the Austrians 50 years after the Treaty of Campo Formio in 1797 ● *34,* to link Venice with Milan. The bridge ended the thousand-year separation from the mainland and shook the city's economy to its roots as Venice, already in the throes of the industrial revolution, saw

Half a day

**Bridges to Venice**

# NATURE

Early explorers and traders from the Orient have long known and respected the force of the monsoon.

The climate of Singapore and Malaysia is dominated by the monsoon – a term derived from the Arabic word *mausim*, meaning season – which represents a major change of wind direction and humidity associated with widespread temperature changes over land and water. Three important causes of the monsoon are the differential effects of heating and cooling of landmasses and areas of sea, the northward movement of the Inter-Tropical Convergence Zone, ITCZ (where the tradewinds meet) during the summer and the interference to atmospheric circulation caused by the Himalayas. Southeast Asia experiences monsoon seasons winter and summer. Combined with intermittent local and regional storms, the monsoons have played an important role in shaping both the human and the natural faces of Singapore and Malaysia.

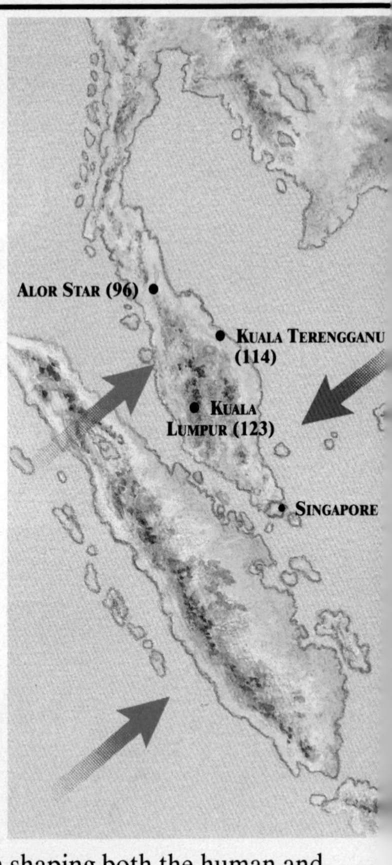

**1. The northeast or winter monsoon**
In winter as the overhead sun moves south so does the ITCZ. The central Asian landmass cools, causing high pressure and monsoon winds to blow southwards. The winds bring dry, cool air to much of central and eastern Asia, but collect moisture over the sea, which they shed on Thailand, Malaysia, and Indonesia.

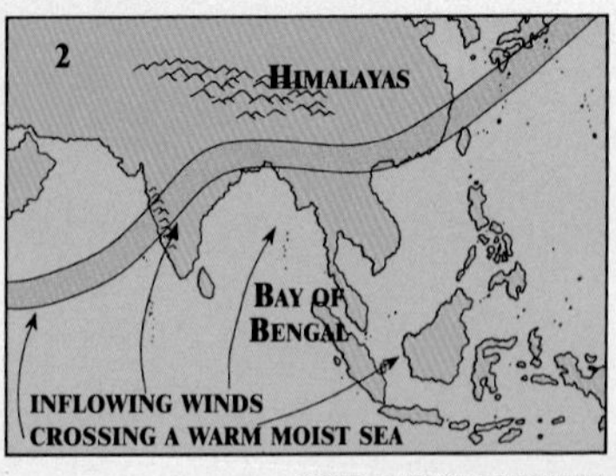


**2. The southwest or summer monsoon**
As the overhead sun appears to move northwards during the summer, it draws with it the ITCZ. Warm, moist air from the Indian Ocean is drawn into mainland Asia, first north and then northeastwards as the Coriolis effect comes into play. The air is humid and unstable and results in heavy rainfall over the sub-continent. In Southeast Asia the wind is less marked and brings lighter rainfall, but nevertheless a discernible monsoon is experienced.

Cold = High pressure
Low pressure ITCZ
Seasonal equatorial jet stream

"THE MONSOON THRESHES ACROSS THE SEAS, KEEPING THEM FRESH AND FREE FROM THE DINGY MANGROVE SWAMPS AND HIDEOUS BANKS OF MUD...."

HUGH CHARLES CLIFFORD, *IN COURT AND KAMPUNG*

A waterfall in the Pahang interior carries silt from the mountains of the Main Range.

Monsoon fury : lashing of the waves against the sea wall off the Chendering, Terengganu coast.

A flooded street in Kanowit, Sarawak, leaves villagers and vehicles stranded after the downpour.

**MONSOON FOREST**

This is also known as tropical deciduous forest. Trees usually shed their leaves during the dry season and come into leaf at the beginning of the rainy season. These forests are characterized by an abundance of tall trees such as teak and bamboo thicket, lianas and epiphytes such as orchids.

**ORCHIDS**

This orchid, *Dendrobium anosmum*, flowers profusely. Over one hundred Dendrobium species are found in Peninsular Malaysia.

## Coastal Reef and Shoreline

**Eurasian curlew**

**Lesser frigate bird**

The palm-fringed coastlines of Singapore and Malaysia have long been the breeding and feeding grounds for a diverse array of wildlife that rely on the daily ebb and flow of the tides to renew the nutrients they feed on. Coastal wetlands are extremely important for migrant birds, providing a sheltered, nutrient-rich base for exhausted arrivals. Complex offshore coral reefs are among the richest ecosystems on earth.

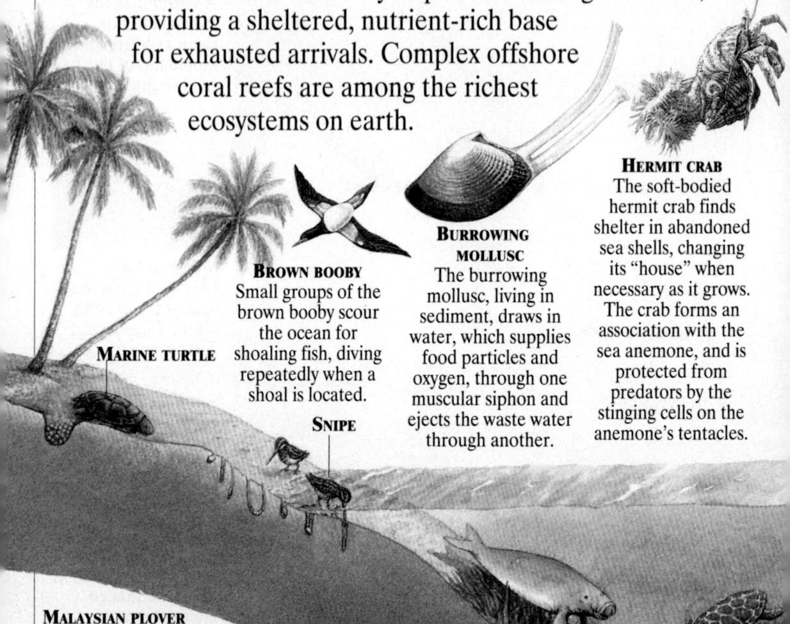

**Hermit crab**
The soft-bodied hermit crab finds shelter in abandoned sea shells, changing its "house" when necessary as it grows. The crab forms an association with the sea anemone, and is protected from predators by the stinging cells on the anemone's tentacles.

**Burrowing mollusc**
The burrowing mollusc, living in sediment, draws in water, which supplies food particles and oxygen, through one muscular siphon and ejects the waste water through another.

**Brown booby**
Small groups of the brown booby scour the ocean for shoaling fish, diving repeatedly when a shoal is located.

**Marine turtle**

**Snipe**

**Malaysian plover**

**Great crested tern**

Large mixed flocks of wading birds, such as the Malaysian plover and the great crested tern, feed on a variety of worms and shrimp-like crustaceans. The size and shape of the bird's beak determine the exact type of prey and at what stage of the tidal cycle the species will feed.

**Dugong**
The dugong is a vegetarian mammal, feeding almost exclusively on sea grasses. Because of its low reproductive rate and late maturity, as well as its slow pace of life, it is especially vulnerable to extinction.

**Green turtle**
Green turtles lay their eggs on deserted tropical beaches. Wary of predators, they emerge from the sea at night. Using their flippers, they dig a deep flask-shaped nest and lay up to 100 eggs. The nest is covered with sand and incubation takes several months.

**Parrotfish**

**Orange clownfish**

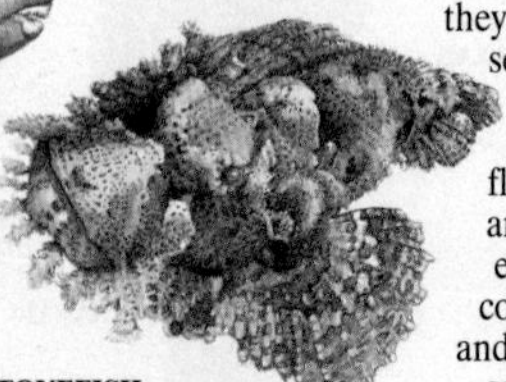

**Stonefish**

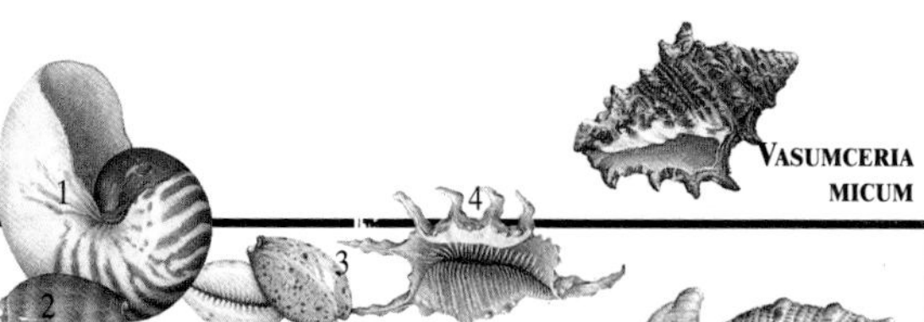


**VASUMCERIA MICUM**

**CORAL REEF**
The coral reef ecosystem has great biological diversity. Coral colonies are composed of countless individual polyps that feed on microscopic plankton. The reefs can cover a large area, but grow very slowly – a yard a thousand years.

**(1) NAUTILUS POMPILIUS (2) CYPRAEA CARNEOLA (3) CYPRAEA LYNX (4) LAMBIS SCOLPIUS**
The elaborate, sculpted beauty of sea shells is most evident in the tropics and sub-tropics. Unfortunately, the beauty of these shells has led to the over-exploitation of many species, especially for jewelry and the tourist trade.

**CASSIS CORNUTA**

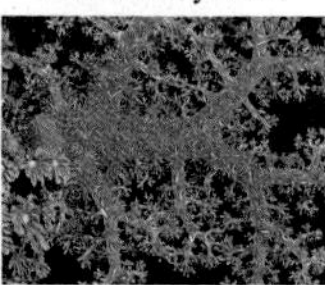

**SOFT CORAL**

**HARD CORAL**

**SEA CUCUMBER**
The sea cucumber lives on the sandy base of the ocean floor, feeding on detritus and algae. Occurring in a wide range of colors and sizes, many of the larger species are collected for human consumption.

**SPONDYLUS REGIUS**

**MITRA MITRA**

**RAY**
The broad and pointed fins of the ray allow it to glide effortlessly through the oceans. Its thin, elongated tail is armed with razor-sharp, tooth-like structures for defense. The ray's skeleton is made of cartilage rather than bone, to diminish its weight.

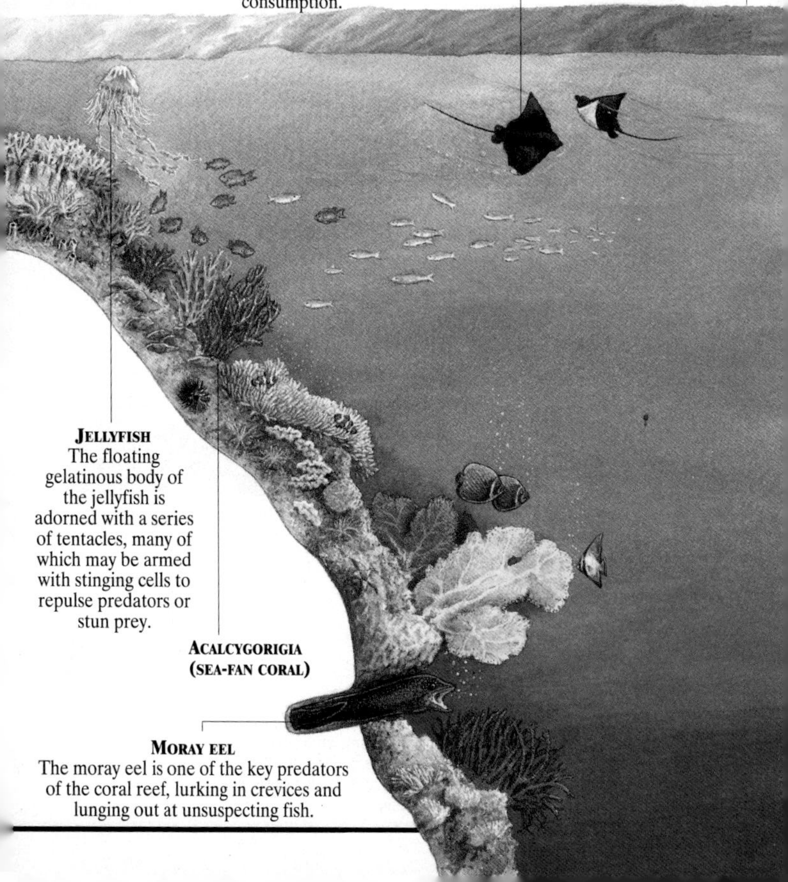

**JELLYFISH**
The floating gelatinous body of the jellyfish is adorned with a series of tentacles, many of which may be armed with stinging cells to repulse predators or stun prey.

**ACALCYGORIGIA (SEA-FAN CORAL)**

**MORAY EEL**
The moray eel is one of the key predators of the coral reef, lurking in crevices and lunging out at unsuspecting fish.

Characteristic of muddy estuarine shores in the tropics and sub-tropics, mangrove forests with their dark, closed canopy and tangled mass of roots appear to be a hostile and barren environment. However, they support a rich selection of wildlife. Mangrove trees and nipa palms form a link between land and sea. The vegetation helps to prevent coastal erosion, helping form new land by trapping sediment. In many areas mangrove forests are disappearing as marginal land is cleared and reclaimed for construction, trees felled for woodchips and aquaculture enterprises, such as shrimp farming, established. The mangrove forests are important roosting and feeding grounds for many migrating birds escaping the harsh winter in Siberia.

Aerial roots provide support and absorb oxygen.

**NIPA PALM**
Nipa palms often border the many tidal channels that criss-cross mangrove swamps. The fruit (top left) is edible.

**WHITE-THROATED KINGFISHER**

**LESSER ADJUTANT STORK**
The distinctive lesser adjutant stork probes the murky waters and mud with its strong beak in search of crabs and fish.

**MUDSKIPPER**
Although reliant on water to keep its skin and gills moist, the mudskipper searches for food out of the water, walking with its crutch-like fins or jumping about on mudflats.

**FIDDLER CRAB**
The brightly colored male fiddler crab uses its enlarged claw to intimidate and fight other males and to attract females.

**RHIZOPHORA MUCRONATA**
The mangrove tree, *Rhizophora mucronata*, propagates by producing spikes which are instant seedlings, germinating while still attached to the parent tree, before dropping into the mud and taking root. It also produces more conventional seeds.

**Long-tailed macaque**
The long-tailed macaque is commonly seen in mangrove forests, usually in groups of up to thirty individuals.

**Milky stork**

**Archer fish**
The archer fish lives on insects and other small animals that feed on the surfaces of leaves and branches overhanging the water. It has a novel way of catching its prey: by ejecting a jet of water that knocks the prey into the water, from where it is easily caught.

**Estuarine crocodile**
The salt-water crocodile lives mainly in the ocean, but is also found in swamps and rivers until the salt water gives way to fresh water.

The tropical forests of Malaysia form one of the richest assemblages of wildlife that can be found on this planet. From the upper reaches of the forest canopy to the depths of the forest floor, life abounds in an array of shapes, sizes, and colors. The upper canopy is governed chiefly by the birds, mammals, and insects which coexist, feeding on the riches of fruiting trees. On the forest floor, numerous beetles, termites, ants, and fungi continuously toil to recycle the fallen leaves, fruit, and branches into the valuable nutrients that are the key to sustaining the biological diversity of the forests.

**RHINOCEROS HORNBILL**

**BORNEAN GIBBON**
The resounding calls of the Bornean gibbon carry far over the forest canopy, announcing the presence of a troop feeding in a tree.

**COLUGO (FLYING LEMUR)**
The colugo or flying lemur glides from tree to tree with the aid of a membrane of skin which extends between its limbs and body.

**ORANG UTAN**
The largest and most intelligent of all Asian primates, the orang utan occurs in the swamp and river forests of Sarawak and Sabah.

**BRUSH-TAILED PORCUPINE**
The porcupine is a nocturnal animal and feeds on fruit, small mammals, and insects.

**BINTURONG**
The binturong (bear-cat), a thickly furred mammal with a bushy tail, is found in tall secondary forests. It is usually nocturnal and arboreal and lives on fruit and small mammals.

**FUNGI**
Fungi thrive under warm moist conditions. They do not photosynthesize but obtain nutrients by growing on dead matter. Clockwise from top far left are the *Russula*, the Sunburst Fungus, the *Xeromphaline* and the *Entoloma*.

**BULWER'S PHEASANT**
Female Bulwer's pheasants are usually dull in color to provide camouflage when incubating; the male's bright colors attract the female.

**NUTRIENT STORAGE**
In temperate forests most nutrients are held in the soil (left-hand bar); in poorer tropical soils, they are held in the biomass (right-hand bar). As scarce nutrients occur at the surface, tree roots seldom grow deeper than 26 feet. To compensate many develop large buttress roots at the trunk base for extra support.

**EPIPHYTES**
In the high forest canopy epiphytes festoon the branches and climbers, adding to the splendor of the forest. Most epiphytes, such as ferns and orchids, are non-parasitic.

**LEOPARD**
One of the main predators of the forest, the leopard preys on mouse deer, hogs, and tapirs.

**PANGOLIN**
Feeding on ants and termites, the pangolin sports a scaly armor allowing it to roll into a tight ball when threatened.

**WHITE-BELLIED WOODPECKER**
Woodpeckers feed on caterpillars, and create crevices in tree trunks for other nesting birds, or for epiphytic plants to grow from.

**BANTENG**
The banteng is nocturnal and shy, and feeds on grasses, young leaves, and shoots.

**RAFFLESIA**
The parasitic *Rafflesia,* the largest flowering plant in the world, attracts insects to feed on its nectar.

Few human activities have had a greater impact on the landscape in Southeast Asia than the development of plantations for commercial exploitation. Vast areas of natural forest have been cleared during the last 100 years. Two trees in particular, neither native to the region, are involved: the rubber tree and the oil palm. Rubber and oil-palm plantations combined cover 8000 square miles of Malaysian territory today. Ecologically there is wide-scale loss of wildlife, and many species cannot exist in these vast areas of monoculture owing to a lack of vegetation cover and food. Many plantations use fertilizers and pesticides, further reducing the possibilities for wildlife.

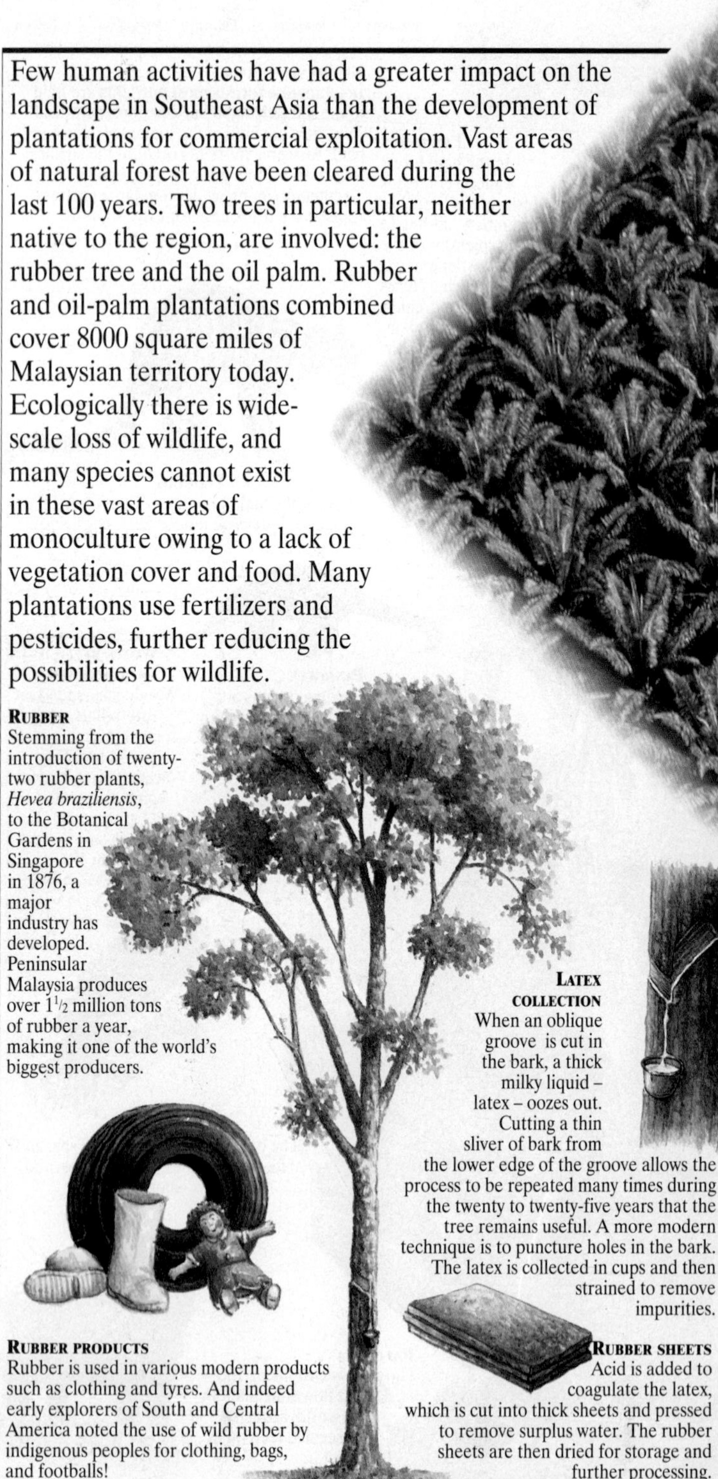

**RUBBER**
Stemming from the introduction of twenty-two rubber plants, *Hevea braziliensis*, to the Botanical Gardens in Singapore in 1876, a major industry has developed. Peninsular Malaysia produces over $1^1/_2$ million tons of rubber a year, making it one of the world's biggest producers.

**LATEX COLLECTION**
When an oblique groove is cut in the bark, a thick milky liquid – latex – oozes out. Cutting a thin sliver of bark from the lower edge of the groove allows the process to be repeated many times during the twenty to twenty-five years that the tree remains useful. A more modern technique is to puncture holes in the bark. The latex is collected in cups and then strained to remove impurities.

**RUBBER PRODUCTS**
Rubber is used in various modern products such as clothing and tyres. And indeed early explorers of South and Central America noted the use of wild rubber by indigenous peoples for clothing, bags, and footballs!

**RUBBER SHEETS**
Acid is added to coagulate the latex, which is cut into thick sheets and pressed to remove surplus water. The rubber sheets are then dried for storage and further processing.

**OIL PALM**

The oil palm (*Elaeis guineensis)*, a native of West Africa, was brought to Singapore in 1870, from where seeds were distributed to surrounding countries. It is used extensively as a source of oil and is also grown as an ornamental tree in many sub-tropical locations.

**FRUIT OF THE OIL PALM**

Oil palms have tiny flowers which develop into a cluster of fruits, eventually turning black when ripe. Two to six bunches are produced each year. These are harvested and the outer flesh of the fruit streamed and pressed to recover the oil. Oil is also extracted from the kernel of the fruit.

**KERNEL PRODUCTS**

The oil from the kernel is used in a variety of products, such as margarine, chocolate, and pharmaceuticals. The residue after the kernel oil has been extracted is used in cattle feed.

**OIL-PALM PRODUCTS**

The oil is used for making soap, candles, and lubricating greases and also in the processing of tinplate and coating ironplate.

**COCONUT**

Coconut palms, *Cocos nucifera*, are widely found in coastal areas and are planted mainly for their fruit. However, coconut products are also used in a wide variety of produce.

**FRUIT (KERNEL)**

**COCOA**

Cocoa is Sabah's leading export crop. It has to be planted in the shade of other trees and takes two years before the crop comes into fruit, reaching its full potential after three years.

**COCONUT PRODUCTS**

The kernel is used in edible products, including the oil extract. The oil is also used in pharmaceuticals and cosmetics. The husk is used to make ropes and mats. The construction industry makes use of the trunk and the palm leaves are traditionally utilized for hat- and basket-making.

**COCOA PRODUCTS**

Cocoa pods are usually harvested by hand and collected for processing. Wet beans are fermented for one week, during which time the flavor develops. The beans are then dried and used in the production of chocolate products.

HORNBILL FEATHERS

Tropical forests are far more than a source of timber: throughout the world they are home to thousands of plant and animal species and hundreds of native tribes. These people rely on the good health of the forest for their daily survival, not only in providing sources of food, but also for shelter, medicines, clothes, and recreational opportunities. Forest-dwelling tribes live in harmony with their environment, carefully managing the limited, fragile natural resources that supply so many of their needs and ours in our modern societies.

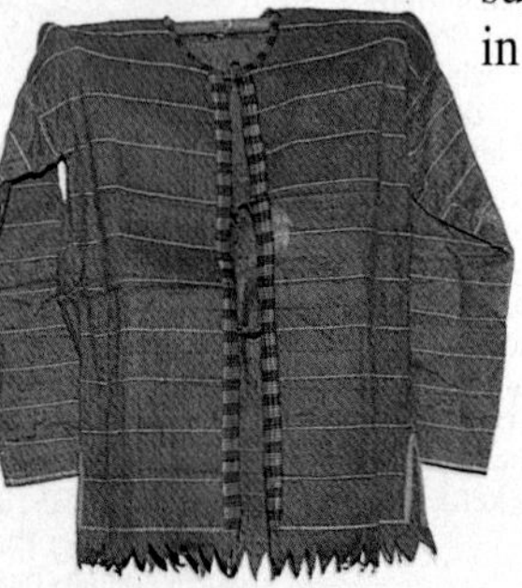

The tropical forests of Malaysia are like a giant fruit bowl. Common species include: mango, fig, durian, rambutan, mangosteen, jambu batu (guava), jackfruit (nangka), starfruit, pomelo, buah duku, buah susu (passion fruit), soursop, and ciku.

SOURSOP

MANGO

JAMBU BATU (GUAVA)

STARFRUIT

Many forest products are used for clothing: the Dayak people make jackets from the bark of trees.

Wild honey is a prized delicacy of the forest. To avoid being stung, human gatherers build a fire below the nest, the smoke temporarily lulling the bees into a torpor.

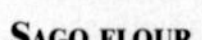

SAGO FLOUR

**SAGO PALM**
The sago palm grows in swampy places where there is little competition from weeds. Sago is widely used as animal food, and the pith is also ground to make sago flour, the staple diet of many tribes.

**SOFT-SHELLED TURTLE**
Eggs of the soft-shelled turtle are gathered from the sandy banks adjoining rivers and swamps.

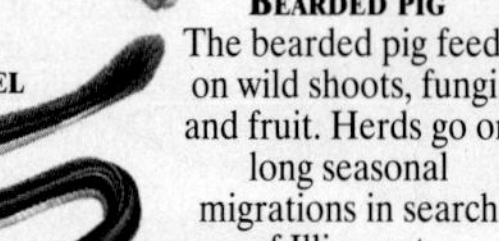

EEL

**BEARDED PIG**
The bearded pig feeds on wild shoots, fungi, and fruit. Herds go on long seasonal migrations in search of Illipe nuts.

**DAMAR**
Damar (resin) is obtained from the dipterocarp forests of Malaysia and is used in varnishes and paints.

**CAMPHOR OIL**
Produced from the wood of the camphor laurel, camphor oil is used in medicines and the manufacture of celluloid.

**DRESSING RATTAN**
This photograph, taken around 1900 in the Malay peninsula, shows rattan undergoing the process of being sorted, straightened, and stripped in preparation for delivery to the next stage of production.

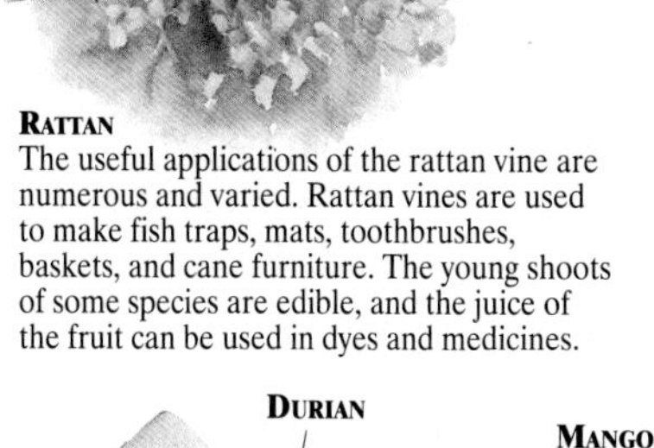

**RATTAN**
The useful applications of the rattan vine are numerous and varied. Rattan vines are used to make fish traps, mats, toothbrushes, baskets, and cane furniture. The young shoots of some species are edible, and the juice of the fruit can be used in dyes and medicines.

**DURIAN**

**MANGOSTEEN**

**PALM TREES**
Palm trees are a source of wood and thatch for construction and of food – palm hearts for example are widely eaten.

**PALM HEARTS**

**BUAH DUKU**

**POMELO**

**CHILI AND PEPPER**
These two spices are a must in many local dishes in Singapore and Malaysia. The cultivated chili plant is just over 1 foot tall, with long narrow leaves. Pepper (right) is grown on the fertile slopes in Sarawak, a major world producer of the crop.

**MALAYSIAN PEACOCK PHEASANT**
The Malaysian peacock pheasant and the great argus are widely hunted gamefowl of the forest.

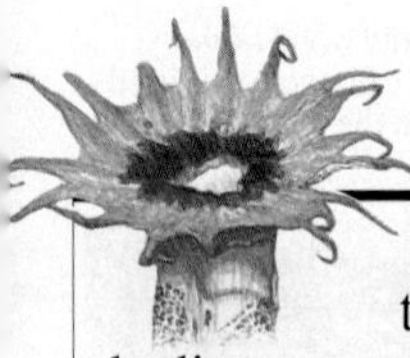

Fungi thrive in Mount Kinabalu's moist climate. The sunburst fungus is particularly spectacular.

The mountains of Malaysia are home to some of the richest wildlife anywhere on this planet. From the limestone pinnacles of Sarawak to the heights of Mount Kinabalu, at 13,455 feet the highest peak in Southeast Asia, there are natural wonders at each turn. The highest mountain between the Himalayas and New Guinea, Mount Kinabalu is renowned for the sheer diversity of plant and animal species it supports, many of which are found nowhere else in the world. Plant and animal species vary with the elevation – at 4000 feet lowland rainforest covers the landscape. From there to around 6000 feet a rich montane oak forest dominates. At 6500 feet the cloud forest is eerily spectacular, with gold and green mosses draping the trees. Above 8500 feet strange gnarled trees are found where the soils begin to thin and become alkaline. Above 11,000 feet there is no soil layer and a few mosses and sedges are all that can be found in terms of vegetation. The last few hundred feet of the ascent are barren, austere granite.

**PITCHER PLANT**
With its colorful serrated pitchers, *Nepenthes villosa* is the highest-growing plant of its type. It survives in poor soils, supplementing its diet with insects caught in the digestive fluid at the base of the pitcher.

**SLOW LORIS**
The nocturnal slow loris is a gentle, thick-furred primate that feeds on insects, small mammals, and fruit. It can be found in the forest canopy and in the cocoa plantations in Sabah.

**YELLOW-BREASTED WARBLER**

**KINABALU FRIENDLY WARBLER**

**MOUNTAIN BUSH WARBLER**

Only a few species of birds live above 8000 feet; these include the mountain bush warbler, the Kinabalu friendly warbler, and the mountain blackbird. The latter two are only to be found on Mount Kinabalu.

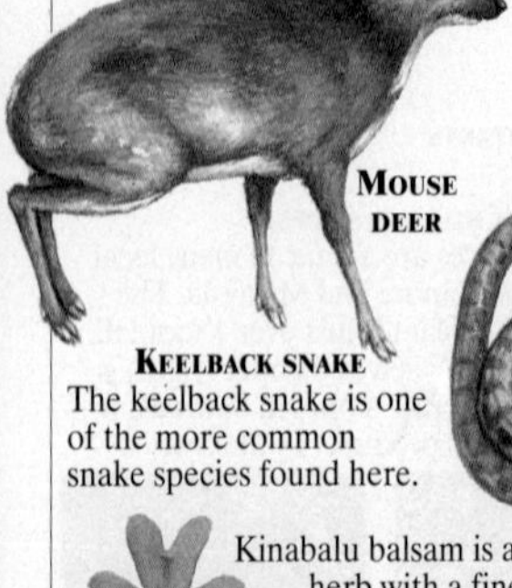

**MOUSE DEER**

**KEELBACK SNAKE**
The keelback snake is one of the more common snake species found here.

Kinabalu balsam is a delicate herb with a fine purple flower that grows around 6500 feet.

Even at 12,500 feet, a lovely white-flowered orchid, the mountain necklace orchid, covers the rock crevices in November when it is in full bloom.
SILVER POTENTILLA
MOUNTAIN TRACYMENE
A few species survive at the highest elevations – mainly grasses and sedges.
*Tracymene saniculifolia* is a colorful red and white species.
The Kinabalu buttercup is found in the wetter areas of the summit slopes.
MOUNTAIN BLACKBIRD
The vegetarian, mountain blackbird lays only one egg at a time in its large nest.
Mount Kinabalu is home to a number of species of squirrel. The Borneo mountain ground squirrel lives in the scrubby vegetation of the higher elevations at around 11,000 feet.
Compact clumps of *Stapf's vaccinium* occur at around 9500 feet.
Wild raspberries are found at around 8500 feet.
Rhododendrons are typical flowering plants of high altitudes. Thirty-five species are found in Sabah alone, and display an immense selection of shapes, sizes, and colors to passersby. Many rhododendrons have complex symbiotic relationships with sunbirds and other species that act as pollinators.

**WHITE-HEADED MUNIA**
The white-headed munia is common in grasslands and *padi* fields.

Kedah on Malaysia's northwest coast is known as the rice capital of the country. Here there are vast areas of flat land where, with the help in recent years of an irrigation scheme on the Muda River, Kedah's rice production has soared. The wetland permanent cultivation of rice on the peninsula differs from that found in Sabah and Sarawak, where dryland *padi* is grown. In remote areas, land is prepared by slash and burn and then planted with rice seeds. Following a modest harvest, tapioca will be grown and the land then abandoned to recover its fertility.

**STAGES OF RICE CULTIVATION**

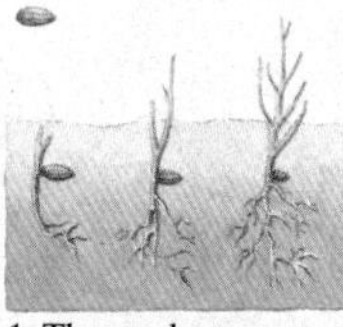

1. The seed germinates and forms its early growth in a nursery bed for wetland rice cultivation. This takes between fifteen and forty days.

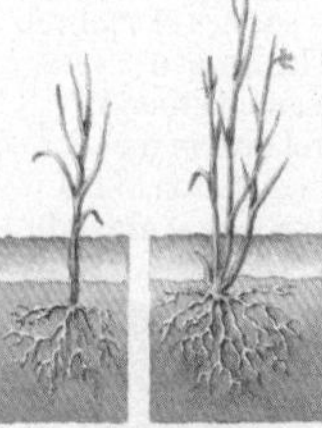

2. The rice plant is then transplanted and grows to its full height of around 2 feet.

3. Mature plant, with grains of rice ready for harvesting.

**BUFFALO**
The buffalo is still used in Malaysia, although mechanical means of plowing are becoming much more common.

**DRYLAND CULTIVATION**

Clearing the forest.

Harvesting.

Winnowing.

**WETLAND RICE CULTIVATION**

Preparing the land.

Transplanting the seedlings.

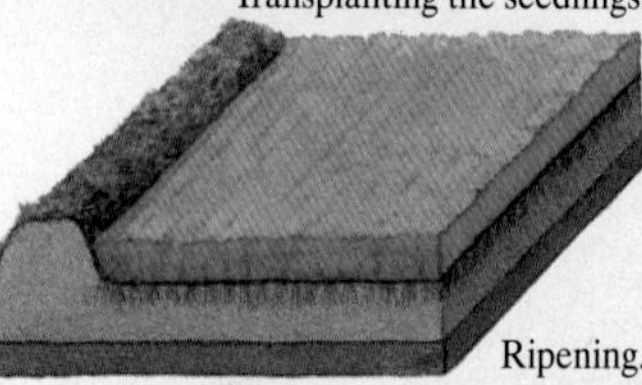

Ripening.

Harvesting.

# HISTORY

## EARLY HISTORY

***70,000 BC***
*Neanderthal Solo Man in Java, Indonesia.*

***20,000 BC***
*Pioneer settlers in the Philippines.*

Neolithic footed dish.

***18,000 BC***
*Paleolithic art flourishes.*

***8000 BC***
*Invention of the wheeled cart and ox-drawn plow.*

***6000 BC***
*Rice farming begins in Southeast Asia.*

The founding in c. AD 1400 of the Melaka sultanate, the state which grew to become one of the greatest trading centers in Asia and the source of Malay culture and tradition, conventionally marks the beginning of the modern history of the territories which constitute present-day Malaysia and Singapore. Yet clearly Melaka and its greatness were built upon political traditions and commercial networks that had evolved over earlier millennia. Thus, it is far more difficult to reconstruct the prehistory of this region than that of almost any other country in Southeast Asia. There are no great temple complexes, no vast collections of stone inscriptions, no court annals. The principal historical sources are scattered archeological remains and, in particular, references to the region in contemporary Indian, Chinese, and Arab writings. The Niah Caves in Sarawak were the site of some of the earliest finds of human habitation, dating back to 35,000 BC. In Peninsular Malaysia the first evidence appears around 10,000 BC–12,000 BC, and a few Neolithic and Bronze Age finds have been made.

## TRADE IN THE MALAY ARCHIPELAGO

***AD 30***
*Crucifixion of Jesus Christ in Jerusalem.*

***AD 150***
*Trade contacts are established between South India and Indonesia.*

Container from the Bronze Age.

The earliest history of these territories was shaped principally by trade. Lying along the great sea lanes between India to the west and China to the east, the region's ports allowed Indian and Chinese traders to trans-ship their cargos and provision their vessels. But perhaps more importantly, those traders were also attracted by the region's own great wealth. The forests were a rich source of aromatic woods (camphor, for example), resins, and rattan; the earth yielded substantial deposits of iron, tin, and gold; the seas provided pearl oysters, shellfish, edible seaweeds, and cowrie shells (used as currency in many parts of Asia before coins became common).

**THE ARRIVAL OF TRADERS FROM INDIA AND CHINA.** In time, as commerce and production expanded, traders coming to the region from India and China brought with them ideas of government and statecraft, as well as religious beliefs. The earliest trading contacts between the Malay world and India appear to have taken place around AD 300. Inscriptions in Malay dating from the 7th century reveal a considerable Sanskrit influence; and a substantial part of the Malay concept of kingship, as well as court ritual and language, is to this day clearly of Indian origin. A number of Indian stone

An old painting of a river scene of Kuching, Sarawak.

inscriptions and Hindu and Buddhist images, some dating from as early as the 4th century AD, have been found at several sites on the west coast of Peninsular Malaysia. Chinese sea trade with the Malay world began in the 5th century, driven in large part by Chinese demand for local aromatic woods, ivory, wax, and resins. In return, Chinese merchants brought silk, lacquerware, and pottery. Evidence of that trade can be seen in the pottery fragments recovered from sites across the region. The large number of natural harbors and inlets along the coastlines of the Malay archipelago provided the centers for this growing trade, the points at which cargo from west or east Asia might be trans-shipped, and the points at which local products from the vast hinterland would be gathered. That commercial base then provided the foundation for the formation of states. The central theme in the prehistory of the Malay world (and indeed in much of its subsequent history) is, therefore, of an almost incessant struggle between the numerous trade-based states for political and economic domination of the region. Commonly, hegemony was fragile and short-lived. But one state achieved an unrivalled domination.

Inscribed stone tablet, 7th century.

***AD 150***
*The use of Indian Sanskrit by Malay rulers.*

***AD 180***
*The decline of the Roman Empire begins.*

***AD 320***
*Unification of India by the Gupta dynasty.*

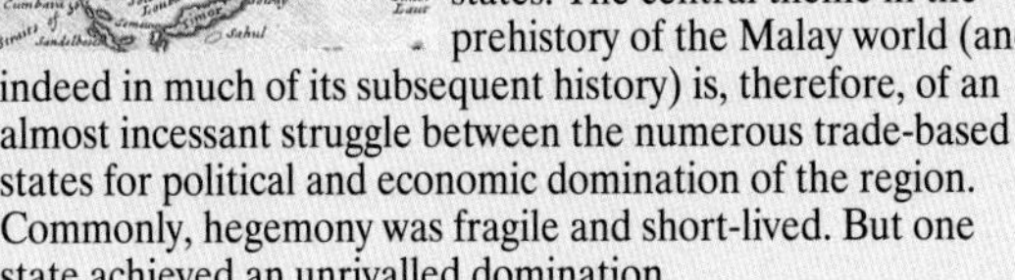

## The Rise and Fall of Srivijaya

The state of Srivijaya, located, it is believed, in Palembang in southeast Sumatra, emerged in the 7th century and maintained a commercial and political pre-eminence in the Malay world until about the 13th century. Srivijaya was not only a great trading center, a mighty emporium offering luxurious commodities from India, the Arab world, and China as well as from Srivijaya's own domains, but also, as a result of its great wealth, a center of advanced learning and refined culture. It was also renowned for the study of Mahayana Buddhism, attracting scholars from China and India. However, it is in the disintegration of Srivijaya's pre-eminence, under increasing challenge from neighboring states from the 12th century onward, that the origins of the rise of Melaka (formerly Malacca) are to be found. The new state, on the west coast of the peninsula, was established by a refugee prince from Palembang, Paramesvara, and it clearly saw itself as the heir to Srivijaya's power. In some respects, the eclipse of Srivijaya and the founding of Melaka lie firmly within the, by that time, well-established pattern of Malay history. But, in another important respect, Melaka marks a significant break with the past. That break was the conversion of the state to Islam.

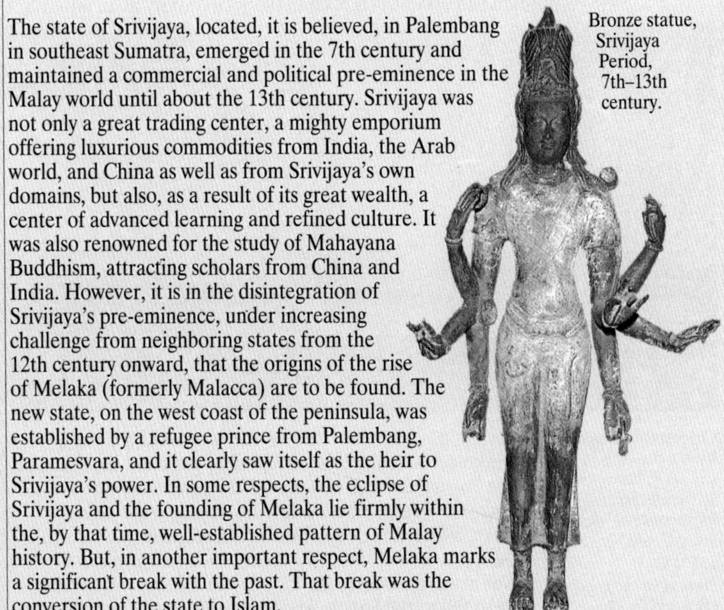

Bronze statue, Srivijaya Period, 7th–13th century.

An Indian Muslim merchant from Bombay, India.

## MELAKA IN THE 15TH CENTURY

*1291*
*Marco Polo reaches Sumatra. Two years later, the Mongols invade Java.*

*1364*
*The Siamese kingdom of Ayutthaya is founded.*

*1431*
*Joan of Arc is burned at the stake.*

*1445*
*Europe's first book is printed by Gutenberg.*

*1488*
*Bartholomew Diaz reaches the Cape of Good Hope.*

*1492*
*Christopher Columbus discovers the West Indies.*

Muslim traders from the Arab world and increasingly from India had long been familiar in ports throughout the Malay archipelago. If not directly seeking conversions, these traders at least provided local peoples with an insight into Islamic values, attitudes, and beliefs. At the beginning of the 14th century, one of the earliest of the Melaka rulers (the historical record is too thin to be more precise) embraced Islam. That conversion provided a strong impetus to the rise of Melaka as a great trading center, for it brought into the port large numbers of Indian Muslim merchants whose cargoes of textiles were the basic item of trade, drawing in a vast range of other commodities and traders. Like Srivijaya before it, Melaka was not simply a trading state, but an important center of culture and statecraft. During the 15th century, it extended its powerful influence throughout the peninsula and beyond, bringing smaller states within its authority and advancing conversion to Islam. Perhaps more importantly, Melaka, in its greatness, fundamentally shaped Malay traditions and institutions: literature, administration, social behavior, and practice. All Melaka's successor states sought to match its power and influence: none succeeded.

## THE PORTUGUESE AND THE DUTCH

Melaka's political domination was relatively short-lived. The state had established itself in the 15th century as an important

Chromolithograph from a drawing of a sea battle between the Spaniards and the Portuguese at Melaka Straits, dated 1606.

*1577–80*
*Francis Drake goes on his world voyage.*

collecting point for the valuable spices produced in the islands of the eastern archipelago. It therefore attracted the attention of the Portuguese and in August 1511, after a month's siege, Portuguese forces under Afonso de Albuquerque seized Melaka, establishing one of the first European territorial possessions in Asia. But, in January 1641, as Portuguese power in Asia waned in the face of new European arrivals, Melaka fell to the Dutch. The three centuries from the fall of

> "The Portuguese and the Spaniards were truly wonderful conquerers and colonizers. They effected more rapid changes in the countries they conquered than any other nations of modern times." Alfred Russel Wallace

Melaka to the Portuguese until the arrival of British power in the peninsula toward the end of the 18th century can be seen as a period of almost unending struggle for pre-eminence between the various states of the peninsula. This is a common theme in the history of the Malay world from the earliest times. That period, however, had one important feature distinguishing it from earlier and subsequent periods: external powers were intimately involved in the politics of the Malay peninsula, but essentially as equals of the local states. Unable to dominate them and impose a new pre-eminence, they did, however, possess sufficient strength to prevent any of the indigenous states from doing so either. Those external powers were, of course, the Portuguese and then the Dutch, but also the Thai state of Ayutthaya which, with its long-standing interest in the Malay states of the northern peninsula, re-exerted its authority in that area primarily from the middle of the 17th century. The most powerful Malay polity in this period was Riau-Johor, whose rise in the 17th century owed much to an alliance with the Dutch.

Dutch tombstone, Melaka.

## The British

BORN 1820
and, like the British Empire
Still going Strong!

Advertisement, *Straits Produce*, 1926.

Britain's territorial advance in the region began in 1786, when the sultan of Kedah, threatened by possible attacks from the Burmese and the Thais, leased the island of Penang to the English East India Company in the hope of securing British protection. Then, in 1795, the British took possession of Melaka, fearing that the territory would fall to the French following Napoleon's occupation of the Netherlands. It was returned to the Dutch at the conclusion of the French Wars. But in 1824, as part of a general settlement of Anglo-Dutch interests in the Malay world, Melaka became an undisputed British possession. The final element in Britain's initial territorial advance had occurred a few years earlier. In 1819, Stamford Raffles, a clerk with the English East India Company, secured permission from the sultan of Riau-Johor and the local chief to establish a trading post on the island of Singapore, once a commercial center but now, after some four centuries, largely deserted except for small communities of fishermen, pirates, and petty traders. In 1824 the two Malay rulers ceded Singapore to the East India Company in perpetuity, in return for payments and pensions. In 1826, the Company brought together Singapore, Melaka, and Penang to form the Straits Settlements. By the mid-19th century, Singapore had, in the tradition of Srivijaya and Melaka, established itself as a great trading center, although in scale it easily eclipsed its predecessors.

***1775–6***
*The American Revolution and the Declaration of Independence.*

***1789***
*The start of the French Revolution. George Washington is first president of the USA.*

***1804***
*Napoleon Bonaparte becomes emperor.*

***1807***
*The slave trade is abolished in the British Empire.*

***1811–16***
*The British take over Java after defeating Franco-Dutch forces.*

***1815***
*Battle of Waterloo.*

Painting of the Penang waterfront.

## THE STRAITS SETTLEMENTS

*1837*
*Queen Victoria ascends the throne.*

*1839*
*Outbreak of Opium Wars.*

*1841*
*Hong Kong is acquired by Britain.*

In the period between the middle of the 19th century and World War One, British administration was extended from the Straits Settlements to embrace all the territories which constitute present-day Malaysia and Singapore. However, that advance took place in a very piecemeal manner and resulted in an extraordinary diversity of administrative structures and constitutional arrangements. The Straits Settlements, comprising the islands of Singapore and Penang, and the small enclave at Melaka, was from 1867 a crown colony under direct British rule.

## THE MALAY STATES

Frank Swettenham.

*1848*
*Gold is discovered in California.*

The major extension of British administration to the peninsula began in January 1874 when, under the Pangkor Treaty, the sultan of Perak agreed to accept a British resident whose advice "must be asked and acted upon on all questions other than those touching Malay religion and custom". The residency system was then extended to Selangor, Negeri Sembilan, and Pahang. In 1896 those four states were brought together in the Federated Malay States (FMS), with the federal capital in Kuala Lumpur. The first resident of the FMS was Frank Swettenham. The remaining five states in the peninsula constituted the Unfederated Malay States (UMS). Perlis, Kedah, Kelantan and Terengganu, dependencies of Thailand through to the beginning of the 20th century, were transferred to British authority in 1909, and Johor accepted a British adviser in 1914. The sultans in the UMS maintained a considerably greater degree of administrative independence under British authority than the sultans in the FMS.

## THE BORNEO TERRITORIES

*1861*
*Abraham Lincoln becomes President of the USA.*

*1868*
*Meiji Restoration in Japan.*

*1869*
*Opening of the Suez Canal.*

British administration in the Borneo territories (now East Malaysia) took yet another quite distinct form. In 1841 an English adventurer, James Brooke, was appointed rajah of Sarawak by the sultan of Brunei, thus founding a dynasty of "white rajahs" who would govern that territory for a century. The rule of the Brookes was highly paternalistic, not least in protecting the local peoples from rapid economic change and commercial exploitation. In the other Borneo territory, at the northeast corner of the island, concessions granted by the sultans of Brunei and Sulu were, in 1881, acquired by the newly formed British North Borneo Company, chartered in London and thus enjoying the protection of the British crown.

View overlooking a river in Borneo, from an early engraving.

## COMMERCE AND TRADE

Under British rule, economic change was very rapid but was restricted largely to the west coast of the peninsula and the Straits Settlements. By the final decades of the 19th century, Singapore was by far the most important trading center in the region, one of the great Eastern ports. Primary commodities from a hinterland extending to Thailand in the north and embracing the huge archipelago of the Dutch East Indies (now Indonesia) came into the port for processing, repackaging and despatch to the industrial markets of the West. In return, Singapore received Western manufactures for distribution throughout its hinterland, including the west-coast states of the peninsula. The period from about 1870 saw a rapid expansion in the exploitation of the area's exceptionally rich tin deposits, at first by Chinese mining entrepreneurs, then by highly capitalized Western mining companies. In the late 19th century, Malaya was by far the most important producer of tin in the world. The first years of the 20th century saw the establishment of rubber cultivation in the west-coast states, utilizing the infrastructure of roads, railways, and ports that had been created for the tin industry. Commercial rubber cultivation was first undertaken by European planters, and while large Eastern rubber companies held a dominant position in the industry, Malay smallholders were soon also planting the crop on a wide scale. Malaya was clearly the world's most important producer of rubber in the early decades of the 20th century.

Satirical cartoon from *Straits Produce*, 1927.

***1900***
*Boxer Rebellion uprising in China.*

***1901***
*Queen Victoria dies on January 22 after a reign of sixty-five years.*

***1909***
*Henry Ford produces Model T motor car.*

***1914–18***
*World War One.*

## DEMOGRAPHY

Close on the heels of economic growth came demographic change. The local Malay population, engaged mainly in the subsistence cultivation of rice, had little economic reason to offer their labor for the mining of tin or the plantation cultivation of rubber. Consequently, the final decades of the 19th century saw large-scale immigration of Chinese coolie labor into the tin districts, and the early 20th century the recruitment of Tamil laborers from South India to tap plantation rubber. In addition, Indian and, in particular, Chinese traders and moneylenders came to dominate the commercial sectors of the economy. Reflecting the location of economic activity, the Chinese and Indian communities too became geographically concentrated. In the west-coast states, by the 1930's, those communities outnumbered the Malays, while Singapore and Penang were overwhelmingly Chinese towns.

***1927***
*Lindbergh undertakes a solo flight across the Atlantic on May 21.*

Chinese worker at a tin mine in Selangor.

Currency note during the Japanese occupation, 1942–5.

**1927**
*Mussolini assumes power in Italy.*

**1929**
*The Great Depression following the Wall Street Crash.*

**1932**
*Manchuria becomes a puppet state of Japan on February 18.*

The processes which brought British rule to an end in its Southeast Asian territories were, in a number of important respects, quite distinctive, and occasionally unique, in the history of European decolonization in Africa and Asia. The complex juxtaposition of administrations and constitutional arrangements already described inevitably meant that British withdrawal would frequently be a tangled affair. The large-scale immigration of Chinese and Indians into the peninsula, and their clear establishment as settled populations by the 1930's and 1940's, would add an important ethnic dimension to the processes by which power would be transferred to local elites. The period between the beginning of serious agitation for the end of British rule and the actual achievement of Britain's withdrawal was remarkably brief.

## THE JAPANESE OCCUPATION

**1933**
*Hitler is appointed Chancellor on January 30, and the Nazi terror begins.*

**1939–45**
*World War Two.*

**1941**
*Japanese sink HMS* Repulse *and HMS* Prince of Wales *off the Melaka Straits on December 1.*

**1942**
*The Battle of El Alamein on October 23. Allied forces invade north Africa on November 7.*

# THE SUNDAY TIMES

*"Singapore Must Stand; It SHALL Stand"—H.E. the Governor*

SUNDAY, FEBRUARY 15, 1942.

# STRONG JAP PRESSURE

## Defence Stubbornly Maintained

## VOLUNTEERS IN ACTION

BRITISH, Australian, Indian and Malay troops, and including now men of the Straits Settlements Volunteer Force, are disputing every attempt, by the Japanese to advance further towards the heart of Singapore town.

### FIRST V'C' WON IN MALAYA

THE first Victoria Cross to be awarded for fighting in Malaya, goes to Lieut.-Col. Wright Anderson of the Australian Imperial Forces, says the B.B.C.

On the eve of the Japanese attack in December 1941, the British position in Malaya appeared to be far more secure than that of any other colonial power in Southeast Asia. The previous two decades had seen major nationalist agitation, and on occasions open revolt, in British Burma, French Indo-China (Vietnam) and the Dutch East Indies (Indonesia). Malaya was remarkably quiescent. The absence of significant agitation against British rule might be explained by two main considerations: as far as the Chinese and Indians were concerned, their political interests in this period remained largely focused on their countries of origin; for the Malay community, the important point was the absence of the substantial, disruptive economic change that might in time have provoked anti-British agitation, together with the protective presence of the sultans. Indeed, in some Malay quarters the British administration was perhaps now seen as a bulwark against eventual domination by the Chinese and Indians. The rapid removal of the British by Japan's advancing forces in late 1941 and early 1942, and the brief period of Japanese administration, brought fundamental political change. Because of the long history of Japanese aggression towards China, the local Chinese communities were implacably anti-Japanese and consequently bore the brunt of Japanese suppression. In the power vacuum that followed the sudden collapse of Japanese power in August 1945, ethnic violence erupted.

The Japanese surrender at Singapore's City Hall, August 1945.

**1943**
*Churchill, Roosevelt, and Stalin meet in Teheran on November 28.*

**1944**
*Warsaw uprising.*

"RECONSTRUCTION WORK WAS ON A COMPREHENSIVE SCALE.... THE REBUILDING OF THE GOVERNMENT SERVICES OCCUPIED MUCH OF THE TIME AND ENERGY OF THE RESTORED COLONIAL REGIME."

GILBERT KHOO AND DOROTHY LO, *ASIAN TRANSFORMATION*

## THE POST-WAR YEARS

The British, returning in September 1945, quickly sought important constitutional reform to bring administrative unity to the peninsula and the settlements. Their first proposals, for a Malayan Union, met fierce Malay opposition and led, in May 1946, to the formation of the United Malays National Organization (UMNO), the first mass Malay political organization. Within a few years, the other races had established their own communal-based parties, the Malayan Indian Congress (MIC) also in 1946, and the Malayan Chinese Association (MCA) in February 1949. The second set of constitutional proposals, for the creation of a Federation of Malaya, was successfully implemented in February 1948. The Federation brought all the states of the peninsula, together with Penang and Melaka, into a single political unit; crucially, Singapore was kept outside the new alignment. The immediate post-war years had also seen rising labor agitation in Malaya, led by the Malayan Communist Party (MCP). In early 1948, faced with increasing suppression on the part of the colonial authorities, the MCP decided to launch an open revolt, concentrating their first attacks upon British plantation interests. On June 18, 1948 the government declared a state of emergency throughout Malaya. The Emergency was not officially ended until 1960, although the revolt was effectively broken by the mid-1950's. At its height, in the late 1940's and early 1950's, it had threatened severe disruption to the export economy but was defeated in part by firm government measures, including the mass relocation of the poor rural Chinese who provided much of the MCP's support, and by the fact that, at least by the early 1950's, it was evident that the British were leaving.

Demonstration against cession of Sarawak to Britain, 1946.

***1947***
*India and Pakistan become two independent sovereign states.*

***1948***
*Burma gains independence as a republic; Mahatma Gandhi assassinated in New Delhi on January 1. The new state of Israel is proclaimed by President David Ben-Gurion on May 14.*

## THE END OF BRITISH RULE

To whom would the British transfer power? In the late 1940's, perhaps mindful of the extreme communal violence that had attended their departure from India, the British administration sought to encourage the emergence of political parties that had no communal identity. Those attempts failed. Instead, the early 1950's saw the emergence, as a result of negotiation within Malayan political circles, of an electoral alliance between the UMNO, MIC, and MCA, under which seats were allocated on the basis of communal strength. The Alliance, led by Tunku Abdul Rahman, decisively demonstrated its strength at federal elections in July 1955.
Independence from British rule came on August 31, 1957, under a constitution which recognized the special position of the Malays as well as the "legitimate interests" of the other communities.

***1950***
*Korean War.*

Federation of Malaya *Merdeka* (Independence) Ceremony, 1957.

Celebrating the birth of the Federation of Malaysia. The words "*Majulah Malaysia*" mean "Progress for Malaysia".

## FROM MALAYA TO MALAYSIA

The withdrawal of Britain from its remaining territories could now proceed, although it was not fully evident precisely how that was to be achieved. In 1959 Singapore was granted internal self-government (Lee Kuan Yew was prime minister), with the prospect of full independence within a short period. The Federation of Malaya viewed the prospect of an independent Singapore, given its large Chinese population and left-wing politics, with considerable alarm. Consequently, in May 1961 the Malayan prime minister, Tunku Abdul Rahman (right), proposed the creation of a wider federation that would embrace Malaya, Singapore, and the Borneo territories. Since 1946, both Sarawak and North Borneo had been crown colonies, on the termination of the rule, respectively, of the Brooke family and of the British North Borneo Company. Although, in the years that followed, the new colonial administrations did little to prepare the territories for self-government, on September 16, 1963 independent Sarawak and Sabah (North Borneo) joined with the Federation of Malaya and Singapore to form the new Federation of Malaysia. The relationship came under immediate strain. The Philippines and Indonesia condemned the new alignment as a neo-colonial construction. Both powers broke off diplomatic relations and Indonesia launched a number of military raids into Sarawak and Sabah. But there were also serious internal strains, as the People's Action Party in Singapore under Lee Kuan Yew made clear its determination to contest for the Chinese vote in peninsular elections, thus threatening the electoral position of the MCA and, in turn, the stability of the Alliance party. In August 1965, Singapore was, in effect, expelled from the Federation. The present-day boundaries were now established.

***1953***
*Eisenhower becomes thirty-fourth president of USA on January 20. Edmund Hillary and Sherpa Tenzing reach summit of Mount Everest (29,002 feet) on May 29.*

***1962***
*The first manned orbital flight by USA.*

***1964***
*The XVIIIth Olympic Games at Tokyo.*

***1965***
*Hindi is established as the official language of India.*

## RECENT YEARS

From 1965, the city-state of Singapore, in a fundamental transformation of its economic structure, achieved rapid expansion of its manufacturing sector, in later years moving into higher and higher technologies. At the same time, the island strengthened its position as a regional center by the development of highly advanced commercial, financial, and communications services. Economic change in Malaysia has been somewhat less dramatic, although recent years have seen the development of a strong export-oriented manufacturing sector. Arguably the more important changes in Malaysia since 1965 have been political in character –

***1965***
*Abortive coup by young military officers leads to downfall of Indonesia's President Sukarno.*

***1966***
*Inauguration of Paris – Shanghai flights on September 19.*

The Association of Southeast Asian Nations (ASEAN) was founded in 1967. Its six member countries are Brunei Darussalam, Indonesia, Malaysia, Philippines, Singapore, and Thailand.

notably the evolution of a firm relationship between the East Malaysian states and the rest of the Federation and, more dramatically, a realignment of communal forces in the politics of the peninsula. The fragile communal political structures of the immediate post-Independence years were badly shaken by rioting between Chinese and Malays in May 1969, following substantial gains by the opposition Chinese parties in federal elections. In the early 1970's, the government sought a fundamental shift in political and economic structures in favor of the Malays. Malay domination of the political processes was strengthened; among the main objectives of the "New Economic Policy", introduced in 1971, were increased Malay participation in the modern sectors of the economy, long dominated by Chinese and Indians, and the expansion of Malay capital ownership; and the language of Malay was now established as the medium of instruction at all levels of education.

***1970***
*Tunku Abdul Rahman resigns as Malaysian Prime Minister on September 22 and is succeeded by Tun Abdul Razak.*

***1971***
*Singapore hosts the Commonweath Conference on January 14.*

***1972***
*Ceylon becomes the Republic of Sri Lanka on May 22.*

***1975***
*Vietnam War ends on April 30.*

## Singapore and Malaysia Today

Modern Singapore is an advanced industrial economy. In a rapidly growing manufacturing sector, electronic products and components, chemical and petroleum products, and machinery and transport equipment are prominent. Industry is export-oriented with the single most important market for Singapore's exports being the United States. Singaporeans enjoy a high standard of living: GNP per capita in 1990 was US$11,160, only just below that of New Zealand. The social and welfare facilities available are also good, with 87 percent of the population living in subsidized housing. The clearing of Singapore's poor housing stock from the 1960's and the creation, by the Housing and Development Board, of modern estates (right) has transformed living conditions for the majority of the population. Singapore's remarkable economic and social advances in the decades since independence have been achieved under a highly paternalistic, interventionist administration which has rarely tolerated outspoken opposition to its vision of the island's needs and future. In recent years, Malaysia too has established a major industrial sector, in which, again, electronic goods and components are prominent. In 1992, manufacturing accounted for 30 percent of Malaysia's GDP. Even so, primary commodity production – tin, rubber, and palm oil – remains important in the economy. Agriculture, forestry, and fishing accounted for 16 percent of its GDP and mining for a further 9 percent. Politics in modern Malaysia remain dominated by the ambition to expand Malay participation in the modern sectors of the economy and to erase the identification of race with occupation and material condition.

***1976***
*Reunification of Vietnam on June 24.*

***1989***
*The Berlin Wall comes down; reunification of Germany.*

***1990–1***
*Iraq invades Kuwait; Gulf War.*

***1991***
*Dissolution of USSR and the birth of the Commonwealth of Independent States.*

An important aspect of the remarkable ethnic diversity of Malaysia and Singapore is that an extraordinary number of languages can be heard within these territories. The Chinese population divides into several linguistic groups – Hakka, Teochew, Hokkien, Foochow, Hainanese, and Cantonese. The Indian population comprises communities which include Tamil, Sikh, and Gujarati. Among the Orang Asli (indigenous) population of the peninsula, about fifteen different languages can be found. In Sabah and Sarawak, there are many indigenous peoples such as Kadazan, Iban, and Murut, each with a distinct language. For centuries the language of commerce throughout the area has been Malay. In Malaysia, since the early 1970's, Malay has been the language of education, administration, and politics and as such is used as a tool in creating a national identity following Independence.

The romanized form of Malay predominates today, although Arabic and Jawi (an Arabic-based script) are still used in some areas.

The Straits Times

联合早报
Lianhe Zaobao

Berita Harian

தமிழ் முரசு
TAMIL MURASU

A number of Chinese dialects are spoken in Singapore and Malaysia, although Singapore has embarked on a nation-wide publicity drive to promote the use of Mandarin among Chinese Singaporeans. All children learn a second language: usually Malay, Mandarin, or Tamil, depending on their race.

**MULTI-LINGUAL REPUBLIC**
In Singapore, newspapers are published in four national languages. The majority of the population is Chinese and, although dialects are spoken among the older generation, Mandarin is the version taught in schools. Malay, Tamil, and English are the other national languages, with English as the language of international commerce and the medium of instruction throughout the education system.

**AN OLD BOYS' SCHOOL**
The Chinese Boys' School in Amoy Street was established in 1854 by a wealthy philanthropist, Tan Kim Seng, and was one of many small Chinese schools funded by wealthy merchants. Classes were conducted in various Chinese dialects at first, and in Mandarin after 1911.

# Arts and traditions

Muslim Indian and Arab traders introduced Islam to the Malay peninsula some time before the 14th century. The faith quickly attracted followers, for not only did it make trade with these merchants easier, thereby bringing prosperity to those ports whose rulers had converted, but its emphasis on the equality of man appealed to the general populace, unlike Hinduism which preached the divisions of caste. The ruler of Melaka converted to Islam in the early 15th century. However, the religion became established on the east coast of the peninsula much earlier, as the "Terengganu Stone" (above left) proves. Found upstream from Kuala Terengganu, this pillar is inscribed with promulgations from a local ruler instructing his subjects to obey Allah's word and Islamic law, and dates from 1303.

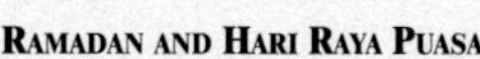

**Ramadan and Hari Raya Puasa**
During the Islamic month of Ramadan (*bulan puasa*), all Muslims, except the very young, the infirm, and pregnant and nursing women, abstain from food and drink between the hours of sunrise and sunset. Ramadan is very special for Muslims as it recalls the period during which the Quran was first revealed to Mohammad. Fasting starts with the new moon and ends with the next. The end of Ramadan is celebrated on Hari Raya Puasa by feasting on traditional foods, wearing new clothes, and visiting friends and relatives.

**Prayer mat**
The prayer mat (*tika sembahyang*) is an essential accessory for all Malays. Before prayer it is placed with the head of the mat facing the *kiblah*, the direction of Mecca. Prayer mats can be simple items of inexpensive cotton or beautifully woven imports from Turkey, Iran, or Pakistan.

### The Haj

The pilgrimage to Mecca used to mean a grueling sea journey, and only a fortunate few ever saved enough money for the trip. However, these days the Tabung Haji, a government-run agency, and Malaysian Airlines have streamlined the operation, and many thousands of Malay Muslims now journey to Mecca every year. Pilgrims wear a simple, unsewn white dress, abstain from sex and disagreements, and join their fellow Muslims to perform the circumambulation of the Ka'aba. Upon completion of the Haj, men often wear a *songkok haji* (below).

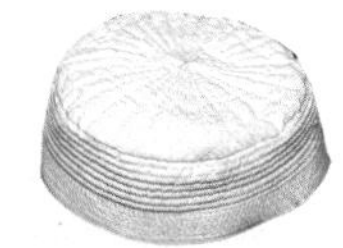

### The five pillars of Islam

The five pillars embody the basic principles of Islam which all Muslims are obliged to follow: to declare the *kalimah shahadah* (Declaration of Faith) which states "there is no god except Allah, and Mohammad is the Messenger of Allah"; to perform the five daily prayers; to pay *zakat*, a charitable tax; to fast in the month of Ramadan; and, once a lifetime, to make the pilgrimage to Mecca, the Haj.

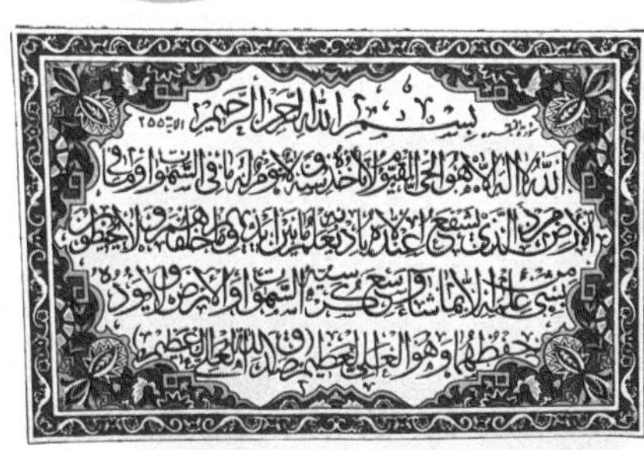

### Daily prayers

Prayers can be performed in the mosque, the house or in any other clean place. Prayers should always be preceded by ablutions which cleanse the mouth, face, hands and arms (up to the elbows), and feet. The five daily prayers are Subuh, just before sunrise, between 6am and 7.15am; Dzohor, the mid-day prayer between 1pm and 2pm; Asar, mid-afternoon, at around 4.30pm; Magrib, just after sunset; and the last prayer for the day, 'Isha, at 8.30pm.

### Masjid and surau

*Masjid*, meaning mosque, comes from the Arabic for a place of worship, but *surau*, meaning "prayer room", is Malay. Mosques (State Mosque of Selangor, above) do not need to be consecrated; the builder merely declares that the building is to be used as a place of worship. Mosques in Malaysia appear in many different styles: some have distinctive pagoda-shaped minarets and tiered Javanese-style roofs, while others are distinguished by their gleaming onion-shaped domes.

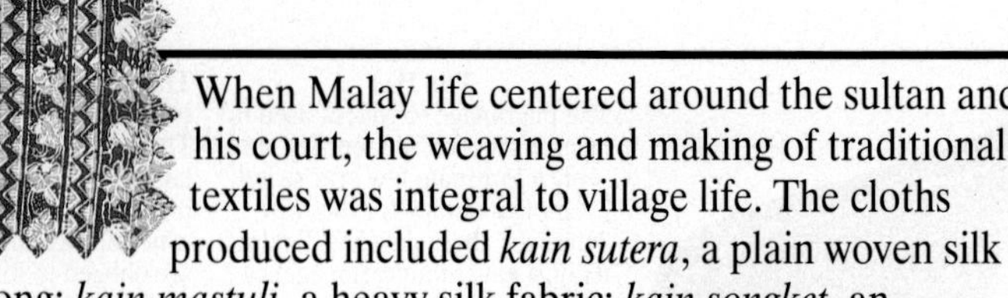

When Malay life centered around the sultan and his court, the weaving and making of traditional textiles was integral to village life. The cloths produced included *kain sutera*, a plain woven silk sarong; *kain mastuli*, a heavy silk fabric; *kain songket*, an elaborate silk brocade; and *kain lemar*, a complete mix of weft *ikat* and gold brocade. Batik became popular in the 1930's as a cottage industry not associated with the courts. Today, most traditional textiles are produced in Kelantan and Terengganu.

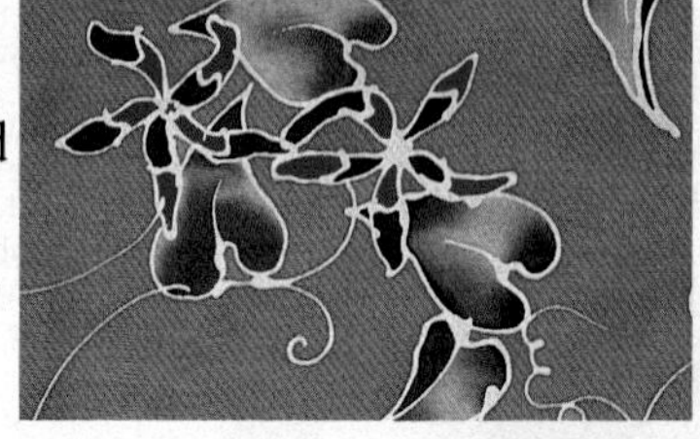

**DESIGNS**
Batik designs follow natural forms and most patterns are inspired by everyday objects. Floral and geometric patterns are common and occur in both stamped and hand-painted batiks, although the latter are more free-flowing and individualistic.

**BATIK**
Batik-making is a comparatively recent craft in Malaysia as most batik cloth was formerly imported from Indonesia. In the 1930s craftsmen began making batik in Kelantan, but the craft only really flourished after World War Two. Batik cloth, in both traditional stamped designs and free-flowing hand-painted styles, is now the most popular of all Malaysian folk arts and is made in all states, although its heartland remains Kelantan.

**BLOCK-PRINTING**
The block, made of bended zinc strips soldered to a handle, is dipped into a hot wax-resin mixture and applied to the cloth. The cloth is draped over moist banana tree stems to prevent the wax from running over the pattern, then put into a dye bath. The process is repeated for the other colors. Finally, the cloth is boiled to extract the wax.

**WAX PEN (CANTING)**
The design is inscribed onto the cloth using a *canting*, a bamboo-handled device with a copper nib-like dipper on the end. It is dipped into the prepared wax and the pattern then drawn on the cloth.

**HAND-PAINTING**
Popular among fashion-conscious Malays, hand-painted batik is used in women's *baju kurung* and men's evening shirts. Applied to either rayon or silk, it is more expensive than stamped batik.

**Weaving the cloth**
The warp providing the colored silk background for the cloth is set up on a hardwood warping frame (*anian*) by a specialist. The warp, comprising 1680 silk threads, is then transferred to the loom and stretched until taut. The weaver sits on a bench built into the end of the loom. The threads of the warp are attached to either of the two sets of heddles, and when the weaver presses on the treadle, one set is depressed while the other is raised. Through the space between the heddles, she throws the shuttle, carrying either silver or gold threads, or plain silk threads. She then reverses the procedure, lowering the raised threads and bringing the shuttle back through the newly created space.

**Traditional kain songket**
This elaborate silk fabric has always been part of the traditional wedding attire and is also worn for ceremonial events. Costing about RM1000, men's outfits consist of a stiffened kerchief or head-wrapper (*tengkolok*); a long-sleeved tunic (*baju*) with a stand-up collar; a tasseled waistcloth; a knee-length sarong (*samping*); and trousers. Women's outfits are either in the *baju kurung* style, with a long tunic over an ankle-length sarong, or in the *baju kebaya* style, where the tunic is replaced by a long silk blouse fastened with gold brooches.

**Kepala**
The *kepala* is the centerpiece, the 18-inch-wide panel that occurs halfway along a 6-foot sarong. It is woven in a more elaborate design than the rest of the length.

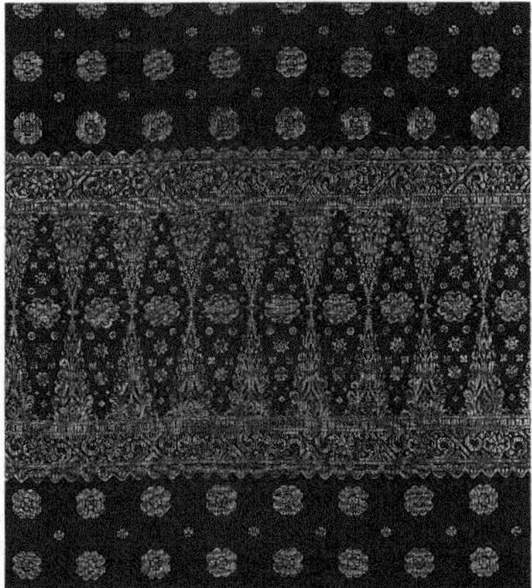

**Kain lemar**
Silk weft threads are pre-dyed, and areas to be left uncolored tied so as to resist the dye. The patterned weft is then woven into the warp with a supplementary warp of gold or other metallic threads to create *kain lemar*, the most technically sophisticated of all Malaysian textiles. Old masterpieces such as the one pictured here cannot be matched by today's weavers.

The Orang Asli of West Malaysia and the numerous peoples of Sarawak and Sabah still rely on forest products, especially for their carvings. Their traditional sculptures are sacred and religious objects. However, recent developments have led to some degree of commercialization, and with the spread of urbanization and tourism the Orang Asli have become more cash-oriented. Not all tribes use wood – some, particularly nomadic groups, use other materials such as bamboo and reeds. Given the ephemeral nature of much indigenous art, wood-carving must be seen as an outstanding form.

**MASKS**
Masks represent spiritual beings and are worn during ceremonies. Most masks are carved from soft woods, usually seasoned by smoking in the kitchen hearth for several months.

**SPIRIT FIGURES**
The Jah-Hut of Pahang create varied, dynamic symmetrical figures in geometric shapes. These are expressions of spirits whose characteristics are represented by symbols. Sometimes the Jah-Hut pile their spirits in a vertical assemblage resulting in a totem pole. A single spirit may be repeated many times to symbolize movement.

**SICKNESS FIGURES**
Small sickness figures worked by the Melanau of Sarawak are summarily expressed because they are meant to be disposed of after use – soft woods serve the purpose. The medicine man "transfers" the illness from the patient to the fetish.

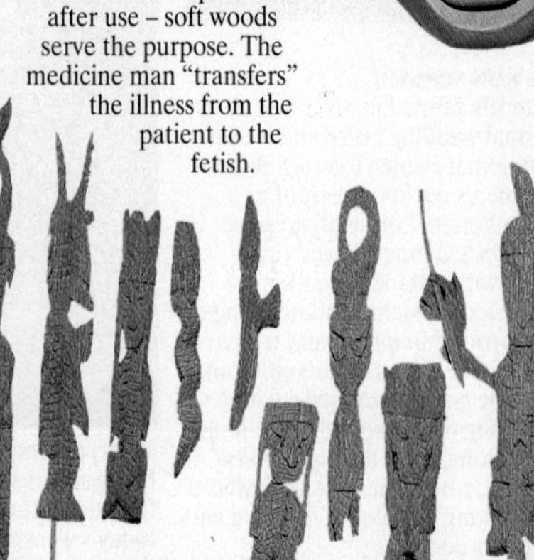

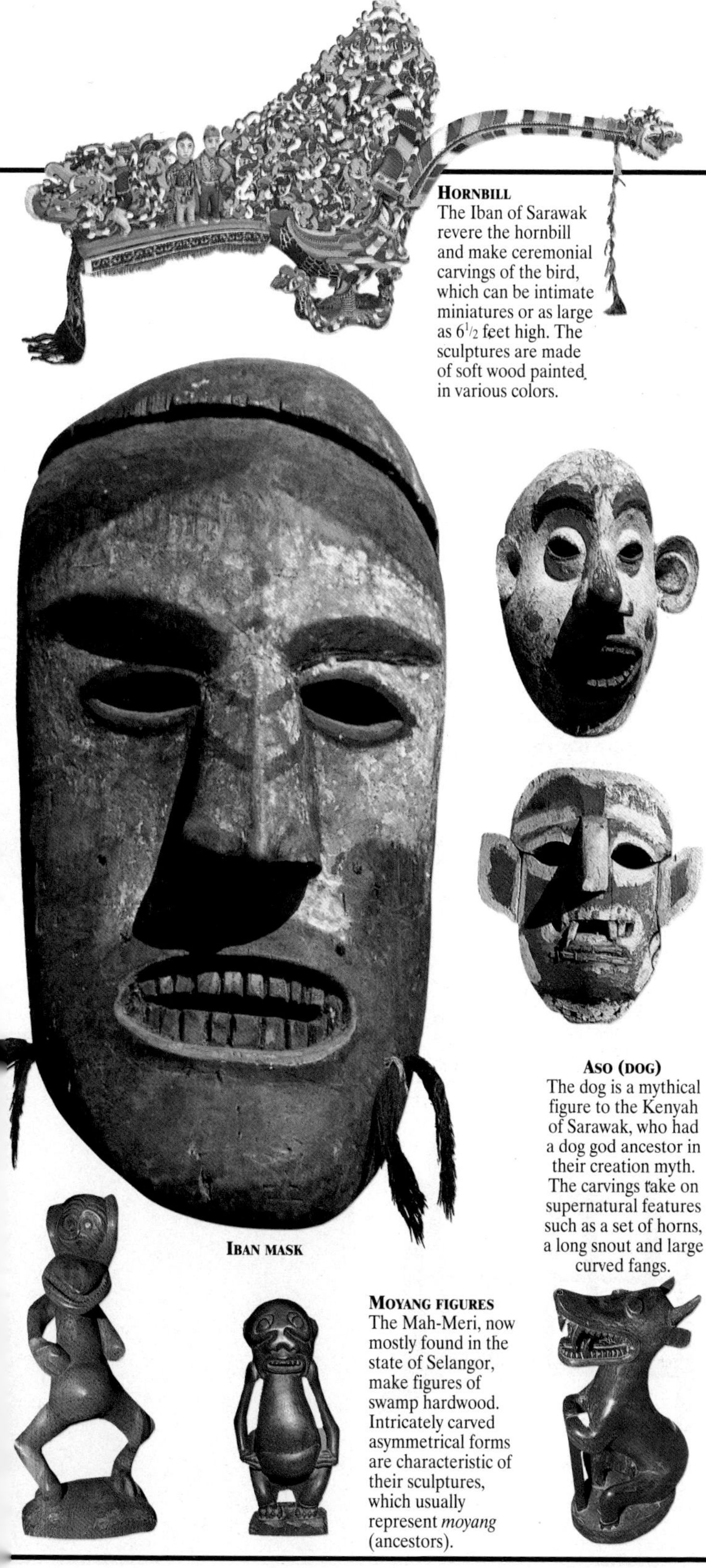

**HORNBILL**
The Iban of Sarawak revere the hornbill and make ceremonial carvings of the bird, which can be intimate miniatures or as large as $6^1/_2$ feet high. The sculptures are made of soft wood painted in various colors.

**ASO (DOG)**
The dog is a mythical figure to the Kenyah of Sarawak, who had a dog god ancestor in their creation myth. The carvings take on supernatural features such as a set of horns, a long snout and large curved fangs.

**IBAN MASK**

**MOYANG FIGURES**
The Mah-Meri, now mostly found in the state of Selangor, make figures of swamp hardwood. Intricately carved asymmetrical forms are characteristic of their sculptures, which usually represent *moyang* (ancestors).

Dr Anton Willem Nieuwenhuis, a physician and explorer who toured Borneo at the turn of the century, noted that "It appears to be members of the upper class families, however, who have the necessary leisure to apply themselves to artistic craftwork seriously." Before the advent of plastic, woven baskets were indispensable for the transportation of goods; floor mats were universally used before the days of beds and other furniture. A few simple tools served to make a great variety of items: a wedge-shaped blade lashed to a haft to make an axe for cutting or an adze for hollowing out, and a long-handled, short-bladed knife for rough shaping and scraping. Today the craft industry is thriving, with many of its products still for local consumption. However, modern wood-carvers are not averse to employing a chainsaw for initial blocking, and files and sandpaper for the final polish.

**MASKS**
Most Borneo people used to make masks – to drive away spirits, to hide their identity when welcoming guests, and for ceremonies such as harvest festivities ● *48*.

**DOMESTIC UTENSILS**
All dishes, containers, baskets, mats, and winnowing trays used to be home-made and beautifully so. Rice mortars, weaving implements, sugar presses, decorative panels, and chiefs' seats – all were carved from wood.

**SWORD DECORATION**
The hilt of a kris is always carved, and some specialists still carve intricate hilts from deers' horns. In the past most men also decorated the sheath of their kris.

"THE GREAT MAJORITY OF MEN AND WOMEN ARE CAPABLE OF PRODUCING WORKS OF ART WITHOUT ANY TUITION OTHER THAN WATCHING THEIR ELDERS."

DR ANTON WILLEM NIEUWENHUIS, *QUER DURCH BORNEO*

**PROTECTIVE FIGURES**

Some longhouses have protective figures placed near the access path or at the face of the stairhead. These human figures were sometimes provided with exaggerated genital organs in the belief that evil spirits would be bewildered by the sight of such peculiar appendages.

**TATTOOS**

Some Orang Ulu women have lacy tattoos covering their legs and forearms, but few young girls now undergo this painful and time-consuming process. Iban men have distinctive throat tattoos and vivid body patterns. Tattoo designs are applied from transfers blacked with soot, then tapped into the skin with a needle.

**TINJAR CARVING**

The Berawans of he Tinjar River stand out among the many excellent craftsmen of the Baram catchment. Their craftwork ranges from dainty household utensils to memorial poles and decorated burial huts for the departed. One of their most important designs is the dragon or water spirit which figures among their mythical ancestors.

**MONUMENTS**

Today earth burials are common, but in the past the bodies of high-ranking people might be deposited in tomb-huts or tomb-pillars containing a slot in the side for the coffin ● *78*. Families were concerned that relatives should be worthily enshrined, and the best craftsmen were employed and generously paid to produce the monuments that still attract our admiration.

Chinese street theater is staged for the enjoyment of saints and deities on their feast days; human audiences are the happy beneficiaries of this entertainment. There is a good chance of catching performances in Chinese urban areas from August to September, during the Hungry Ghosts' Festival. The popularity of street theater declined with the advent of television, but has increased in recent years. Once again, the stage is populated with young stars in bright new costumes. A temporary stage, made of timber planks, bamboo poles, and cloth, is set up in an open space or public road. Chinese opera, puppet theater, and *godai* (musical variety shows) are staged over periods of two days to one week. The afternoon shows are half-heartedly performed, the actors saving their best for the packed audiences of the nightly galas.

**CHILD ACTOR**
Most opera troupes are based in the countryside, where seasonal employment is part of agricultural life. The opera scene is dominated by Teochew troupes from southern Thailand, where child actors are easily recruited.

**TUA HEE**
The grandest form of Chinese street theater is Chinese opera, also called *Tua Hee* (literally, big show) or *wayang*. The plays are excerpts from popular classics such as *The Romance of the Three Kingdoms* and *The Journey to the West*. The set of backdrops is adaptable to various scenarios. The actions are symbolic – a scissored kick means an entry or exit over the threshold – and the fighting is stylized.

**MUSIC**

The musicians are either middle-aged or elderly men, playing the *er-hu* (two-stringed violin), oboe, zither, mandolin, gongs, and cymbals. Following the plot closely, they are responsible for both dramatic music and sound effects.

**PUPPET THEATER**

Puppet shows are traditionally staged for certain deities, such as the Goddess of Mercy. *Por Tay Hee* Glove (puppet theater) originates from Quanzhou, a city in Fujian province. This form of theater derives from the tradition of the puppeteer traveling from village to village with a sack full of puppets. The sack was used as a backdrop, and is still employed today to cradle the puppets backstage.

**MAKEUP**

The actors are heavily made up, each mask-like face representing a character, whether a general, a magistrate, or a jester. Visitors are usually allowed backstage, where actors and actresses are always in the process of applying face paint, dressing up, or rehearsing.

**CHAKARE**

*Chakare* (stringed puppet theater) is usually Cantonese. The characters' faces are expressively sculpted and painted. As in Chinese opera, there are two basic hand positions, the mannered hand and the fighting fist. Instruments such as knives, fans, scrolls, and so forth may be inserted into the fighting hand.

**GODAI**

*Godai* is another form of street theater popularized in the 1950's in the "fun & frolic" arcades such as Great World Park in Singapore. *Godai* is part of the Hungry Ghosts' Festival celebration during the seventh lunar month. The variety show, with a mixture of singing and slapstick comedy, is popular with young people unfamiliar with the legends of traditional theater.

Some Chinese festivals in Malaysia still perpetuate forms already abandoned in their country of origin. Chinese festivals and street processions have taken on a uniquely Malaysian flavor. The most active state for Chinese festivals is Penang, where celebrations occur throughout the year, timed according to the Chinese lunar calendar. All can be witnessed in towns and villages wherever there is a sizable Chinese population. Key dates are the 1st and the 15th of each lunar month.

**CHINESE NEW YEAR**
During the Chinese New Year period, traditional Chinese businesses close for up to two weeks. Firecrackers, now banned, are still exploded. Family visits take place and red packets containing money are exchanged. Lion dances are performed in the streets to encourage auspicious beginnings, inaugurate a business, and start off the New Year. During the first few days of Chinese New Year, lion dance troupes dash noisily about town in lorries to their performance venues.

**CHINGAY PARADE**
The procession of Chingay, "the art of embellishment", originally featured intricately decorated floats. These days, the floats take second place to giant flags originally carried for religious festivals. Then come unicyclists, acrobats, lion dancers and their drummers, and the luminous dragon that weaves through the crowd. Masked clowns add to the carnival element. The Chingay Parade, held on Christmas Day, also includes school bands and cultural groups from non-Chinese communities.

**Festival of the Nine Emperor Gods**
The first nine days of the ninth lunar month mark the Taoist festival of the Nine Emperor Gods, who represent nine stars of a constellation. During this festival, mediums dressed in yellow, the color of the Nine Emperor Gods, undertake pain-defying feats.

**Hungry Ghosts' Festival**
During the seventh lunar month of the Hungry Ghosts, the Gates of Hell are opened and the spirits of the dead are let loose to roam among the living. The Chinese make offerings to the King of Hell, represented by a paper effigy, petitioning him to discipline his underworld subjects. Altars are decked with food offerings such as suckling pigs (bottom, right). The ritual ends with bonfires of giant joss sticks (right, below) and joss paper, and the offerings are distributed among the followers.

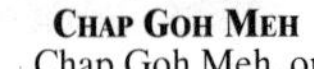

**Chap Goh Meh**
Chap Goh Meh, or the fifteenth night of Chinese New Year, is a romantic Straits Chinese tradition celebrated in Penang. At the Esplanade, young girls cast oranges into the sea, wishing for good husbands. This used to be the only time of the year when maidens were allowed out of the house, to be paraded around the Esplanade in trishaw, buggy, or car – for viewing by prospective wooers.

Bold Chinese characters appear on signboards, banners, and scrolls in the region's Chinatown districts. Traditionally, Chinese words were written in vertical columns, and read from top to bottom, right to left. However, many signs now read from left to right, especially when they occur in conjunction with Malay or English phrases. Individual Chinese characters have remained relatively unchanged through the centuries, with some ancient pictographs retaining both their original form and meaning until today.

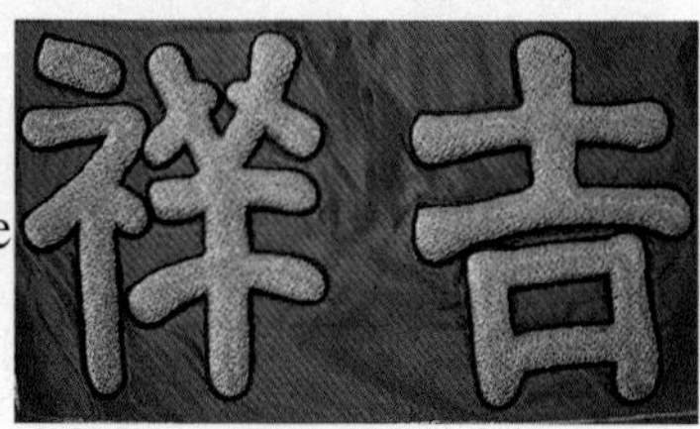


Two characters suggesting happiness embroidered in gold on a red silk banner.

This local vegetarian restaurant uses an ideogram meaning "to set in order" joined with one denoting "demonstration"; the whole character means "abstinence, fasting".

**Goodwill messages**
Brushed messages of goodwill are always written on red paper for sale to those who want passports to happiness, peace or wealth.

**The sign writer**
Itinerant letter and sign writers are now a vanishing breed. However, they still make an appearance at Lunar New Year, dispensing luck, prosperity, and all manner of good wishes. This man is writing the character *shen* (spirit) with a Chinese brush.

**Taoist charm**
This is a blanket charm to cover all types of misfortune. The elongated strokes of the swirling charm characters are intended to evoke the power and force of lightning. Written by a diviner or priest, these charms are burnt and their ashes consumed after mixing with water.

**Characters from a child's copybook**
These two characters, from a beginner's copybook, meaning "grass" (right) and "tea" have the "grass" radical at the top. Small numbers within the outlines of the characters indicate the order of strokes for writing each character.

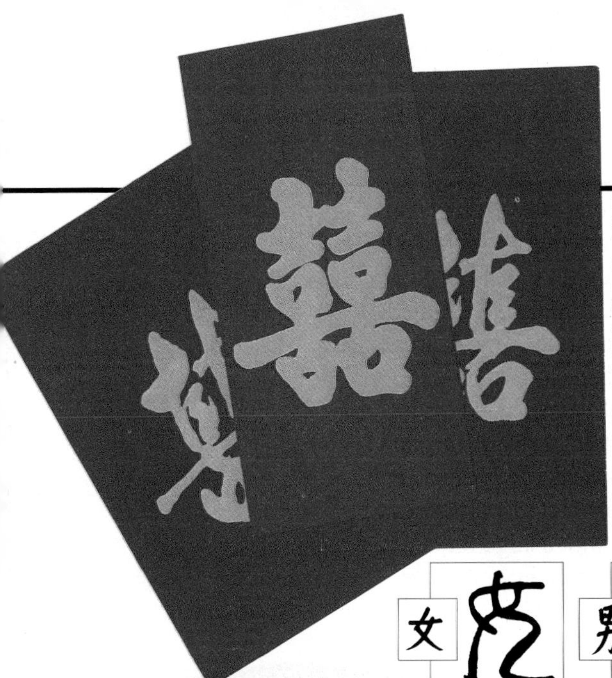

**Double happiness**

The ideograph for "happiness" is repeated to suggest a double amount of joy at marriage. Red envelopes with the *shuangxi* or double-happiness symbol contain presents of money for the Chinese bride and groom.

女

The ancient pictograph of a woman suggests a passive posture.

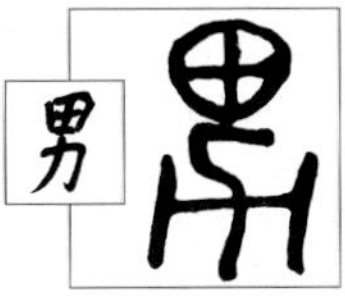

男

The ancient pictograph of a man symbolizes work in the fields.

**Restroom signs**

These signs provide direction to the "Ladies" (left) and the "Gents" (right) in a Singapore entertainment complex.

**Chess pieces**

Pieces from a modern set of Chinese chess show the character for "carriage". It is a stylized version of the ancient pictograph that depicted the body, wheels and axle from above.

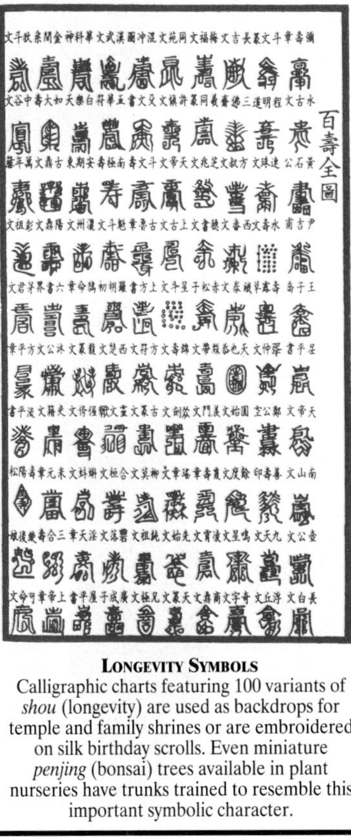

百壽全圖

**Longevity Symbols**

Calligraphic charts featuring 100 variants of *shou* (longevity) are used as backdrops for temple and family shrines or are embroidered on silk birthday scrolls. Even miniature *penjing* (bonsai) trees available in plant nurseries have trunks trained to resemble this important symbolic character.

**South**

The character for "south" often appears in the names of local Chinese establishments, because the popular Chinese term for Southeast Asia is Nanyang or "South Seas".

Dance is a sacred art that has been cherished and preserved in India for over two thousand years. Classical Indian dance grew out of temple rituals and devotions. In Singapore and Malaysia Indian emigrants – mainly from the south of India – introduced a number of dance forms, principally *Bharata Natyam*, *Kathak*, and *Odissi*. Regular performances of these can be seen in cities with a large Indian community, especially Singapore, Kuala Lumpur, and Penang.

**BHARATA NATYAM**
*Bharata Natyam* is firmly rooted in Hinduism and expresses religious themes and devotions. One of the six main dance forms from India, it originated in Tamil Nadu, was first performed by female temple dancers, and was not seen on stage until the 1930's. Characteristic is a variety of movements with emphasis on striking the floor with the feet, jumping and turning, with mime, including hand gestures (*abhinaya*), being used to tell the story.

**ABHINAYA**
The individual finger gestures in *Bharata Natyam* are called *hasta*, a codified language of gestures explained in the *Abhinaya Darpanam*. The gesture shown here depicts the great feet of Krishna as he lifts the lofty mountain peak to shelter his beloved devotees from a huge storm.

**ODISSI**
The classical dance form of *Odissi* evolved in the ambience of the temple. It is a lyrical style of dance with close replication of the poses found on classical temple sculptures. It is predominantly a dance form for women.

**KATHAK**
*Kathak* dance originated in northern India and evolved from the fusion of Hindu and Muslim cultures. A Mughal-style costume is often worn. The dance form is not particularly associated with temple rituals and is performed by both male and female dancers. Technique is less rigid than in *Bharata Natyam*, taking movements from life, stylizing them and adding complex rhythmic movements.

**Indian dancer**
This painting from the Victoria and Albert Museum in London illustrates a *Bharata Natyam* dancer in striking pose wearing the traditional costume. Behind her stand six musicians, each playing a different instrument. The two men playing the cymbals are *nattuvanar*, lead singers. The women at the rear of the procession act as relief dancers, taking the place of the principal dancer when she becomes tired.

**Mridanga**
The *mridanga* is a traditional Indian drum made of a wooden cylinder with leather-covered ends. The strings passing between the two sides control the tonal quality of the sound of the drum. This instrument is considered a very important component of the orchestra.

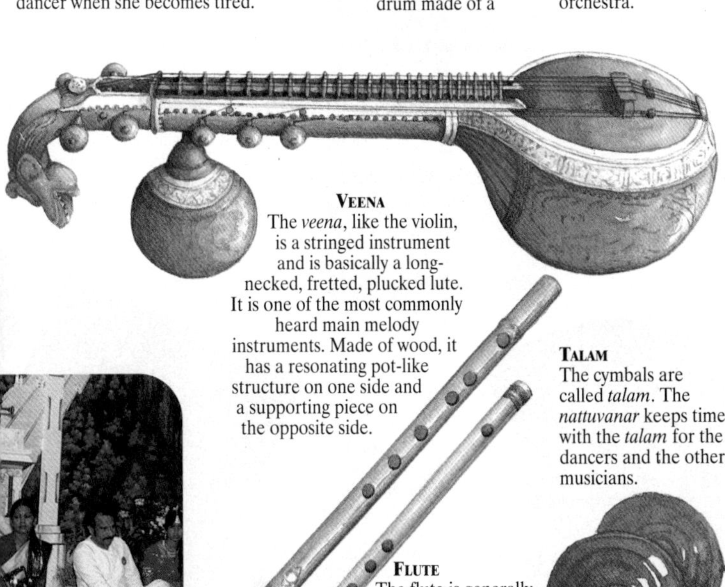

**Veena**
The *veena*, like the violin, is a stringed instrument and is basically a long-necked, fretted, plucked lute. It is one of the most commonly heard main melody instruments. Made of wood, it has a resonating pot-like structure on one side and a supporting piece on the opposite side.

**Talam**
The cymbals are called *talam*. The *nattuvanar* keeps time with the *talam* for the dancers and the other musicians.

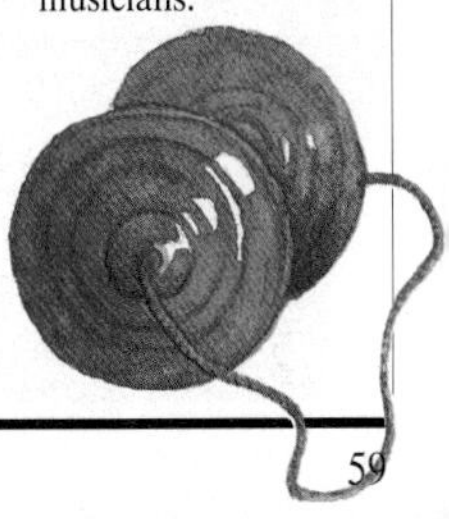

**Flute**
The flute is generally made of bamboo and produces a sweet sound when played by an experienced flautist.

Malaysia's multi-racial composition is reflected in the diversity of costumes of its various ethnic groups. (Apart from the three major urban ethnic groups of Peninsular Malaysia, the Malays, Chinese, and Indians, East Malaysia alone contains no less than sixty tribal groups.) Many garments are simply pieces of cloth folded, wrapped and draped about the body. Tribal groups still wear home-woven fabrics, and some remote tribes still use vegetable dyes for the yarn. Mechanical looms, however, are common in easily accessible villages. The wrap-around skirt, called sarong when sewn into a tube, is universal. Tailored costumes generally reflect foreign influences.

**KENYAH WEAR**
The simplest blouse or jacket (below) is made by folding a rectangle of cloth with a hole or slit for the head. Kenyah men wear such jackets made of bark over their loincloths. The bark is dyed and decorated with designs similar to those on their bodies. The ends of the loincloth drape down to the knees, front and back.

**TRADITIONAL MALAY MALE ATTIRE**
Traditional male attire consists of a wrap-around skirt. The ends of a two-yard-long cloth are sewn together to form a cylinder, a sarong, into which the wearer steps, or are left as a rectangle called *kain lepas*.

**PLAID CLOTH**
Cotton sarongs for men have plaid patterns. The skirt can be worn knee or ankle length. An ensemble requires two more pieces: one, a sash tied around the waist to hold a kris (dagger), is worn with one end hung over the right shoulder; the other piece forms a head-cloth.

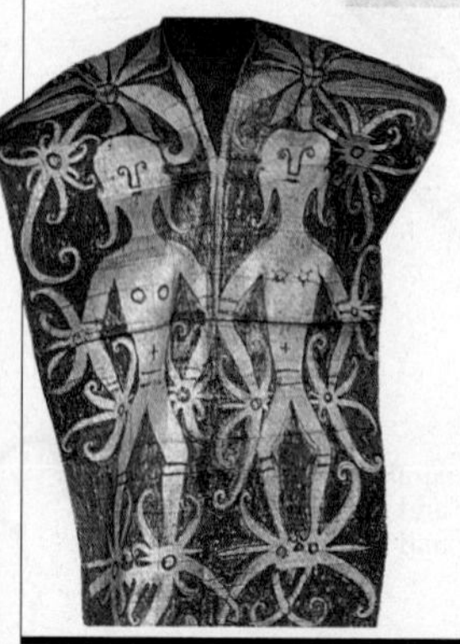

**CLOTHES OF THE RUNGUS**
The untailored clothes of the Rungus of Sabah are made from rectangular 18-inch-wide woven indigo-dyed cotton decorated with bands of zig-zag and other geometric patterns, inspired by the local flora and fauna and by dreams. Such cloths are worn as a wrap-around skirt, breast cloth, or shawl.

> "A good deal of discomfort was obviated by my wearing Malay dress."
>
> Margaret Brooke, *My Life in Sarawak*

**Baju kurung**

The *baju kurung* is "the dress that confines". This tunic, with a slit at the neck, is pulled over the head like a jersey. Such tailored garments became fashionable in the late 19th century. The *kurung* and its variants are worn by both Malay men and women. Women wear the *kurung* with the sarong.

**Tradtional Malay female attire**

Malay women used to wear the *kemban*, a breast or bodice cloth cinched at the waist with a belt which also secured the skirt. The bare shoulders were draped with a stole.

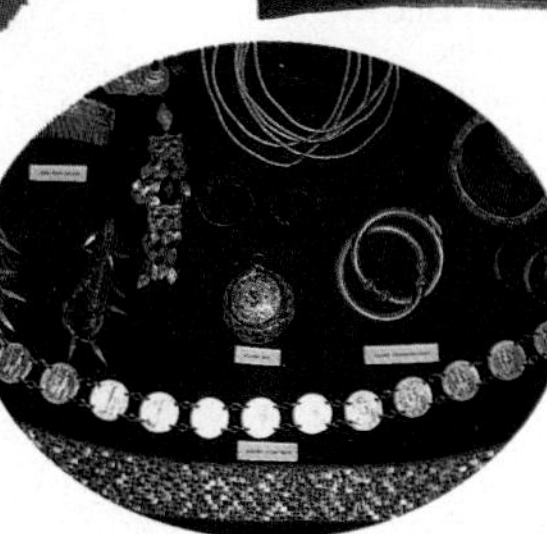

**Iban dress**

The basic garment of the Iban women of Sarawak is the *bidang*, a short tubular skirt made from two lengths of woven cloth. Apart from a sash belt, a girdle adorns the midriff and consists of a series of rattan hoops. The breast cloth, instead of being worn horizontally, is placed criss-cross over the shoulders. Numerous silver ornaments complete the Iban style.

**Rungus colored beads**

The designs appear on headgear, scarves, and baskets. Colored beads are the main form of Rungus accessory.

No fruit in all of Asia provokes such strong reactions as the durian. To some, it's the "King of Fruits"; for others, it's just "Yuk!" True addicts often go on special overnight "pig-out" excursions to Malaysian durian orchards. Novelist Anthony Burgess is not among them. In his novel *Time for a Tiger* he describes the durian as "like eating a sweet raspberry blancmange in a lavatory". Clearly the durian is no ordinary fruit, not like rock melon or even kiwifruit, which taste pleasant and do not provoke violent reactions. People do not remain indifferent to the durian – mainly because of its truly astonishing smell.

**THE DURIAN**
It is usually about the same size as a big pineapple, it's hard and menacingly prickly (a memorable Singapore newspaper headline read: "Man Uses Durian To Threaten Cop"). It tastes creamy and rich, and it is high in protein, calories, fiber, and vitamins A and C.

**THE DURIAN SEASON**
Durians are grown mainly in Malaysia and Thailand (home of some monsters – Thai durians can weigh 26 lb and sell for US$100 each). They are also grown these days in Australia's Northern Territory. In Southeast Asia, durian high seasons come twice a year (roughly, June/July and November/ December). The durian must fall naturally from its tree and then be eaten within five days.

**FOLK TALES**
Such a remarkable fruit comes, naturally, with many tales attached. In Malaysia they say that "When the durians come down, the sarongs go up." An unofficial survey conducted among durian-eaters in Penang revealed a definite upwards jump in the monthly birth statistics – nine months after both durian seasons. The durian can be sampled in other milder forms, such as ice cream and milk shake.

The pungent smell means that the durian stays banned from Singapore's swish MRT, regional airlines, and many hotels.

**RAFFLES AND THE DURIAN**
Those new to the durian (*Durio zibethinus*) should give it a try. But if they really cannot take this "King of Fruits", they are in famous company: even Singapore's illustrious founder Stamford Raffles could not, either. His faithful chronicler Munshi Abdullah recorded an incident in 1819: "…as soon as Mr Raffles caught the smell of the durians, he held his nose and ran upstairs.… 'The smell of these durians has given me a headache!' From then on, no one dared to bring him any more durians."

**DURIAN SELLERS**
During its two short seasons, durian stalls appear along rural Malaysian roads and on the city streets of Singapore. Discerning durian buyers first check that its thorns are firm and resilient to the touch, then that its controversial smell is "fresh"– the sound of loose seeds rattling within indicates ripeness. No sound suggests it is "too old", not yet ready, or, worse still, has been taken off its tree before falling of its own accord – a heinous crime in the durian world.

Street food is an integral part of the Malaysian and Singaporean experience. Hawkers provide freshly cooked food around the clock, at budget prices. In pre-war days, itinerant push-cart hawkers catered for every type of food, each signaling his presence with a unique call. Many hawkers in Malaysia still use push-carts, but those assembled around coffee shops and hawker centers offer a larger choice of dishes.

**LAKSA**
Rice noodles, mackerel, shrimp paste, tamarind, pineapple, ginger flowers, and mint are just some of the ingredients that go into *laksa*, a sweet, sour, and savory concoction that originates from Thailand. It is a classic dish of *nyonya* cooking, a local variation of Chinese and Malay food.

**SATAY**
The region's most famous dish is perhaps *satay*. Meat is seasoned in turmeric and coconut milk, skewered and grilled over a charcoal fire. On the right is an itinerant *satay* man of yesteryear.

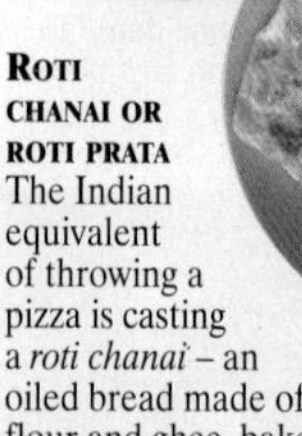

**ROTI CHANAI OR ROTI PRATA**
The Indian equivalent of throwing a pizza is casting a *roti chanai* – an oiled bread made of plain wheat flour and ghee, baked on a flat hotplate.

**ICE KACANG (BEAN ICE-CREAM)**
Some say that finding red beans under a mountain of shaved ice is like finding vegetables in a desert – although in the case of *ice kacang* the tastes blends well. Other ingredients are jelly seaweed, sago, and sweet corn.

**ROJAK**
A typically local dish is *rojak*, which is sold by the Indians, as well as the Chinese. The Indian *rojak* (left) has potato, egg, bean curd, prawn fritters, and squid cut into slices and dipped in gravy prepared from peanuts, sugar, and starch. The word *rojak* has come to mean a hodgepodge.

**WON TON MEE**
*Won ton mee*, that is, noodle soup with meat dumplings, used to be sold by a peddler who went around clacking his chopsticks on a hollow box – thus another name for this dish is *tock tock mee*.

**KELINGA MEE**
Another hybrid food is *kelinga mee* – Chinese noodles and seafood fried with an Indian sauce made from sweet potatoes and tamarind. This dish, originally sold by hawkers along the Penang waterfront, was a favorite among stevedores and sailors.

**TRADITIONAL CAKES**
Many varieties of Malay cakes and *nyonya kueh* are sold at stalls in coffee shops or at hawker centers. Local Indian cakes and cookies are peddled by itinerant hawkers who carry large trays above their heads. These peddlers are a rare sight nowadays in city streets. Wholesome ingredients such as tapioca flour, glutinous rice, mung bean flour, palm sugar, coconut milk, and vegetable dyes from flowers and pandan leaves are used.

**CHINESE BISCUITS**
Chinese biscuits sold in bakeries and stalls are traditionally small pastries filled with thick pastes made from such ingredients as lotus seeds and red beans. These biscuits can either be sweet or savory.

**NASI KANDAR**
Rice and spicy curries were once carried in trays suspended from the shoulder yokes of itinerant hawkers – hence the name *nasi kandar* (yoke rice). The food is sold today at roadside stalls and from push-carts, but its traditional name remains.

**BAK KUT TEH**
Pork rib herbal soup is thought to be good for the constitution. It is served by itself, or with yam rice and vegetables (*chai buay*). *Bak kut teh* stalls open for breakfast or supper.

The typical Chinese coffee shop or *kopi tiam* developed as an urban phenomenon in the early 20th century. It is thought that Hainanese migrants first acquired a taste for this foreign drink while working as housekeepers in the service of Europeans, a job in which their group had specialized. Subsequently, with the growth of the local economy, they opened their own food and beverage businesses, introducing both the drink and its name (which by then had become *kopi*) to the local population.

**SIMPLE PLEASURE**
The coffee shop is an important aspect of social life in Singapore, especially among those who enjoy sipping coffee and watching the world go by.

**A LIVING LEGACY**
The Singapore Foochow Coffee Restaurant and Bar Merchants' Association was formed in 1920, while the Keng Keow (or Hainanese) Coffee Merchants' and Bar Owners' Association was first registered in 1934. A number of the coffee shops in the city are very old. Although the original furniture may have been removed, the coffee shop still plays its role in daily life, as this photograph clearly shows.

**FURNITURE**
Marble-topped wooden tables and black chairs from coffee shops now fetch high prices in antique shops and have become almost a must buy for foreign residents. The chairs were imported from Poland and Czechoslovakia, while the tables, often made of teak, were produced locally in a British-influenced style, combined with a local *savoir-faire* that imparts a unique charm.

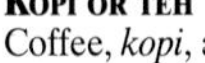

**KOPI OR TEH**

Coffee, *kopi*, and tea, *teh*, served by the cup in coffee shops are often too sweet for Western tastes; sugar and condensed milk are both used as sweeteners, usually in large amounts. *Kopi* is coffee with milk and sugar, *kopi o* is black coffee with sugar, and *kopi kosong* means coffee without milk or sugar.

**CUSTOMARY PRACTICE**

Coffee and tea are usually served very hot. To cool down their drinks quickly, some customers pour the drink into the saucer and then drink from it, as seen in this painting by Ma Geylang.

**THE STOVE**

The essential part of the coffee-shop kitchen is the stove, where water is kept at near boiling temperature. Coffee-shop owners also pride themselves on roasting their own coffee. The old recipe in which coffee powder is mixed with a little margarine is still widely used, giving local coffee a special taste. Coffee is brewed using a sock through which the liquid is poured a few times before being served in the cup.

# Roti prata

Roti prata is a common dish found throughout Malaysia and Singapore. The prata is basically an unleavened bread which has its origins in Indian cuisine. Roti prata is traditionally served in coffee shops and wayside eateries. Although the cook may begin by rolling the dough out on a flat surface, it is common to see it being twirled in the air in the process of thinning and stretching it.

**Preparation**

**1.** Sift the flour. Mix flour, salt, and sugar together. Add the condensed milk and water and knead well.

**2.** Oil hands and make small balls. Coat the balls of dough with oil. Leave in a warm place for two to six hours. Keep covered.

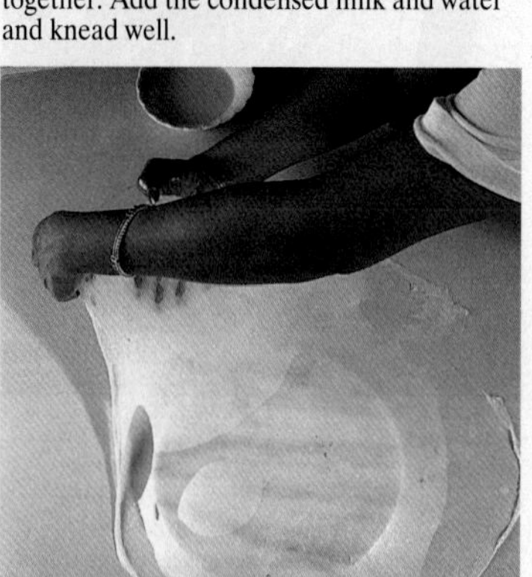

**5.** Oil the top of a table or pastry board and the rolling pin. Gently roll out the dough, stretching it until it is very thin. The rolled dough can contain holes.

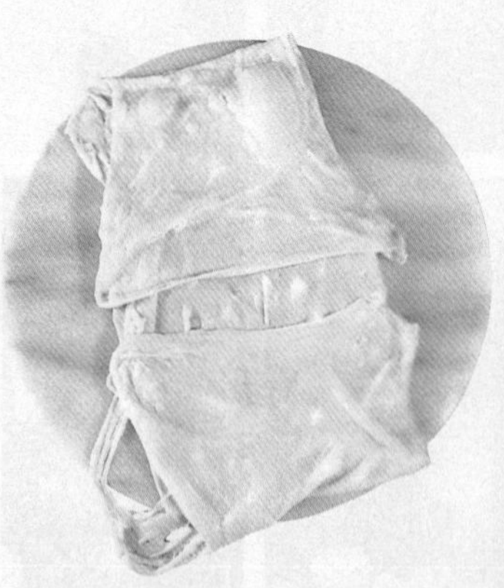

**6.** Add the beaten egg and sprinkle with chopped onions. Fold up the prata.

An Indian hawker waits for customers to buy his bread and cakes.

**INGREDIENTS**

**Roti Prata**

1 lb plain flour
$^{1}/_{2}$ tablespoon salt
1 tablespoon sugar
1 tablespoon condensed milk
9 fl oz water
$2^{1}/_{2}$ fl oz vegetable oil
1 egg beaten
1 onion finely chopped

**Vegetable curry**

$2^{1}/_{2}$ fl oz vegetable oil
1 cinnamon stick
2 cardamom pods
4 cloves of garlic crushed
2 teaspoons puréed ginger
1 onion chopped
1 teaspoon salt
1 sprig mint
3 tomatoes quartered
2 teaspoons garam masala
1 teaspoon chili powder
1 teaspoon turmeric
9 fl oz water
1 lb potatoes boiled, chopped

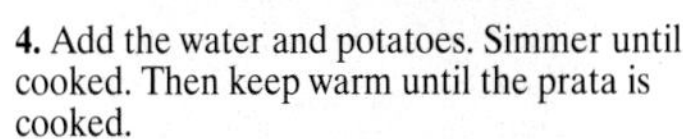

**3.** To prepare the vegetable curry, heat the oil in a pan and add the cinnamon and cardamom. Cook for 2 minutes. Add the garlic, ginger, onion, salt, mint, and tomatoes and cook for 2 minutes. Then stir in the garam masala, chili powder, and turmeric.

**4.** Add the water and potatoes. Simmer until cooked. Then keep warm until the prata is cooked.

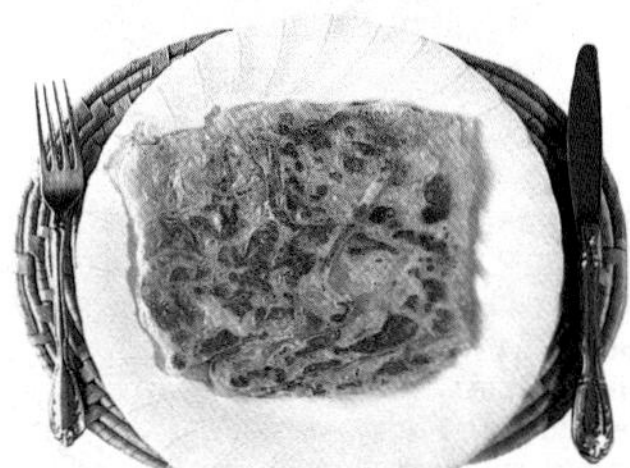

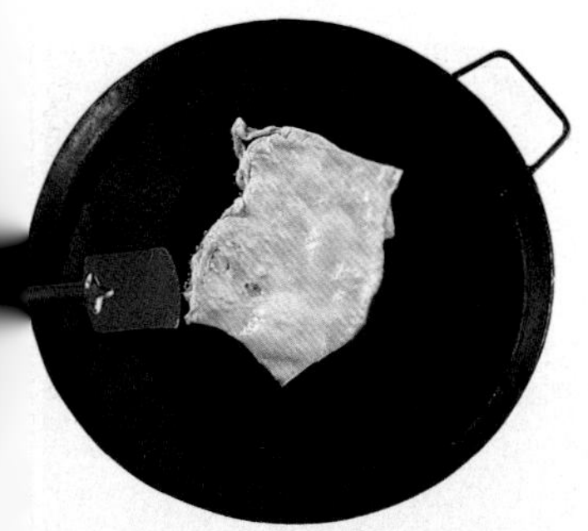

**7.** Heat some oil in a flat, shallow pan or griddle and fry the prata until golden brown.

**8.** Serve the prata and vegetable curry.

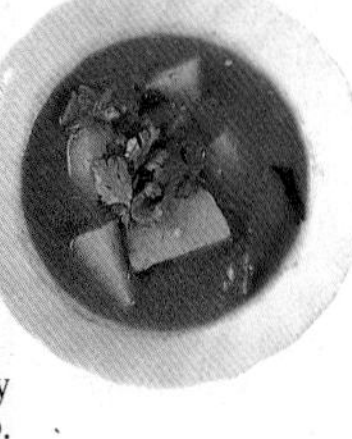

Roti prata can be eaten plain, with a filling, as here, and with a curry sauce or dhal. The curry sauces vary: some contain only vegetables, others include meat, usually minced beef or lamb.

# Songbirds

The keeping and rearing of songbirds is a popular pastime in both Malaysia and Singapore. Bird-singing competitions are big business and prized singers often change hands for thousands of dollars. In Malaysia, the sport is most popular in Kelantan, although contests are also held in the other states. In Singapore, some coffee-shop owners have installed trellises where customers' bird-cages can be hung.

**Magpie robin**
The black-and-white magpie robin is a popular songbird in Singapore, its voice a clear strong whistle.

**Merbuk**
The merbuk (peaceful dove) is the most popular songbird in Peninsular Malaysia. During competitions, their cages are suspended from 26-foot-high poles as the birds are at their most relaxed at this height. The merbuk song is a series of rolling "coos".

**Bird cages**
Trained songbirds live in beautifully crafted bird cages made of split bamboo. Each species has a different cage design that takes its habits into account. The merbuk has a large rounded cage, enabling it to move freely; the bulbul's is square with a high pointed roof, as the bird is very agile. Magpie robins and sharmas have bell-shaped cages, often with a double gate. Kelantanese wood-carvers are famed for their exquisite wooden decorations.

**Bird-singing contests**
Contests take place regularly, for instance on the outskirts of Kota Bharu on Friday mornings, where up to three hundred birds take part, and on Sunday mornings at the Wah Heng coffee shop in Tiong Bahru, Singapore. The judges take account of loudness, length of song, melody, and the bird's physical condition and posture.

# Architecture

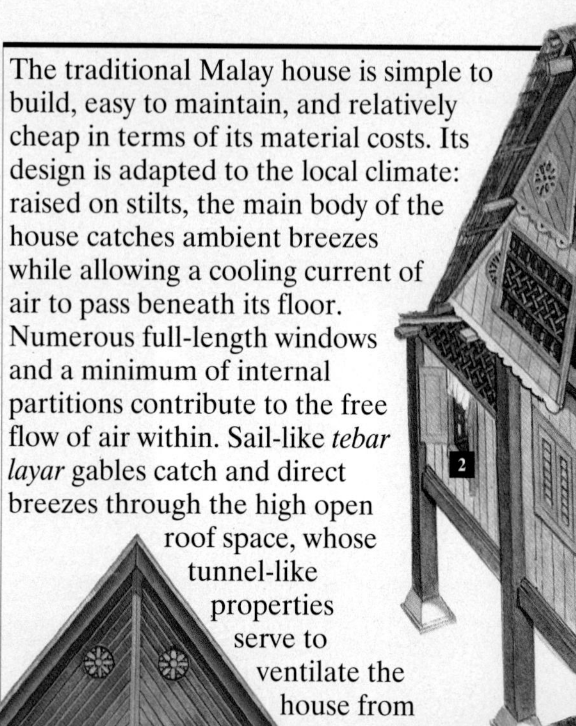


The traditional Malay house is simple to build, easy to maintain, and relatively cheap in terms of its material costs. Its design is adapted to the local climate: raised on stilts, the main body of the house catches ambient breezes while allowing a cooling current of air to pass beneath its floor. Numerous full-length windows and a minimum of internal partitions contribute to the free flow of air within. Sail-like *tebar layar* gables catch and direct breezes through the high open roof space, whose tunnel-like properties serve to ventilate the house from above.

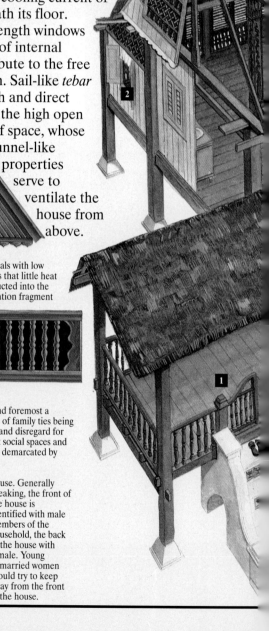

**VENTILATION**

The use of building materials with low thermal properties ensures that little heat is retained within or conducted into the house. Grilles and fenestration fragment the sunlight entering the house, providing illumination but reducing the intensity of the sun's rays.

**FAMILY HOME**

The Malay house is first and foremost a family home, the closeness of family ties being reflected in the open plan and disregard for personal privacy. Different social spaces and areas of activity are clearly demarcated by changing floor levels.

**SEGREGATION**

An important aspect of Malay social life is the separation of men from women in all formal social interactions in accordance with Islamic precepts. This division of male and female finds its expression within the house. Generally speaking, the front of the house is identified with male members of the household, the back of the house with female. Young unmarried women should try to keep away from the front of the house.

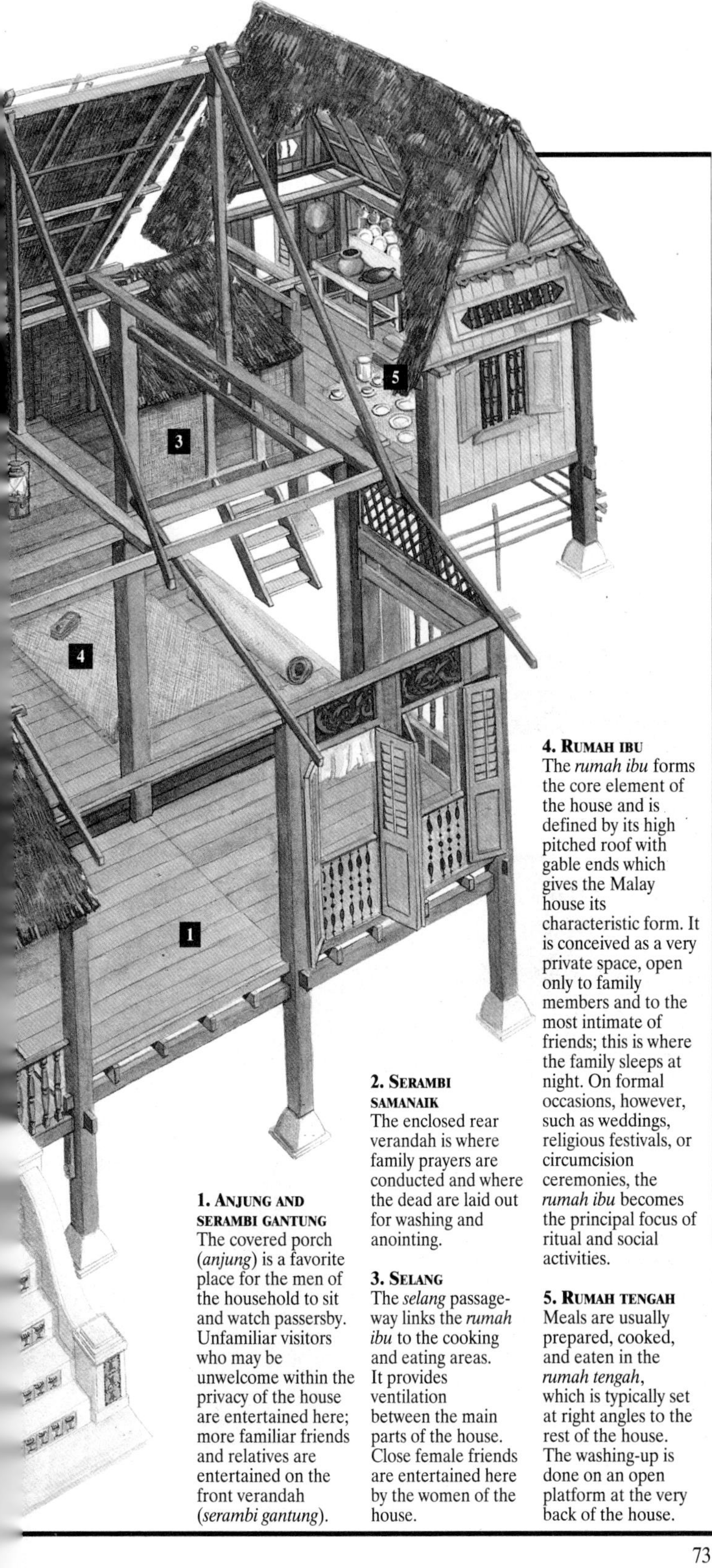


**1. Anjung and serambi gantung**
The covered porch (*anjung*) is a favorite place for the men of the household to sit and watch passersby. Unfamiliar visitors who may be unwelcome within the privacy of the house are entertained here; more familiar friends and relatives are entertained on the front verandah (*serambi gantung*).

**2. Serambi samanaik**
The enclosed rear verandah is where family prayers are conducted and where the dead are laid out for washing and anointing.

**3. Selang**
The *selang* passageway links the *rumah ibu* to the cooking and eating areas. It provides ventilation between the main parts of the house. Close female friends are entertained here by the women of the house.

**4. Rumah ibu**
The *rumah ibu* forms the core element of the house and is defined by its high pitched roof with gable ends which gives the Malay house its characteristic form. It is conceived as a very private space, open only to family members and to the most intimate of friends; this is where the family sleeps at night. On formal occasions, however, such as weddings, religious festivals, or circumcision ceremonies, the *rumah ibu* becomes the principal focus of ritual and social activities.

**5. Rumah tengah**
Meals are usually prepared, cooked, and eaten in the *rumah tengah*, which is typically set at right angles to the rest of the house. The washing-up is done on an open platform at the very back of the house.

Traditional Malay architecture is modular in conception, with extensions being added in response to increasing family size and prosperity. House additions vary regionally, but the core element everywhere is the *rumah ibu* – a simple rectangular structure under a pitched roof with gabled ends. To this may be added a front "hanging" verandah (*serambi gantung*) with full-length windows, and an enclosed rear verandah (*serambi samanaik*). This basic house form predominates in the northern states of Perak, Perlis, Kedah, and Penang.

**GAJAH MENYUSU**
So called because of its resemblance to a suckling elephant (*gajah* – elephant; *menyusu* – to suckle), this is the simplest and most effective way of extending the elementary house form. The main entrance is formalized with the addition of a porch (*anjung*). This type of extension is most commonly found in the northern states of the west coast.

**MELAKAN COURTYARD HOUSE**
Found only in the state of Melaka, courtyard houses such as the one on the right evince several architectural influences: Portugese, Dutch, British, and Chinese. Masonry walls fill the space between traditional structures to form an intimate paved internal courtyard; pantiles are frequently used for roofs. Melakan houses are often elaborately ornamented with Victorian tiles, galvanized-iron roof ridges, and Gothic-inspired filials; glazed Chinese air bricks ventilate the courtyard.

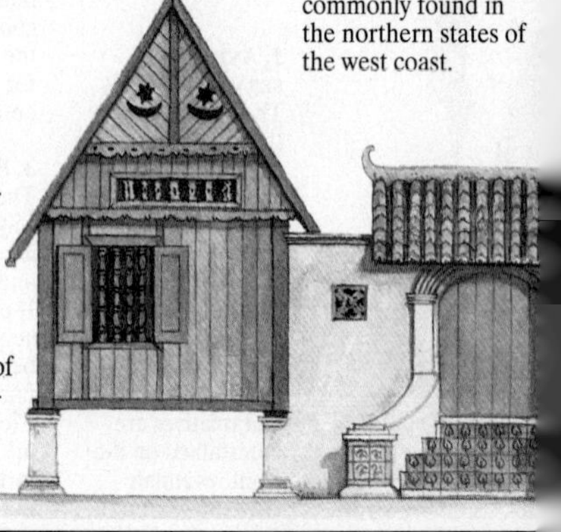

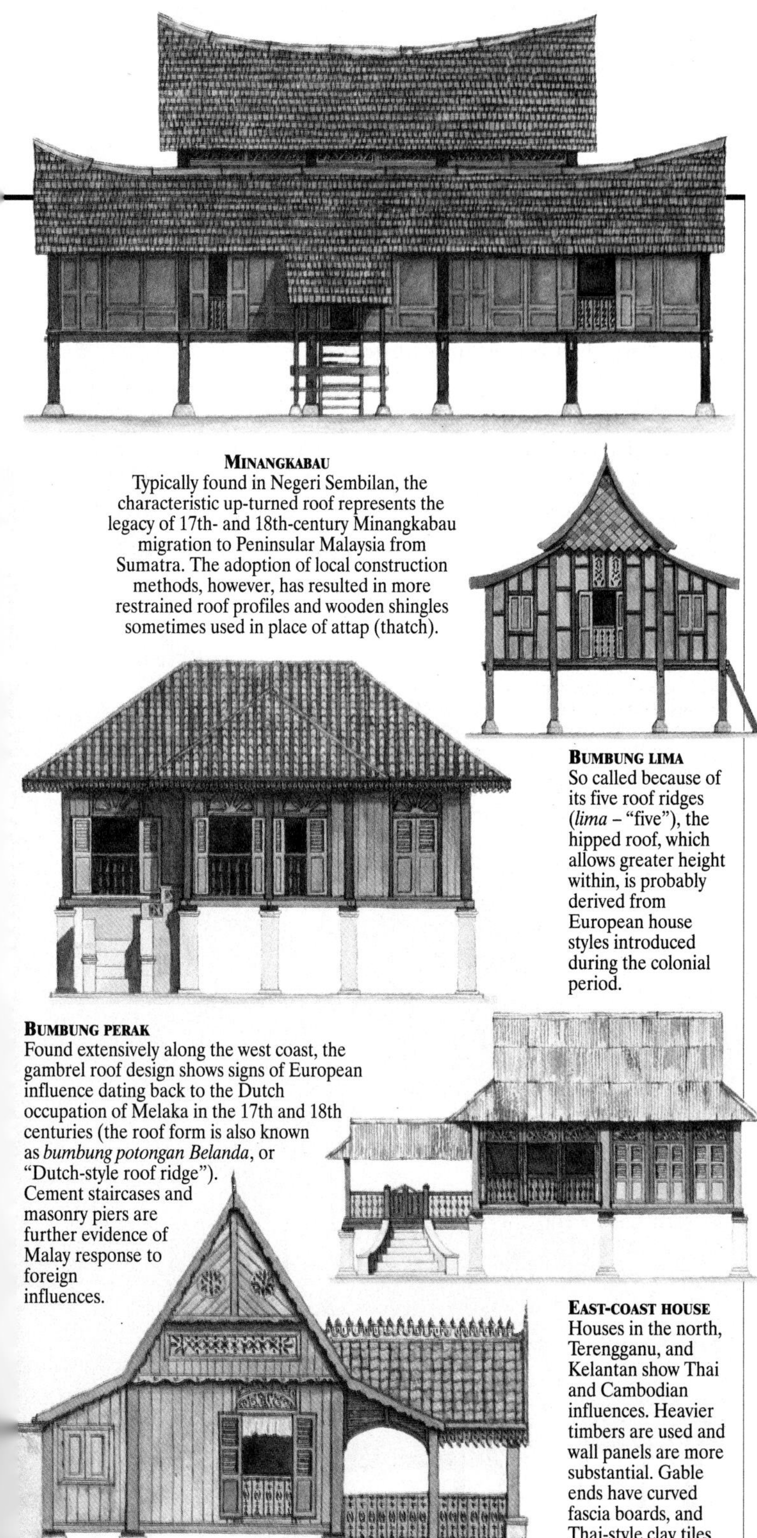

**Minangkabau**
Typically found in Negeri Sembilan, the characteristic up-turned roof represents the legacy of 17th- and 18th-century Minangkabau migration to Peninsular Malaysia from Sumatra. The adoption of local construction methods, however, has resulted in more restrained roof profiles and wooden shingles sometimes used in place of attap (thatch).

**Bumbung lima**
So called because of its five roof ridges (*lima* – "five"), the hipped roof, which allows greater height within, is probably derived from European house styles introduced during the colonial period.

**Bumbung perak**
Found extensively along the west coast, the gambrel roof design shows signs of European influence dating back to the Dutch occupation of Melaka in the 17th and 18th centuries (the roof form is also known as *bumbung potongan Belanda*, or "Dutch-style roof ridge"). Cement staircases and masonry piers are further evidence of Malay response to foreign influences.

**East-coast house**
Houses in the north, Terengganu, and Kelantan show Thai and Cambodian influences. Heavier timbers are used and wall panels are more substantial. Gable ends have curved fascia boards, and Thai-style clay tiles are used for the roof.

Native Bornean society is typified by the longhouse community, made up of autonomous, though interrelated, family units. Each family occupies a separate apartment with independent domestic arrangements, joined together under one roof. The longhouse is raised on piles some 10 to 20 feet from the ground, with a notched log providing access. A notable feature of the longhouse is the covered gallery or verandah running the full length of the building. This provides an important public space for social activities and ritual performances.

**LONGHOUSE TYPES**
Differences in construction reflect different lifestyles: Iban longhouses are generally lightweight, signaling a high degree of physical mobility; Kayan and Kenyah longhouses on the other hand are more monumental in their construction – their occupants have tended to settle in one place for several decades.

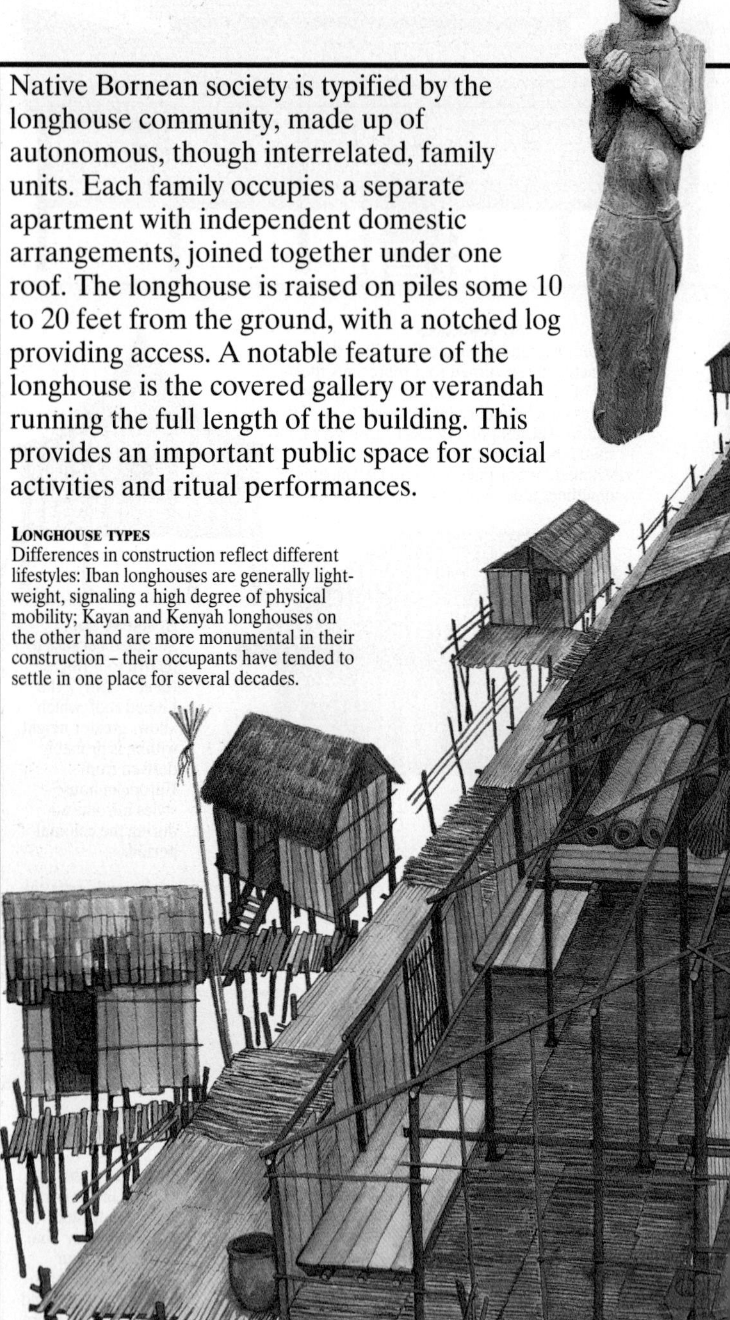

Longhouse at Kanowit, Sarawak.

**Longhouse community**
Longhouse living extends beyond merely practical considerations; it reflects a social philosophy. People live in longhouses because they like to: life in the hereafter is perceived as in a longhouse, perpetually at play, with much feasting, cockfighting, and consumption of alcohol. Though the longhouse offers little in the way of privacy, occupants need never be lonely. Besides, there is always someone in the house to look after the children, the elderly, and the sick.

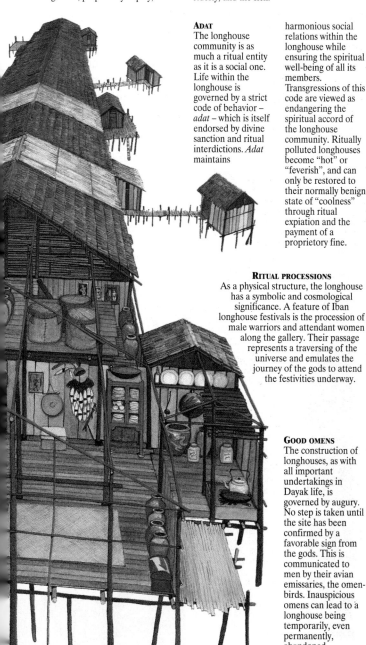

**Adat**
The longhouse community is as much a ritual entity as it is a social one. Life within the longhouse is governed by a strict code of behavior – *adat* – which is itself endorsed by divine sanction and ritual interdictions. *Adat* maintains harmonious social relations within the longhouse while ensuring the spiritual well-being of all its members. Transgressions of this code are viewed as endangering the spiritual accord of the longhouse community. Ritually polluted longhouses become "hot" or "feverish", and can only be restored to their normally benign state of "coolness" through ritual expiation and the payment of a proprietory fine.

**Ritual processions**
As a physical structure, the longhouse has a symbolic and cosmological significance. A feature of Iban longhouse festivals is the procession of male warriors and attendant women along the gallery. Their passage represents a traversing of the universe and emulates the journey of the gods to attend the festivities underway.

**Good omens**
The construction of longhouses, as with all important undertakings in Dayak life, is governed by augury. No step is taken until the site has been confirmed by a favorable sign from the gods. This is communicated to men by their avian emissaries, the omen-birds. Inauspicious omens can lead to a longhouse being temporarily, even permanently, abandoned.

The tribal people of Sarawak have elaborate mortuary rites, including the erection of large-scale memorial structures to house the remains of the dead. Graveyards are sited some distance away from the longhouse. Two characteristic burial structures are the commemorative column (variously known as the *lijeng*, *kelirieng*, *jumuh*, and *jerunan*) and the elevated mausoleum or *salong*, raised on one or more posts. The former tend to commemorate individuals and once erected remain undisturbed, whereas the latter constitute family burial vaults and contain the remains of several related persons.

**KELABIT MEGALITHS**

Kelabit megaliths come in a number of forms; single or paired menhirs, dolmens, stone vats, burial grottos, slab graves, stone seats, and bridges. Paired menhirs are the most common form, consisting of unworked stone pillars, typically about 4 feet high and regular in section. Sometimes they are crudely incised with the outlines of dragon-like creatures, tiger-cats, snakes and spread-eagled human forms. Alternatively they may be decorated with abstract spirals and whorls.

**SARIBAS IBAN SUNGKUP**

The Iban of the Saribas region commemorate their dead with miniature houses or *sungkup* erected over the grave of the deceased. At the death celebration, bamboo containers of rice wine are hung about the *sungkup* and their contents drunk by leading members of the longhouse community in a sacred symposium with the dead.

**BEREWAN LIJENG**

The Berewan *lijeng* is 15–35 feet high by 2–4 feet in diameter and takes several months to carve. The body of the deceased is allowed to decompose, then the bones are washed and placed in a Chinese jar. This is inserted in a niche carved out near the top. Once sealed, the *lijeng* is never tampered with again. It is usually carved out of very heavy ironwood from trees felled as close to the burial site as possible.

**ERECTION OF THE LIJENG**

A ditch is dug halfway along the length of the column and the *lijeng* seesawed into position. Parallel bars inclined at 30° are erected on either side and the *lijeng* levered upright, using the parallel bars as a fulcrum. Once the *lijeng* has reached an inclination of 45°, hawsers, woven from rattan, are used to haul it into a vertical position. This requires about a dozen men.

**Kayan and Kenyah salong**

Among the Kayan and Kenyah strict rules relating to the social status of the deceased govern the design and decoration of *salong*. The mausoleums of aristocrats are the most elaborate, with as many as nine supporting pillars and baroque carvings representing sacred dragon-like serpents (*naga*) adorning the roof. Formerly the *salong* of great chiefs were hung with the heads of enemies, and slaves were sacrificed to accompany the deceased into the after-life.

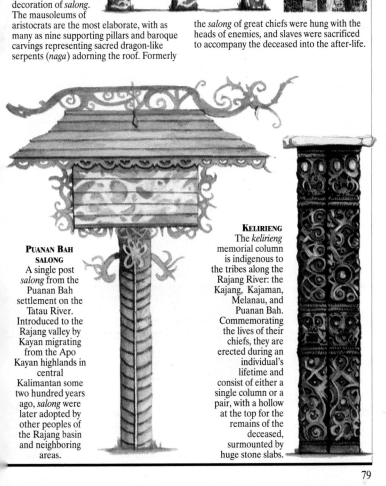

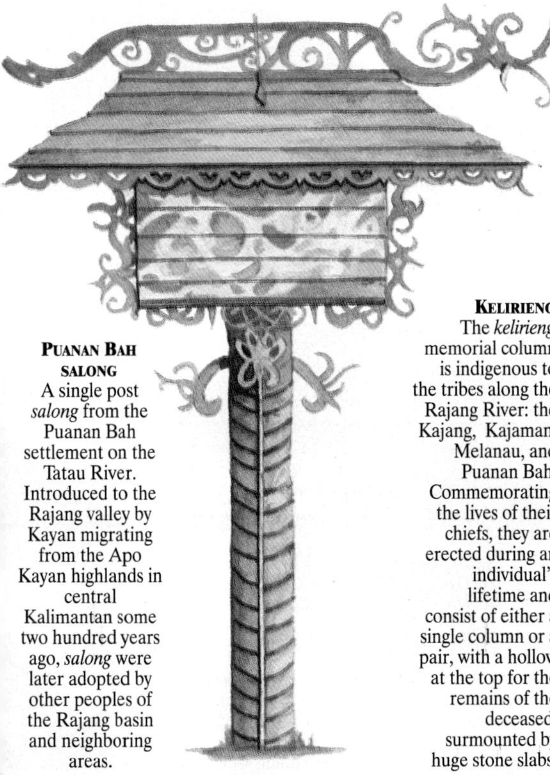

**Puanan Bah salong**

A single post *salong* from the Puanan Bah settlement on the Tatau River. Introduced to the Rajang valley by Kayan migrating from the Apo Kayan highlands in central Kalimantan some two hundred years ago, *salong* were later adopted by other peoples of the Rajang basin and neighboring areas.

**Kelirieng**

The *kelirieng* memorial column is indigenous to the tribes along the Rajang River: the Kajang, Kajaman, Melanau, and Puanan Bah. Commemorating the lives of their chiefs, they are erected during an individual's lifetime and consist of either a single column or a pair, with a hollow at the top for the remains of the deceased, surmounted by huge stone slabs.

The colonial house in Malaysia and Singapore represents a synthesis of European and local architectural styles. Colonial architecture in India, Macau, Melaka, and the Dutch East Indies set a precedent for the Straits Settlements, but many Malay design features were also incorporated. The term "bungalow" comes from the Hindi *bangla* and signals the original inspiration for this house form. Open verandahs and high ceilings provided good ventilation, while deep eaves cut down glare and created shade.

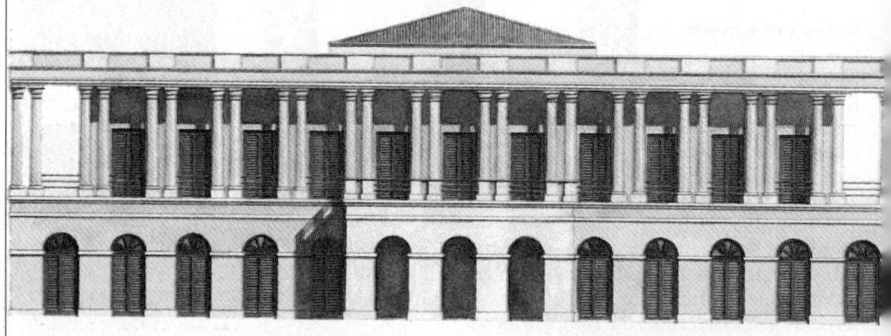

**ANGLO-INDIAN PALLADIAN VILLA**
Renaissance classicist and Palladian architecture was associated with humanism and ideals of rank, prestige and elegance. Penang and Singapore initially followed Anglo-Indian examples, which had their immediate origins in the English Regency style of John Nash (1752–1835). With lofty rooms and colonnaded verandahs, they were well suited to the tropics, once a pitched roof had been added to combat the monsoon rains.

**GEYLANG/KALLANG STYLE**
Popular with Malay and Chinese middle classes, this house style features brick piers, with stairs leading up to a verandah; decorated eaves and fascia boards; and suspended lattice work.

**BLACK-AND-WHITE**
Developed between 1920 and World War Two, the black-and-white house became the prototype for the houses of senior staff in the colonial service, armed forces, and private firms alike. The style takes its name from black-painted timbers with white stucco over timber lathing walls.

**Mock Tudor/half-timbered**
The picturesque ideals of the Arts and Crafts movement in Britain were an important element in Victorian Romanticism. An enthusiasm for Arcadian rusticism gave rise to a "cottage" style of architecture, favored in England for country homes and holiday houses since the 1840's. Typical prominent features include an asymmetrical plan (often with the *porte-cochère* set at 45° to the house), half-timbered elevations, and elaborate ornamentation – scalloped eaves and fascia boards, decorated roof ridges and finials.

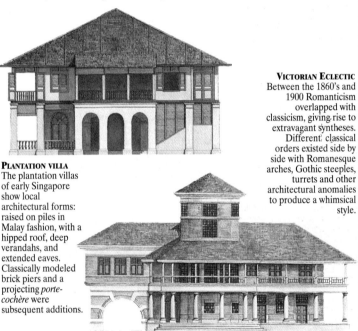

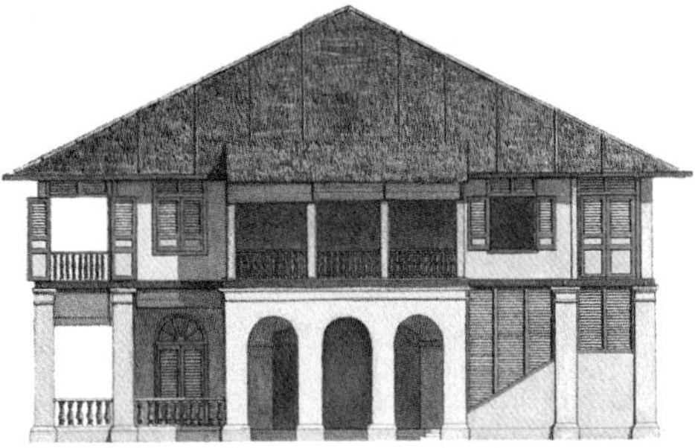

**Victorian Eclectic**
Between the 1860's and 1900 Romanticism overlapped with classicism, giving rise to extravagant syntheses. Different classical orders existed side by side with Romanesque arches, Gothic steeples, turrets and other architectural anomalies to produce a whimsical style.

**Plantation villa**
The plantation villas of early Singapore show local architectural forms: raised on piles in Malay fashion, with a hipped roof, deep verandahs, and extended eaves. Classically modeled brick piers and a projecting *porte-cochère* were subsequent additions.

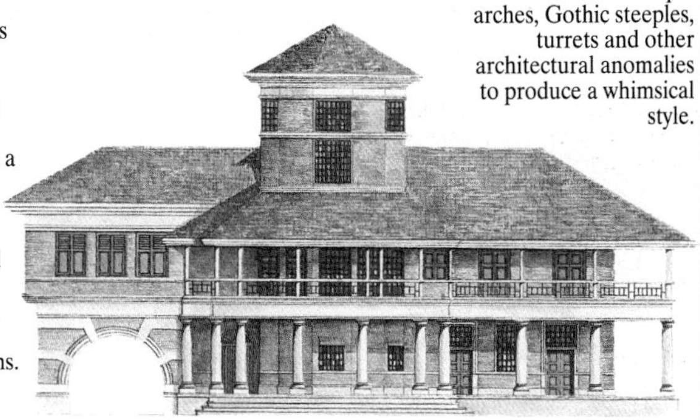

**Transitional modern**
The houses of Frank Brewer (1886–1971) in Singapore feature a steeply pitched roof with overhanging eaves; a bold horizontal line with windows as voids defined by the roof soffit; exposed brick buttresses and arches; arches linked through continuous brick banding; oriole windows and rough-cast plastering.

Islam arrived in the Malay peninsula some time before the 14th century. The earliest type of mosque in Malaysia is Javanese. The prototype seems to have been the Royal Mosque (Masjid Agung) at Demak on the northeast coast of Java, built by an Islamic ruler in 1428, and is square in plan with a tiered, trapezoidal roof. This form, with its crown-like ornamentation, has been known in China for centuries and is associated with the construction of pagodas.

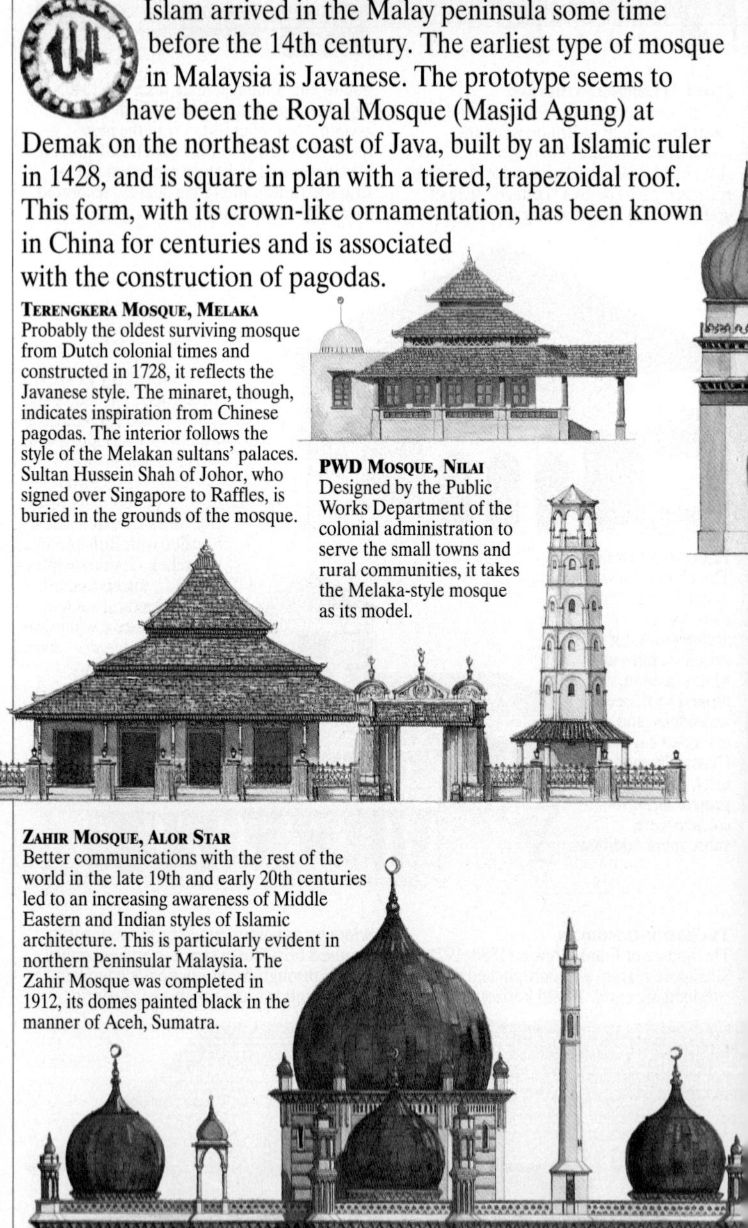

**Terengkera Mosque, Melaka**
Probably the oldest surviving mosque from Dutch colonial times and constructed in 1728, it reflects the Javanese style. The minaret, though, indicates inspiration from Chinese pagodas. The interior follows the style of the Melakan sultans' palaces. Sultan Hussein Shah of Johor, who signed over Singapore to Raffles, is buried in the grounds of the mosque.

**PWD Mosque, Nilai**
Designed by the Public Works Department of the colonial administration to serve the small towns and rural communities, it takes the Melaka-style mosque as its model.

**Zahir Mosque, Alor Star**
Better communications with the rest of the world in the late 19th and early 20th centuries led to an increasing awareness of Middle Eastern and Indian styles of Islamic architecture. This is particularly evident in northern Peninsular Malaysia. The Zahir Mosque was completed in 1912, its domes painted black in the manner of Aceh, Sumatra.

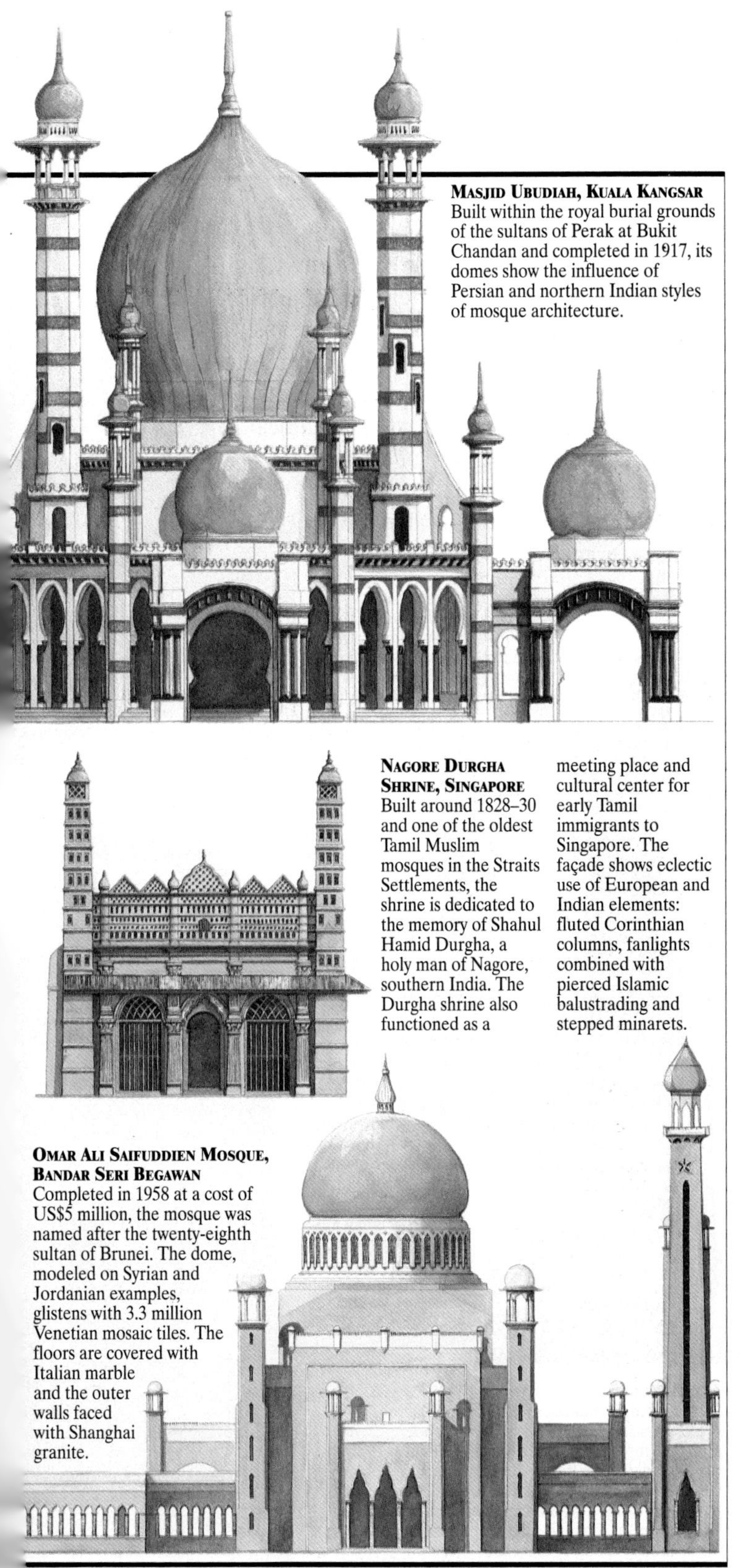

**Masjid Ubudiah, Kuala Kangsar**
Built within the royal burial grounds of the sultans of Perak at Bukit Chandan and completed in 1917, its domes show the influence of Persian and northern Indian styles of mosque architecture.

**Nagore Durgha Shrine, Singapore**
Built around 1828–30 and one of the oldest Tamil Muslim mosques in the Straits Settlements, the shrine is dedicated to the memory of Shahul Hamid Durgha, a holy man of Nagore, southern India. The Durgha shrine also functioned as a meeting place and cultural center for early Tamil immigrants to Singapore. The façade shows eclectic use of European and Indian elements: fluted Corinthian columns, fanlights combined with pierced Islamic balustrading and stepped minarets.

**Omar Ali Saifuddien Mosque, Bandar Seri Begawan**
Completed in 1958 at a cost of US$5 million, the mosque was named after the twenty-eighth sultan of Brunei. The dome, modeled on Syrian and Jordanian examples, glistens with 3.3 million Venetian mosaic tiles. The floors are covered with Italian marble and the outer walls faced with Shanghai granite.

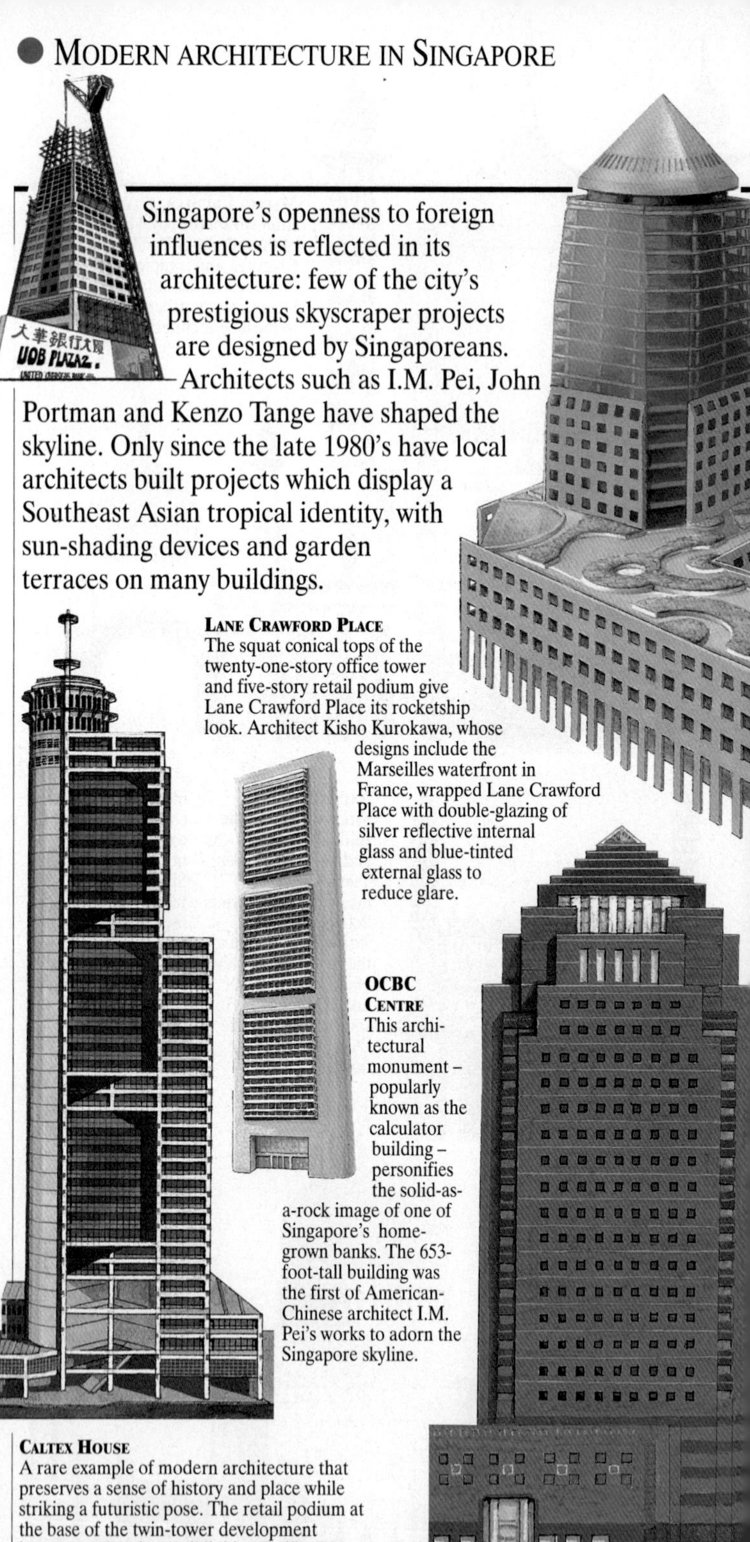


Singapore's openness to foreign influences is reflected in its architecture: few of the city's prestigious skyscraper projects are designed by Singaporeans. Architects such as I.M. Pei, John Portman and Kenzo Tange have shaped the skyline. Only since the late 1980's have local architects built projects which display a Southeast Asian tropical identity, with sun-shading devices and garden terraces on many buildings.

**LANE CRAWFORD PLACE**
The squat conical tops of the twenty-one-story office tower and five-story retail podium give Lane Crawford Place its rocketship look. Architect Kisho Kurokawa, whose designs include the Marseilles waterfront in France, wrapped Lane Crawford Place with double-glazing of silver reflective internal glass and blue-tinted external glass to reduce glare.

**OCBC CENTRE**
This architectural monument – popularly known as the calculator building – personifies the solid-as-a-rock image of one of Singapore's home-grown banks. The 653-foot-tall building was the first of American-Chinese architect I.M. Pei's works to adorn the Singapore skyline.

**CALTEX HOUSE**
A rare example of modern architecture that preserves a sense of history and place while striking a futuristic pose. The retail podium at the base of the twin-tower development boasts a pedestrian mall linking Raffles Place to Collyer Quay. This is an updated replica of its predecessor, Change Alley, once famous for its money-changers and exotic shops.

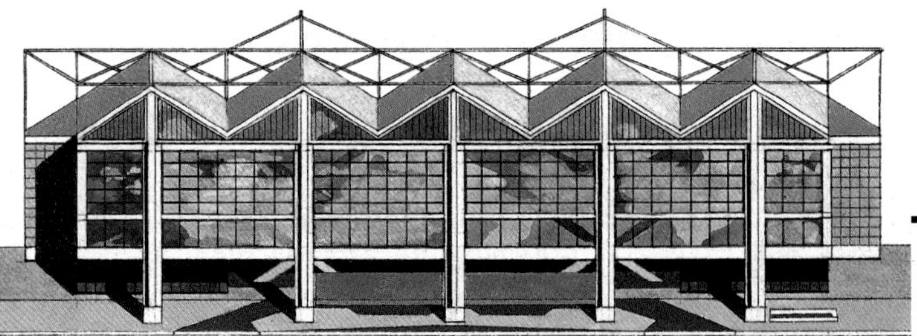

**Suntec City**
The first noticeable feature of Suntec City is its space-frame roof, a series of glass and steel pyramids. Measuring 571 feet by 237 feet, the roof ranks among the largest space frames in the world. The exhibition centre development is scheduled for completion in 1997.

**The Concourse**
This 223,579 square feet complex on Beach Road has the unfortunate distinction of a long gestation period, from its initial design in 1979 to final completion in end 1994. Designed by American architect Paul Rudolph, as a response to tropical light and heat, The Concourse is known for its zig-gurat profile and acutely inclined window panels.

**Singapore Marriot Hotel/Tang's Plaza**
This pagoda-inspired thirty-three-story high octagonal tower is embellished with a Chinese roof of bright green porcelain tiles and red rafters. It has become a landmark at the junction of Scotts Road and Orchard Road.

**Ngee Ann City**
A colonial edifice of strength and dignity is how Singapore architect Raymond Woo describes the reddish-brown granite-clad building occupying 2.8 hectares of prime land in Orchard Road which he designed for Chinese clan organization the Ngee Ann Kongsi. A pair of office towers with pyramidal summits flanks the six-story retail podium which occupies the center of the building. Fronting the retail podium is a semi-circular plaza while colonnaded walkways running the entire 825-foot length of the frontage. Glass pyramidal roofs cover the external walkways and escalator walls.

Malaysia's urban architecture was pioneered mainly by colonial administrators and Chinese immigrant settlers. In the post-Independence building boom of the 1960's and 1970's, local architects were looking for a modern style that would express a local identity. One such successful exponent was the National Mosque. Later examples include Moorish and Mughal architecture and the traditional Malay house.

**Perpustakaan Negara Malaysia (National Library), Kuala Lumpur**
The architect of the National Library has taken the *songket tengkolok* (folded brocade headgear), as the inspiration for this building. The traditional symbol of status, the *tengkolok* is seen as an appropriate emblem for the library. The *songket* pattern is replicated by diagonally laid, paint finished, cement tiles. The complicated form of the building incorporates glazed atria and landscaped courts.

**Dayabumi**
Perhaps the most elegant local interpretation of an Islamic style, the Dayabumi (right) is extruded from a 12-point star shaped plan, each face veiled in 35-storey high lattice grilles, reminiscent of the alabaster grilles in Moorish mosques. The grilles provide a delicate solar shading by day.

**Mesiniaga**
The Mesiniaga building is an unmistakeable futuristic looking structure which one encounters just after leaving Subang Airport. The building, designed by Ken Yeang, embodies his theories of the tropical skyscraper. Heliotropic planted terraces spiral up the building within the expressed frame and various shading devices culminate in the construction at the top.

**Kuching Civic Centre**
The complex comprises three pavilions amidst a spacious landscaped garden setting. The main structure is a 162-foot tall observatory tower-cum-aerial restaurant, which gives a bird's eye view of Kuching. It is linked by sheltered walkways to the other pavilions.

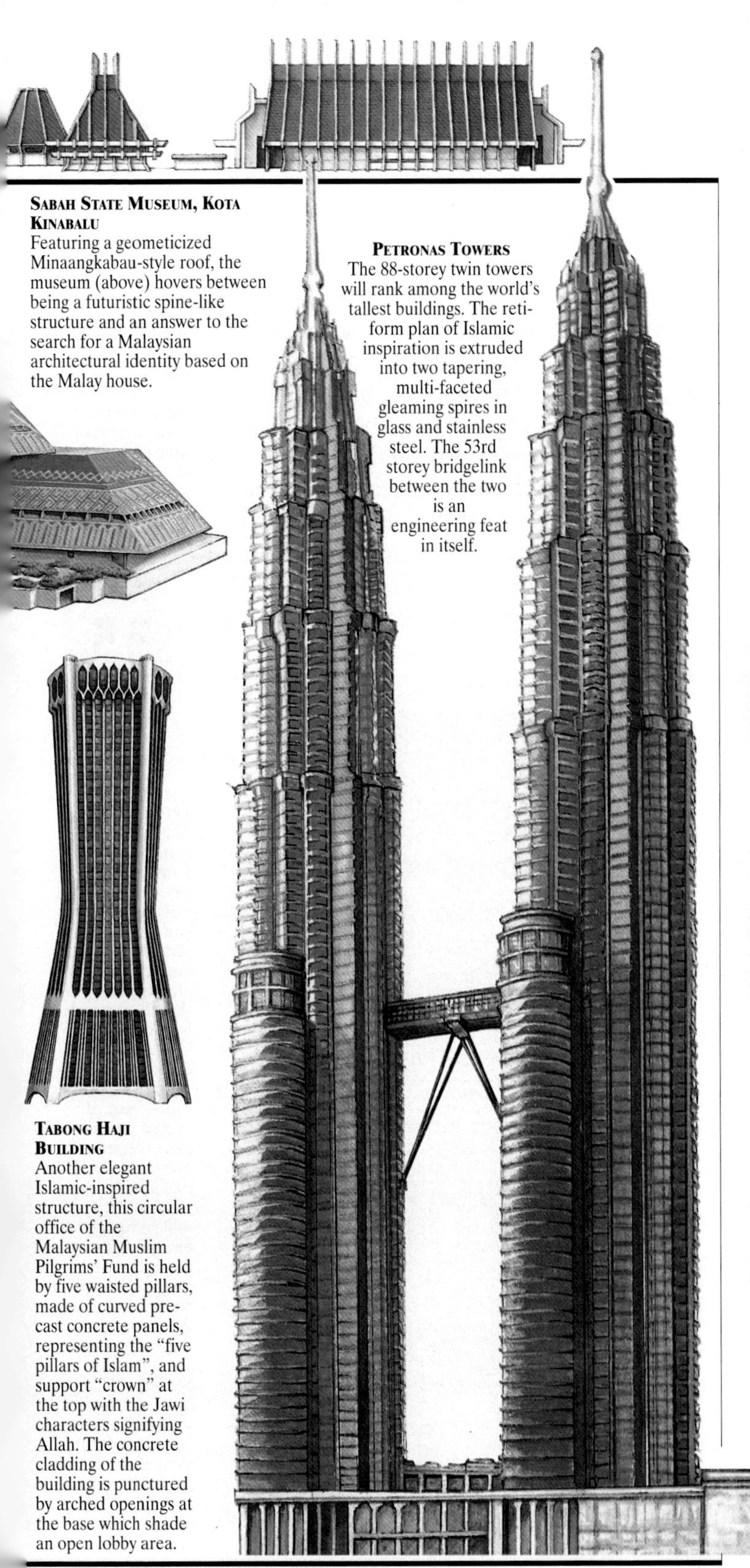

**Sabah State Museum, Kota Kinabalu**
Featuring a geometicized Minaangkabau-style roof, the museum (above) hovers between being a futuristic spine-like structure and an answer to the search for a Malaysian architectural identity based on the Malay house.

**Petronas Towers**
The 88-storey twin towers will rank among the world's tallest buildings. The reti-form plan of Islamic inspiration is extruded into two tapering, multi-faceted gleaming spires in glass and stainless steel. The 53rd storey bridgelink between the two is an engineering feat in itself.

**Tabong Haji Building**
Another elegant Islamic-inspired structure, this circular office of the Malaysian Muslim Pilgrims' Fund is held by five waisted pillars, made of curved pre-cast concrete panels, representing the "five pillars of Islam", and support "crown" at the top with the Jawi characters signifying Allah. The concrete cladding of the building is punctured by arched openings at the base which shade an open lobby area.

**WINDOWS**
Windows are ornamented in a variety of classical styles, with louvered shutters in the Portuguese jalousie manner. Venetian fanlights alternate with Malay-inspired carved grilles.

The first permanent shophouses in the Straits Settlements were designed by immigrant Chinese master-builders from Guangdong. Load-bearing gable walls rise above the roof line; large, single wooden beams and roof purlins span the width of the building; roof ridges are decorated with friezes. The typical shophouse also owes much to Raffles' directive that all such buildings in Singapore should have "a verandah of a certain depth, open to all sides as a continuous and open passage on each side of the street".

**19TH CENTURY**
The classic Straits Settlements shophouse, c.1840, has a narrow street frontage. Air-wells give light and ventilation to the interior. Gable ends are stepped, bow-shaped, or rounded in traditional Chinese manner. The roof ridge is typically decorated with a frieze of broken ceramic pieces cemented over a bas-relief. The roof is laid with Chinese clay tiles, while green glazed tiles may decorate the margin of the roof projecting over the five-foot way. Windows may be square-topped, arched or round headed with fan lights. The external walls are ornamented with painted scrolls. The ground floor serves as shop and storage; upper storeys are dwelling spaces.

**TERRACE HOUSES**
Terrace houses follow a design similar to that of shophouses, except that the open shopfront is replaced by a centrally situated door with windows on either side. The symmetrical arrangement of doors and windows is a feature of traditional Chinese architecture.

**DECORATION**
Using the exterior of the house as a means of ornamentation was a novel idea to Chinese master-builders. Exposure to colonial architecture soon encouraged Chinese builders to adapt European forms of decoration. Chinese elements gave way to a variety of neo-classical features. The adoption of Ionic and Corinthian pilasters and pediments, egg-and-dart moldings, wreaths, festoons, and swags as decorative elements led to increasingly elaborate façades and the evolution of an eclectic local vernacular sometimes called "Chinese Baroque Mannerism".

**PINTU PAGAR**
The Peranakan townhouse typically has two sets of doors. During the day, the full-length main doors are kept open to allow a through breeze, while the half-doors (*pintu pagar*) are closed to shield the house occupants from the gaze of passersby.

**HOE KEE CLUB**
The shophouses of mainland China had already long been subject to European influences before being introduced to Southeast Asia: the Portuguese trading post at Macau was established in the 15th century, and before 1760 English and other European companies traded in an irregular manner at Guangzhou (Canton), Kiamen (Amoy), and other coastal cities. The Hoe Kee Club at Keong Saik Road, in Singapore's Chinatown, however, represents the ultimate extension of European influences, recalling the villas of Palladio in its restrained use of classical forms.

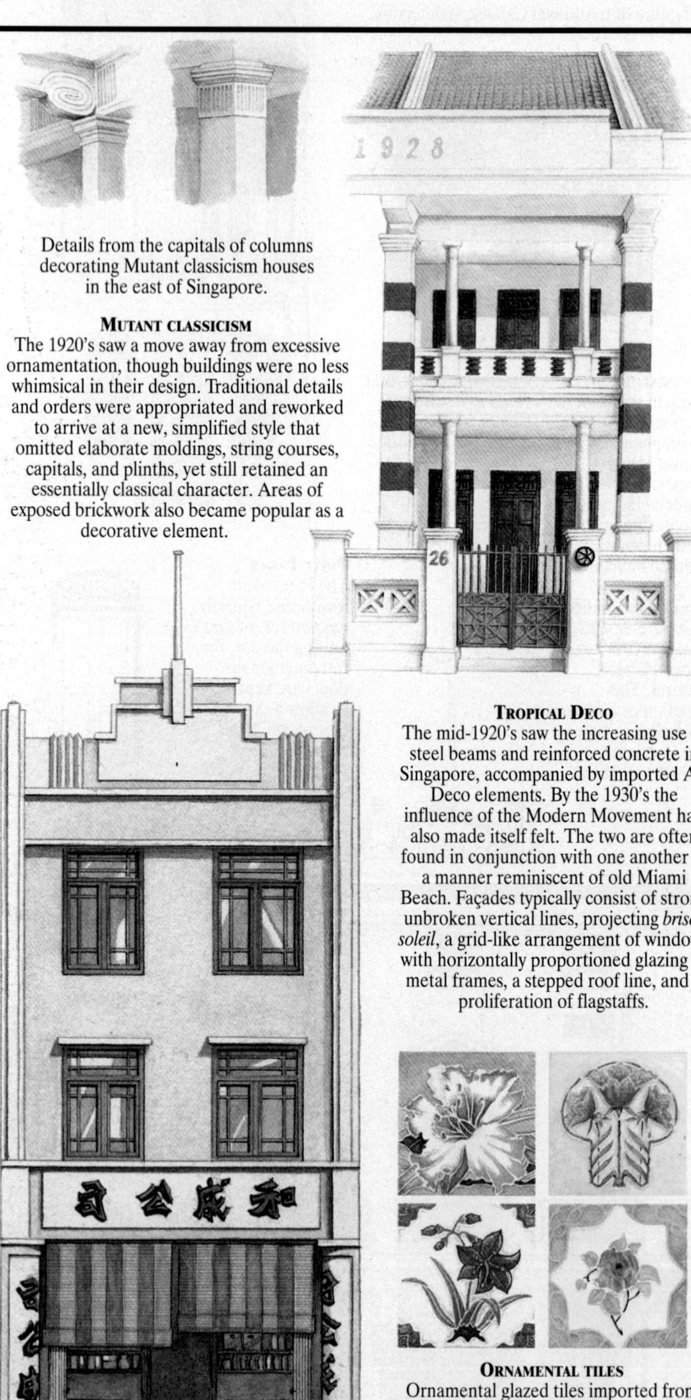


Details from the capitals of columns decorating Mutant classicism houses in the east of Singapore.

**MUTANT CLASSICISM**

The 1920's saw a move away from excessive ornamentation, though buildings were no less whimsical in their design. Traditional details and orders were appropriated and reworked to arrive at a new, simplified style that omitted elaborate moldings, string courses, capitals, and plinths, yet still retained an essentially classical character. Areas of exposed brickwork also became popular as a decorative element.

**TROPICAL DECO**

The mid-1920's saw the increasing use of steel beams and reinforced concrete in Singapore, accompanied by imported Art Deco elements. By the 1930's the influence of the Modern Movement had also made itself felt. The two are often found in conjunction with one another in a manner reminiscent of old Miami Beach. Façades typically consist of strong unbroken vertical lines, projecting *brise-soleil*, a grid-like arrangement of windows with horizontally proportioned glazing in metal frames, a stepped roof line, and a proliferation of flagstaffs.

**ORNAMENTAL TILES**

Ornamental glazed tiles imported from Europe were a favorite decorative device for interiors and façades alike. Colorful flowers are a common motif.

# Seen by painters

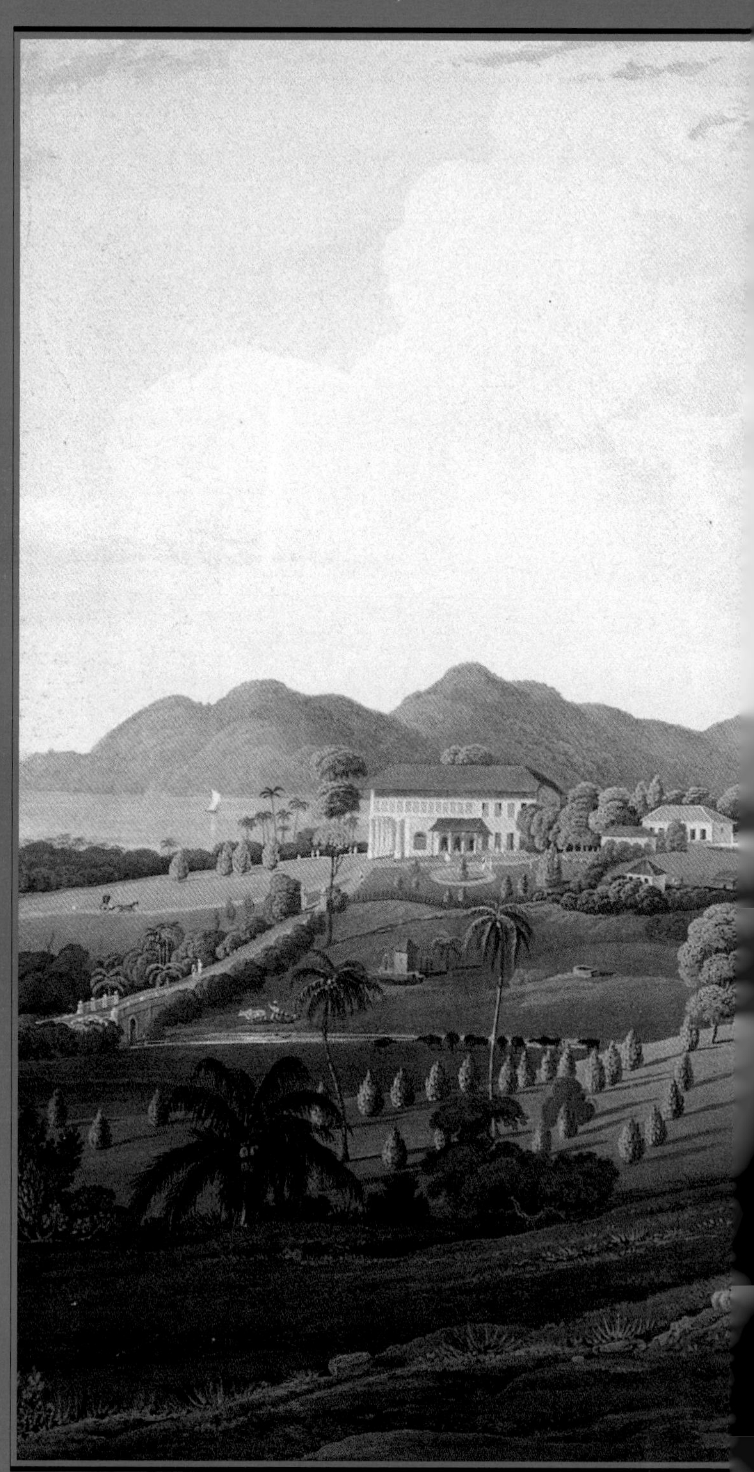

"HOWEVER PATCHED-LIKE THE PENANG HILLS APPEAR FROM THE SEA, THEIR TOPS AFFORD MOST DELICIOUS RETREATS FROM THE SCORCHING HEAT OF THE PLAINS."

JOHN TURNBULL THOMSON, 1864

William Daniell's (1769–1837) hand-colored aquatint, *View of Glugor House and Spice Plantations, Prince of Wales' Island*, was one of a series that he engraved after Robert Smith's oil paintings of Penang in 1818. Daniell and his uncle, Thomas, were well known through their many fine engravings of India, China, and Java. Most of the

engravings were the result of their travels in the East (1785–94), but others, such as the engraving on the left, were made of places they had not visited, based on drawings by artists on the scene. It captures the majesty of the view and conveys a sense of the exotic plants on the slopes surrounding the estate. In the 1820's, Glugor House was one of the largest mansions on the island, and its proprietor, David Brown, owned large estates of pepper, betelnut, and nutmegs. John Crawfurd, the resident of Singapore (1823–6), visited the property in 1821 and said that although the estate had "a poor soil, Mr. Brown had planted it with nutmeg and clove trees, which are in full bearing, and have a very thriving appearance".

# A Chinese temple in Singapore

"IN FRONT OF THE ALTAR STANDS A GREAT BRONZE VASE FILLED WITH SAND, IN WHICH...JOSS STICKS ARE GLIMMERING, WHOSE SCENT FILLS THE TEMPLE AND PREVAILS PRACTICALLY EVERYWHERE THAT THE CHINESE LIVE." EDUARD VON RANSONNET, 1869

Eduard von Ransonnet spent seven weeks in Singapore in 1869. He was part of an Austro-Hungarian expedition that was exploring trade possibilities with Asia. Not content with following commercial paths, he explored and recorded many areas of Singapore, not just the town, traveling on foot and by boat around the countryside to visit Bukit Timah, Changi, Seletar, and the offshore island of Pulau Tekong. A man of many talents, he personally transcribed his sketches into colored lithographs for his book, using blocks in the three primary colors and black. Ransonnet's artistic skills are demonstrated in this view of the interior of the Thian Hock Keng Temple in Telok Ayer Street; certainly one can recognize the carved granite pillars covered with dragons that Ransonnet depicted, and the smoke from joss-sticks in front of the gilded altar with statues. The temple was built with materials sent from China and was completed in 1841, standing on the site of an earlier temple. This was the first place that Chinese immigrants went to after disembarking, to give thanks for a safe journey. Telok Ayer Street originally ran along the shoreline, and the temple faced the sea on the water's edge. Over time, land reclamation has left the temple far from the coast, but it remains a living testimony to Singapore's origins.

"WITHOUT FEAR OF BEING ACCUSED OF EXAGGERATION, ONE CAN SAY THAT SINGAPORE IS MARKED OUT FOR A MOST BRILLIANT COMMERCIAL FUTURE."

AUGUST-NICHOLAS VAILLANT, CAPTAIN OF *LA BONITE*

These two lithographs are based on sketches made by Barthélémy Lauvergne, the artist on board the French corvette *La Bonite*, which visited Singapore in 1837 on its voyage around the world. Although the setting is not precisely identified by the inscription, the first scene shows a canal at low tide, probably a tributary of the Singapore River (1). This is crossed by a bridge and is flanked by the backs of warehouses. Behind the bridge the view looks towards Chinatown in the distance. There is an interesting contrast between the curved roofs of the "godowns", or warehouses, and the colonial lines of the buildings behind the bridge. Artists were often drawn to the prosperous buildings that surrounded the Padang, such as this view (2) taken from the seashore, looking northwards across the open space, which is still known as the Padang. On the right is St Andrew's Church, designed by George Coleman, who was responsible for many of Singapore's earliest colonial buildings. On the right are private houses, and behind rises Government Hill, with the governor's bungalow and the flagstaff, used for signaling the arrival of ships in the harbor.

1

2

"WHEREVER A DAYAK CAN GO, AN ENGLISHMAN CAN FOLLOW."
SPENSER ST JOHN

Spenser St John was consul-general in Borneo for more than ten years. He had a lively interest in exploring the country and its cultures, and traveled by boat and on foot, recording his impressions in a daily journal. These accounts were collated in his book *Life in the Forests of the Far East*. In 1851 he organized a trip up the Sarawak River to inspect the Land Dayaks, reaching the limit of navigation at Santubong. There he was joined by another intrepid traveler, Ida Pfeiffer, whom he took to a Dayak village on the slopes of Mount Siramban. While Pfeiffer visited the Dayak village, the rest of the party stayed in Rajah Brooke's cottage, where they had an unsurpassed view of Mount Santubong surrounded by undulating land and the winding Sarawak River (1). On another expedition up the Limbang River in 1858, St John took nineteen men and trade goods. His aim was to reach the Murut tribe in the interior. Tabari was one of St John's Murut guides, and the group reached his village after a month, on the verge of starvation. The village had twenty-three families, and was reached by a suspension bridge made of bamboo and wood (2).

1

2

# A VILLAGE MARKET

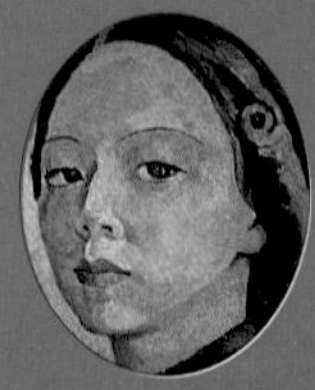

Georgette Chen (1907–93) was born in Paris of Chinese parents and grew up in a scholarly and artistic family. Her self-portrait, made in 1934, shows the influence of the French artists Redon and Moreau. Her *Terengganu Market Scene* is one of a series made during a visit to the region in 1961. Chen said that "common subjects like potatoes and ordinary people appeal to me". The canvas reflects her enthusiasm and evokes the brilliance of a sun-drenched day; an effect produced by using minimal shadows, allowing the light to fall directly onto the figures. The scene shows women at a market on the east coast of Peninsular Malaysia, and evokes the color and bustle of an open-air market. The artist plays with the repetition of triangular roof shapes in umbrellas, hats and even the positioning of rambutan baskets.

# Seen by writers

## MALAYA – THE EARLY YEARS

### THE FOUNDATION OF MELAKA

*The* Malay Annals (Sejarah Melayu) *are a history of the Malay people and the Melaka Royal House. According to an author's preface, Bandahara Sri Narawangsa Tun Mambang compiled this record at the order of Sultan Abdullah, son of Sultan Ajel Abdul Jalil Shah, received on the twelfth day of Rabiul-awal in the year of the* hijra *1021 (AD 1643). The text is believed to have been revised and possibly amplified at the Johor court in later years. Dr John Leyden was a Malay scholar and friend of Sir Stamford Raffles, who succumbed to the rigors of an insalubrious climate; his English translation was published posthumously.*

“Raja Secander Shah returned to the shore of the sea, to the banks of a river named Bartam, where he hunted, standing himself to see the sport from under shade of a spreading tree. One of his dogs roused a white pelandok (mousedeer) which, attacking the dog, drove it into the water. The raja was pleased, and said: ‘This is a fine place, where the very pelandok are full of courage. Let us found a city here.’ To this all his head men assented, and the raja, enquiring the name of the tree under which he was standing, was informed that it was named the malaca tree. ‘Then,’ said he, ‘let the name of the city be called Malaca.’ Raja Secander Shah now settled in Malaca, having remained in Singhapura thirty-two years, which he deserted for Malaca when Singhapura was conquered by Java….

The city of Malaca increased greatly and acquired a numerous population, and merchants resorted to it from every quarter. After a long time that Raja Kichil Besar [Secander Shah's grandson] had reigned, he dreamed one night that he saw Nabi [prophet] Muhammed, who said to him: ‘I testify that God is the one God, and that Muhammed is his prophet’; and Raja Kichil Besar did as he was directed by the prophet, who conferred on him the name of Sultan Muhammed. Next morning, said the prophet, at day break, there will arrive a ship from Jidda, and will land on the shore of Malaca and perform Namaz, listen to their words. Raja Kichil Besar said, very well, he would do so, and not neglect, and immediately Nabi Muhammed vanished…. The vessel arrived at the appointed time, and landed the crew to say their prayers ashore. The raja quickly mounted his elephant and went out to them, followed by all his great men, and perceived that they were the same whom he had seen in his dream, and mentioned it to the bandahara [minister] and chief men. When the crew had finished their devotions, the raja made his elephant sit down, and took up the Makhdum upon his own elephant and carried him to the city; and the bandahara, with all the chief men, adopted Islam and their example

An old engraving of merchants and junks bound for Singapore waters.

was followed by the rest of the people, at the order of the raja, and the Makhdum was their guru [teacher] and he conferred on the raja the name of Sultan Muhammed Shah.”

MALAY ANNALS (*SEJARAH MELAYU*), MELAKA, C. 1643

**THE JUNK TRADE BEFORE EUROPEAN CONTACT**

*Zhao Rugua was superintendent for merchant shipping in the province of Fujian during the latter part of the Southern Sung dynasty. Practically no biographical details are known, except that he was a descendant of the Sung Emperor Taizong. Drawing on previously published guidelines for mariners about to venture across the seas, the* Zhufan zhi (Records of Foreign Peoples) *in its turn has been copied, and incorporated wholly or in part into later works of the same nature. The first selected passage is accepted by most scholars as describing Kuantan on the east coast of the Malay peninsula. Tan-ma-ling is read as a transliteration of Tembeling (romanized spellings vary), a tributary of the Pahang River.*

“The kingdom of Tan-ma-ling is under a ruler who is addressed as Siang-kung. The city is surrounded by a palisade six or seven feet thick and over twenty feet high, strong enough to be mounted for fighting purposes. The people of this country ride buffaloes, wear their hair done in a knot behind, and go barefooted. Officials live in wooden houses, the common people in bamboo cottages, the walls being filled in with leaves and the poles fastened with rattan. The native products comprise yellow wax, laka-wood, the su variety of gharu wood incense, ebony, camphor, elephant's tusks and rhinoceros horns. The foreign traders barter for them with silk parasols, kittysols, silks and Ho-ch'i, samshu, rice, salt, sugar, porcelain basins, bowls and the like common and heavy articles, and bowls of gold and silver. The country of Tan-ma-ling collects together such gold and silver vessels as it receives, while Ji-lo-t'ing and the other countries make assorted collections, and these they offer to San-fo-ts'i (Palembang) as tribute….

The si, or rhinoceros, resembles domestic cattle, but it has only one horn. Its skin is black and its hair scanty; its tongue is like the burr of a chestnut. Fierce and violent in its temper, this animal runs so quickly that you may imagine it is flying. Its food consists solely of bamboo and other woods. Since he rips up a man with his horn, none dare come near him. Hunters shoot him with a stiff arrow from a good distance, after which they remove the horn, which in this state is called a “fresh horn”, whereas if the animal has died a natural death the horn obtained from it is called “dropped-in-the-hills horn”. The horn bears marks like bubbles; the horns which are more white than black are the best.”

ZHAO RUGUA, *RECORDS OF FOREIGN PEOPLES*, FUJIAN, C.1225

## MALAYAN IMPRESSIONS

**THE LOVE OF PROGENY**

*John Crawfurd was an observant and articulate visitor to the Indies. His* Traveller's Tales *are well researched; he spoke and understood Malay sufficiently to question his informants in all the detail he required. Crawfurd's early economic reports on the resources and production of a region considered (erroneously, alas) to be immensly wealthy are a standard source of information for the modern scholar.*

“The endless variety of ceremonies at births it would little interest the reader to repeat, and the detail would afford him no insight into the character of the people. When a woman quickens of her first child, this is the occasion of a festival. When the seventh month of her pregnancy is successfully passed, this is one for another; when the umbilical cord drops off, this is the occasion of a third. It is on this last that the child receives a name; but they have no solemnity corresponding to our baptism. A native, accustomed to our manners, told me that they bestowed names upon their children with as little ceremony as we did upon our dogs or horses!

Those who have a smattering of Arabic, and make pretence to superior piety, give Arabic names to their children. This is common with the Malayan tribes. The Javanese content themselves with native names. The love of progeny with all is declared in the frequency of the practice among the lower order, throughout the different countries of the Archipelago, of the father and mother dropping their own names as soon as their first child, particularly if a boy, is born. If the child, for example, be called, as is frequent enough, by such names as 'the Handsome One', or 'the Weak One', &c. the parents will be called the 'father and mother of the handsome one, or the father and mother of the weak one,' &c. The names bestowed among the Indian islanders may frequently be considered as titles, and are changed at every promotion of one's state or circumstances. From the age of eight to twelve years, the ceremony of circumcision is performed on the male children, and in Java, I do not know whether the custom be general, a corresponding ceremony is observed in regard to young women.”

JOHN CRAWFURD, *HISTORY OF THE INDIAN ARCHIPELAGO*, EDINBURGH, 1820

**WHAT THE MUNSHI SAW**

*Abdullah Abdul Kadir was called* munshi *(language teacher) by the India troops in Melaka. Abdullah was of Arab-Indian descent; he has been thus described by a contemporary: "In physiognomy he was a Tamilian of southern Hindustan: slightly bent forward, spare, energetic, bronze in complexion, oval-faced, high-nosed, one eye squinting outwards a little. He dressed in the usual style of the Melaka Tamils; he had the vigour and pride of the Arab, the perseverance and subtility of the Hindoo – in language and national sympathy only was he Malay." Munshi Abdullah was one of the first Malay writers, as opposed to composers of court records and poetry; many of his works are critical of Malay society. His fervent commendation of Lady Raffles and the comparison with high-class Malay women is a case in point.*

“Mr. Raffles' wife was unlike ordinary women. She shared her husband's charm, the modesty and prudence in everything that she did.... It was her nature, I noticed, to do all her work with the greatest alacrity, never wasting a moment in idleness, but forever working away at one thing or another. In their attitude towards work there was, I found, a very great difference between Malay women and white women. For it is the custom of Malay women, when they have become the wives of important people, to grow more conceited and lazy, becoming haughty in manner and magnifying their own importance in every word they utter. They consider manual labour as beneath their dignity.... They rise at ten o'clock in the morning and take a little refreshment, then sit about for a while before retiring again until the afternoon, when they toy with a betel nut. That is the lot of the fortunate woman who is married to a man of high standing. But I noticed that Mrs. Raffles was as active as the cockroach which has no tail, doing one thing after another; after tidying the house she would sew and after sewing she would write letters. May I be blinded if my eyes ever saw her retire or compose herself for rest in the middle of the day. She was up and about all the time, Allah alone knows!”

ABDULLAH ABDUL KADIR, *HIKAYAT ABDULLAH*, SINGAPORE, 1849

"ALL THE EUROPEAN HOUSES SEEM TO HAVE VERY DEEP VERANDAHS, LARGE LOFTY ROOMS...WINDOWS WITHOUT GLASS, BRICK FLOORS, AND JALOUSIES AND 'TATTIES' TO KEEP OUT THE LIGHT AND THE FLIES."

ISABELLA BIRD, *THE GOLDEN CHERSONESE*

## THE COLONIAL EXPERIENCE

### DAILY LIFE IN SINGAPORE

*Singapore had newspapers early in its history. George Windsor Earl, while a travel writer in the modern sense too, frequently contributed to the* Journal of the Eastern Archipelago *edited by John Logan. Much of Earl's writing is didactic: when describing daily life in Singapore's European community, he cannot resist making a rather snide comparison with Batavia, the commercial center of Java which the British returned to the Dutch after the Napoleonic Wars.*

"The European mode of life, as far as regards the general routine of occupations, is precisely similar to that of Batavia, but there the resemblance ends. At Singapore there exists no political bar to social intercourse; no dread that private conversations may be reported to a jealous and unforgiving government; indeed, the contrast altogether is so great, that I have often felt surprised that a British resident of Batavia who visits Singapore on commercial business, or for the recovery of his health, can ever prevail upon himself to return to that pestilential and misgoverned city. Amusements of an active nature in which the gentlemen engage, consist chiefly of boat-sailing and shooting, and the former, so decidedly British, is carried to a greater extent than in any other part of India. Sailing and rowing matches between the sailing-boats of the merchants, and also between the sampans of the Malays, occur almost daily, the native boatmen taking quite as much interest in them as the Europeans. Those who delight in field-sports find ample amusement in the low lands at the back of the town, which abound in snipes and plovers, or in the creeks on the east side of the harbour, where flocks of pigeons assemble every evening from all parts of the island, to roost on the trees in the little detached islets, where they are free from the attacks of smaller beasts of prey. Wild pigs and deer are to be met with in the wilder parts of the interior, but the jungle is too thick for the chase. Tigers occasionally visit the island from the Malay Peninsula, there being no difficulty in crossing the narrow strait; but as they resort to the neighbourhood of the settlement in quest of food, they are generally caught soon after their arrival by the Malays, who are very skilful in entrapping them.... Among the amusements of the Europeans may be included the paper warfare carried on by individuals through the medium of two public journals, and a single glance will shew to what an extent it prevails. 'Libertas' inserts a letter in the Free

Press concerning some grievance, probably a decision of the Court, and his arguments and assertions are refuted in the next Chronicle by 'Philo Lex'. 'Agricola' and 'Agricola Secundus' maintain a discussion concerning the agricultural capabilities of the island; and the letter of 'A Tory' is speedily answered by 'Anti Humbug'. As the parties are generally those best acquainted with the subjects under review, this exchange of opinions is found both amusing and instructive, for the inhabitants are enabled to see both sides of the question, and may therefore judge for themselves. The two journals are, of course, ministerial and opposition. From the talent and liberality with which they are conducted, and from the fund of information they contain concerning the affairs of Eastern India, they are justly held to be inferior to few periodical publications in the East.”

GEORGE WINDSOR EARL, *THE EASTERN SEAS*, LONDON, 1837

### TO EAT LIKE A NATIVE

*Spenser St John came to Borneo with Rajah James Brooke; during his variegated career in the East he traveled widely and kept copious notes. An astute, sometimes malicious commentator, he was a careful enough observer – as his curry recipe proves.*

“My cook Ahtan, who was very much annoyed last night by having to set before me so poor a dinner as stale bread and salt fish, determined, as he had a long afternoon before him, to devote it to cooking, particularly as I always divided it into two portions, one for him, and one for myself. The curry he produced was admirable, and having secured a cucumber last night, he was enabled to add what the Malays call a sambal, of which there are many kinds; the one he made was of sliced cucumber, and green and red chillies cut into fine threads; others are of dried salt fish finely powdered, or fish roes, or hard-boiled eggs, or the tender shoots of the bamboo, but with nearly all, red or green chillies are added. The most delicious I have seen put on table was made of prawns about an inch long, partly boiled, then seasoned with freshly prepared curry mixture, and at last slightly moved over the fire in a frying-pan, taking care not to burn it; if chillies are added judiciously, so as not to render it too fiery, it causes a keen appetite to all but a confirmed invalid.... The triumph of Malay cookery is the sambal, particularly the one called blachang; the best is composed of the very finest prawns, and pounded up with red chillies, and a little ginger. Coarser kinds are made from the larger prawn, or even from the smallest fish caught on the river's banks. Sometimes the material is first exposed to the sun in order to be completely dried, or it would not keep or mix very well, though it is often soaked till nearly decomposed, and that is

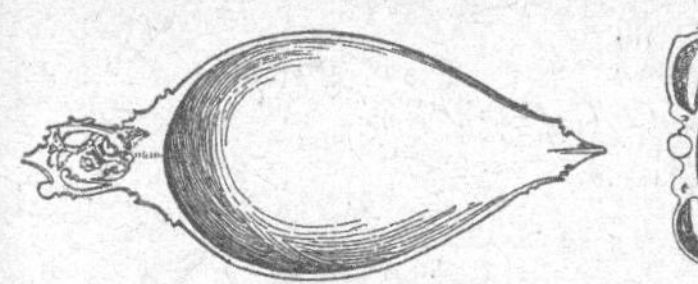  

perhaps the favourite way when it emits a rather powerful scent, but it is very tasty. I have mentioned the admirable curry which Ahtan put before me; perhaps I ought to explain how we make that dish in the Far East; it appears a very different thing from what I have tasted in England under the name of curry: a fowl is cut up into small pieces, and four dried and two green onions, five chillies, half a turmeric, one teaspoonful of coriander seed, one of white cumin, and one of sweet cumin are provided. You must well pound the seeds, turmeric and chillies, and slice the onions fine; then take the saucepan, and after buttering it, slightly brown the onions, add the pounded ingredients with just sufficient water to reduce them to a paste, and throw in the fowl and well mix them up, till the meat has a yellow tint, and lastly, add the cocoa-nut milk, and boil till the curry be thoroughly cooked. I hope my teaching is sufficiently clear to be understood, but I must add, the cocoa-nut milk is made by scraping the meat of half of an old nut very fine, then soaking it in warm water, and after squeezing out the milk, throw the fibre away. I watched the whole process of cooking with great interest, and almost fancy I could make a curry myself.”

SPENSER ST JOHN, *LIFE IN THE FORESTS OF THE FAR EAST*,
LONDON, 1857

•

**THE POLITICS OF INTERVENTION**

*Isabella Bird was a Victorian lady tourist of awsome range: she had been to Canada and America, to Japan, China, and Vietnam before reaching Malaya; she visited Australia, New Zealand, and Hawaii; and she was to become famous for her 1000-mile camel ride through Morocco when she was over seventy! An astute observer and recorder, Bird made efforts to understand something of the countries she visited, beyond their mere tourist attractions. The passage selected here shows that while she does not pretend to understand the intricacies of British intervention in the Malay peninsula, neither does she approve it blindly.*

“The Pangkor Treaty was signed in January 1874. On November 2nd 1875 Mr. Birch, the British Resident who had arrived the evening before at the village of Passir Salah to post up orders and proclamations announcing that the whole Kingdom of Perak was henceforth to be governed by English officers, was murdered as he was preparing for the bath. On this provocation we entered upon a ‘little war’. Perak became known in England, and the London press began to ask how it was that colonial officers were suffered to make conquests and increase Imperial responsibilities without the sanction of Parliament.... As the sequel to the war and Mr. Birch's murder, Ismail, who had retained authority over a part of Perak, was banished to Johore; Abdullah, the Sultan, and the Mentri of Larut, who was designated as an ‘intriguing character’, were exiled to the Seychelles, and the Rajah Muda Yusuf, a prince who by all accounts was regarded as exceedingly obnoxious, was elevated to the regency, Perak at the same time passing virtually under our rule. A great mist of passion and prejudice envelopes our dealings with the chiefs and people of this State, both before and after the war. Sir Benson Maxwell, in *Our Malay Conquests*, presents a formidable arraignment against the Colonial authorities, and Major M'Nair in his book on Perak justifies all their proceedings. If I may venture to give an opinion upon so controverted a subject, it is that all Colonial authorities in their dealings with native races, all Residents and their subordinates, and all transactions between ourselves and the weak peoples of the Far East, would be better for having something of ‘the fierce light which beats upon a throne’ turned upon them. The good have nothing to fear, the bad would be revealed in their badness, and hasty counsels and ambitious designs would be held in check. Public opinion never reaches these equatorial jungles; we are grossly ignorant of their inhabitants and their rights, of the manner in which our interference originated, and how it has been exercised; and unless some fresh disturbance and another 'little war' should concentrate our attention for a moment on these distant States, we are likely to remain so, to their great detriment, and not a little, in one aspect of the case at least, to our own.”

ISABELLA BIRD, *THE GOLDEN CHERSONESE*, LONDON, 1883

### A MISFIT PRINCE

*Hugh Clifford was a colonial civil servant who turned to writing later in life. He wrote many short stories on life in Malaya, not all of them as pessimistic as* Saleh, A Prince of Malaya. *The main theme of this work is that "the native" is not suited for an English education. In this extract the hero, Tungku Saleh, has just returned after five years in England. He is taken into the civil service as a cadet officer; the story comes to an unhappy end with Saleh's rebellion against both the sultan, his father, and the British, and his violent death.*

“'It is a thousand pities, to my thinking that he (Saleh) was ever taken out of his proper environment. The Malay guided by white influence is all right; the denationalized Malay is the devil. Anyway, he must begin by fitting back into his own groove before we try to work him on European lines....'
...He rose from his chair, shook hands with Saleh, and bade him be seated.
'What's the news?' he said in the vernacular. Then he added in English: 'Look, it's absurd for me to talk to you in Malay. You speak English as well as I do, I suppose.'
'Yes, I speak English all right', said Saleh.
'Well then,' said Baker, throwing himself back in his chair and lighting a cigarette, 'how do you like Pelesu?'
'Pretty well,' said Saleh feebly.
'A bit of a change after England, isn't it?'
'Yes,' said Saleh....
'I tell you what,' continued Baker. 'You might cast your eye over these papers and see if there are any about which you could say a word to the king if the chance offers. I wish you would like a good fellow.'
Saleh took the bundle of dockets, pleased to think that he might perhaps be of use, and began to read them. They were all petitions addressed to the Resident by people who claimed that they had been aggrieved by the king. Here was one from a man who said that his wife had been lured into the house of Che'Jebah and had there undergone treatment which may not be more particularly described; here was another complaining that while upriver snaring doves the king and his youths had stripped his fruit trees of their crop; and there were a half a dozen others, all

"(PANTUN) IS THE PLAY ON WORDS, THE EQUIVOCATIONS, THE TENUOUS ALLUSIONS, THAT CONSTITUTE THEIR SPECIAL CHARM FOR THE MALAYS."

HENRI FAUCONNIER, *THE SOUL OF MALAYA*

containing charges ranging from petty theft to aggravated assault. They were not pretty tales to read about one's father, and the worst of it was that Saleh's instinct told him that they were true. He laid the papers back on Baker's table without finishing his perusal of them.

'Oh, have you read them?' asked Baker, glancing up from the writing which he had resumed. 'Some of them,' said Saleh. 'But... I do not think you understand. I cannot speak to the king about such things. You forget that he is my father.'"

HUGH CLIFFORD, *SALEH, A PRINCE OF MALAYA*, NEW YORK, 1926

### MALAY PANTUN

*Henri Fauconnier was a rubber planter;* The Soul of Malaya *records his fascination with the country even while the depression was gnawing at the plantation industry. The book is written in the form of a novel; Rolain explains the land and its people to the newly arrived narrator.* The Soul of Malaya *was awarded the Prix Goncourt in 1930.*

"'Smail's brother has come to see him,' said Rolain, 'and there they are weltering in poetry...Smail!' The verse was finished calmly, fervently, and then the intonation of the voice changed and sounded as profane as a motor-horn outside a church after the hymn has stopped.

'Tuaaan!'

'Come along both of you, and bring the book of pantuns.' Smail entered, followed by his duplicate on rather a reduced scale: the same ease mingled with reserve, the same look of grave and set surprise, the same liquid eyes. The two came and squatted on the mat near us. Rolain turned the leaves of the brown volume.

'Here you are. This expresses what we were saying:

*Asam kandis asam gelugur*
*ketiga dengan asam rembunia*
*Nyawa menanggis di-pintu kubur*
*hendak pulang k-dalam dunia.'*

'Can't understand a word,' said I.

'The two first lines of a pantun,' explained Rolain, 'are only a preparation for the idea that is to develop in the succeeding ones. They create the atmosphere without the crudity of metaphor. Here are bitter-sweet fruits, plants with an acid savour. It is to introduce what follows, as a heart is offered after fruits and flowers, leaves and branches:

The soul weeps at the gate of the tomb;
She so longs to come back to the world...'

'And again:

*Nasi basi atas para*
*nasi masak dalam perahu*
*Puchat kaseh badan sengsara*
*hidop segan mati ta-mahu'*

'So short a poem needs to be read slowly as a still life should be looked at for a long while. Indeed it is a still life: stale rice left in a boat. We think of a voyage or of an adventure, of him who was in the boat, and cooked the rice, and was hungry at that time – and yet the food is left untouched, and we scent a drama. Or perhaps this white rice that no one wants is in itself symbolic. The two last lines reveal the soul-state of the picture:

Lividness of love, tortured flesh,
Life is insipid and death is distasteful...

'It is the expression of so deep a disillusion that no desire survives, not even the desire of death.' Smail had taken back the book and was reading; he appeared to choose the erotic pantuns – which most of them are – and his brother's eyes glittered with pleasure.

*Kerengga di-dalam buloh*
*serahi berisi ayer mawar*
*Sampai hasrat di-dalam tuboh*
*tuan sa-orang jadi penawar*
Red ants in the hollow of a bamboo
Vessel filled with essence of roses…
When lust is in my body
Only my love can bring appeasement.'”

HENRI FAUCONNIER, *THE SOUL OF MALAYA*,
LONDON, 1931

### LOST IN THE JUNGLE

*Best known as a novelist, Somerset Maugham wrote almost one hundred short stories. Several are based on tales he heard during his travels in China and the Far East. Two volumes of "Malayan" stories were published under the titles* The Casuarina Tree *and* Ah King. *This harrowing description of a naturalist lost in the Borneo jungle is from* Neil MacAdam.

“I walked for some time and it struck me I'd come a good deal farther than I knew. Suddenly I caught sight of an empty match-box. I'd thrown it away when I started to come back. I'd been walking in a circle and was exactly where I was an hour before. I was not pleased. But I had a look round and set off again. It was fearfully hot and I was simply dripping with sweat. I knew more or less the direction the camp was in and I looked about for traces of my passage to see if I had come that way. I thought I found one or two and went on hopefully. I was frightfully thirsty. I walked on and on, picking my way over snags and trailing plants, and suddenly I knew I was lost. I couldn't have gone so far in the right direction without hitting the camp. I can tell you I was startled. I knew I must keep my head, so I sat down and thought the situation over. I was tortured by thirst. It was long past midday and in three or four hours it would be dark. I didn't like the idea of spending a night in the jungle at all. The only thing I could think of was to try and find a stream; if I followed its course, it would eventually bring me to a larger stream and sooner or later to the river. But of course it might take a couple of days. I cursed myself for being such a fool, but there was nothing better to do and I began walking. At all events if I found a stream I should be able to get a drink. I couldn't find a trickle of water anywhere, not the smallest brook that might lead to something like a stream. I began to be alarmed. I saw myself wandering on till at least I fell exhausted. I knew there was a lot of game in the forest and if I came upon a rhino I was done for. The maddening thing was that I knew I couldn't be more than ten miles from my camp. The day was waning and in the depths of the jungle it was growing dark already. If I'd brought a gun I could have fired it. In the camp they must have realised I was lost and would be looking for me. The undergrowth was so thick I couldn't

see six feet into it and presently, I don't know if it was nerves or not, I had the sensation that some animal was walking stealthily beside me. I stopped and it stopped too. I went on and it went on. I couldn't see it. I could see no movement in the undergrowth. I couldn't even hear the breaking of a twig or the brushing of a body through leaves,but I knew how silently those beasts could move, and I was positive something was stalking me. My heart beat so violently against my ribs that I thought it would break. I was scared out of my wits....”

SOMERSET MAUGHAM, *BORNEO STORIES*, LONDON, 1975

### THE BATTLE OF TANJUNG KIDURONG

*Thomas Francis McDougall, a FRCS as well as a clergyman, started the Anglican Mission in Sarawak in 1848; he was consecrated Bishop of Labuan in 1855. McDougall had spent his youth in the military garrisons of the Mediterranean, where his father was an officer, and he was always ready to fight the good fight, whether against worldly or spiritual foes. In 1862, the Bishop found himself on Mr Brooke's yacht the* Rainbow *when it was attacked by pirates. He lent a hand with the fighting until his medical duties called him below deck. He wrote a graphic description of the incident to* The Times *– and soon found himself under fire again, this time from his brethren of the cloth. Victorian public opinion was not ready for a double-barrelled Terry's breech-loader in episcopal hands.*

“...Brooke asked the Datu Bandar and Pengeran Matusin (Malays who were on board the Rainbow) if they were perfectly certain that these were Illanun pirates. 'Perfectly so; there is not a shadow of doubt,' all said. So we took our stations, loaded our guns and prepared for action.... Our plan of action was to silence the brass guns with our rifles, to shake them at the oars with grape and round shot, until we could run into them without their being shot, until we could run into them without their being strong enough to board us.... we opened all the guns we got to bear, and kept on full power until we ran into her, struck her midships, our stem running right over her, and then backed off again. We called out to the slaves and all who were not pirates, or who wished to surrender, to hold on by the wreck until we could take them off, and then steamed away after the remaining vessel.... After the first prahu was run down I had to go below to attend to our own wounded as they came in.... I asked many of those I was dressing if their wounds hurt them much, and they said, 'Yes, they hurt, but nothing hurts us so much as the salt water the Illanuns made us drink; they never gave us fresh, but mixed three parts of fresh water with four of salt, and all they gave us to eat was a handful of rice or sago twice a day.' The captives state that when the pirates take a vessel they kill every

one who makes any resistance.... those they spare are first taken aboard their own prahus, they put a rattan or a black rope halter round their necks, beat them with a flat piece of bamboo on the elbows and knees, and the muscles of the arms and legs, so that they cannot use them to swim or run away. After a while they are made to row in gangs.... if he does not do this effectually he is "krissed" and thrown overboard, and another man put in his place.... I must mention that my double-barrelled Terry's breech-loader...proved itself a most deadly weapon from its true shooting and certainty and rapidity of fire. It never missed fire once in eighty rounds, and was then so little fouled that I believe it would never have fired eighty more rounds with like effect....”

THOMAS FRANCIS MCDOUGALL, LETTER TO *THE TIMES*, MAY 27, 1862

**IBAN LOVE SONG**

*This is an extract from* Renong Indu Merindang Ati *(Girls' Pastimes), a cycle of songs recorded at Rumah Jantan, Suri, Debak, in July–September 1973 by Carol Rubenstein. The singers were Enteri anak Gawing and his son, Gudom anak Enteri. Renong are songs about love as much as they are love songs proper, highly stylized, usually very long poetic works passed to the younger generation by elders. Ms Rubenstein has collected and preserved thousands of lines of Sarawak indigenous poetry.*

“They go thru an uncut island of bushes;
and then reach totally untouched forest;
and then pass newly growing jungle,
crossed with many tracks and junctions.
Losing speed and strength, their hips aching,
they sit and rest, the wise young girls,
like the adong fish keeping still
in order to snatch the little petutu fish.
They sit unmoving at the raised root of the tree,
their legs folded up like the double fold of the male sarong.
Looking to the front and to the back of them,
the still-dependent young girls, lovely as Kumang,
see the last rays spreading from the edge of the sky,
touching the ferns and orchids high in the trees and setting them gleaming.
'Let us stay here, my dear yearning friend.'
Then they take the fruit of the empadi tuba tree,
the tree whose bark is prickly with curved thorns.
And then they grip the fruit of the planted empadi tuba tree,
their hands curling around it
Then they crush them together in an old coconut husk,
and the two of them pound it further on a smooth hard stone.
'Life for us is useless, unwanted as we are,
no beloved sweetheart joining us inside the mosquito net.
It is best for us to separate from the others,
to leave their day behind us,
to join the souls of the dead at Mandai Gulong.
It is very pleasant, the path to paradise, the path
is broad as the huge padi container of the sedong padi.
For the pathway of our lives is narrow, tiny as the fibres of the coconut husk.'
Then the two mix the poison
within the smooth inner husk of the coconut,

"PRESENTS GIVEN TO A GIRL DURING COURTSHIP CAN NEVER BE RECOVERED WHATEVER THE EVENT."

BROOKE LOW, FROM HENRY LING ROTH'S *THE NATIVES OF SARAWAK AND BRITISH BORNEO*

kneading it further within the coconut,
whose husk is rough.
They gaze out before them,
the developing young girls, lovely as Kumang,
towards the clouds moving in the sky
where constellations of stars are hanging.
The two are about to drink it in,
lifted to their mouths, to go between their lips,
to slip past the notches of their teeth –
when suddenly they hear waves of sound
made by small brass bell which is hung
among the colorful strands of a sword's
belt, the bell sounds lightly bouncing
above the sword's curved handle.
They see a young man who is beyond
merely handsome!
He is dressed in a singlet and a thin smooth
loincloth, a sword tied around his waist,
on his head a thick bunch of plumes,
topped with long gracefully waving feathers of the
hornbill.”

ENTERI ANAK GAWING AND GUDOM ANAK ENTERI, (RECORDED BY CAROL RUBENSTEIN), *SARAWAK MUSEUM JOURNAL SPECIAL MONOGRAPH NO. 2, 1973,* SARAWAK MUSEUM

**RIVER TRAVEL IN SABAH**

*Sandakan, the North Borneo Company's trading town on Sabah's east coast, was founded by William Pryer with a staff of three, seventeen fowls, and a barrel of flour. Those were the days of the Wild East – Sandakan's first census lists "actor, brothel keeper, prostitute, gambler" as professions, besides more staid employments such as "butcher, baker, charcoal burner, porter, shipwright". Mrs Pryer stood by her husband's side. Her writings reveal a sensible lady with the true pioneering spirit. As this extract from her diary of an adventurous journey inland shows, she was not sentimental.*

“The usual accounts of tropical scenery are much overdrawn, so far as my experience extends; at any rate, with regard to the number of flowers to be met with. As a rule, the forest itself is one uniform dark green. Orchids are often to be seen, but their flowers are rarely conspicuous. There are, of course, exceptions, but they grow so high up in the forks of the trees that unless the tree is felled or a ladder made there is no getting at them, climbing being practically impossible for the great forest trees grow from 100 feet to 150 feet before they spread out a single branch in their search for light and air, their trunks being as straight as the columns of a cathedral aisle. On the river bank, however, one tree was often seen which proved an exception to this rule, this being doubtless the season for its blooming; rising to a height of 30 feet or so,it was smothered in flowers of a bright lilac hue, and looked not unlike a rhododendron… On and on we went, wearily and slowly, our boatmen always good-tempered, and ready to make the best of a bad situation, never a grumble, never a murmur, making fun of each other when a companion sank to his armpits in soft ooze, pulling and tugging and laughing and swimming by turns. We passed no houses; we met no boats for days, except at a small village called Blut. In this campong there is only one decent house, but we found the proprietor at home, who showed us his new domicile with great pride. He had recently paid Elopura a visit, and had become inspired with a desire to possess a better abode than his neighbours, so had erected one on the Sandakan model. This man had a wonderful tale about a coal mine, which W. [William Pryer] promised to inquire further about on the first possible occasion.”

WILLIAM B. PRYER (MRS), *A DECADE IN BORNEO*, LONDON, 1894

## Post-war and Independence

### A slave girl in Singapore

*Janet Lim belonged to the last generation of girls to be sold to wealthy families as* mui tsai *(little sister) domestic slaves. Born in China, Janet had the misfortune to lose her father at an early age; when her mother remarried, the in-laws sold the unwanted eight-year-old to a trafficker who disposed of her in Singapore.*

"I was looked at, criticised, and after much bargaining sold for $250. My master was an old man. Living with him was his second wife, who had been his former servant, and their son, who was about my age. His first wife, who had several grown-up children, lived about five miles away. In our house there were also two servants and two other girls, one a slave like myself and the other a distant relation.... Mostly I was given housework to do. I also had to look after the poultry. This I did not mind; indeed the geese were my great friends. I talked to them about my sorrows and worries, and, turning their heads this way and that, they seemed to understand me. It was in this household that I learned to cook, sew and swear! I had no friends except the geese and although the other slave was my equal, yet we had little to do with each other, for she was the mistress' favourite.... In China, the slave girl system had been a recognised institution for centuries.... Such a girl was not given regular wages, and was not at liberty to leave her employer's family of her own will or the wish of her parents. A document was drawn up on red paper – as I witnessed in my own case – and the purchase money was handed over.... In my own case the transfer was made indirectly through a trafficker in girls. Girls were bought by the trafficker from destitute parents or from those who, for some reason, wished to get rid of a girl. The girls were then transported elsewhere, often overseas to Malaya, and sold at a profit. These traffickers also dealt in girls destined for brothels, but although some *mui tsai* did eventually become prostitutes the two uses of girls were distinct. In Singapore, at the time I arrived there, it was not illegal for a family to have a *mui tsai*, but if cruelty or ill-treatment were proved the employer could be prosecuted; the girls involved in prostitution were dealt with separately under various ordinances for the protection of women and girls. Obviously, the *mui tsai* system was open to abuse and although many of the 'slave girls' were treated well, everything depended on the character of the master. My master was a rich man, a landowner, and he had many friends. He often had parties and got drunk, but he was not violent. More often he suffered from insomnia, and then he would walk around the whole house visiting all the women's rooms. After about three months he started trying to visit me at night. I cannot express my terror when I heard his footsteps. I crawled anywhere, inside cupboards, under beds, outside windows, anywhere, as long as I could get out of his reach. I never slept twice running in the same place. Luckily for me the house was very large. Many a night I slept with my friends, the geese, but more often in a bathroom."

Janet Lim, *Sold for Silver*,
London, 1958

Malay village scene from an old postcard.

## Goat village

*Abdul Samad Said was born in Singapore, and his novel* Salina *is set in the urban kampungs, the slums of that city. In the years just after the war, when accommodation was scarce, the burgeoning city's poor were prepared to pay rent for empty goat sheds, now dignified by the name "house".*

"Most of the houses were crowded. The inhabitants' former houses had, in most cases, been bombed or rented by their landlords to richer tenants. The old woman had been to the kampong a week ago, after a friend told her that there was an empty shanty. She had been lucky enough to rent one which had just been vacated. It was not easy. The house cost fifty dollars 'coffee money' and the promise of twenty dollars on the correct day. Then it was hers, with its roof of iron, palm thatch and plank, and layers of rubber and fresh pumpkin leaves, its walls of plywood, iron, plank and board, and its earth floor, to protect her from the heat and the rain.

The water taps at the Public Works Department barracks were guarded by a Bengali. 'More work for me,' he said to no one in particular. 'When Palimah left, I didn't think anyone else would want the place. But now here's another.' ... A tall thin Indian in a worn white singlet and faded blue trousers nodded as he served his customers. As he finished wrapping the dried chillies, he replied: 'Yes, but not so many. Two. A boy and his mother. She was here a week ago. I told her Kurupaya had a place. She took it.'

'Oho,' said the watchman in a loud harsh voice. 'How much for a room now? Did he put the rent up again?'

'Of course. Palimah paid eighteen dollars for the five of them. I hear Kurupaya put it up to twenty a month,' the merchant replied, shaking his head and rubbing his palms as he always did when he talked.

'My God, that Kurupaya is a smart fellow! He's got a lot of money and he wants a lot more.' The watchman spat and turned to sit on his woven bench. 'How much for coffee money?'

'Fifty dollars,' the merchant replied, turning to serve another customer. When he had finished he continued: 'Fifty dollars is nothing. They pay up. It's so hard to get a place, people would pay a hundred dollars!'

'Yes, yes, yes. But it's not right to ask poor people to pay so much.' The merchant said nothing. Kurupaya was a relative of his."

Abdul Said Samad, *Salina*,
Kuala Lumpur, 1975

### THE BROTHERS

*Stella Kon is one of Singapore's most noted modern playwrights; with* Emily of Emerald Hill *she gained international renown. In this excerpt from* Trial, *career politician Ximeng declines to help his musician brother who is in trouble; the fact that he was engaged to Rosa before she eloped with Bobby throws another light on the scene.*

"Ximeng: What happened?
Rosa: We decided to play his Lion City Symphony in public, free for everyone to hear.We took the speakers and equipment down to Orchard Road and set them up and started the music; people stopped to listen, they seemed interested, a crowd gathered. Then some policemen arrived and asked to see our performing licence, and when we said we didn't know we needed one they said we'd have to stop. Bobby was upset, because we were getting a good response from the crowd, and he tried to argue about it.Then the policeman said that we were creating a public disturbance and obstructing traffic, and we'd have to go to the police station. Bobby wouldn't stop the music so they started switching off the power, pulling out the cables, knocking the equipment around. Bobby lost his temper and struggled with them.
Ximeng: He shouldn't have done that.
Rosa: He was holding a long aerial rod. One of the policemen claimed that Bobby hit him with the rod, but I know he didn't intend to – if he did, it was an accident.
Ximeng: Striking a police officer is a serious offence.
Rosa: And we have been told he could be jailed for it. If it were a fine your father would pay it at once. But he couldn't stand being put in jail. You know him, he's your brother… he's so responsive, so sensitive, he'd be terribly hurt by the trauma and humiliation. It would destroy him.
Ximeng: Because of his fine artistic temperament.
Rosa: Ximeng, you must do something to help us. You don't resent us, do you, for loving each other? You are not holding a grudge against us?
Ximeng: I don't hold grudges. I don't let personal relationships influence my decisions, one way or another. Rosa, surely you see that I can't intervene in this case? What do you expect me to do, have a little word with the magistrate and ask him to let my brother off, as a favour to me? I couldn't do that kind of thing.
Rosa: There must be some acceptable way you can help.
Ximeng: I am not going to be involved in this matter. The nation will fall into chaos if every leader starts using his position to assist his own family. Bobby will have to accept that the laws which apply to other citizens also apply to him. Please don't ask me again.
Rosa: Ximeng, for the sake of anything you ever felt for me.
Ximeng: I think you'd better leave now."

STELLA KON, *TRIAL*,
SINGAPORE, 1986

# ITINERARIES

▲ Empress Place and Singapore River, Singapore.

▲ Tanjong Pagar conservation area, Singapore. ▼ Pulau Ubin village, off Singapo

▲ City skyline, Singapore.

▲ Chinatown and Shenton Way skyline, Singapore. ▼ Port containers, Singapore.

▲ Kuala Lumpur, capital city of Malaysia.

▲ Parit, near Ipoh, West Malaysia. ▼ Kuala Besut in Terengganu, West Malaysia

▲ Penang Hill, West Malaysia.

▲ Rubber plantation, West Malaysia.

▼ Old Melaka town, West Malaysia.

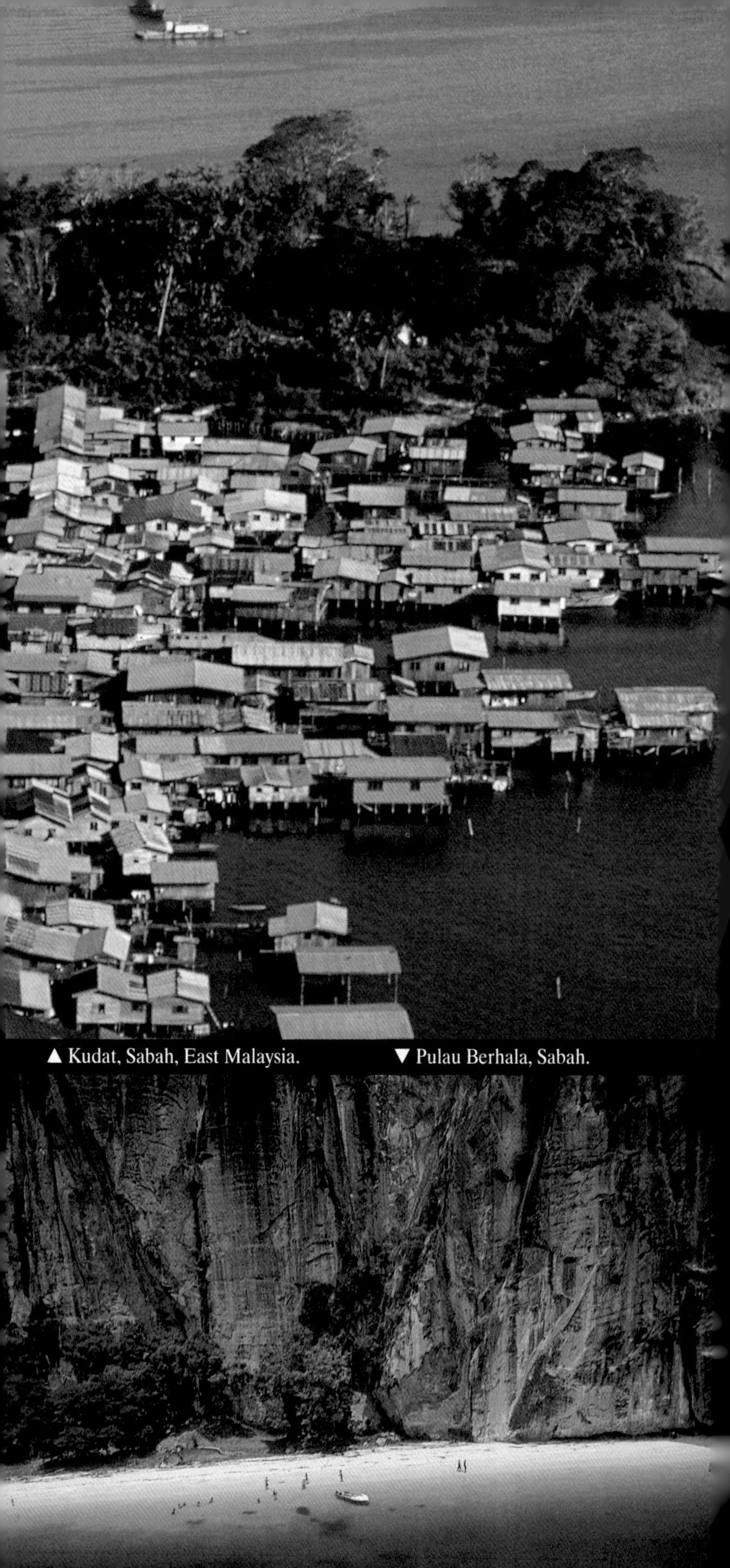

▲ Kudat, Sabah, East Malaysia. ▼ Pulau Berhala, Sabah.

▲ Sibu waterfront, Sarawak in East Malaysia. ▼ Mulu caves, Sarawak.

▲ Omar Ali Saifuddien Mosque.

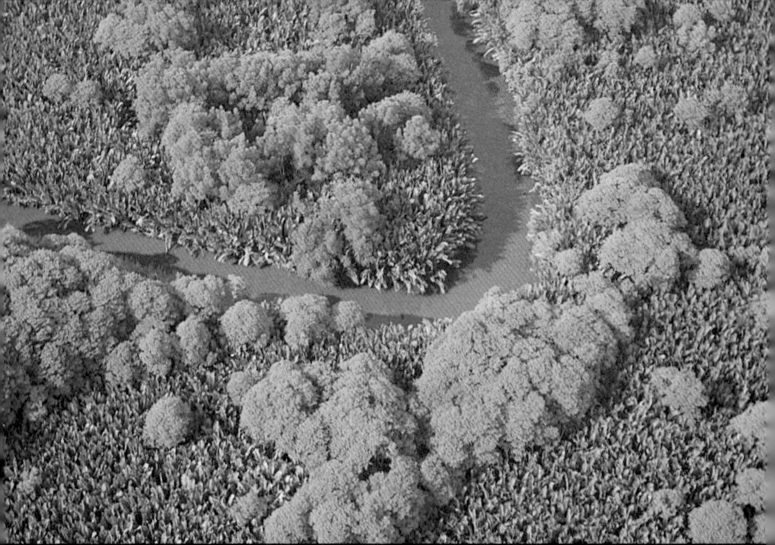

▲ Forest reserve in Temburong.

▼ Oil rigs, Brunei Darussalam.

# SINGAPORE

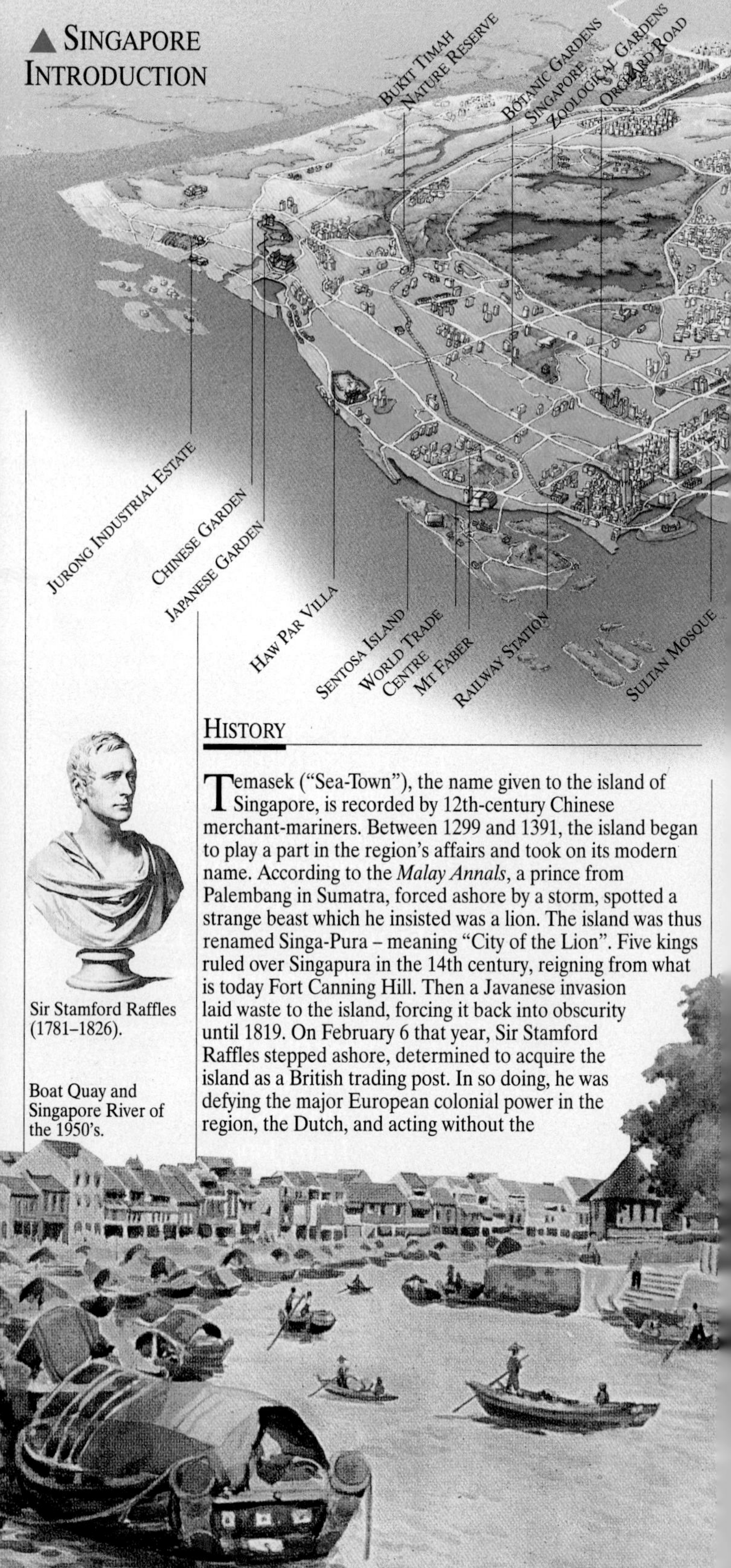


## History

Temasek ("Sea-Town"), the name given to the island of Singapore, is recorded by 12th-century Chinese merchant-mariners. Between 1299 and 1391, the island began to play a part in the region's affairs and took on its modern name. According to the *Malay Annals*, a prince from Palembang in Sumatra, forced ashore by a storm, spotted a strange beast which he insisted was a lion. The island was thus renamed Singa-Pura – meaning "City of the Lion". Five kings ruled over Singapura in the 14th century, reigning from what is today Fort Canning Hill. Then a Javanese invasion laid waste to the island, forcing it back into obscurity until 1819. On February 6 that year, Sir Stamford Raffles stepped ashore, determined to acquire the island as a British trading post. In so doing, he was defying the major European colonial power in the region, the Dutch, and acting without the

Sir Stamford Raffles (1781–1826).

Boat Quay and Singapore River of the 1950's.

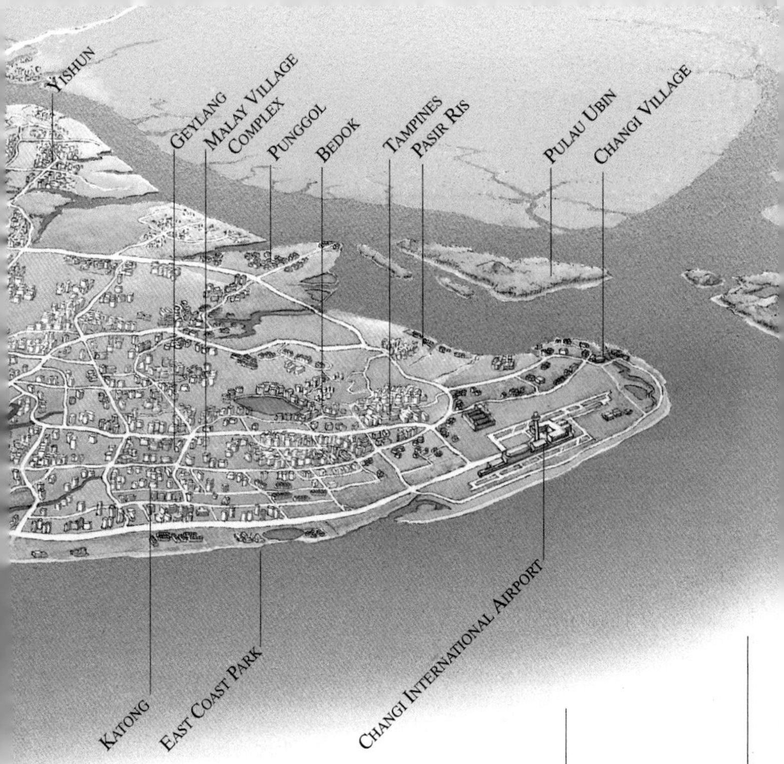

YISHUN
GEYLANG
MALAY VILLAGE COMPLEX
PUNGGOL
BEDOK
TAMPINES
PASIR RIS
PULAU UBIN
CHANGI VILLAGE
KATONG
EAST COAST PARK
CHANGI INTERNATIONAL AIRPORT

political backing of London or the support of his employer, the East India Company. His object was "not territory but trade" and he gave Singapore free-port status (which it still has today) and issued invitations for others to join him. The Chinese came from the poverty-stricken southern seaboard regions of China, and were joined by Indians, Arabs, Jews, Europeans, and Armenians. Raffles quickly designated town areas for the various ethnic groups and set in motion many of today's institutions (from the five-foot way to the Sultan Mosque). In 1824, the Anglo-Dutch Treaty legitimized this British intrusion. Ruffled Malay princelings had been bought off, the harbor was full of boats, the town had taken shape, the population had risen to 11,000 – Singapore Inc. was up and running.

## MODERN SINGAPORE

Today, growth in Singapore is still remarkable, not just in economic terms, but in such projects as large-scale land reclamation which have given Singapore an extra 52 square miles of territory. Growth has been equally impressive in tourism. In 1957, assemblyman William Tan opposed a S$300,000 tourism promotion budget, insisting Singapore had just three attractions to offer visitors: "swamplands, some fine buildings, and the death houses of Sago Lane". At that time Singapore attracted 150,000 tourists each year. By 1995, the figure had soared to over 7 million. This quantity of tourist arrivals brought about S$9 billion of revenue. Many Asian tourists come on designer brand-name shopping sprees. Caucasian tourists are often disappointed by such modern trappings and come hoping instead to see Far East exotica. Indeed, the joy for many is the intricate mixture of old and new, East and West, lashings of lush tropical greenery and telephones that work. Away from Shenton Way and Orchard Road, much of Singapore still reflects Raffles' original vision.

**FOUNDERS' MEMORIAL STONE**
The island's early commercial success was built on the efforts of thousands of anonymous migrants. At Collyer Quay, opposite Fullerton Building, is the Early Founders' Memorial Stone. It originally intended to be the cornerstone of a larger memorial honoring the early migrants. Sadly, the "Unknown Immigrant" project ran out of money. At night the area is attractively lit by gaslight.

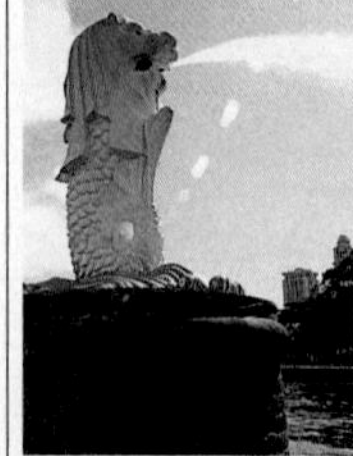

**MERLION**
Singapore's official tourism emblem – the half-lion, half-fish Merlion statue – has been spouting water from its position at the mouth of the Singapore River since 1972.

**SINGAPORE RIVER MUSEUM**
Alongside Merlion Park is the Singapore River Museum, which houses engrossing displays including reconstructions of a coolies' room and an old-style waterfront shophouse office. Most vivid of all, however, are samples of the river's bed before and after the "big clean-up" in the 1980's by the Ministry of Environment. The difference is amazing. Admission is free, and underneath the museum is a small souvenir shop.

## COLLYER QUAY

**CLIFFORD PIER.** Almost the last remnant of the old seaport's bustling waterfront, Clifford Pier would still make a fine spot for visitors to set foot on Singaporean soil. The human activity here can still mist the eyes of those with nostalgic notions of a long-gone Far East nautical era, even though the area is overshadowed by the financial district's soaring modern buildings and the swirling road traffic of Collyer Quay. The pier inspired the storyline of Joseph Conrad's classic novel, *Lord Jim*, which was based on the roving adventurers, yarns, and incidents he encountered along the Singapore waterfront in the 1880's. It is still a lively area, with Neptune Theatre the only Singaporean venue allowed to stage topless shows by international dance troupes. The aerial link from the pier over Collyer Quay houses the modern version of the once-famous Change Alley. The deft-fingered money-changers who gave the alley its name can still handle any currency on the spot, usually offering better exchange rates than the banks nearby. The location is appropriate, too, for this area is close to the center of modern Singapore's thriving financial and business district. The north end of Change Alley leads to Raffles Place, a square and a delightful pedestrian mall complete with neo-classical structures which mark the entrance to the main downtown MRT station.

## RAFFLES PLACE

Number One Raffles Place is the address of the striking OUB (Overseas Union Bank) Centre. Designed by the Japanese architect Kenzo Tange, it houses a shopping center with a comfortable outdoor cafe (known as Chatterbox) and, at the top of its sixty-four

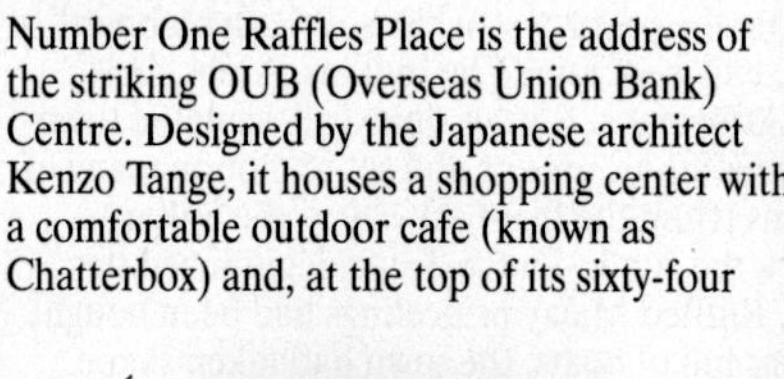

stories, the expensive Pinnacles restaurant has sweeping panoramic views and offers French and Cantonese menus. The OUB tower is exactly the same height as its nearby "rival" UOB (United Overseas Bank) Plaza – 918 feet. This is the maximum height permitted for buildings in Singapore: any higher and they become an aviation hazard and obstruct telecommunications. These soaring bank towers are the highest in the world outside the United States and Japan. The third local major bank is the OCBC (Overseas Chinese Banking Corporation) skyscraper, designed by the well-known Chinese-American architect I.M. Pei; its looks have earned it the wry local tag of "the pocket-calculator building".

## Boat Quay and Clarke Quay

Singapore River's two biggest draws are Boat Quay and Clarke Quay. Boat Quay, along the southern flank of the river, is a glorious stroll in the early morning or at dusk. Lining one side of the riverbank is a row of pubs and a wide variety of eating outlets that offer alfresco dining until late in the evening. This section of the river was the original Singapore port, with *tongkang* (lighters) and bum-boats ferrying cargos to and from the ships moored out at sea. Colorful Clarke Quay has attracted both tourists and locals since November 1993. One of the largest conservation projects in Singapore, it cost S$190 million and took about four years to complete. The family-style riverside village is open all day until late evening and has street bazaars, boutique shophouses, live stage performances, an amusement arcade and a department store.

**Curry Puffs**
OUB Centre's shopping complex basement is home to a great Singapore snack – Polar curry puffs. Made since 1926 to a still-secret recipe, with fillings of mashed potato, egg and chicken, these crispy puffs have a unique flavor and must be tried. Polar Puffs & Cakes was once located at High Street where, under the name of Polar Cafe, it became a popular meeting place for lawyers and bankers whose offices were nearby. Polar has other outlets along Orchard Road, selling its curry puffs and cakes.

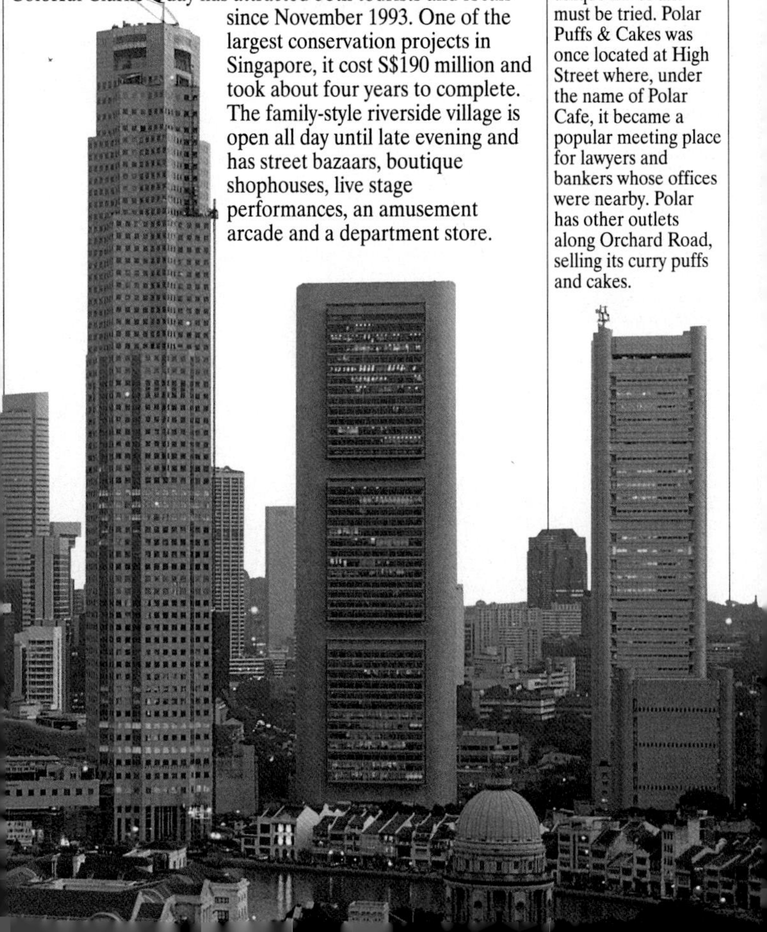

# ▲ Singapore The Waterfront

1. Adelphi, the
2. Anderson Bridge
3. Apollo Centre
4. Asia Insurance Building
5. Beach Road
6. Boat Quay pubs and restaurants
7. Bras Basah Complex
8. Caltex House
9. Cavenagh Bridge
10. Change Alley Aerial Plaza
11. Chinatown Point
12. City Hall
13. Clarke Quay
14. Clifford Centre
15. Clifford Pier
16. Coleman Bridge
17. Coleman Street
18. Colombo Court
19. CPF Building
20. DBS Building
21. Elgin Bridge
22. Ellenborough Market
23. Esplanade, the
24. Excelsior Hotel
25. Exchange, the
26. Funan Centre
27. Furama Hotel
28. Gateway, the
29. Fullerton Building
30. High Street Centre
31. Hongkong Bank Building
32. Hong Leong Building
33. Hong Lim Complex
34. ICB Building
35. International Plaza
36. John Hancock Tower
37. Liang Court
38. Marina House
39. Marina Mandarin
40. MAS Building
41. Maxwell Road
42. Ministry of National Development Building
43. National Archives
44. North Bridge Road
45. Ocean Building
46. Octagon, the
47. Odeon Tower
48. The Oriental Singapore
49. OUB Centre
50. Padang, the
51. Pan Pacific Hotel
52. Parliament House

Goodwood Park
RAFFLES HOTEL
Hard Rock CAFE

**Boat Quay**
Once occupied by small trading companies, the shophouses along Boat Quay have been given a new lease of life. Pubs and restaurants today line the river bank,

**Waterfront, early 1900s**
An early view of the waterfront, c. 1900-30, showing Johnston's Pier, now known as Clifford Pier.

roviding a lively and
nternational
ackdrop for alfresco
ining and dining
nder the stars.

**The Gateway**

This landmark at Beach Road stands out as a pair of razor-edged office building thirty-seven stories high, blending glass with aluminium to give a crystalline exterior. At a glance, the twin towers appear to resemble a common feature in Bali: the *candi bentar*, split gate to a temple entrance.

**UOB Plaza**

Completed in 1992 and standing at 918 feet by the Singapore River, the sixty-six-story UOB Plaza ranks among the tallest buildings in the island republic. On the thirty-eighth story is a sky lobby – the first in this region – where the express double-decker mid- and high-rise lifts meet and transfer passengers.

CENTRAL
FIRE STATION
L TAILOR
大中央洋服

# ▲ Singapore
# The civic and cultural center

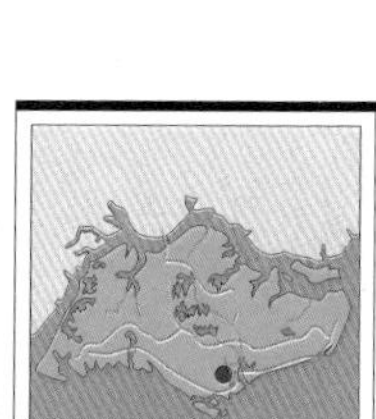

◷ 1 day

**The Esplanade**
A series of memorials lines the Esplanade. These include the World War One Cenotaph and the Tan Kim Seng "water fountain", which honors a rich merchant who, in 1857, donated $13,000 to set up a municipal drinking-water system. However, this opportunity was wasted, with the donation being spent largely on the memorial itself. This is also the site for Singapore's lavish new Arts Centre (scheduled for decade-end), called The Esplanade.

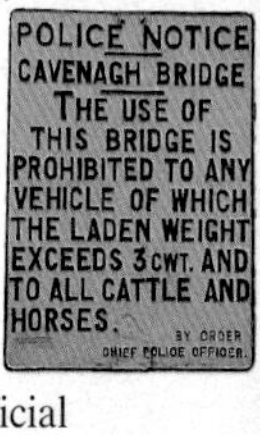

**Lim Bo Seng**
The most notable war memorial on the Esplanade is the pagoda-like Lim Bo Seng Memorial, guarded by its four bronze lions. This commemorates a Chinese Singapore war hero, who was tortured to death by the Japanese secret police in 1944.

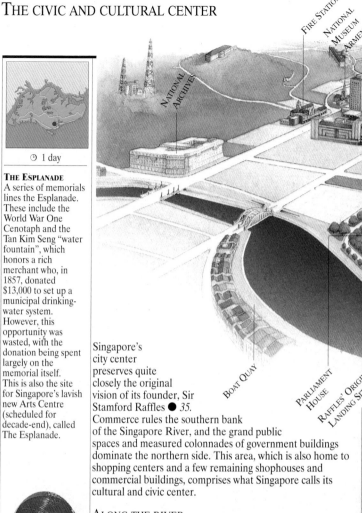

Singapore's city center preserves quite closely the original vision of its founder, Sir Stamford Raffles ● *35.* Commerce rules the southern bank of the Singapore River, and the grand public spaces and measured colonnades of government buildings dominate the northern side. This area, which is also home to shopping centers and a few remaining shophouses and commercial buildings, comprises what Singapore calls its cultural and civic center.

## Along the river

Parliament House, built in 1827, was originally a merchant's private house, and has undergone several extensions and adaptations to make it a home fit for independent Singapore's Parliament. Victoria Memorial Hall and Theatre also serves as a home for major local cultural bodies such as the Singapore Symphony Orchestra formed in 1978, and for more popular cultural activities. Local television made its debut outside the building in February 1963, with about five hundred people watching a fifteen-minute film called *TV Looks At Singapore,* on seventeen monochrome TV sets. The Hall's clock tower has served as Singapore's "Big Ben" since 1906. The statue of Raffles outside was unveiled in 1887, stunning the Malays at the official reception. This became clear from one quoted reaction to the bronze statue's color: "He was a black man, like us!" The statue was hidden from the Japanese during their 1942–5 occupation, when it was wanted for a proposed Tokyo museum of Imperial conquests. One question has plagued the

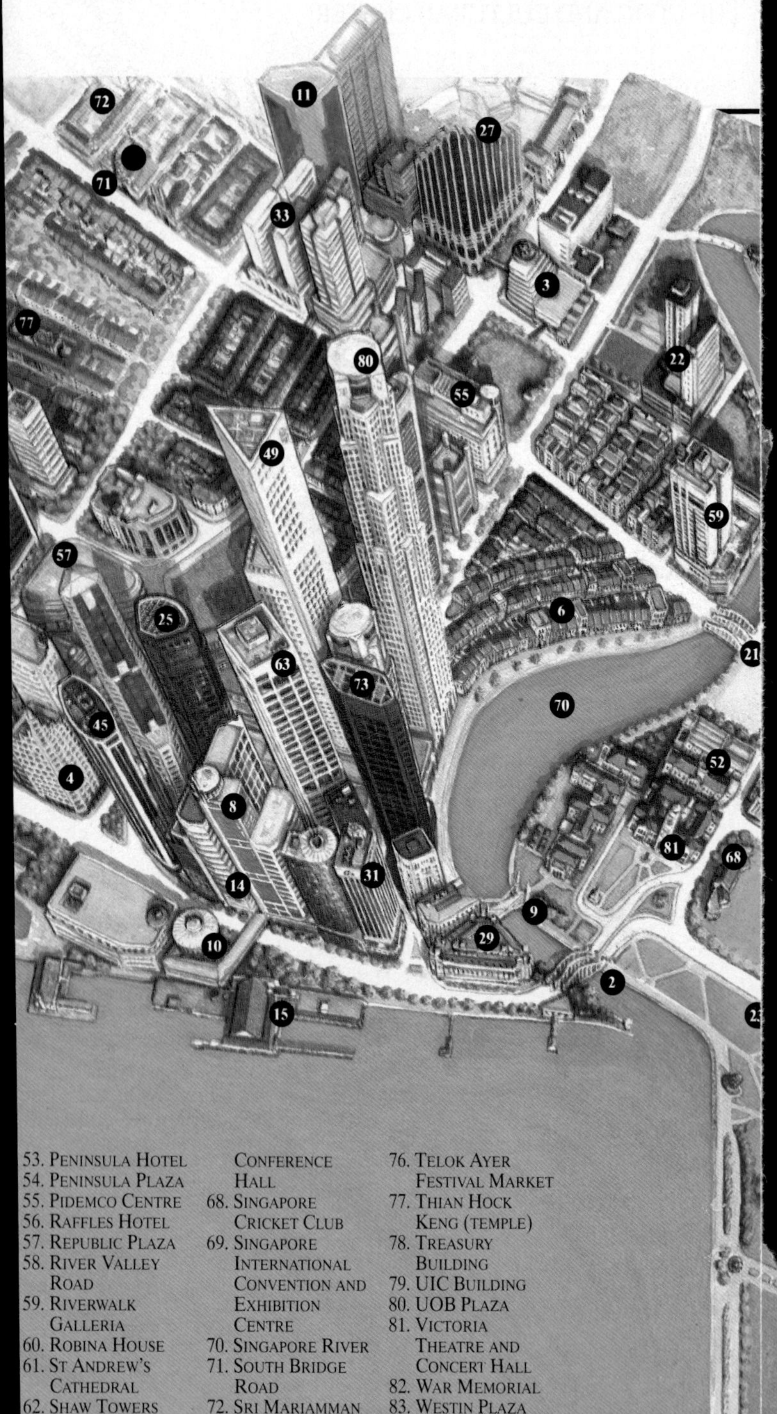

53. Peninsula Hotel
54. Peninsula Plaza
55. Pidemco Centre
56. Raffles Hotel
57. Republic Plaza
58. River Valley Road
59. Riverwalk Galleria
60. Robina House
61. St Andrew's Cathedral
62. Shaw Towers
63. Shell Tower
64. Shenton House
65. Shenton Way
66. Shing Kwan House
67. Singapore Conference Hall
68. Singapore Cricket Club
69. Singapore International Convention and Exhibition Centre
70. Singapore River
71. South Bridge Road
72. Sri Mariamman Temple
73. Standard Chartered Bank
74. Supreme Court
75. Tanjong Pagar MRT station
76. Telok Ayer Festival Market
77. Thian Hock Keng (temple)
78. Treasury Building
79. UIC Building
80. UOB Plaza
81. Victoria Theatre and Concert Hall
82. War Memorial
83. Westin Plaza
84. Westin Stamford

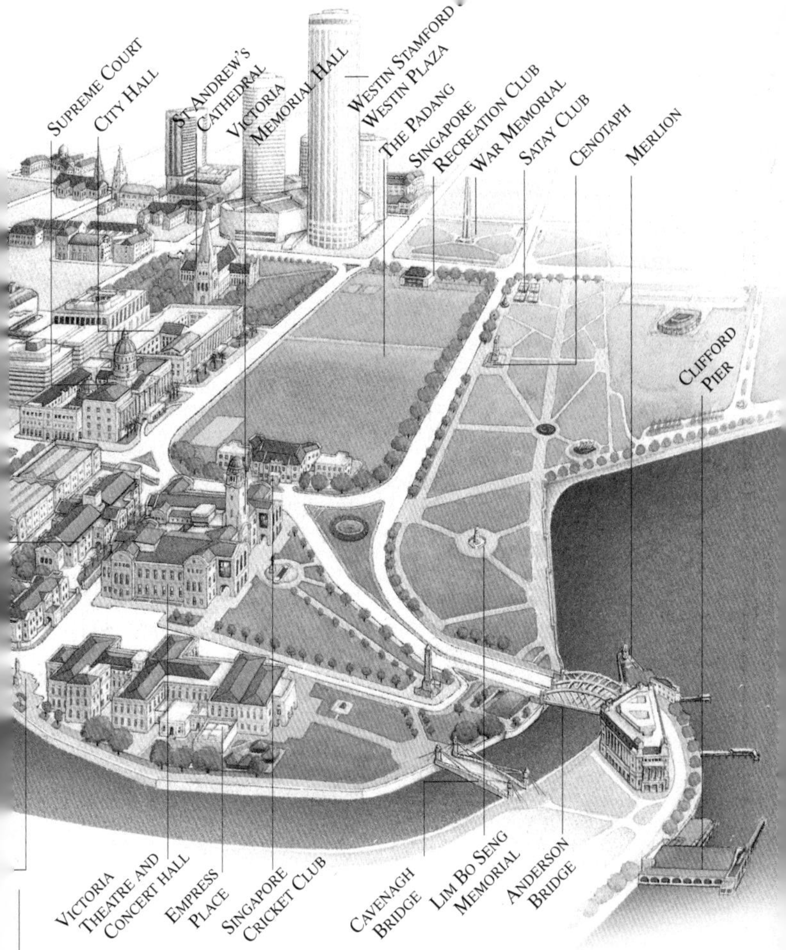

Dalhousie Memorial, modeled after an Egyptian obelisk, since it was unveiled in 1850 in front of the Victoria Concert Hall. It commemorates an obscure British colonial overlord's visit and, even today, this question is still asked – why?

**THE PADANG.** An open field near the center of power is a feature of many ancient cities. But the Padang is now a spot where English sports such as rugby, cricket, and lawn bowls are played under a tropical sky, even as peak-hour traffic crawls by around them. The Singapore Cricket Club, at one end of the Padang, still serves traditional English food to its members; at the other end stands the newly-rebuilt Singapore Recreation Club complex. The dignified public buildings that line the Padang – the Supreme Court, with its agreeable 1930's murals by Italian artist Rodolfo Nolli, and City Hall – have been the scene of major events in Singapore's history: Lord Louis Mountbatten received the official Japanese "return" of Singapore on September 12, 1945, at City Hall, and independent Singapore's early National Day festivities were centered on its sweeping steps. The main public activity is now the human drama in its Divorce Court, mirrored by the weekend troupes of wedding parties who find this a favorite spot for their photographs.

**THE SIAMESE ELEPHANT**

Outside Parliament House stands a little bronze elephant. The inscription on its pedestal explains that the statue was a gift from King Rama V of Thailand (then Siam), as a token of gratitude for his visit in 1871. Singapore had become the first foreign country visited by a reigning Siamese monarch.

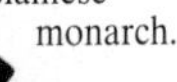

**ST ANDREW'S CATHEDRAL.** The current cathedral was built in 1861, modeled on Netley Abbey in Hampshire. It is the third Anglican church to stand on this central site (allocated by Stamford Raffles). As with so many 19th-century public buildings, it was constructed using Indian convict labor. The secret of its bright whiteness is, allegedly, the plaster with which it is coated; known as *madras chunam*, it is a mixture of shell lime, egg white, coarse sugar, and water from soaked coconut husks.

**SUNTEC CITY.** This is the largest privately owned commercial complex in Singapore, with its centrepiece – the 100,000 sq.m. Singapore International Convention and Exhibition Centre (SICEC) – coming onstream in 1995. It includes a 12,000 sq.m. convention hall, office towers, Suntec City Mall and the Fountain Terrace, dense with eateries and bars grouped around Suntec's trademark brash fountain-cum-sculpture.

**THE MEMORIAL.** Between Marina Square and Raffles City stands the Memorial to the Civilian Victims of the Japanese Occupation. There is an urn at its center, containing the ashes of a few of the many Asian, Eurasian, and Western casualties of the 1942–5 war years ● *38*. It is estimated that up to fifty thousand people were killed by the Japanese while Singapore was Syonan (Japanese for "Light of the South"). This is their memorial. Its four tapered 219-foot-high columns have earned it the local tag "chopsticks memorial".

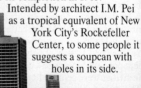

**MARINA SQUARE.** This complex is American architect John Portman's contribution to the republic's cityscape. A shopping mall housing several restaurants, two cinemas, and three hotels, each with its own character, demonstrate Portland's "trademark" – soaring internal atria. The Oriental Hotel is first cousin to Bangkok's more famous hotel of the same name and succeeds in combining modernity with personality and good taste. The tall one is the Pan-Pacific with its external bubble lifts and its female doormen. The third one is the Marina Mandarin. The newest hotel here is the 610-room deluxe Ritz-Carlton Millenia Singapore.

**RAFFLES CITY.** This building has provoked arguments ever since its completion in 1985. Intended by architect I.M. Pei as a tropical equivalent of New York City's Rockefeller Center, to some people it suggests a soupcan with holes in its side.

**A CHIP OFF THE OLD BLOCK**

"In December 1890, the building was ready to be used, and there was some correspondence in the paper about the delay in opening it…owing to the windows and lamps not having arrived from England, which some of the congregation thought to be a bad excuse, and offered to pay for temporary screens until the stained-glass windows arrived. There was such a great demand for seats that a ballot was held at the Masonic Lodge.... Applications could be made at $1 or 50 cents a month, according to their position.... On the occasion of the Memorial Service on the day of Queen Victoria's funeral, there were about 1,400 persons in the congregation."

"TO HAVE BEEN YOUNG AND HAD A ROOM AT RAFFLES WAS PROBABLY LIFE AT ITS BEST."

JAMES MICHENER

Others regard it as a grossly out-of-proportion behemoth. The complex houses the world's tallest hotel, the seventy-three-story Westin Stamford, which has become noted for its annual "vertical marathons". The current record for running up its 1336 steps is 6 minutes and 55 seconds. The high-speed lift takes 34 seconds to reach the Compass Rose restaurant at the top. Here diners can also enjoy superb 360-degree views of Singapore and the surrounding islands. When Queen Elizabeth II dined at the restaurant in 1990, her main course was grilled veal tenderloin, coated with a light anise sauce. Former US President George Bush dined here in early 1992. His main course was grilled (American) filet mignon, topped with fresh goose liver and a light port-wine sauce.

**CHICKEN RICE RESTAURANTS.** Just a block away from Raffles City stand two rather more modest Singaporean institutions, the old-fashioned Swee Kee (51 Middle Road) and Yet Con (25 Purvis Street) restaurants. Both specialize in a local dish called chicken rice, which has been perfected by cooks from the southern Chinese island of Hainan.

**THE RAFFLES.** As befits one of the world's most famous hotels, and although overshadowed (literally) by towering Raffles City, the Raffles is still in a class of its own. It reopened in September 1991 in a blaze of publicity after a S$160 million restoration. However, some critics suggest Raffles has been over-restored, thus losing a lot of its raffish character – but it is often forgotten that the Raffles only became raffish in the 1950's. Before then, it served as a snobbish, whites-only hotel – which it certainly was in the era of writers such as Somerset Maugham and Noël Coward.

The "new" Raffles is now once again Singapore's most expensive hotel, with its renowned Tiffin Room, Writers' Bar, Long Bar, and Palm Garden, and its Singapore Sling gin cocktails as popular as ever. The rear section of the hotel complex is devoted to food outlets such as the Empire Café and the Seah Street deli and designer shops; the 392-seat Jubilee Hall Theatre Playhouse in late Victorian-style and a Raffles Hotel Museum and shop are here, too. Singapore's colonial core continues northwards from the Raffles, taking in the Cathedral of the Good Shepherd, the charming former St Joseph's Institution – now Singapore's Art Museum – and Chijmes (formerly Convent of the Holy Infant Jesus) now intended as a local equivalent to London's Covent Garden.

**OPENING CRUSH**
The anchor tenant of the Raffles City shopping complex is the Japanese department store, Sogo. On its opening day in October 1986, over 200,000 shoppers crowded in and police were needed to control the crush – over S$1.5 million was spent on that first day. Shopping is one of the two major Singaporean leisure activities (the other is dining).

**"WHEN AT THE RAFFLES, WHY NOT SEE SINGAPORE?"**
The Raffles Hotel's roll-call of famous guests is impressive. Rudyard Kipling insisted "the food is as excellent as the rooms are bad", while German writer Herman Hesse later took a contrary view, insisting the Raffles' food was "miserable". Actors, as well as writers, have stayed here – Marlon Brando, Orson Welles, and Elizabeth Taylor, to name but a few. The British ex-Prime Minister Harold Wilson threw a Raffles party for his wife's sixty-second birthday. Uganda's Prime Minister Milton Obote was lunching at the Raffles in 1971 when informed he was out of office – Idi Amin had taken over. And ex-Beatle John Lennon called the hotel "Rattles" in its guest book.

To many, Raffles is the quintessence of the grand Oriental hotel. The opening of the Suez Canal in 1869 stimulated trade and travel between Europe and the Far East. This in turn led to a demand for better-class accommodation. Four Armenian brothers, the Sarkies, were to prove particularly successful at providing this, opening hotels in Penang, Rangoon, and, in 1887, Singapore. The first Raffles Hotel was a modest bungalow on Beach Road, with a commanding view of the sea. However, plans were soon laid for expansion.

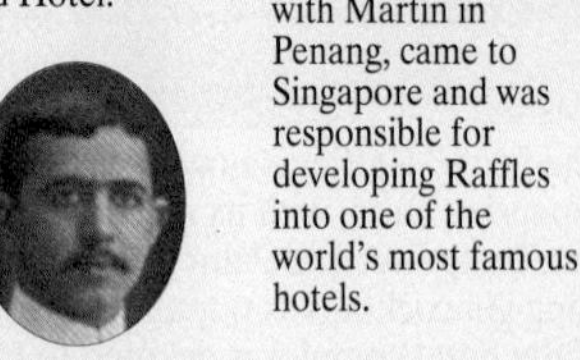

**THE SARKIES BROTHERS**
Having left Persia and settled in the East, the Sarkies brothers were, by the 1880's, busy laying the foundations for the development of a number of the East's great hotels. Martin Sarkies began the process and was the proprietor of the Eastern and Oriental in Penang. When he retired, Arshak, his youngest brother, took over, becoming well known throughout the Straits Settlements for his generosity. Aviet was destined for Rangoon, the principal city of Burma, where at the end of the century he opened the Strand Hotel. Tigran, after working with Martin in Penang, came to Singapore and was responsible for developing Raffles into one of the world's most famous hotels.

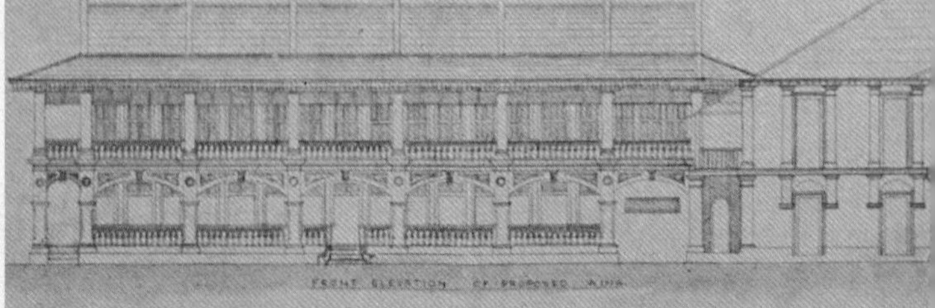

**EARLY DEVELOPMENTS**

In the decade after it opened, the original bungalow saw constant expansion and improvement. First, two-story wings were added. They provided Raffles with twenty-two new suites, all of which faced the sea and had their own shaded verandah. A little later, the famous Billiard Room was erected on the corner of Beach Road with Bras Basah, and then in 1894 came the Palm Court Wing.

**CUISINE**

Apart from increasing the size and grandeur of the hotel, Tigran also took great interest in building up the hotel's reputation for serving fine food and wine, and even opened Raffles Tiffin Rooms in the commercial district so that residents could "tiffin in Town!" The culmination of Tigran's achievements came in 1899 with the opening of the Main Building, an elegant three-story structure fitted with the latest electrical systems, powering a myriad lights, fans, and call bells.

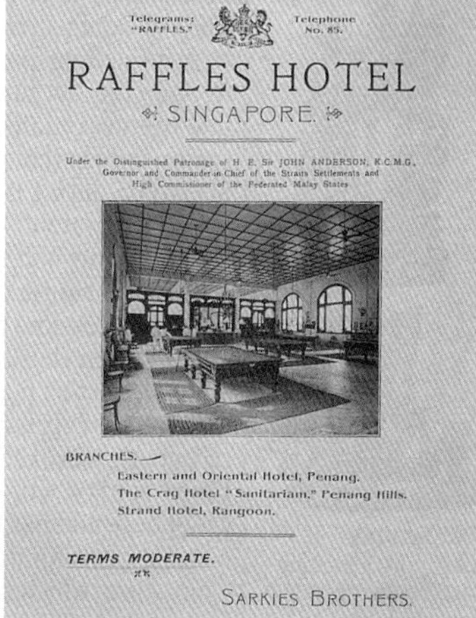

Telegrams: "RAFFLES." Telephone No. 85.

RAFFLES HOTEL

SINGAPORE.

Under the Distinguished Patronage of H. E. Sir JOHN ANDERSON, K.C.M.G., Governor and Commander-in-Chief of the Straits Settlements and High Commissioner of the Federated Malay States

BRANCHES.—

Eastern and Oriental Hotel, Penang.
The Crag Hotel "Sanitarium," Penang Hills.
Strand Hotel, Rangoon.

TERMS MODERATE.

SARKIES BROTHERS.

The grand Dining Room occupied much of the ground floor, seating five hundred.

A 1905 booklet boasted: "The Hotel commands an area of 200,000 square feet and faces the sea, has a commanding view of the Harbour, and the adjacent islands... whilst that which may well recommend it most to the weary traveller arriving from a long sea voyage is its home comforts, which may be attested by the records of its visitors' books, proving that some of the most distinguished Royalty and European personages have often made use of the Raffles Hotel whilst sojourning in Singapore.... Every effort is made to ensure first class accommodation in every respect for families and the travelling public." The legend had begun.

## STAMFORD ROAD

**THE NATIONAL MUSEUM.** Permanent exhibitions at the museum include its Straits Chinese collection, the highlights being a traditional bridal chamber, a set of twenty "educational" miniature dioramas portraying the nation's history, and the Jade Gallery. Over three hundred jade carvings and objects were donated to the museum by the Aw family, which became wealthy through its Tiger Balm "cure-all" ointment. The carvings in the Jade Gallery are not to everyone's taste: some may find them over-elaborate, but they do intrigue. The collection was gathered mainly in late-1930's Hong Kong, as rich Chinese families fleeing the Japanese advance traded in their jade for sorely needed cash. The Aw family then shifted its newly acquired jade to the "safety" of Singapore. But in 1942 the Japanese ● *38* arrived to claim the Aw jades as war booty, packing the collection into twenty containers ready for shipment to Tokyo. For reasons which remain unclear, the collection remained in Singapore during the war years and was afterwards returned intact to a grateful Aw family. It was then put on display at the Aw family home on Nassim Road, which became known as the Jade House (now demolished, with its site covered by swish new condos) before being presented to the nation in 1980. The much traveled jade items now have a permanent, dignified resting place in the National Museum. The museum also has exhibits tracing Singapore's pre-1819 history. A more recent era is evoked by the Thian Hiang Tea Shop. This has been based on a turn-of-the-century traditional Chinese tea shophouse and has been faithfully reconstructed using original items found in a tea-shophouse in Merchant Road in Chinatown, which was demolished in 1986. This exhibit features the shop's teak shelves, chests, chairs, and tables and a whole range of tea-trade paraphernalia, such as weighing scales, pewter tea canisters, and sign boards, all of which were made in China. Another important exhibit at the National Museum is its 18th-century Paul Revere Bell – the only one outside the US. As well as making his midnight horseback ride to warn fellow-Americans that "The British are coming!", the Boston-based Revere was a noted bell-maker. The Singapore bell was commissioned to sound the night-time curfew by his daughter Maria, who had married Joseph Balestier, first American

**EXCAVATIONS**
Singapore's exciting 14th-century history is constantly evoked by regular finds of small Javanese gold items, porcelain pieces, pottery, and coins during excavations in the city-center area. Significant finds are displayed in the National Museum.

consul in Singapore. The bell is large and heavy – it weighs 1 ton – and it took more than ten men to move it during the museum's 1990 renovations. The bell no longer tolls, for it cracked in 1911 and has not sounded since. Attached to the museum is the National Art Gallery, which, like the museum itself, features regular exhibitions with a Southeast Asian theme. The National Museum is the centerpiece of an ambitious project to create a new museum-rich Civic District by 1999. New museums will include Asian Civilizations, Fine Arts, Singapore History, and a children's museum, with a new road tunnel underneath Stamford Road to relieve the present heavy traffic congestion in the area. The National Library (formerly Raffles Library) will be demolished, and its books relocated at Victoria Street.

## Armenian Street

**The Armenian Church.** The Church of St Gregory the Illuminator at Armenian Street bears witness to the artistry of the early colonial architect George Coleman, an Irishman, and to the small but significant presence of Armenians in 19th-century Singapore (the founders of the Raffles Hotel, the Sarkies, were Armenian). Finished in 1835, it is the oldest intact church in Singapore and, although small and seating only fifty-two, it is regarded as Coleman's masterpiece.

**The Substation.** Located also on Armenian Street, the Substation has rapidly become Singapore's home for the modern arts and, by local standards, is daringly unconventional. It hosts a wide range of activities, with the emphasis on performing arts, and has an open backyard which turns into a lively "Left Bank" rendezvous spot at weekends. Opposite the Substation is one of the city's best bookstores, MPH, located in one of the last few handsome Edwardian commercial buildings that once housed Singapore's finest shops and emporia. Nearby, up a gentle slope off Stamford Road, is the National Library.

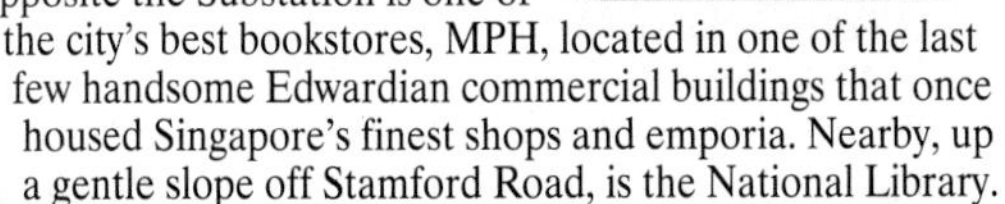

**The Chamber's dragons**
The pagoda-roofed Singapore Chinese Chamber of Commerce and Industry is protected by two glazed porcelain nine-dragon mural walls (above) along its Hill Street entrance. These were faithfully modeled from the nine-dragon mural in Beijing's Beihai Park, a ceremonial structure found also within the Forbidden City itself. The artwork is so realistic that these traditional Chinese dragons look almost alive.

**MRT** ◆ *324-5*
The ultra-modern Mass Rapid Transit public rail travel system, or MRT as it is known in this acronym-loving country, has made a considerable difference to Singapore's quality of life since it opened in 1988. The only transport system of its kind in Southeast Asia, it is a must for visitors from Indonesia, Malaysia, and Thailand, who regard an MRT ride as an essential part of their itineraries. Others value it for its coolness, speed, cleanliness, safety, and comfort. The MRT links central Singapore's key locations, with the newest link taking in more northern stops and the proposed new northeast line running from World Trade Center, following the line of Serangoon Road. Reasonably priced short-term tourist fare-cards are available at MRT station ticket offices.

**A VIEW FROM GOVERNMENT HILL**
Many of the early views of Singapore were taken from Government Hill. Below is the earliest published one, dating from the 1820's. The accompanying inscription was inspired by the struggle between Raffles and his lieutenant, William Farquhar, who took over the running of Singapore from Raffles. Farquhar's knowledge of the Malay world was as deep as Raffles'. One factor that led to their breakup may have been Raffles' disapproval of Farquhar taking a Malay wife. The inscription reads: "The Flourishing Settlement was formed in 1819 under the auspices of Lt Col Wm Farquhar, many years Resident and Governor of Malacca, equally esteemed for his hospitality and Talents as for his knowledge of and attention to the Natives and so much respected by them that in the Course of Five Years a little village containing only a few mean Huts surrounded by an uninhabited Jungle, through his exertions and those of his followers from Malacca, has become a large and populous Town of the utmost Importance."

## FORT CANNING PARK

Once known in Malay as "Forbidden Hill", Fort Canning Park is the focal point of Singapore's past. Small gold ornaments from 14th-century Java unearthed during digs on the hill and now on display in the National Museum, prove that Singapore enjoyed a flourishing ninety-two years (1299–1391), when it was ruled by five successive kings, before its "disappearance" from the history books until 1819.

**GOVERNMENT HILL.** When Stamford Raffles arrived in Singapore, his sensitive feel for history – and desire to escape the sea-level humidity – made him choose its summit (giving it the name of Government Hill) for his official residence and for Singapore's first, short-lived botanic garden. Local Malays were not prepared to clear the trees and scrub from the hill for that residence – the fearsome reputation of the "Forbidden Hill" proved too strong – and laborers had to be imported from Malacca. Stern British action (running up the Union Jack and firing a cannon a dozen times) dispelled any lingering mystique about the hill.

**THE KRAMAT ISKANDAR SHAH.** The Malay reluctance was provoked by the discovery of what they regarded as the royal tomb of Iskandar Shah, the last of those five kings of ancient Singapore (then known as Temasek). This tomb (*kramat*) now has a wooden shelter held up by twenty carved wood columns engraved with fighting-cock motifs. It was erected in 1990 by Melakan craftsmen, but it is unlikely that Iskandar Shah's remains do lie here – he was forced to flee Temasek by an invading Javanese army, retreating to Malacca where he set up that city's sultanate and launched what is regarded as its Golden Era. Fort Canning Park's *kramat* is still well maintained and people go there to pray or pay homage (childless couples, it is said, come to pray for fertility).

**THE CEMETERY.** Not very far away from the *kramat* is the old Christian cemetery (1822–65) with its Gothic gateways and decaying tombstones that tell sad stories

Earpieces unearthed in 1926 were part of a significant find, which added weight to the evidence of the *Malay Annals* that the kings of Singapore reigned over the Malay world for five generations.

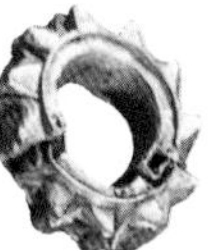

of Europeans of all ages, who died in a foreign land for reasons and from diseases they would not have encountered had they stayed at home.

**THE FORT.** The hill became known as Fort Canning when in 1861 its top was flattened and Raffles' residence demolished, to make way for a fort that would command the harbor area. It ceased its military function in 1907 and by 1927 had been converted into the reservoir that it still is. The hill took on military importance again in the mid-1930's, as the Japanese threat became apparent. An elaborate underground bunker was dug into the hilltop and became known as the "Battle Box" when World War Two broke out. It was here in February 1942 that the British military authorities decided that the island had no alternative but to surrender to the invading Japanese. The bunker remained undisturbed and flooded until 1991, when it was pumped out and refurbished as an authentic display to mark the fiftieth anniversary of the British surrender. Modern Fort Canning Park includes a cultural centre for Singapore's dance company and TheatreWorks drama group, a country club adapted from one-time British army offices, an Asean sculpture garden and a Garden of Fragrance.

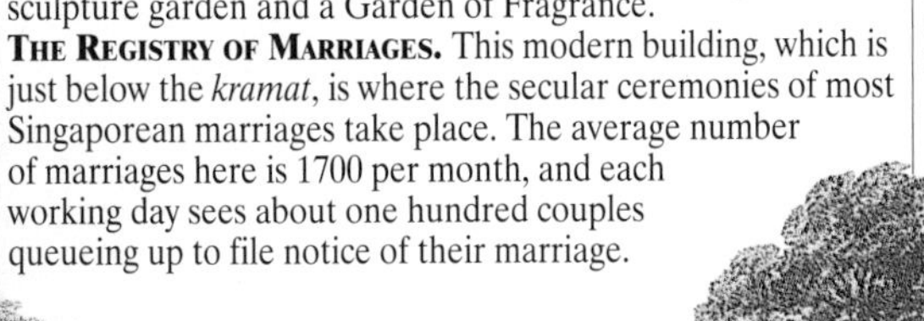

**THE REGISTRY OF MARRIAGES.** This modern building, which is just below the *kramat*, is where the secular ceremonies of most Singaporean marriages take place. The average number of marriages here is 1700 per month, and each working day sees about one hundred couples queueing up to file notice of their marriage.

**A GOLDEN TALE**
A gold bracelet and simple earpieces were discovered at Fort Canning in 1926 by workers digging the reservoir. The bracelet and other finds from Fort Canning are now in Singapore's National Museum, where a permanent display details the pre-Raffles history of the island. The bracelet dates stylistically to the 14th century.

# ▲ Singapore
# The Eastern & Oriental Express

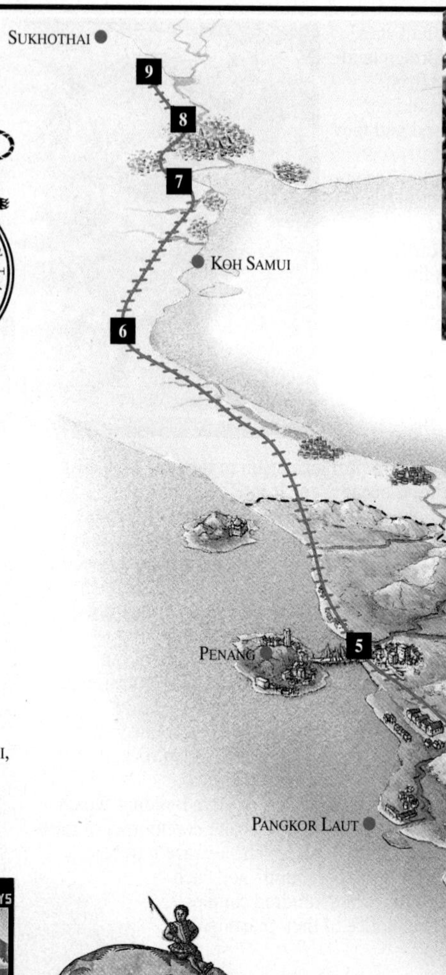

SUKHOTHAI
9
8
7
KOH SAMUI
6
PENANG
5
4
PANGKOR LAUT

**Stops along the main route**
1. Singapore
2. Tampin
3. Kuala Lumpur
4. Ipoh
5. Butterworth
6. Surat Thani
7. Hua Hin
8. Bangkok
9. Phitsanulok

**Extensions/ side trips**
In Malaysia: Melaka, Pangkor Laut and Penang.
In Thailand: Phuket, Koh Samui, Kancanaburi, River Kwai and Sukhothai.

The first railway in Malaysia was built by the sultan of Johore in 1869 and by 1909 the Federated Malay States Railway had connections north of Kuala Lumpur to Penang, south to Seremban and through the state of Johor to the tip of the peninsula.

During the late 19th century, railway mania spread to Southeast Asia. In both Thailand (then Siam) and Malaya, railways opened up previously inaccessible areas for cultivation and settlement, and also provided a new mode of leisure transport. Thailand's royal family traveled by train to their summer palace at Hua Hin, and in British Malaya the railway took government officials and rubber planters to resorts on Penang and in the Cameron Highlands.

"THE SCENERY ALONG THE LINE WILL GIVE THE TRAVELLERS A GOOD IMPRESSION OF BRITISH MALAYA AND SIAM."

1928 RAILWAY PAMPHLET FOR PASSENGERS

The Eastern & Oriental Express, its name inspired by the E & O Hotel in Penang, is the first train to transport passengers directly from Singapore to Kuala Lumpur and Bangkok. An agreement signed in 1991 between E & O and the Malaysian and Thai railways now allows a single luxury train to travel the whole length of the 1200-mile peninsula in three days, leaving Singapore every Sunday and Bangkok every Wednesday.

The Railway Hotel at Hua Hin (number 7 on map) in Thailand.

Veneers of wooden marquetry emphasize the opulence of the state compartments.

**LUCKY NUMBERS** Each of the twenty-two carriages bears a four-digit ID number formed of the numbers 2, 3, 6, 8, and 9 in order to avoid (for Chinese travelers) unlucky 4 (signifying death), 5 (negative), and 7 (erratic).

# ▲ Singapore
# Orchard Road

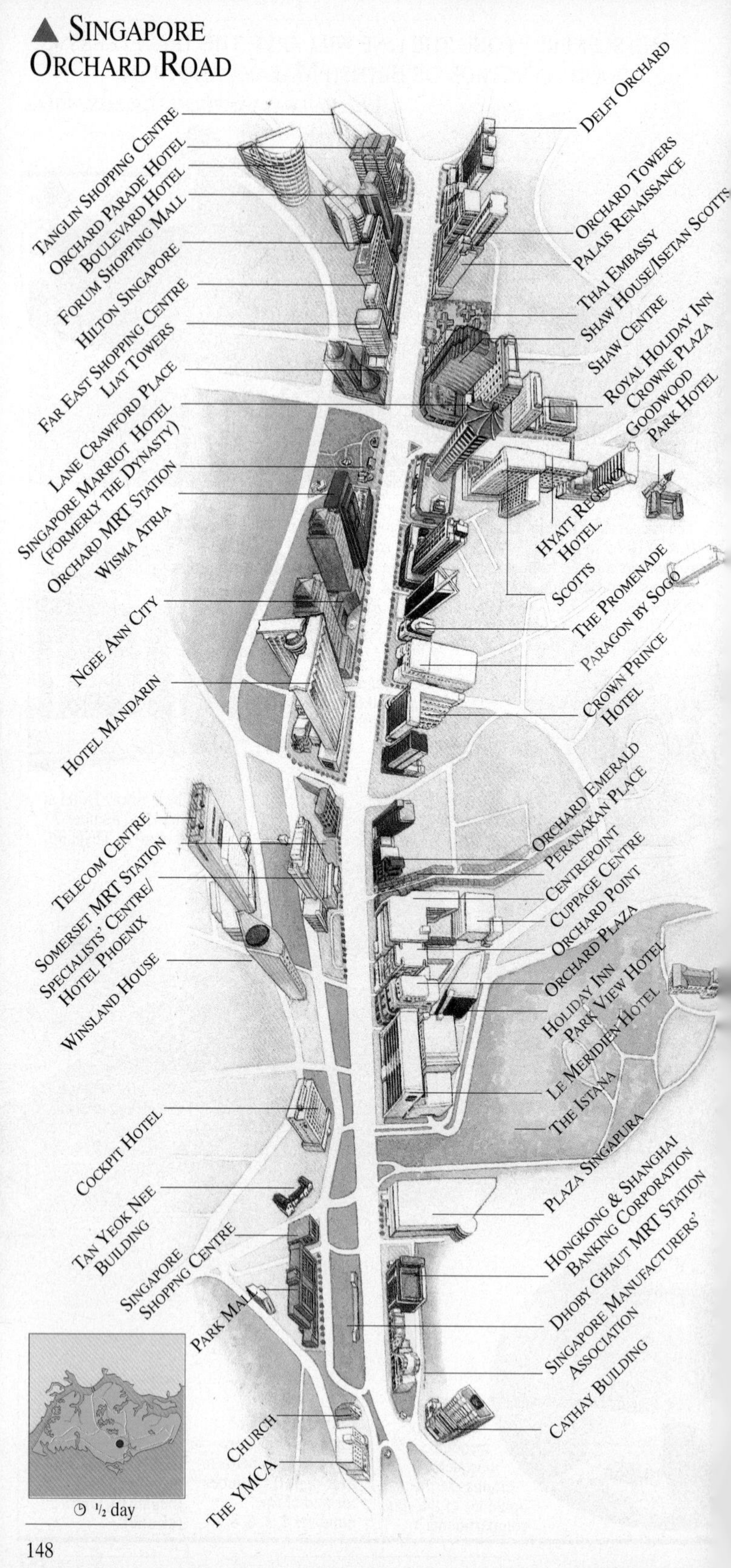

Tanglin Shopping Centre
Orchard Parade Hotel
Boulevard Hotel
Forum Shopping Mall
Hilton Singapore
Far East Shopping Centre
Liat Towers
Lane Crawford Place
Singapore Marriott Hotel (formerly the Dynasty)
Orchard MRT Station
Wisma Atria
Ngee Ann City
Hotel Mandarin
Telecom Centre
Somerset MRT Station
Specialists' Centre/ Hotel Phoenix
Winsland House
Cockpit Hotel
Tan Yeok Nee Building
Singapore Shopping Centre
Park Mall
Church
The YMCA
Delfi Orchard
Orchard Towers
Palais Renaissance
Thai Embassy
Shaw House/Isetan Scotts
Shaw Centre
Royal Holiday Inn Crowne Plaza
Goodwood Park Hotel
Hyatt Regency Hotel
Scotts
The Promenade
Paragon by Sogo
Crown Prince Hotel
Orchard Emerald
Peranakan Place
Centrepoint
Cuppage Centre
Orchard Point
Orchard Plaza
Holiday Inn Park View Hotel
Le Meridien Hotel
The Istana
Plaza Singapura
Hongkong & Shanghai Banking Corporation
Dhoby Ghaut MRT Station
Singapore Manufacturers' Association
Cathay Building
½ day

"THE NATIVE STREETS MONOPOLISE THE PICTURESQUENESS OF SINGAPORE WITH THEIR BIZARRE CROWDS."

ISABELLA BIRD, *THE GOLDEN CHERSONESE*

Orchard Road was not always the glossy Fifth Avenue/Ginza-style hotel–shopping–entertainment center it is now. As its name suggests, this was once a mere country lane flanked by fruit orchards and pepper and nutmeg plantations. It served as a link between the colonial-era commercial shopping center of Raffles Place and the European residential areas of Tanglin and Holland. The opening of the first Tangs department store in 1958 (where the Singapore Marriot Hotel/Tangs Plaza complex now stands) heralded the start of Orchard Road in its current form, with gleaming rows of competing shopping complexes and hotels – all boasting they have Singapore's "most prestigious location". Despite the humidity, Orchard Road is still a strollers' boulevard: at weekends, it becomes almost a fashion catwalk as modern Singaporeans put on their most stylish wear and go "on parade" (be seen here in beach shorts and tattered T-shirts only if you don't care!). New subways have been put under Orchard Road to dissuade pedestrians from crossing this busy one-way street. Once, on National Day (August 9), Swing Singapore – tagged as "Southeast Asia's largest street party" – took place at night here with 400,000 Singaporean revelers.

## THE LOWER STRETCH

**THE ISTANA.** This is the official residence of Singapore's presidents. It is a handsome building, in even more handsome grounds which include a landscaped nine-hole golf course. Built by Indian convict labor, it opened in 1869 as the colonial era's Government House. The Istana (Malay for "palace") is normally closed to the public, but on four public holidays each year (New Year's Day, Chinese New Year, Hari Raya, and Deepavali) the grounds are opened, a military band plays and the president mingles with his "guests".

**TAN YEOK NEE'S MANSION.** The old mansion, perched precariously above the CTE (acronym for CenTral Expressway) road tunnel entrances on Clemenceau Avenue, is a unique asset for Singapore – the last remaining example of a wealthy southern Chinese merchant's mansion. Between 1940 and 1991, it served as the local Salvation Army headquarters, and its harmonious, dignified interior was left untouched (if badly in need of restoration). Now owned by the neighboring Cockpit Hotel, the future role of this structure built during 1865–85 remains unclear. The mansion has been gazeted as a national monument.

**CATHAY BUILDING.** At the southern tip of Orchard Road, the Cathay Building ranks as Singapore's first skyscraper. It was completed in 1939 and immediately had to change its function from civil to military, used first by the British, then by the Japanese. Now the building includes Singapore's first art cinema, the Picturehouse, alongside its two mainstream cinema halls, Cathay 1 and Cathay 2.

**YESTERYEAR'S ORCHARD ROAD**
Fruit trees, bungalows, and a cemetery made up Orchard Road in its early years. The area's transformation has been swift, leaving few reminders of the days of ox carts. Clemenceau Avenue, off the lower stretch of Orchard Road and facing the Istana, was named after the World War One French prime minister ("Tiger of France") Georges Clemenceau, who visited Singapore in 1920 to officiate at the foundation stone ceremony for the Esplanade's Cenotaph.

**DHOBY MEN**
The street name Dhoby Ghaut evokes the 19th-century character of this area. *Dhoby* means washermen. Here along the grassy banks of the then Stamford River (now a covered canal) washing was left out to dry by Indian laundry-men.

**PERANAKAN FAÇADES** The shophouse façades and doorways of Emerald Hill Road are some of the finest examples of Peranakan (Straits Chinese) architecture. Built for wealthy Peranakans, they show a marvelously eclectic appreciation of detailed ornament. In these buildings the shophouse form has been adapted for residential use.

## THE MIDDLE STRETCH

**EMERALD HILL ROAD.** Hemmed in beside and behind Centrepoint, and with Peranakan Place as its Orchard Road "shop-front", Emerald Hill Road is a preserved colony of Chinese-Malay shophouse architecture ● *88–90*. It is a highly sought-after area for commercial outlets and for discerning residents, delighted to have the opportunity to restore these lovely ornamented houses back to their original (1900–30) finery.

**MANDARIN HOTEL.** The Mandarin, with its two blocks and 1100 bedrooms, was the first huge hotel built in anticipation of Singapore's modern tourism era. Opened in 1973, the hotel has spent millions on ensuring its interior makes an impact, mainly of a chinoiserie nature, with its décor, carpets, and works of art. The Mandarin is also noted for its policy of employing attractive female staff, whom it dresses in *cheongsam*. Its Top of the M rooftop revolving restaurant makes an excellent viewing deck for diners.

## THE UPPER STRETCH

**TANGLIN ROAD.** Smokers will appreciate the outdoor hotel restaurants and bars at the turn between Orchard and Tanglin roads – for only in the open air can they smoke when food is present, because of Singapore's severe anti-smoking laws. Many of Singapore's antique shops and a specialist bookstore are in Tanglin Shopping Centre. Nearby is the Regent Hotel, an early John Portman design and the upscale Tanglin Mall.

**ORCHARD TOWERS.** This shopping complex turns into an entertainment center at night, with its clubs and pubs. Orchard Towers has a food center in its basement and a supermarket at the rear podium.

**HARD ROCK CAFÉ.** Singapore has a Hard Rock Café – a trendy nightspot on Cuscaden Road opposite Orchard

**The Hanging Gardens of Shangri-La**
The landscaping and gardens of the Shangri-La Hotel, off Orchard Road, are an impressive sight.

Towers – with a collection of rock memorabilia to rival any other Hard Rock Café. The collection includes some local touches, such as a bra worn by the ample-bosomed singer Anita Sarawak now based in Las Vegas. More familiar names are celebrated in Eric Clapton's Special Strat guitar, Elton John's 1975 sequined headdress, and Gold albums of the Beatles. Not far away, at Liat Towers, is Planet Hollywood.
**Orange Grove Road.** This road leads to the Shangri-La, one of Singapore's most acclaimed hotels. "The Shang", as it is known locally, is proud of its Rose Veranda afternoon high-tea lounge which serves over forty varieties of tea. Surrounded by the lush tropical greenery of 15 acres of gardens with 133,000 trees and plants and a waterfall, the hotel describes its grounds as "Singapore's other Botanic Gardens".

## Scotts Road

**Goodwood Park Hotel.** Once the Teutonia Club, the Goodwood Park Hotel anchors the Scotts Road end of the Orchard Road district. The building served the German community in 1900, which explains why its picturesque tower resembles a Rhineland turret, but at the outbreak of World War One it was seized as enemy property by the British authorities. It became a hotel in 1929, launching a "grand old hotel" rivalry with the Raffles. It is now noted for the luxurious Sultan of Brunei Suite in its tower, its durian mousse cake, and its charming coffee lounge, where Taiwan porridge is a local late-night favorite. It is also the only hotel in Singapore which can (with 24 hours' notice) cook up a Scottish haggis.
**Singapore Marriott Hotel/Tangs Plaza.** Diagonally facing the recently completed Lane Crawford Place, this complex is probably the most photographed building on Orchard Road. In fact, the hotel's thirty-three-story tower block, under its former name, the Dynasty, is a familiar landmark in Singapore. After extensive internal alterations, the hotel reopened in 1995 as the Singapore Marriott Hotel. The adjoining Tangs Plaza is one of the oldest department stores in Singapore, first established by a door-to-door salesman Tang Choon Keng.
**The Hyatt Regency Hotel.** The Hyatt Regency Hotel is a modern building, and much effort is spent to ensure that it stays that way. Yet it contains a typically Singaporean blend of state-of-the-art and superstition. Hyatt's front entrance doors stand at a slight angle to Scotts Road, for a reason: geomancer's advice. When the hotel opened in 1971, a geomancer warned that the hotel's wealth could "flow out" from the cashier's desk straight through its front doors, if there were no "obstacle" to such a flow. So the doors were shifted to an angle, thereby stopping the hotel's profits from sliding away. A fountain was also built at the entrance, apparently to "pool" the hotel's fortunes. The hotel has indeed proved to be a profitable enterprise.

**Meridian line at the Forum**
For visitors feeling lost in Orchard Road, the Forum Shopping Mall can help. Outside its entrance stands a meridian line locating this spot at precisely 103 degrees, 49 minutes, 50.4 seconds east of Greenwich. And its latitude is 1 degree, 17 minutes north.

**"Door Gods"**
The "Door Gods" outside the Hilton International Hotel are ferocious-looking 9-foot-high ceramic statues, said to represent two generals from the Chinese Tang dynasty (AD 618–806) who stood guard at the emperor's bedroom to protect him from malicious ghosts. (Miniature versions of this protective duo can be found in many traditional Chinese homes.) The "Door Gods" once graced the Hilton's lobby, but were relocated as their presence was considered intimidating to guests.

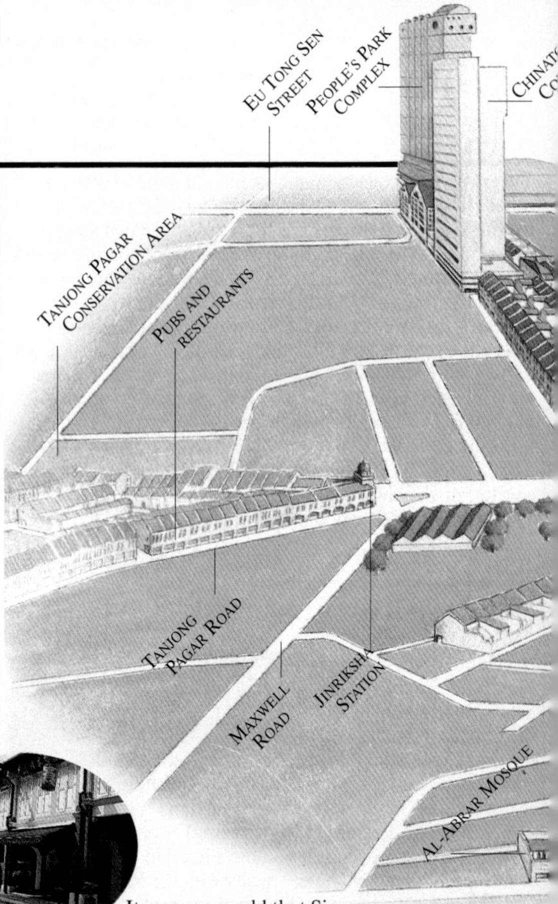

# ▲ Singapore Chinatown

Eu Tong Sen Street

People's Park Complex

Chinatown Co[mplex]

Tanjong Pagar Conservation Area

Pubs and Restaurants

Tanjong Pagar Road

Maxwell Road

Jinriksha Station

Al-Abrar Mosque

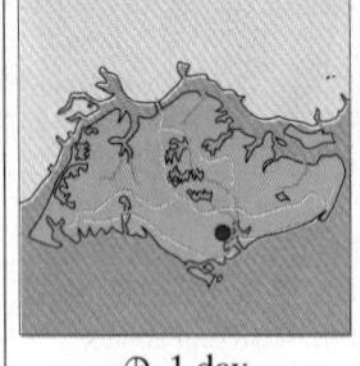

◷ 1 day

**Lunar New Year in Chinatown**
Chinese New Year occurs during January or February. Houses are cleaned, all old debts are settled, and festive items such as sweetmeats, candies, and cookies are bought, mainly from Chinatown, which really comes alive at this time of the year. Street lights and a night bazaar bring large crowds of shoppers from all over the island to enjoy the lively and colorful atmosphere.

**Foot reflexology**
There is a traditional Chinese belief that an ache in any part of the body can be soothed by massaging the right spots on the soles of a person's feet. This belief has come back into fashion in today's Singapore, and many foot-reflexology centers have sprung up as a result. The advice includes recommending that people go barefooted, as this stimulates the sole-zones of the feet, but this is obviously not always practical. A short foot-reflexology session, accompanied by sipping warm water, can prove most restorative.

It may seem odd that Singapore, a predominantly Chinese city, should have a Chinatown – and one of the world's most vibrant at that. Plans for Chinatown's future thrust straight into the heart of Singapore's Great Conservation Debate. In the post-1965 rush to modernize, the building boom was ruthless, obliterating anything that stood in its way – much of old Singapore just disappeared. Then, in the mid-1980's, a halt was called and, with typical thoroughness, conservation became a keyword in Chinatown and its neighboring area, Tanjong Pagar. The debate centres on whether restoring tumble-down shophouses ● *88–90* to visual splendor while driving out traditional small-scale economic activity and families is good or not. Shophouses are a case in point: people actually lived out their lives in the upper stories. But preservation costs money, and the new rentals for restored shophouses are often beyond the means of those living in them prior to restoration. The result is ruthless gentrification, so that some of the restored shophouses in Chinatown resemble a movie lot, housing small executive concerns – the color and vitality of streets where Chinese familes live and work in their shophouses is, however, rapidly disappearing.

## Telok Ayer Street

Running parallel to and very near the business district highways of Shenton Way, Robinson Road, and Cecil Street, Telok Ayer Street still retains many of its charming 19th century features, though modern businesses are taking over

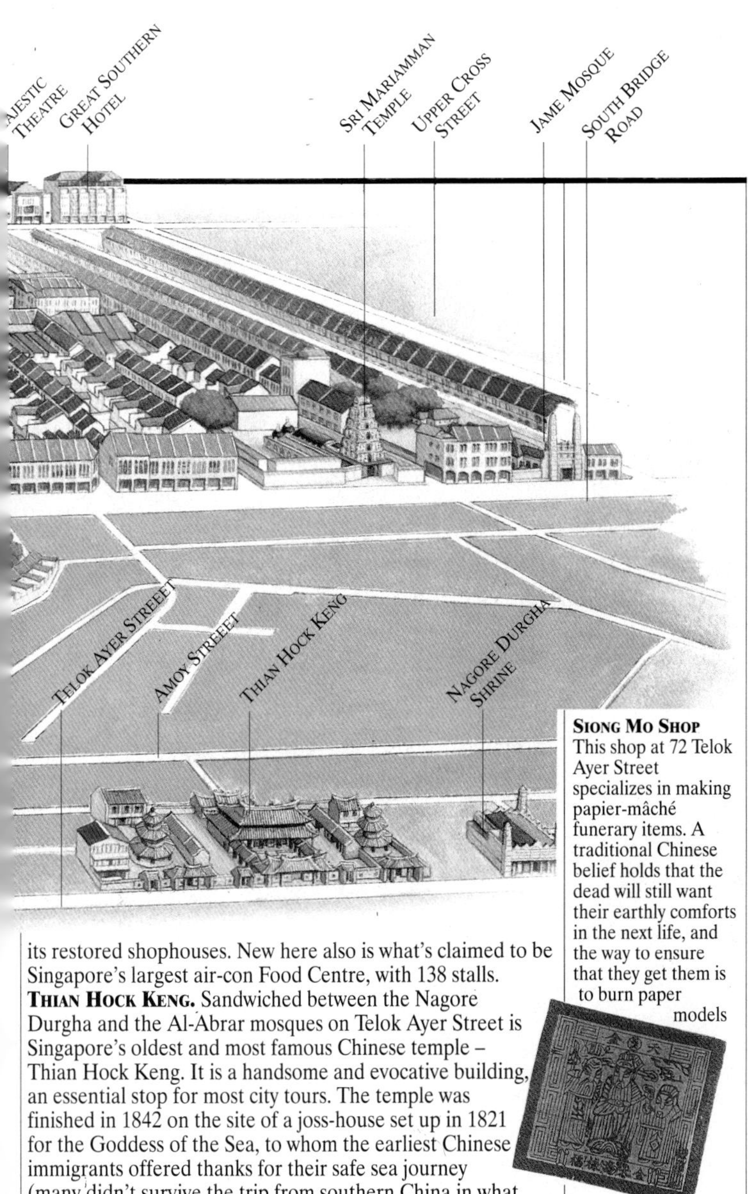


its restored shophouses. New here also is what's claimed to be Singapore's largest air-con Food Centre, with 138 stalls.

**THIAN HOCK KENG.** Sandwiched between the Nagore Durgha and the Al-Abrar mosques on Telok Ayer Street is Singapore's oldest and most famous Chinese temple – Thian Hock Keng. It is a handsome and evocative building, an essential stop for most city tours. The temple was finished in 1842 on the site of a joss-house set up in 1821 for the Goddess of the Sea, to whom the earliest Chinese immigrants offered thanks for their safe sea journey (many didn't survive the trip from southern China in what have been termed "coffin ships"). The temple is an ensemble of painted deities, dragon statues, burning incense, peaceful courtyards, and Chinese architectural and religious motifs.

**SIONG MO SHOP**
This shop at 72 Telok Ayer Street specializes in making papier-mâché funerary items. A traditional Chinese belief holds that the dead will still want their earthly comforts in the next life, and the way to ensure that they get them is to burn paper models of favored items at cremation time. Models include mansions, jumbo jets, cars (usually Mercedes), hand-phones, television sets, video recorders, credit cards, and even *karaoke* sets. The most popular of the funerary items sold in such shops like Siong Mo is paper money for the spirits of the dead. Burning delivers the money to the spirits in the after-life.

# ▲ Singapore Thian Hock Keng

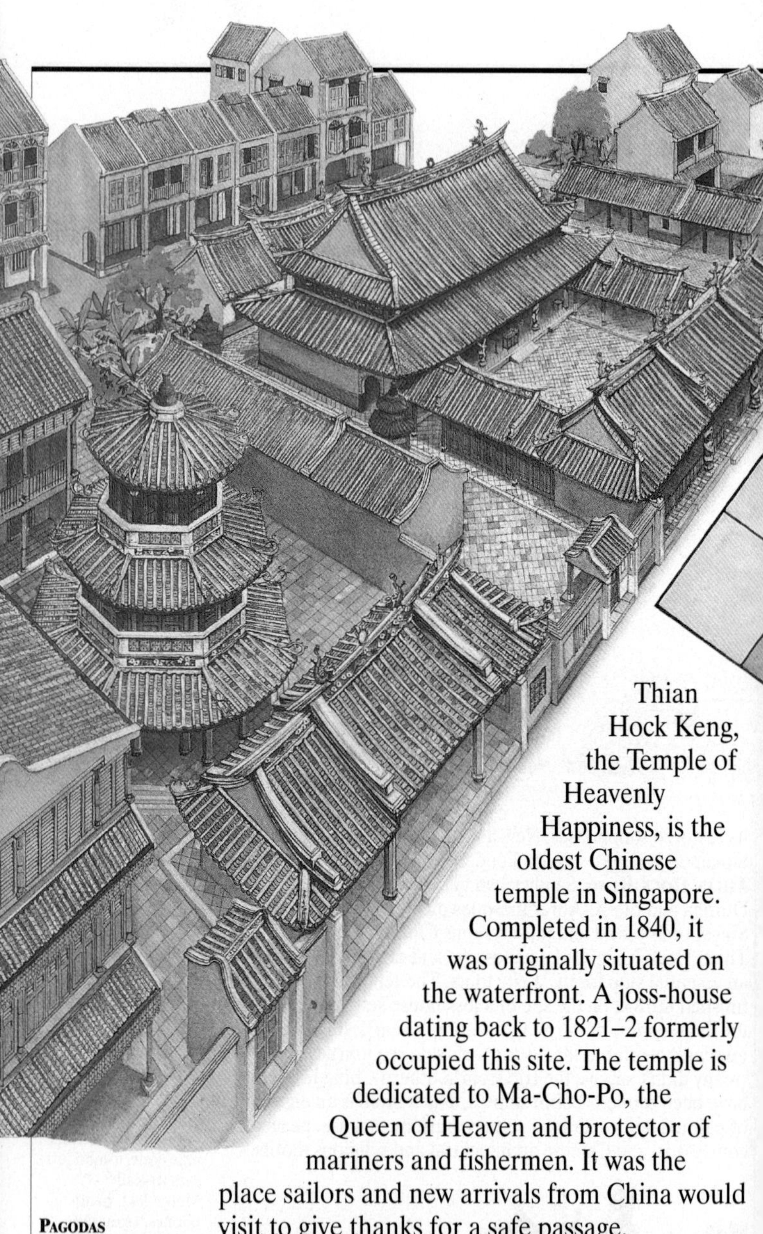

Thian Hock Keng, the Temple of Heavenly Happiness, is the oldest Chinese temple in Singapore. Completed in 1840, it was originally situated on the waterfront. A joss-house dating back to 1821–2 formerly occupied this site. The temple is dedicated to Ma-Cho-Po, the Queen of Heaven and protector of mariners and fishermen. It was the place sailors and new arrivals from China would visit to give thanks for a safe passage.

**Pagodas**
Originally intended to house relics of the Buddha, pagodas became the tombs of celebrated Buddhist priests. At Thian Hock Keng, they house the ancestral tablets of former monks, and their enclosures are the most sacred part of the temple complex.

**Ancestor tablets**
Many Chinese believe that the dead should be venerated and worshiped. Ancestors are credited with wisdom and experience beyond that of their descendants. The soul of the deceased takes on three aspects: one part follows the body to the grave; a second commences its journey to the underworld; and the third enters the ancestral tablet (**3** on plan).

**THE TEMPLE DONORS**
Construction of the temple was paid for by individual contributions, the principal donor being the Hokkien leader Tan Tock Seng (1798–1850).

**ROOF RIDGES**
The roof spirals are sculpted from cement and ornamented with glazed tile chips.

**MAIN SHRINES**
The image of Ma-Cho-Po occupies the place of honor in the temple, and was brought from China (1 on plan). To her right is Kuan Kung, the God of War, and to her left, Pao Sheng Ta Ti, the Protector of Life. The temple also has a shrine to Tua Peh Kong, the God of Prosperity and guardian deity of overseas Chinese.

**DRAGONS**
The paired dragons on the roof ridges embody the principles of *yin* and *yang*. Between the two cavorting dragons is a bluish glass globe elevated on a pedestal surrounded by a ring of fire. This is the "night-shining pearl", a Taoist symbol representing the sun and symbolizing the positive *yang* principle. Dragons are said to worship the pearl.

**TEMPLE DOORS**
The doors at the main entrance of the temple have guardian figures from Confucian mythology painted on them.

**CARP**
Carp, found on the roof ridge, are a symbol of success, their struggle against river currents representing man's endeavor to succeed in life. Legend has it that if a carp were to leap the Longmen (Dragon Gate) Rapid of the Yellow River, it would become a dragon. Like the carp, man is believed to have the potential to acquire knowledge and achieve wealth.

**SECONDARY SHRINES**
Behind the main building is an altar to Kuan Yin, the Goddess of Mercy. She is flanked by the sun and lunar deities Tai Yang Xing Jun and Tai Yin Xing Jun respectively. To the left of the main courtyard stands the Temple of Success, housing the Fa Zhu Gong, the Lord of Laws. On the right are shrines dedicated to Prince of Prominence, Za Si Xian Hem, and the Lord of Man's Origin, Jia Lan Ye.

**GRANITE PILLARS**
The granite pillars at the main entrance and those supporting the main roof came from China. The roof structure and projecting eaves consist of a beam-frame construction, with the transition from vertical pillar to horizontal ties and cross-beams being achieved by cantilevered brackets.

**CHINESE MEDICAL HALLS**
The intricacies of traditional Chinese medicine and herbal cures baffle Singaporeans as much as they do visitors. But, partly in reaction to a worldwide shift against high-tech Western medicine and encouraged by modern explanatory packaging, including take-away, ready-to-mix herbal preparations, Chinese medical halls are finding new customers all the time.

**"GOLDSMITH'S ROW"**
The concentration of goldsmith shops along South Bridge Road once earned this street the nickname "Goldsmith's Row". The shops are owned mainly by Chinese and, unlike the West, which prefers 9-, 14-, or 18-carat gold, the goldsmiths here trade in 22-carat and sometimes even full-purity 24-carat gold, giving a greater resale value. The charges for the workmanship involved in crafting gold items such as bracelets, necklaces, and earrings are much lower than those in the West.

## THE HEART OF CHINATOWN

The square-shaped zone formed by Mosque, Pagoda, Temple, and Smith Streets is where Chinatown really buzzes during the Lunar New Year. Here, tiny shops sell a wide variety of festive household items and knick-knacks that continue to delight Singaporeans and tourists. Street vendors display edibles such as Taiwanese sausage, waxed duck, sea coconut, candied fruit, and durians. Mosque Street is graced with old-style Chinese tea-shops which, like some British pubs, serve as men-only social clubs. Two such tea-shops are Tai Tong Hoi Kee and Da Nan Tang, but the only real physical difference between these and the typical Singaporean coffee shop is that green Chinese tea, not coffee, is the main drink.

**EU YAN SANG.** At 269 South Bridge Road stands the shop of Eu Yan Sang, one of the leading local traditional Chinese herbal medicine specialists. The firm's wide range of medicines includes ginseng, deer antler, powdered pearl, herbal soups, and tonic teas. Although not as popular overall as Western medicine, traditional Chinese herbal treatments still play a part in modern Singapore, with medicine halls scattered all around the island's housing estates. Bilingual staff at Eu Yan Sang are better than most at explaining to puzzled tourists what might be good for them.

**SRI MARIAMMAN TEMPLE.** South Bridge Road may be in the heart of Chinatown but its "star"– in true multi-religious and multi-cultural Singaporean style – is an Indian Hindu temple built in 1843. Sri Mariamman is a goddess credited with the power to cure epidemic diseases such as smallpox. The temple's *gopuram* (gateway tower) features seventy-two deities, and its walls are topped with white cows, while inside it has numerous sheltered courtyards, religious carvings, and a main ceiling painted with elaborate frescoes. Visitors are welcome.

**JAME MOSQUE.** Nearby is the Jame Mosque, which dates from 1835 and is distinguished by twin entrance towers.

**PIN-UP GIRL**
During the 1950's and 1960's, framed pictures of popular Chinese movie stars adorned thc walls in the lobby of movie houses in Chinatown.

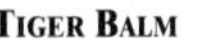

**CHINAMAN SCHOLARS' GALLERY.** At 14A Terengganu Street is the Chinaman Scholars' Gallery, a small privately owned display of paraphernalia from Chinese homes of the 1920's and 1930's, along with many traditional Chinese musical instruments. Old-style tea ceremonies are also performed here for visitors.

## EU TONG SEN STREET

**THE GREAT SOUTHERN HOTEL.** This hotel along Eu Tong Sen Street has been called "The Raffles of Chinatown" because of its characterful past. Built in 1936, it's been newly restored as an office-shopping centre. It is still a good example of the Modern Movement and was the first Chinese hotel to feature an elevator. Alongside it is a Chinese cinema, the Majestic, with its fanciful frontage. Meng Kee Eating House, a Cantonese restaurant on nearby Upper Cross Street claims an unusual distinction: the unswerving admiration of former Canadian Prime Minister Pierre Trudeau – they know exactly Trudeau's favorite menu: an eight-course meal that includes crab pincers and roast suckling pig. Trudeau's letters and photos adorn its walls.

**PEOPLE'S PARK COMPLEX.** Adjacent to the Great Southern Hotel, this complex was the first trend-setting shopping center of its kind in Southeast Asia; it still has the bustling street atmosphere of old Chinatown at its adjoining food center. People's Park Centre, another pioneer shopping complex on the same stretch, has an emporium, a food center, shoe shops, and tour agencies among its tenants.
**CHINATOWN POINT.** Across the street and opposite People's Park Centre, the modern face of Chinatown is symbolized by the blue cladding of Chinatown Point, interesting mainly because it houses the sixty-odd shops of the Singapore Handicraft Centre and because its air-conditioned interior provides an excellent cooling-off spot.
**THONG CHAI MEDICAL INSTITUTION.** Further up Eu Tong Sen Street is the Thong Chai Medical Institution, an impressive building dating from 1892, with authentic Chinese features such as inner courtyards, decorative carvings, and air-wells. It served as a free hospital until 1973, when it was declared a national monument. Now "rehabilitated", its continued existence may be assured, but its future role is uncertain.

**TIGER BALM**
Along with the Singapore Sling cocktail, this medicated herbal remedy ointment (label shown below) – "Works where it hurts" is its slogan – may well be Singapore's most noted contribution to world health. Its distinctive little glass pot with the leaping tiger logo is now on sale in sixty-eight countries. Its formula, using only natural ingredients, including camphor, menthol, clove, and peppermint oils, was devised a century ago in Rangoon by the Aw brothers, who adapted it from a balm used since ancient times in China. The Aws – Boon Haw and Boon Par were their given names – later based themselves in Singapore, where the balm is still made, and the success of their Tiger Balm has led to spin-offs such as the famous Tiger Balm Gardens, which preceded the Haw Par Villa theme park.

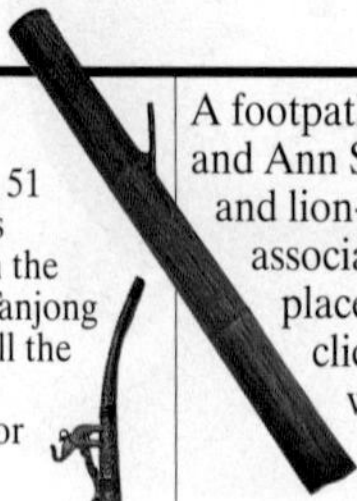

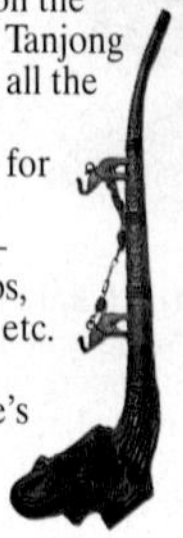

**OPIUM EXHIBITS**
On show at 51 Neil Road's museum on the history of Tanjong Pagar are all the items necessary for opium smoking – pipes, cups, oil-lamps etc. Since Singapore's earliest times, opium was the favored "escape route" for rich and poor alike, with the British administration leasing out the right to distribute and sell the destructive drug, usually at special opium houses which were open from 6am to 10pm. In 1911, the government took over this lucrative business, and opium was not finally banned until 1946.

A footpath runs from Telok Ayer Street up to the Club Street and Ann Siang Hill maze of small roads – a focus for pugilist and lion-dance troupes, temple carvers, tiny clubs, trade associations, mutual-help bodies, and family clan meeting places. Elderly people get together there, and the clicking of mahjong pieces can still be heard. At weekends, Club Street plays host to an unofficial and unusual flea market. This characterfull area is also popular with advertising agencies, creative enterprises and the like, happily installed within its restored houses. Ann Siang Hill reflects Chinatown's gentrification at its best. Several galleries and tea-houses are located here. Demonstrating that sensitive preservation can work, the Inn of the Sixth Happiness, on Erskine Road, has taken over a row of fourteen shophouses and created an appealing example of chinoiserie. This small hotel includes among its forty-eight rooms a Mandarin Duck Suite for honeymooners, who are treated to a huge two-hundred-year-old Qing dynasty rosewood bed, and a VIP room called the Opium Suite. This features an antique blackwood opium bed, though use of the drug itself is not encouraged.

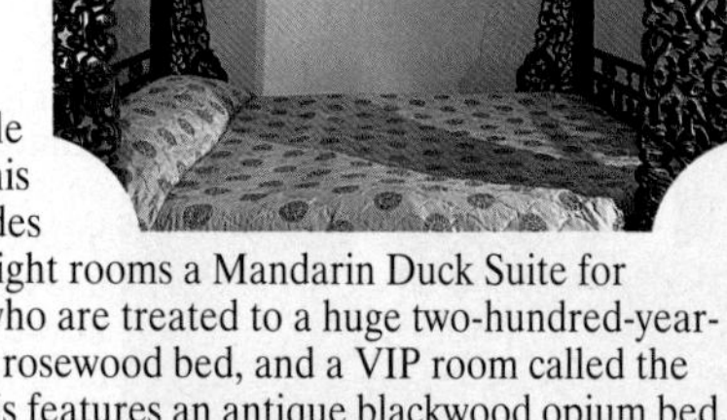

## TANJONG PAGAR

The constituency of Singapore's first prime minister, Lee Kuan Yew, for over thirty-five years, Tanjong Pagar was the first of the old neighborhoods to be restored. Tanjong Pagar

translates as "Cape of Stakes", referring to a 14th-century incident during the reign of ancient Singapura's fourth king, when there was a seafront invasion of "flying" swordfish. Under attack from these dangerous fish, the inhabitants erected wooden barricades with sharpened stakes on top, upon which the fish would impale themselves. So they did, and the name Tanjong Pagar has been used ever since. On Duxton Road stands the interesting Royal Selangor Pewter Museum and the intimate Duxton Hotel. On Neil Road, there are a number of upmarket traditional Chinese tea-houses, the best known of them being the Tea Chapter at 9A–11A, and many arts and crafts shops. Overall, Tanjong Pagar is visually attractive but, despite its expensive and sensitive restoration, it cannot be said to have yet found a satisfactory role in modern Singapore. At present, it is mostly visited for its choice of night-time pubs and bars, which are popular with the local expatriate community. At 51 Neil Road is a restored complex that tries to please everyone: it has a Fountain Food Court, mini shopping bazaar, and a little Tanjong Pagar museum. At the narrow corner of Neil and Tanjong Pagar roads is the Jinriksha station which, until the 1930's, was the hub for Singapore's many rickshaws. To be a rickshaw coolie was one of the more desperate choices available to Chinese immigrant men. It was a hard life, and opium addiction and indebtedness to rickshaw owners were the usual fates of those seeking to earn a fortune with their footpower.

**Keong Saik Road.** Linking Chinatown with Tanjong Pagar is Keong Saik Road, which at first glance merely looks battered, if characterful, with its Chinese shophouses. But look closer at those house numbers in little lightboxes over most doorways. These lights go on and off to denote whether the "working girl" upstairs is receiving gentlemen visitors – or whether she is already busy. Keong Saik Road is a concentrated Chinese-only red-light strip, and has been so for a long time. It is the center of what was called the "Blue Triangle", an area which dates from the 1870's (when the Chinese gender ratio was one woman to thirty men). The atmosphere here is friendly and easy-going; the road's several little coffee shops are fine spots at which to linger a while and undertake some serious social observation. Gentrification, mainly in the form of boutique hotels, is changing the street's old risque atmosphere.

**Good Luck**
A *hong bao* is a small red envelope (below) containing an undisclosed sum of money, to be given away as a token of good luck to the recipient during the Lunar New Year. After an exchange of Lunar New Year greetings, the *hong bao* giver presents it to someone younger in the home, often a child, a teenager, or even a young unmarried adult. Sometimes, as a gesture of appreciation for work done, the Chinese employer gives his or her employee a *hong bao*. It would, of course, be quite improper to open the envelope in front of the giver.

Keppel Road was named after Admiral Sir Henry Keppel, scourge of the Borneo pirates.

**THE RAILWAY STATION**
"It is the most pleasing railway station you will ever visit, and it will leave you without that shattered feeling which New York Central or Euston (in London) or the Gare du Nord (Paris) inflict on one."

Roland Braddell, *The Lights of Singapore*, 1934

Even if the long-term future of Singapore's main railway station is uncertain, it should enjoy a few more twilight years thanks to the arrival of the Eastern and Oriental luxury Singapore–Bangkok rail service. This is an offshoot of the restored Venice Simplon Orient Express train, based at London's Victoria Station.

## THE PORT AREA

The Port of Singapore Authority (PSA) container port that stretches from Tanjong Pagar to well beyond the World Trade Centre is one of Singapore's success stories, with those round-the-clock "giraffes" (yellow container-hoisting cranes) making it one of the world's busiest ports. The patient queue of huge ships moored at sea waiting to unload testifies to this.

**KRAMAT HABIB NOH.** Situated between the financial district and the container port, this eccentric Malay shrine, dating from 1880 and reached by a long flight of steps, covers the tomb of Habib Noh al-Habshi, a holy man who died in 1866. He allegedly had the supernatural power to transport himself to any place he wished (including Mecca, every Friday).

**THE RAILWAY STATION.** Marooned among such symbols of modern transport as the Ayer Rajah Expressway (AYE) flyover and the lorries pulling out of the container port, Keppel Road railway station is a building that will delight railway buffs – if they hurry. For its future is uncertain, with Malayan Railways (who own it and the lucrative land on which the station and its tracks stand) is anxious to sell it off. If it is demolished, it will be a real loss for Singapore, as the station is a building of genuine character. It was opened in 1932, with its modernist, almost Bauhaus, styling and barrel roof all said to be inspired by Helsinki's railway terminus. One interesting feature is its six paintings-on-tiles, portraying idealized European images of typical Malayan life. The train trip across Singapore and over the Causeway is an easy and cheap way of getting to Johor Bahru.

**CHURCH OF ST TERESA.** Passengers pulling out of Keppel Road station soon see a church they may suspect is a transplanted Sacré Coeur, the hilltop Montmartre church in Paris. This is St Teresa's Catholic Church, perched on a gentle slope off Kampong Bahru Road. It was designed by a French architect in honor of the Parisian landmark.

**ALKAFF MANSION.** Once an out-of-town home for local wealthy Arab traders in the 1920's, Alkaff Mansion is noted for high-society gatherings in its ample gardens, and

**Cable Car Rides** Viewing the port area by cable car atop Mount Faber.

commands sweeping views of the harbor from its site atop Bukit Jagoh (formerly Mount Washington). Now restored as a fancy restaurant, Alkaff Mansion (below) specializes in traditional Dutch colonial *rijstafel* spreads, with ten attractive waitresses, dressed in traditional Malay *sarong kebaya*, bringing the meal – item by item, with the bearer carefully explaining each dish – to the table. Alkaff Mansion is an elegant house, sensitively restored inside and out, and its garden terraces are also a delight for afternoon tea.

**World Trade Centre.** This large complex of offices, exhibition halls, and shops is also Singapore's cruise center, with large visiting liners mooring here and smaller ferries leaving for the neighboring Indonesian islands and for the Singaporean "fun island" of Sentosa. The various WTC halls house major exhibitions virtually every week, while in the building proper there is a Guinness World of Records Exhibition.

## Sentosa

The cable cars that operate at 266 feet above the water are one way of getting to the island. Non-stop ferries or a bridge to the island are the alternatives. The paddle-steamer moored by the island's terminal is the Sentosa Riverboat, with American and local fast food, and entertainment on its deck. Sentosa's attractions include its Underwater World, Insectarium, Coralarium, Musical Fountain, a round-trip monorail, swimming lagoon, golf courses, nature trails, beaches and indigenous wild monkeys. There is also a 37m-high Merlion, with viewing gallery in it's lions head, eyes that shoot laser beams and nostrils breathing smoke; Fantasy Island water adventure park; VolcanoLand; Maritime Museum; Asian Village; and the Beaufort and Rasa Sentosa hotels. Historic exhibits worth seeing are Fort Siloso and the waxwork displays of Pioneers of Singapore and Surrender Chambers.

**Fort Siloso.** This fort was a major part of Britain's "Fortress Singapore" plan, but in 1942 its guns faced the wrong way to deter the invading Japanese (although one supply ship was sunk by a Fort Siloso gun). The fort's past, with its tunnels, guns, and ramparts, now makes for an interesting tour. The fort was a British PoW camp during the Japanese occupation, and a permanent Behind Bars exhibition here evokes this period with a reconstruction of two prison cells, lifesize model PoWs, and a show of their artworks.

**State of Johor Mosque Complex** Directly opposite the World Trade Centre's exhibition halls, this charming, recently restored complex is at the very heart of the Malay tradition in post-1819 Singapore. For, in 1824, the descendants (and their followers) of the present sultan of Johor were "evicted" by their new British overlords from central Singapore and transfered to this area, where as far as the British were concerned they would be "out of sight and out of mind". Yet, by 1840, the site was taking on its current harbor and dockyard role and the banished Malay community found itself occupying valuable land which it sold off parcel by parcel, keeping a central compound for itself. In 1885, the principal leader succeeded in being recognized by Britain as sultan of Johor (the title had fallen vacant), and the royal focus shifted north across the water to Johor Bahru, by then the capital of a flourishing prosperous Malayan state. The current sultan's family still recognizes its Singaporean roots, and every year a royal party crosses the Causeway for a religious ceremony at the mosque complex. Traces of the original *istana* (palace) still remain, such as brickwork from the walls that once enclosed the royal baths (to the right of the Malay cemetery).

**TIGER BREWERY**
At Tuas, near the western tip of the island, one of Singapore's two lager beers (the other is Anchor) is brewed. Tiger Brewery organizes tours of the brewing process, after which visitors are led to the English pub-style Tiger Tavern, where they can sample lagers, stouts – or even soft drinks. Tiger has won many international beer awards – and launched the extensive literary career of writer Anthony Burgess: his first published novel was *Time for a Tiger*, set in British Malaya, with its title referring to Singapore's lager beer rather than the big cats of the jungle.

The Chinese Pagoda within the grounds of the Chinese Garden in Taman Jurong.

## JURONG

**HAW PAR VILLA.** Haw Par Villa took what was superb from the old Tiger Balm Gardens – its array of "morally uplifting" painted concrete-and-wire tableaux – and surrounded them with sub-Disneyland trickery to make up a Chinese mythological theme park.

**MING VILLAGE.** This art-curios center makes accurate porcelain replicas of artifacts from ancient China using traditional methods. Its showrooms display hundreds of replicas from the Sung, Yuan, Ming, and Qing dynasties.

**SINGAPORE MINT COIN GALLERY.** The gallery has a display of coins, medals, and medallions from Singapore and around the world, plus a shop for coins and currency souvenirs. Visitors can also watch minting operations in progress.

**JURONG BIRD PARK.** Set in 50 landscaped acres of grounds, the park features over five thousand birds from 450 species, with an emphasis on tropical and sub-tropical specimens, although there is also a penguin enclosure. The shows make it more of a theme park than a proper bird sanctuary. There is a Nocturnal House with owls, kiwis, etc., and a walk-through open-air aviary topped off by invisible netting – which free birds are always trying to get in through! Its latest attraction is a Parrot Paradise section, with over 500 parrots – of the world's 358 species, Jurong now has 108.

**JURONG CROCODILE PARADISE.** Close by the bird park is Jurong Crocodile Paradise, which may not be how the 2500 crocodiles themselves would regard it – especially when they're summoned into the Crocodile Wrestling Arena.

**JURONG HILL.** This hill is a good viewing point from which to observe the outline of Sumatra and of Jurong, the industrial heartland of Singapore. It is also close to two Gardens of Fame, where visiting dignitaries are invited to plant a tree (usually the one with the poisonous fruit and the funny name – Pong-Pong). Notable tree-planters here have included the shah of Iran and Kurt Waldheim.

**SINGAPORE SCIENCE CENTER.** Popular with college students and visitors from abroad, the center has over six hundred exhibits on display in seven galleries, and is intended as a "hands-on" venue. It is best known locally for its Omnimax movies, which project five-story-high, 75-feet-wide images through a 180° fish-eye lens to fill a vast dome screen, engulfing its audience. When a "Ring of Fire" movie on volcanic activity was screened here, the slogan went: "The closest you'll ever get to an erupting volcano".

**TANG DYNASTY CITY.** One of Singapore's latest large-scale (30-acre) attractions. This theme park recreates the 7th-century Chinese city of Chang'an, now Xian, an important trading post on the Silk Road and an imperial capital during the Tang dynasty. The City includes scale reconstructions of the Great Wall of China and the terracotta warriors of Xian.

**CHINESE AND JAPANESE GARDENS.** The attractive Chinese and Japanese gardens adjoin each other, and both afford tranquility amid the built-up surroundings of Jurong. The Chinese Garden, dotted with pagodas and pavilions, looks exotic, while the Japanese Garden reflects the Japanese love of order and serenity.

"...HALFWAY BETWEEN INDIA AND CHINA. THIS WILL BE THE GREAT HALTING-PLACE ON THE TRADE ROUTE TO THE FAR EAST."
J.G. FARRELL, *THE SINGAPORE GRIP*, 1978

**COURTS OF HELL**
The folksy Chinese Buddhist homilies of Haw Par Villa's tableaux include one which insists that men merrymaking at nightclubs are wasting their time and money: "It is better to enjoy the warm comfort and care of the wife at home." The Courts portray frighteningly gruesome punishments for "offenders" such as quack geomancers, loan sharks, exploitative pimps…

**PENJING DISPLAY, CHINESE GARDEN**
New to the Chinese Garden is a 7000-square-yard garden devoted to *penjing,* the Chinese art of miniaturization perfected during the Tang dynasty, and better known by its Japanese name *bonsai.* Over three thousand *penjing* samples are here, arranged in Miniature, Tree, Masterpiece, Rockery, and International sections. The style of the garden is based on that developed in Suzhou, a 2500-year-old city near Shanghai, celebrated for the beauty of its landscape, rockeries, gardens, and ornamental lakes.

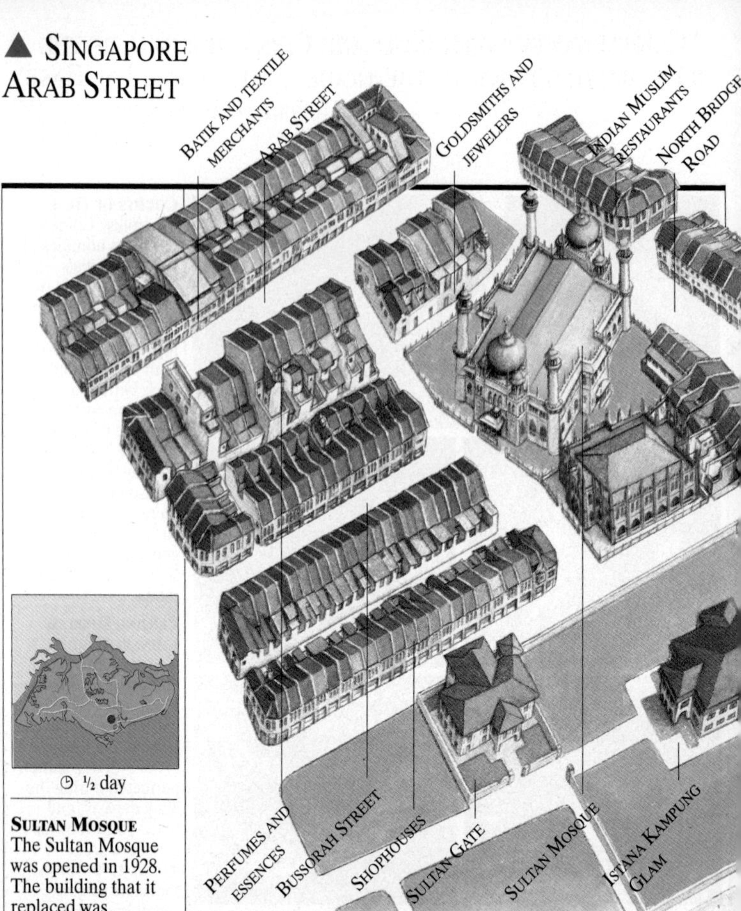


½ day

**SULTAN MOSQUE**
The Sultan Mosque was opened in 1928. The building that it replaced was constructed in the more Southeast Asian "Javanese" style developed in the early days of Islamic influence, in the 15th and 16th centuries ● *82–3*. Singapore's mosque architecture tends to be Arabic or Indian influenced, but one of the largest mosques on the island, in Still Road, retains the style adopted by the original Sultan Mosque.

Sir Stamford Raffles was precise about the area in Singapore he would designate for Malays, Arabs, Bugis traders (from Sulawesi), and others linked by their Islamic faith. He wrote: "The Arab population will require every consideration...." And they would have a 57-acre plot between the Rochor River (today, a canal) and Beach Road, then, as its name suggests, the seafront. The area's twin focal points would be Sultan Mosque and Istana Kampung Glam, the seat of local Malay royalty. They still are. The street names of today's Kampung Glam area reflect Raffles' town planning: Arab, Haji, Jeddah, Bussorah, Baghdad, Muscat, Sultan Gate. They evoke a casbah transferred to the Far East and form an area drenched in atmosphere, dispelling the notion that all of modern Singapore is sterile and bland.

**KAMPUNG GLAM.** It is indeed surprising that Kampung Glam has escaped the wrecker's hammer, and now the area is designated a conservation zone. The best way to start a walking tour of Kampung Glam is to stand on Beach Road facing north, down Bussorah Street, with the Plaza Hotel and the glinting twin towers of the Gateway at your back. This reveals a low-rise vista that culminates in the dull-gold onion domes and minarets of Sultan Mosque. The atmosphere of Kampung Glam is exciting and magnetic. Enter and enjoy its cluster of shops of textiles, basketware

"CHINESE JOSS-HOUSES, HINDU TEMPLES, AND MOHAMMEDAN MOSQUES ALMOST JOSTLE EACH OTHER…THE SHRILL CRY FROM THE MINARETS CALLING THE FAITHFUL TO PRAYER."

ISABELLA BIRD, *THE GOLDEN CHERSONESE*

and rattanware, batik, sarongs, beads, carpets, rugs, lace, brassware, synthetic gems, all the perfumes of Arabia, Malay scents, and spices, as well as eating houses. The Habib and Rahmath basketware shops at 20 and 22 Arab Street are among Singapore's most-photographed shop exteriors, so appealingly do their cane, straw, rattan, and pandan-leaf goods spill over the sidewalk. Batik is popular in this area too. Aljunied's House of Batik at 91 Arab Street is one such specialist batik outlet. Colorful synthetic gems at Mohd. Haniffa, 119 Arab Street; rugs and carpets at Vipin, 54 Arab Street. Especially interesting are those shops at which men and women can customize their own (alcohol-free) perfumes. The essences include attar of rose, jasmine, sandalwood, basil oil, honeysuckle – up to one hundred basic ingredients are available, and many are ready-mixed so that individuals can simply adjust the perfume's "tone". These are pure essences, and thus more intense than the usual cologne or toilette strengths. Kazura at 755 North Bridge Road is one such essence shop, and Haji V. Syed at 718 North Bridge Road another. If, by now, you are wilting in the heat, cooling relief can be found in the modern Golden Landmark Hotel and shopping center which, in keeping with the area, has window motifs with an Islamic influence.

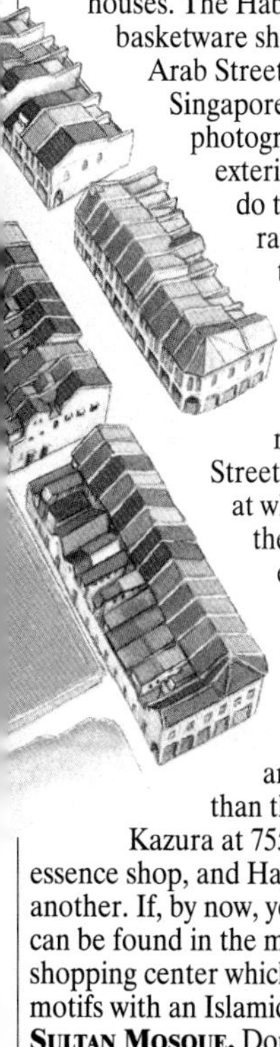

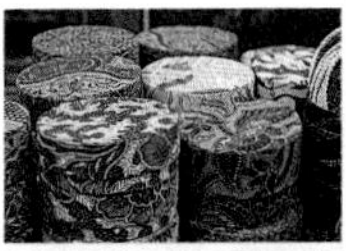

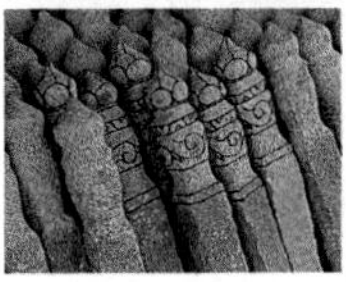

**SULTAN MOSQUE.** Dominating this huddled area is Sultan Mosque, which, ever since the site was allocated by Raffles in 1822, has been the island's principal place of prayer for the Muslim community (Singapore has over eighty mosques). The present building, opened in 1928, was designed by British colonial architects who employed various Middle East and Arab themes to create a dignified whole. A light-hearted touch is the way its dome bases are decorated with glass bottles. Subject to the normal courtesies (no shorts, no shoes, no photos), visitors are welcome to enter via the rear Bussorah Street entrance. Two other notable mosques in this area are Malabar Jama-Ath Mosque at the junction of Victoria Street and Jalan Sultan, a vividly blue-tiled building, close to an old cemetery with frangipani trees and the "Tombs of the Malayan Princes"; and along Beach Road, Hajjah Fatimah Mosque, which is known as "The Leaning Tower of Singapore" for the way its Christian Gothic-styled spire leans at 6 degrees, which was probably unintentional.

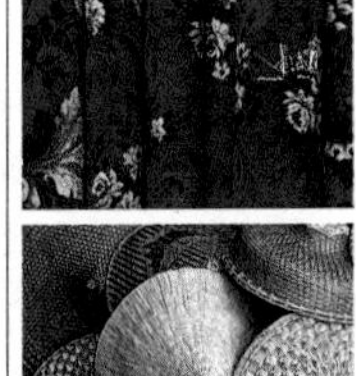

**SARONG**
The wrap-around sarong is practical, tropical unisex wear and comes in many colors and patterns. It makes an excellent present too.

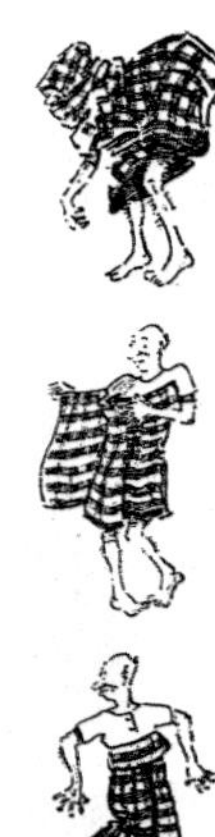

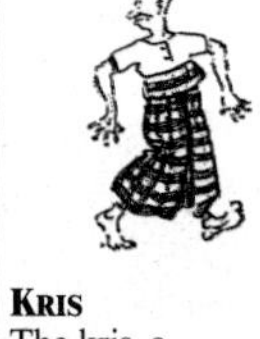

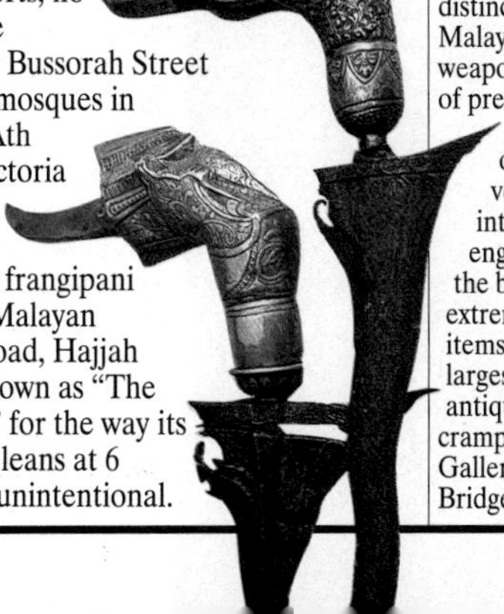

**KRIS**
The kris, a distinctively curved Malay knife, is both a weapon and a symbol of prestige and status. Hand-crafted ornamental versions, with intricate engravings along the blade, are extremely handsome items. Singapore's largest collection of antique kris is in the cramped Malay Art Gallery at 737 North Bridge Road.

**GLAM**
Kampung Glam got its name from the Gelam tree, which once flourished in this area. From its leaves comes Cajupute oil, a crucial medicinal ingredient of the Boxing Ring brand embrocation oil. This was first prepared in a Kampung Glam shophouse, where the secret formula was devised forty years ago, until the family firm finally outgrew the premises in 1991. The lotion is widely available at medicine halls and chemists, and is recommended for sporting aches and sprains (local women who have just given birth rub it on their stomachs, too).

BOXING RING BRAND
*Embrocation.*

On North Bridge Road opposite Sultan Mosque are three jolly eating houses, the rival Zam-Zam, Victory, and Singapore restaurants. Their specialties include *prata* (Indian pancakes), *murtabak*, and *teh tarik*, Malay for "stretched tea", referring to the way milky sweet tea gets poured from one mug to another – to cool and mix it – with such speed and accuracy that it does look like it's being "stretched" ● *67*. Further along, at 797 North Bridge Road, is a food institution, the two-story Islamic Restaurant, founded in 1921 and probably Singapore's oldest still in family hands, which provides a spicy range of curries, *murtabak*, *biryani*, *sambal*, *kurmas*, and *rendang*. It even offers its own invention – *roti Mariam*, a Malay-flavored flat wheat pancake – and packs its own curry spices for aficionados to use at home.

Another good eating place in the area is the Sabar Menanti (Malay for "wait patiently!") coffee shop at 66 Bussorah Street, behind Sultan Mosque, which specializes in chili-hot *nasi padang* (rice with spicy food dishes) and *ikan bakar* (baked fish).

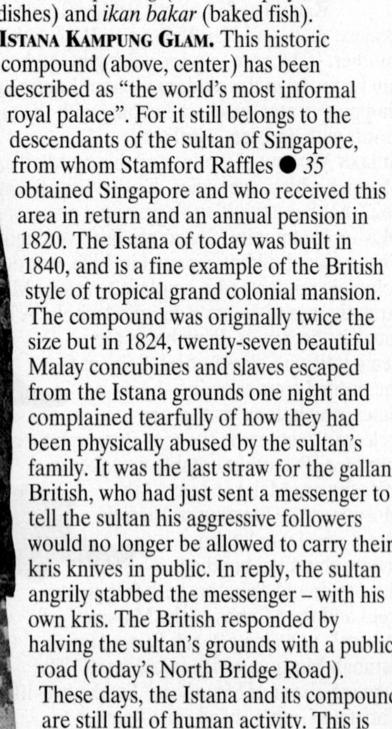

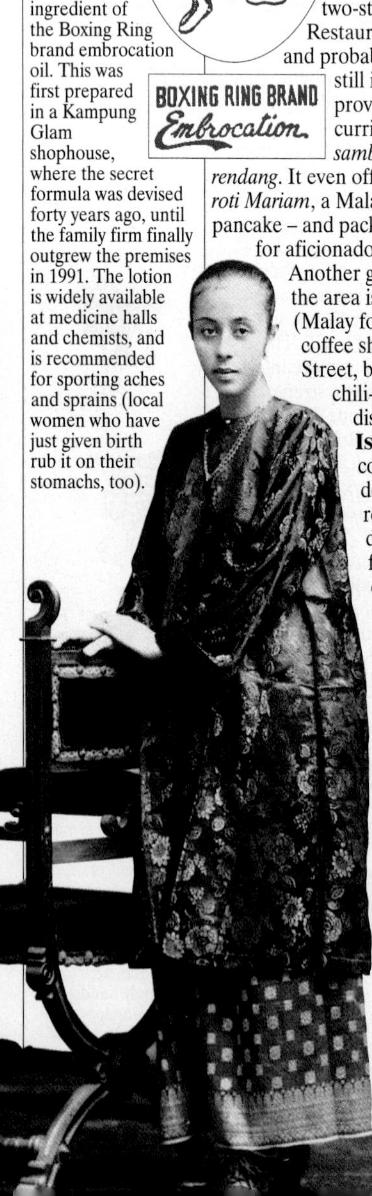

**ISTANA KAMPUNG GLAM.** This historic compound (above, center) has been described as "the world's most informal royal palace". For it still belongs to the descendants of the sultan of Singapore, from whom Stamford Raffles ● *35* obtained Singapore and who received this area in return and an annual pension in 1820. The Istana of today was built in 1840, and is a fine example of the British style of tropical grand colonial mansion. The compound was originally twice the size but in 1824, twenty-seven beautiful Malay concubines and slaves escaped from the Istana grounds one night and complained tearfully of how they had been physically abused by the sultan's family. It was the last straw for the gallant British, who had just sent a messenger to tell the sultan his aggressive followers would no longer be allowed to carry their kris knives in public. In reply, the sultan angrily stabbed the messenger – with his own kris. The British responded by halving the sultan's grounds with a public road (today's North Bridge Road).

These days, the Istana and its compound are still full of human activity. This is because anyone who can claim a family

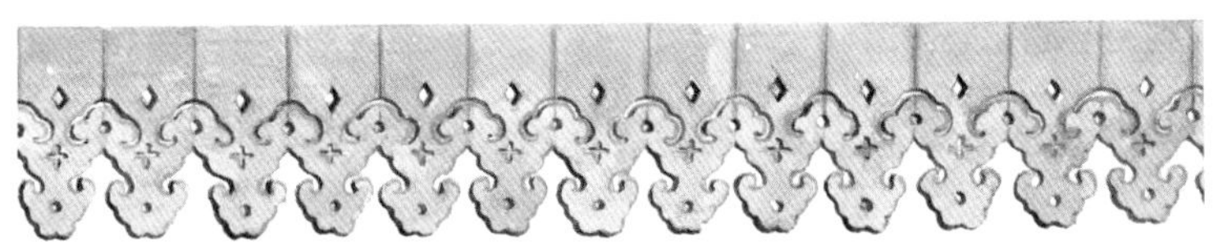

link – no matter how distant – with the first sultan's family is entitled to move in. Visitors are welcome to enter through the imposing gateposts and stroll around the grounds; it is a fascinating, friendly place and an authentic piece of Singaporean history. Back outside the Istana, along Pahang Street, note the traditional tombstone makers and carvers, practicing a craft that is clearly not dying out.

## BUGIS STREET

A couple of blocks away, near Bugis MRT station, is the restored version of the world-famous Bugis Street. A perfect replica of what was demolished in 1985, the tourist attraction features almost every aspect of the old one – except perhaps what had made the street world-famous: the "anything can, and probably will, happen" late-night atmosphere aided by "les girls", glamorous transvestites and transsexuals who made Bugis Street their playground. "Les girls" are now scattered around town, from Orchard Towers to Changi Village. But remember: caveat emptor!

**PARCO BUGIS JUNCTION.** This shopping complex has a Bugis *prahu* trading boat on display and includes two restored (covered-over and airconditioned) old shophouse "streets", with the Hotel Inter-Continental alongside.

**PERFUMES**
The perfumes of Arab Street do not use alcohol and are a fantastic evocation of the exotic. Customers can make their own blend of essential oils, and keep it in glass bottles.

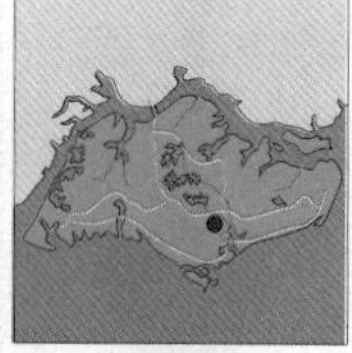

◷ ½ day

**SPICES**
The aroma of spices mingles with the smell of incense and flowers around Little India. One store that has specialized in a wide variety of food flavorings since 1920 is P. Govindasamy's at 46–52 Serangoon Road. The spices come from India and are ground in Singapore. It is claimed that only three people in Singapore know the precise recipe for Govindasamy's renowned curry.

## SERANGOON ROAD

A local saying goes: "There are three ways to get to India from Singapore – one, by air; two, by sea; and three, by taxi to Serangoon Road." Why Serangoon Road became so Indian is unclear, for the island's earliest Hindu temples were built in the town center. One theory is that the brick kilns and lime pits set up in the swampy mid-19th-century Serangoon Road area attracted Indians, given their association with the early building industry, plus the fact that ample grass and water here encouraged another early Indian business – rearing cows for their milk. The vast majority of early Singapore's Indians were effectively convict slave building laborers. In 1841, there were about 1200 Indian convicts, comprising 10 percent of Singapore's population then, making roads, digging canals and clearing jungle. They built St Andrew's Cathedral ▲ *138*, and it is still remarked how well the Indian foremen and laborers were able to recreate such a perfect replica of an English-county-town Anglican church. The last major projects undertaken by Indian laborers, who were kept in chains when not at work, were the Government House (now the Istana at Dhoby Ghaut) in 1868 and Cavenagh Bridge over the Singapore river in 1869. The latter project used pre-cast steel shipped out from Glasgow and it stands today as Singapore's oldest major bridge (for pedestrians only), a point further emphasized by its quaint signboard,

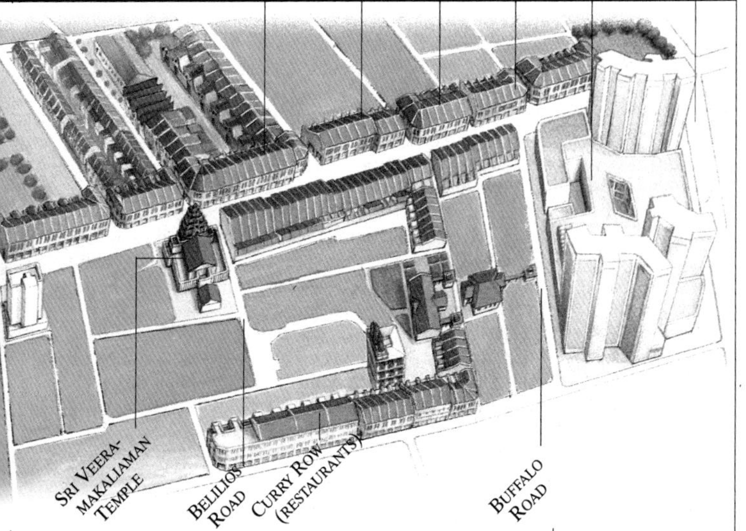


which bans all cattle and horses. In 1870 Britain's penal policy for India saw long-term convicts being held in the grim prison cells at Port Blair in the Andaman Islands. Indian convicts in Singapore serving shorter sentences were given the option of either returning to India or "trying their luck" as free men in Singapore. Most stayed. However, not all Indians who came here were prisoners or slaves – there was a healthier trading community too. Serangoon Road had first been cut through the jungle in 1828, and it was during the 1870's that the cattle-buffalo business took root here with such big traders as I.R. Belilios, a Venetian Jew, encouraged by the ample water, grass, and bamboo clumps then around this stretch of Serangoon Road. Both Belilios and the cattle business itself are recalled today by street names in the area, such as Belilios, Buffalo, Lembu, and Kandang Kerbau. The festive months of October–November are the season of Deepavali – the Festival of Lights – when the stretch of Serangoon Road between Bukit Timah and Kitchener roads is lit up and the whole area goes *en fête* for three weeks. Hindu and Sikh temples, cakeshops, vegetarian restaurants, saris, Punjabi suits, dhotis, spices, jasmine garlands, gold, jewelry, fabrics, incense, brass items, Madras movie videos, Tamil movie-star pin-up posters, Indian music cassettes and tapes, roadside barbers, and fortune-tellers who use parakeets to pick a card foretelling the fate of curious clients – all these make up the distinctive sights, sounds, smells, and tastes of Little India.

**SRI VEERAMAKALIAMMAN TEMPLE.** This temple, with its handsome *gopuram*, was built in 1881 by indentured Bengali laborers, and was recently restored. It is dedicated to Kali the Courageous, a ferocious incarnation of Siva's wife. Inside is a shrine to the elephant God of Wisdom, Ganesh.

**PERFUMED GARLANDS** The Indian word for these attractive garlands with their delicate perfume is *malai*, and they are sold at many of the shops in Little India. Generally made from jasmine flowers that are either just in bud or in full bloom, they are carefully strung together on a cord made from the fiber of the banana tree. The garlands are worn at weddings and on other auspicious occasions.

**THE EARLY DAYS IN SERANGOON ROAD**
Serangoon Road was one of the first cross-island roads to be built after the major city roads had been completed. The photograph above is a reminder of a time when buffaloes were kept not only for their milk and meat, but to provide the main form of transport. Cattle were also used to turn grinding machinery in the food industry.

An old area that has, by and large, escaped modernization, Serangoon Road and its many adjoining lanes are rich in examples of distinctively Singaporean, two-story turn-of-the-century shophouses. Bright shades of green and blue predominate.

**SRI SRINIVASA PERUMAL TEMPLE.** Serangoon Road's most notable temple is Sri Srinivasa Perumal Temple, with its modern (1979), 66-foot-high monumental gateway *gopuram* (above) supporting intricate pastel-colored god and goddess statues. The temple really comes alive during two Hindu religious festivals: Thaipusam, in January, and the Thimiti firewalking festival in October–November.

**CENTRAL SIKH TEMPLE.** This center for a deeply traditional religion is visually exciting because of its modernist break with traditional Sikh style. The three-story building was completed in 1986 and won a prestigious architectural design award for its entrance canopy and gateway. Inside, the spacious prayer hall has no columns, and is air-conditioned and fully carpeted. The dome is 42 feet high and covered with white and gold mosaic tiles. The whole complex contains many community facilities, including a Sikh library-cum-museum, a dining hall, and a kitchen. There are also communal pools, symbolizing the ritual importance of bathing. The temple cost S$6.5 million to build, and has been described as the most impressive Sikh temple outside the Punjab.

**KOMALA VILAS RESTAURANT.** Food is why most non-Indians come to Little India. Komala Vilas at 76 Serangoon Road is an institution, specializing in south Indian vegetarian dishes since 1947. The restaurant's very popular *thali,* or set meals, usually based around a vegetarian curry, have won it an international reputation – even in India itself. Prices are low and opening hours long (7am to 10.30pm). Its bustling atmosphere makes the unassuming Komala Vilas a must-visit.

**FISH-HEAD CURRY**
Curry Row's eateries are the best places to sample yet another contender for Singapore's national dish – the Fish-Head Curry. This is indeed a fish head (massive, usually grouper or red snapper), which is served floating in chilli-hot curry sauce. The sight of the fish-head's "accusing" eyes may alarm some first-timers, but devotees of this dish regard the flesh behind them as the crowning delicacy of the meal.

## RACE COURSE ROAD

Race Course Road faces Farrer Park, now a field but one which has witnessed many major events in Singapore's social history (including its first horse race-track, golf course, and polo pitch). On December 4, 1919, Farrer Park became an airstrip, when a Vickers Vimy made a "pitstop" there during a historic Britain–Australia flight in under thirty days.

**CURRY ROW.** Race Course Road, one block away from Serangoon Road, is better known as "Curry Row" because of its concentration of crowded, informal south Indian banana-leaf curry houses. Banana leaf refers to the "plate" on which these spicy meals are served.

**TEMPLE OF 1000 LIGHTS.** At the other end of Race Course Road from Curry Row stands the Temple of 1000 Lights, built in 1927 by a Thai monk. Its name comes from the light bulbs surrounding its huge seated Buddha statue, 50 feet high and weighing 300 tons. The bulbs are switched on each time a donation is made.

"SOME (STATUETTES) WERE SUPPORTED BY A COUPLE OF ATTENDANTS WHO PREVENTED THEM FROM FALLING AS THEY TOTTERED ON IN FRENZIED GYRATIONS."

DELIGHT SWEETSER, *ONE WAY ROUND THE WORLD*, 1898

**THAIPUSAM**
This extraordinary Hindu annual festival is usually held in January. A ceremonial procession moves from Sri Srinivasa Perumal Temple on Serangoon Road south across Dhoby Ghaut and Orchard Road to the Chettiar Hindu Temple on Tank Road. The most striking aspect of Thaipusam for visitors is the way devotees pierce parts of their bare bodies with sharp skewers, steel spears, barbs, and the like – and show no pain nor blood. The elaborate body-piercing devices borne by intense devotees are called *kavadi*, and preparation for this ceremony requires fasting and abstinence from bodily pleasures for a month before Thaipusam. There are various metaphysical explanations for the "rising above bodily pain" aspects of the ceremony which is as extraordinary as it is genuine and sincere. Tourists are welcome to watch the ceremony, but if they also go into the temples, they should leave their doubts outside – along with their shoes.

**KRANJI WAR MEMORIAL**
This is a moving memorial to those who lost their lives during World War Two. Over twenty thousand men and women with no known graves are commemorated by name here, while over four thousand tombstones (all of similar design) spread out over a hill overlooking the Strait of Johor. Annual remembrance ceremonies are held here. Kranji also has a Singapore State Cemetery in which its deceased presidents are buried.

**BUKIT TURF CLUB.**
The club is Singapore's horse-racing venue, with thirty-two race days each year. Its annual big event is the Gold Cup in September–October, attracting up to fifty thousand spectators. Horse-racing tours are arranged for visitors. A new race-course will open in 1998 at Woodlands (close to Kranji MRT), leaving the current Bukit Timah site clear for private housing.

## ALONG BUKIT TIMAH ROAD

**NEWTON CIRCUS.** Singapore's best-known open-air food center, Newton Circus serves meals until at least 2am. Its large size and near-town location make it popular with a wide cross-section of locals, and a must for those on "Singapore by night" tours. The center's informal, bustling atmosphere is as much a lure as the food on offer. Complaints have been made about aggressive touting by its hawkers, but visitors can sit anywhere, and choose whatever dish they want. If only one food-center visit can be made, Newton Circus would be a good choice (though its future is now in some doubt because of how valuable the central site it occupies has become). Further west, Adam Road Food Centre (known as "Adams") operates round the clock and serves local fare. One of its stalls used to be known for offering "penis soup" until stern authorities ordered a name change to "goat's organ soup".

## BETWEEN THOMSON AND SEMBAWANG

MacRitchie, Peirce, and Seletar Reservoir parks form part of Singapore's large central water-catchment area, and are popular with joggers. During weekends, families and youth groups picnic here
**SUN YAT-SEN VILLA.** This is not just a pleasing Victorian villa, it is a building of historic significance. Here, between 1906 and 1908, Dr SunYat-sen and his supporters plotted the downfall (as in the movie *The Last Emperor*) of Qing Manchurian dynastic rule in Beijing and planned the establishment of a modern Chinese republic in 1911. The villa was built in the 1880's as a "love-nest" for the favored singing concubine of a rich Chinese merchant, before being made available for Dr Sun's many semi-secret visits to Singapore. In this building, the "Tong Oath" was sworn by local wealthy Chinese businessmen who gave financial support to several uprisings in China in 1912. Dr Sun was briefly installed as modern China's first president. The villa now features a vivid exhibition devoted to the 1942–5

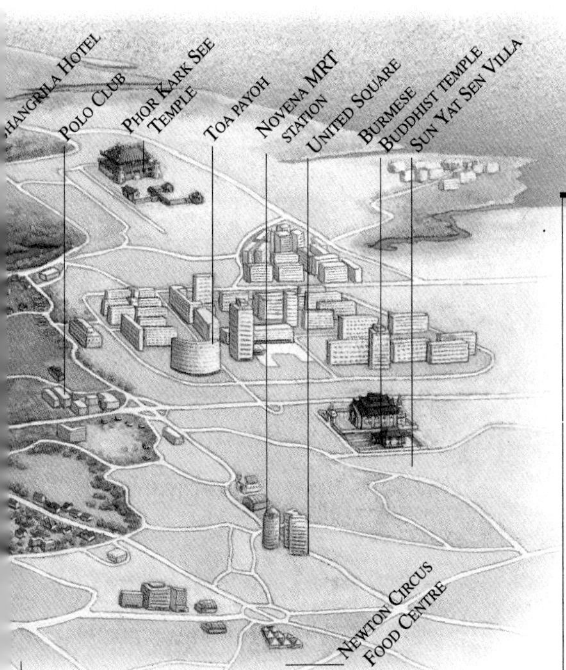

Shangrila Hotel
Polo Club
Phor Kark See Temple
Toa Payoh
Novena MRT Station
United Square
Burmese Buddhist Temple
Sun Yat Sen Villa
Newton Circus Food Centre

Japanese occupation years, and much material relating to Dr Sun's political career. Close by is the Burmese Buddhist temple, one of the most lavish outside Burma, with many traditional Burmese features and an 11-foot-high Buddha statue, brought here from Burma in 1921.

**Toa Payoh.** Another temple, called Siong Lim and noted for its marble Siamese Buddha statues, heralds the start of Toa Payoh from Lorong 8, one of the oldest HDB (Housing and Development Board) estates, in which more than 85 percent of Singaporeans live. Toa Payoh ("big swamp", which it was before large-scale landfill) is the new town most often explored by visitors as it is convenient to get to on the MRT and also gives a feel of the "real" Singapore. It offers typical neighborhood hawker food centers, and good-value shopping.

**Bishan.** Just north of Toa Payoh, Bishan is a showpiece new town. At Bishan's Bright Hill Drive, sprawling over 30 acres, stands Phor Kark See, Singapore's most astonishing Buddhist temple complex, housing statues, pagodas, huge joss-columns, murals, monks, dragons, gardens, old peoples' homes, and vegetarian restaurants with geomancy-inspired designs. At the crematorium, tourists are allowed to watch from a distance during funeral rituals. Several cremations take place daily, after which temple guardians place the remains in urns inside the temple's pagoda, which has a capacity for 300,000 urns.

**Admiralty House.** Built as an official Royal Navy residence in 1939, the building (elegantly designed by Sir Edwin Lutyens) was completed just in time for it to be taken over by the Japanese. In 1945, some two hundred Japanese PoWs dug its swimming pool, now one of the range of amenities offered by the country golf club, for which Admiralty House serves as a handsome clubhouse.

**Sembawang.** Effectively the "end of the line" when heading north in Singapore, Sembawang town, with its park facing the Strait of Johor, is one of Singapore's few remaining rustic corners.

◷ 1 day

**Phor Kark See Turtle Pond**

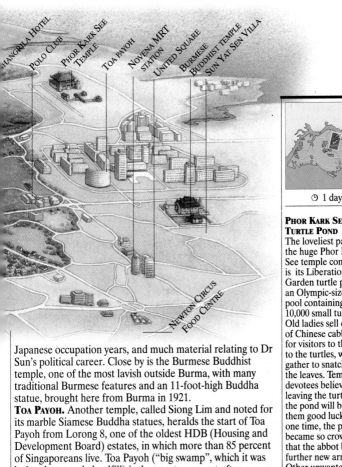

The loveliest part of the huge Phor Kark See temple complex is its Liberation Garden turtle pond, an Olympic-sized pool containing over 10,000 small turtles. Old ladies sell clumps of Chinese cabbage for visitors to throw to the turtles, which gather to snatch at the leaves. Temple devotees believe that leaving the turtles in the pond will bring them good luck. At one time, the pond became so crowded that the abbot banned further new arrivals. Other unwanted animals such as dogs and rabbits also wander freely in the Liberation Garden.

## PARKS AND GARDENS

**THE BOTANIC GARDENS.** Singapore's Botanic Gardens ▲ *176–7* are one of the world's best: not only is it a superb collection of tropical plantlife (over two thousand species – with an excellent research section on orchids), it has also played a crucial role in the development of Southeast Asian botany. The rubber seedlings brought here (from Brazil, via London's Kew Gardens) in 1877 and the trees that were grown from them launched the lucrative regional rubber industry. One such "pioneer" rubber tree (*Hevea brasiliensis*) is still flourishing at the Botanic Gardens, which was set up on this site in 1859 and now covers 80 acres. Unusually for a Singaporean attraction, entry to the Botanic Gardens is free. In 1995, a National Orchid Garden opened inside the Gardens, with over 700 orchid species (180 native to Singapore) and 2,100 hybrids, resulting in some 600,000 orchids for show in varying seasonal displays. Admission is charged.

**BUKIT TIMAH NATURE RESERVE.** The nature reserve contains 200 acres of primary rainforest ■ *22–3* and could be how Singapore looked when Raffles and his men arrived in 1819 ● *35*. The reserve is so tropical and fertile that a claim has been made that the number of plant species growing on just one of its acres exceeds the entire number of species in all of Britain. The reserve is left untouched, but there are four walkways, including one that leads to the top of the hill (the highest – natural – point in Singapore at 581 feet). Trekkers should appreciate that it gets hot and sticky in this denseness, and that mosquitoes and snakes are ever-present. Watch out also for cheeky monkeys and the great racquet-tailed drongo bird. Singapore's oldest tree (almost four hundred years and belonging to the *Shorea curtisii* species) is located just inside the reserve.

**SINGAPORE ZOOLOGICAL GARDENS.** Singapore's zoo uses its natural setting by Seletar Reservoir to excellent effect. By and large, its animals roam free (barriers are discreet) in a forest-and-lake landscape that feels right in this age of eco-consciousness. As the management says: "Our reward is happy animals. The proof lies in the zoo's good breeding record: unhappy animals do not make love!" It has 1700 individual "happy" animals. Prize exhibits include its Primate Kingdom for monkeys, its Komodo dragons (indigenous to the Indonesian island of Komodo), and the largest social colony of orang utans on display in the world. Visitors can take breakfast or high tea with some of them. The zoo stages animal shows and, unusual in a tropical climate, even has polar bears on view (in a refrigerated pool). Singapore's single most famous animal, however, must be Ah Meng, the zoo's mascot mega-star female orang utan – lover of three, mother of four, and herself a granny. Ah Meng's services to the zoo have proven so valuable that she was

**FLORA AND FAUNA**
"The vegetation was most luxuriant, comprising enormous forest trees, as well as a variety of ferns, caladiums, and other undergrowth, and abundance of climbing rattan palms. Insects were exceedingly abundant and very interesting, and every day furnished scores of new and curious forms. In about two months I obtained no less than 700 species of beetles."
Alfred Russel Wallace, *The Malay Archipelago*, 1869

**BOTANIC GARDENS' EARLY HISTORY**
The idea to create a botanic garden in Singapore came as early as 1819, when Stamford Raffles established a garden at his home on Government Hill. This was expanded into a botanical and experimental garden, which became the foundation for the spice plantations which were scattered across the island. By 1875 the gardens had expanded and land was found for them on Tanglin Road.

taken to a 1992 Tourism Ball and given an official award: a scroll and a hand of bananas. The Zoo's innovative Night Safari has proved popular with locals and visitors alike. It has over 1,200 animals of 110 species roaming freely around an open-air nocturnal 100-acre habitat – but please note, no flash cameras or torches. Open till midnight, the Night Safari has restaurant facilities.

**Mandai Orchid Gardens.** This is a private enterprise, spread over a 10-acre hillside and exporting over four million sprays of orchids a year to thirty countries around the world. Visitors can see thousands of orchids here, including the purple-and-white Vanda Miss Joaquim. The gardens were started as a hobby in 1960 by two British botanists.

**Sungei Buloh Nature Park.** A growing local concern for environmental issues – and a new reluctance to destroy ecosystems to create golf courses – is behind the establishment of Singapore's first protected nature park at Sungei Buloh ▲ *341* in Kranji, near the causeway to Malaysia. Its untouched swamps, groves, scrubs, and ponds play host to over 100 species of birds. Nine concealed viewing hides allow serious bird-watchers to observe all this wildlife (as well as squirrels, mouse-deer, reptiles, and lemurs) at close quarters without scaring the creatures away.

**Other wildlife.** Wildlife abounds around the northern part of Singapore, especially at Senoko (Sungei Sembawang). This is mainly mangrove swampland ■ *20–1* and extremely rich in birdlife, with two of the world's endangered bird species – the Chinese egret and the Asian dowitcher – often spotted here. "Unofficial" wildlife are the wild crocodiles that turn up occasionally in places like the Kranji and Seletar reservoirs.

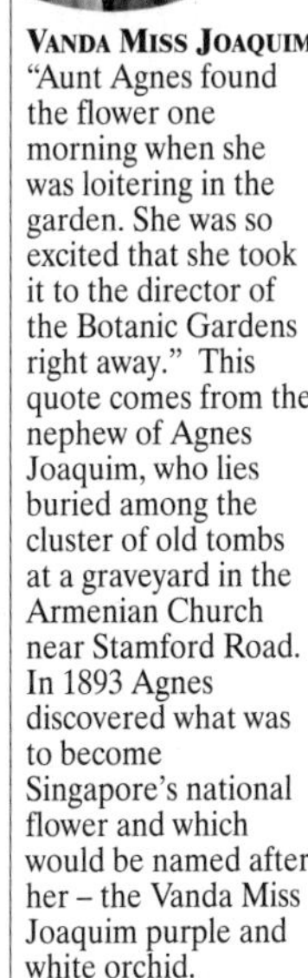

**Vanda Miss Joaquim**
"Aunt Agnes found the flower one morning when she was loitering in the garden. She was so excited that she took it to the director of the Botanic Gardens right away." This quote comes from the nephew of Agnes Joaquim, who lies buried among the cluster of old tombs at a graveyard in the Armenian Church near Stamford Road. In 1893 Agnes discovered what was to become Singapore's national flower and which would be named after her – the Vanda Miss Joaquim purple and white orchid.

**Mynahs**
Singapore's most numerous common birds, the mynahs, need neither bird park nor reserve to thrive. They adapt so well to today's urban environment that they now easily outnumber sparrows and pigeons. Introduced as a caged bird from India and Indonesia during the 1920's, the 6-to-9-inch-long mynah, with its black and white patches on its wings, plus distinctive yellow beak and claws, is a cheeky, fearless bird. Mynahs can roost just as easily in air-conditioning vents as in trees, and forage in garbage for their food.

Singapore's Botanic Gardens comprise the Central Core, the Tanglin (Heritage) Core, and the new Bukit Timah Core. The Central Core contains most visitor amenities, including the orchid garden center. Conceived as a focal point and orientation area, this core also introduces visitors to the Gardens' research activities and recreational features. The Tanglin Core is the oldest part of the Gardens, close to the original entrance at the junction of Holland and Cluny Roads. A tranquil tropical garden, this core contains the Gardens' offices, library, and herbarium. The recently developed Bukit Timah Core is an active recreation area, with its "eco-lake" aquatic garden, a natural habitat for aquatic plants and wildlife, and a plant resources center.

CENTRAL CORE

TANGLIN CORE

**TRAVELER'S PALM**
Not a true palm at all, this plant is actually a member of the banana family.

**GETTING THERE**
The Botanic Gardens are open from 5am to 11pm on weekdays and until midnight on weekends and eve of public holidays. They are within walking distance of the eastern end of Orchard Road, and can be reached quickly by taxi or by SBS bus nos 7, 105, 106, and 174. The entrance (left) faces the T-junction of Cluny, Holland and Napier Roads.

"...And add to these retired Leisure, that in trim gardens takes his pleasure."
John Milton

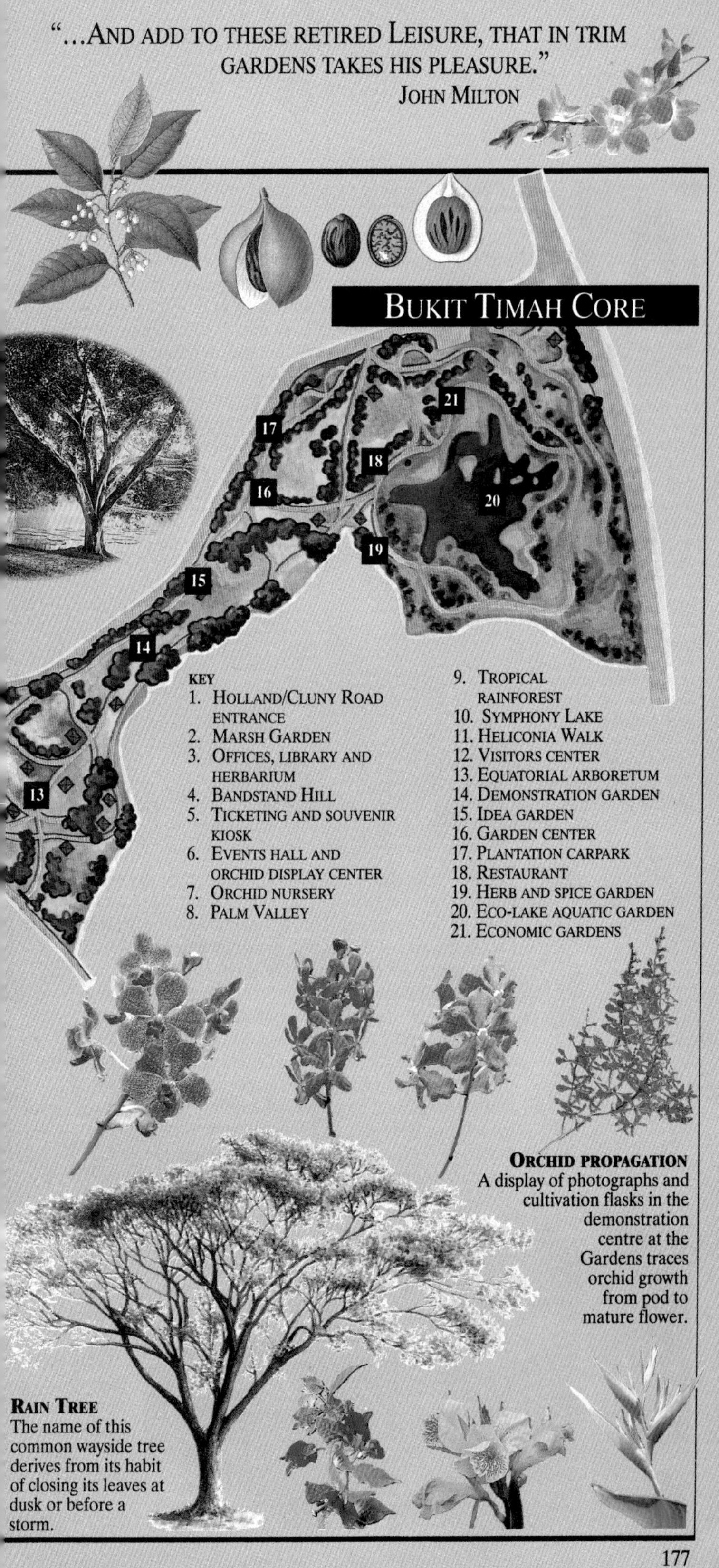


## Bukit Timah Core

KEY
1. Holland/Cluny Road entrance
2. Marsh Garden
3. Offices, library and herbarium
4. Bandstand Hill
5. Ticketing and souvenir kiosk
6. Events hall and orchid display center
7. Orchid nursery
8. Palm Valley
9. Tropical rainforest
10. Symphony Lake
11. Heliconia Walk
12. Visitors center
13. Equatorial arboretum
14. Demonstration garden
15. Idea garden
16. Garden center
17. Plantation carpark
18. Restaurant
19. Herb and spice garden
20. Eco-lake aquatic garden
21. Economic gardens

**Orchid propagation**
A display of photographs and cultivation flasks in the demonstration centre at the Gardens traces orchid growth from pod to mature flower.

**Rain Tree**
The name of this common wayside tree derives from its habit of closing its leaves at dusk or before a storm.

**JAMU**
Watch out for the *jamu* stalls around Geylang Serai. *Jamu* means medicine and is based on (mainly Indonesian) traditional herbal folk wisdom. Powdered *jamu*, mixed with water and, usually, a raw egg, though often vile-tasting, is claimed to satisfy many requirements, from sexual potency or bigger breasts, through to relief from rheumatism. *Jamu* is also made into beauty preparations for rubbing into the skin. Try some. At least it won't do you any harm.

## GEYLANG

This area began as a small Malay settlement in the mid-1840's, when the government of Singapore decided that the Malay village at the mouth of the Singapore River was obstructing harbor traffic and could well be a haven for pirates. About 450 Orang Laut moved to Geylang, and the coconut plantations surrounding the area gave it the name of Geylang Kelapa (*kelapa* meaning coconut). Since the beginning of this century, however, the name has changed to Geylang Serai (*serai* is Malay for lemon-grass). Although the Istana Kampong Glam and Sultan Mosque area may be the

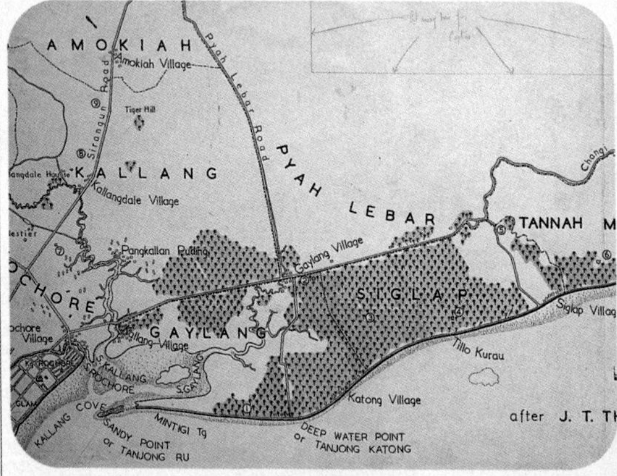


original historical Malay center, the heart of the modern Malay community lies at Geylang – or more precisely, Geylang Serai market. This is most obvious on Hari Raya Puasa, the end of the fasting month, when a stretch of Geylang and Changi roads is lit up in festive style, and Muslims from all over the island converge on Geylang Serai market for its many temporary night bazaar stalls and for the bustling, friendly atmosphere, not to mention tasty food items such as *ketupat* (boiled rice-cake wrapped in strips of young coconut leaf) and *kueh-mueh* (assorted cakes and snacks), and the Joo Chiat Complex, where the main attraction (apart from its air-conditioned coolness) is its wide range of materials for making end-of-Ramadan clothes, wall decorations, new curtains, and the like for traditional Malay homes. Much money is spent at Geylang Serai during Hari Raya.

**MALAY VILLAGE.** The idea of a replica Malay village came from Malay members of parliament, who in 1984 urged that Geylang should have a permanent memorial to the Malay community. The village opened in 1990 but

closed soon afterwards following lukewarm public response; it reopened in early 1994. The revamped 33-acre attraction features a reconstructed kampung setting, which includes handicraft stores, souvenir shops, and food stalls. Craftwork demonstrations and cultural shows are also staged there.

**RED HOUSE**
A familiar landmark along East Coast Road (noted for many informal eating places), the Katong Bakery ,or "Red House", still makes its own bread and cakes and has a characterful, old-fashioned coffee-shop interior.

## KATONG

**JOO CHIAT.** Between Geylang and the sea in the east-coast area is the Joo Chiat neighborhood, which is traditionally associated with the old wealthy Eurasian/Peranakan (Straits Chinese) communities. Katong still has many delightful bungalow houses in ample grounds, especially along Mountbatten Road (which also has exciting modern homes and downright eccentric ones). Parallel to Mountbatten is Meyer Road, which presents the modern face of affluent Singapore. Known locally as "Condo Valley", Meyer Road has new and old condominiums rising side by side, each with their swimming pools, children's playgrounds and floodlit tennis courts. Occupants on the upper floors enjoy sweeping views across to Indonesia from their balconies.

**PARKWAY PARADE.** On Marine Parade Road is the multi-story Parkway Parade shopping complex, whose occupants are a mix of furniture stores, specialty shops, fast-food outlets, an amusement center, and a supermarket. With a traditional wet market and hawker center outside, Parkway Parade is usually lively till late in the evening.

**EAST COAST PARK.** This park is one of Singapore's over-organized designated leisure zones, but it is nonetheless likeable, especially at weekends, when Singaporeans do relax and unwind here (large family groups come for picnics). East Coast Park has many appealing attractions, including stretches of sandy beaches, chalets for rental, swaying coconut trees, jogging and cycling tracks, the Crocodile Farm and Big Splash swimming pools, the East Coast Sailing Centre (for windsurfing and canoeing), and quiet corners. There is also the open-air, good-value Seafood Centre, which houses eight restaurants offering similar seafood menus.

**JAMES CLAVELL**
His Selarang Barracks prisoner-of-war years launched the writing career of American blockbuster specialist James Clavell. His gritty, every-man-for-himself *King Rat* novel was based on a real-life character, who spent 1942–5 as a "fellow-guest" of the Japanese.

**JAPANESE OCCUPATION PHOTO EXHIBITS**
Le Meridien Changi Hotel has a permanent display of photographs taken at great personal risk by Australian PoW George Aspinall during the Japanese occupation. With a folding Kodak 2 camera, Aspinall – then a teenager – took vivid photos of a battered Singapore, prison-camp conditions and suffering inmates.

Changi to most people now means one of the world's very best airports, but for those with longer memories, Changi – its prison, its barracks, its very name – is synonymous with the collapse of Britain's "Fortress Singapore". Yet Changi also means, to Singaporeans, a soothing escape from the city and the housing estates, as they enjoy its beaches, its sea breezes, its bars and eateries, and its decidedly holiday atmosphere. Changi would not exist at all, however, were it not for the British military. It was carved out of the jungle, then fortified in the 1930's as Japan moved into China; from 1940–1, it was where Allied forces (mainly Australian) were billeted when rushed to Singapore to repulse the anticipated Japanese advance. After their failure to do so in 1942, Selarang Barracks and Changi Prison were where 85,000 of these forces and Singapore's Caucasian population spent the occupation years ● *38*. The main memorials to that era are the Changi Murals (five religious paintings by a British PoW), which are preserved in St Luke's Chapel, off Cranwell Road; and Changi Prison Museum and Chapel, a replica building inside today's actual prison, which can be visited for its display of PoW "souvenirs". During the Fiftieth Anniversary commemorations in 1992 of the Fall of Singapore, a Memorial Grove was established just outside the prison where many veterans planted trees to honor the war dead. Tanah Merah Ferry Terminal, off East Coast Parkway and close to Changi Airport, opened in 1995 primarily to forge a new link with Indonesia's neighbouring islands of Bintan and Batam. This terminal also has car-loading facilities.

## CHANGI VILLAGE

Changi Village is especially enjoyed today for its beach, which faces Pulau Ubin ("bumboat" ferries from Changi Harbor) and the Johor coastline. Families picnic here at weekends. There are modest good-value shops in Changi Village, while nightspots include the lively Europa Lounge and Charlie's Snack Bar, which specializes in beers from most parts of the world and British favorites such as fish and chips. More ethnic food can be had at the superb Ikobana (Minangkabau for authentic) *nasi padang* restaurant (daytime only).

# West Malaysia



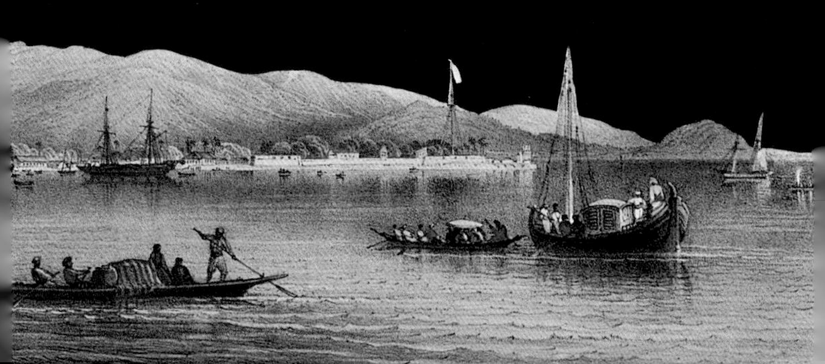

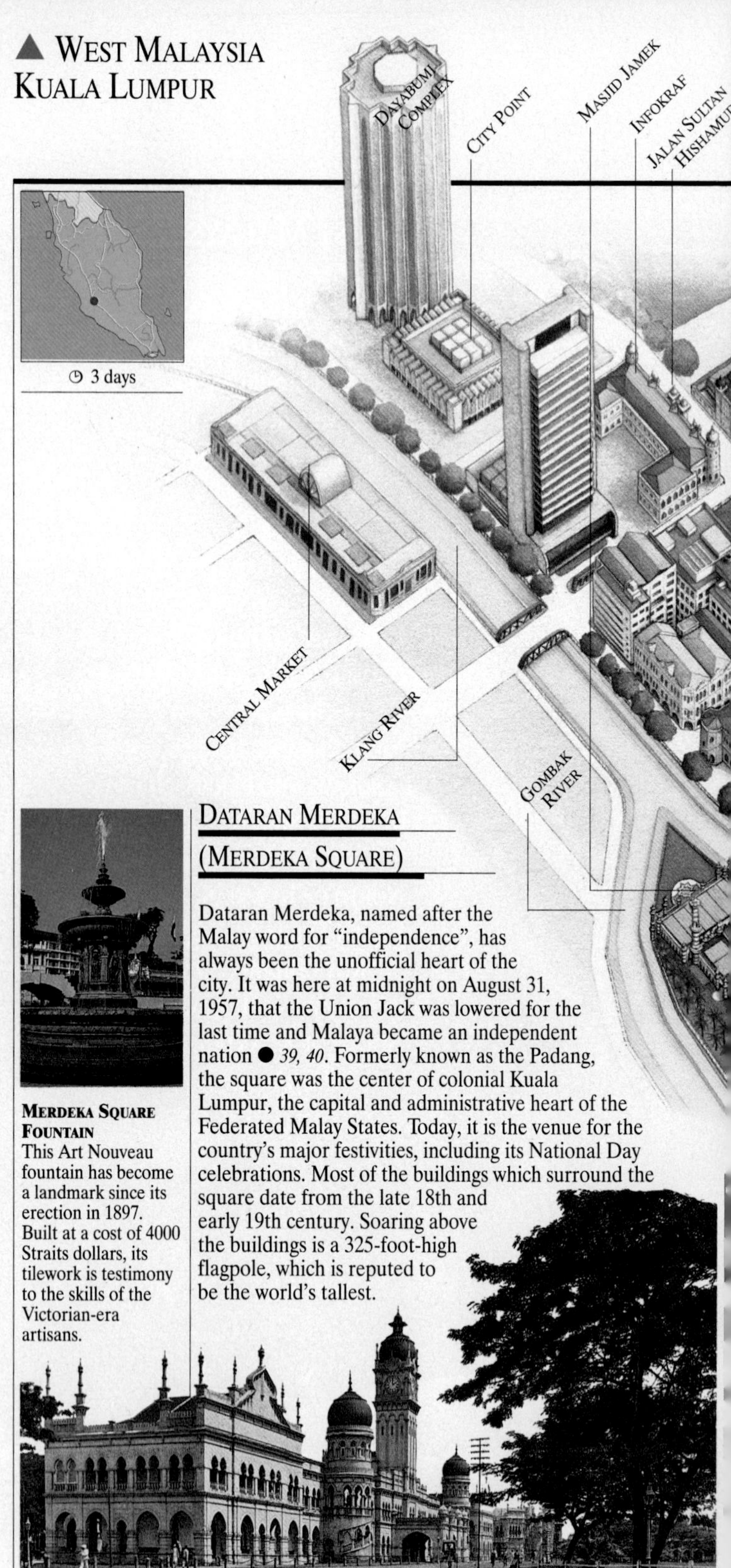


## DATARAN MERDEKA (MERDEKA SQUARE)

Dataran Merdeka, named after the Malay word for "independence", has always been the unofficial heart of the city. It was here at midnight on August 31, 1957, that the Union Jack was lowered for the last time and Malaya became an independent nation ● *39, 40*. Formerly known as the Padang, the square was the center of colonial Kuala Lumpur, the capital and administrative heart of the Federated Malay States. Today, it is the venue for the country's major festivities, including its National Day celebrations. Most of the buildings which surround the square date from the late 18th and early 19th century. Soaring above the buildings is a 325-foot-high flagpole, which is reputed to be the world's tallest.

**MERDEKA SQUARE FOUNTAIN**
This Art Nouveau fountain has become a landmark since its erection in 1897. Built at a cost of 4000 Straits dollars, its tilework is testimony to the skills of the Victorian-era artisans.

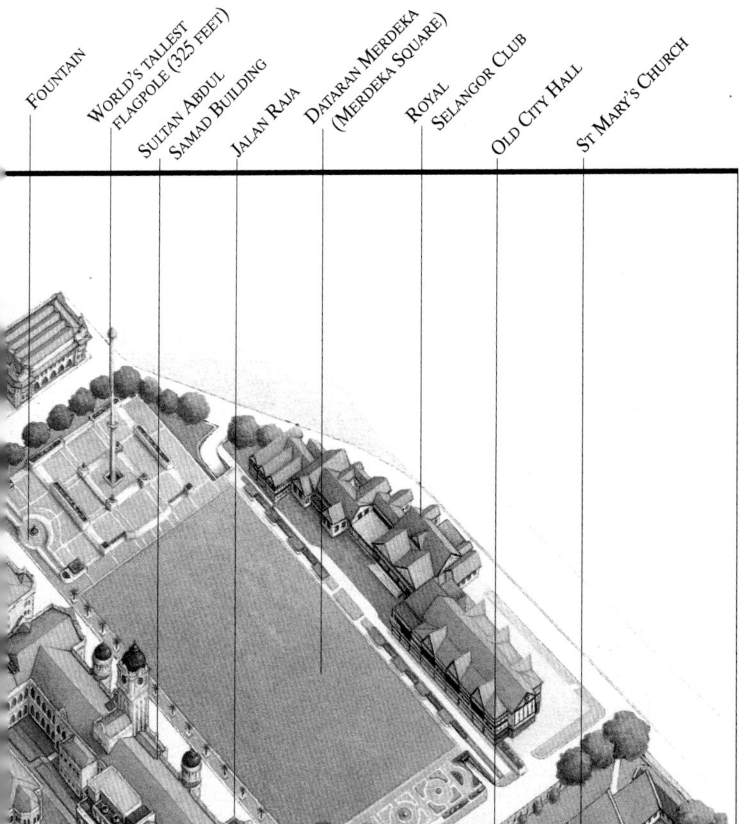

FOUNTAIN

WORLD'S TALLEST FLAGPOLE (325 FEET)

SULTAN ABDUL SAMAD BUILDING

JALAN RAJA

DATARAN MERDEKA (MERDEKA SQUARE)

ROYAL SELANGOR CLUB

OLD CITY HALL

ST MARY'S CHURCH

**SULTAN ABDUL SAMAD BUILDING.** Gleaming copper domes, a 133-foot clock tower, and arched colonnades characterize the former Secretariat Building, Malaysia's most photographed edifice. As the forerunner of the capital's famed Mughal-style buildings, it was almost built in Renaissance fashion but for the timely intervention of C. E. Spooner, the state engineer, who told the architect to redesign it as it was not suitable for the government offices of an Islamic country. Construction began in 1894 when the governor placed some tin, coins, and a copy of *Selangor Journal* beneath the foundation stone. Kuala Lumpur's premier landmark was completed three years later. Today it houses the Judicial Department and the High Court.

**THE ROYAL SELANGOR CLUB.** Once the bastion of British power in Malaya, this mock-Tudor club, facing the Sultan Abdul Samad Building, was where rubber-plantation owners used to relax over their *stengah* (half-whiskies and water) and play cricket on the Padang, while their pale wives gossiped over gin. Founded in 1884, the club's original plank and thatch building was eventually replaced by the Tudor-style one which dates from 1922. The building was badly damaged by fire in 1970, and only a small portion of today's club predates the blaze. Theories abound over how the club's nickname, "the Spotted Dog", came about. One popular tale relates that the police commissioner's wife used to bring her black-and-white dalmatians to the club; some see it as a thinly veiled reference to its mixed-race membership. Yet another hypothesis suggests that the club's first tiger emblem was so badly drawn it resembled a spotted dog.

## ALONG THE RIVERBANK

From its earliest beginnings Kuala Lumpur grew up around the historic confluence of the Klang and Gombak rivers, for until the railway was completed from Port Klang, they provided the main links with the outside world. The two rivers also served as an ethnic boundary separating the colonial masters and official Kuala Lumpur on the west bank from the Asian section on the east bank, symbolizing the divide-and-rule attitude of the times.

**CENTRAL MARKET.** This pastel-colored, Art Deco edifice was once the capital's wet market – a haunt of fishmongers and fruit sellers. Thanks to some forward-thinking bureaucrats who saved it from demolition, the building has been refurbished into a lively maze of shops and restaurants. This complex is not the average sterile shopping mall, for the city's budding artists and craftsmen have been encouraged to set up shop here. During the market's opening hours, shoppers can watch glass-blowers, batik-painters, key-chain engravers, portrait artists, and fortune-tellers at work, or perhaps catch a traditional dance performance.

**THE GREAT FLOOD OF 1926**
Floods were an annual affair in the city's earlier days before the Klang River was diverted. Record depths were reached in the floods of 1926, causing extensive damage to property. Adventurous members of the Selangor Club even swam across the Padang (as it was then known) to the bar. When the floods receded, several million dollars of soggy bank notes from the flooded strongroom of the nearby Chartered Bank were laid out to dry on the cricket field, under the watchful eyes of the police, of course.

**MENARA DAYABUMI.** Connected by footbridge across the river from Central Market is the city's latest Moorish-style edifice, the Dayabumi Complex, which houses the headquarters of Petronas, Malaysia's national oil corporation.

**JALAN SULTAN HISHAMUDDIN.** South of Dataran Merdeka, along Jalan Sultan Hishamuddin are some of the city's best-known sights, including Infokraf, a handicrafts exhibition center housed in the old building complex at the corner of Jalan Raja, the National Mosque, and, opposite, the Pusat Islam, the nation's Arabian-style Islamic Center, which houses an impressive collection of ancient Muslim manuscripts.

**MASJID NEGARA (NATIONAL MOSQUE).** Beside the hall are reflecting pools and fountains, shaded by a massive umbrella-shaped dome; a 238-foot-tall minaret stands above the mosque. Constructed in 1965, the 13-acre complex also houses a mausoleum where many national heroes and past prime ministers are buried.

**MASJID JAMEK.** Shaded by palms and topped by silvery domes and pink-and-white minarets, this turn-of-the-century mosque is not only graceful, but also marks the historic site of Kuala Lumpur's first settlement on the promontory between the Klang and Gombak rivers. Tourists are welcome to visit the mosque, except at prayer times, and shorts-clad visitors can don more modest robes for a small donation. They should leave their footwear at the entrance. Modeled after a North Indian mosque, the Masjid Jamek was designed by the talented A.R. Hubback, who was also the architect of the famed Moorish-style railway station and the Sultan Abdul Samad Building.

**NATIONAL ART GALLERY.** The National Art Gallery was formerly the Hotel Majestic, a grand colonial hotel in the tradition of Singapore's Raffles Hotel. Temporary exhibits are housed in the old lobby and dining room, while the former guestrooms, now extensively renovated, house the nation's permanent collection by Malaysian and overseas artists.

**RAILWAY STATION.** An architectural feast of domes, cupolas, and keyhole archways characterizes the Kuala Lumpur Railway Station built in 1911. The station rivals its forerunner, the Sultan Abdul Samad Building ▲ *183*, as the city's premier landmark. Opposite the station is the impressive graystone Railway Headquarters Building, the last of the official buildings designed in Arabian Nights style.

**MENARA DAYABUMI**
Thirty-four stories high, this gleaming white building has thirty-two sides and, to contribute to the striking Islamic architecture, high vaulted arches and open fretwork. The building is floodlit at night and the fretwork gives it a lacy, delicate quality.

An undated old postcard of Masjid Jamek and its ancient splendor reflected on the Gombak River.

**MOORISH CHARMS**
Travelers visiting Malaysia have waxed lyrical over the Moorish architectural charms of the railway station ever since 1911; Paul Theroux called the it "the grandest station in Southeast Asia".

**Pavement medicine men**
A fast patter and a flair for the dramatic are necessary attributes for these sidewalk vendors of alternative medicine. Popular venues include the pavements along Jalan Melaka and Jalan Masjid India. Their mainly male clientele clusters around while the medicine man extols the virtues of his oils, and herbal remedies which can allegedly heal everything from flagging sexual prowess to cobra bites and fungal infections. Spread around them are the seeds, barks, leaves, and ointments that constitute their pharmacy, and in addition there are usually photographs which depict in graphic, gory detail the "before" and "after" phases of various illnesses.

**Coliseum Restaurant**
Once the haunt of famed novelist Somerset Maugham, and more recently of Malaysia's leading cartoonist, Lat, the Coliseum still retains its original façade and an unmistakable aura from the city's colonial past. Built in 1928, the restaurant is famed for its sizzling steaks.

## Chinatown

Heart of the city's oldest settlement, Chinatown hums with activity 24 hours a day. In the grid of streets around Jalan Petaling, turn-of-the-century shops shelter traditional family businesses. At medicine shops known as *sinseh*, Chinese druggists weigh out herbal preparations on their old brass scales. Dry-goods stores display exotic but essential ingredients in Chinese cuisine, including eggs preserved in horse urine, birds' nests, and sharks' fins. After dark, Jalan Petaling is closed to all but pedestrians and metamorphoses into a frenetic night market famed for its pirated wares and bargain-basement shopping.

**Chan See Shu Yuen Temple.** Glazed ceramic carvings in the Guangdong style decorate the roof ridges of this elaborate Chinese temple located at the southern end of Jalan Petaling. Terracotta wall friezes depicting scenes from Chinese mythology add to the opulence of the exterior walls of the temple, which has changed little since its construction in 1906.

**Tze Ya Temple.** Tucked away in an alley off Jalan Tun H.S. Lee, formerly Jalan Bandar, is one of the city's oldest temples. Its curious siting is apparently in accordance with auspicious *feng shui* principles. An old portrait of Yap Ah Loy, the famed Chinese Kapitan who was responsible for the temple's construction, is still displayed on an interior wall.

**Sri Maha Mariamman Temple.** An opulent *gopuram*, the tiered tower bedecked with colorful statues of deities characteristic of Hindu temples towers above the entrance to the Sri Maha Mariamman Temple on Jalan Tun H.S. Lee. The temple houses a silver chariot which is pulled during the annual Thaipusam procession from the temple to the Batu Caves. Built originally at the site of the Central Railway Station in 1883 by Indian laborers who worked on the rubber plantations, the shrine was moved to its present location in 1885. The temple was founded by Tambusamy Pillai, a civil servant turned businessman. He was famed for his extravagant "curry tiffins".

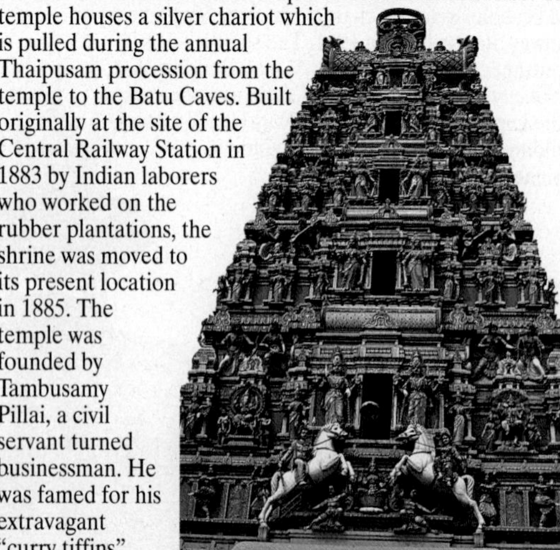

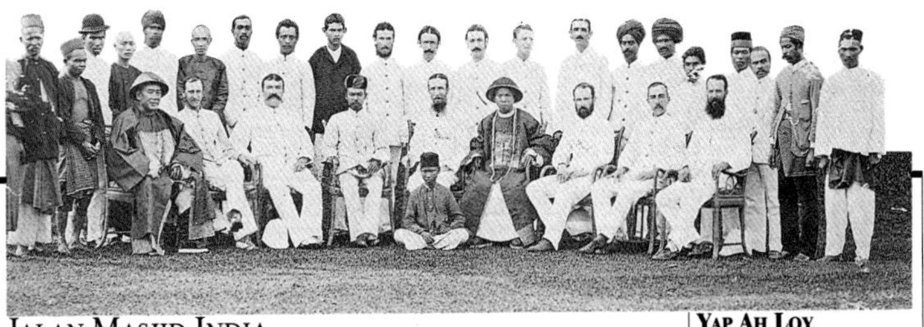

**Yap Ah Loy**
Lured to Malaya like many Chinese immigrants by the promises of abundant wealth, Yap Ah Loy (above, seated center with conical hat), a Hakka from Guangdong, was one of the lucky few who fulfilled their dreams. The seventeen-year-old was quickly disenchanted toiling in the tin mines, and with great cunning wheeled and dealed his way to the top in a town where only the toughest survived. In 1868, at thirty-one years of age, Yap Ah Loy became the Kapitan Cina, the head of the Kuala Lumpur Chinese community. Under his fierce and determined leadership the warring secret societies were brought under control. During his momentous seventeen-year tenure, Kuala Lumpur emerged from a shanty town to become the busy capital of Selangor.

## Jalan Masjid India

One of Kuala Lumpur's most fascinating ethnic hubs is the area around Jalan Masjid India, often known as "Little India" for its preponderance of traders from the sub-continent. Opposite the North India-style mosque, which the street is named after, is Wisma Yakin, a cluster of Malay shops specializing in traditional outfits, velvet fez-like *songkok*, prayer rugs, PLO-style headwraps, and herbal *jamu* preparations from Indonesia. Further along are Indian shops perfumed with incense, draped with dazzling saris and crammed with brasswares and household paraphernalia. Indian Muslim and Malay restaurants are abundant here, and open-air stalls specialize in lunchtime *nasi campur*, a selection of cheap and delicious curries and rice.

## Jalan Tuanku Abdul Rahman (Batu Road)

Kuala Lumpur's most popular shopping street was named after the nation's first prime minister. It was formerly known as Batu Road and is famed for its fabric, clothing, and shoe shops, as well as its horrendous traffic jams – both vehicular and pedestrian – a typical KL experience. Come festival time, whether it is Chinese New Year, Hari Raya, Christmas, or Deepavali, the street is jammed with bargain-hunters, itinerant food vendors, and blind organ-playing buskers.

Some popular local shops along this stretch include Globe Silk Store, Peiping Lace, Mun Loong, and Royal Selangor.

**Wisma Loke (Artiquarium).** Extensive renovations have transformed this former mansion behind Medan Tuanku into an art and antiques gallery. This was previously the home of Loke Yew, one of the city's pioneers and richest businessmen. The turn-of-the-century mansion is an eclectic combination of architectural styles and features decorative gables, fine craftsmanship, and a courtyard with a Chinese moon gate. The elaborate mansion took twelve years to build and was the city's first private residence to boast electric lights.

**Five-Foot Way**
Known in Malay as *kaki lima*, the five-foot way is an integral part of Malaysian and Singaporean pre-war architecture. Originally conceived by Sir Stamford Raffles, the founder of Singapore, the arched walkway provided shade to pedestrians from the equatorial heat.

**Malaysia's 10-sen coin**
Immortalized on the 10-sen (cent) coin is the nation's Parliament House, built in 1963.

**National Monument**
Dedicated to those who fell in the twelve-year Emergency proclaimed after a communist insurrection in 1948, this bronze memorial in the northern corner of the Lake Gardens was created by Felix de Weldon, the American who designed the Iwo Jima Memorial in Washington, DC, which probably accounts for the unmistakably Caucasian faces of the Malaysian security forces depicted on the monument.

## Around Taman Tasik Perdana (Lake Gardens)

Once the haunt of wild pigs and the occasional tiger, the 172-acre Lake Gardens was opened to the public in 1889 and has been the city's most popular parkland ever since. The artificial lake, created by damming the Sungei Bras Bras, was originally named Sydney Lake, the maiden name of Resident-General Sir Frank Swettenham's wife, but today it is known as Tasik Perdana. Nearby, overlooking the gardens, is Sri Taman, the former official residence of the prime minister.

**Muzium Negara (National Museum).** Sweeping Minangkabau-style roofs and a 115-foot-long tiled mural are striking architectural features of the National Museum located on Jalan Damansara near the southern entrance of the Lake Gardens. Renowned as one of Southeast Asia's premier museums, it houses rich archeological, ethnographical, and natural-history collections. Dioramas complete with wax models depict cultural aspects, including a Straits Chinese house and a Malay circumcision ceremony.

**Bird Park, Butterfly Farm, Orchid Gardens, and Deer Park.** These attractions are located on the east side of the Lake Gardens approached from Jalan Perdana. The Bird Park, enclosed by a vast plastic net roof, is best visited in the early morning, when the birds are most active in the walk-in aviary. Species include Malaysia's unique hornbills, including the fabulous rhinoceros hornbill, the "talking" tiong, and imported flamingos and African macaws. The Orchid Gardens house an exotic collection of Malaysian orchids, while at the nearby Deer Park children can hand-feed deer and catch a glimpse of the *kancil*, the legendary mouse-deer of Malayan folk tales. At the Butterfly Farm, visitors can enjoy watching Malaysia's prodigious butterfly species without even having to set foot into the jungle.

**Bangunan Parlimen (Parliament House).** Towering over the northwest corner of the Lake Gardens is Bangunan Parlimen, the

"THE IMPRESSION LEFT BY THE TOWN...IS OF PERPETUAL FRESHNESS...OF BRIGHT LIGHTS AND SCENTED BREEZES, AND OF A SPACIOUS PICTURESQUENESS VERY GRATEFUL TO THE EYE."
CUTHBERT WOODVILLE HARRISON, *FEDERATED MALAY STATES,* 1923

nation's power hub, an eighteen-story complex housing the Dewan Rakyat (House of Representatives) and the Dewan Negara (the Senate). Visitors are allowed to attend parliamentary sessions with prior permission.

**CARCOSA SERI NEGARA.** Room rates start from RM850 per night at Kuala Lumpur's ritziest hotel. For the well-heeled an evening in the Seri Ehsan suite, where Queen Elizabeth once spent the night, can cost as much as RM2500. Originally the official residence of Sir Frank Swettenham and subsequent colonial governors, Carcosa became a Japanese officers' mess during World War Two, and later, the residence of the British high commissioner. Recently, the historic building was transformed into a luxurious five-star hotel. Each of the thirteen suites has its own butler, and spacious verandahs provide sweeping views across the lush tropical gardens. During the day, high tea – complete with silver, linen, and elegant service – and Sunday's inviting curry-tiffin lunches are affordable luxuries for those who yearn for a glimpse of the grand life, but cannot afford to stay a night.

## KUALA LUMPUR'S GOLDEN TRIANGLE

Kuala Lumpur's most expensive real estate, hub of five-star hotels, multi-national corporations, and shopping malls, is bordered by Jalan Ampang, Jalan Tun Razak, and Jalan Imbi. Karyaneka Handicraft Centre, at the junction of Jalan Bukit Bintang and Jalan Raja Chulan, has an extensive range of Malaysian crafts including silk *songket* cloth, batik, basketwork, and silver jewelry.

**BUKIT BINTANG SHOPPING COMPLEXES.** Lot 10, a green-hued, multi-story shopping complex, complete with stainless-steel palm trees, is a recent addition to the growing number of malls which have contributed to making Bukit Bintang a shoppers' paradise. Starhill Center, which includes the Marriot Hotel, is another. Department stores in Bukit Bintang Plaza and adjoining Sungai Wang Plaza offer attractive bargains in cut-price clothes, electrical goods, and leatherware. The small but no less busy Imbi Plaza is a center for computer products.

**LE COQ D'OR**
As a poor youth Chua Cheng Bok was denied marriage to the rich girl he loved, so he spent the rest of his life amassing a fortune to make the girl's father regret his decision. His elaborate Victorian mansion (below), crammed with European artworks, easily outshone neighboring residences, including that of his lost childhood lover. According to the tin magnate's will, the house could not be sold, but so long as the interior remained unchanged the building could become a restaurant. Le Coq d'Or Restaurant on Jalan Ampang is well known for its old-world interior as well as for its Western cuisine.

**TABUNG HAJI BUILDING**
Easily distinguished by its unique hour-glass shape, the futuristic Tabung Haji Building, on the corner of Jalan Tun Razak and Jalan Ampang, a fusion of Islamic styles and contemporary design, is the administrative center for organizing the annual pilgrimage to Mecca.

KUALA SELANGOR
LIGHTHOUSE
BUKIT MELAWATI
NATURE PARK
RAWAN

**MALAYSIAN AGRICULTURAL PARK (TAMAN PERTANIAN)**
At Bukit Cerakah, in north Shah Alam, a pocket of rainforest and plantation land has been developed into a recreational area. Taman Pertanian provides an encapsulated look at rice-planting – from sowing to harvesting, and exhibition crops of oil palm, rubber, cocoa, and coffee. When the park authorities announced that their Temperate House, a closed-environment, experimental building which follows the same seasons as the temperate realms of the southern hemisphere, was under winter snow, massive traffic jams resulted as urban dwellers, who had lived all their lives in the mono-season of equatorial Malaysia, flocked to catch a glimpse of a white winter.

## SHAH ALAM

Passing through the ceremonial gate (Kota Darul Ehsan), the Federal Highway enters Selangor, Malaysia's most prosperous and industrialized state. Eighteen miles from Kuala Lumpur is Shah Alam, the new state capital. Built on former plantation land, this planned town features spacious parklands, high-rise office blocks, an international motor-racing circuit, Malaysia's largest mosque, and the royal palace of the sultan of Selangor, whose Bugis ancestors, famed warriors, navigators and merchants from Sulawesi, founded the sultanate in the 18th century. Malaysia's own car, the Proton Saga, is manufactured in the town's industrial belt.

**MASJID SULTAN SALAHUDDIN (SELANGOR STATE MOSQUE).** Blue-and-white zigzag patterns decorate the four 132-foot-high minarets (the highest in the world), which tower over a computer-designed dome reputed to be the largest of its kind. Built to hold twenty-thousand worshipers, the dome has a unique pinpoint lighting system, described as providing a "starry night in the desert" effect. Special water-saving taps for prayer ablutions are operated by a sensor which cuts off the flow automatically when hands or feet are withdrawn.

## KLANG

**MASJID SULTAN SULAIMAN.** Architectural styles blend at the Masjid Sultan Sulaiman, where the angular minaret shows early Art Deco influences and the dome is reminiscent of Turkish mosque design. Sultan Sulaiman's own creative ideas influenced the mosque's British architect and may have been the inspiration for the juxtaposition of Eastern and Western designs. Built by the British, it was presented to the sultan in the late 19th century.

**GEDUNG RAJA ABDULLAH (TIN MUSEUM).** Klang's oldest building has had a chequered history. Built by Raja Abdullah as a residence and tin warehouse in 1856, it was later besieged and taken by Raja Mahadi, Abdullah's opponent in the Selangor Civil War. In 1874 it became the State Treasury, and later the Central Police Station. In 1984, during its restoration by the historical buildings conservation group, the Badan Warisan, early drawings of paddle-steamers were discovered beneath its layers of whitewash. It now wears a new hat as the Tin Museum, where displays chronicle the industry that shaped the early fortunes of Klang and Selangor state.

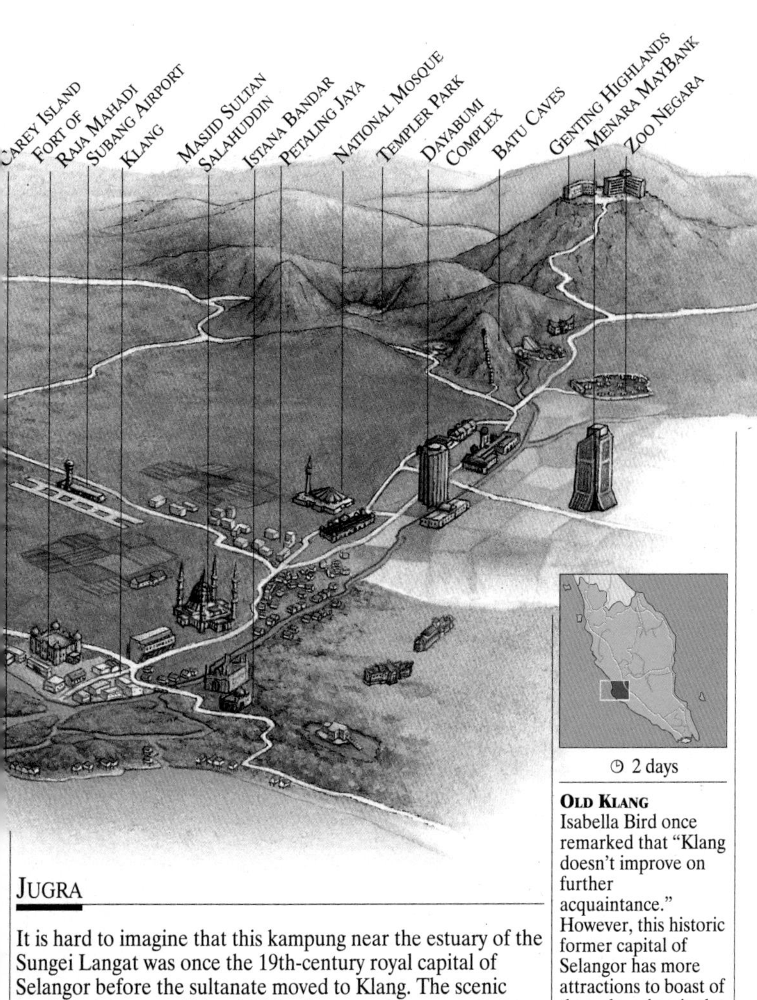


## Jugra

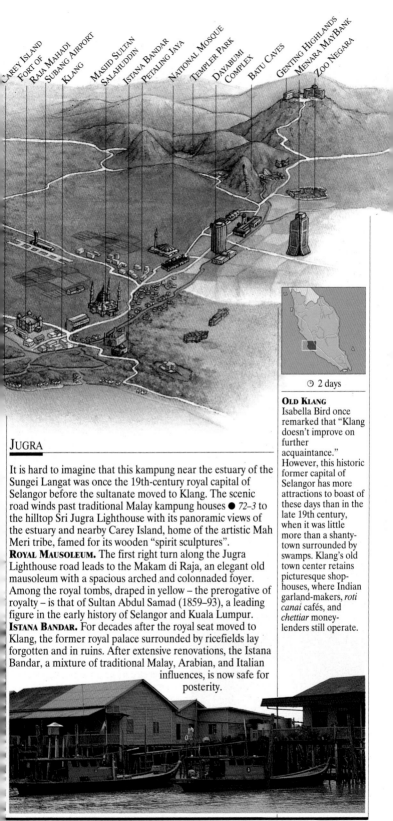

It is hard to imagine that this kampung near the estuary of the Sungei Langat was once the 19th-century royal capital of Selangor before the sultanate moved to Klang. The scenic road winds past traditional Malay kampung houses ● *72–3* to the hilltop Sri Jugra Lighthouse with its panoramic views of the estuary and nearby Carey Island, home of the artistic Mah Meri tribe, famed for its wooden "spirit sculptures".

**Royal Mausoleum.** The first right turn along the Jugra Lighthouse road leads to the Makam di Raja, an elegant old mausoleum with a spacious arched and colonnaded foyer. Among the royal tombs, draped in yellow – the prerogative of royalty – is that of Sultan Abdul Samad (1859–93), a leading figure in the early history of Selangor and Kuala Lumpur.

**Istana Bandar.** For decades after the royal seat moved to Klang, the former royal palace surrounded by ricefields lay forgotten and in ruins. After extensive renovations, the Istana Bandar, a mixture of traditional Malay, Arabian, and Italian influences, is now safe for posterity.

◷ 2 days

**Old Klang**
Isabella Bird once remarked that "Klang doesn't improve on further acquaintance." However, this historic former capital of Selangor has more attractions to boast of these days than in the late 19th century, when it was little more than a shanty-town surrounded by swamps. Klang's old town center retains picturesque shop-houses, where Indian garland-makers, *roti canai* cafés, and *chettiar* money-lenders still operate.

**Blowpipes of the Orang Asli**
Made either of wood or bamboo, *sumpit* (blowpipes) are still used by some Orang Asli for hunting small game. About 6 foot 6 inches long, and accurate 33 feet away, this weapon delivers a wooden dart, usually tipped with poison from the deadly Ipoh tree. Old blowpipes are often intricately carved and the rarest fitted with mouth-pieces made from "golden ivory" – hornbill beaks.

**Thaipusam at Batu Caves**
Malaysia's most spectacular religious event, the annual Thaipusam festival, which commemorates Subramaniam's victory over evil, attracts 100,000 pilgrims. As repentance for past sins, thousands of Hindu devotees carry ornate *kavadi*, metal frames decorated with sacred peacock feathers, which are attached to the wearer's body by metal spikes. To demonstrate suffering, others pass skewers through their cheeks and tongues.

## Ulu Klang

**The Klang Gates.** In the early 1960's, before the Klang Gates dam closed off the ancient animal trails from Pahang to the Klang Valley, the Ulu Klang backwaters were still home to a large herd of elephants. Today, suburbia sprawls across these former marshlands and up into the foothills at the head of the Klang Valley. Spectacular quartz ridges, popular with weekend hikers, rear above Taman Melawati, a new satellite suburb renowned for its Saturday-night market and its prolific *kueh* (cake) stalls during the Ramadan fasting month.

**Zoo Negara (National Zoo).** Follow the large road signs to Zoo Negara on Jalan Ulu Klang, but avoid the weekend crowds. Although not as harmoniously laid out as Singapore's open-plan zoo, it is a good spot to view Malaysia's renowned indigenous species, which are becoming increasingly rare in their native habitat. Exhibits include the "King of the Jungle", the Malaysian tiger, the shy Malaysian elephant, Borneo's "Man of the Forest", the orang utan ▲ *308–9*, the Malayan honey bear, the tapir, and the white-handed gibbon. Don't miss the unique mousedeer, a hero of Malay jungle tales. Malaysia's smallest hoofed animal, a mere 8 inches high, is actually not a deer at all, but a distant relative of the camel. Other attractions include the aquarium and the elephant and seal shows.

## Gombak

Although suburbia is rapidly encroaching on Gombak, the district still offers some interesting sights and excellent rainforest escapes for city dwellers. A Malay kampung ambience still prevails along the Old Pahang Road, which was the only road to Kuantan before the new Karak Highway was built. Traditional wooden houses line the banks of the Gombak River at Kampung Sungei Chin Chin, noted for its exotic wild durians collected by the Orang Asli in the surrounding jungle.

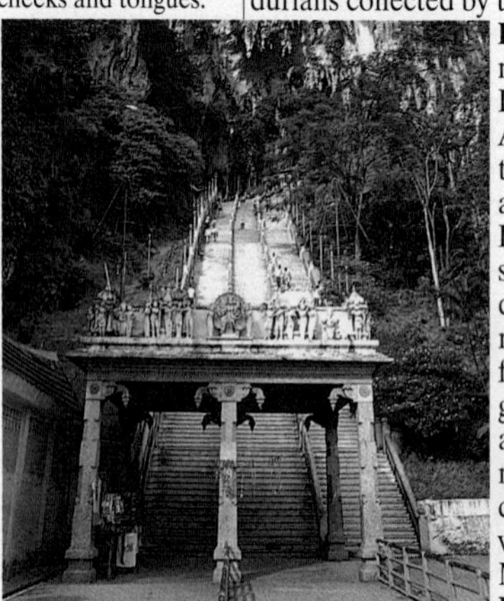

**Batu Caves.** Located inside a limestone massif, nearly 8 miles north of Kuala Lumpur, are the spectacular Batu Caves. An arduous ascent up 272 steps leads to the Temple Cave, the main cavern, where a hundred-year-old shrine devoted to Lord Subramaniam attracts a steady stream of devout Hindus. Stalactites decorate the 330-foot-high ceiling. In the rear of the cavern the light streams in from a hole in the roof, lighting up the gloomy interior. Nearby is the locked access to the Dark Cave which is over a mile long. This underground network of caves is home to unique fauna. Intending visitors need prior permission from the Malayan Nature Society.

**Mimaland.** A children's favorite, this

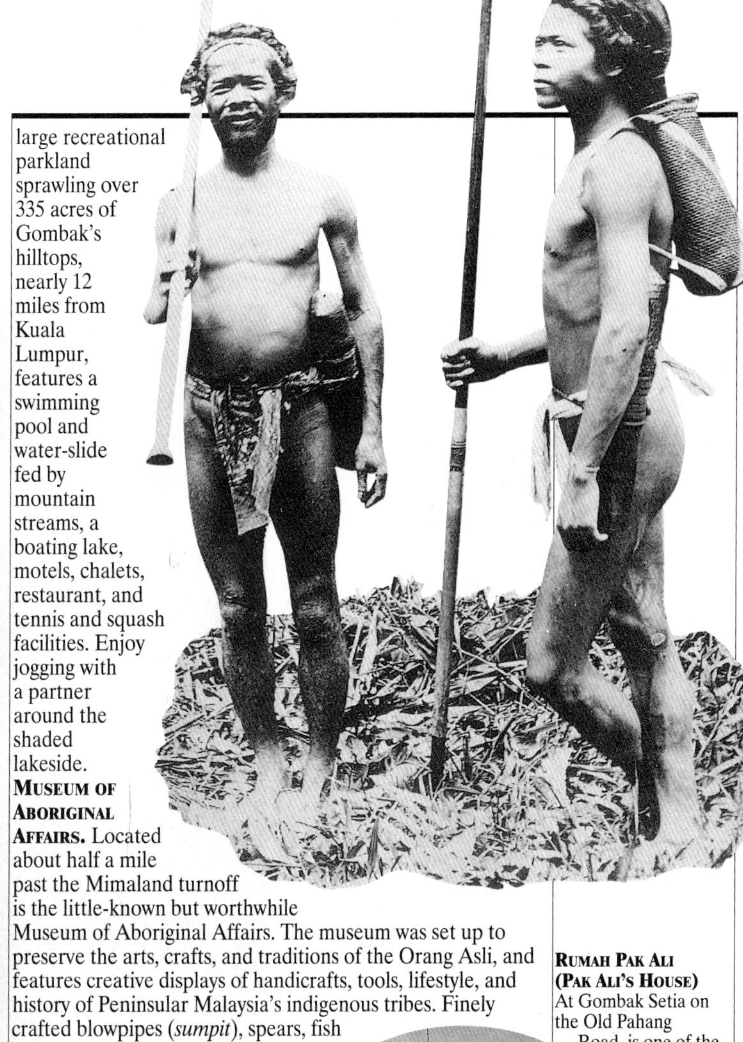

large recreational parkland sprawling over 335 acres of Gombak's hilltops, nearly 12 miles from Kuala Lumpur, features a swimming pool and water-slide fed by mountain streams, a boating lake, motels, chalets, restaurant, and tennis and squash facilities. Enjoy jogging with a partner around the shaded lakeside.

**MUSEUM OF ABORIGINAL AFFAIRS.** Located about half a mile past the Mimaland turnoff is the little-known but worthwhile Museum of Aboriginal Affairs. The museum was set up to preserve the arts, crafts, and traditions of the Orang Asli, and features creative displays of handicrafts, tools, lifestyle, and history of Peninsular Malaysia's indigenous tribes. Finely crafted blowpipes (*sumpit*), spears, fish and bird traps, and intricate basketwork are among the many crafts represented. The museum is located in the heart of an Orang Asli settlement, at the foot of the jungle-clad Main Range (Barisan Titiwangsa). While some Orang Asli have opted for an urban lifestyle, other tribal members still hunt and gather rattan, durians, and traditional herbs from the nearby mountains.

**TEMPLER PARK AND KANCHING FALLS.** Originally mooted as "a vast jungle retreat for the public", Templer Park is now one of Kuala Lumpur's favorite weekend picnic areas. Trails lead off into the rainforested interior to the landmark Bukit Takan, a 1000-foot-high limestone massif popular with rock climbers. At the adjoining Hutan Lipur Kanching, a forest reserve, are the spectacular multi-tiered Kanching Falls set amid towering jungle. Avoid the weekends and local public holidays and go early to appreciate the rainforest ■ *22–3* and its fascinating monkeys at their best.

**RUMAH PAK ALI (PAK ALI'S HOUSE)**
At Gombak Setia on the Old Pahang Road, is one of the best surviving examples of a traditional Malay house in Selangor. Built early this century as the residence for the local *penghulu* (regional chieftain), this elegant wooden home has recently opened to the public. Stained and not painted, in the traditional fashion, the house features long shuttered windows with carved balustrades and an airy front verandah known as a *serambi* ● *72–3*.

**Malaysia's best satay**
Mention Kajang to any Malaysian and their first thought will be of satay, the tasty, skewered-meat dish cooked over charcoal, which the town is renowned for. It all started in 1917, when Haji Tasmin set up a stall selling satay prepared with a secret marinade. His fame spread and customers now come from all over the peninsula to enjoy the age-old recipe, still faithfully adhered to by his descendants. The satay stalls ● *64–5* are located in the old Kajang town center at the corner of Jalan Besar and Jalan Sulaiman.

**Nine pillars of the State Mosque**
The design of this contemporary-style mosque centers around nine lofty pillars representing the original states of Negeri Sembilan (meaning "nine states" in Malay). Of the nine, only six are still recognizable districts: Sri Menanti, Sungai Ujong, Johol, Jelebu, Rembau and Tampin.

## Ulu Langat

Heading south from Kuala Lumpur, take the old highway through Cheras to Batu Sembilan, then turn left for the Ulu Langat district. A meandering kampung road follows the Sungei Langat, and at Dusun Tua, once a colonial jungle retreat, hot springs can be seen in the shallows. The road forks at Batu Lapan Belas. Continue straight for riverside picnic areas at Pangsun and, at the end of the road, the start of the summit trail to Gunung Nuang (4900 feet), one of Selangor's highest peaks. Turn right at Batu Lapan Belas for waterfalls at Sungai Gabai and Sungai Tekala.

## Kajang

Approached either by the Lebuhraya (Expressway) or the Old Seremban Highway, Kajang is fast becoming a commuter suburb of Kuala Lumpur. However, the town center still maintains an old-world charm. Turn-of-the-century shophouses shaded by chick-blinds line Jalan Tukang, and beside the river is the Shen Sze She Yar Temple built in 1898, featuring painted "guardian" doors and an untouristy ambience. Turn off at Semenyih, 5½ miles south of town, for a scenic drive through the Negeri Sembilan villages of mountain-backed Broga and Ulu Beranang with its historic wooden mosque.

## Seremban

Negeri Sembilan's state capital, Seremban, was originally the main town of Sungai Ujong, the largest of the nine original self-governing districts pioneered by the matriarchal Minangkabau of Sumatra. Six of these districts united in 1895 to form today's state. A mid-19th-century tin rush was followed by a short-lived civil war which disrupted the tin trade, and was just the excuse needed for the British to intervene, resulting in the establishment of a British resident in 1874 ● *36*. After this, peace prevailed, and the township flourished in the early-19th-century rubber and tin booms. Elegant public offices were constructed,

and a bustling Chinatown emerged at the hub of town. Today, many of the new buildings are out of town, and as a result there are still a number of old buildings to be seen.

**STATE MUSEUM CULTURAL COMPLEX.** Situated beside the expressway entrance to Seremban town, near the toll house, is the Taman Seni Budaya, a museum and cultural complex. Striking Minangkabau roofs characterize the traditional architectural style of this museum built in 1986 to house ethnographic and historical displays of the region's colorful past. State-made handicrafts and souvenirs are on sale at the Cultural Complex.

**ISTANA AMPANG TINGGI AND RUMAH MINANGKABAU.** These two superb examples of traditional Minangkabau architecture ● *75* stand in the State Museum grounds. Istana Ampang Tinggi, originally a royal wedding present, was built without the use of nails in Kuala Pilah in 1861 and later reconstructed at its present site. Intricate wood carvings of Koranic verses decorate the dark-stained walls of the Rumah Minangkabau, a former royal residence built in 1898. This famous house was disassembled and shipped to England, where it formed part of the Malayan display at the 1924 Wembley Exhibition.

**JALAN DATO' HAMZAH.** The British colonialists always preferred to build on hills and Seremban is no exception, for the most impressive government buildings, both past and present, are located at the highest point of the town. Gracious columns and arched verandahs are a feature of the former State Secretariat, now the State Library, built in the same neo-classical style as the neighboring District Land Office (Pejabat Daerah Tanah). On adjoining Jalan Bukit is the new State Secretariat, built in modern Minangkabau style, and crowning the hill is the Istana Hinggap, one of the royal residences of the Yang di-Pertuan Besar, the ruler of Negeri Sembilan.

**TAMAN TASIK (THE LAKE GARDENS).** Seremban's recreational parklands, centered around two lakes below Jalan Dato' Hamzah, provide a welcome retreat from the equatorial sun. Within a short walking distance from the center of town, Taman Tasik is a favorite lunch-time escape for the town's workers, and a popular dawn and dusk jogging venue. Attractions include weekend cultural shows, a small bird park, and a 5-acre nature reserve.

## ULU BENDOL

Winding through scenic jungle-clad hills, the road to Kuala Pilah leads 11 miles east of Seremban to Ulu Bendol, a forest reserve where the picturesque Bendol River cascades over a series of rock pools. This popular picnic spot is crowded on weekends, but quiet and peaceful throughout the week. Trails wind through the rainforest, one of them providing an arduous hike to the summit of Gunung Angsi.

**MINANGKABAU ROOFS**
Nothing symbolizes Negeri Sembilan more aptly than the upswept roofs which occur not only on traditional kampung houses, but on most modern government buildings, and even gas stations and bus-stops. According to Minangkabau lore, these peaked roofs represent the horns of a victorious (*minang*) buffalo (*kabau*) calf, the winner of a legendary match with a Javanese buffalo, staged to settle a longstanding territorial war. In earlier times, most roofs were covered with *attap*, a type of thatch made with interwoven fronds of the nipah, a trunkless palm which grows in swampy regions. The Istana Ampang Tinggi (above) still boasts a roof in the traditional style, but today most Minangkabau houses are roofed in galvanized iron, like the one shown below, at Kuala Pilah. The upper roof, a characteristic found only on Minangkabau houses, covered the *lonteng*, an attic where the unmarried girls slept. Today, this top floor serves as a storage area.

**MYSTERY STONES OF PENGKALAN KEMPAS**
At Pengkalan Kempas are a collection of megalithic stones beside the grave of Sheikh Ahmad Majnun Shah, a 15th-century religious leader who rebelled against Melaka's Sultan Mansur Shah. The 6-foot high stones, known as the "Sword", the "Spoon" and the "Rudder", predate the tomb and are apparently vestiges of pre-Islamic culture. An inscribed rectangular piece ("The Ordeal Stone") has a 4½-inch-diameter hole through its center. Legend relates that when false oaths were uttered, the hole would tighten around the culprit's arm.

## SRI MENANTI

In the heart of Minangkabau country is Sri Menati, the royal capital of Negeri Sembilan. Surrounded by forested hills, the sleepy one-street town seems to have been lost in time. In the surrounding villages are beautiful examples of traditional Malay architecture, particularly in the area close by the royal palaces. This serene valley has been the home of Minangkabau settlers since they fled Melaka when the Portuguese invaded in 1511 ● *34–5*, and has been a royal seat for four hundred years. The Minangkabau follow a matriarchal system known as *adat perpateh*, where ancestry is traced through the female line and the women inherit the family wealth. This is opposite to the patriarchal *adat temenggong*, which is followed by other Peninsular Malay societies.

**ISTANA LAMA.** Built to replace a former palace destroyed by the British during the Sungai Ujong uprising, this four-story palace dating from 1905 was the home of the Yang di-Pertuan Besar, the royal ruler of Negeri Sembilan until 1931. Constructed entirely of *cengal* hardwood in the traditional style using no nails, the palace features central pillars over 65 feet high, and exquisite carved panels. An unusual addition is the *tingkat gunung*, a central three-tiered tower.

**ISTANA BESAR.** Impressively sited in the Sri Menanti valley is the current residence of the royal head of Negeri Sembilan, whose descendants have ruled this region for four centuries. The grandiose 1930's-style palace features a dazzling white exterior and an azure-blue tiled roof. Visitors are allowed with prior permission from the State Secretariat in Seremban.

## KOTA LUKUT

Just outside the town of Lukut, 13 miles from Seremban, is historic Kota Lukut. Overlooking the Lukut River, this hilltop fort was built by Raja Jumaat, a son of a Riau prince, in 1847 to defend the area's rich tin trade. Remains of massive laterite walls and moats can still be seen – evidence of the fortifications needed to protect the river, a vital access to the upstream tin mines. After Raja Jumaat's death, his son Raja Bot made additions to the fort and was reputed to have even engaged the services of Arab mercenaries.

"IT IS TIN MINING WHICH HAS BROUGHT THE CHINESE TO THESE STATES, AND AS MINERS AND SMELTERS THEY ARE EQUALLY EFFICIENT AND PERSEVERING."

ISABELLA BIRD, *THE GOLDEN CHERSONESE*

## PORT DICKSON

For travelers in search of an idyllic tropical beach, Port Dickson falls short compared to the vastly superior east-coast shores. However, for those in need of a seaside retreat within a short drive of Kuala Lumpur, it certainly fits the bill. Originally founded as a health resort for Europeans in colonial days, Port Dickson is even more popular today than it was then. For those in search of peace and quiet it is best to avoid going at the weekend, when it seems as if half of Kuala Lumpur has turned out. The actual center of Port Dickson, about 19 miles from Seremban, is very much a working town with a bustling port, oil refineries, and massive oil tankers waiting offshore to refill. However, along the 11-mile coastal drive south of town are good golden-sand beaches, resort hotels, and cheap seafood restaurants. Pantai Bagan Pinang is a favorite beach for windsurfers and is good for swimming at high tide. Nearby is a useful tourist information office and a handicrafts shop stocking local wares. Further along, at Teluk Kemang on the beach opposite the Ming Court Hotel, is a bazaar selling souvenir T-shirts and local crafts, including colorful woven food-covers, often mistaken for conical hats. Another pretty beach is Blue Lagoon, a small bay with condominium-style accommodation.

**TANJUNG TUAN (CAPE RACHADO).** Raja Jumaat, a benevolent local chieftain, donated the land that this lighthouse stands on to the Melaka state back in the mid-19th century, thus explaining how the lighthouse occupies Melakan territory in the middle of the Negeri Sembilan state. The dramatic lighthouse hill offers panoramic views of the Melaka Straits and, on clear days, vistas of Sumatra. Thick jungle, home to a lively band of monkeys, surrounds the colonial-style lighthouse, while the cape, Tanjung Tuan, is an important stopover for migratory birds. Hawks and eagles are also spotted from September to October and from March to April.

**THE MINANGKABAU**
Minangkabau culture originates in the central highlands of west Sumatra, and is characterized by its architecture, its spicy cuisine, particularly the rice and curry meal *nasi padang,* and its unique matrilineal society. Minangkabau women inherit property and family riches and, partly as a result of this tradition, the men seek their fortunes abroad. Today, many Minangkabau still emigrate to Malaysia to find employment.

**WHEN THE BRITISH BLEW UP A FAMOSA**
During the Napoleonic Wars the English took temporary occupation of the fort from the Dutch, but when their tenure was over, they decided to destroy it lest the Dutch use it against them. First coolies with pickaxes were used to try and break the walls, but they were unsuccessful. Then gunpowder was brought in, the area cleared and the fuse lit. Munshi Abdullah, Raffles' scribe, recalls the event: "The gunpowder exploded with a noise like thunder, and pieces of the Fort as large as elephants, and even some as large as houses, were blown into the air and cascaded into the sea." Luckily Raffles stepped in and saved the last remaining gate, Porta de Santiago, but the famous fort was gone forever. "For the Fort was the pride of Melaka and after its destruction the place lost its glory...."

## BUKIT ST PAUL (ST PAUL'S HILL)

Commanding a strategic position overlooking the Melaka River and the Melaka Straits, St Paul's Hill predates its Portuguese name by at least two centuries. Originally, on this auspicious site stood the palace of the Melaka sultanate ● *32–3* from its inception in c. 1403 by the fugitive Sumatran Prince Parameswara. A 16th-century Portuguese writer named Barros confirmed this, saying that, "The first settlement which they (the Malays) made was on a hill above the fortress which we now hold...." St Paul's Hill offers a peaceful respite from the crowded town, and sometimes, like a phantom of the past, you can even see a *perahu*, its sails filled with the tradewinds, plying the Melaka Straits.

**ST PAUL'S CHURCH.** Constructed with stones from the demolished foundations of the Melaka sultanate palace, St Paul's Church was built by the Portuguese in 1521. The present name, however, dates from the Dutch era, as the original church was called Nossa Senhora da Annunciada

(Our Lady of the Annunciation). In 1566 the Jesuits enlarged the building to its present size and in 1590 the tower was added. Opponents of Catholicism, the Dutch pulled down the roof to build catwalks for their soldiers, and the altar was used as a cannon embrasure. Around the walls of the still roofless St Paul's are some massive granite tombstones dating from Dutch times.

**PORTA DE SANTIAGO.** Below St Paul's Hill is the Santiago Gate (Porta de Santiago), the last remnant of the great Portuguese fortress A Famosa, which once encircled the entire hill, encompassing the area now bordered by Jalan Kota, Jalan Gereja, Jalan Mahkamah, and Jalan Istana. Center of the Portuguese administration, the

"MELAKA IS A CITY THAT WAS MADE FOR MERCHANDISE, FITTER THAN ANY OTHER IN THE WORLD."

TOME PIRES, *SUMA ORIENTAL*

massive fortress, according to Eredia, a 16th-century author, contained "the castle, the Governor's Palace, the Bishop's Palace, the State Council Hall, the Hall of the Brotherhood of Mercy, five Churches... and two hospitals". The Dutch East India Company's coat of arms and the date 1670 which appear above the Santiago Gate were added by the Dutch when they were restoring the fort.

**MELAKA SULTANATE PALACE.** Reconstructed in 1985 from written accounts in the *Sejarah Melayu*, a 16th-century court history, and using traditional construction methods, the Melaka Sultanate Palace at the base of St Paul's Hill is a replica of the legendary istana of Sultan Mansur Shah. Although built at considerable cost, and reputedly the largest wooden palace in Southeast Asia, the new version still pales by comparison with the description of the original palace. According to the historical text in the *Sejarah Melayu*, "So fine was the workmanship of this palace that not another royal palace in the world at that time could compare with it." Inside the new palace is a Cultural Museum depicting dioramas from the golden days of the Melaka Sultanate.

**OLD DUTCH CEMETERY.** Follow Jalan Istana past the Melaka Sultanate Palace to Melaka's oldest Protestant cemetery containing graves from the Portuguese, Dutch, and English colonial eras. A 19-foot-high monolith marks the graves of British soldiers, victims of the short-lived Naning War when Minangkabau Malays rose up against their colonial masters in protest against tax laws.

**MELAKA'S MISSING TUNNELS**

According to legend, a mile-long tunnel runs from Porta de Santiago to St John's Fort. The "lost" tunnel was apparently secretly built when the Dutch were repairing the Santiago Gate. The rationale for this theory is that the gate took over twenty years to repair, whereas the building of the Stadthuys took less time. Apparently the authorities bricked over the entrance and sealed it with a metal plate.

This view of Melaka (left), from Middleton's *Complete System of Geography*, has been reversed by the publishers. The original was printed backwards, with St Paul's Hill on the right side of the river. Publishers at the time often lifted such illustrations from earlier sources. In most cases they took care to change a few details on the new engravings. But Middleton was apparently idle: he made his engraving directly from the earlier illustration, thus reversing it. The mistake was perpetuated in several published views of Melaka.

**Maugham at the Malacca Club**
Now the Independence Museum, the onion-domed former Malacca Club opposite the Porta de Santiago features in one of Somerset Maugham's best short stories. In his reminiscences, Maugham describes how his American traveling companion, Gerald Haxton, was late for dinner at the club. When he eventually arrived he said, "I'm sorry, I know I'm drunk, but as an apology, I've got a corking good story for you…" The tale was told and became "Footprints in the Jungle", a true murder story of a wife and her lover, who killed her planter husband. The Club still survives, but is now housed in modern premises, and the short-story quote about the club still hangs proudly on the wall of the conference room.

## Town Square

Hub of the town since its earliest days, the Town Square is the focus of Melaka's historical center. Often known as Red Square because of the distinctive hue of its buildings, it boasts some of the most superb examples of Dutch colonial architecture in the Far East. The nearby bridge across the Melaka River marks the site of the original 14th-century covered bridge destroyed by the conquering Portuguese in 1511. Downstream, sailing *perahu* from Indonesia still barter cargoes of charcoal for rice – shades of the past when Melaka was known as "the richest sea port with the greatest abundance of shipping that can be found in the whole world".
**The Stadthuys.** This former home of the Dutch governors, built between 1641 and 1660, and recently restored to its former glory, is one of the oldest Dutch buildings in Southeast Asia. Constructed on the foundations of the former Portuguese fort walls, the Stadthuys features solid masonry walls, and one room still contains an original carved-wood ceiling. Since 1982, the Stadthuys has housed the Historical Museum (Muzium Sejarah) and exhibits from Melaka's six-hundred-year-old past, including a blackwood cupboard bearing the monogram of the Dutch East India Company, 15th-century Portuguese costumes (plus Malay and Chinese wedding clothes), and coins dating from the Melaka sultanate.
**Christ Church.** Bricks were shipped specially from Holland to build the massive walls of Malaysia's oldest Protestant church, constructed between 1741 and 1753. Spanning the nave are seventeen beams, each hewn from a single hardwood tree, and measuring 48 feet 9 inches long. The church's original features include the carved wooden pews and a tiled frieze of the Last Supper, which adorns the altar. Set in the floor are Portuguese tombstones inscribed in Latin and one in memory of an Armenian merchant from Persia. Records at the church date back to 1641.
**Clock tower and fountain.** Centerpoint of the Town Square is the Tan Beng Swee Clock Tower,

built by a wealthy Straits Chinese philanthropist in 1886. Another landmark is the Queen Victoria Fountain, carved from red English marble and constructed in 1901 to commemorate the Diamond Jubilee – the sixty-year-long reign of the British monarch.

## Jalan Tun Tan Cheng Lok (Heeren Straat)

Named after Melaka's most famous *baba* son, this historic street lined with Chinese-style townhouses was formerly known as Heeren Straat, the Dutch for "Noble Street". Some houses date from the Dutch era, and others, including some of the most decorative, were built during the 19th-century rubber boom when the street was nicknamed "Millionaires' Row". The narrow house frontages are deceptive, as these homes of wealthy Peranakans ("born here" in Malay) are often astonishingly long. Typical features of the buildings include footways tiled with hand-painted Delft and Wedgwood tiles; carved front doors surmounted by the family motto in gold calligraphy on a black lacquered board; Corinthian columns; and opulent bas-reliefs of bats, phoenixes, flowers, and dragons.

**The Baba and Nyonya Heritage Museum.** Millionaire *baba* planter Chan Cheng Siew built this flamboyant townhouse, now a private museum, in 1896. Located at 48–50 Jalan Tun Tan Cheng Lock, the double-frontage Straits Chinese townhouse offers a superb glimpse into a little-known and vanishing lifestyle ▲ *202–9*. Furnished with original pieces, the interior decoration is overwhelmingly ornate. Among the features in the museum are a gilded teak staircase; an ancestral altar embellished with dragons; delicate carved and gold-leafed screens; blackwood furniture inlaid with mother-of-pearl; embroidered silk paintings; and an original kitchen complete with traditional utensils for *nyonya* cuisine. For a small fee, tours with a fascinating narrative are organized through this exquisite home.

**Chee Mansion.** A central tower, once the highest point in the old town of Melaka, crowns the roof of this palatial Peranakan mansion which, unlike neighboring townhouses, is set back from the road on Jalan Tun Tan Cheng Lock. An eccentric mix of Dutch, Portuguese, Chinese, and English architectural styles, the mansion was built by a Eurasian architect in 1919 for the wealthy Chee family.

**Symbolic fish**
The interior courtyard, or air-well, a dominant feature of Melaka's *baba* townhouses, had a dual function, for not only did it light and ventilate the house, it also facilitated the collection of rainwater which *feng shui* adherents believe brings luck to the household. Air-well drainpipes were invariably fish-shaped, as this symbolized "plenty", and in many old townhouses today these porcelain fish are still in use.

**Straits Chinese silver** ▲ *207*
A curious blend of Chinese motifs and Islamic design, Straits Chinese silver, the preferred jewelry of 19th-century *nyonyas*, is now a fashionable collectors' item. Much sought after by antique dealers, this ornate silverware was produced locally by immigrant Chinese craftsmen. Although many of the motifs were Chinese, only in Straits Chinese silver do such weird and wonderful pieces as pillow ends and curtain hooks appear.

The Straits Chinese or Peranakans who settled in the British Straits Settlements trace their descent from South Chinese ancestors. Peranakan men are known as *babas* and the women as *nyonyas* and they speak patois Malay. Dutch accounts confirm that a permanent Chinese settlement of shopkeepers, craftsmen, and farmers existed in Melaka by the early 17th century. The early settlers came without their families, and it is highly probable that many formed unions with Malays or women of other races who had emigrated from the outlying islands. At the beginning of the 19th century, many Melakan Chinese flocked to the bustling new settlements of Penang and Singapore. These Peranakans or "local-born" Chinese were relatively well-to-do, unlike the flood of new immigrants from Fujian Province in South China.

**CHERKI CARDS**

Family fortunes were occasionally put in jeopardy by *nyonyas* who were cherki fanatics. With cards made in Germany carrying Chinese ideographs, the *nyonyas* played the game using a combination of Chinese and Malay terms.

**CUSTOMS AND BELIEFS**

The early settlers in Melaka brought with them folk beliefs and customs from South China, hence most rituals of worship, birth, marriage, and death remained faithful to Chinese tradition. However, they also prayed at Malay *kramat* and used Malay as well as Chinese herbal medicines. Many Singapore *babas* today are Christians.

**A STRAITS CHINESE FAMILY**

This photograph, taken around 1900, shows mixed Chinese, Malay and European influences in the daily dress of the Straits Chinese or Peranakans. The father and son wear Chinese jackets and loose trousers with Western hats. The mother and daughter wear the long Malay-style tunic over their sarongs, but have embroidered Chinese shoes on their feet.

**WEDDING GROUP 1929**
Though the Peranakans borrowed much from the Malays in cuisine, dress and language, they upheld Chinese custom for ceremonial occasions. This wedding party is attired formally in elaborate Chinese costumes: the groom has donned a Manchu-style hat and cloth shoes with his Chinese gown and jacket. The bride wears a heavy headdress and embroidered Chinese tunic with voluminous sleeves, more suited to the cooler climate of South China.

**SIREH LEAVES**
Sireh, the leaf of the betel tree, played an important role in local wedding rituals. Chewing sireh also became an absorbing daily pastime for the *nyonyas*. The leaves were wrapped around areca nut shavings, bits of gambier, and strands of tobacco, with a dash of lime for added bite.

**NYONYA CUISINE**
Peranakans incorporated the local methods of preparing foods with different spices with Chinese cooking styles to form the unique "*nyonya* cuisine". Informal meals were eaten with fingers in the Malay manner, but ritual meals for the bridal couple and table offerings for the gods and ancestors were laid out with Chinese bowls and chopsticks.

**LANGUAGE**
As a result of early marriage and working ties with the local population, the Peranakans in time developed a distinctive patois of Malay interspersed with Hokkien dialect words and phrases. By the end of the 19th century, this polygot language had also absorbed many English expressions.

**ROMANIZED MALAY BOOKS**
Though few Peranakans could read or write Chinese, they were interested in classic Chinese romances and adventure stories. Chinese epics translated into Romanized Malay thus found a large and faithful reading public.

From the tender age of eight or nine, a young *nyonya* girl began learning needlework. By the time she reached puberty, she would usually be ready to start preparing her wedding trousseau. Large embroidered items such as door-curtains and bed-panels for the bridal chamber were the work of professionals, and were generally ordered from China. However, a host of smaller intimate articles were expected to be made by the *nyonya* herself. The motifs were generally Chinese designs with happy associations – birds, butterflies, mythic creatures, flowers, and fruits which suggested a successful marriage blessed with prosperity, long life, and many children. When English magazines and pattern books became easily available in the early 20th century, some *nyonyas* borrowed Western designs like roses and golden-haired girls, swans and cavorting puppies. Drawing on Malay as well as Chinese needlework traditions, the *nyonya* used silk and metallic thread on silks and velvets and created rich contrasts of textures. However, it is beadwork for which the *nyonya* is perhaps best known. Using cut-glass beads called *manek kaca*, and tiny metallic beads called *manek perigu*, she was able to achieve a lively, shimmering effect on her work.

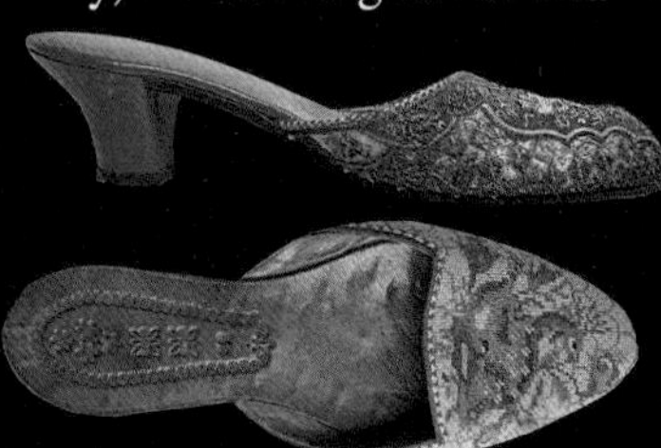

**WEDDING PURSES**
Small wedding purses held a token sum of money to suggest that the bridal couple would never be in want. These charming beaded or embroidered purses were usually more fanciful in shape than traditional Chinese purses.

**BEADED SLIPPERS**
The *nyonya* made slippers not only for herself and female relatives but also for her husband or fiancé. The *baba*'s slippers were equally decorative but cut in a different style from those intended for women.

**EMBROIDERED WEDDING SHOE**
Of rich red velvet, this shoe was made and worn by a Peranakan bride. Auspicious peonies on the shoe are executed in opulent metallic thread embroidery.

**GROOM'S KNEE PADS**
The bridegroom could look forward to painless kneeling during the tedious wedding ceremonies as he was cushioned by these padded knee-pads sewn by his bride.

**Sangkut baju**
This arrowhead-shaped shoulderpiece probably had Malay/Indonesian origins. It was an accessory used by early *nyonyas* who wore the *baju panjang* or long tunic. Elaborate versions like this were reserved for ceremonial occasions.

**Bed ornament**
Suspended embroidered or beaded ornaments, gaily festooned with colored tassels, enhanced the Peranakan bridal bed. This example features the Chinese *bagua* (eight trigrams).

For gatherings on festive occasions such as weddings, birthdays or the Lunar New Year, the Peranakans brought out their best porcelain. Dinner sets could run from several hundred to a few thousand pieces. Those who wished to impress their guests displayed entire assemblages of fully enameled porcelain imported from China. Wealthy families also had specially commissioned sets carrying the family hallmark. The shapes of this decorative porcelain, made from the mid-19th century to the early 20th century, were generally Chinese but it is the striking color combinations that impart a charmingly distinctive character to what is now popularly known as *nyonya* porcelain.

**KAM CHENG**
Echoing the shape of functional vessels in the South Chinese kitchen, these jars with lids were decorative enough to appear on the sideboard at great family feasts, or be displayed in glass-fronted cupboards.

**WEDDING WASHBASIN**
A pair of decorative porcelain washbasins formed part of the furnishings of the wedding chamber. The bride rose early to prepare a basin of warm water not only for her new spouse, but also for her mother-in-law.

**PHOENIX AND PEONY**
Two favorite motifs appear on *nyonya* porcelain: the phoenix, emblem of the empress, which also denotes fertility, and the peony, symbolic of wealth and marital happiness.

**JOSS-STICK HOLDER**
Faithfully following the practice of ancestral worship, the devout *nyonya* would light joss-sticks every morning before going about on her chores. A porcelain joss-stick holder was placed centrally on an altar table laid with food offerings.

**WEDDING TEAPOT**
Pairs of diminutive enameled teapots like these were used in the Chinese tea ceremony held at Peranakan weddings, when the bride served tea to her new in-laws.

The Straits Chinese relished the opulence of precious metal, using it for many types of personal ornaments and objects for household display. These articles were crafted in silver, but wealthier patrons had ceremonial items made in gold. Gilding was also widely employed in Peranakan silverwork to simulate the richness of gold. Craftsmen included Malay and Indian as well as Chinese silversmiths who had migrated to the Straits Settlements. Chased and repoussé work, which produced the richness that the Peranakans liked, were the most common techniques employed. Designs were generally auspicious and symbolic Chinese motifs joined together in a complex manner.

**BRIDAL SAPU TANGAN**
Most of the ritual handkerchiefs of *nyonya* brides were of embroidered silk or velvet. The *sapu tangan* was used on the third, fifth, and twelfth day of the celebrations.

**SIREH BOXES**
The Hindu-Malay custom of chewing betelnuts wrapped in *sireh* adopted by the Peranakan led to the making of many silver articles. Among the most engaging are the globular and cylindrical containers fashioned to hold the various ingredients.

**GROOM'S BELT BUCKLE**
The silver belt buckles worn by both *babas* and *nyonyas* were adaptations of the prominent ceremonial buckles of the Malays. A silver buckle and belt were a customary gift from the bride's family to the new son-in-law.

**GILDED BANTAL**
This octagonal *bantal* featuring a *qilin* or unicorn, was used to adorn the end of the big bolster on the bridal bed.

**ANKLETS**
The *nyonya* practice of wearing anklets was of Hindu-Malay origin. This pair has an Islamic-style foliate pattern. Chinese patterns such as bamboo stems can also be found on Peranakan anklets.

# PERANAKAN TERRACE HOUSE

The façades of Peranakan terrace houses give a highly picturesque character to Singapore, Penang, and Melaka. The houses evolved from utilitarian two-story dwellings. In the late 19th century, the simple shophouse rows developed into more ornate residential terrace houses. To traditional Chinese features such as the rounded roof gables and painted scrolls were added European features. By 1918, the use of European classical orders became bolder. Chinese craftsmen freely adapted Renaissance, Mannerist, or Baroque elements in the plasterwork columns and pilasters. Malay-inspired timber fretwork under the eaves also contributed to the eclectic mixture of styles.

**1. PSEUDO-CLASSICAL ORDERS**
Plasterwork pillars and pilasters seen on the façade have a delightful and surprising character. This arises from the fanciful and unorthodox use of European architectural idioms by Chinese craftsmen, catering to the ornate taste of the Peranakan client.

**2. LOUVERED WINDOWS**
A feature of Portuguese colonial architecture found first in Melaka, these jalousies have shutters to reduce the sun's glare on hot afternoons, yet allow the passage of air. They also permitted modest *nyonyas* to catch a glimpse of activities in the street without being seen. Above the windows are carved fan-shaped panels inspired by the timber panels of Malay houses.

**3. PINTU PAGAR**
The swinging *pintu pagar* or gate-doors of terrace houses are set beyond the imposing entrance doors inscribed with Chinese couplets. The short leaves of the *pintu pagar* provided the household with a measure of privacy in the daytime, when the tall paneled Chinese doors were left open.

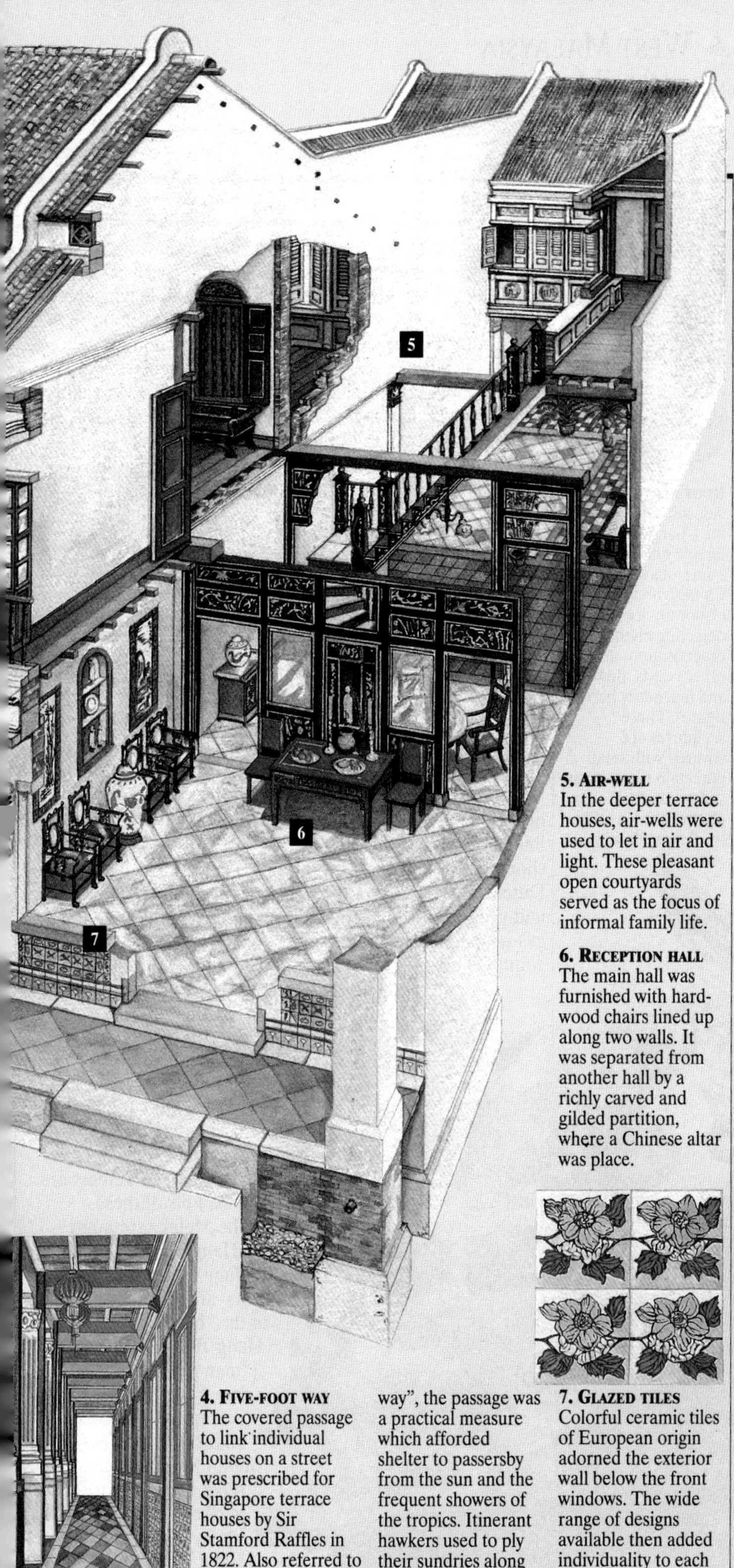


**5. Air-well**
In the deeper terrace houses, air-wells were used to let in air and light. These pleasant open courtyards served as the focus of informal family life.

**6. Reception hall**
The main hall was furnished with hardwood chairs lined up along two walls. It was separated from another hall by a richly carved and gilded partition, where a Chinese altar was place.

**4. Five-foot way**
The covered passage to link individual houses on a street was prescribed for Singapore terrace houses by Sir Stamford Raffles in 1822. Also referred to as the "five-foot way", the passage was a practical measure which afforded shelter to passersby from the sun and the frequent showers of the tropics. Itinerant hawkers used to ply their sundries along this stretch.

**7. Glazed tiles**
Colorful ceramic tiles of European origin adorned the exterior wall below the front windows. The wide range of designs available then added individuality to each terrace house.

**ROOF CARVINGS**
Adorning the roof of the Cheng Hoon Teng temple and Melaka's numerous other Chinese temples are elaborate decorations depicting mythical dragons, lions and other beasts, flowers, and legendary heroic figures. These sculptures are covered with small porcelain tiles, which still retain their color after centuries under the fierce equatorial sun.

## JALAN HANG JEBAT (JONKERS STREET)

"Young Nobleman's Street", as Jonkers Street translates in Dutch, was also a high-profile residential area for Straits Chinese families. Many beautiful town houses still line both sides of this bustling thoroughfare renowned for its antique shops, and one *baba* house has been converted into a restaurant with marble-topped tables and original décor. Other interesting buildings include the Hokkien Merchants Guild (*Huay Kuan*), which features fine wood and stone carvings artistically decorated with gilt and lacquer.

**ANTIQUE SHOPS.** The late T. J. Kutty, an Indian Muslim from Kerala, started the first Jonkers Street junk shop in 1936. Many *baba* families had lost their fortunes when the price of rubber plummeted in the Great Depression and were forced to sell their precious heirlooms just to survive. Kutty bought up their treasures and started the antiques business that his descendants still run today. Wares three hundred years old cram the many curio shops lining the street. Enterprising shoppers bargain aggressively and good buys include carved Dutch sideboards, red-and-gold Melaka opium beds, pink-and-green *nyonya* porcelain, Straits Chinese silver, Victorian gas-lamps, charcoal-burning brass irons, sandalwood chests – countless other souvenirs from Melaka's chequered past.

**HANG KASTURI'S MAUSOLEUM.** To the right, before the Jalan Tokong intersection with Jalan Hang Jebat, is an ancient whitewashed mausoleum believed to be that of Hang Kasturi, one of the five warriors attached to the court of Sultan Mansur Shah. As famous in Malaysia as the Three Musketeers are in the West, the exploits of these warriors of the Melaka sultanate – Hang Tuah, Hang Kasturi, Hang Lekir, Hang Lekiu, and Hang Jebat – are legendary. Leader of the "blood-brothers" was Hang Tuah, an Orang Laut ("man from the sea") who rose from obscurity to become Laksamana, admiral of the fleet, under Sultan Mansur Shah, whose reign from 1459 to 1477 marked the golden age of Malay power and culture. Hang Tuah was not only a mighty warrior, but also an

Porcelain used in a Peranakan home.

idol of the harem, and tales abound of his dashing good looks: "Wives and maidens alike were all a-flutter at the sight of Hang Tuah passing by." The warriors' popularity with the ladies was also their undoing, and a duel between Hang Tuah and Hang Jebat remains one of the best-known stories in Malay literature.

## Jalan Tukang Emas

In the heart of Melaka's old town, running parallel to Jonkers Street, is Jalan Tukang Emas, or Goldsmith Street, renowned for its many religious houses of worship, proof, Melakans say, of the town's harmonious and tolerant character. Tinsmiths, blacksmiths, cobblers, coffin-makers, paper-artists, and basket-weavers still ply their trades there and in adjoining Jalan Tukang Besi.

**Kampung Kling Mosque.** Corinthian columns, a Victorian chandelier, Portuguese tiles, a pagoda-style minaret, and a three-tiered Javanese-style roof feature in this elegant mosque built in 1748. Located on the corner of Jalan Tukang Mas and Jalan Lekiu, the mosque is named after Kampung Keling, the original residential area of Muslim Indian traders (*kling*) at the time of the Melaka sultanate ● *34*.

**Sri Poyyatha Vinayagar Moorthi Temple.** On the same street as the mosque is Malaysia's oldest Hindu temple, built in 1781. Sacred to both the Chettiar (traditional Hindu moneylenders) and the Chitty (Peranakan Indians who claim to have been in Melaka five hundred years), the temple is dedicated to the deity Vinayagar, represented by an elephant's head made of black stone imported from India. At the annual Masi Magam festival, a sacred statue of Lord Subramaniam is conveyed on a silver chariot to the Nagarathar Temple at Cheng, about 6 miles from Melaka town.

**Cheng Hoon Teng Temple.** For over three hundred years, Malaysia's oldest Chinese temple on Jalan Tokong has been the principal place of worship for Melaka's Chinese. The temple was founded by Li Kup, who fled China when the Manchus toppled the Ming dynasty. A picture of the revered founder hangs in the hall of the Sin Chew or "soul tablets", a room behind the main temple, where past leaders are honored.

**A tale of Melaka**
In the late 14th century a Sumatran prince named Parameswara was looking for a site for his new capital. According to one version, his hunting dogs were accosted by a fierce mouse deer, and this auspicious sign made the prince select the small fishing village of Melaka for his capital. Within a few decades the village grew into a major trading center, and wealthy merchants from India, Arabia, and China flocked to the city. It was an ideal location, for the calm Melaka Strait was protected from the monsoons, and boats could anchor there and wait for the winds to change before sailing home. During the reign of Sultan Mansur Shah, the town became one of the major ports on the ancient spice route. However, the Portuguese were keen to wrest the control of the lucrative spice trade from the Malays. With superior firepower, they attacked in 1511 and Melaka fell to Portuguese rule for the next 130 years. They were in turn ousted by the Dutch, who remained in power until 1824, when they swapped Melaka with the English for Bencoolen in Sumatra. When Melaka was finally returned to the Malayans in 1957, the town again became independent after 450 years under the colonial yoke.

## Genting Highlands

From Kuala Lumpur on a clear day, Genting Highlands, the nearest hill resort to the nation's capital, can be seen perched on a mountain top 5850 feet above sea level. From the Karak Highway turn off at Genting Sempah at the top of the range, where an 11-mile four-lane highway winds to the resort. Taxis and buses service the route and, for the well-heeled, a helicopter service provides a fast link with Kuala Lumpur's Subang International Airport. Although the resort offers plenty of other attractions, Malaysia's only casino is undoubtedly its biggest lure. Gamblers flock here from all over Southeast Asia to try their luck at baccarat, roulette, blackjack, Tai Sai, and keno, or take a fling on the one-armed bandits. Malaysia's Muslims are not allowed into the gambling halls. At the Genting Theatre Restaurant, up to a thousand diners can enjoy the cuisine and watch Las Vegas-style floor shows. The resort also boasts two luxury hotels, an indoor swimming pool, and boating and bowling facilities. A cable car connects the resort with the Awana Country Club with its golf course and equestrian center. The mountain-top is often shrouded in clouds and the nights are cool enough for sweaters. Views of the Klang Valley and the surrounding jungle-clad hills are spectacular.

## Janda Baik

For those who like to escape the crowds, Janda Baik offers a pleasant alternative. Take the right-hand turn at Genting Sempah, continue past the food stalls on the Old Bentong Road, and follow the signs to Janda Baik. This picturesque highland valley is home to a number of city dwellers' weekend retreats, but it still has a kampung ambience. Cattle wander across the road, and the only signs of commercialism are a dry-goods store and a laid-back coffee shop. Janda Baik's main

**Bullock carts**
Before the advent of the motor car, the ubiquitous *kereta lembu*, or bullock cart, served as a multi-purpose vehicle on the peninsula' s early thoroughfares. Used for transporting everything from lumber to passengers, bullock carts, which usually featured a distinctive thatched roof to offer shade, were controlled by Indian or Sikh drivers who seemed to have a magical way with their stubborn beasts of burden. Well-to-do travelers journeyed by *gharry* (cart), but for most of the population the bullock cart was the only long-distance means of transport on the winding route leading through the interior from Kuala Lumpur to Pahang.

> "IN THESE SHADOWED AMPHITHEATRES SPLASHED BY WATERFALLS, A CARPET OF GREEN AND BLACK BUTTERFLIES, WITH GREAT FRINGED WINGS, ROSE UP BEFORE US.... "
>
> HENRI FAUCONNIER, *THE SOUL OF MALAYA*

attraction is its boulder-strewn river, which cascades along beside the road offering some excellent picnic spots and swimming holes to cool off in.

## TASIK CINI

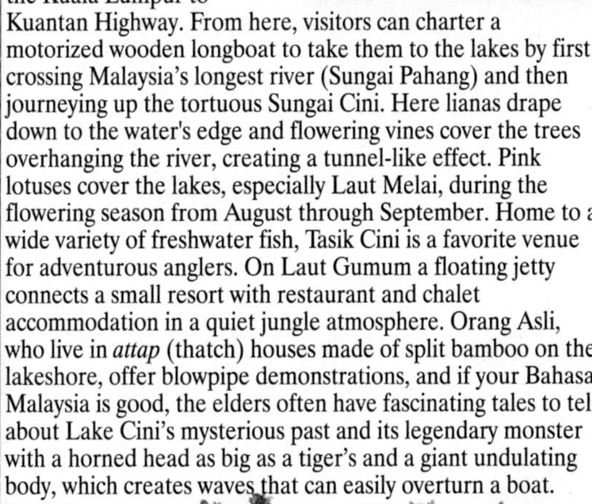

Believed by the local Orang Asli to be the home of a legendary Loch Ness-type monster, Tasik Cini is a series of lakes, known as *laut*, in the backwoods of Pahang state. The lakes can be approached via the town of Cini off the Segamat to Kuantan Highway, but the classic way is via Kampung Belimbing, a village on the Sungai Pahang, 16 miles from the turnoff on the Kuala Lumpur to Kuantan Highway. From here, visitors can charter a motorized wooden longboat to take them to the lakes by first crossing Malaysia's longest river (Sungai Pahang) and then journeying up the tortuous Sungai Cini. Here lianas drape down to the water's edge and flowering vines cover the trees overhanging the river, creating a tunnel-like effect. Pink lotuses cover the lakes, especially Laut Melai, during the flowering season from August through September. Home to a wide variety of freshwater fish, Tasik Cini is a favorite venue for adventurous anglers. On Laut Gumum a floating jetty connects a small resort with restaurant and chalet accommodation in a quiet jungle atmosphere. Orang Asli, who live in *attap* (thatch) houses made of split bamboo on the lakeshore, offer blowpipe demonstrations, and if your Bahasa Malaysia is good, the elders often have fascinating tales to tell about Lake Cini's mysterious past and its legendary monster with a horned head as big as a tiger's and a giant undulating body, which creates waves that can easily overturn a boat.

**SUBMERGED KHMER CITY**

Orang Asli elders maintain that underneath the waters of enigmatic Tasik Cini there is a submerged Khmer city. Legends tell that when the city was in danger of attack the inhabitants flooded the town. In the last encounter, they must have all perished in battle, for the town has remained submerged ever since. No serious search has ever been mounted for the ancient remains, reputed to lie deep under the silt which covers the lake bed. However, aerial photographs have indicated straight lines, which could be ancient canals, and linguists point to similarities between the local Senoi dialect and that of the ancient Khmer of Cambodia.

The domestic use of pewterware in the Malayan peninsula was extensive under Portuguese then Dutch rule beween the 16th and 18th centuries. However it is thought that a domestic pewter industry was established only in the late 19th century, after the discovery of tin mines in Perak and Pahang. The first pewterer in Kuala Lumpur was Yong Koon, who came to Malaya from Swatow in China in 1885. Yong started a one-man industry, Selangor Pewter (later Royal Selangor), specializing in oil lamps, incense burners, and candelabra for Chinese temples, later graduating to teapots, tobacco boxes, and wine jugs.

**EARLY PEWTER-MAKING**

1. Casting pewter sheets between firebricks, expelling the excess molten material by rocking forward on the top brick.

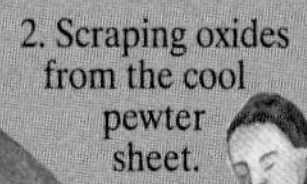

2. Scraping oxides from the cool pewter sheet.

3. Forming a tea-pot body by hammering the sheet around a mandrel.

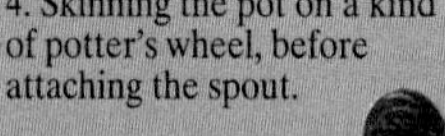

4. Skinning the pot on a kind of potter's wheel, before attaching the spout.

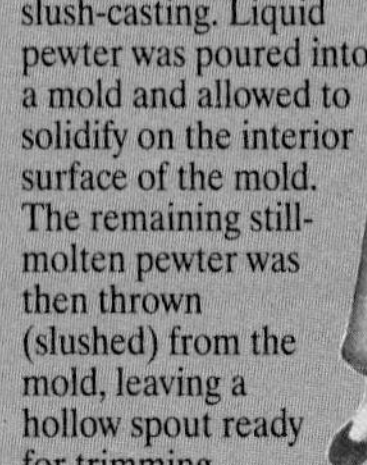

5. Making the spout by slush-casting. Liquid pewter was poured into a mold and allowed to solidify on the interior surface of the mold. The remaining still-molten pewter was then thrown (slushed) from the mold, leaving a hollow spout ready for trimming.

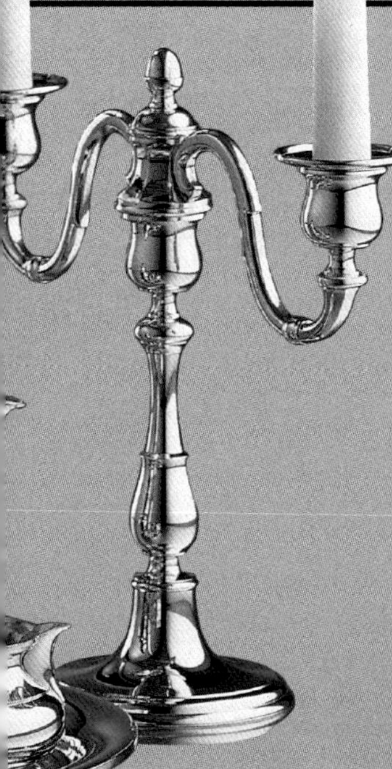

**Modern pewter-making**

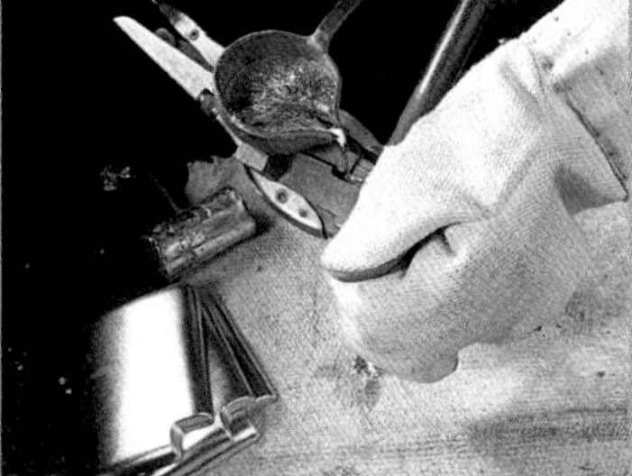

1. Molten pewter is hand-cast into steel molds.

2. Castings are molded separately, then soldered together such that the joints are virtually invisible.

3. A hipflask is polished on a buffing wheel.

4. Items are checked for weight, finish quality, and adherence to specifications.

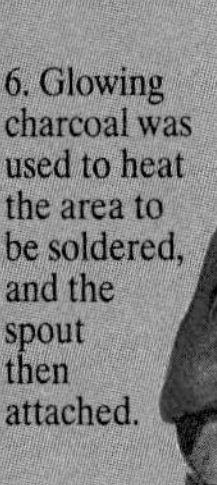

6. Glowing charcoal was used to heat the area to be soldered, and the spout then attached.

7. The cover would be made of another sheet of pewter, placed over a former and beaten to the desired shape.

**ELEPHANT LORE**
Great mounds of steaming elephant dung or huge footprints in the mud are all that visitors are likely or lucky to see of Malaysia's largest mammals. Even in the early days hunters were extremely fortunate to catch a glimpse of these mighty creatures that seemed to be blessed with a sixth telepathic sense. To remain undetected, one must always be down wind – difficult in the jungle with its ever-changing eddies. Elephants' silence is legendary and except when they are eating, which is usually at night, it is difficult to approach them without their sensing it and taking flight. They move in annual cycles and regularly visit the same feeding grounds, moving along their ancient forest paths. Orang Asli can tell how near elephants are by the warmth of their dung and the freshness of their tracks, and it's a lucky sign if swarms of gadflies are present, for these insects always accompany the giant mammals.

## TAMAN NEGARA

Located in the heart of Peninsular Malaysia, the nation's oldest and largest national park, Taman Negara, covers more than one million acres of what is reputed to be the world's oldest jungle. Travelers journeying there by car turn off the Kuala Lumpur–Kuantan highway at Temerloh for Jerantut. Kuala Tembeling, the start of the 4-hour boat journey to Taman Negara, is 9 miles from Jerantut. All visitors must enter the park by boat as there is no other alternative, a situation which has undoubtedly helped to maintain Taman Negara's primeval aura. Stretching over three states, Pahang, Terengganu, and Kelantan, the park is home to much of Malaysia's rapidly disappearing wildlife, including tigers, elephants, tapir, and seladang (the indigenous cattle). Many of the larger mammals tend to roam in the far interior of the park, and even when at close range are difficult to spot because of the dense rainforest. Specially erected hides offer opportunities to see wildlife, although elephants and tigers are rarely encountered. However, most visitors can expect to see sambar and barking deer, wild pigs and often tapir (below, right). The forest is a fascinating experience ■ *22–3, 26–7* and apart from the extra bonus of glimpsing animals in the wild, this green world offers primeval rainforest, wild rivers, mountain-climbing, caving, prolific bird-life, the hypnotic "jungle-chorus", and a chance to be alone in an unsurpassed natural setting. Intending visitors should first obtain permits and book motels (above) at the Taman Negara counter, Malaysian Tourist Information Centre (MATIC), Jalan Ampang, Kuala Lumpur.

**KUALA TAHAN.** At the end of the 35-mile boat journey, located where the Sungai Tahan meets the Sungai Tembeling, is Kuala Tahan, Taman Negara's Park Headquarters. At the reception visitors pay for boat rides and accommodation at either the resthouse, motel, chalets, hostels, or campsites. Restaurants specialize in Malay food and packed lunches for trekkers and meals for overnight stays in the hides. At Tahan Hide, a short walk from the Headquarters, wild pig and deer can be seen at dawn and dusk.

**GUNUNG TAHAN.** Taman Negara's crowning glory is the 7107-foot-high Gunung Tahan, West Malaysia's highest peak. Ten-day summit treks can be organized at Park Headquarters although it's best to plan in advance. The ascent is not

“THE FAUNA… IS MOST REMARKABLE AND ABUNDANT; MUCH OF ITS FOREST-COVERED INTERIOR IS INHABITED BY WILD BEASTS ALONE, AND GIGANTIC PACHYDERMS… ROAM UNMOLESTED OVER VAST TRACTS OF COUNTRY.” ISABELLA BIRD, *THE GOLDEN CHERSONESE*

difficult and the 30-mile trek up to the remote peak is an adventure in itself, involving several river crossings and an arduous up-and-down trail through the humid lowland jungles and across dry mountain ridges. After Kuala Teku (fourth day) the trail ascends through oak forest where pitcher plants can be spotted. On the fifth day, from the summit plateau, a climb through stunted moss-forests leads to the top where temperatures can drop to 40° Fahrenheit.

**BUKIT TERESEK.** Gunung Tahan can be seen from the look-out atop Bukit Teresek, on a steep but popular trail from Kuala Tahan. For short-term visitors this trek offers a good look at the rainforest ■ *22–3*, with opportunities for sighting white-handed gibbons, giant squirrels, and prolific bird-life, including the sweet-voiced, white-rumped sharma.

**OVERNIGHT HIDES.** Hides built beside grassy clearings overlooking salt-licks offer the best opportunity for sighting wildlife, as animals frequent these spots to obtain essential body salts. Most hides offer overnight accommodation and at those farthest from Park Headquarters visitors are more likely to see more exotic wildlife. Jenut Tabing (one-hour walk) is good for wild pigs, barking deer, and tapir; Jenut Belau and Jenut Yong (two-hour walk) for tapir, sambar deer, barking deer, and civet cats; Jenut Kumbang (five-hour walk) for tapir; and Cegar Anging (one-hour walk) for seladang. For overnight visitors, here are some useful hints to maximize the chances of seeing wildlife: everyone should be in the hide and quiet by 5pm and no one should leave until the following morning; there are no cooking facilities in the hide because cooking smells keep game away; it is best to bring food along, but if you must cook, do so a long way from the hide; take turns to stay on the night watch – it's worth it as you just may be rewarded.

**SACRED TUALANG TREE**

Towering above the rainforest canopy are the distinctive tualang trees, forest giants which often attain heights of 260 feet. The cylindrical trunk grows for more than 97 feet before the first branches interrupt its smooth girth. It is easily recognizable by its gray-green foliage. Malays believe that it is favored by bees and the word *bertualang* “to swarm (bees)” is taken from the tree's name. These trees are often found by the roadside with a Chinese or Hindu shrine at their base, for their extreme old age and height often give rise to tales of their “sacred” powers.

**TAPIR**

The tapir (*badak murai*) is an unusual looking mammal, with its long trunk-like proboscis and its two-tone body. Its forequarters and legs are black and its rear is white. Out in the open the coloring seems brilliant but in the shadows of the gloomy rainforest, its markings become camouflage. This shy creature weighs about 990 pounds and relies on its patterning and its ability to remain underwater for long periods for survival. The aboriginal Negritos used to trap and snare it for food, and it is also an occasional meal for tigers. The Malays believe that this creature has the ability to walk along the bottom of riverbeds, completely submerged, feeding on aquatic grasses.

# Kuala Selangor to Pulau Pangkor

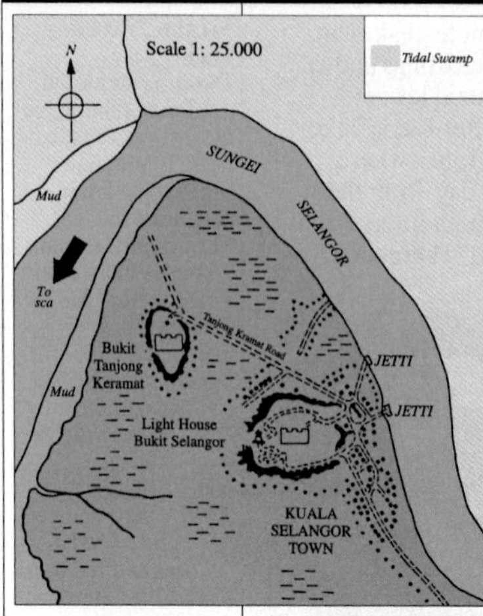


## Kuala Selangor

From Kuala Lumpur, travelers can reach Kuala Selangor either by turning north at Klang onto Route 5, or by taking the more scenic Route 54 from Kepong. Located beside the estuary of the Selangor River, this old port is home to a large fishing fleet. Wooden trawlers with their distinctive red cabins can be seen lining the foreshores of the town. Settled by Bugis immigrants from Sulawesi since the 17th century, Kuala Selangor was once the royal capital of the Selangor Sultanate.

**Bukit Melawati.** Strategically sited, with panoramic views of the river and the Melaka Strait, Bukit Melawati, the hill above Kuala Selangor, was the site of Malay forts. The largest, Kota Melawati, still retains its execution block and some grand old cannons on the seaward side. Crowning the hill is the Altingsburg Lighthouse. Other attractions include parklands shaded by towering raintrees, the Kuala Selangor Museum, and the Royal Mausoleum – the burial place of Selangor's Bugis sultans.

**Kuala Selangor Nature Park.** Comprising coastal wetlands and mangrove swamps, the 650-acre Kuala Selangor Nature Park, located at the base of Bukit Melawati, is a new conservation project designed to heighten awareness of the world's shrinking wetland habitats and plant life. Home to 130 bird species and stop-over for an estimated 100,000 wading birds, Kuala Selangor is unique for its birdlife. Man-made lakes and observation hides enable visitors to get a closer look at the wildlife, including leaf monkeys, otters, squirrels, and flying foxes.

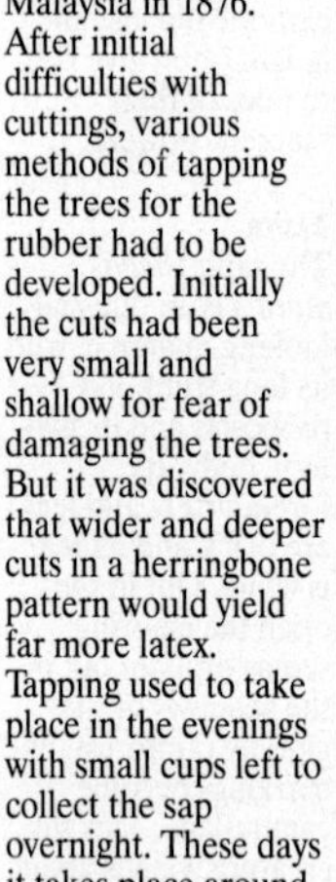

**Rubber-tapping**
Rubber ▲ *222–3* was first introduced into Malaysia in 1876. After initial difficulties with cuttings, various methods of tapping the trees for the rubber had to be developed. Initially the cuts had been very small and shallow for fear of damaging the trees. But it was discovered that wider and deeper cuts in a herringbone pattern would yield far more latex. Tapping used to take place in the evenings with small cups left to collect the sap overnight. These days it takes place around dawn and the latex is collected by mid-morning.

## Lumut

The jump-off spot for Pulau Pangkor, this peaceful riverside town also offers its own attractions and boasts a colonial-style resthouse and a stylish country resort for overnight visitors. Despite the presence of Malaysia's largest naval base, Lumut has a relaxed ambience. South of the base is Teluk Batik, a palm-fringed beach with golden sands facing the Manjung Straits. Formerly the Dindings, the beach provides excellent swimming and views of Pulau Pangkor. Late July/August, Teluk Batik hosts the Pesta Laut Lumut, a sea carnival with water-sports competitions and cultural events.

## Pulau Pangkor

Emerald waters and white-sand beaches characterize Pulau Pangkor, Perak's popular island resort located a short ferry-

Pulau Pangkor boat-builders put the finishing touches to the skeleton of a barge.

ride from Lumut port. Ferries run to the island from 6.45am to 7.30pm and land at the island's main town of Pangkor. From here it is a short taxi ride to Pasir Bogak, the most popular beach with hotel and chalet accommodation. The best beaches are found on the west side of the island, while on the east shore are some interesting fishing villages set on stilts. At Pangkor, and further north at Sungai Pinang Besar and Sungai Pinang Kecil, are excellent seafood restaurants. Traditional wooden boat-building is still carried out at Sungai Pinang Kecil. Lush rainforest ■ *22–3* covers the island's interior, and hornbills and monkeys are easily sighted in the early morning and late afternoon. The best way to explore the island is to hire a motorbike in Pangkor. On weekends and public holidays, the island is crowded with tourists and accommodation is hard to find.

**KOTA BELANDA.** At Teluk Gedong, nearly 2 miles south of Pangkor, are the remains of Kota Belanda, a fort built by the Dutch in the 17th century as a foothold in their bid to monopolize the rich Perak tin trade. Restored by the National Museum in 1973, this brick bastion was the scene of many fierce battles between the Dutch, the Malays, and the Bugis from Sulawesi.

**PANTAI PUTERI DEWI.** According to local legend, Pantai Puteri Dewi, "The Beach of the Fairy Princess", was where a broken-hearted Sumatran princess leapt to her death upon hearing the news that her beloved had died.This scenic beach is now part of the Pan-Pacific Resort.

**CORAL BAY.** Sun-lovers can beat the crowds at Pasir Bogak by hiking or riding a motorcycle or bicycle to Coral Bay. This isolated beach, as yet unspoilt by commercialism, is situated at the northern end of Teluk Nipah. Backed by jungle-covered hills, the clear waters are excellent for swimming, and the tree-shaded beach an inviting locale for lazing on the clean white sands.

## PULAU PANGKOR LAUT

Now the exclusive domain of the Pansea Pangkor Laut Resort, this idyllic island off the southwest tip of Pulau Pangkor is reached by ferry from either the jetty at the Seaview Hotel on Pasir Bogak Beach or direct from Lumut. On the west coast of the island is Emerald Bay, a beach renowned for its deep-green waters and talcum-white sands.

**BATU BERSURAT**

Just past Kota Belanda at Teluk Gedung is the curious Batu Bersurat, a boulder inscribed with the words "Ifcralo 1743" and a carving of a child being attacked by a tiger. According to folklore, a Dutch boy disappeared and was believed to have been attacked by a tiger. The soldiers manning the fort carved the stone as a memorial to the boy.

**THE LEANING CLOCK TOWER**

Detour off Route 5 to Teluk Intan, a riverside market town famed for its unusual leaning clock tower. The pagoda-shaped tower, apparently built in 1885 by the Chinese contractor Leong Choon Chong, has a tilt, reminiscent of the Leaning Tower of Pisa. However, its curious angle is not the result of faulty construction, but merely evidence that the town is subsiding.

**HENRI FAUCONNIER AT THE GAP**
In his prize-winning 1930s novel *The Soul of Malaya,* Henri Fauconnier's heroes turn up at the Gap Resthouse for dinner, but the menu then was a far cry from the fried noodles which constitutes today's fare. "A resplendent table had been prepared; all the government crockery and silver with the bull's head crest, the whole stock of bottles arrayed like skittles on the sideboard... cocks, ducks, a suckling pig were laid before us."

**THE GAP ROAD AMBUSH**
Along Gap Road, a sign marks the spot where in 1951, during the Emergency, Sir Henry Gurney, the British high commissioner, was ambushed and killed by communists.

## BUKIT FRASER (FRASER'S HILL)

Perched 4950 feet above sea level, Fraser's Hill is a cool escape from the equatorial lowlands. It was built by the British as a colonial retreat within easy reach of Kuala Lumpur (60 miles). Spread over seven hills, the resort is named after a reclusive mule-skinner and tin-trader, Louis James Fraser, who ran a hilltop gambling shack for miners in the last century. Fraser's Hill still retains an English ambience. Stone bungalows with lead-light windows boast gardens of chrysanthemums, and Devonshire Tea is served at the old Tudor-style Tavern in the heart of the village and at Ye Olde Smokehouse on the road to Jeriau Waterfalls, a picnic and swimming spot. The golf course, picturesquely set in a valley between two hills, was once pock-marked with tin mines, until a far-sighted colonial administrator had it leveled and turfed. As the day temperature hovers around 75° Fahrenheit and 25° lower at night, Fraser's Hill is ideal for jungle hiking, and well-made trails wind around forested hills. Other attractions include horseback riding, bird-watching, or just sipping tea in your bungalow and watching the evening mist move across the mountains. From Gap Road, a one-way road connects with Fraser's Hill. The gates open for 40 minutes each way, with odd hours for ascending and even hours for descending.

**THE GAP RESTHOUSE.** There are about a dozen colonial resthouses left in Malaysia. Some have been rebuilt and revamped, but a few, like the Gap, have survived almost intact from an age which vanished thirty-five years ago at Independence. Astride a promontory, surrounded by jungle, the resthouse is a favorite stop-over for travelers en route to Fraser's Hill.

## CAMERON HIGHLANDS

Malaysia's premier hill resort is located in the far northwest corner of Pahang state, but is only approachable from the Perak side of the Barisan Titiwangsa, the mountain range

"In Malaya the seasons are hardly distinct. You do not die a little every year, as in Europe at the end of autumn. You cease to think of date or time."

Henri Fauconnier, *The Soul of Malaya*

which runs like a spine through the center of Peninsular Malaysia. At an altitude of between 4875 and 5850 feet, temperatures can drop to 50° Fahrenheit at night, making an evening beside a roaring log fire an unusual experience for the tropics. After Tapah on the Ipoh road, the 36-mile drive from the plains to the Highlands is one of Malaysia's most scenic. Thickets of bamboo and tree ferns crowd the roadside and, the road ascends, the view across the jungle-clad hills is superb. Along the way, keep a look-out for the indigenous Orang Asli, who can sometimes be seen hunting with their blowpipes. Their thatched-roof houses perch on hills beside the winding road, and just beyond Batu 7, villagers stage blowpipe demonstrations and sell "golden chickens" (tree-fern heads).

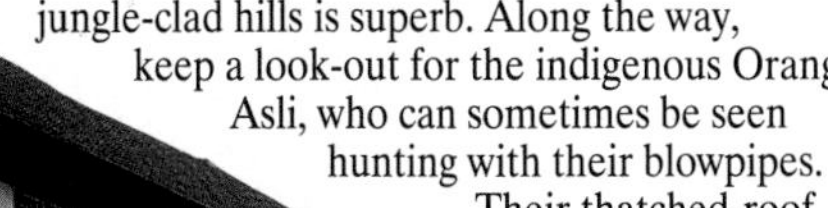

**Ye Olde Smokehouse.** One of Cameron Highlands' most famous buildings, Ye Olde Smokehouse Hotel provides the ultimate in colonial ambience at a price to match. Ivy snakes across the Tudor-style walls, the garden is a picture-postcard copy of an English country garden, and wood fires warm the chilly evenings while diners enjoy real roast beef and dumplings. Devonshire Tea with real home-made strawberry jam is also served on the flagstone patio.

**Sam Poh Temple.** Just before Brinchang, the third and highest town in the highlands, take a right turn to the ornate Sam Poh Buddhist Temple, the principal place of worship for the Highlands' Chinese. Gilded Buddha statues adorn the central altar of the main hall, which is supported by red-tiled columns on lotus-shaped marble bases.

**Sungai Palas Tea Plantation.** Manicured tea bushes carpet the rolling hills of the Sungai Palas Tea Plantation ■ *24–5*, about 3 miles from Brinchang. Home of the renowned Boh Tea, Sungai Palas and the older Boh Tea Estate, outside Ringlet, have been owned by the Russells since the 1930's.

**Robertson's rose gardens**
Set above the winding Sungai Palas road is an old-style bungalow surrounded by terraces of carefully clipped and tended rose bushes. Dating from colonial days, Robertson's is renowned for their distinctive home-made marmalade, rose-jam, and syrup. From its hilltop vantage point are spectacular views of the countryside.

**Bird-watching**
An annual contest held in early June, the Fraser's Hill International Bird Race, sees competitors racing against the clock to see how many bird species they can record within the allotted time-span. The forested heights around Fraser's Hill are noted for their birds. The best place to bird-watch on an early morning is along the road from the Gap Resthouse to Fraser's Hill.

# ▲ The Economic Boom in the Early 1900's

**Tin mining in Perak**

From the establishment of British rule in the mid-1870's, the peninsula experienced a sustained period of remarkably high growth. That growth was built initially on the extraction of tin from the rich seams that ran down the west coast. The industry was built exclusively on Chinese capital and business drive. In the early 1900's, Malaya became the world's most important producer of tin and rubber. Around 1910, European mining companies with huge dredges moved in and by the late 1920's European capital dominated the industry. The rubber industry was first established by European capital and business skill, although an important Malay smallholder rubber sector rapidly emerged.

**Rubber estates**
The vast European rubber plantations employed teams of Indian laborers who would begin tapping latex from the trees at the break of dawn and end the chore by late morning.

**Chinese mining**
Chinese mining methods were extremely labor-intensive, employing large gangs of imported coolies from China, using simple implements to extract the tin from the ground and transport it for initial sorting and washing. The photograph shows open-cast mining, c. 1907.

**WESTERN MINING**
European tin mining was highly capital-intensive. The bucket-dredge could shift huge volumes of tin-bearing soil in a day, and made possible the exploitation of less rich seams. A 1927 *Straits Produce* cartoon takes a satirical look at this development.

**INDUSTRIAL GROWTH**
The profits from the two major and profitable industries of tin and rubber enabled the colonial administration to build an infrastructure of roads, railways, and ports, probably unrivaled in colonial Southeast Asia, and made possible the construction of imposing commercial buildings in Singapore and luxurious planters' houses.

**BOOM TOWN**
The Western trading houses, plantation companies, and banks maintained imposing offices in Singapore's commercial district. The port of Singapore was one of the great trading centers in the East, through which most of Malaya's tin and rubber entered the world market.

1.

**RUBBER PROCESSING**
Much skill was required to tap the latex and produce the maximum yield without damaging the rubber tree ■ *24*. Coagulating latex (1). Pressing the latex into sheets (2).

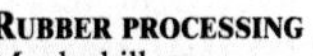

2.

**J.W.W. BIRCH CLOCK TOWER**
A victim of early nationalist sentiment, J.W.W. Birch, the first British resident of Perak, was murdered in 1875 while posting unpopular tax notices along the Perak River. Birch was an arrogant man who had very little regard for Malay custom. He is seen by today's historians as a hostile administrator, who was looking for trouble. However, the colonial government at the time regarded him as a hero. A Victorian-style clock tower commemorating Birch stands behind the State Mosque on Jalan Dato Sagor.

Recently designated a city, Ipoh was little more than a market village in 1884 when de Morgan, a French tin prospector, marked it on his Kinta Valley map as a Malay kampung. However, as the highest-navigable point on the Kinta River, the village had been settled a long time before this, when the river was explored to that point by a Sumatran sea-captain in the 15th century. At the time of British intervention in Perak around 1879, Ipoh was part of the fief of Dato' Panglima Kinta, a territorial chief under the Perak Sultanate. The mosque he built still stands on Jalan Masjid. The city's unusual name derives from the *ipoh* or *upas* tree, which yields a poisonous sap used by the Orang Asli on their blowpipe darts. Once plentiful, only two old trees still remain, one in the Taman D.R. Seenivasagam and one in front of the railway station. By 1890, Ipoh's population had expanded considerably: the town had become the hub of the Kinta Valley, and a center for tin collection and smelting. Many of the buildings in the old colonial center date from Ipoh's days as "The Town That Tin Built".

**RAILWAY STATION AND HOTEL.** Undoubtedly, Ipoh's Moorish-style railway station, topped with domes and cupolas, is the city's best-known colonial edifice. It is known to the local residents as the Taj Mahal of Ipoh. An advertisement from a 1923 guidebook promises "First Class Accommodation", "Excellent Cuisine", "Electric Light, Fans & Lift". The latter still applies at today's Station Hotel, which is being upgraded to an international hotel. From the 595-foot-long verandah one can enjoy panoramic views of Ipoh and its limestone crags. With some imagination one can also imagine the old hotel in its heyday, when planters stretched out in their rattan chairs and surveyed the very same view.

**CITY HALL AND HIGH COURT.** Ipoh's colonial administrators were far-sighted enough to build some enduring public buildings during their tenure. The neo-classical City Hall (Dewan Bandaraya) opposite the railway station, and the neighboring High Court (Mahkamah Tinggi) built in 1881 are two such architectural treasures.

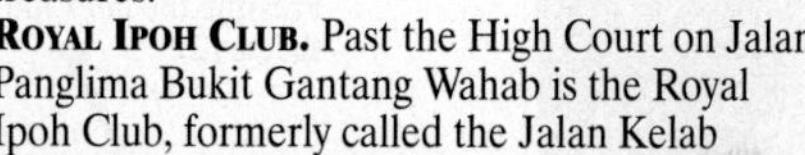

**ROYAL IPOH CLUB.** Past the High Court on Jalan Panglima Bukit Gantang Wahab is the Royal Ipoh Club, formerly called the Jalan Kelab (Club) for obvious reasons. Facing the Padang, the green playing fields, the black-and-white Tudor-style clubhouse architecture is reminiscent of Kuala Lumpur's Royal Selangor Club, which dates from the same era.

**ST MICHAEL'S SCHOOL.** Opposite the Royal Ipoh Club on Jalan S. P. Seenivasagam is the imposing three-story St Michael's School, which has been designated a historical

"THE TIDE WAS HIGH AND THE RIVER BRIMMING FULL, LOOKING AS IF IT MUST DROWN ALL THE FOREST, AND THE TRESTLE WORK ROOTS ON WHICH THE MANGROVES ARE HOISTED WERE ALL SUBMERGED." ISABELLA BIRD, *THE GOLDEN CHERSONESE*

building on the nation's conservation listing. The school features decorated gables and wide arched verandahs that run the entire length of the building.

## OLD CHINATOWN

As the original mercantile center of Ipoh, Chinatown began when Dato' Panglima Kinta, the district chieftain, sold land lots to the Chinese for RM25 a block. In 1882 there were only four thousand Chinese miners in the Kinta, but six years later their numbers had swelled to 38,000. Chinatown prospered, and by the turn of the century the road grid between the railway station and the river was lined with shophouses. Today, many of these buildings are still in their original state because Ipoh town expanded across the river and into the suburbs, thus sparing the old center from demolition. About forty late-19th- and early-20th-century shophouses have been listed as historical buildings.

**JALAN LEECH SHOPHOUSES.** Original shophouses on Jalan Leech still use split-bamboo chick-blinds painted with garish advertisements to shade their wares from the sun, and pedestrians can stroll along the sidewalk, a covered passage designed to keep out the heat and traffic. One of Ipoh's best-known food treats is the delicacy *popiah*. Bean sprouts, grated radish, carrots, chopped prawns, and crab meat form the filling of this spring-roll-type snack, which is wrapped in a thin pastry mantle and eaten with a tasty sauce made of chili, tamarind, and sweet potatoes. Shophouses on Jalan Leech are renowned for this delicacy. At the Hall of Mirrors, a barber shop turned coffee house, patrons can also enjoy caramel custard, another Ipoh favorite.

**FMS BAR**
Conveniently situated across the road from the Padang, Ipoh's old playing fields, and the venue for cricket and football matches, is the FMS Bar. A landmark since colonial days, when rubber planters, merchants and mining bosses rubbed shoulders at its renowned bar, the FMS, short for Federated Malay States, still retains an aura of the old days.

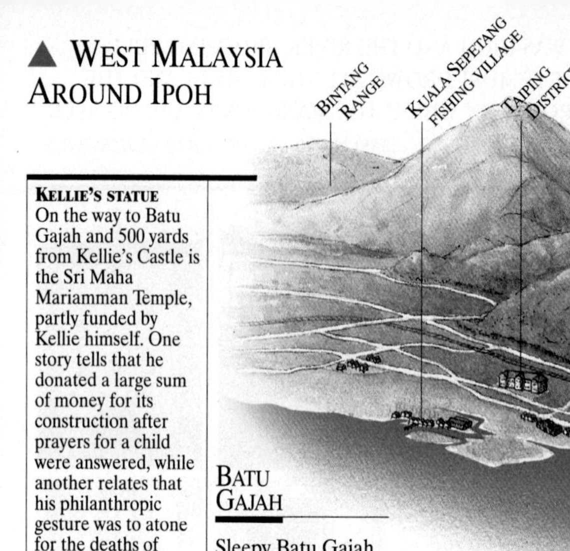


**KELLIE'S STATUE**
On the way to Batu Gajah and 500 yards from Kellie's Castle is the Sri Maha Mariamman Temple, partly funded by Kellie himself. One story tells that he donated a large sum of money for its construction after prayers for a child were answered, while another relates that his philanthropic gesture was to atone for the deaths of Indian laborers working on his dream castle. An image of Tuan Kellie, clad in his typical planter's attire of "Bombay Bloomer" shorts and solar topee, shares the temple's roof frieze along with Indian deities.

## BATU GAJAH

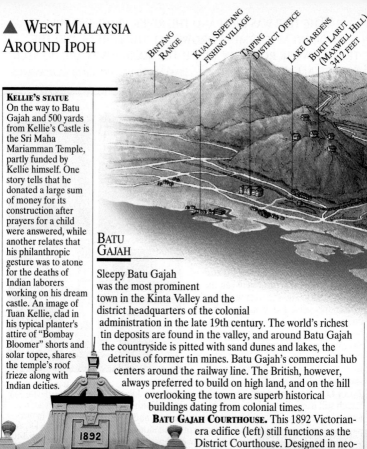

Sleepy Batu Gajah was the most prominent town in the Kinta Valley and the district headquarters of the colonial administration in the late 19th century. The world's richest tin deposits are found in the valley, and around Batu Gajah the countryside is pitted with sand dunes and lakes, the detritus of former tin mines. Batu Gajah's commercial hub centers around the railway line. The British, however, always preferred to build on high land, and on the hill overlooking the town are superb historical buildings dating from colonial times.

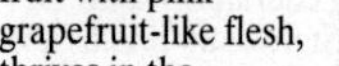

**BATU GAJAH COURTHOUSE.** This 1892 Victorian-era edifice (left) still functions as the District Courthouse. Designed in neo-classical style, it is the most imposing of Batu Gajah's colonial buildings. Architectural features include keystone arches, decorated gables (below), and a covered walkway between the courts.

**KELLIE'S CASTLE.** This unfinished palatial folly, located just outside Batu Gajah on the Gopeng Road, was the brainchild of William Kellie Smith, a Scottish-born rubber baron who first arrived in Malaya in 1900. The two-story brick mansion, with its square tower, ramparts, and arched Moorish-style hallways, was almost completed, when Kellie died of pneumonia while on vacation in Europe. Apparently he had made the trip to buy elevators for his lavish castle-like home, which still remains incomplete today.

**POMELOS OF TAMBUN**
The pomelo, a citrus fruit with pink grapefruit-like flesh, thrives in the limestone soil at Tambun, east of Ipoh. Prized by the Chinese as religious offerings, their prices fluctuate according to the festival calendar. Orchards sell the fruit fresh from the tree, but it is also available from stalls lining the south-bound road from Ipoh just past the Sam Poh Tong cave temple.

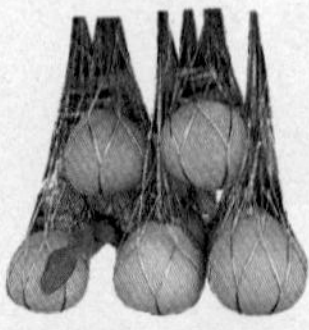

## PAPAN

Chinese shophouses ● *88–90* predominate in this old tin-mining town on the Pusing road south of Ipoh. The future of Papan is uncertain, as recent discoveries of rich tin deposits under the town center have prompted suggestions that the entire town be removed to allow the tin to be mined. Conservationists oppose the move because Papan's old center contains many historical buildings.

**ISTANA RAJA BILAH.** On the outskirts of Papan there is an old two-story residence which was once the home of Raja Bilah, a

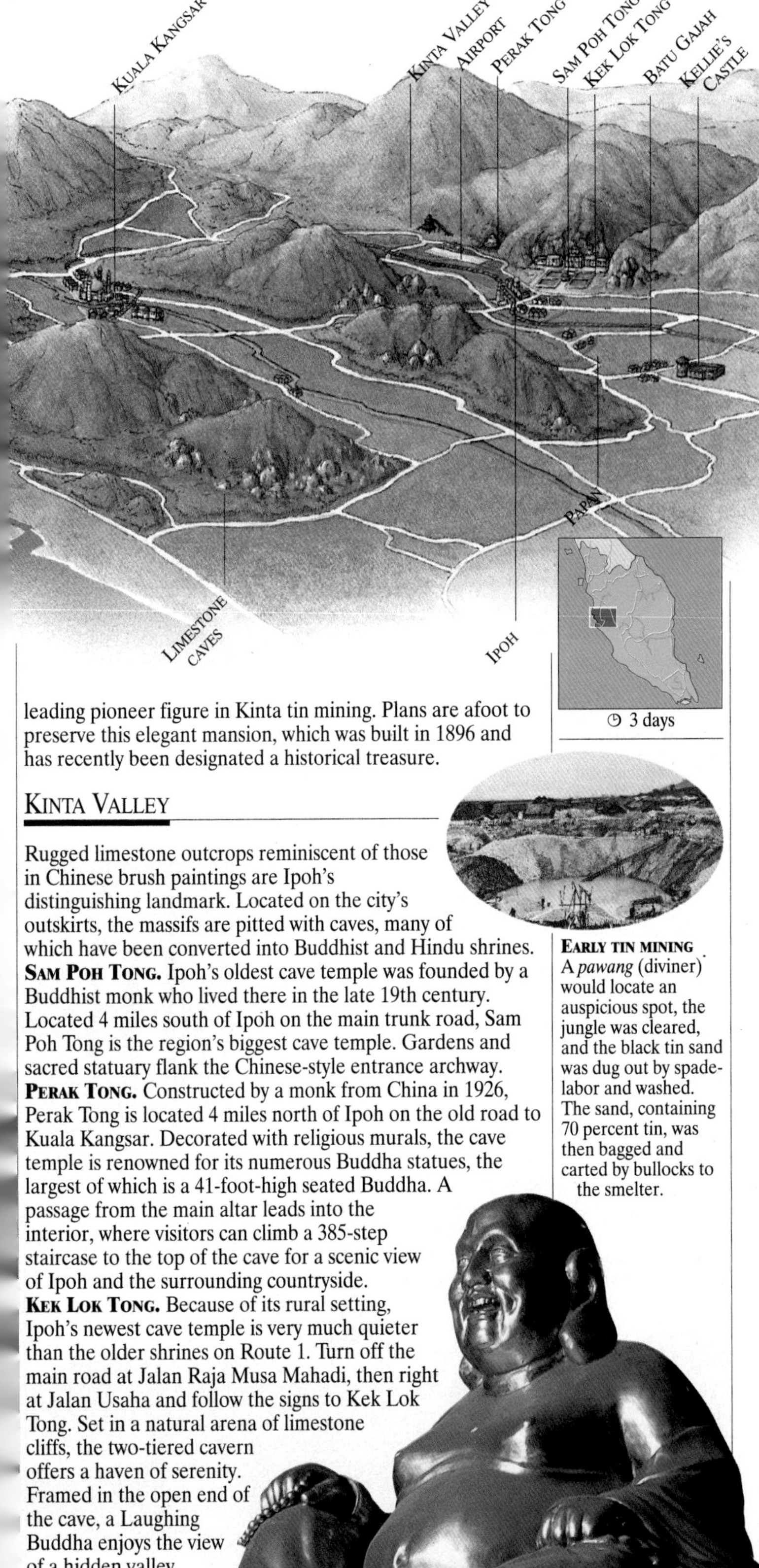


leading pioneer figure in Kinta tin mining. Plans are afoot to preserve this elegant mansion, which was built in 1896 and has recently been designated a historical treasure.

## Kinta Valley

Rugged limestone outcrops reminiscent of those in Chinese brush paintings are Ipoh's distinguishing landmark. Located on the city's outskirts, the massifs are pitted with caves, many of which have been converted into Buddhist and Hindu shrines.

**Sam Poh Tong.** Ipoh's oldest cave temple was founded by a Buddhist monk who lived there in the late 19th century. Located 4 miles south of Ipoh on the main trunk road, Sam Poh Tong is the region's biggest cave temple. Gardens and sacred statuary flank the Chinese-style entrance archway.

**Perak Tong.** Constructed by a monk from China in 1926, Perak Tong is located 4 miles north of Ipoh on the old road to Kuala Kangsar. Decorated with religious murals, the cave temple is renowned for its numerous Buddha statues, the largest of which is a 41-foot-high seated Buddha. A passage from the main altar leads into the interior, where visitors can climb a 385-step staircase to the top of the cave for a scenic view of Ipoh and the surrounding countryside.

**Kek Lok Tong.** Because of its rural setting, Ipoh's newest cave temple is very much quieter than the older shrines on Route 1. Turn off the main road at Jalan Raja Musa Mahadi, then right at Jalan Usaha and follow the signs to Kek Lok Tong. Set in a natural arena of limestone cliffs, the two-tiered cavern offers a haven of serenity. Framed in the open end of the cave, a Laughing Buddha enjoys the view of a hidden valley.

**Early tin mining**
A *pawang* (diviner) would locate an auspicious spot, the jungle was cleared, and the black tin sand was dug out by spade-labor and washed. The sand, containing 70 percent tin, was then bagged and carted by bullocks to the smelter.

## KUALA KANGSAR

Situated on a bend beside the broad Perak River, with views beyond to the mauve mountains of the main range, Kuala Kangsar, the state's royal capital, is a most picturesque town. From Ipoh, travelers can take the old highway via Sungai Siput, dominated by a conical limestone hill, or the alternative route via the new expressway (*lebuhraya*) which climbs the hills outside Ipoh and burrows through a jungle-clad mountain. This riverine town has been the seat of Perak's royalty since Sultan Muzafar's reign in the 1740's. Previously, there had been various royal capitals further downstream on the Perak River. The town center – a collection of old shophouses – clusters on the northern bank of the small Sungai Kangsar, the river which gave the settlement its name. Apart from its major attractions, Kuala Kangsar also boasts Malaysia's oldest rubber tree, one of the original experimental trees that initiated the nation's phenomenal rise to become the world's top rubber exporter. The tree that changed the face of Malaysia stands beside the District Office at the corner of Jalan Raja Chulan and Jalan Tun Abdul Razak. Another old rubber tree can be found beside the former Residency, now a girls' school.

**ISTANA KENANGAN.** More like a gingerbread house than a palace, the whimsical Istana Kenangan is a showpiece of Malay traditional architecture. Located near the mosque on Jalan Istana, the palace now serves as the state's Royal Museum, housing royal heirlooms, exhibits, and historical photographs of the Perak Sultanate. Istana Kenangan was built in 1931 as a temporary palace for Sultan Iskandar and was constructed without the use of nails. Above the shuttered windows are masterful wood carvings in floral designs. Beside the Palace Museum is the old royal barge once used for boating parties on the Perak River.

**UBUDIAH MOSQUE.** Gleaming onion domes and black-and-white marble minarets create an esthetic combination at Kuala Kangsar's splendid Ubudiah Mosque (top, left) located south of town, on Jalan Istana. Sultan Idris laid the foundation

Ubudiah Mosque in Kuala Kangsar.

**ISTANA KENANGAN WALL PANELS**
Wall panels made of split bamboo or the bark of the bertam palm are a feature of many traditional houses, including the Istana Kenangan, which was built without using nails. Woven into decorative designs, these panels could be prefabricated and then merely slotted into place when the house frame was constructed. The intricate panels of Kuala Kangsar's old palace have been enhanced by the brilliant yellow, black, and white color-scheme which graphically highlights the different designs.

stone for the town's most famous landmark in 1913 but died before its completion. World War One interrupted construction, as did a couple of rogue royal elephants who apparently ran amok, ruining the Italian-marble floor. Sultan Abdul Jalil officially opened the Moorish-style mosque in 1917. The mosque is reputably one of the most beautiful in Malaysia today. The pool for ablutions before prayers is a separate domed pavilion supported by red marble pillars. Beside the mosque is the Royal Mausoleum, the final resting place of Perak's rulers since the mid-18th century.

**Istana Iskandariah.** Splendidly sited on a hilltop overlooking the Perak River, the Istana Iskandariah is the residence of Sultan Azlan Shah, Perak's reigning head of state. A mixture of Islamic and Art Deco styles, the grandiose palace was constructed in the 1930's to replace the temporary Istana Iskandariah. Surrounded by spacious grounds, the palace is closed to the public, but views of it can be had from the gates on the Perak River side.

**The Malay College.** Facing a swathe of playing fields is Malaysia's premier residential school for boys, opened in 1905. Once the prerogative of royal offspring, the College is now open to all boys provided they demonstrate the academic excellence for which the school is famed. The colonnaded, brick neo-classical institution was originally red, but today is a dazzling white, providing a splendid contrast against the green of the spacious fields. The college register reads like a "Who's Who" of Malaysian public life, and includes prominent politicians, numerous judges, and royal leaders.

**Isabella Bird in Kuala Kangsar**

When intrepid adventuress Isabella Bird arrived in Malaya in 1879, the British were just beginning their push into the interior. After a twelve-hour journey on elephant-back (below), Bird stayed with Hugh Low, the British resident, who shared his house and his dinner table with two apes. Her stay in the royal town makes one long for those days: "Three days of solitude, meals in the company of apes, elephant excursions, wandering about alone, and free, open air, tropical life in the midst of all luxuries and comforts, have been very enchanting."

## TAIPING

Center of the rich tin-mining district of Larut, Taiping's main claim to historical fame was the fierce inter-clan fighting which erupted there between rival Chinese factions and resulted in colonial interference and the appointment of a British resident. Backed by a series of forested hills which trap the moisture-laden coastal clouds, Taiping has the heaviest rainfall in Peninsular Malaysia. In fact, betting in its coffee shops centers around what time the daily downpour will take place. The regular afternoon showers make for cool and pleasant evenings, when the nightlife revolves around the prolific outdoor eating stalls. Downtown Taiping has an unhurried air, for much of the state's industry is concentrated around Ipoh and the Kinta Valley. Streets of old shophouses, 19th-century townhouses, temples, mosques, and colonial buildings contribute to Taiping's old-world charm.

**MUZIUM PERAK (PERAK MUSEUM).** Malaysia's oldest museum is located on Jalan Taming Sari opposite the nation's oldest prison. Housed in a classical-style colonial building, the museum owes its inception to Hugh Low, the third British resident of Perak who presided at the opening in 1883. The exhibits include a fascinating weapons gallery, with spears for tiger-driving and a collection of krises including one magical blade with forty-seven waves, prehistoric stone and iron implements, handicrafts of the Negrito and Orang Asli, and a popular natural-history section.

**LARUT AND MATANG DISTRICT OFFICE.** Taiping's most outstanding example of neo-colonial architecture is the imposing district offices on Jalan Kota. Built in 1879, the two-story edifice was formerly the state council chambers, when Taiping was the administrative center of Perak. Decorative gables and scalloped archways contribute to the overall richness of this handsome public building.

**BUKIT LARUT (MAXWELL HILL).** Taiping seems to have more than its fair share of Malaysia's oldest institutions (railway, prison, museum), and in addition it

**MALAY KRIS AND SHEATHS**
The kris is considered by the Malays as a sacred heirloom. It is believed that the dagger protects its owner, usually the head of the house, and his family members.

also boasts the nation's oldest hill resort. In contrast to Fraser's Hill and the Cameron Highlands, little has changed at Bukit Larut - the bungalows atop the 3412-foot hill are still in their original state and there has been no redevelopment or commercialization. Private cars are not allowed up the steep approach. On clear days, the panorama extends from Penang to Pulau Pangkor. A resthouse and bungalows provide overnight accommodation.

**LAKE GARDENS.** Created from an exhausted tin mine in the 1890's, Taiping's Lake Gardens are its crowning glory. Huge *angsana* (rain trees) shade the park's road from the equatorial sun and, when in bloom, shower the pavements with "golden rain". On the lawns beside the lake, t'ai chi enthusiasts keep fit, and the park's trails are busy with joggers. One of Malaysia's oldest zoos is located in the 155-acre gardens along with a golf course and a floating restaurant. The resthouse overlooks the Lake Gardens.

## MATANG

On the way to Kuala Sepatang from Taiping, the road passes through delightful kampungs. During the mid-1800's, Matang was under the control of Long Ja'afar, a Malay chieftain, who was responsible for opening up the Larut area for tin mining.

**KOTA NGAH IBRAHIM.** The walls of this former fort at Matang date back to the 1860's and 1870's, when Long Ja'afar and his son Ngah Ibrahim were embroiled in the Larut Wars. Ngah Ibrahim was implicated in the murder of Perak's British resident J. W. W. Birch and exiled to the Seychelles, where there is still a Malay community that traces its roots back to these times. Maharaja Lela, another chief involved in the assassination, was reportedly hung from the tree which still stands in the fort's grounds.

**KUALA SEPATANG.** Once a bustling port for the rich tin-mining region of Larut and connected by rail to Taiping, Kuala Sepatang is now a ghost of its former self ,when it was known as Port Weld. However, it is an interesting fishing town on an estuary surrounded by mangrove forests ■ *20–1*. A nature park with boardwalks over the wetlands is in the making. The riverside restaurants are renowned for their fresh seafood.

**EARLY HISTORY OF TAIPING**

In the early 1800's Larut was controlled by Malay chiefs under the rule of the Perak sultanate, but it was known for its rich alluvial tin. The Chinese arrived in 1848, when Long Ja'afar, the chief of Larut, opened up the region and invited miners to work in the district. His son Ngah Ibrahim, who later figured in the assassination of Perak's first British resident, took over the mines in 1858, but by then the population had swelled and a few years later struggles broke out between the various Chinese clans. These feuds developed into fierce inter-clan fighting, and both the lucrative tin and opium trades suffered. The quarrels also affected the Malays, who were having succession problems in the Perak sultanate. Eventually the British intervened by taking a gunboat up the Perak River, and installing a resident to look after their affairs at Larut. Chinatown was renamed Taiping, and true to its name, which means "everlasting peace", the feuding between the clans stopped. Taiping developed into an attractive and peaceful colonial town.

**THE SPICE TRADE**
The name Penang derives from the Malay word for betel nut. Pulau Pinang means "island of the betel nut". The tree from which the nut is obtained, *Areca catechu*, once thrived there. During the days of the spice trade, Penang was a trading center for cloves, nutmeg, cinnamon, betel nut, and Acehnese pepper, first planted in 1790. The southern hills of Penang are redolent of clove and nutmeg to this day.

**LIGHT'S LANDING**
When Francis Light took possession of Penang in 1786, landing at Cape Penaigre (now Georgetown), he found the cape covered with tough ironwood trees, leaving no open land on which to establish camp. Light is said to have filled a cannon with coins and fired it into the jungle. He then equipped the onlooking natives with sturdy Dutch axes. The campsite was cleared in record time.

## HISTORY

Ever since its foundation two centuries ago, Penang has been a favored destination of travelers, as much for its scenic beauty as for its places of ethnic and colonial interest. Penang state consists of two separate portions – the island and a strip of the adjacent mainland. The two are connected by ferry and the Penang Bridge. Penang's capital, Georgetown, lies on the northeast cape of Penang Island. The city, sometimes referred to simply (and erroneously) as "Penang", is today the second largest in Malaysia. The historic center comprises a large number of elderly shophouses, dating mostly from the 19th or early 20th century. Their architecture, often called "Straits Eclectic", is a rich mixture of European, Arabic, Chinese, Indian, and Malay influences. Scattered among the shophouses are some fine Art Deco and Early Modern buildings. Penang was the first British settlement in the Melaka Straits ● *35–6*, established to provide the East India Company's vessels with a necessary port of call on the long voyage to China. The island offered both a safe harbor and a commanding strategic position at the northern end of the Melaka Straits. It was ceded in 1786 by the sultan of Kedah to the East India Company's representative, Captain Francis Light, who named it Prince of Wales Island. To increase the island's scanty population, Light, as Superintendent of Penang, gave land away to anyone who would settle there. Penang attracted large numbers of Asians: Indians, Chinese, Malays, Burmese, Thais, Sumatrans, and Javanese. Soon immigrants began to arrive from farther afield: the island's early population included substantial communities of Armenians, Jews, and Persians and dozens of other races. During the Napoleonic Wars control of the China trade became the East India Company's first priority. The need for shipyards in the Straits grew increasingly urgent. Penang was named the Fourth Presidency of British India in 1805 and a governor appointed to administer the settlement. Hopes for the new presidency ran high, but Penang was soon to be overshadowed by

the success of Singapore. By 1819, the focus of trade and power had shifted southwards, to the other end of the Melaka Straits. Penang remained a backwater for the next half-century, until British intervention in the affairs of the Malay States brought growth and prosperity to the island once more. The development of tin mining and plantations ■ *24–5* in the hinterland of Malaya gave new impetus to trade, and Penang became an important regional and international port. The boom in trade was accompanied by a great increase in population, both of which continued until the Rubber Crash of the late 1920's and the outbreak of World War Two several years later. Penang experienced its golden age during the early 1920's. Travelers came by steamship and the white-hulled cruisers of the P&O Line to visit the famous "Pearl of the Orient". Favored arrivals would be taken up by Penang society and experience a way of life far beyond the means of most people in Europe and America – a life conducted among cosmopolitan people of every nationality, in airy, sprawling mansions and luxurious clubs. They would pass their days in an endless round of riding, swimming, cricket, motoring expeditions, and parties by the score. During World War Two, Penang became Japanese-occupied territory ● *38–9*, along with the rest of Malaya. After liberation by Allied forces in 1945, the Municipality of Penang continued to grow. Georgetown was declared a city in 1957. During the 1960's and 1970's, however, the focus of attention shifted to Malaysia's new capital, Kuala Lumpur, and Penang began to stagnate once again. The final blow came in 1974, when the island's status as a free port was withdrawn. Under Malaysia's then Chief Minister, Dr Lim Chong Eu, Penang was declared an industrial free-trade zone, and the island's second reawakening began. In spite of growing industrialization, the island's fascinating mix of history and scenic beauty survives, making it a continuing favorite destination with vacationists from neighboring countries as well as those from faraway places.

**The E & O Hotel**

The focus of Penang's glittering 1920's society was the Eastern & Oriental Hotel, established in 1885. Managed by the Sarkies brothers (who also owned Singapore's famous Raffles Hotel), the E & O, with its immaculate lawn along North Beach, boasted "the longest seafront east of Suez". Arshak

Sarkies, the manager, was an indulgent man who would much rather run a fine hotel for pleasure than for profit; the E & O was soon widely known as the "Eat and Owe". Not surprisingly, bankruptcy was declared in the 1930's. The hotel now turns a profit under new management, but its days of glory seem to be well behind it – at least for the present.

**MALAYAN RAILWAYS**
The staid and handsome Customs Building near the waterfront, with its prominent clock tower, was originally the Malayan Railway Building. Opened in 1905, it was known as "the only railway without a rail". Tickets were sold at the station for journeys all over Malaya. A traveler would catch the ferry to Butterworth Terminal on the mainland, from where the rest of the journey could be accomplished by train.

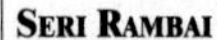

**SERI RAMBAI**
Among the cannons at Fort Cornwallis is Seri Rambai, a 17th-century Dutch piece seized from Kuala Selangor. It was presented to the sultan of Selangor by the sultan of Aceh, whose forefather had captured it in an attack on the Johor sultanate.

The original colonial town was planned by Francis Light. South of Fort Cornwallis, a grid was mapped out to create quarters for the Asian population. The site was swampy and polluted, a hotbed of contagious tropical diseases. Assessment was based on every 20 foot of frontage, encouraging the development of shophouses, with their high, narrow fronts. "Five-foot ways" introduced by regulation in Raffles's Singapore also became a typical feature here. Trade was carried on along Beach Street. During the late 19th century, the eastern waterfront was gradually extended by the addition of reclaimed land up to Weld Quay, as new shipping offices and warehouses were built. The town spread haphazardly beyond the initial grid as far as the mid-19th-century boundaries of Prangin Canal and Transfer Road – the latter named after the transfer of colonial rule from the Indian office to the Straits Settlements in 1867 ● *35–6*. Later on, the town was subjected to serious planning, with new residential districts and tree-lined roads leading to the interior of the island. The European settlement moved from its original site on the North Beach to new suburbs around the Residency at the end of the 19th century. Both these areas are still characterized by charming bungalows, often with mews and servants' quarters and usually surrounded by extensive gardens.

“PINANG (PENANG) CAME INTO OUR POSSESSION IN 1786, THROUGH THE ENTERPRISE OF MR. LIGHT...”

ISABELLA BIRD, *THE GOLDEN CHERSONESE*

## CAMPBELL STREET

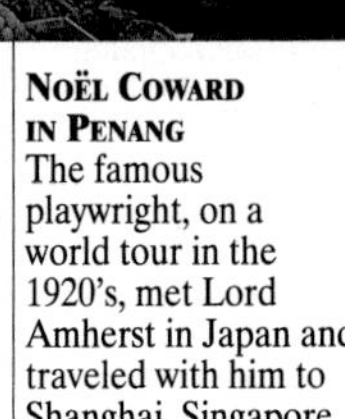

Penang’s “wet markets” promise a lively morning. The turn-of-the-century Campbell Street Market spills out on to nearby Carnarvon Street, and coffee shops ● *66–7* in the vicinity provide a variety of breakfasts.
**KOMTAR.** The Kompleks Tuan Abdul Razak (KOMTAR) is a sixty-five-story government building housing state and municipal offices and a shopping complex. The viewing gallery and restaurant at the top offer spectacular views of Georgetown.

**NOËL COWARD IN PENANG**
The famous playwright, on a world tour in the 1920’s, met Lord Amherst in Japan and traveled with him to Shanghai, Singapore and Penang before proceeding west to Colombo. In Penang, they visited the Snake Temple and the zoo, which was then run by a Buddhist monk.

## LIGHT STREET

**FORT CORNWALLIS.** A stockade of nibong palm trees was erected on the tip of the cape where Francis Light first landed. Fort Cornwallis was rebuilt in 1805 as a star-shaped brick structure with a surrounding moat and cannons pointing out to sea. As the first building of the East India Company, the fort accommodated offices, a chapel, a signal station and quarters for the provosts and Indian sepoys.
**THE PADANG.** Facing the fort was the Padang, an open ground used for military exercises, and later by cricket and football clubs. At the other end is the Town Hall, built in 1880. However, Penang’s administration soon expanded beyond the confines of the building and the City Hall, adjacent to it, was erected in 1903. Facing the sea are the State Assembly buildings, formerly the Recorder’s Courts, built in the early 19th century. The adjacent bank building was once a private mansion owned by a Chinese notable, Foo Tye Sin. Koh Seang Tat’s fountain, next to the Town Hall, and Cheah Chen Eok’s Victoria Jubilee Clock Tower on the roundabout are two monuments donated by Chinese gentlemen to the Penang Municipality in 1883 and 1897 respectively.
**CONVENT OF THE HOLY INFANT JESUS.** At the end of Light Street is the Convent of the Holy Infant Jesus, a French mission started by three sisters in 1852. Near the entrance is the New Chapel, consecrated in 1932, whose prominent feature is a set of French stained-glass windows. The convent was used as a Japanese base during World War Two; captured officers of the USS *Grenadier* were tortured in the school’s Block C classrooms. Also within the grounds is the Government House of the British East India Company, the best surviving example of Anglo-Indian architecture in Georgetown, built by Lt-Governor Robert Farquhar in 1805.
**SUPREME COURT AND DEWAN SRI PINANG.** The Supreme Court at Light Street was built in 1904. In the grounds is a memorial to James Richardson Logan, a Scottish lawyer well known for defending Asian causes. Opposite the courthouse is Dewan Sri Pinang, the city’s main performance hall, designed and erected by the Public Works Department.

A French stained-glass window in the Convent of the Holy Infant Jesus.

**Secret-society wars**
The early colonial government was ill-equipped to handle Penang's heterogeneous Asian populace, and the communities lived largely by their own laws. Secret societies proliferated. Later they controlled the island's gambling, prostitution, opium smuggling and labor recruitment rings. During the secret-society wars of 1867, the Hokkien-dominated Khian Teik and the Malay Red Flag societies were pitted against the mainly Cantonese Ghee Hin and a Malay-led society, the White Flag. The societies were dissolved in 1890 and their assets transferred to the management of newly formed religious, charitable, and mutual benefit associations.

**Clan jetties**
Along Weld Quay, 19th-century *attap*-roofed houses on stilts recall the clan villages of southern China. Each jetty is populated by relatives of the same surname – Chew, Lim, Tan etc. At the end of Chew Jetty, Burmese trawlers bring in timber and low-grade rubber to barter for bicycles and other Western goods. The jetties' inhabitants were traditionally fishermen and stevedores.

## Lebuh Acheh and Armenian Street

**Khoo Kongsi Temple.** Since the 1830's, Hokkien Chinese traders, many of whom had ties with north Sumatra across the Strait, moved into this part of Georgetown. They built a stronghold, with majestic clan temples sited in large courtyards whose narrow entrances, flanked by the clansmen's humble row houses, belied the magnificence within. The five most powerful Hokkien clans, Yeoh, Cheah, Khoo, Lim, and Tan, were involved in the Hokkien-dominated secret society; each clan had its own clan temple and enclave in this medieval-style quarter. The newest and most imposing of the clan temples is the Khoo Kongsi, built in 1907 in late Ching dynasty style. It stands in the granite-paved compound known as Cannon Square, a name that recalls the damage caused by

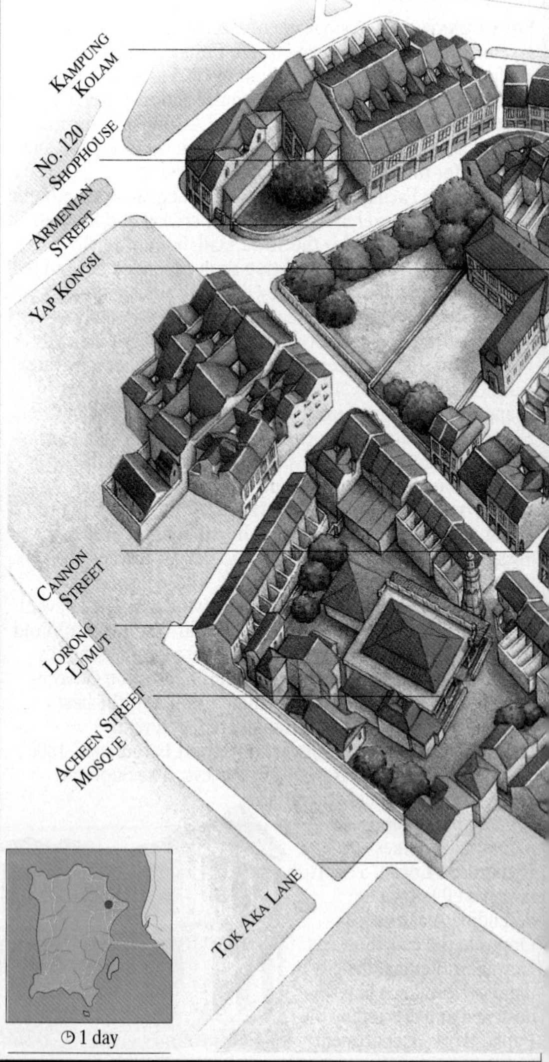

"THIS IS A TRULY BRILLIANT PLACE (GEORGETOWN) UNDER A BRILLIANT SKY, BUT OH I WEARY FOR THE WILDS!"

ISABELLA BIRD, *THE GOLDEN CHERSONESE*

cannon fired in this direction to quell the street battles of the Penang riots. The temple faces a stage where *wayang* (Chinese opera) performances take place on auspicious occasions such as the birthdays of the deities.

**ACHEEN STREET MOSQUE.** The mosque was built in 1808 by Tengku Syed Hussain, an Acehnese pepper trader of royal descent who settled in Penang in 1792. He became a great leader in the island's first urban Malay community. The early brick-and-timber houses in the walled mosque compound are survivors of the time when the surrounding area, south of the official British settlement, was a large kampung.

**NO. 120 SHOPHOUSE.** At 120 Armenian Street is the shophouse where Dr Sun Yat-sen and his supporters in Penang planned the Canton Uprising of 1911, a historic event which contributed to the overthrow of the Manchu dynasty.

**ROADSIDE TREES**
Many of Penang's avenues are lined with trees over a century old: angsana or rain trees (*Pterocarpus indicus*) and Cuban royal palms.

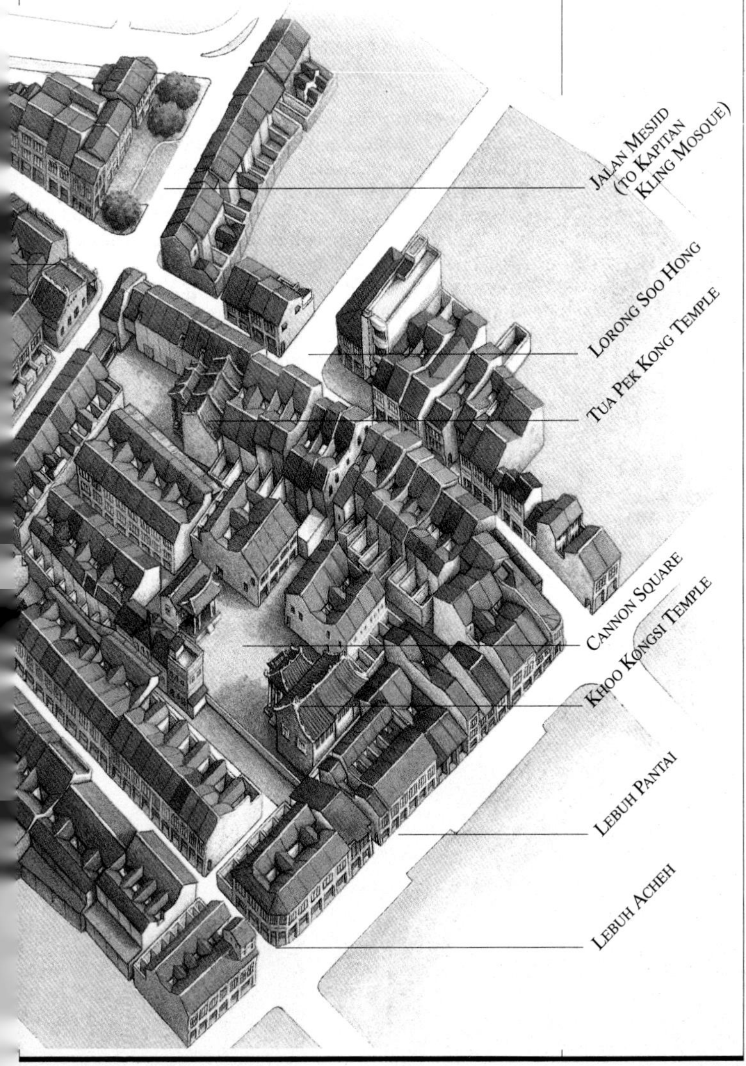

JALAN MESJID (TO KAPITAN KLING MOSQUE)
LORONG SOO HONG
TUA PEK KONG TEMPLE
CANNON SQUARE
KHOO KONGSI TEMPLE
LEBUH PANTAI
LEBUH ACHEH

Two Indian dancers on the door of a jewelry shop welcome customers.

**Kapitan Kling**
The early Indian Muslim settlers who came from British India were called Chulia or Kling after two ancient South Indian kingdoms. Their first leader was Kapitan Kling, founder of the famous mosque.

## Pitt Street

Pitt Street, at the edge of Light's old town, contains Penang's oldest places of worship. Christianity, Chinese traditional religion, Hinduism and Islam are all represented here, their shrines standing within yards of each other. Interestingly, they line up in rough correspondence to the historically ethnic character of the streets. St George's Church stands at the end of Bishop and Church Streets, where the European and Eurasian communities resided; Goddess of Mercy Temple is at the end of China Street, Mariamman Temple near Market Street (Penang's "Little India"), and Kapitan Kling Mosque at the end of Chulia Street, where many Indian Muslims took up residence.

**St George's Church.** This, the first Anglican church in Malaysia, was designed and built in 1817–18 by the military engineer Captain Robert Smith, who also painted a series of magnificent views of Penang. Smith's oil paintings are among the historic views of the island on display at the Penang State Museum and Art Gallery.

**Goddess of Mercy (Kuan Yin) Temple.** The temple was founded in 1800 as the seat of a Chinese tribunal which represented both the Hokkien and Cantonese communities. Chinese opera and hand-puppet theater performances are staged several times a year on the granite-paved square in front of the temple. At one corner of the square stands an octagonal public well, no longer in use.

**Mariamman Temple.** On Queen Street stands the Mariamman Temple, religious focus of the surrounding Hindu community. The temple was built in 1833 and houses images of the goddess Mariamman in her various aspects, sculpted by artists from Madras. Several times a year, the goddess' chariot passes in procession from the temple and through the streets of Little India.

**Kapitan Kling Mosque.** This mosque (below) has been enlarged several times over the years, gradually being transformed into a striking example of colonial-Mogul architecture. In the grounds are early graves, a cannon, a public well, and a minaret.

## OTHER CITY SIGHTS

**THE PENANG BUDDHIST ASSOCIATION.** Located on Anson Road, this unusual colonial-style (1925) Buddhist temple complex contains a miniature Chinese pagoda, mother-of-pearl furniture, Victorian cast-iron, and Czech glass chandeliers, reflecting the eclectic taste of the Straits Chinese *baba* and *nyonya* ▲ *202–9*.

**PULAU TIKIS.** This historic community has grown to form a part of Georgetown over the years. It incorporates the Eurasian village Kampung Serani, founded around 1810 by refugees from religious persecution in Siam during the reign of Phya Tak. Some timber houses of unique character survive on land once reserved for poor Catholics. The adjacent Church of the Immaculate Conception was built in 1899.

**WAT CHAYAMANGKALARAM.** A Burmese village once existed at Pulau Tikis; its oldest building, still standing, is the stupa, built in 1800. The Burmese community was superseded by a Thai one, which built its own temple, Wat Chayamangkalaram (1845) across the street. In the main hall is one of the world's largest reclining Buddhas, and a wheel which tells your fortune for a coin. Bangkok Lane, adjacent to the temple, is a charming street of shophouses with colored glass window panes.

**NATTUKOTTAI CHETTIAR TEMPLE.** Managed by the South Indian moneylending clan known as the Chettiar, this temple is similar to others of its kind in Melaka and Singapore. It features two main aisles and a cross-axis hung with paintings, wooden figurines, and chandeliers.

## FURTHER ALONG THE COAST

**TANJUNG TOKONG.** This is the site of a fishing village established several years before Light's landing by refugees from Manchu China. A temple is dedicated to the founder of the settlement, deified as Tua Pek Kong. Around it are several excellent seafood restaurants.

**TANJUNG BUNGAH.** The "Cape of Flowers" marks the beginning of Penang's most famous beach, which continues along the coast to Batu Ferringhi. The beach is lined with jungle and casuarina trees. A complex of hotels front the sea at Batu Ferringhi, where skiing, windsurfing, and sailing are popular.

**QUEEN VICTORIA STATUE**
This bronze statue at Victoria Green was paid for by public subscription, and erected by members of the Chinese Recreation Club. During the Japanese occupation most of the town's cast-iron gates and balconies were plundered for scrap, but the statue survived. Two conflicting stories account for this: a Japanese officer wrote that he concealed the statue with a huge signboard, while a contractor claimed he had carried it away and hidden it in a chicken-coop.

**GURNEY DRIVE FOOD CENTER.**
Morning joggers habitually reward themselves here with a breakfast of herbal pork soup; evening strollers have a wide variety of hawker foods ● *64–5* to choose from.

**BATU FERRINGHI**
Portuguese sailors arriving from India in the 16th century obtained fresh water at a small rocky island off the Penang coast. Batu Ferringhi, or Foreigner's Rock, has lent its name to the beaches facing it. These same beaches now constitute Penang's prime tourist destination.

**CLIMBING PENANG HILL**
For nearly a century, the approved methods of ascent were by sedan chair and Acehnese pony, along a road from the Botanic Gardens, built and maintained with Indian convict labor. In 1922, after several fiascos, the funicular railway from Ayer Itam was opened. This "modern convenience" fueled a small building boom. The entrance to the Botanic Gardens is located on the jeep track leading to the top of the hill.

**BOTANIC GARDENS WATERFALL**
The garden's Great Waterfall was the first tourist attraction in Penang.

**TELUK BAHANG.** Around Teluk Bahang are a batik workshop, where visitors can watch this Malaysian craft form, and the Penang Butterfly Farm, which features a landscaped enclosure containing thousands of butterflies representing dozens of tropical species.

**MUKA HEAD.** Serving seafood dishes, the rustic Hai Pin (which means "end of the world") Restaurant is located near a fisherman's jetty right at the end of the road. From here you have to walk or take a boat to the lighthouse on Muka Head, or to secluded Pantai Kerachut (Monkey Beach).

## PENANG HILL AND VICINITY

**PENANG HILL.** The first impulse of European settlers in swampy, tropical Georgetown was to head for the hills – specifically, Penang Hill. The high summit of the island, which is really several hills, was already settled by 1810, predating the Indian "hill stations" which it so much resembles. The higher slopes were reserved for important civil servants, the medical officer, and other leading lights; at the very summit, Flagstaff Hill, was the governor's residence, Bel Retiro. Its high flagpole was used to signal to the town. Lower down, the hills were terraced and planted with temperate fruits (hence Strawberry Hill), and the mercantile community built stone cottages into which they would retreat, full of nostalgia, during the hottest months of the year. In the late 1820's, the Asian municipal commissioners' bungalows on the lower terraces became the first non-European residences on the Hill. Today, Penang Hill is highly cosmopolitan, though the atmosphere of a colonial hill station, dotted with historic bungalows and walking trails, still lingers.

**BOTANIC GARDENS.** Penang's Botanic Gardens lie in a deep valley, at the head of which is a magnificent waterfall, the subject of many early-19th-century paintings. In 1884 the

surrounding rock quarry was transformed into "a nursery for the planting of colonial products". Horticultural and economic plants were regularly introduced into Malaya from Kew Gardens in London via the Singapore and Penang botanic gardens. The intent behind the layout of the gardens themselves was to create a seemingly natural yet civilized landscape – a jungle trail to the Lily Pond, a grass mound that served as a bandstand, wooden bridges and bamboo groves along the river that meanders through the Gardens. Today the Gardens have a very good collection of palms, bamboos, flowering trees, and exotic plants. Long-tailed macaques roam freely through the 72-acre grounds, which are surrounded by tropical forested hills.

**TITI KERAWANG AND FISHING VILLAGES.** The hub of Titi Kerawang is the historic village of Balik Pulau, with its old convent. Pulau Betong, Teluk Kumbar, and Gertak Sanggul are pleasant fishing villages from which visitors can hire a boatman to ferry them to quiet, secluded beaches.

**AYER ITAM.** A historic village at the foot of Penang Hill, Ayer Itam is the marketplace for the surrounding poultry and vegetable farms. The area is said to be geomantically auspicious, and the hill is studded with small temples reached by granite stairways. The Buddhist monastery (Kek Lok Si) features landscaped terraces and a beautiful pagoda whose architecture blends Burmese, Chinese, and colonial influences. It is believed to contain ten thousand Buddhas.

## SOUTHERN SIGHTS

**KAMPUNG SERONOK.** The name, which means "happy village", commemorates a historic celebration held here after the liberation of Penang from the Japanese ● *38*. This highly motivated community has its own cultural music and dance troupe, a library, a commercial printing press, and even a model kampung house which is a miniature museum of traditional building materials, household utensils, and farming implements.

**SNAKE TEMPLE.** This Chinese temple was erected in 1850 by followers of the Taoist deity, Chor Soo Kong. Located in the southeast of the island and about 3 miles from the airport, the temple features dozens of snakes, including vipers, coiled around the furniture and sacred objects. They are said to be kept drowsy and harmless by the fumes from the burning incense and joss-sticks. The snake population in the temple is said to increase each July on the birthday of the deity.

**PENANG BRIDGE**
Spanning 4.2 miles, Penang Bridge is the longest in Asia and the third longest in the world. It links Penang with the mainland's north–south highway.

**MALAYSIA'S BIGGEST BUDDHIST TEMPLE**
Commonly known as Kek Lok Si, which means "Temple of Paradise", this place of worship was built in 1890 and took about twenty years to complete. It was founded by a Chinese Buddhist priest from the province of Fujian, China, who reached the shores of Penang in 1887. The seven-tier 100-foot-high pagoda (above) itself was completed only in 1930. A major tourist attraction in Penang, it is the biggest Buddhist temple in Malaysia.

The Snake Temple, Penang.

Chromolithograph by Vincent Brooks from John Cameron's *Our Tropical Possessions in Malayan India*, 1815.

## Butterworth

The journey to Langkawi begins at Butterworth, where the Penang ferry docks. Butterworth is a small bustling mainland town whose focus is its railway station. The Royal Australian Air Force once had a base here, and a 1950's-vintage fighter aircraft, an F-86 Sabre, is displayed beside the main highway.

## Kedah

Kedah is the rice-bowl of Malaysia, a predominantly agricultural state, where rice farmers practice double cropping and enjoy two harvests a year. Houses surrounded by clusters of trees resemble atolls in a sea of ricefields. The state has seen considerable development in recent years, especially in and around the tourist resort of Langkawi. The route from Butterworth to the state capital of Alor Setar passes through Kuala Muda, where the gateway of an 18th-century fort remains, but no trace at all of the 11th-century kingdom once established here; Sungai Patani, Kedah's second-largest town, with its clock tower and Sunday farmers' market; and Langgar, with its royal mausoleum.

**Merdeka Bridge.** The Muda River, which forms the boundary between the states of Penang and Kedah, is spanned by the Merdeka Bridge, built in 1957, the year of Malaya's Independence (*merdeka*).

**Gunung Jerai.** Also called Kedah Peak, this dramatic 3900-foot limestone outcrop is visible from Penang Island and far out to sea, where it is used as a landmark by ships entering the Melaka Strait from the north. A pre-dawn climb promises breathtaking views of the Kedah plains, with ricefields stretching to the horizon.

**Lembah Bujang (Bujang Valley).** At the foot of Gunung Jerai is the Bujang Valley, a rich archeological site dotted with remnants of a Malay Hindu civilization dating from pre-Islamic times. The Archeological Museum at Merbok documents finds from

**Nobat**
*Nobat* performances are intrinsic to the royal ceremonies of the Kedah sultanate. The music is played on the instruments of the royal orchestra – three drums, a gong, and a flute. The *nobat* tradition is hereditary – playing skills and privileges are handed down from father to son. When not in use, the instruments are covered with a cloth of royal yellow. The orchestra is housed in this unusual octagonal building, which stands opposite the Zahir Mosque.

“WHEN THE CANOE REACHED…THE LANGKAWIS, THE GIG GAVE UP THE CHASE. THE CANOE DISAPPEARED SUDDENLY ‘LIKE MAGIC’, THE LABYRINTH OF ISLANDS AND CHANNELS AFFORDING HIDING FOR A FLEET OF A THOUSAND PRAHUS.” JAMES F. AUGUSTIN, 1839

about fifty sites. Candi Bukit Pahat, the “temple of the hill of chiseled stone”, is believed to date from AD 700.

**KUALA KEDAH.** Red trawlers sail home with their catch to this picturesque fishing village at the mouth of the Kedah River, which can be reached by a bridge or by a short sampan ride to the north bank. The remains of an 18th-century fort still stand here, though the fort eventually failed to defend Kedah, which fell to Siamese invaders in 1821. Francis Light is said to have met the sultan of Kedah here to negotiate the cession of Penang.

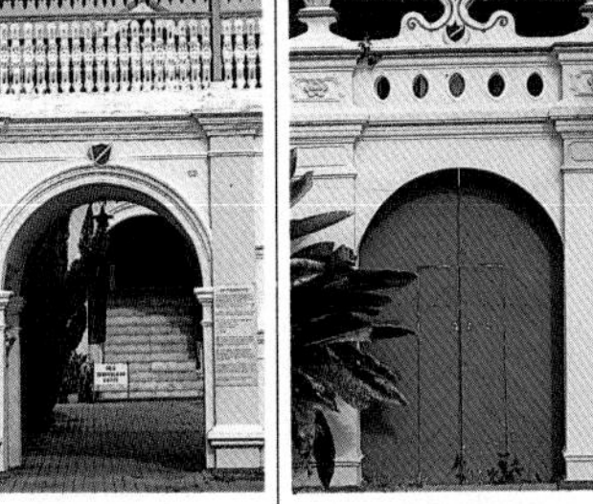

The entrance arches of four of Alor Setar’s major attractions depict various influences. Top left, Zahir Mosque (Mughal); top right, Balai Besar (Thai); bottom left, the Royal Museum (Indian); and bottom right, the Royal Mausoleum (colonial) at Langar.

## ALOR SETAR

Kedah’s capital, Alor Setar, is a fast-growing town whose main attractions are the Royal Museum, Balai Besar, Balai Nobat, and Zahir Mosque, all built around the padang, a large field used for public assemblies. The Kedah State Museum on Lebuhraya Darulaman exhibits prehistoric artifacts, archeological finds, cultural, natural, and ethnographical collections.

**ROYAL MUSEUM.** The museum, formerly the palace of the sultans of Kedah, was opened in 1983 after restoration. It was the site of royal residences from 1763 to 1941; the present building dates from 1851. The grandest occasion in its history was the simultaneous wedding of five princes and princesses in 1904, a ceremony lasting sixty days and nights.

**BALAI BESAR.** The Great Hall or Balai Besar was also rebuilt in 1904, in time for the royal weddings. The two-story audience hall is an interesting blend of Thai, Malay, and colonial architecture. Nearby is the Balai Nobat, which houses the sacred instruments of the royal orchestra.

**KEDAH STATE ART GALLERY.** Originally the Kedah High Court, this 1912 building was designed as a single-story structure so as not to obstruct the view from the Istana Pelamin. It was used for various official purposes until 1983, when it was reopened as an art gallery.

**ZAHIR MOSQUE.** Construction of the mosque was completed in 1915. It is designed to resemble the architecture of a mosque in Langkat, north Sumatra.

**WAYANG GEDEK**
The shadow theater of Kedah tends to be more modern and more comical than the better-known *wayang kulit* of Kelantan. Performances take place during traditional festivals. The characters speak Malay or Thai, and the dialogues often involve risqué jokes as well as popular tunes from Malay or Hindi movies. The minor comic characters may include mini-skirted beauties, cowboys, or soldiers who ride on stage in cars and aeroplanes.

DATAI
AIRPORT
TELAGA TUJUH
PANTAI KOK
PULAU REBAK
FIELD OF BURNT RICE
PULAU BERAS BESAR

**LANGKAWI MARBLE**
The limestone hills of Langkawi yield a fine marble, comparable with Italian Carrara, which has been used on the walls of many famous buildings, including those of the Blue Mosque in Shah Alam, Selangor.

**THE CURSE OF MAHSURI**
About 6 miles from Kuah is the Tomb of Mahsuri (below). The Malay princess was wrongly accused of adultery and condemned to death. In revenge, she cursed the people of Langkawi for seven generations. The eighth generation has just been born, and the curse has now been officially lifted. It is said that Mahsuri became pregnant by drinking from Tasik Dayan Bunting (hence the lake's name). Some believe the princess was not executed but banished by her father, and ended her life by drowning herself in the lake. Her baby is said to have turned into a crocodile.

## LANGKAWI

Langkawi is the largest of 104 islands, collectively also known as Langkawi. Beach lovers come for the white sands and the best swimming, snorkeling, and coral diving ■ *18–19* on the west coast of Malaysia. The limestone landscape features hot springs, caves, and coves. Ferries from Kuala Perlis and Kuala Kedah land at a jetty near Kuah, the main town of the island whose principal landmark is a seaside mosque.

**PANTAI CHENANG.** The best beaches on Langkawi line this protected cove. Watersports, boat trips to nearby islands, and diving expeditions are all on offer. Telaga Tujuh, the "Seven Wells", is a 295-foot waterfall, cascading over seven naturally formed limestone basins.

**OTHER BEACHES.** On the north coast is Pasir Hitam, the Beach of Black Sand, where there is a jetty used by Thai boats. At Tanjung Rhu, visitors can take a boat to Gua Cerita, the Cave of Legends, with its old Arabic inscription. The best snorkeling and coral diving area is to the south, in the marine reserve between Pulau Segantang, Paya, and Lembu.

**THE INTERIOR.** There are several attractions in the interior of Langkawi. These include an ancient Acehnese grave not far from the Tomb of Mahsuri. Also near Mahsuri's tomb and about 12 miles from Kuah is Padang Matsirat (Field of Burnt Rice). Villagers believe that this is proof that the Malay princess' curse was effective for, shortly after her death, Thai warriors invaded the region and the villagers set their ricefields alight rather than leave them to the invaders. At Gunung Raya, a 2600-foot peak crowns the island. Nearby is Durian Perangin, with its cooling jungle waterfall and hot springs. At Rumah Bangsai is a traditional Malay house complex where villagers demonstrate their craft skills. The wildlife sanctuary at Pulau Dayan Bunting offers glimpses of mouse deer and several bird species, and Tasik Dayan Bunting (Lake of the Pregnant Maiden), where legend tells that after a childless couple drank from the lake, the wife became pregnant. Gua Langsir (Banshee Cave) is 295 feet high, full of bats, and believed to be haunted.

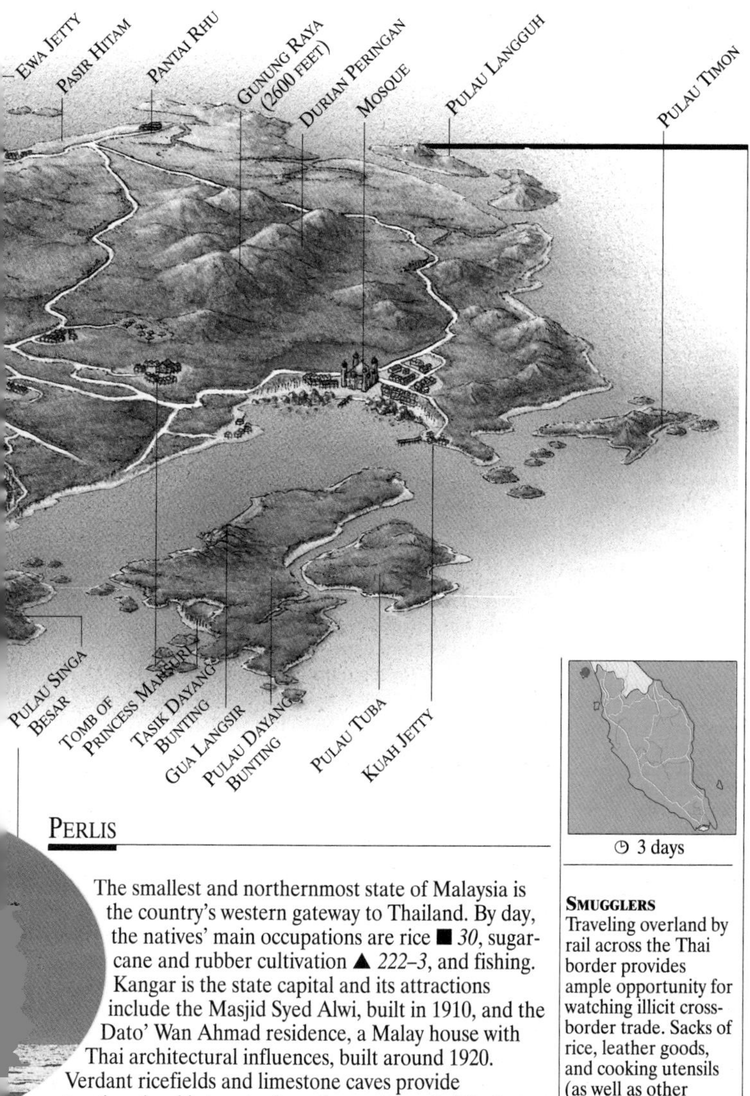


3 days

## Perlis

The smallest and northernmost state of Malaysia is the country's western gateway to Thailand. By day, the natives' main occupations are rice ■ *30*, sugar-cane and rubber cultivation ▲ *222–3*, and fishing. Kangar is the state capital and its attractions include the Masjid Syed Alwi, built in 1910, and the Dato' Wan Ahmad residence, a Malay house with Thai architectural influences, built around 1920. Verdant ricefields and limestone caves provide contrasting visual interests along the route north. The last stop on the Malaysian side of the border is Padang Besar, a town of wide-open spaces with ample parking for Haadyai-bound motoring visitors who leave their vehicles here. A duty-free store caters to shoppers at this checkpoint.

**Other attractions in Perlis.** In the town of Arau are the Royal Mosque and the beautiful palace of the sultan of Perlis. Kuala Perlis, at the mouth of the Perlis River, is a departure point for visitors taking the express ferry to Langkawi. The trip to the island resort takes only 45 minutes. Other attractions, west of Padang Besar, are the limestone formations of Kaki Bukit, a village once active in the tin-mining industry. Here, too, is the Gua Kelam, Kaki Bukit ("Dark Cave at the Foot of the Hill"), a 1300-foot limestone cave traversed by a walkway suspended over an underground stream.

**Smugglers**
Traveling overland by rail across the Thai border provides ample opportunity for watching illicit cross-border trade. Sacks of rice, leather goods, and cooking utensils (as well as other contraband) are dropped off at pre-arranged locations when the train slows down, and are picked up by waiting motorcyclists, who then speed away with their booty.

**SALTED FISH**
Most Malaysians now own refrigerators, but salted fish, which evolved as a method of preserving seafood during the monsoon when fishermen couldn't get to sea, is still just as popular in local cuisine as in

former years. Fish ranging in size from the tiny anchovy-like *ikan bilis* to large red snapper are dropped in tubs of salted water, then dried on racks in the sun. After five days under the sun, they are dry enough to be sent to market.

**CHEMPEDAK**
Teluk Chempedak is named after one of Malaysia's many delicious fruits. The chempedak is a member of the *Artocarpus* genus, along with the jackfruit or nangka (*Artocarpus heterophyllus*) and the breadfruit or sukun (*Artocarpus incisa*) cultivated in Malaysia. Their fruits are large and fleshy (the breadfruit contains up to 20 percent starch) and can be eaten raw or cooked into curry. The chempedak is tasty and refreshing.

## KUANTAN

Although Kuantan only became Pahang's state capital in 1955, some colonial buildings date from well before this period, although the origins of the old fishing port remain unknown. Historians relate that Pam (Pahang) was inhabited by Malays before the foundation of Melaka, and 12th-century manuscripts identify Kuantan as Tan-ma-ling, a vassal of the legendary trading kingdom of San Fo-ts'i. Today, Kuantan is the bustling hub of the mid-east coast with sprawling suburbs and the odd high-rise. The old town, with its ubiquitous Chinese shophouses, hugs the northern banks of the river of the same name. Shaded pathways run alongside the river and there are plentiful outdoor eating establishments. At the center of town is a tree-lined padang (playing field), a colonial-style courthouse, and the elegant new State Mosque. There are many recreation areas beside the river at Taman Gelora, and from there a long sandy beach stretches alongside the Royal Pahang Golf Club to Tanjung Tembeling.

**TELUK CHEMPEDAK.** Kuantan's favorite attraction is the golden-sand beach at Teluk Chempedak, 3 miles from the city center along the street of the same name. The beach hosts two luxury hotels, numerous more modest establishments, nightclubs, and restaurants. A plaza with handicraft shops, food stalls and a shaded beachside promenade occupies the popular northern end of the beach. Although the beach can be packed at weekends, the sands are still spacious and the abundant jungle shrouding the surrounding hills gives a feeling of communing with nature within a stone's throw of five-star luxury.

**BESERAH FISHING VILLAGE.** Acres of raised platforms for drying fish front the picturesque village of Beserah just north of Kuantan. It is best to visit the village early in the morning when the inhabitants lay the salt fish out to dry. Wander around the beachside streets where traditional wooden homes on stilts above the sand are shaded by groves of towering coconut palms. During mid-afternoon, depending on the season, patient travelers are rewarded by a unique scene, for when the fishing boats return, buffalo carts are driven down to the shoreline and the fish are unloaded directly from the boats into baskets on the carts. Beserah village also boasts a batik factory north of the river. The beaches north of town are clean and beautiful, and the waters here ideal for swimming and windsurfing.

**SUNGAI PANDAN WATERFALL.** Surrounded by lush jungle, the 488-foot-high Sungai Pandan Waterfall cascades down a near

"THE TIN IS SMELTED DURING THE NIGHT IN A VERY RUDE FURNACE, WITH MOST INGENIOUS CHINESE BELLOWS, IS THEN RUN INTO MOULDS MADE OF SAND, AND TURNED OUT AS SLABS."

ISABELLA BIRD, *THE GOLDEN CHERSONESE*

vertical rockface. These spectacular falls are approached from either the Sungai Lembing road (turnoff before Panching) or from the Highway 1 turnoff near Kuantan Airport. Follow the signs to Air Terjun Sungai Pandan.

**SUNGAI LEMBING TIN MINE.** Most tin in Malaysia is mined by the alluvial method, but at Sungai Lembing is the country's biggest and only major underground tin mine. When in operation, it was reputed to be the deepest such mine in the world but the slump in tin prices forced the mine to close more than a decade ago, and the town of Sungai Lembing went to sleep when the mine did. To visit, check with the tourist information center in Kuantan.

**GUA CHARAS.** A solitary limestone massif outside Panching is the site of Gua Charas, a revered Buddhist sanctuary. Climbing up the steep cliff-face beside a Buddhist temple, 220 stone steps lead to the hill-top limestone caverns festooned with stalactites. One cave contains a 33-foot-long Reclining Buddha, the life-time labor of a wandering Thai monk who once lived here. Monks still occupy nearby cells and maintain the shrines at this temple sited 3 miles from the turnoff at Panching Police Station on the Sungai Lembing Road.

Workers packing tin ingots for onward delivery.

## SNAKE ISLAND

Sungai Ular, 19 miles north of Kuantan, is the quintessential east-coast fishing village – uncommercialized and traditional. Fishing boats crowd a picturesque estuary, tall coconut palms sway in the tradewinds, and fishermen mend their nets. Snorkeling is possible at nearby Pulau Ular, an island which legend tells was created by a giant serpent, hence the name "Snake Island".

## CHERATING

Once a sleepy fishing village, Cherating, 28 miles from Kuantan, is now a popular holiday resort renowned for its spacious golden-sand beaches and its lazy tropical ambience. Asia's first Club Med is to the north of the village and spreads across 3 miles of private beach front. But for travelers seeking a beach stay in more traditional Malay style there is plentiful thatched-roof chalet accommodation in the village and south along the beachfront. Windsurfers can be hired at the beachside. A favorite with backpackers, budget-travelers, and Malaysians alike, Cherating also boasts small restaurants serving Malay and Western dishes. The village also features a handicraft center where visitors can participate in batik making and pandanus-leaf weaving.

**INTERNATIONAL BOARDSAILING REGATTA**

Every year in January, Bachok Beach, just north of Kuantan, is the venue for the Kuantan Challenge, the International Board Sailing Regatta. This is when the world's top windsurfers gather for a thrilling contest. The South China Sea is usually at its calmest in January and at its best for board-sailing, for the annual monsoon can often whip up waves to well over a 6-foot surf. This is a challenge to the best of wave jumpers.

Gua Charas (above), a limestone cave towers above the rubber and oil-palm plantations near Sungai Lembing.

**TURTLE-WATCHING**
One of Terengganu's greatest tourist attractions is found at Rantau Abang, 11 miles north of Kuala Dungun, where a long sandy beach harbors one of the world's few remaining nesting places for the giant leatherback turtle. In the past, onlookers sat on the turtles, played radios, stole their eggs, and managed to whittle turtle numbers down until they reached endangered levels. Today, although all these former pursuits are banned, and the nesting process documented, with hatcheries ensuring that baby turtles get out to sea, numbers are still dwindling. However, for the lucky visitor who waits up all night for the chance to see one of the mighty turtles weighing around 770 pounds and measuring nearly 5 feet, the vigil is amply rewarded. Nesting time occurs between May and September and there is ample beachside accommodation in chalets, and 19 miles of beaches on which you can relax and stroll for an hour or two while awaiting the grand event.

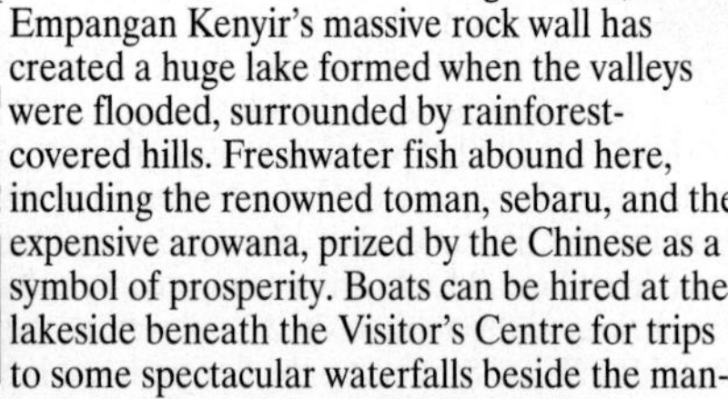

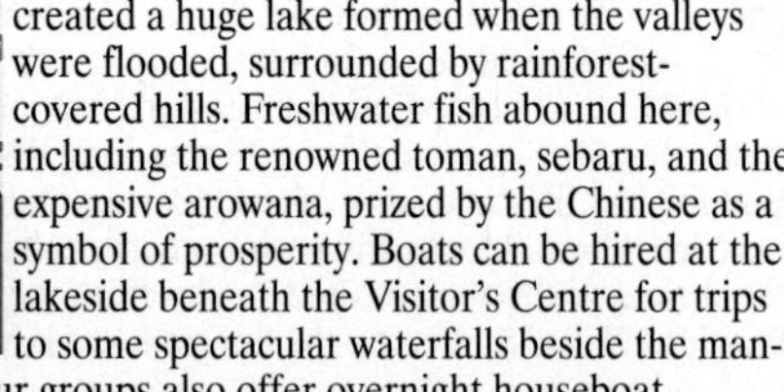


## KUALA DUNGUN

An old fishing port, Kuala Dungun is 82 miles north of Kuantan. The estuary bustles with maritime action although the town was once busier when the port served the now dormant iron-ore mines at Bukit Besi. The riverside market and a stroll through the old town offer a glimpse into the lifestyle of a typical Terengganu town. North, over the river, is the Tanjung Jara Resort, a picturesque hotel complex which has won many awards for its traditional Malay architecture.

## KUALA BERANG

Terengganu's vast interior is still little known to most travelers but offers forest parks, spectacular waterfalls, a huge dam, and excellent fishing. Kuala Berang, the gateway to the state's inland attractions, is reached either by taking the inland route from Kuala Dungun or, alternatively, by turning off at Marang further up the coast.

**EMPANGANG KENYIR (KENYIR DAM).** Located east of Kuala Berang and reputed to be Southeast Asia's largest dam, Empangan Kenyir's massive rock wall has created a huge lake formed when the valleys were flooded, surrounded by rainforest-covered hills. Freshwater fish abound here, including the renowned toman, sebaru, and the expensive arowana, prized by the Chinese as a symbol of prosperity. Boats can be hired at the lakeside beneath the Visitor's Centre for trips to some spectacular waterfalls beside the man-made lake. Tour groups also offer overnight houseboat holidays and trips to Taman Negara (National Park), entering via the lesser-known Terengganu side of the park.

**SEKAYU WATERFALL.** South of Kuala Berang, 33 miles from Kuala Terengganu, are the nature park and waterfalls of Air Terjun Sekayu. Trails lead through the jungle to the falls which cascade down a series of rockfaces. Along the boulder-strewn stream are small pools ideal for a dip in the icy spring waters flowing from the mountains. Accommodation is available at the park's resthouse or chalets, which must be booked in advance through the Forestry Department in Kuala Berang.

**TERENGGANU STONE.** Terengganu is often referred to as the country's "Cradle of Islam" for it was near Kuala Berang in 1897 that the historic "Terengganu Stone" was discovered. Inscribed with 14th-century Islamic writings, the oldest yet found in Malaysia, the monolith proved that the east coast was already inhabited by Muslims even before Melaka was founded. The stone fragment tells of a ruler named Raja Mandulika and outlines a set of Muslim laws.

"HERE THE LOVER OF THINGS AS THEY ARE, AND OUGHT NOT TO BE, MAY FIND A DWELLING AMONG PEOPLE WHOSE LIVES ARE BUT LITTLE RUFFLED BY THE FEVER-HEATED BREATH OF EUROPEAN PROGRESS." HUGH CLIFFORD, *IN COURT AND KAMPUNG*

**MASJID KAMPUNG TUAN.** Long renowned for its religious teachers, the east coast also lays claim to many historic mosques. At Kampung Tuan, just north of Chukai, is a unique wooden mosque, reputed to be more than three hundred years old. The building features a four-tiered roof reminiscent of ancient Javanese-style mosques and Pattani-style roof tiles which are overlapping square slabs of terracotta.

## MARANG

Malaysia's most photographed east-coast fishing village, Marang, lies 9 miles south of Kuala Terengganu. Few coastal vistas can equal the view across the estuary where traditional, crescent-shaped *kolek* boats ply the waters against a background of white sandy beaches and a far-off tropical isle on the horizon. Marang is a working fishing port and the dockside is a fascinating place to watch the boats coming and going and unloading their catch; it is also the gateway port to nearby Kapas Island. South of Marang at Kampung Rhu Muda are some well-known small beach resorts which offer island trips, and north of town there are inexpensive thatched-roof chalets near the footbridge leading to the beachside kampung across the lagoon.

## PULAU KAPAS

Terengganu's most accessible tropical isle, Pulau Kapas, is located about 4 miles offshore from Marang. Fishing trawlers-cum-passenger ferries make the mainland-to-island run in about 30 minutes, but departure times usually depend on the tides. The return trip from Marang jetty costs RM15. The small wooded isle offers white sandy beaches, clean turquoise waters, and swimming and snorkeling in the tepid tropical sea. Overnight accommodation is easily available at three small resorts which offer chalets and small wooden huts. Each resort has its own restaurant providing basic Malay cuisine.

**KUINI**
At Kijal, a fishing village 11 miles north of Chukai, makeshift stalls line both sides of the highway. Kijal is the center for the delicious local mango known as kuini, which has sweet tender flesh and a heady aroma.

**"MUSIM TUTUP KUALA"**
Literally "the season when the estuaries close", this annual event is also known as the northeast monsoon. Kelantan bears the brunt of the wind and rain which arrive in force from October to March. Some years the monsoon is moderate but at other times it can cause severe flooding. Fishermen haul their boats into the sheltered lagoons and use their leisure time to repair and paint their boats and mend their nets.

**Bell on Bukit Puteri**
Atop Bukit Puteri, in the grounds of the old fort, is a large bell which dates from the era of Baginda Omar (1839–76), Terengganu's long-reigning sultan, who once resided in the stone hilltop fort. Known by its Malay name of *genta*, the bell, measuring 3 feet across, was formerly used to signal the time for the daily breaking of fast – *berbuka puasa* – during the month of Ramadan, when Muslims the world over abstain from food and drink between the hours of dawn and dusk.

**Batik and brassware**
For visitors curious to see Terengganu's traditional crafts being made, watch out for signs saying "*batik dan tembaga*", which, translated, means "batik and brassware". Located in Kampung Ladang at the eastern end of Jalan Sultan Zainal Abidin, these workshops offer visitors a fascinating look at the state's time-honored crafts.

One of Peninsular Malaysia's oldest ports, Kuala Terengganu was mentioned as early as the 13th century on Chinese mariners' maps, and could have been a trading center centuries before this date. Capital of Terengganu state, Kuala Terengganu is also the royal seat, and the current sultanate traces its roots back to the 16th century. Built at the entrance to the Terengganu River, the town is located on the promontory between the river and the South China Sea and is a combination of old-world charm and modern high-rise office blocks, symbols of the state's new-found petroleum riches. Batik and *songket* – silk woven cloth with gold threads – are traditional Terengganu crafts and can be bought at the riverside Central Market or at the Karyaneka Handicraft Centre at Rhusila, south of town. At the Suterasemai Centre at Chendering, locally grown and woven silk cloth is hand-painted with batik designs.

**Istana Maziah.** Designed in the French style, this former royal palace (right) was constructed in 1894 for Sultan Zainal Abidin III, who ruled for thirty-seven years and witnessed the state's change in status from being under nominal Siamese rule to being an Unfederated Malay State under British protection. Elegantly painted in the royal shade of yellow, the Istana Maziah, once the seat of power, is still used for royal weddings and investitures.

**Abidin Mosque.** Originally a wooden structure dating from the reign of Sultan Zainal Abidin II (1793–1808), the Masjid Abidin was reconstructed with bricks by his descendant and namesake, Sultan Zainal Abidin III, in the late 19th century. Located at one end of Jalan Masjid, the mosque has undergone even more extensions although much of the central structure is still original.

**Bukit Puteri.** On Jalan Sultan Zainal Abidin, beside the Post Office, a flight of steps climbs Bukit Puteri, a small hill overlooking the Terengganu River estuary. On top is Kota Bukit Puteri, a recently restored fortress which dates from the early 19th century, and contains several fine cannon, a small armory which originally had a cannonball-proof roof, and the ruins of an old stone palace.

## Pulau Duyung

Traditional boat-building still flourishes on Pulau Duyung, the largest of the islands in the

middle of the Terengganu River. The new bridge over the river connects with the island; however, the easiest and most picturesque approach is by ferry-boat from the town's jetty. Power saws have replaced hand tools, but the techniques remain unchanged in the island's workshops, where craft from fishing trawlers to ocean-going yachts are constructed. Orders pour in from international boating enthusiasts as the red *cengal*, a rainforest hardwood used by Pulau Duyung's craftsmen, is renowned by mariners the world over for its seaworthiness and durability.

## CHINATOWN

Hugging the shores of the Terengganu River, with their back rooms built on piers above the water, are the rambling shophouses of Kuala Terengganu's historic Chinatown. Lining both sides of Jalan Bandar, these two-story buildings dating from the 19th century feature original red-tiled roofs with characteristic Chinese-style roof ridges, arched and shuttered windows, and a shaded five-foot way. Trishaws ply this fascinating old street which still supports traditional family businesses such as laundry service (far left) and Chinese restaurants. Huge chick-blinds (near left), split bamboo awnings, hang in front of all the shops to protect them from the merciless equatorial sun. These are colorfully hand-painted with the name of the shops and often feature advertisements for medicine, and men's sarongs, known as *pelikat*. Popular brand names include *Cap Gajah* (Elephant Brand) and *Cap Kuda* (Horse Brand). Terengganu crafts, including the brasswares made in nearby Kampung Tanjung, are on sale here. Blue and white Terengganu batiks, silk brocades known as *songket*, and colorful silky lengths to make the Malaysian women's *baju kurung* cram the textile shops along both sides of Jalan Bandar. Heading toward Jalan Sultan Ismail, the visitor comes across an old Chinese temple on the left with an ornate altar and its old roof with beams blackened from decades of incense smoke.

**TOK DUYUNG**
On Pulau Duyung's neighboring isle, Pulau Duyung Kecil, linked by ferry-boat from the town jetty, is the ruined house of Tok Duyung. Dating from the late 19th century, all that is left today are a few columns and part of the outer building, which shows fine carpentry, a hallmark of Terengganu's traditional wooden buildings. Tok Duyung was a charismatic religious leader and an Islamic teacher during the reign of Sultan Zainal Abidin III, who was himself well known for his piety and religious studies. Terengganu has long been renowned for having the most zealous Muslims on the peninsula and is famed for its Koran readers and its *pondok* schools, such as that of Tok Duyung, where students live in small huts around the teacher's house.

# Around Kuala Terengganu

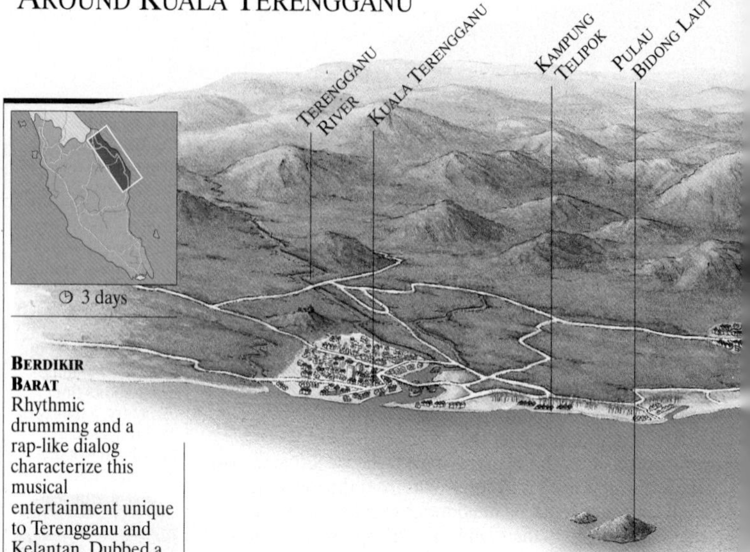

Terengganu River
Kuala Terengganu
Kampung Telipok
Pulau Bidong Laut

◷ 3 days

**Berdikir Barat**
Rhythmic drumming and a rap-like dialog characterize this musical entertainment unique to Terengganu and Kelantan. Dubbed a "verbal art form", Berdikir Barat is a relatively recent phenomenon compared to the east coast's more ancient musical traditions. Basically, it is a matching of wits between two teams, which usually consist of ten people per side. The impromptu verse often ridicules the opposition, and much depends on the virtuosity of the leaders. Berdikir Barat Asli is the more original version as compared to the new forms, which are even used as propaganda songs on television. East-coast night markets sell a variety of Berdikir Barat cassettes – ask for "Asli" if you want the best singers and original style.

## Kampung Merang

Some of Terengganu's best beaches line the South China Sea north of town. Instead of taking the highway to Kota Bharu, turn off after the new bridge onto Route T1. Kampung Merang, 17 miles away, is a scenic fishing village on the edge of a long white-sand beach with views over an island-studded horizon. Hotel and chalet accommodation is available north of town beside Pantai Merang, the town beach, which is usually deserted and ideal for travelers wanting solitude.

## Pulau Redang

This pristine isle, 30 miles from Kuala Terengganu, has been carefully monitored by conservationists since construction began on a multi-million-ringgit resort complex there. Plans are also afoot to pipe freshwater to it under the sea, as most of Terengganu's islands are notoriously short of drinking water. White sandy beaches, crystal clear waters and accessible coral reefs ■ *18–19* contribute to the island's popularity with travelers who enjoy getting off the beaten track and roughing it. Passenger boats ply from Kuala Terengganu, but many charters and tours depart from Merang, the port closest to Pulau Redang.

## Kuala Besut

Turn off the main highway north just after Jertih for Kuala Besut, an old fishing town close to the border with

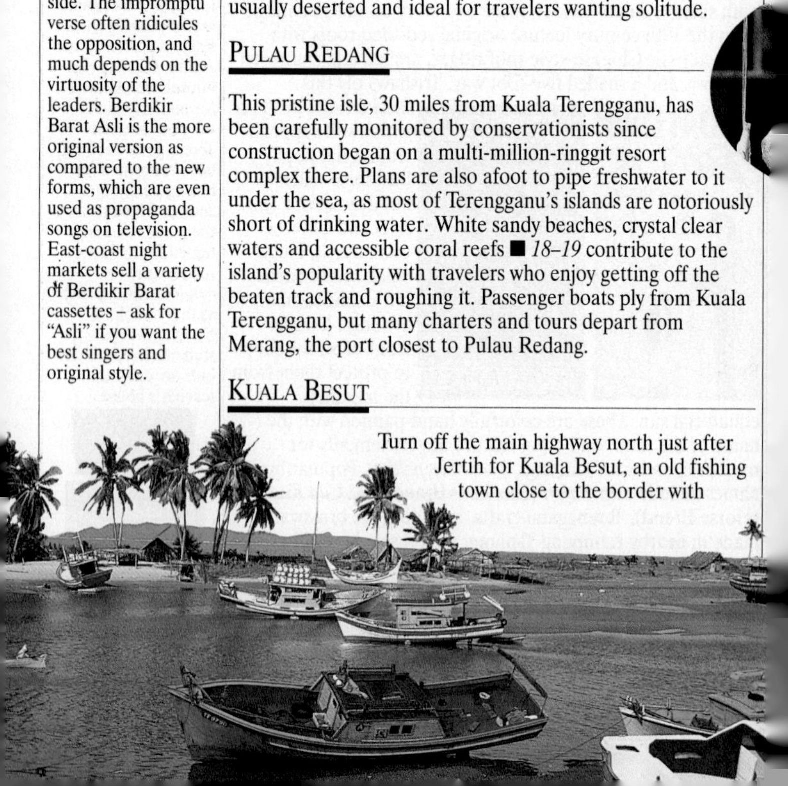

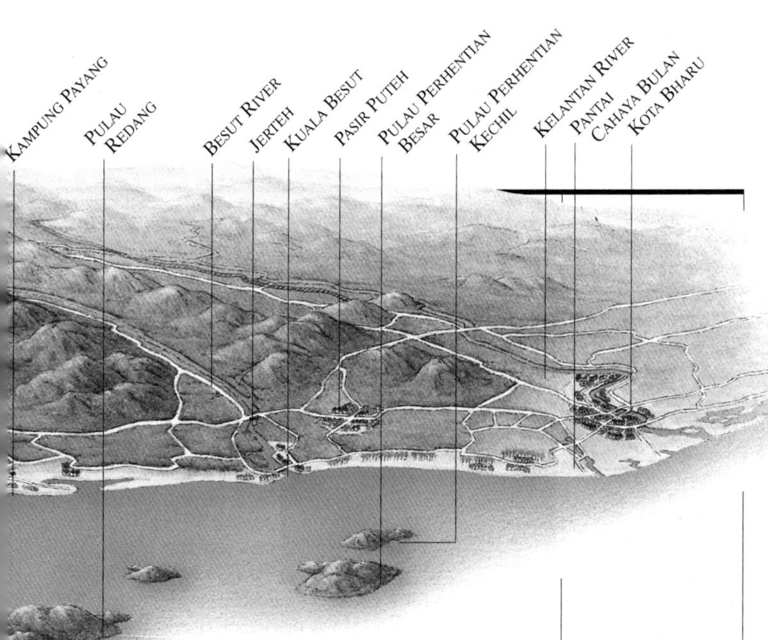


Kelantan. It seems the further north one travels, the more uncommercialized the ports become, and Kuala Besut is no exception. Goats roam downtown streets lined with old wooden shophouses where Malay businesses are the norm, not a rarity as on much of the west coast. The harbor throbs with action as deep-sea fishing trawlers and traditional east-coast *kolek* boats come and go from the bustling town jetties. Just south of Kuala Besut is picturesque Pantai Air Tawar, a long beach with resthouse accommodation.

## PULAU PERHENTIAN

Terengganu's most northerly isles, the picturesque Perhentian group, are located 13 miles offshore, a 90-minute boat ride from Kuala Besut jetty. Boats leave daily, and more often on Thursday and Friday. The one-way fare is RM15. En route to the islands, the boat passes tiny, deserted Pulau Ru, flying fish skip across the sparkling waters, and the keen-eyed may even spot dolphins. Visitors disembark at Pulau Perhentian Besar, where the jetty leads to a beachside resthouse which must be booked in advance at the district office in Kuala Besut. Further along the beach are simple, thatched-roof chalets and a resort with chalets, dormitories, and camping facilities. A couple of beachside restaurants offer meals. Perhentian's beaches are pristine, the waters crystal clear, and the coral and fishlife are excellent and easily accessible for snorkelers. Masks and snorkels are available for hire at the chalets. Across the channel is Pulau Perhentian Kecil, which supports a large fishing village. Boatmen ferry visitors across the strait and back again for a small fee, and the island kampung is an interesting diversion from sun and sea. Lush rainforests cover the island's interior, and trekking trails offer good short hikes.

**VIETNAMESE BOAT PEOPLE**

Easily seen off the Terengganu coast near Merang is Pulau Bidung Laut, which has only recently been returned to the Malaysian government after years of being under the auspices of the United Nations, for this was formerly the home of thousands of Vietnamese boat people. At one stage, up to forty thousand refugees were housed here. In the monsoon season, when the Northeast Trades were blowing, overloaded Vietnamese boats would converge on Malaysia's east coast after a wind-aided journey which took only five days. During their stay on the island, much of the jungle was cleared and the former idyllic isle became unrecognizable. However, the land heals quickly in the tropical climes. Plans are afoot to build a small resort, and fishermen are now allowed back into the surrounding waters.

**GIANT DRUM FESTIVAL**
Every year around May, Kota Bharu is awash with the sounds of the annual celebration of Pesta Rebana, the Festival of the Giant Drums. The roll of these drums, made from chisel-cut logs and measuring 2 feet in diameter, can be heard for miles. Contestants come from all over the Kelantan Basin, and teams consist of twelve men, two to a drum. Points are given for rhythm, tone, decoration, and the players' skill at utilizing the two different drumming methods: bare fingers or padded drumsticks.

**KITE-MAKING**
Dating back to the 15th-century Melaka sultanate, kite-flying is a passion for many Kelantanese, who create their kites in workshops around Kota Bharu. Made by applying waxed and colored paper over a split-bamboo frame, the kites are then decorated with cut-out flowers and motifs. Kites come in many sizes and shapes, resembling the peacock, the swallow, the cat, and the moon.

## KOTA BHARU

Capital of Kelantan state, and the royal seat, Kota Bharu is also known as the cradle of traditional Malay culture. Largely spared the influx of immigrants who came to work the mines and plantations during the colonial era, Kota Bharu has remained uniquely Malay. Batik sarongs are still popular wear for both sexes, men continue to wrap their heads in turban style, crafts flourish in the town's cottages industries, and traditional pastimes such as *silat* (Malay martial arts), kite-flying, top-spinning, and *rebana* (giant drum) playing are still keenly pursued. Kota Bharu hugs the banks of the Kelantan River, which flows through the fertile basin of the same name, the source of much of the state's rice, tobacco, and vegetables. During the annual monsoon, the river often overflows its banks and the Kelantanese take to boats to get around the flooded streets. However, it is not all bad, as after the floods the farmlands are covered with mineral-rich silt. Farming communities around Kota Bharu are surrounded by ricefields ■ *30*, alternately lushly green or glittering with water, and many of the fishing villages are picture-postcard scenes of tall swaying coconut palms, long sandy beaches, and estuaries full of painted fishing boats.

**ISTANA BALAI BESAR.** In the center of town, beside the Istana Jahar, is the former palace of Sultan Muhammad II. Its name translating as "The Palace with the Large Audience Hall", the Istana is encircled by the original wooden fort wall which predates the palace built in 1844. The Throne Room and the Hall of Audience are still used for important royal occasions.

**ISTANA JAHAR.** Formerly the palace of Raja Bendahara, the Istana Jahar was built by Kelantan's top craftsmen in 1887. Evidence of the wood-carver's skill is seen in the palace's intricate fretwork and carved wooden beams. Since 1991 the Royal Customs Museum has been housed there and features displays of old brasswares, traditional kitchen utensils, jewelry, krises, and the *singakerti* – a carriage shaped in the form of a legendary beast and used in old royal ceremonies.

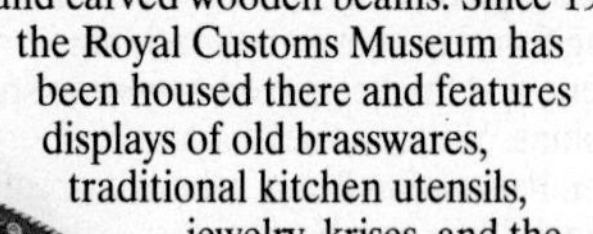

**CENTRAL MARKET.** Proof of the Kelantan Basin's fertility is the astonishing variety of produce on display at the town's Central Market, an octagonal building lit naturally by a translucent roof which filters the

A *wayang kulit* puppet of Kelantan.

sunlight. Under this soft, yellow light, surrounded by their wares, sit the batik-clad female hawkers who monopolize the fruit and vegetable business. Great prickly durians, bananas ranging in size from sweet *pisang mas* to long green plantains, gleaming red chilis, riverside greens wet with dew, and other fresh edibles too numerous to mention are artfully displayed on the market floor. Behind them are the "wet" markets for fish and meat, and upstairs are eating stalls, shops selling dry goods and *wayang kulit* figures, and garments stalls.

## Pantai Cahaya Bulan

Kelantan's famed "Moonlight Beach" – Pantai Cahaya Bulan – is located along the street of the same name 6 miles from Kota Bharu. Winding through fishing villages, past batik and *songket* workshops, sweetcorn and *agar-agar* street vendors, this scenic road offers a glimpse into Kelantanese kampung life. A sea-breeze always seems to be blowing on the coast, permanently bending the lofty coconut palms and clouding the air with a fine salty mist. Makeshift stalls with sand floors offer deep-fried *keropok* (fish crackers) and prawns in batter.

## Pantai Dasar Sabak

About 6 miles from Kota Bharu is the fishing village of Pantai Dasar Sabak, set on a sand spit between the sea and a lagoon. Renowned for its decoratively painted boats, the village comes alive every afternoon, when the fishermen return with their catch. The chanting crews then lend a hand to haul the wooden boats out of the surf and roll them on coconut palm trunks up the sandy beach.

**Japanese Landing Beach.** Pantai Dasar Sabak was shaken from its bucolic reverie on December 7, 1941, when the Japanese landed on the beach and began their thrust down the peninsula to Singapore. A war-time bunker marks the spot of this historic landing.

**Cottage crafts**
Along the road to Pantai Cinta Berahi are dozens of small backyard workshops specializing in traditional crafts. Excellent buys in batik are found in the roadside showrooms between the beach and Kampung Badang. At the latter village are several renowned kite-makers who specialize in the popular *wau bulan* or "moon kite". In Kampung Penambang, 2 miles from Kota Bharu, visitors will notice cottage factories with petite village girls hand-weaving *songket*, a silk cloth shot with silver and gold thread.

KUBU YANG DIGUNA
UNTUK MEMPERTAHANKAN
SERANGAN JEPUN 1941

## TUMPAT

Sited at the termination of the East Coast Railway, Tumpat seems still to be firmly rooted in the past, with its old railway buildings and the shophouses that line the sleepy main street. The scenic drive from Kota Bharu passes rice paddies ■ *30* and tobacco fields, and just outside of town on a small rise overlooking the rural vista is the pastel-colored Istana Bukit Tanah, a royal residence built in the late 19th century.

**THE DISTRICT OFFICE.** Tumpat's neo-classical district office, built in 1927 when the town was in its heyday, has remained practically unchanged from that date. Lovingly maintained, the beige-and-white office building features a semi-circular foyer graced with elegant archways, while columns and plaster rosettes in bas-relief decorate the upstairs walls.

**PANTAI SRI TUJUH.** Malaysia's longest lagoon nestles behind the Tumpat region's most popular beach, Pantai Sri Tujuh. Located 4 miles from town, the casuarina-shaded sands are excellent for picnics and the beach is good for swimming and windsurfing. Chalets and camping facilities are available. The beach is the venue for the annual International Kite Festival in May, attracting many foreign kite enthusiasts to Tumpat.

**A BARON IN TUMPAT**
Patrick Balfour, later 3rd Baron Kinross, visited Tumpat in the 1930's and recorded his memorable journey through Kelantan in his entertaining travel book *Grand Tour*: "I crossed the frontier back into Malaya, and Nigel met me. That night he killed a fatted calf (which is to say, in the East, that he opened a tin of *pâté de faisan truffée* from Fortnum's) in Tumpat, for travelers rarely come to this out-of-the-way spot.…It is a tranquil spot. In its sandy main street are cafés and Chinese shops… and its side-streets peter out into coconut groves, where the poorer Malays inhabit dwellings of plaited straw, on piles."

## PASIR MAS

Kelantan is famous for its pretty women and Pasir Mas is renowned throughout Malaysia as the home of the prettiest. Surrounded by ricefields and kampungs, the town is the hub of an old rural settlement on the west bank of the Sungai Kelantan, about 9 miles south of Kota Bharu. The local restaurants and food stalls at Pasir Mas serve Kelantanese delicacies which are sweeter and more easily palatable to the Western tongue than the chili-scorching food of the south. A local favorite is *ayam percik* – grilled chicken marinated with a mix of coconut milk, chili, onion, and cardamom sauce. Also try the *nasi dagang* – glutinous rice with prawn curry gravy, and *jala mas* ("golden fishing net"), a sweet.

**WAT PHOTHIVIHAN.** Apart from sharing a common border, Kelantan has a long association with Thailand, for the sultan paid tribute to Siam up until British intervention in the early 1900's. Kelantan's Thai minority trace their roots back through several generations, and although they are hardly distinguishable from other Kelantanese by their dress, they still are ardent followers of Buddha. At Wat Phothivihan, a Thai temple

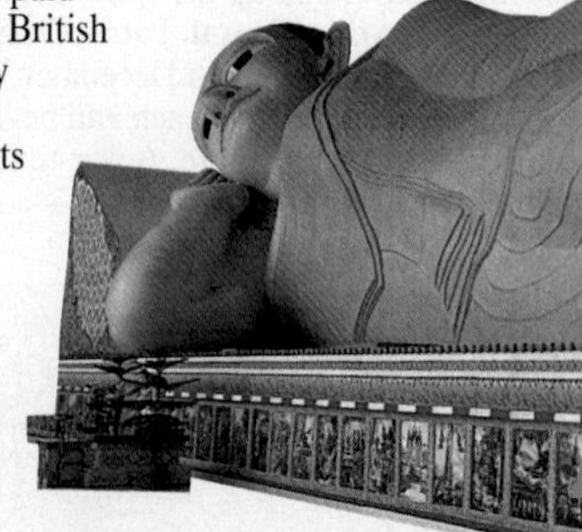

Wat Uttamaran Temple in Repek, Pasir Mas.

north of Pasir Mas via Meranti, is Malaysia's biggest reclining Buddha, measuring 120 feet long.

**WAT UTTAMARAN.** Picturesquely sited in a serene rural setting, this beautiful old Thai temple is located outside of Repek and approached from the Rantau Panjang road. Elaborate gilt decorations and layers of upswept roofs characterize Kelantan's oldest functioning Thai temple, which dates from the turn of the century.

## THE EAST–WEST HIGHWAY

Since 1982, when the East–West Highway opened, travelers have been able to drive directly from the northern west coast to Kota Bharu without having to undertake the previous lengthy detour via Kuantan. This engineering marvel traverses the mountain tops of some of Peninsular Malaysia's wildest country which, being out of bounds during the Emergency, has been spared from rampant logging, and most of the forests are still in a pristine state. Travelers entering the highway from Kota Bharu drive south to Tanah Merah, 28 miles away. From there it is 101 miles to Grik across the Main Range in Perak. Accommodation is available at the resthouse on Pulau Banding, an island in the vast man-made lake of Tasik Temengur, formed during the construction of the Temengur Dam.

**BATU MELINTANG.** Past Jeli, just before the highway climbs to cross the Barisan Titiwangsa (Main Range), is Batu Melintang, a small village beside Sungai Pergau. Dominating the rural settlement is a solitary limestone massif called Gunung Reng, pitted with numerous caves reputed to be the dwelling places of Stone Age man.

**SUNGAI PERGAU WATERFALLS.** Climbing the hills from Batu Melintang, the road winds beside the wild waters of Sungai Pergau, as it makes its way from the mountains down to the lowlands. At Batu 14, where the highway crosses the river, a path leads down to the waterfalls and adjacent picnic grounds. During the dry season the pools are good for a dip, but not during the monsoon, when the waterfalls are thunderous and a swim would be nothing less than suicidal.

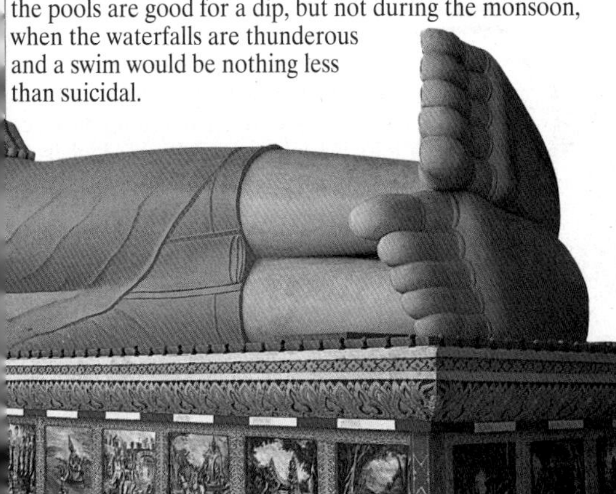

Of the village scenery, Patrick Balfour wrote in *Grand Tour*: "We drove through the liquid shade of woods, where the sarongs and parasols of the natives made drops of colour on the road. We came out into ricefields, glistening with water, seldom rectangular but curving like emerald rivers between banks of palms."

**TUDUNG SAJI**
Along the back roads of Kota Bharu and in the kampungs, itinerant hawkers are often seen with a load of *tudung saji* – conical food-covers suspended from a sturdy pole slung across their shoulders. Usually painted in a blaze of colors, the covers are woven from split pandanus leaves which are then dried, dyed, and woven. The leaves are also used to make baskets and matting.

**Old Chinese settlement**
One of Peninsular Malaysia's oldest Chinese settlements, Pulai traces it roots back several generations. Settled by Hakka Chinese, the village is about 6 miles from Gua Musang, and contains a Buddhist temple.

**Hugh Clifford**
In 1887 Governor Weld broke down Pahang's resistance to colonial interference and installed his nephew Hugh Clifford as the first British agent at the royal capital of Pekan. Clifford played an active role in the Pahang War, a series of uprisings against British rule. Stamford Raffles' tutor, Munshi Abdullah, later wrote that Clifford "showed his courage and complete indifference to the menacing weapons that were brandished in his face".

## Kuala Krai

Previously, travelers wanting to visit Kelantan's untamed interior had no alternative but to go by rail, but with the recent opening of the road from Gua Musang to Kuala Lipis all this has changed. Now visitors from the southern states can opt for this new route or take the old coastal road. The scenery is vastly different on the inland road, which cuts through primeval forests, although these must now be viewed from afar as the accessible land closer to the highway has been opened up for oil-palm and rubber plantations ■ *24–5*. Heading south from Kota Bharu, Kuala Krai (41 miles), at the meeting of the Kelantan and Pergau Rivers, is the springboard for some spectacular waterfalls and forest regions ■ *26–7*. The town's other claim to fame is a set of steps beside the river, where the height of the annual monsoonal floods is recorded.

**Lata Berangin and Lata Rek.** South of Kuala Krai, take the turn at Lalok for two of Kelantan's prettiest waterfalls, Lata Berangin and Lata Rek. Set in scenic forested hills, the waterfalls are easily accessible and offer spectacular views of the surroundings.

## Dabong

Turn off south of Lalok for Dabong, a riverine town on the main railway to Kota Bharu. About 3 miles out of town, viewed from Route 66 (the road to Jeli), is Peninsular Malaysia's highest waterfall, Lat Jeri, also known as the Gunung Stong Waterfall, which drops 250 yards down a granite mountain face. Inquire in Dabong for guides to assist in the 1-hour trek.

**Gua Ikan.** The "Fish Cave", Gua Ikan, is located less than 2 miles from Dabong on the Lalok road and derives its name from the river running through its spacious limestone cavern.

**Gua Musang.** Rugged limestone

"THESE FORESTS ARE AMONG THE WONDERFUL THINGS OF THE EARTH. THEY ARE IMMENSE IN EXTENT, AND THE TREES WHICH FORM THEM GROW SO CLOSE TOGETHER THAT THEY TREAD ON ONE ANOTHER'S TOES." HUGH CLIFFORD, *IN COURT AND KAMPUNG*

peaks characterize the distinctive scenery around Gua Musang, a remote frontier town in the far south of Kelantan. The rocky hills are pitted with caves, where artifacts have been found dating back to the Stone Age. Beyond the town is Gunung Ayam, a hill believed to be the legendary home of Cik Siti Wan Kembang, a 14th-century warrior-queen of Kelantan. Trips from Gua Musang can be organized to Taman Negara (National Park), only 12 miles from town. Out of town near the resthouse is a traditional-style royal residence of the sultan of Kelantan.

## KUALA LIPIS

Pahang's capital under the former British administration, Kuala Lipis, 71 miles from Gua Musang, still retains an ambience from those colonial times. Shophouses, built in the early 1900's, line the main road through the town, which is perched above the swift-flowing Sungai Jelai. On the hills outside are some fine examples of colonial architecture. Painted a distinctive pink and white, the Lipis District Office (below), a neo-classical architectural gem built in 1919, seems quite out of place surrounded by forest-clad hills. The Clifford School, where royalty and well-known politicians were schooled, has had extensive renovations, but the original block built in 1913 still survives. On another hill on the outskirts of town is the Moorish-style Istana Hinggap, a royal residence built in 1926.

**RESTHOUSE-CUM-MUSEUM.** Once the home of the British resident, the Kuala Lipis Resthouse atop a hill overlooking the town, is Peninsular Malaysia's most grandiose resthouse. Built in 1922, the two-story structure boasts an impressive arched foyer. A sunken living room surrounded by a wide open verandah plays host to the Kuala Lipis Museum. On the walls are collections of memorabilia from the region's historical past, including Neolithic tools, an elephant's tooth, krises and swords, finely woven *kain limau* (royal cloth), and historical photographs spanning several generations of Pahang royalty.

**KENONG RIMBA JUNGLE PARK.** Kuala Lipis is the gateway to Pahang's designated wilderness region. Limestone peaks, lush rainforest, and prolific wildlife abound in this State Park located at the southwest corner of Taman Negara. The limestone caves include Gua Batu Tinggi, a large cavern through which the Kenong River flows; Gua Batu Tangga, with its unusual step formations; and Gua Batu Telahup, where the limestone has been rubbed smooth by elephants that sheltered in these caves during the monsoon. Trekking tours can be organized through tour operators in Kuala Lipis. Independent travelers can make the 3-hour boat journey downstream from town, or alight from the train at Batu Sembilan and organize boatmen from there.

**EAST COAST RAILWAY**
Getting tin ore to the markets was an immense problem, which the British overcame by building railway links from the mines to the ports. By 1910, tracks reached from one end of the west coast to the other; in 1920 a track was built linking Gemas in Johor with Kuala Lipis. In 1931 the line was extended to its present length, running all the way to Tumpat in Kelantan. The early engineers faced a huge task: the forests first had to be cleared, and then bridges built over the broad jungle rivers, which rise to dangerous levels during the monsoon ■ *16–17*. The East Coast Railway remains as a testimony to those skilled technicians and the thousands of laborers who laid the tracks through some of the world's most difficult terrain.

**POLO AT PEKAN**
The Royal Polo Field at Pekan, set against a backdrop of coconut palms and traditional Malay villages, may seem like an unlikely spot to host a world-class tournament. For the people of Pekan who have been bought up with the game, such an event would be just another polo match which the royal line of Pahang have been playing there for generations. The current ruler, Sultan Haji Ahmad Shah, is possibly Malaysia's best player ever; he once boasted a five-goal handicap and only ended his career in 1986 at the age of fifty-five. His two sons, Tengku Abdullah and Tengku Abdul Rahman, are also excellent players, and they conduct a course at Pekan to train local Malay youths in the royal sport.

## PEKAN

As the exclusive abode of Pahang's royal line, Pekan, or "The Town" as its name translates, has been home to the sultanate for at least five hundred years. Located upstream from the mouth of Sungai Pahang, Peninsular Malaysia's longest river, Pekan was where Melaka's Sultan Mahmud fled when the Portuguese conquered Melaka in 1511 ● *34*. The shophouses of Pekan Baru, or Chinatown, face the river, while the royal residences surrounded by Malay kampung houses ● *72–3* are located behind the town. The original wooden resthouse overlooks the padang, as do many old royal homes and buildings, including Istana Mangga Tunggal on Jalan Istana Abu Bakar, Istana Permai, near the current palace, and the sultan's former offices on Jalan Sultan Ahmad.

**MASJID ABDULLAH.** Just past the State Museum is an Art Deco mosque built during the reign of Sultan Abdullah (1917–32). Although it has been superseded by the larger Abu Bakar Mosque, the building is more pleasing architecturally.

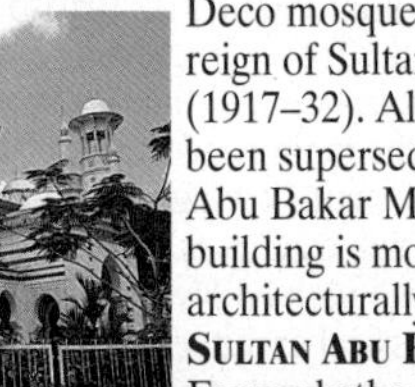

**SULTAN ABU BAKAR MUSEUM.** Formerly the British resident's house, then the Japanese headquarters, and later the residence of Sultan Abu Bakar, this historic building became the State Museum in 1976.

“In Pahang was a settlement called Pura (Pekan).... The jungles are stocked with elephants, and bison, said to be not very much smaller than elephants, deer and monkeys....” *Sejarah Melayu*

Open daily except on Mondays, the museum’s galleries house remarkable collections of traditional textiles, weapons, ceramics (including recent finds from a sunken junk in the South China Sea), prehistoric artifacts, models of Pahang fishing craft, a diorama of shaft-mining in Sungai Lembing, and a royal gallery featuring the outsize uniforms of the late Sultan Abu Bakar, who was unusually tall for a Malaysian monarch.

**Istana Abu Bakar.** This opulent royal palace is the home of the present sultan of Pahang, Sultan Haji Ahmad Shah. It was built in contemporary style during the latter part of the reign of his father, Sultan Abu Bakar (1932–74). The palace overlooks the expansive Royal Polo Field, the focus of annual feasting on the sultan’s birthday.

**Pulau Keladi Silk Weaving Centre.** Beside the river, about a mile from the Kuantan turnoff, the ancient art of silk-weaving survives at the Pahang Silk Weaving Centre. Skilled female weavers turn out the plaid and striped patterns that are indigenous to Pahang. Scarves and lengths of silk are on sale at the center.

## Endau Rompin

Peninsular Malaysia’s last untrammeled wilderness region, soon to be designated a State Park, covers a vast area of rainforest straddling the Johor–Pahang border. Home to prolific wildlife and virgin forests, the region offers wild rivers, gruelling hiking, excellent fishing, and the chance to be totally at one with nature. Gibbons are heard often, and tigers’ trails can sometimes be spotted, as can elephant, tapir, and deer tracks. Hornbills are usually seen at dusk and mixed flocks of birds at dawn. A rare fan-palm forest thrives on Gunung Janing; a steep trek leads to the Buaya Sangkut waterfall. Wild bananas grow alongside the trails. Endau Rompin is also home to the peninsula’s largest population of Sumatran rhinoceros, estimated at twenty. These rare mammals are among the world’s most endangered animals. Four-wheel-drive vehicles can be taken from Kahang, a small town on the road between Kluang and Mersing, to Kampung Peta, an Orang Asli village on Sungai Endau.

**Tun Abdul Razak’s birthplace**
Known as “Bapa Pembangunan” (Father of Development), Tun Abdul Razak, Malaysia’s second prime minister (1970–6), was born in Pekan on March 1, 1922. A reconstruction of the house he was born in, built by traditional carpenters to the exact plan of the original, is located just past the turnoff to the Silk Weaving Centre. Inside are photos of the late prime minister’s life and times, and original pieces of furniture.

**Istana Leban Tunggul**
This former royal residence just off Jalan Rompin Lama, was built in the late 19th century, but has for decades been unoccupied and in a state of ruin. Plans are now afoot to revamp the building, which has come to be considered a historical treasure. Its unusual architectural style features superb wood-craftsmanship and unique Moorish-style domes which crown the two-story mansion’s roof.

# JOHOR – AROUND MERSING

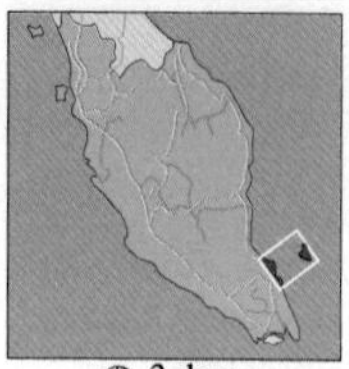

◷ 3 days

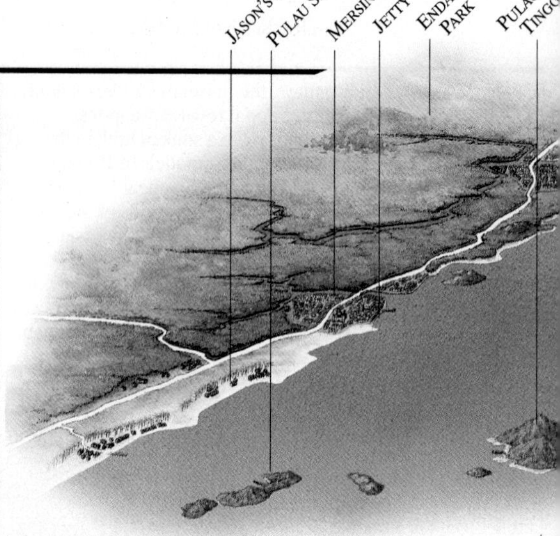


**HOLLYWOOD COMES TO TIOMAN**
In the late 1950's, the beach south of the present Tioman Island Resort and the waterfall behind Mukut (below) were two of the locations used in the shooting of *South Pacific*. Elderly villagers at Mukut still remember when the "Happy Talk" sequence was shot using their waterfall as a backdrop.

**ANCIENT CERAMICS AT JUARA**
The National Museum carried out excavations at Juara in 1976, unearthing pottery dating from the 12th-century Sung dynasty to the 17th century – evidence of the island's importance as a major stopover when sails ruled the sea.

## MERSING

As the gateway port to Johor's resort islands and mountainous Pulau Tioman, Mersing comes alive on weekends and public holidays, when the town is awash with tourists heading to and from the islands. The bustling river port is not only the hub for passenger boats, but has also been home to a large fishing fleet for several decades. Scenically located overlooking the river and the South China Sea, Mersing town offers cheap accommodation, good seafood restaurants, and is the place to organize boat trips and book accommodation for the numerous island resorts nearby, all of which have offices in the town or at the jetty. Shaded by whispering casuarina trees, a paved walkway which follows the shoreline around town and past the estuary is an excellent place for an evening stroll to the resthouse set on a hilltop overlooking the island-studded horizon.

## PULAU TIOMAN

Spectacular rocky peaks, virgin rainforests, white sandy beaches, and turquoise waters combine to make Pulau Tioman one of Malaysia's better-known tourist destinations. Regular

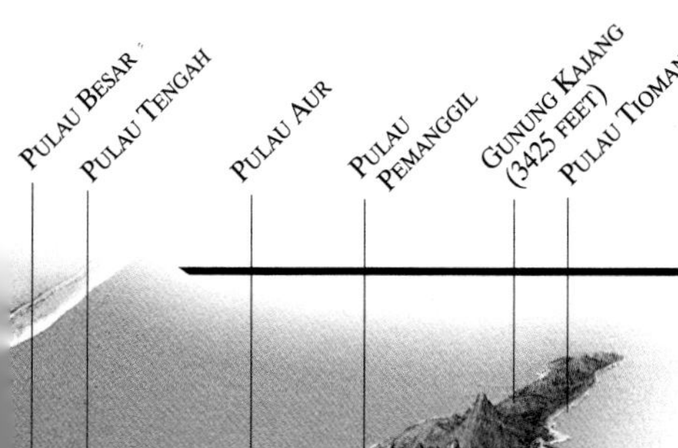


boat services ply the waters between Mersing and Tioman, and visitors have the choice of the "slow-boat" (fishing trawler-cum-passenger boat) which takes 4 hours, or the faster boats which cut the time to about 2 hours. Daily flights also connect the island with Kuala Lumpur and Singapore. Long known by mariners as a source of fresh-water, plentiful timber, game, and sheltered coves, Pulau Tioman is the largest and highest island on Peninsular Malaysia's east coast. Thatched houses and wooden chalets line the shoreline north and south of Tioman village, and a small climb over the hill at the north end of the beach leads to Ayer Batang, a shaded beach with offshore corals, renowned for its cheap accommodation and restaurants, and a favorite venue for international backpackers. A trail leads through the mountainous interior to Juara, a village on the eastern side of the island. Other kampungs, each with chalets and excellent beaches, include Genting, Teluk Nipah, and Mukut, which are accessible only by boat.

## Pulau Rawa

The forerunner of Johor's island resorts, Pulau Rawa, an idyllic isle, is 70 minutes by boat from the jetty at Mersing. This well-established resort, popular for weekend stays, has been run by the Johor royal family since its creation in 1971, and maintains a tradition of excellent service. The beach is talcum-white and the water clear and inviting. Fishing, snorkeling, and scuba-diving equipment can be hired at the resort.

## Pulau Sibu

Located south of Mersing, Pulau Sibu has resort and chalet accommodation, good beaches, and coral reefs ■ *18–19*. The boat ride from Mersing to the island takes less than 3 hours. The water around Pulau Sibu, however, is not as clear as that near Pulau Tioman, which is further off the coast and away from the mainland rivers. Sibu's village is still inhabited by fishing families, and its power supply comes from a pilot project using solar cells. The island can be explored on foot and has a wide variety of resorts and seafood restaurants.

**Kelong**
Looking like a wooden house perched on stilts high above the sea, the *kelong* is actually a large offshore fish trap. Stakes are driven into the sea floor, and the fish are driven into the center, where a generator-driven light lures them into the net. After the *ikan bilis* (tiny anchovies) are hauled to the surface, they are cooked in sea-water and loaded onto trawlers for transport to the mainland, where they are dried in the sun.

**Poh Keh's Shophouse**
Distinguished by a circular upstairs verandah supported by columns, and decorated with floral plaster bas-reliefs, this shophouse in Mersing was built by Poh Keh, an enterprising immigrant from China. He was awarded the contract to build the first road linking Johor Bahru to Mersing. Later on, Poh Keh took his fortune with him back to China, but lost it all when the communists took over the country. Returning to Malaya undaunted, he started again from scratch and moved his sundry shop to the ground floor of what is now Mersing's most famous shophouse.

**Aw Pottery**
Minangkabau-style roofs and porcelain-studded walls are the distinctive hallmarks of the Aw Pottery at Kampung Macap, an area of abundant clay deposits some 3 miles south of Ayer Hitam. Visitors and pottery enthusiasts are welcome to watch the potters at work in the large workshops and to browse through the wares (some of which are pictured below) in the adjoining showroom.
About two thousand pieces of pottery are produced at each firing from a giant brick kiln which is 158 feet long and resembles a fire-spouting dragon. Although the industry is now modernized and has expanded internationally, much of the work is still done manually. Founded in 1940 by Aw Eng Kwang, an immigrant from China, the pottery business is still run by his descendants.

## Batu Pahat

This old town, also known as Bandar Penggaram, has been settled since the days of the Melaka sultanate ● *34*, although few monuments of antiquity remain. The only indication of the old river port's history is at Minyak Beku, where on the flat rocks near the shoreline is a well believed to have been made by the Thais before their 15th-century attack on Melaka. Situated beside the river of the same name, Batu Pahat is the hub of Malaysia's textile industry and is rapidly becoming a center for the electronics industry, with new factories springing up in the adjoining former plantation land. In the old town there are still several old shophouses, a decorative Chinese Chamber of Commerce on Jalan Rahmat, and Art Deco mosque Masjid Jamek on Jalan Ampuan. Batu Pahat is also renowned for its cheap food: oyster omelette and pork satay at Glutton's Corner; *nasi biryani* at the stalls near the bridge; fried bananas opposite the Immigration Office; and chicken fried rice at Pak Jonid's on the Kluang Road.

## Ayer Hitam

This bustling crossroads town, about 56 miles from Johor Bahru, is a favorite stopover for long-distance coaches and local tourists. The town is a mere jumble of old wooden shophouses fronted by market stalls, but no one comes here for the architecture. Ayer Hitam's attraction is in its fantastic array of dried food; from roasted banana chips and shrimp paste, otherwise known as *belacan* (right, above) to Malay cakes and dried cuttlefish (right, below). The open-air markets are popular for fresh fruit, such as rambutans and durian brought in from the surrounding countryside, and pottery produced at nearby Macap.

## Pontian Kecil

This untouristy town situated on the Strait of Melaka is an interesting place to spend a few hours while en route north or as a break on the way to Kukup for a seafood meal. The river, which runs through the center of town, is crammed with colorful fishing trawlers. The main street is typical of Johor's rural towns; Chinese shop houses are shaded by chick blinds advertising the stores' wares, and at coffee shops ● *66–7*, customers in singlets and flip-flops sip their drinks at marble-topped tables. A scenic drive parallels the coast, where shaded parklands give a panoramic view of the Strait and Pulau Pisang, a wooded offshore island. At the Meden Selera, food stalls offer a wide variety of Johor-style cuisine, and a sea-front resthouse provides accommodation.

At the time it was built in 1851, this pleasure boat (above) of the sultan of Johor embodied the latest in boat design, with its "wave principle" hull.

## Kukup

An unpretentious fishing village of wooden houses set on stilts above the water is the setting for Johor's most famous seafood hub. Located on the southern end of the state's west coast, Kukup's cluster of restaurants serve hot and spicy chili crab, barbecued fish, garlic prawns, and squid sambal. They are the *raison d'être* of this village frequented by locals, Singaporeans, and ever-increasing bus-loads of international tourists keen to sample fresh seafood as close to its source as possible, and at economical rates, too. From Johor Bahru, turn off Route 5 for Pontian, then take the coast road to Kukup 11 miles from Pontian.

**Masjid Jamek Benut**
Built in early 20th century, this mosque stands out among the kampung houses at Benut, a fishing village 14 miles north of Pontian. Painted in a pale blue and cream, it features a squat dome and a minaret decorated in floral bas-reliefs. Stained-glass windows dominate the prayer hall, and each cupola and the central dome bear finials with the Islamic symbol – the crescent moon and five-pointed star.

## Tanjung Piai

Thrusting out from the tip of the Malay peninsula is Tanjung Piai, the most southerly point on the Asian mainland. It is located south of Kukup, after a right turn at the Serkat mosque. A wooden jetty marks the spot, and views of Singapore can be had from the seafood restaurant at the end. Along the foreshore, fishermen string nets then wait for the tide to go out before plucking the trapped fish from their nets. Village women bargain with fishermen over the day's catch, as monkeys swing about in the mangrove forests.

**SULTAN ABU BAKAR**
Skilful at political maneuvers, Johor's Sultan Abu Bakar (top) improved the administrative system in 1858. He was adept at both getting along with the colonial powers and keeping the integrity of his own state intact. By the 1870's Johor boasted a treasury, police force, judicial system, and secular schools, and Abu Bakar was considered by Ord, the Straits governor, to be "the only Raja in the whole peninsula... who rules in accordance with the practice of civilised nations". However, his popularity in Singapore and London did nothing to endear him to other Malay sultans, who considered him too European, and merely the son of a Temenggung (above) – a high-ranking official.

## THE STRAITS WATERFRONT

"New Johor", as Johor Bahru translates, is the most recent seat of the Johor sultanate, although the old port on the north side of the Johor Straits predates its former name of Tanjung Petri given it in 1866, when Sultan Abu Bakar chose it as his capital. Today suburbs sprawl into the former plantation land, and ports and refineries have sprung up in the mangrove swamps. However, much of the old royal part of the city along the waterfront, nicknamed "The Lido", still remains. Overlooking the Johor Strait, with Singapore in the background, the shaded parklands that rim the shoreline are a pleasant spot to picnic, watch people, jog, or engage in a favorite Johorean pastime – snacking at food stalls. Further down the sea-front restaurants specialize in fresh seafood and cater to hordes of Singaporeans, who flock to Johor Bahru on weekends for cheap food, bargain shopping, and the now not so naughty nightlife.

**ISTANA BESAR AND ROYAL MUSEUM.** "In his tastes and habits he is an English gentleman," wrote a colonial governor of Sultan Abu Bakar of Johor, who not only spoke English well, but played cricket and even journeyed to England to meet Queen Victoria. On his European trips the Sultan collected furniture and artifacts for his royal abode, Istana Besar (the Big Palace, above), which was completed in 1866, equipped with all the latest in Western comforts. Overlooking the Strait, this grand palace has recently been restored and is now the Muzium Di Raja, the Royal Museum, which displays the staggering antique collection of Sultan Abu Bakar and his son Sultan Ibrahim. Features of the opulent interior include the Reception Room, with its exquisite crystal furniture, the Throne Room, with its golden thrones, and the Hunting Room, with trophies from the days when tigers roamed the outskirts of Johor Bahru.

**SULTAN ABU BAKAR MOSQUE.** Commanding a hilltop position overlooking the Johor Straits is one of Malaysia's loveliest mosques – Masjid Sultan Abu Bakar. Construction began in 1892, during the reign of Sultan Abu Bakar, "The Father of Modern Johor", who died before its completion in 1900. The cream-and-white mosque, which can

The star-and-crescent symbol stands out as an impressive feature on the gate of a Johor Bahru shop.

accommodate up to two thousand worshipers, features decorative plaster work, splendid archways, and hexagonal minarets topped with black domes.

**JARO.** Short for Johor Area Rehabilitation Organization, JARO is regionally renowned for its excellent handicrafts. At its new shop near the resthouse off Jalan Abu Bakar are a variety of crafts made by the handicapped and ex-leprosy and TB sufferers. Good buys include woven basketware, furniture, soft toys. A special section specializes in leather bookbinding. All proceeds go to the organization.

**ISTANA BUKIT SERENE.** At the far end of the seafront, sprawling across spacious grounds with magnificent hilltop views of the Johor Strait, is Istana Bukit Serene, the official residence of the current sultan of Johor. Built in 1933, the palace is surmounted by a 100-foot tower which has become a regional landmark. Within the attractive grounds are the sultan's famed orchid garden, private zoo, and antique-car collection – all out of bounds except for the privileged few.

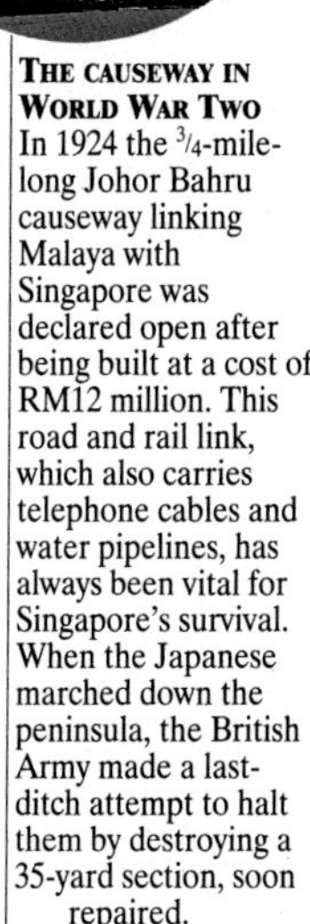

**THE CAUSEWAY IN WORLD WAR TWO**
In 1924 the 3/4-mile-long Johor Bahru causeway linking Malaya with Singapore was declared open after being built at a cost of RM12 million. This road and rail link, which also carries telephone cables and water pipelines, has always been vital for Singapore's survival. When the Japanese marched down the peninsula, the British Army made a last-ditch attempt to halt them by destroying a 35-yard section, soon repaired.

## DOWNTOWN JOHOR BAHRU

As the gateway to Singapore, Johor Bahru is often jammed with traffic – the causeway linking the city (inaugurated on January 1, 1994) with the island republic begins in the downtown area at the end of Jalan Tun Razak. Singaporeans flock to Johor Bahru, as their strong currency buys a lot more north of the border. Old shophouses and coffee shops still cluster around the city center, although they are increasingly giving way to new skyscrapers, fast-food restaurants, and shopping complexes. Shop for tropical fruit at the market on Jalan Wong Ah Fook, try the spicy *nasi padang* at Hwa Mui on Jalan Trus, and the hot South Indian food of the Kerala on Jalan Ibrahim.

**SULTAN IBRAHIM BUILDING (THE FORT).** This building (top right) on Bukit Timbalan is named after the monarch (right) and houses the State Government offices. Constructed in 1940 of gray stone in Saracenic-style, the imposing building contains fine mosaics in the Grand Hall, and its 195-foot tower is one of Johor Bahru's landmarks.

# JOHOR – THE SOUTHEAST

**THE LAST OF THE MELAKA SULTANS**
By all accounts, Sultan Mahmud, the last direct descendant of the Melaka sultans, who trace their lineage back to Raja Iskandar Zulkarnain (Alexander the Great), was a sadist. Well-known for killing at whim, "the royal lunatic," as one historian dubbed the late sultan, was murdered in 1699 by a noble whose pregnant wife had been knifed to death at Mahmud's request. Although his gross behavior was legendary, in Malay *adat* (code of ethics) to kill a ruler was tantamount to treason, and as a result, the entire Malay world was shattered by the regicide. The royal houses of Palembang in Sumatra and Perak, who were related to the late sultan, were incensed at the murder, and some historians believe that this one event symbolized the decline of the Malay trading kingdoms than any other.

## KOTA TINGGI

Located 24 miles north of Johor Bahru at the head of Sungai Johor, Kota Tinggi serves as the gateway to the beach resort of Desaru and the nearby waterfalls, ancient tombs and forts that the region is well-known for. As an ancient seat of the Johor sultanate, Kota Tinggi served as a royal capital and predates Johor Bahru, the present capital, by centuries.

**LOMBONG WATERFALLS.** Undoubtedly Kota Tinggi's major attraction, the Lombong Waterfalls are reached by taking Route 91 out of town and then following the signs to "Air Terjun Lombong" about 9 miles further on. Plan your trip during the week if you enjoy nature in the quiet, as on the weekends the falls are packed with holiday-makers.

## DESARU

Southern Johor's best-known beach resort is 32 miles from Kota Tinggi along a highway which cleaves the vast oil-palm estates. Two luxury resort hotels overlook a spacious beach shaded by murmuring casuarina trees which account for the name Desaru, meaning "place of casuarinas". Attractions include golf, jungle trekking and horse-riding.

## JOHOR LAMA

Remnants of this once great fort and former capital of the Johor sultanate still survive beside Sungai Johor downstream from Kota Tinggi. Known as Kota Batu (Stone Fort), it can be reached either by boat from Kongkong or by taking the Desaru road and turning off to Kampung Teluk Sengat. Enraged by Johor's blockades against Melaka, the Portuguese attacked Johor Lama in 1587. Although their cannons wreaked damage estimated at 200,000 cruzados their first attempt ended in failure, since the fort was stoutly defended by 8,000 Malays, including warriors from Terengganu, Java and Sumatra. Two weeks later, the Portuguese returned in renewed force and after nine days of intense fighting, Kota Batu fell to the infidel Iberians. Dom Paolo de Lima, the conqueror, set fire to the town and made off with the spoils of his conquest, including treasures that had been hastily buried by the Malays, 2,000 sailing craft, 1,000 guns and 1,500 muskets. Even more treasures, buried after the battle, were unearthed this century when archeologists uncovered bronze objects, coins and amulets dating from the Majapahit empire, and shards of Chinese porcelain.

A Malay house near Johor Lama.

# EAST MALAYSIA

**SARAWAK'S BROOKE DYNASTY**
The Victorians perceived Rajah Sir James as a hero of the Byronic and romantic kind. At his death in 1867 he left a much enlarged Sarawak to his nephew Charles. Sir Charles had a natural son, too, but dynastic considerations prompted him to marry Margaret de Windt. The couple had three sons, of whom the eldest, Charles Vyner, succeeded in 1917. Rajah Charles didn't trust his heir and disapproved of his daughter-in-law. Neither of the parents made a secret of their preference for the younger son, Bertram, who was vested with power under the terms of his father's will. The behavior of Sylvia, the last rajah's wife, and her flapper daughters made waves in the 1930's, when misalliances and multiple divorces were not at all the thing in the best families. There was scant sympathy for the dynasty when Sir Charles Vyner abdicated in 1946, ignoring the claims of his nephew and heir, Anthony, Bertram's son.

## HISTORY

In Malay "serawak" means "antimony", although the place-name cannot have conveyed much to readers of J. de Barros' 15th-century work *Décadas de Asia*, which mentions "Cerava, the place antimony comes from". The Sarawak and other river systems on the northwest coast of Borneo once lay under the suzerainty of the sultan of Brunei. Inhabited by Bidayuh tribesmen and under the fitful government of a few Malays along the coast, Sarawak was for centuries no trouble to anyone – nor any great use. The rise of Singapore put a market within reach. In the 1820's, a handful of Brunei nobles moved to Kuching, intent upon selling Sarawak's gold, antimony, and jungle produce to the growing emporium. Their less than tactful policies soon provoked a rebellion which dragged on for years. In 1839, an English gentleman–adventurer named James Brooke happened by. Invalided out of the East India Company's army, Brooke had visited Singapore in his private yacht, and was asked to take a letter to the Brunei viceroy in Kuching. Here he was persuaded by Rajah Muda Hassim, heir apparent to the sultan of Brunei, to help quell the uprising, which he did quickly. To the viceroy's considerable surprise, Brooke won the war by

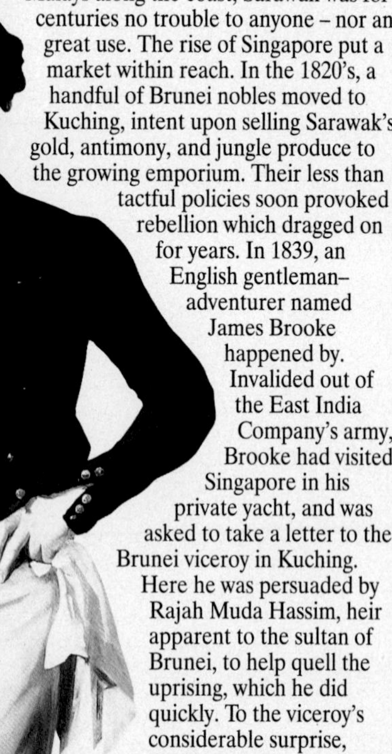

showing mercy and understanding to the rebels. The offshoot of the tangled story is stranger than fiction: James Brooke found himself rajah of the obstreperous little province in 1841! Some of Sarawak's population may have "blessed the name of Brooke", to quote Sir James, and appreciated his efforts to abolish piracy and headhunting; others resented his infringement of what they considered to be their traditional rights. The Chinese rebellions in 1857 were a dramatic challenge to Brooke authority. The early years of the raj were troubled by conspiracies of dispossessed Brunei nobles and local leaders. Without money to retain a standing army, the rajahs often incited friendly tribes to administer hefty doses of "pacification" to unfriendly ones – a strange stratagem for a government dedicated to the abolition of inter-tribal warfare. Sarawak's international position was secured by British protection in 1888. To the rajah's chagrin, Brunei was similarly protected, frustrating any designs of absorbing his former overlord's land. By the turn of the century, Sarawak was mostly peaceful, and had reached its present size. It dozed through the years between the wars, when newly arrived civil servants were assured that "Here we all take it easy."

## Black gold

Oil was discovered in 1910, and four years later Sarawak started to export the precious commodity. The only serious fighting during World War Two took place in Miri, in 1941 and 1945, when the Japanese and the Australians, respectively, bombed the oil fields. Kuching's old-world townscape escaped almost unscathed. Early reports of Borneo's untold riches proved to be canards. There had been considerable gold mining activity in the 18th and 19th centuries, but today Bukit Young in Bau is one of the few mines still operating. Jungle produce and sago yielded more revenue than "Sarawak diamonds" ever did; much of the country's soil is unproductive if cleared of its forest cover. The Japanese invasion in 1941 ended Brooke's rule. The third rajah, Sir Charles Vyner, visited his country to announce its cession to the British crown in 1946. Sarawak was a colony until 1963. At the turn of the century, the discovery of petroleum near Miri in eastern Sarawak had put the quaint principality on the map in another sense. Miri was fiercely fought over in World War Two; the presence of oil was a major consideration when the concept of Malaysia was mooted in the early 1960's. In 1963, Malaya, Singapore, Sabah, and Sarawak joined to form Malaysia ● *41*. The sultanate of Brunei opted to remain outside this federation.

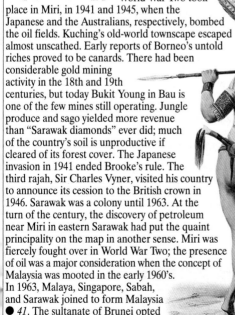

**The end of an era**
The Brookes were an anachronism in their own time. A white rajah who was chief justice and court of appeal in one person offended 20th-century notions of democracy. Rajah Charles Vyner spent more time in England than in Sarawak, leaving the administration to a civil service recruited on the basis of being "gentlemen, and jolly good fellows".

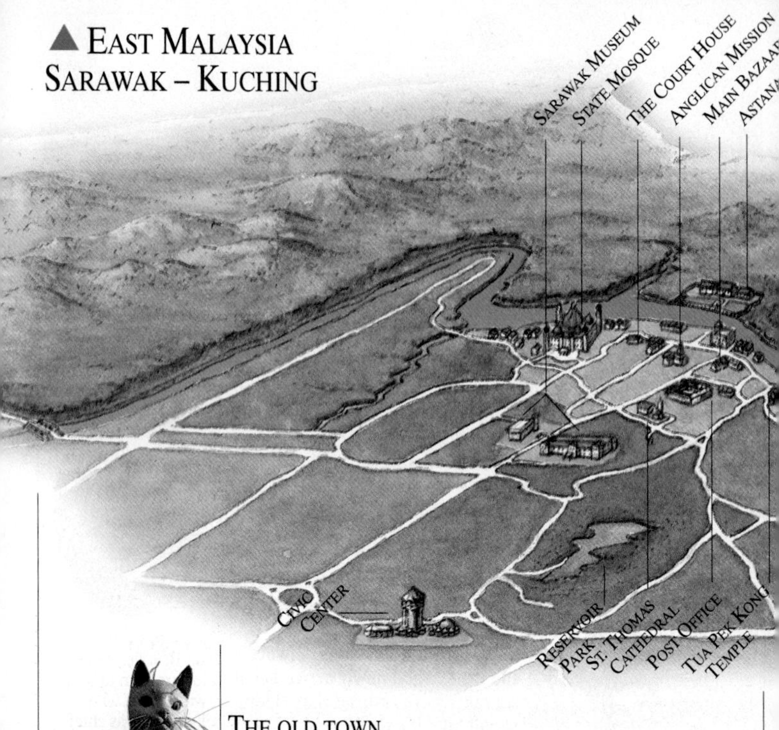


*Kucing* means "cat" in Malay, and there is no shortage of quaint stories explaining the origin of the town's name. James Brooke once asked his trusty Malay boatsman: "What's that?" pointing at the town; the local yokel saw a cat on the river shore and answered: "*Itu kucing.*" ("That's a cat.") However, Kuching had its name long before Brooke was seen or heard of, and Sarawak Malay for cat is *pusa*, not *kucing*.

## THE OLD TOWN

From a one-boat town on a muddy river, Kuching has grown into the capital of Malaysia's largest state. Visitors don't always recognize the town's mixed population. Satin, beads, and feathers are reserved for festival wear; when they walk down the street on a workday, Sarawak's Chinese, Malays, and Borneo natives look pretty much alike! The old town follows the river, the lifeline and sole traffic route in the old days. Attractions such as Fort Margherita, the Astana, and the Court House are within hailing distance of each other, literally: in the rajahs' days the watchmen at these three bastions had to call to each other every hour. Gambier Road and Main Bazaar, together with India and Carpenter Streets, are lined with South Chinese-style shophouses. Several carpenters' shops still operate in Carpenter Street. Around the corner hangs the tile of a "Maker of Fancy Coffins". Tinsmiths hammer in adjoining shops, and goldsmiths and watchmakers testify to the town's prosperity.

**FORT MARGHERITA.** This fort sits on Fort Hill opposite Kuching, ready to defend the town at all costs. Cannons stand behind battened-down gun ports, trained on the river and the town. Yet the venerable fort has not had a shot fired at it in all the years of its existence. The Japanese bombed it in 1941 – and missed! Fort Margherita was built in 1879 as the headquarters of the Sarawak constabulary. It is still in police service today, as a museum. The building is best approached from Pengkalan Sapi, the ferry jetty opposite the vegetable market, though it may also be reached by road. Entry is free. As the fort is situated inside a police school, visitors must produce some form of identification to the sentry post at the entrance.

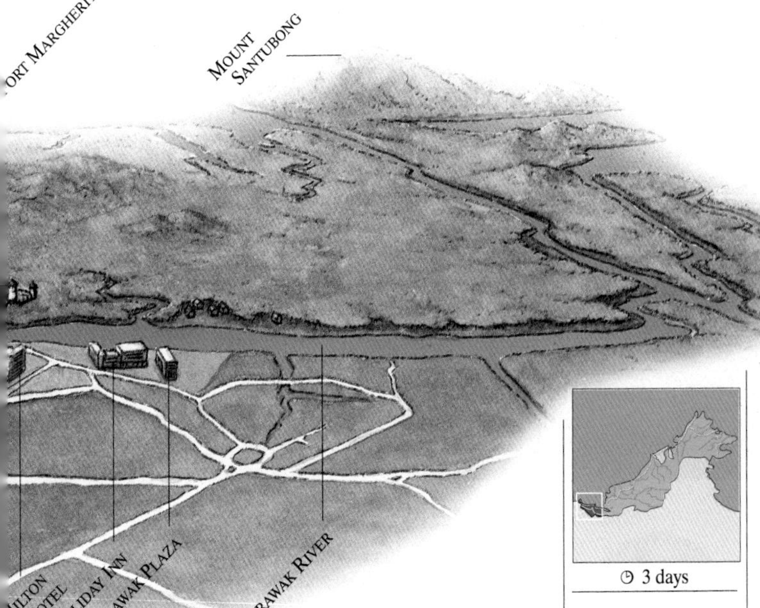


**The Astana.** This palace (pictured below) was built by Rajah Charles in 1870, after his marriage to Margaret de Windt. It consists of three substantial bungalows linked by verandahs, and a keep crowned with battlements which served both as defense and ornament. Its setting on a hillock opposite Kuching town provided the wide-roofed building with adequate ventilation and shade; with its high stucco ceilings it was a pleasantly cool building even before the advent of air-conditioning. The Astana is now the official residence of the governor of Sarawak, and is closed to the public.

**The Court House.** The present Court House was built in 1874 as a secretariat. Its situation permitted Rajah Charles to supervise the arrival of his government officers, which he often did, gold watch on the table, from the breakfast room at the Astana across the river. It was one of the strong points of Brooke's rule that the rajah was available to his subjects whenever he was in the country. He sat in court personally and heard cases, petitions, and appeals, advised by local community leaders well versed in their own codes of law. Today this dignified building (above) houses the High Court of East Malaysia. The Court Chamber ceiling is of special interest, being decorated with panels of native designs representing various tribes. The magnificent hardwood shingle roof was replaced in 1988 at great expense: skilled workmen who know how to make and fit wooden shingles are scarce. The Charles Brooke Memorial in front of the Court House was unveiled in 1924, as a tribute to the "old rajah" who had steered the ship of state with an iron hand for forty-nine years. It is decorated with four bronze plaques depicting the four main races of Sarawak, and a marble medallion of the "old lion's" impressive profile.

**"Tuan DO"**
Before telegraphic communications, a district officer (DO) was indeed monarch of all he surveyed. Omni-potence, coupled with loneliness, bred a race of eccentrics. A well-known anecdote tells of a DO who arraigned himself for wrecking furniture when drunk and, after pleading guilty in the dock, went up to the bench and sentenced himself to pay a fine.

One of the four bronze plaques on the Charles Brooke Memorial.

## THE MAIN BAZAAR

The Main Bazaar and Gambier Road are the scene of the weighing, sorting, loading, and unloading of double- and triple-parked lorries for most of the day. Sacks and bundles are hauled into commodious storage lofts with overhead pulleys. Two men support a strong beam which holds a spring scale now that the *dacing* (steelyard) is no longer legal for trade. They are probably weighing sacks of pepper or bundled rubber sheets, commodities which founded many a Hokkien or Teochew family firm three or four generations ago. Kuching is linked to the other towns of Sarawak by road, air, river, and sea. Kuching port can take vessels of up to 12,500 tons, and today handles an increasing number of containers.

**INDIAN MOSQUE.** A stroll from Kuching's hotels along the waterfront and main landmarks may well end in India Street. Kuching's cloth merchants are concentrated in the old *kling* (Indian) bazaar, now a pedestrian mall. The Indian mosque is hard to find, as it is hemmed in by houses. Between houses No. 37 and No. 39, stone steps form the entrance to a narrow lane, which leads to the mosque. Visitors are allowed in but are reminded to take their shoes off before stepping into this place of worship. Slim visitors can go on past the mosque, into the ever-narrowing lane until they find themselves squeezed between two walls, and in the back of a spice shop in the Main Bazaar.

**TUA PEK KONG TEMPLE.** There is some controversy about the actual age of the Tua Pek Kong. This Chinese temple was built in 1876, but on a site that

**THE ANGLICAN MISSION**
Thomas Francis McDougall was a parson–surgeon posted to Sarawak in 1848. He combined piety and charity with an honest fighting spirit. Traveling in a boat which was attacked by pirates off Bintulu, he aided the crew until he was required below deck to treat the wounded. This unepiscopal performance earned him much criticism in ecclesiastical circles.

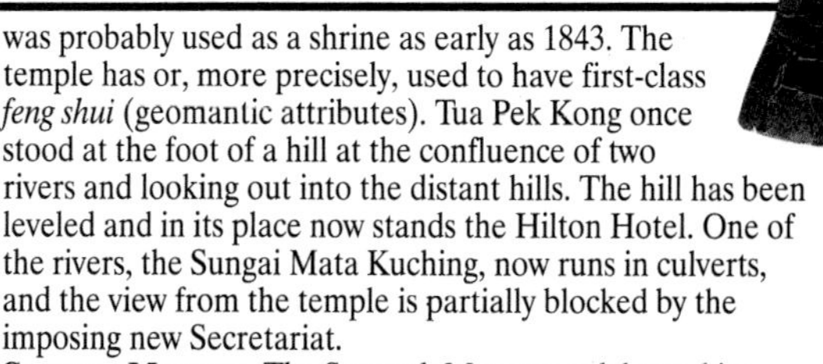

was probably used as a shrine as early as 1843. The temple has or, more precisely, used to have first-class *feng shui* (geomantic attributes). Tua Pek Kong once stood at the foot of a hill at the confluence of two rivers and looking out into the distant hills. The hill has been leveled and in its place now stands the Hilton Hotel. One of the rivers, the Sungai Mata Kuching, now runs in culverts, and the view from the temple is partially blocked by the imposing new Secretariat.

**SARAWAK MUSEUM.** The Sarawak Museum celebrated its centenary in 1991. For one hundred years it has instructed, amused, and amazed visitors from all over the world. Ever since its inception, the museum has been well patronized by locals. Museum visits are a form of instant quality control – an Iban weaver would not feel shy to voice criticism if she saw inferior textiles on display; nor would an Orang Ulu carver confronted with a poorly made artifact supposedly from his tribe keep his comments to himself. There is some doubt about the origin of the museum building. Of course Rajah Charles chose the design personally, some say after a town hall in Normandy, others after a girls' school in Australia. The museum has long been the only institute of higher learning in Sarawak, and its *Sarawak Museum Journal* is a highly respected publication of Borneo research. The Sarawak Museum now occupies three buildings: the Old Building, Tun Abdul Razak Building immediately across the road and, behind the latter building, the old Malay School. The museum collections will be extended into the present post office after a new one has been built.

**THE POST OFFICE.** This was built during the reign of Rajah Charles Vyner. Constructed on an impressive scale, its Greek-style portico is supported by Corinthian columns. Besides its usual function as a post office, it is the point of origin of the only trunk road in Sarawak. A letter addressed to "Mile 6" or "Mile 57" will be delivered!

**BORNEO CANNONS**
Antique cannons are found in various places in Sarawak. Many of them are from Brunei, once a famous center of brass-casting. These old symbols of warfare and piracy are usually held in high esteem by their present owners. *Bujang sambong*, the "welded bachelor" in Kampong Sibuyau at the mouth of the Batang Lupar River, is credited with supernatural powers. People in distress make a vow which they redeem in the form of cakes, chickens, or even a goat. The *bujang sambong* is appealed to in cases of illness or peril at sea.

**Pottery kilns**
When James Brooke arrived, there was already a Chinese pottery kiln on the banks of the Sarawak River producing utilitarian vessels for the local market. Such wares were finished with a honey-brown glaze of iron oxide. A pottery's name plate may proclaim Wong or Sim; the master potter is nearly always a Teochew called Ng. Having made his fortune in Southeast Asia, an aging Mr Ng would retire to China to be succeeded by a younger family member from his village. Today, pottery businesses pass on to Sarawak-born sons and grandsons, who tend to replace the wood-fired "dragon kilns" with the gas-fired variety.

The Sarawak River delta is now accessible following the construction of roads and bridges there. Facilities such as beach hotels and an adventure camp and lookout are expected to stimulate tourism in the area.

## Bako National Park

Less than 2 hours from Kuching, Bako National Park preserves 6750 acres of mangroves ■ *20–1*, peat forest, dipterocarp rainforest ■ *22–3*, and the heath vegetation known locally as *krangas*. Besides a troop of cheeky monkeys, who loiter around the holiday bungalows in the constant hope of getting fed, the park is home to a tribe of *Larvatus nasalis* or long-nosed monkeys, a leaf-eating species that can be seen breakfasting among the trees at dusk. Wild pigs in the park have picked up the unporcine habit of wading into the gentle surf to root for crabs and shellfish. Bako peninsula is mostly sandstone, worn and weathered to fantastically tinted cliffs and sea stacks by the waves and tides. Some of the higher ground has been eroded by rain and wind to form a *padang batu*, an almost barren flat rock plain covered with scanty scrub vegetation.

This is where pitcher plants or monkey cups flourish. A number of scenic and educational trails permit access to all the nooks and crannies of Bako National Park. They range from a half-hour stroll to a day-long trek, which necessitates camping overnight at Telok Limau or Telok Kruin. Visitors can book comfortable bungalows for overnight stays in the park.

## Mount Santubong

Mount Santubong stands like a beacon. For centuries it has guided traders, and pirates, into the mouth of the river. Celebrated in legend and song, Santubong is the mystical home of Kuching's Malays, who trace their descent to a hero, Datu Merpati, who lived here "long long ago". Mount Santubong is only 2740 feet high, but it supports some

highland vegetation ■ *28–9*. Rhododendrons bloom on its windswept upper slopes and there is moss forest near the summit pool. A well-marked trail takes visitors up a fairly steep hike to the peak. It is well worth the effort for an all-round view of the Sarawak River basin on a fine day. On any other day, some rain protection should be taken along. The squalls never last long, but they come on very suddenly – this region has 200 inches of rainfall a year!

**THE MYSTERIOUS BATU GAMBAR.** An interesting find near Mount Santubong was made in a nearby creek called Sungai Jaong. It is a mysterious boulder decorated with a spread-eagled human figure in bas-relief, apparently unconnected with Indian or Chinese trading or cultural activity. A cast of the *batu gambar* (literally, picture stone) can be seen in front of the old Sarawak Museum in Kuching.

## LUNDU AND SEMATAN BEACHES

Between the Sarawak delta and the Borneo promontory, Cape Datu, are the beaches of Lundu and Sematan, and the newly gazetted National Park of Gunong Gading with its gushing waterfalls and easily accessible Rafflesias. 60 miles of good road make Lundu a popular weekend spot for Kuching townees. The beaches vary from mangrove flats ■ *20–1* to sandy strands shaded by tall casuarina trees. Lofty apong palm fronds deck the swamp between streams and inlets. Here a few old-timers ply their trades: the tapper and boiler of palm sugar, the maker of leaf thatch, the charcoal burner.

**DAMAI CULTURAL VILLAGE.** Situated within walking distance of the beach resorts, the Damai Cultural Village contains Sarawak in miniature. Longhouses ● *76–7* of the major tribal groups are on display, staffed by guides who explain and demonstrate the culture of their people to visitors. Dance and music performances are staged regularly, and handicrafts are produced and offered for sale.

**THE SANTUBONG BUDDHA**

Santubong was a trading town from the 10th century to the 14th century, and was frequented by Chinese and Indian seafarers. A Tantric shrine has been uncovered half a mile from the present Santubong village, near the river's edge, where ancient mariners made their landfall after an adventurous voyage. The stone paving of the temple concealed a vertical shaft which held a ritual deposit box containing gold-foil figures and stone beads. The Santubong Buddha was found on the hill behind the shrine. This little statue has been identified as a cave-temple type of the Gupta Buddha, possibly dating from the 9th century. It is believed to have been brought to Santubong from India in the 10th or 11th century. A.D.

KAMPUNG SIGI
PALOH
IGAN RIVER
KAMPUNG KUALA MATU

**"SICKNESS IMAGES"**
These "sickness images" were carved by Melanau healers after diagnosis of the illness of the patients. Fashioned from soft sago pith, such images are the focus of night-long ceremonies.
At dawn the symbol of illness is placed in a provisioned little boat and floated down the river, on a journey of no return. Doctors are baffled by recoveries of seemingly hopeless cases after the *dukun* or *bomoh* (shaman) has been summoned.

The Rajang, at 338 miles, is Malaysia's longest river. From high in the central mountain range of Borneo, its tributaries gush over spectacular rapids on their way off the plateau. They unite above Kapit, then the majestic river rolls down through an ever-widening valley. After Sibu it divides into the meanders typical of a large watercourse pushing through its own alluvium bed towards the sea. The fertile lowlands between the Rajang and smaller rivers to the east support the Melanau people, a group spread much further up and down the coast in past times. The Melanau differ from other indigenous Borneo peoples in their staple: sago. They live amphibiously between the open sea and the brackish swamps, where the sago palm grows. Sago is harvested by felling the palm, splitting the trunk to expose the pith, rasping it, and washing out the starch by pressing it through coarse mats into sedimentation troughs. The starch is spread on mats to dry, producing raw sago flour. Sago mills, most of them in the Mukah/Oya region, produce RM17 million worth of refined starch each year.

## SIBU

Below this bustling town the river frays into a multitude of estuarine courses lazily rolling through the plains. In 1900, Chinese Methodists from Foochow (Fuzhou) disembarked at Sungai Merah, a few miles from present-day Sibu, invited to settle there by Rajah Charles Brooke, who envisaged a rice-producing area to provision his state, but rice-growing was

**THE SIBU PAGODA**
The landmark seven-story Sibu pagoda, built in 1989, stands on an old temple site by the waterfront. A wooden shrine was rebuilt in brick and stone in 1897. World War Two bombs destroyed the temple but the statue of *Tua Pek Kong* ("Great-Uncle", the resident deity) remained unharmed.

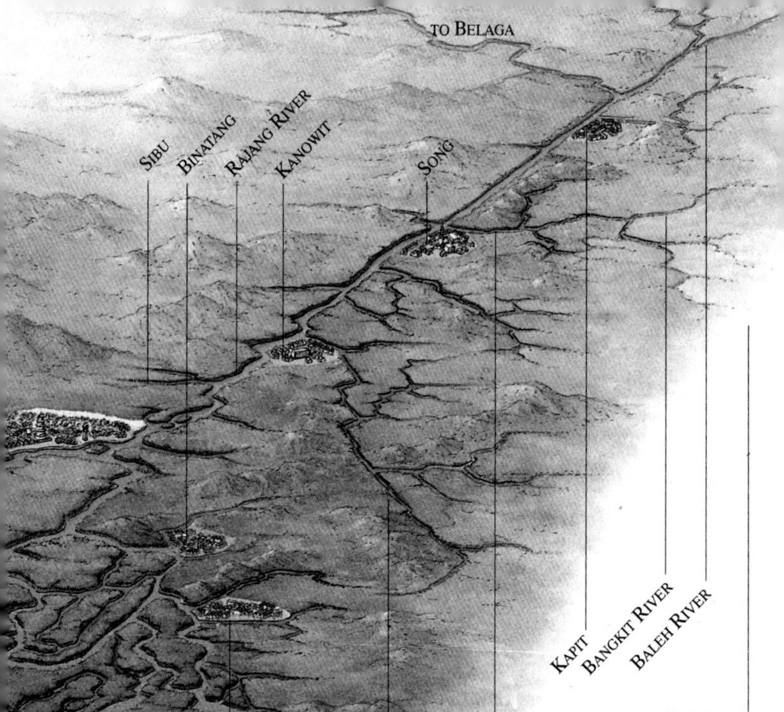

TO BELAGA
SIBU
BINATANG
RAJANG RIVER
KANOWIT
SONG
KAPIT
BANGKIT RIVER
BALEH RIVER
JERIJEH
SARIKEI
KANOWIT RIVER
KATIBAS RIVER

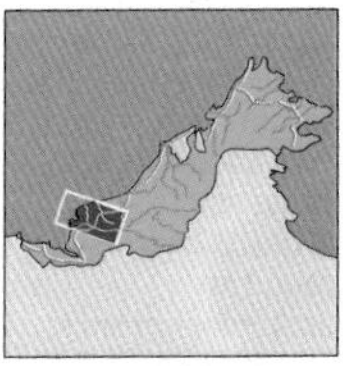

⏱ 4 days

soon abandoned for cash crops such as rubber. Sibu court records of this period are liberally peppered with cases such as "Serin of Telok Selalo vs Wong Eng Guan" and "Kriak vs Ah Chai", as the newcomers wrested land from the Iban who traditionally occupied the Lower Rajang. Unlike 19th-century Chinese immigrants, the Foochows arrived with their families. They did not have to look to the local population for marriage partners; in the early years they would have disdained such unions! Land laws were enacted to cope with this unprecedented situation, but very often the local district officer, unhampered by much legal knowledge, settled cases using just his own ideas of justice. "The whole of the trouble in this district", wrote one, "is that they [Foochows] don't know the language or customs of the Dayaks; they come in and see old padi land which is free from all large timber and very easily cleared and naturally settle there. They do not seem to be able to distinguish between ordinary trees and fruit trees. I feel none of the damage done to Dayak fruit trees is wilful, but merely out of pure ignorance...."

## KANOWIT AND KAPIT

Trading junks used to sail upriver as far as Kanowit, where the river narrows to 250 yards wide. Chinese shopkeepers settled here in the 1870's, and the township might have become the commercial center of the Upper Rajang had Rajah Charles not settled upon Kapit as the administrative headquarters. Kapit is the staging point for adventurous journeys to the interior, but the town, with a population of ten thousand, can only be reached by river or by air.

**GOLD BUTTON**
The top, bottom, and side views of a gold button used to adorn the sleeve of a Melanau woman's jacket.

**BEADS**
The Orang Ulu and Lun Bawang have elevated a common Borneo predilection for beads to a fine art. Nimble fingers decorate any article of daily use with fine beadwork. Larger beads, some considered very valuable because of their age, are strung into necklaces proudly worn by both sexes. Knowledgeable elders can distinguish several dozen types of beads, unhesitatingly separating antiques from modern fakes – and, as with ceramics, there's no shortage of those! Glass and stone beads have come to Borneo by way of trade since very ancient times. Bone and stone artifacts have been found at archeological sites, mostly in caves. Then small Chinese and Indian opaque glass beads arrived, Indian carnelian, translucent West Asian glass, and, from around 1400, polychrome confections from Venice, Amsterdam, Bohemia, and even Birmingham. A new trend is to make clay beads for common use, thus preserving valuable antiques. Since the 1980's, wearing grandma's beads with a modern outfit has become "in" with the smart young set. Beads may have lost their magical significance, but their beauty is timeless.

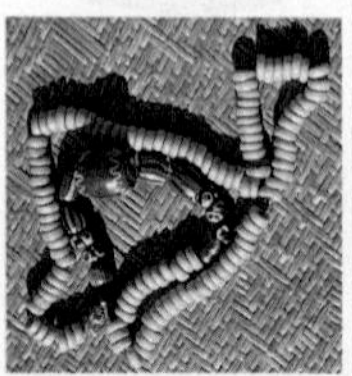

## KAPIT

Strong rapids separate the Upper from the Lower Rajang. Until quite recent times, these roaring obstacles served as an effective barrier for the upriver peoples, the "Orang Ulu". Above the rapids lie the mountains of central Borneo, hemmed in by a highland plain in many places, fended by cliffs and gorges that only the nimblest feet can traverse. Kapit, at the foot of the rapids, was founded to prevent land-hungry Ibans from moving upriver and into the Balleh region. As a crowd-control operation it was a flop; the Ibans simply crossed the watershed from the Ulu Ai and settled in the Balleh anyway. But the settlement around the fort grew. Today it is one of Sarawak's largest inland towns, the very heartland of a pioneering Iban population. Any upriver trip from Kapit is bound to be long and tiring, and may be difficult. If the water level is too high or too low, not even the most daring boatman will shoot the rapids to Belaga, the main town of the Upper Rajang.

**RUMAH GARAI.** This longhouse stands at Kaki Wong, and is accessible only by express boat. Visitors are welcome, provided they contribute towards their own provisioning, on the understanding that they observe Iban longhouse manners, and that they will not resent their hosts' absence in the rice fields during the agricultural seasons. Instead of the standard gifts of sweets and tobacco, bring tinned foods, biscuits, and fresh fruit as healthy additions to the family diet. A longer-staying guest could bring his hostess a sarong, toys for the children, or books and magazines, all of which are almost unobtainable in *ulu* (interior) areas.

## BELAGA DISTRICT

When you reach Belaga, you are in another world. This predominantly Kayan area has preserved a traditional way of life while adopting innovations such as electricity, piped water, schools, and clinics.

Longhouses ● 76–7

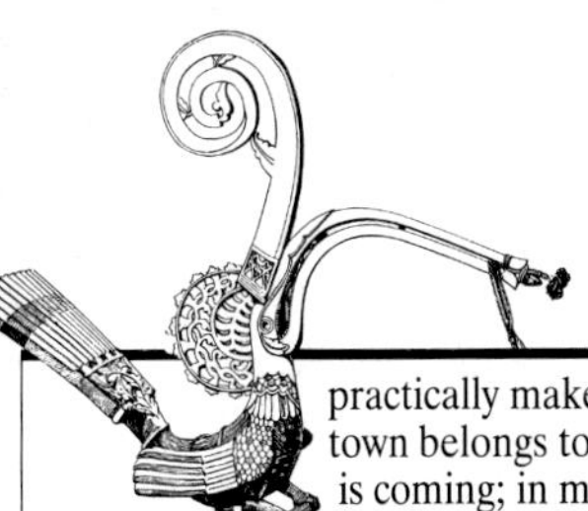

practically make up the town, just as the town belongs to the longhouses. But change is coming; in many communities the young and able-bodied men have migrated downriver in search of paid employment, while their wives, children, or parents wait in the longhouse for their seasonal visits. The center portion of a Kayan longhouse is embellished with wall paintings of traditional designs, such as the Tree of Life surrounded by "good" animals, suited to the aristocracy who live there. The middle and lower classes have their rooms farther away from the center, in roughly descending order. Kayan society, and indeed all Orang Ulu society, was strongly stratified in the past. Certain ornaments in clothing, house decoration, and tattoos could only be used by the upper class. The lower classes owed their masters corvée labor. They could not leave the longhouse without the chief's permission, or dare to marry into a higher class without incurring severe sanctions. The advent of education, Christianity, and a reformed version of the traditional religion softened the rigors of the old system. Traditional observation of omens and taboos is relaxed or ignored. It is illegal, in all of Sarawak, to allude to a person's supposed "slave descent"! Foreigners are

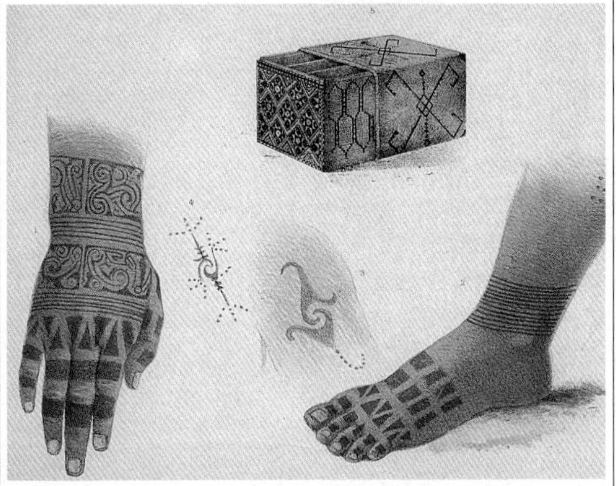

often surprised to see Christian chapels and churches in Borneo's interior, many of them beautifully decorated with traditional native designs. The mostly evangelical communities frown upon smoking, drinking, and pop music on a Sunday, but do not discourage the artistic and cultural traditions which are such an integral part of Ulu life. However, changes in fashion and lifestyle are brought about by outside influences, not religion. Very few native girls have their arms and legs tattooed these days. Some women are even having their elongated ear lobes snipped off by a doctor, but this is done for personal reasons: "I hate getting stared at and photographed each time tourists come up here!" one matron in Wong Murum confessed. Handicrafts, beadwork, smithcraft, and wood-carving are the natural artistic expression of most Orang Ulu, and nowadays there is the bonus of earning extra money by producing for the local market. Like the Iban, many Orang Ulu are risking life and limb to earn good money in the logging camps, despite the threat tree-felling poses to their own environment.

**ORANG ULU CRAFTS**
The Orang Ulu devoted huge efforts and expenditure to the construction of tomb monuments commensurate with the departed's status. Aristocrats were obliged to employ the best craftsmen, to feed and pay them royally while they carved grandpa's tomb post. Economy in such an essential matter would have reflected badly on the family.

# THE WARPATH OF WOMEN

The Iban say that when a child is conceived, the as yet unsexed embryo is offered the choice of a spear (*sangkoh*) or weaving heddle (*letan*) to hold. Should it choose the former, then its sex will be male; the latter, female. The spear is identified with warfare and headhunting, while the heddle represents weaving, the female counterpart to the taking of heads. In Iban oral literature the legendary headhunters of Panggau Libau marry the weavers of Gellong. Women who are skilled at weaving are compared with men who have been on the warpath and taken heads; those who are experienced in the ritual preparation of dyes and mordants are identified as the female equivalent of great war leaders. And just as young men were traditionally considered ineligible for marriage until they had taken a head, or at least participated in a headhunting raid, neither could Iban maidens be properly considered for marriage until they had demonstrated their competency at weaving.

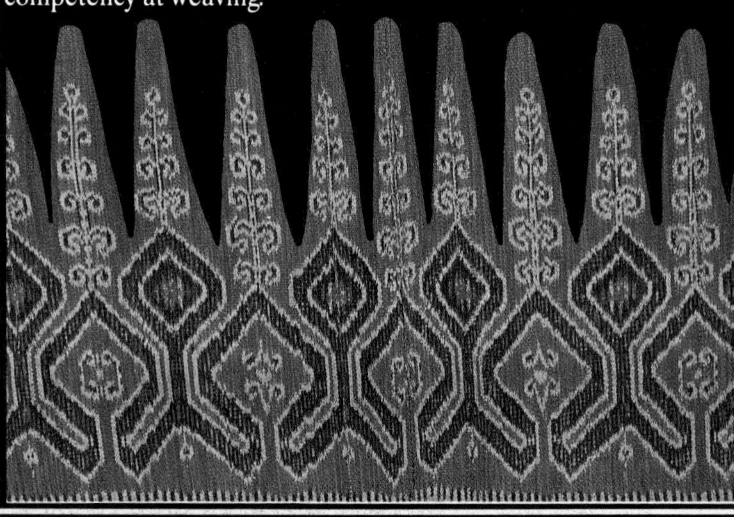

"THE WOMAN SITS ON THE GROUND WITH THIS LOOP AROUND HER WAIST, AND THUS MAINTAINS THE NECESSARY TENSION ON THE WEB."

CHARLES HOSE, *NATURAL MAN, A RECORD FROM BORNEO*

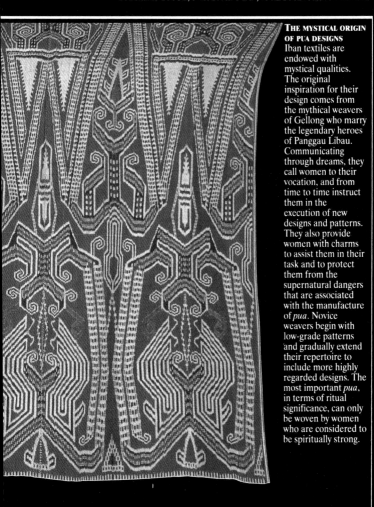

**THE MYSTICAL ORIGIN OF PUA DESIGNS**
Iban textiles are endowed with mystical qualities. The original inspiration for their design comes from the mythical weavers of Gellong who marry the legendary heroes of Panggau Libau. Communicating through dreams, they call women to their vocation, and from time to time instruct them in the execution of new designs and patterns. They also provide women with charms to assist them in their task and to protect them from the supernatural dangers that are associated with the manufacture of *pua*. Novice weavers begin with low-grade patterns and gradually extend their repertoire to include more highly regarded designs. The most important *pua*, in terms of ritual significance, can only be woven by women who are considered to be spiritually strong.

**BACK-STRAP LOOM**
So-named because of a strap that is attached to the breast beam of the loom which passes around the back of the seated weaver. The weaver maintains an appropriate tension on the warp yarns by leaning backwards. The far end of the warp encircles a bar, or warp beam, which is attached to some part of the longhouse structure. The warp is continuous, making a loop between the breast beam and the warp beam. A shed stick separates half the warp elements and allows for the insertion of weft, which is beaten down into place by a smooth wooden batten or "sword stick". When the completed weaving is removed from the loom, it has a tubular shape. A small section remains unwoven and it is here that a cut is made, creating fringes.

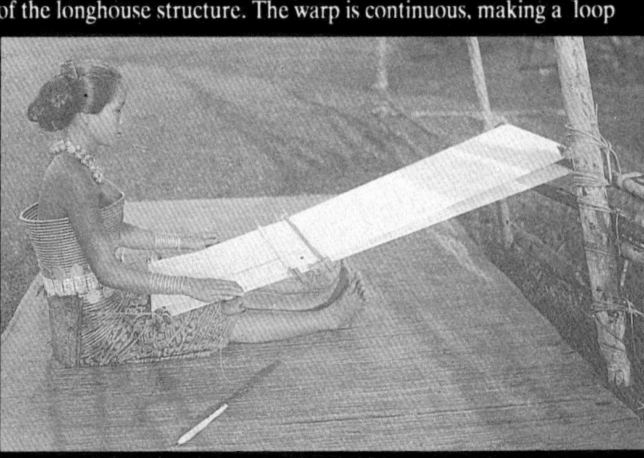

# PATTERNS

Iban textile patterns are characterized by branching geometric designs, angular whorls, pendants, triangles, and diamonds. Imageries of crocodiles (*buaya*), mythical serpents (*nabau*), and anthropomorphic figures (*engkeramba*) are also common, the latter being identified as ancestor figures. The patterns are executed by the warp *ikat* method, where selected warp fibers (*ngebat*) are tied together with natural fiber in a pre-established configuration prior to their immersion in a mordant (*selup*). The bound sections do not take up the dye and constitute a light beige figure set on a terracotta background. The process is repeated to provide different accents in various shades of brown and black. The weft fibers do not register as part of the pattern when subsequently woven into the fabric. Vegetable dyes are obtained from forest plants and are mixed with lime.

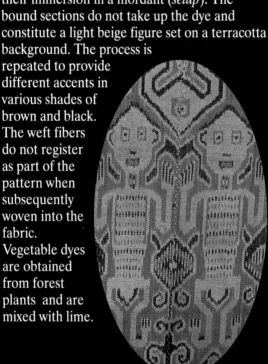

"I LOVED WEARING THE DRESS BECAUSE OF ITS BEAUTY, BUT... A TALL ENGLISHWOMAN CANNOT EXPECT TO WEAR IT WITH THE GRACE WHICH BELONGS TO THOSE TINY FRAIL-LOOKING DAUGHTERS OF THE SUN." MARGARET BROOKE, *MY LIFE IN SARAWAK*

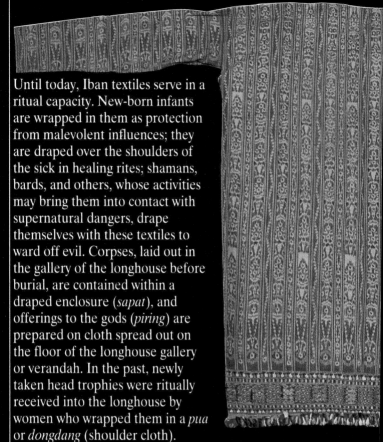

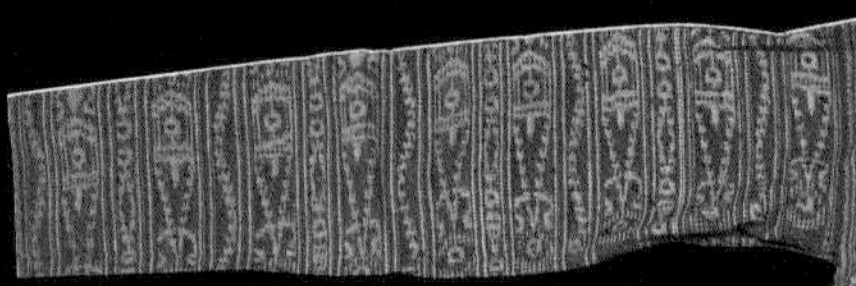

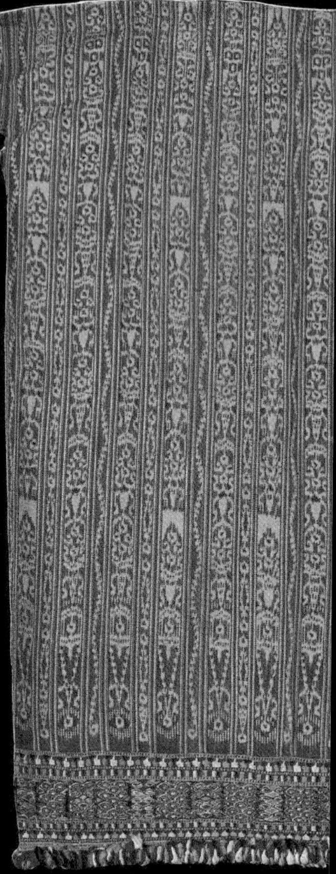

Until today, Iban textiles serve in a ritual capacity. New-born infants are wrapped in them as protection from malevolent influences; they are draped over the shoulders of the sick in healing rites; shamans, bards, and others, whose activities may bring them into contact with supernatural dangers, drape themselves with these textiles to ward off evil. Corpses, laid out in the gallery of the longhouse before burial, are contained within a draped enclosure (*sapat*), and offerings to the gods (*piring*) are prepared on cloth spread out on the floor of the longhouse gallery or verandah. In the past, newly taken head trophies were ritually received into the longhouse by women who wrapped them in a *pua* or *dongdang* (shoulder cloth).

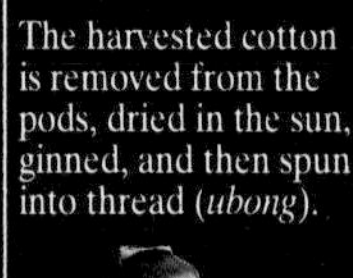

The harvested cotton is removed from the pods, dried in the sun, ginned, and then spun into thread (*ubong*).

**Supplementary Weft**

This skirt in a supplementary weft on a plain ground is similar in technique and design to cloths from Sumatra, Bali, and Laos. Scholars can only speculate on the connections.

The *kalambi* (jacket) worn by the Iban is made from yarn spun from home-grown cotton (*taya*).

**OTHER TECHNIQUES**
Iban weavers are skilled in techniques besides the warp ikat for which they are famous. Sungkit, or supplementary weft, (right) involves weaving differently colored weft threads on top of the body of the cloth. Elaborate tapestry weaves and needle weaves are often used for panels in jackets (below).

**JACKET DETAILS**
The bodice is one continuous piece of fabric, folded at the shoulder line, with the sleeves cut from extra fabric woven at one end of the bodice piece. In this respect, the entire garment must be conceived during the actual weaving of the fabric. *Baju* were worn by Iban warriors, the supernatural qualities of the fabric conferring immunity to injury on the wearer. Long coats with sleeves are worn by shamans and bards during ritual performances.

# SARAWAK – THE BARAM RIVER

**THE FORMIDABLE DR HOSE**
Dr Charles Hose was as great as he was large. Many tales are still told of his remarkable wit and resource, and his girth. Here is one: In 1904 a roving group of Iban took some Penan heads. Within two weeks of the unprovoked attack, Dr Hose had the culprits arrested, tried, and sentenced. Besides prison terms and fines, one of their tribe had to bring compensation to the injured Penan. But would the timid nomads let him into their camp? Dr Hose gave the messenger one of his shirts to present as credentials, and it was immediately accepted. "Yes, we believe you come from Tuan Hose. Nobody else in Sarawak has a shirt this big."

The Baram River is one of the most interesting routes into the interior of Sarawak, the land of the Orang Ulu. The term "Ulu" describes a location – "upriver". The Kayan, Kenyah, and their many sub-tribes are upriver peoples, or Orang Ulu. So, too, are the Kelabit who are ethnically related to the Lun Bawang and the Lun Dayeh of the lowlands, and the settled Punan and their nomadic cousins, the Penan. The Orang Ulu of Borneo's interior live an independent life. Irrigated ricefields make a search for new jungles to fell for farmland unnecessary. Orang Ulu longhouses ● *76–7* are built to last, with solid uprights and axe-hewn hardwood planks. Trade goods have long made their way into the high plains, but for centuries the natural barriers almost excluded the outside world. Dutch and British territorial stakes did not mean much in the highlands; at the time of World War Two, some Orang Ulu were mildly surprised to hear that they were citizens of Sarawak. These peoples governed themselves for centuries without much outside interference. In the mid-19th century the Kayan threatened to attack Brunei, and devastated nearby areas just to show that they could if they wanted to. When Aban Jau, a Sebop chief from the Baram tributary Tinjar, heard that the sultan of Brunei had generously transferred the whole of Baram to the rajah of Sarawak, he burst out angrily: "Why should I accept the rajah's flag? I have no need of it. What right has the sultan of Brunei to hand us over to the rajah? We are wild creatures of the forest, none of his poultry yard." Once upon a time, forays into neighboring territories were an accepted sport for the young bloods; Malay and Chinese traders did not venture far up the Baram in those days. Even with motorboat and airplane, some Ulu locations remain remote. Low or high water can double traveling time, or make a journey impossible. A holiday traveler with an onward reservation should leave several spare days in his itinerary before venturing too far above Marudi. Bario in the highlands, the home of the Kelabit, can be cut off from the rest of Sarawak if poor visibility prevents the Twin Otter from landing. The land route, on foot, takes over a week.

## MARUDI

Fort Hose stands on a hillock above Marudi, where the Baram Regatta was founded in 1899. This was the brainchild of Dr Charles Hose, the resident who had two assistants, fifteen policemen and thirty Sarawak Rangers to govern a huge,

restless district. He persuaded the belligerents to bring their swift war boats to Marudi. The results were encouraging. Firstly participants let off steam peacefully, and secondly they covered a course of 3.5 miles in 15 minutes 10 seconds, "somewhat faster than the Oxford–Cambridge boat race". It wasn't all picnic baskets on the lawn, however. When former enemies met, they used the occasion to stage a display battle which, on one occasion, nearly got out of hand. "The Lirongs were in full war dress, their feathered coats of leopard skin and plumed caps.... and very effective they were as they came swiftly on over the shining water. Sixty or seventy warriors in each canoe raising their tremendous battle cry.... those on the hill took it up, answering shout for shout, and the forest across the river echoed it, until the whole place was filled with a sonorous roar. The Kenyahs ran hastily to their huts for their weapons, and by the time they had grouped themselves on the crest of the hill, armed with sword and shield and spear and deadly blow-pipe, the Lirongs had landed on the bank below and were rushing up the hill to attack. A few seconds more and they met, a clash of swords and shields and great shouting, and in the semi-darkness a noisy battle raged. After some minutes the Lirongs drew off and rushed back to their boats as wildly as they had come.... it was a token fight or jawa which achieved two useful ends: it let off superabundant high spirits, and it 'saved the face' of the injured party by showing how wrathful they were" (Dr Charles Hose, *Pagan Tribes of Borneo*, 1912). In later years, other events were added to the canoe races. Wheelbarrow, three-legged, blindfold, and sack races amused the populace; the 1906 record tersely states that the animal race was "won by a duck; second place went to a fox terrier".

**WOOD-CARVING TOOLS**
Some of Sarawak's best artists are Orang Ulu, though most Borneans could in the past produce wood-carvings for utilitarian or religious purposes. Tools were simple: a wedge-shaped blade that was lashed to a haft to make an axe or an adze, and a long-handled knife.

## BARIO

Bario is home to the Kelabit people, rice farmers who have lived in near seclusion for centuries. (The painting on the right shows a Kelabit woman playing the flute.) A sophisticated irrigation system permits them to farm the same plot of land year after year efficiently; unlike most other Sarawakians, they have long used buffaloes for puddling the wet ricefields. By Borneo standards, the Kelabit people are wealthy – rich in antique jars, heirloom beads, gongs, and livestock, and amply provided with rice reserves. Few Sarawakians visit this remote community, but many relish its most famous production: fragrant Bario rice.

**A PUNAN TALE OF THE NIAH CAVE**
Once, Niah was a longhouse. In it lived a poor old woman and her grandson. The people erected an extension to the longhouse. One evening, the grandson didn't return home: he had been sacrificed to ensure the safety of the new extension! The bereaved grandmother could only think of revenge. In her room, she dressed a frog in a skirt with dancing bells. Then she beat the gongs. The people pushed open her door and saw the frog leaping about, the bells tinkling each time it moved. They burst into loud laughter, which was an insult to the frog. The spirits were furious and wrought vengeance. The sky darkened. A hailstorm soon burst upon the longhouse, and the building turned to stone. Stone it has remained to this day.

## BINTULU

What oil was to Miri, natural gas is to Bintulu. From a sleepy village has sprung a town of 63,000, most of the newcomers working in the gas, chemical, or related service industries.

## SIMILAJAU NATIONAL PARK

Similajau, Sarawak's newest national park, was opened in 1978. Covering an area of 18,600 acres, it lies 12 miles of reasonably good road from Bintulu, making it one of the most accessible parks in a state where most beautiful experiences have to be paid for in hours of uncomfortable travel. Similajau is a favorite spot for visitors to observe sea eagles and Brahminy kites. The clear sea invites swimmers – but they should note that the saltwater crocodile (right) is also among the local wildlife! This may account for the "Similajau ghost" yarns that circulated among oil prospectors in the 1950's. Oil-exploration crews used to see a mysterious person, just out of clear viewing distance, disappearing if anyone came too close. Local laborers who know a ghost when they see one preferred to stay off the wharf after dusk.

## NIAH CAVE NATIONAL PARK

Niah National Park is situated between Miri and Bintulu, a 3-hour road trip from either town. Accommodation is available at the National Park, but during busy seasons it is advisable to reserve from Miri or Kuching. A special permit is needed to visit the Painted Cave. Niah

"In 1947 I visited Niah; I was amazed by the splendour, beauty, prodigious size and myriad life of the Great Cave."
Tom Harrisson, *Borneo Writings and Related Matters*

National Park was opened in 1975, though the Niah Cave area had been under protection by the Sarawak Museum since the 1960's. Most visitors make a beeline for the West Mouth, eager to get underground, but the 7848-acre park is well worth a leisurely walk. Niah itself is a clump of limestone riddled with caves, sitting in a bed of peat swamp. Before the area became a national park, access was difficult; during the bird-nesting season, nesters and buyers of this expensive commodity used to camp inside the caves for weeks or even months. The accepted currency in this strange community was the bird's nest: so many for a cup of coffee, a plate of rice, a bunch of candles. Nowadays, plankwalks keep the hiker above the squelch. The occasional nature enthusiast may, however, stray off the walks in quest of the particularly beautiful butterflies that seem to love disporting themselves in little forest clearings among the tree trunks. The West Mouth of Niah Cave is reached after Traders' Cave. It is here that the Niah Deep Skull was found, the oldest human relic in Southeast Asia and dated to c. 38,000–35,000 BC. The cave trail passes through the West Mouth. There are well-marked paths in the caves, and steps where they are needed, but nobody should attempt Niah in sandals. A good grip is needed, especially on the guano beds, which get very slippery if above-ground rainfall results in water entering through the cave ceiling.

**Kain Hitam, the Painted Cave.** In the old days, cave nest-collection rights were items of trade. The cave portrayed below has a local name, Kain Hitam, which suggests it was once sold for a bolt of black cloth. That was a poor bargain because Kain Hitam is a high, dry cave open to the occasional ray of sunlight; swiftlets prefer near darkness. Kain Hitam was once a burial cave, decorated with mysterious hematite paintings of boats and dancing figures. None of the local residents saw fit to tell inquisitive foreigners about them in the 19th and early 20th centuries, and the wondrous site was only rediscovered in 1958 by Barbara Harrisson, a member of the Sarawak Museum's Niah team. On the sandy ground below the paintings lie boat-shaped coffins, carbon-dated to between 2000 BC and AD 500. Grave-gifts of crockery and beads lay scattered, undisturbed for ages. In recent years, the walls of Kain Hitam have been affected by a greenish type of moss that disfigures other light caves in Niah, too. While measures are taken to preserve these unique paintings, the cave may have to be closed to the public.

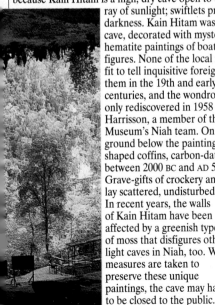

**Birds' nests**

Locals were once strangely reticent about the Niah Caves if any foreign explorer asked about them. The caves were associated with burials; they also produced a commodity that the initiated few did not want to advertise too openly: birds' nests. The cave swiftlet makes its nest of gelatinous saliva, and today's retail price for this traditional Chinese delicacy ranges between US$250 and US$375 per 4 ounces, depending on the grade and quality of the product. Nesters climb flimsy bamboo poles to 200 feet above the cave floor in their quest for nests. Each man carries a long stick with a sharp blade at the end to prise the nests off the cave ceiling. In recent years, ruthless poachers ripped off nests still containing eggs or baby birds, but nesting has been strictly controlled since 1991 in an attempt to rehabilitate the dwindling bird population.

**THE MIRI DISCOVERIES**

"The No.1 Well was spudded in Miri on the August 10, 1910. Early days were very different from today's Miri with its manicured lawns and company housing – reed mat huts, isolation, even food shortages if bad weather prevented the steamer from landing, disputes with local laborers who had never seen a dollar coin and feared they were being cheated on their first pay day. Wild pigs roamed around the tatty bungalows, rats and cockroaches held high revel at night. But the oil continued to flow. A sealine, to permit offshore loading, was built in 1914, a refinery at Lutong in 1917" (source: Shell Publicity). Offshore production in Miri started with the Baram field, which lurched off to an inauspicious start. Baram 1 was abandoned after costly equipment had been damaged by heavy storms, and then the pipe of Baram 2 was twisted by howling torrents and had to be plugged for safety. But Baram 3, aided by a bit of Borneo magic, opened the Baram field.

## MIRI

Say "Miri" and the average Sarawakian adds "Oil Town" by conditioned reflex. The Grand Old Lady overlooks the town like a guardian spirit: Sarawak's first oil well has been accorded National Monument status and is well worth a visit for the beautiful view from Canada Hill, where she stands on sturdy hardwood legs.

Travelers know Miri as a staging point; up-the-Baram trips start here, excursions to Niah Cave or to Brunei by road, to Limbang and Lawas in East Sarawak by Twin Otter. Petroleum and related products now account for over half of Sarawak's exports. The inland wells have practically ceased production, and black gold is now wrested from the shallow continental shelf. Work on the first offshore field, Baram, was difficult. To quote a 1964 article on Miri by Shell Berhad, Sarawak: "By now word had got round, and the roughnecks were determined to summon some good luck on their side first. With drilling bit poised for spudding-in, a *bebiau* (traditional blessing) ceremony with a chicken was performed on the drilling floor. And lo and behold, the weather suddenly became unusually rough for the time of year, got so bad at one point that the sidewinder (drilling vessel), after drilling 4,013 feet, had to move off location! But worse was to come: when drilling resumed, a blowout threatened. When that was brought under control it was decided that the well should be abandoned, and all operations at Baram be postponed until the arrival of the SEDCO Alpha. But the chicken had done its job. Baram 3 had discovered the Baram field."

## MOUNT MULU NATIONAL PARK

Having viewed the Mulu travelog and obtained permits from the Miri district office, travelers take a river express to

"THIS (BARAM) RIVER HAS AN EVIL REPUTATION; IT IS VERY BROAD, AND A SANDBANK LYING ACROSS ITS MOUTH ONLY PERMITS OF THE PASSAGE OF SHALLOW SHIPS."

MARGARET BROOKE, *MY LIFE IN SARAWAK*

Marudi. After lunch in the bazaar there, they endure three more hours of in-boat video film to Long Panai, then another hour to Long Terawan ("Long" is the confluence of two rivers). From there on, the River Tutoh is too shallow for the express. A longboat takes over, traveling up the Melinau River to park headquarters. From Miri to the park is a long day's trip. There is, however, an alternative route: since the opening of the Mulu airstrip in 1992, it is possible to fly in by Twin Otter in 45 minutes. This air service was not without its teething problems: the last plane at night, scheduled to leave at 5pm to permit passengers to get back to Miri before dark, used to be prevented from taking off by clouds of bats emerging from Deer Cave for their evening flight. Wildlife has the right of way in a national park – it is also notoriously difficult to reschedule! There are now no passenger flights after 4.30pm. Chalets can be reserved at the National Park Services in Miri, and some travel agencies maintain lodges just outside the park area. Tourists are not allowed to roam Mulu National Park without an official guide. The park and its caves are well marked and maintained, but huge enough to easily get lost in. The cave tour is a strenuous hike, up and down steep slopes. In some caves, shafts of light from holes high in the ceiling illuminate the magnificent limestone formations and rockfalls. Elsewhere, only hikers' flashlights stab thin holes in the darkness. Electricity has been installed in some caves to light the more difficult passages. Only skilled, well-equipped cave climbers can stray from the beaten path with impunity. For this reason, visitors intending to undertake one of the more difficult treks in Mulu National Park should consider taking out temporary accident insurance. Emergency rescues from Miri by helicopter cost RM3000 per hour.

**MULU BIODIVERSITY**
At least fifteen types of virgin forest are found within Mulu's 217 square miles. The Mulu massif consists of sandstone and shales, which support lowland mixed dipterocarp and montane forests below 4000 feet. Trees 180 feet tall tower above a canopy made up of three hundred species; buttressed forest giants achieve a girth of more than 100 inches. In the higher regions, vegetation – sedge, dense shrubs, orchids, and lichen – becomes increasingly stunted by wind and weather.

**INSECTS OF MULU**
The Mulu caves are deep and silent – but you are not alone! Swiftlets navigate around obstacles by sonic "click-click". Bats cling to the ceilings, making their presence known by deep beds of guano on the floor below. An army of cockroaches shows a healthy interest in the bird and bat guano. Red earwigs (below) are well adapted to a twilight existence, as are centipedes, pale spiders, and crickets. There is a white crab in the dark caverns of Mulu and even a fish that has lost its sight – useless under the circumstances – and navigates by natural "radar".

## THE MULU CAVES

The maze of limestone caverns at Mulu invites superlatives: the largest cave, Sarawak Chamber, is 1980 feet long, 1485 feet wide, and 330 feet high; the longest, Clearwater Cave, is a passage which spans 36 miles. The latter is also the biggest, grandest, most spectacular, and wildest. Mulu was formed about five million years ago, when the formerly submerged area of sand- and limestone was lifted from the sea. Heavy tropical rainfall has been wearing away the massif ever since, eating deep holes into the limestone and surface-polishing the sandstone which is Mount Mulu. Over the centuries, caves formed; dripping water subsequently formed their stalactites and stalagmites. The pinnacles themselves are exposed limestone surfaces honed to razor sharpness by centuries of heavy rainfall cascading down the rock plateaux above them. Some caves collapsed, leaving deep valleys with towering cliff-sides scarring the surface. Tropical rainforest ■ *22–3* grew over it all, deeply penetrating roots aiding the water's corrosive force in molding its stunningly beautiful, nearly inaccessible scenery.

**SARAWAK CHAMBER.** The largest cave is only accessible with a special research permit and an experienced guide. It is not yet fully explored and is considered too dangerous to open to the public. Its claim to fame is its enormous size – it has been calculated that it could accommodate eight Boeing 747s nose-to-tail, with another thirty-two parked at both sides! The experiment has yet to be carried out.

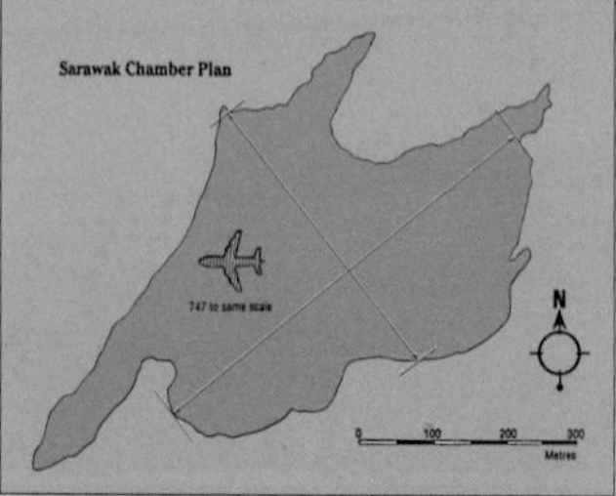


**CLEARWATER CAVE.** An underground river flows through Clearwater

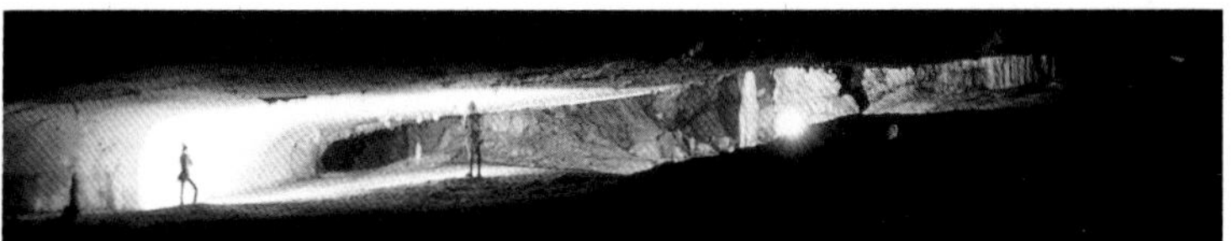

Cave and emerges as a sun-dappled pool beside the cave entrance. Visitors climb up a seemingly endless flight of steps on the mountain face, entering the cave from above to catch a glimpse of the still waters in the dim interior. At 36 miles, Clearwater is the longest cave system in Southeast Asia.

## Mount Mulu

Visible from Bandar Seri Begawan in Brunei, Mount Mulu has never been an "unknown" mountain. It was pointed out to early European visitors as the abode of dwarfs and ghosts, a place to be shunned. Spenser St John, the British consul in Brunei, was told: "Sharp axes below, pointed needles above, such is the mountain of Molu!" He tried to conquer the giant more than once, but his 1857 expedition, having scaled almost vertical cliffs using rotting roots and creepers, had to turn back because there was no water. The second attempt in 1858 fared no better. A downpour, dramatically raising water levels, nearly cost the traveling party their lives. When they came closer to the mountain, they found it impossible to pitch tents on the bare rock. Mulu's "sharp axes and needles", the 150-foot pinnacles, repulsed this attack too. Not even Charles Hose, who generally had his own way in the Baram, could conquer this mountain. During the 1920's a way up Mulu's forbidding sandstone face was discovered by Tama Nilong, a Berawan. Tama Nilong was a rhino hunter, not a mountaineer – one imagines a resigned shrug when he was approached by Shackleton to guide the Oxford University expedition to the summit in 1932. But guide them he did, in pouring rain and chilly mist, across mats of decaying vegetation precariously suspended over the mountain's precipitious side, and through moss forest so thick that a trail had to be hacked through it. The summit of Mulu was reached on November 18, 1932, uselessly as far as Tama Nilong was concerned, for the party didn't bag a single head of game. Three years later, a Sarawak Museum expedition climbed Mount Mulu and placed a survey point on the summit, after the mountain was accurately measured and found to be 7840 feet high. Nearby Murud, at 7922 feet, is the highest mountain in Sarawak.

## Gunung Api and the pinnacles

Unlike Mount Mulu, Gunung Api is a peak of limestone. The famous "axes and needles" belong to Api, pinnacles washed and sharpened by 200 inches of annual rainfall over a period of five million years. Climbing in this terrain is made more hazardous by the absence of water; the copious rain quickly disappears underground. Blocks of limestone can be dislodged by a slight touch. A moving boulder nearly crushed a party from the Royal Geographical Society and Sarawak Government expedition which conquered the mountain in January 1978. One of the guides in the expedition was Tama Bulan, grandson of Tama Nilong, who had led Shackleton to Mount Mulu in 1932.

**Deer Cave**

This cave contains the largest passage known to man, tunneling through one of the hills of Mulu. Both cave-mouths admit enough light to make this a twilight cave except at its very center. After heavy rainfall (which is quite often) a waterfall cascades 400 feet through an opening in the roof. Beyond Deer Cave lies the idyllically named Garden of Eden. Deer Cave is home to a dozen species of bat, of which the freetailed bat is the most spectacular. Many visitors await dusk at the Bat Observatory – irreverently dubbed the "Battarium" – to see them emerge for their nightly flight in search of food. On a fine evening, observers are rewarded by the sight of thousands of bats wheeling and twisting against the evening sky (left). In bad weather the show is cancelled. The mostly fruit- and insect-eating bats prefer to starve rather than venture out into heavy rain, which may force them to the ground, where they would become easy prey to carnivorous enemies.

The pinnacles of Gunung Api.

**The early years**
"The coast runs to Mangkabung Bluff: the river of this name being about two miles to the S.W. of it. It can be entered by boats, or small traders; the inhabitants, which appear to be of a friendly disposition, have a small village within, on the right. They offered us dried fish and fowls, but I suspect them to be very poor....
We now come to the Pulos Gaya, one of the best and most completely land-locked harbours on this coast. It is formed by a high bluff on the east, to which I have given the name of Tanjong Gaya; by the Great Gaya Island on the west; and by the smaller Islands of Sapangar, Manukan, Manukan-Kichi and a third nameless rock stretching across the mouth."

Captain Sir E. Belcher, *Voyage of HMS Samarang,* 1848

Kota Kinabalu has an eventful history. Its early name, Api-Api ("fire"), says it all: besides suggesting volcanic activity in the remote past, Api-Api is also a mangrove shrub which grows in shallow water. The North Borneo Company ▲ *298, 316* wanted a settlement near the British colony of Labuan, but Api-Api didn't have a deep harbor. A trading post on Pulau Gaya opposite Api-Api was burnt by rebel Mat Salleh; after this the NBC decided to shift the township to the mainland after all. Jesselton (named after one of the company's governors) was to be the railhead of the Trans-Bornean Railway from the west coast to Sandakan. The railway never materialized, but Jesselton grew big enough to attract the attention of the invading Japanese forces in 1941: the town was razed to the ground. Then the Australians, liberating Borneo, twice bombed what had been rebuilt of the town in 1945. Maybe this answers the question: "Why aren't there any quaint old buildings in this town?" All that was left standing was the post office (now a tourist information center) in Gaya Street, the clock tower, and one government office. The town became Sabah's capital after the war, and was renamed Kota Kinabalu in 1967. It is laid out on modern lines, its main roads either parallel to the coast or leading to the waterfront.

**The waterfront.** And what a waterfront it is! Pleasure, fishing, and commercial craft line the jetties, the fishmarket teems with marine freaks of every imaginable kind, traders, hawkers, beggars and others throng the bazaar. Handicraft stalls on the waterfront do good business, especially in the evening, when half the town dines alfresco in the market

place. Shell and reed artifacts mingle with banana fiber textiles and gaily colored embroidery. There is a constant coming and going of small craft between the southern Philippines and Sabah, especially the east coast. Nobody would like to guarantee that proper customs duties have been paid on all the merchandise exhibited in Kota Kinabalu's waterfront market.

**Lookout point.** The steep hill behind the town offers a few lookout points for a grandiose view of Kota Kinabalu and the scattered islands of Tunku Abdul Rahman National Park. The Sabah Foundation's futuristic glass tower gleams tall on the eastern margin of the town.

**Sabah Museum.** This modern building stands on Bukit Istana Lama, a slight hill behind the State Mosque. The museum is a treasure house of Sabah's past, present, and future. Its exhibits include prehistory and early history, Borneo ethnography, natural history, and a fine array of the handicrafts of Sabah's many indigenous tribes. The ceramics gallery is highly esteemed by connoisseurs. Sabah Art Gallery, where many well-known local artists got their first exposure to the public, is situated next to the museum.

**Shangri-la Tanjong Aru Resort (or STAR).** This hotel enjoys the advantage of being sited practically in a national park of islands, blue waters, and white beaches.

**Tunku Abdul Rahman National Park.** The park is unique for two reasons: it is a 121,185-acre marine park, and it is a mere 20 minutes by speedboat from Sabah's capital. The idyllic islands the visitor glimpses from Kota Kinabalu's waterfront belong to it, both above and under water. Tunku Abdul Rahman National Park's five islands could have been specially made for trekking, lazing, and sunbathing on the clean white beaches, or swimming, snorkeling, underwater photography, and nature observation in the water. Bungalows are available on Pulau Mamutik and Pulau Gaya; some of the islands have resident populations that were there before the Park was established, so they are allowed to remain.

**Pulau Tiga Nature Reserve.** Further westward and off the peninsula at Kuala Penyu is the Pulau Tiga Nature Reserve. It covers 39,660 acres and is noted for its mud volcanoes. About knee-high, these strange mounds well up with hot grey mud fairly constantly. The National University of Malaysia is conducting scientific investigations here. The reserve is accessible by prior arrangement with the Sabah Parks Department in Kota Kinabalu.

**Rafflesia**

"The first species of Rafflesia known to Europeans was found by Raffles and Arnold in Sumatra in 1816. What they saw was a monstrous flower, a yard across, and some flower-buds, emerging from the stem of a vine. The species was named Rafflesia Arnoldii.... It is the most specialized of all parasitic flowering plants as it has neither stem, leaves, nor roots. Apart from its flowers, it consists of strands of tissue growing inside the living substance of its host.... The bud swells until it is the size of a small cabbage. It is dull, dark purplish. Then it opens, and gives forth a foul odour which attracts flies. The giant flower has five petal-like organs, and in the center is a large basin-shaped cavity. In the cavity is a broad disc bearing slender projections on its upper surface. Under the edge of the disc are either stamens or stigmas; the flowers are either male or female and pollen has to be carried from one to the other, presumably by flies."

R.E. Holttum, *Plant Life in Malaya*

The Rafflesia plant (**1**), section through the male flower bud (**2**), and some unopened buds (**3**).

(2)

(3)

(1)

A pair of Dusun women at work and a type of pan pipe (below).

**THE RUNGUS**
The Rungus of northern Sabah cling to their traditional lifestyle with more tenacity than some other Orang Dusun. They include farmers, traders and fruit vendors at the market. The Rungus women are well known for bead-craft and needle-weaving. Antique beads are treasured and worn, new seed beads are threaded into decorative strips and sashes.

Kota Kinabalu lies in a fertile lowland plain. Large irrigated ricefields stretch on both sides of the road quite close to town. The colonial name for Kadazan, Dusun, means orchard or garden in Malay; Orang Dusun refers to the farmers and gardeners there. Several pleasant country towns can be reached in short drives from Kota Kinabalu. Menggatal and Penampang are slowly becoming suburbs of the spreading state capital. A few potters between Menggatal and Tuaran produce colorful souvenir wares as well as vessels and flower pots for local use. Kota Belud lies farther away from Kota Kinabalu, on the way to Sabah's northern peninsula. Tamparuli, with its famous Long Bridge, lies at the turnoff to Mount Kinabalu, a popular stopping place for tour coaches.

## MENGKABONG WATER VILLAGE

The Sabah coast is fringed with "water villages". One of the most accessible is Mengkabong, half an hour's drive from Kota Kinabalu. The inhabitants here are Bajau Laut, sea Bajau, the sea gypsies of the past, who lived more or less on boats, or in flimsy huts over the shallow tides. Nowadays, the people of villages such as Mengkabong engage in agriculture or work in towns, like most Sabahans. In the past some villagers are said to have visited dry land only to bury their dead in traditional burial grounds ● *78–9*, marked by streamers on the riverside trees.

## KUDAT

Little disturbs the peace of this country town, though over a hundred years ago it was the capital of Sabah. The North Borneo Company had its origins in a series of complicated deals with the sultans of Brunei and Sulu. Neither of these potentates had much power in the areas they so generously leased or ceded. The businessmen who held the concessions considered them as investments, to be resold when opportunity offered. London financier Alfred Dent had all the rights in his hands in 1880, and founded the North Borneo Chartered Company. With Dent as manager, the company went into

business in 1883. Some areas were already under administration. Kudat was declared the capital in 1881. Sabah's north never became a commercial center. Did local shipping find it too close to Marudu Bay, the former pirate stronghold? Did a hostile Spanish presence in Manila keep country traders away? The Lotud and Rungus were left to their coconut groves and longhouses, to eke out a living as best they could, when Sandakan was made capital in 1884. It is only since World War Two that Kudat has proper road access to Kota Kinabalu by the West Coast Highway.

## TAMU

The *tamu* is a Sabah institution that existed before the days of the North Borneo Chartered Company, but was fostered by its officers. *Tamu* means "meeting" as well as "market"; if the district officer needed to convey a message to many people at once, he could conveniently meet them next *tamu* day. In the countryside, an exchange rate for jungle produce and the blandishments of civilization – iron, beads, cloth, salt – was often fixed by the supervising officer. This was to prevent town-wise traders from cheating unsophisticated country folk!

**TUARAN TAMU.** Tuaran is a charming seaside town, where a *tamu* is held every Sunday; many Kota Kinabalu residents use the occasion for a trip to the countryside. Apart from making a pleasant outing there is little that cannot be bought at a *tamu* – food, vegetables, fish, clothing and shoes, battery-operated appliances, music tapes, comics, and magazines. Handicrafts are on sale at the market, but the prospective buyer of handwoven Bajau kerchiefs and Kadazan skirt panels, Bajau pottery and fine mats, and colorful Lotud bead-work had better be on time. Tuaran *tamu* starts soon after 7am, and these items being popular among the villagers as well as tourists, they are usually the first to go.

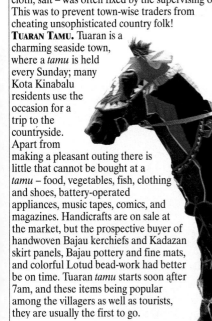

**TAMU SCHEDULE**
Wednesday: Tamparuli
Thursday: Keningau, Tambunan
Saturday: Penampang, Beaufort
Sunday: Tenom, Tambunan, Kota Belud, Papar, Tuaran, Gaya Street (Kota Kinabalu).

**THE BAJAU**
The Bajau are Sabah's second-largest indigenous group. Older Bajau men wear their elegantly draped *destar* headdress at a social occasion such as a *tamu*. The *destar* is a folded, peaked kerchief, woven on a simple backstrap loom by women. A tradition of stylized animal and human figures has survived the sturdy seafarers' conversion to Islam; mounted men usually take up the center of the *destar* (center of page). A Bajau horseman may be seen attired in a gilt-buttoned black jacket. Bajau horsemen add a distinctively Sabahan touch to local festivities as they ride at a gallop, barefoot in brass stirrups, through the surf.

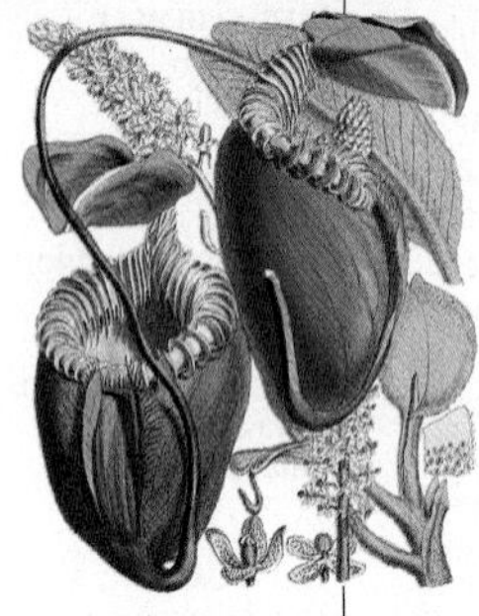

Pitcher plants (above and following page, top, on Mount Kinabalu.

## MOUNT KINABALU

Kinabalu is said to mean "Chinese widow" in pidgin Malay. A touching story about a Kadazan maiden who married a Chinese prince (it always is a prince!), lost when trying to climb Mount Kinabalu, has been associated with the mountain ever since foreign explorers asked their Malay guides what the name signified. The people who named the towering mass of rock were Kadazan, formerly called Dusun. Aki-nabalu is the "resting place of ancestors", the abode of the departed, which few approached for any reason except to die – as a 1957 climbing party found out when they stumbled upon the neatly blanketed body of a man wanted by the police for murder! If superstition didn't keep the local population off the mountain, the cold did. Icy winds howl over the bare rockfaces, making it quite impossible for a lightly dressed lowlander without shoes to spend more than a few hours at the higher altitudes. When getting ready for his 1851 expedition, Hugh Low found it difficult to recruit men. Local villagers were reluctant to sell supplies to the travelers, and vexed the good Mr Low with their unreasonable demands. Low made camp at Paka Cave. Few of his porters dared to accompany him on the last climb to what he thought was the summit, twin crags called "Donkey's Ears". The next expedition, led by Spenser St John, had a sizeable armed escort. St John records they spent a night at Mengkabong village where: "… the old Datu of Tamparuli was at first uninterested and scarcely noticed us, his eyesight weak, and he appeared dull and stupid. A glass of whiskey and

**KINABALU SACRIFICE**
Panar Laban, high on the summit trail, means "place of sacrifice", where in the past the mountain spirits had to be appeased by offerings and gunshots designed to make them ignore human trespassers. Individual climbing parties no longer stop for this rite. An annual sacrifice is made by a *bobolian*, often a retired park guide, on behalf of all who enter the abode of the departed: eggs, chickens, tobacco and matches, betel nut and sireh leaf, rice, the sort of tidbits mountain spirits are known to be partial to.

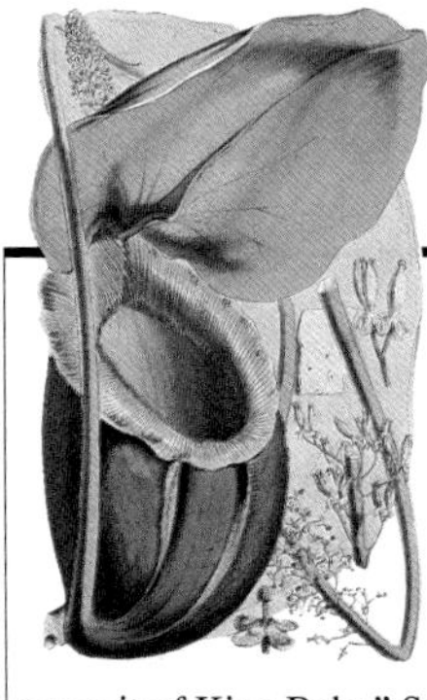

water revived his energies and his recollection. He shook Mr Low warmly by the hand, and then turning to the assembly told them in an excited voice of the wonderful feats he had performed on the old journey, and how he had actually reached the summit of Kina Balu." St John and Low reached the northwest peak, but found that "a heap of stones which looked like a cairn from below" was higher. In 1888 a scientific explorer, John Whitehead, discovered that "a large loose pile of rocks" was in fact the highest point of the massif. Mount Kinabalu provides an impressive backdrop to Kota Kinabalu – when it can be seen. The Monarch of Borneo is often swathed in cloud, swirling in the high winds of the morning or settled white and solid at noon. The best chance for catching a glimpse of Kinabalu's craggy crest is between 6am and 8am and also in the late afternoon. Serious mountaineers dressed in climbing gear and warm woollies devote two or three days to the ascent of Mount Kinabalu. Not everyone, however, takes the mountain all that seriously! There are large crowds of frolicking day-trippers.

**Sabah's First National Park.** Mount Kinabalu was the first National Park to be opened in Sabah, in 1964. It attracts thousands of visitors yearly, not all of whom climb Southeast Asia's highest peak. Many simply enjoy the cool climate, clean air and unique scenery, or come for some brisk haggling over farm vegetables at the village *tamu* and the roadside stalls in Kundasang and Ranau, or to buy mushrooms fresh from the farm. There are also the researchers, who spend weeks and months studying the mountain's many varied types of vegetation, wildlife, and meteorological phenomena.

**Kinabalu wildlife**

To the layman, the birds of Kinabalu have whimsical names: black-breasted triller, short-tailed bush warbler, Bornean mountain whistler, Kinabalu friendly warbler – all promise a chorus of bird melody in the cool mountain dawn. According to naturalist Tom Harrisson, however, the Kinabalu friendly warbler produces a "hissing note and a weak single whistle"; noted ornithologist E.B. Smythies dismisses the bird as "normally silent, but utters a single chuck note if disturbed". The Kinabalu friendly warbler is only found on the higher slopes of this mountain and neighboring Trusmadi. It is a cinnamon-brown, lively bird with a white-spotted throat, noticed by early climbers for its friendly and fearless nature. The mountain blackbird shares with the Kinabalu friendly warbler the distinction of being found on Mount Kinabalu and nowhere else in Borneo.

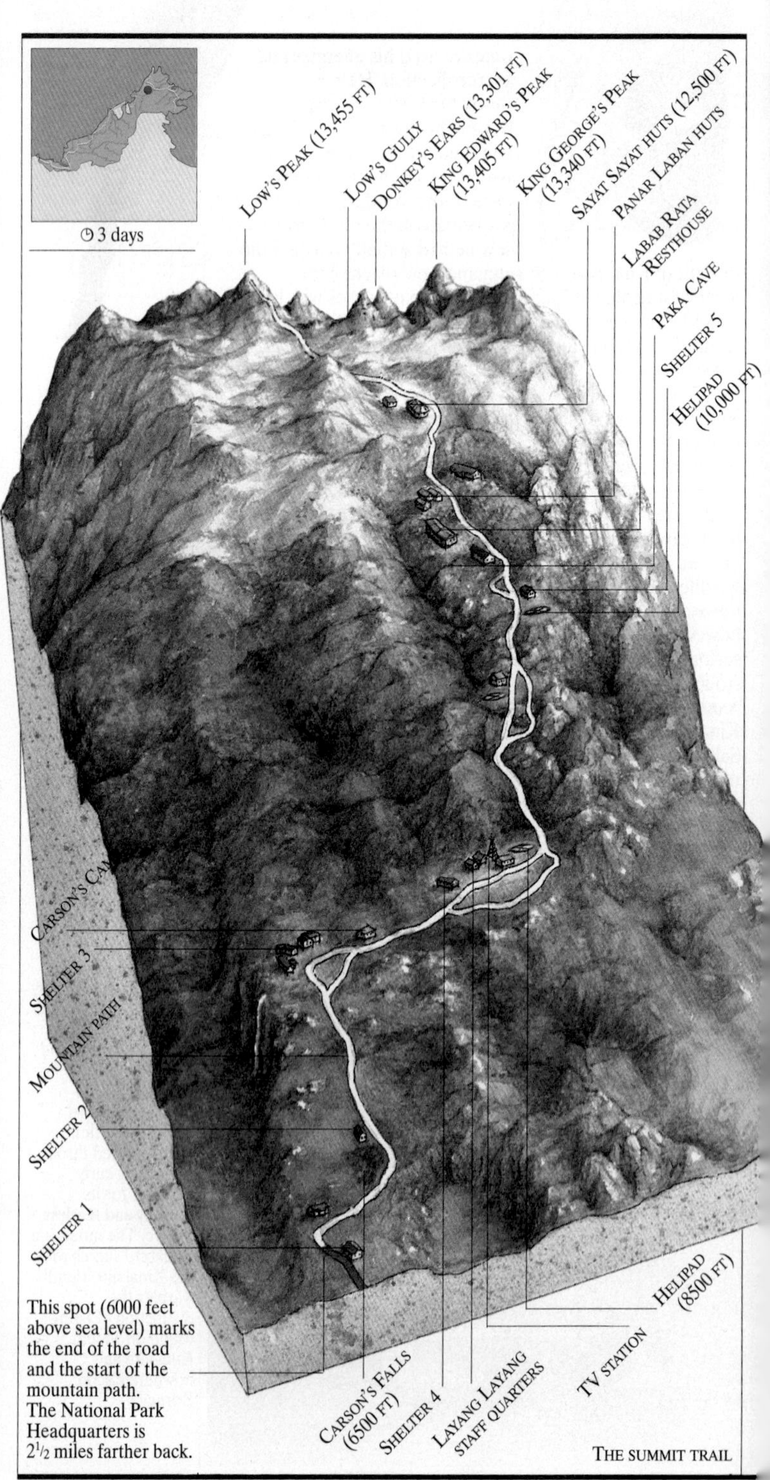
◷ 3 days
Low's Peak (13,455 ft)
Low's Gully
Donkey's Ears (13,301 ft)
King Edward's Peak (13,405 ft)
King George's Peak (13,340 ft)
Sayat Sayat huts (12,500 ft)
Panar Laban huts
Labab Rata Resthouse
Paka Cave
Shelter 5
Helipad (10,000 ft)
Carson's Cam
Shelter 3
Mountain path
Shelter 2
Shelter 1
This spot (6000 feet above sea level) marks the end of the road and the start of the mountain path. The National Park Headquarters is 2½ miles farther back.
Carson's Falls (6500 ft)
Shelter 4
Layang Layang staff quarters
TV station
Helipad (8500 ft)
The summit trail

**RAFFLESIA**
The parasitic *Rafflesia* depicted on a Malaysian postage stamp.

## CLIMBING MOUNT KINABALU – KOTAL'S ROUTE

It is a curious fact that the people who live near mountains have no desire to climb them. The Swiss saw the Alps as an obstacle to profitable traffic until the English started the (profitable) craze for mountain climbing. The man who found a way up Mulu was actually on a rhino hunt. The man who discovered the eastern route up Mount Kinabalu in 1963 was looking for caves that might contain valuable birds' nests. He was Kotal bin Mondial, a Kadazan from Kundasang at the foot of Mount Kinabalu. Kotal knew the hunting path that ran from behind his village into the rock face of Mesilau; one day in 1963 he walked farther than he ever had before. Darkness overtook him, and he spent a freezing night huddled over a little fire in the valley he later named "Mekado" ("cold, hard place"). The next morning he climbed up a rockface straight ahead and found himself on Mount Kinabalu's eastern plateau. As he later confessed to John Briggs, author of *Mountains of Malaysia*, he did not find any birds' nests. Kotal led an expedition of the Royal Geographical Society up the route now named after him. Kotal's Route is not a hike: the trip from Kundasang Golf Course to the summit of Mount Kinabalu and back takes nine days! It involves stiff climbing, adept mountaineering skills, good and reliable equipment, and a specific permit from the director of Sabah Parks. There are no shelter huts on this trail, no water tanks; because the whole area is in a National Park campers are not allowed to make fires of protected plants. Sturdy, low tents and sufficient warm, waterproof clothing are useful in keeping out the cold. The first two days lead past rocky cave shelters and dense stands of rhododendrons; the second night on this trail is usually spent just below a peak called the Rhino Horn. There is no vegetation at all after Mekado Camp, that "cold, hard", and – according to seasoned mountaineers – "damp and windy" place. Food, water, and cooking fuel have to be carried by the climbers themselves. Above 10,000 feet there is no earth to fasten the tent pegs; the ropes have to be secured to rocks or wedged into clefts. The final ascent of the eastern peaks – King George's and King Edward's – involves walking rather than climbing, on a glacier-worn high plateau. Rain or falling mist can make this a very dangerous promenade; most climbing parties walk roped. Daring mountaineers might want to venture to the edge of Low's Gully and look down a 3300-foot drop.

**THE SUMMIT TRAIL**
The well-marked trail begins $2^1/_2$ miles from National Park Headquarters. From Carson's Falls, it climbs through moss and rhododendrons. At 6500 feet Shelter 1 is reached. The moss forest gets thicker and damper to Shelter 2 at 7000 feet. Carson's Camp, at 8600 feet, is usually reached at lunch time; hikers fortify themselves before the steeper climb to Shelter 4 at 9200 feet, where glimpses of Kinabalu's crest and neighboring mountains are possible.
Shelter 5 is at Paka Cave, a rock shelter where early expeditions camped. From February to April, this area is abloom with rhododendrons. At Panar Laban there are huts, where hikers spend the night, leaving at dawn to arrive on the peak at sunrise. The summit plateau itself is a rock slope.

# SABAH – THE KADAZAN HEARTLAND

**THE BEAUFORT–TENOM LINK**
Borneo's only commercial railway is found in Sabah. Built at the turn of the century by the North Borneo Company, the Beaufort–Tenom link did much to open up the interior, cut off from the coast by the rugged Crocker Range. The railway is narrow-gauge and the rolling stock not exactly new, though the line is now electrified. Passenger carriages are equipped with wooden seats and cooling fans. The train stops for a lengthy lunch break at Beaufort before resuming the spectacular part of the journey, the passage through Padas Gorge. The Beaufort–Tenom line is an engineering feat that took five years to complete. The 92-mile trip from Kota Kinabalu's Tanjung Aru Station to Tenom in the Murut heartland takes about 6 hours.

Tambunan and Keningau form the center of the Kadazan region. It is accessible from Kota Kinabalu by vans stationed in the town center, which have the destination written on their sides in foot-high letters. When the driver judges he has a good load he sets off across the Crocker Range; passengers shout when they wish to alight. Tourists should make their destination known beforehand – Tambunan (Bamboo Village) or Keningau. The Tambunan–Keningau area is Kadazan heartland. Fertile soil and adequate water reward the farmer's and gardener's toil. In East Malaysia a distinction is made between farms that grow *padi*(rice), and "gardens" for everything else: rubber garden, cocoa garden, pepper garden. The most beautiful *padi* farms ■ *30*, terraced into gentle hillsides, are found at Sinsuran. Seeds sprout in a nursery bed and are planted out in autumn; there is no greener green on earth than the emerald silk of young rice! The water level is controlled to nourish the plants and keep weeds down; as the grain matures, the fields are drained. Keningau is the meeting place of the Kadazan and the Murut (or Tagal, or Lundayeh). South of Keningau the mountains start; Nabawan is an outstation and the end of the road as far as "civilized" vehicles are concerned. A four-wheel drive will make it to Sapulut, or to Agis south of the watershed, but from here on it's boats or boots all the way to Kalimantan. Keningau is the center of the Interior Division, shut off from the coast. The Crocker Range with its steep gorges keeps this high plateau isolated from the outside. Waterfalls and rapids are common tourist attractions here. The dawn view from the main peak, Mount Trusmadi, offers a spectacular picture of Mount Kinabalu against the pale pink of sunrise. In colonial times, the Interior Division was governed by officers of the North Borneo Company ▲ *298, 316*, with little to assist them except a few native policemen and their wits.

## THE SABAH RAILWAY

One railway line was supposed to link Jesselton with Sandakan; a glance at a map will explain why it was never built. The other, from Jesselton to Beaufort on the west coast and then to Tenom in the Interior

Division, posed almost equal engineering problems, but was built. The railway was the talk of North Borneo during the company's second decade; the 1899 Report is studded with pictures of rail buildings, rail heads, temporary rail bridges at Padas Gorge, and a close-up of the locomotive. Once the local people grasped the connection between good transport and the possibility of selling their farm produce to the markets, they began to flock to the new townships that mushroomed along the line. With the rail came the telegraph, and the outside world began to intrude, just a little bit, into the Interior Division.

## Padas River

Some people do not call it a sport unless it requires a safety helmet. They ought to appreciate rafting down the Padas Gorge. Rafters reach their starting point by getting off the train at Tenom, an isolated village. Rafts are inflated, safety gear loaded, and the craft launched into the deceptively calm waters of a tributary. Once in the mainstream, the crew find what white-water rafting really means: exhilaration, terror, speed, and excitement!

## Tambunan

"There's a bamboo-weaver on a bamboo chair eating bamboo shoots at a bamboo table in a bamboo house..." At Tambunan Village Resort Centre there is an annual bamboo festival. Once you put your mind to it, there's nothing that cannot be made of bamboo. Flattened bamboos are used for building. Bamboo makes cooking pots and musical instruments, hats and baskets. At Tambunan Village, young people learn handicrafts, *tapai*-brewing, and farming. There is lodging here too for guests who want to spend a few days in idyllic rural seclusion. Warning: the still-room is separated from the village by a high suspension bridge. *Tapai* (fermented glutinous rice) connoisseurs maintain that the bridge sways a lot more on the way back.

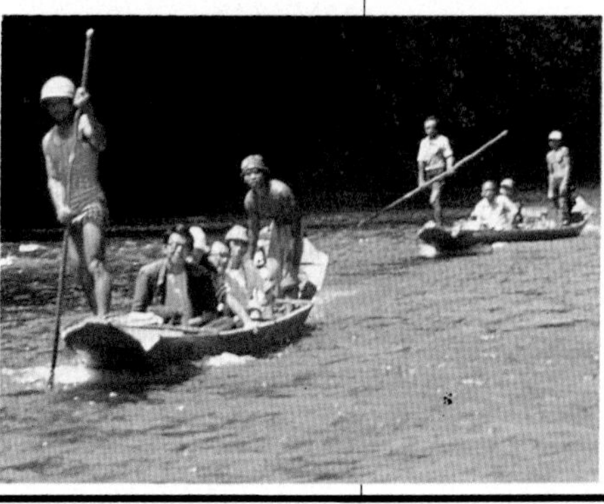

**Padi terraces and buffaloes**
The flat highlands in the Pagalan River valley are tailor-made for *padi* farming. Buffaloes puddle the fields before planting. Bunds and sluices are carefully maintained by farmers whose ancestors ate the rice from these very fields over centuries.
In many parts of Sabah, buffaloes are an essential way of life. The thick-skinned beast is draft animal, mount, status symbol, bride wealth, or food, as required; buffalo horn is fashioned into decorative items for domestic use or sale. "Beware the Buffalo" signs remind motorists that the beast has right of way on Sabah roads. Injury to such a valuable creature usually brings instant justice from enraged villagers on the unwary driver!

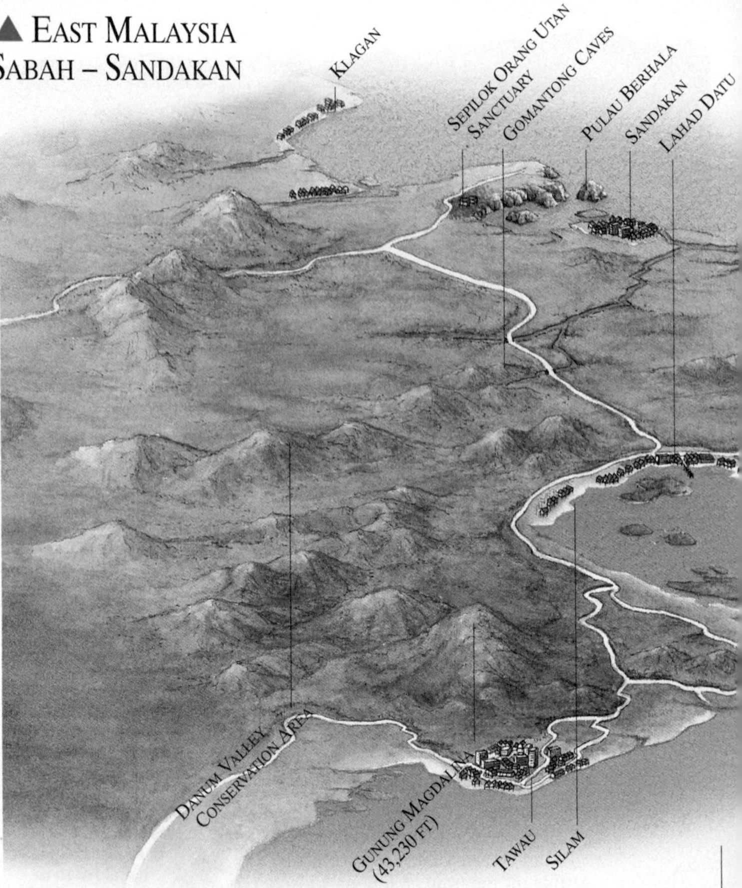

KLAGAN
SEPILOK ORANG UTAN SANCTUARY
GOMANTONG CAVES
PULAU BERHALA
SANDAKAN
LAHAD DATU
DANUM VALLEY CONSERVATION AREA
GUNUNG MAGDALENA (43,230 FT)
TAWAU
SILAM

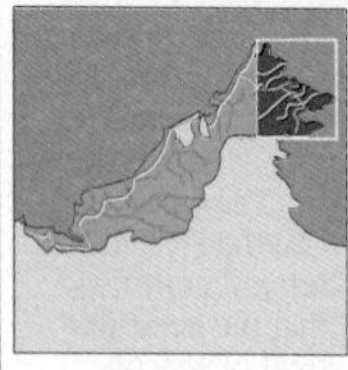

◷ 4 days

## MELISAU

The Crocker Range Crossing opened the temperate Melisau plateau to the outer world. Vegetable and fruit production in the Kundasang–Ranau area shot up after its completion; lorries laden with farm produce and flowers growl over the passes in the night, to the Kota Kinabalu market. Flowers produced on the Melisau plateau are sold to Japan and Hong Kong as well as locally. Australia assisted the Malaysian government to complete the highway by linking Ranau at the foot of Mount Kinabalu to Sandakan on the east coast. It is now possible to drive from Kota Kinabalu to Sandakan, with a few scenic stops on the way, in one day.

A Sandakan village scene from a postcard dated 1915.

## SANDAKAN

The spectacular harbor of Sandakan made it an obvious shelter, a hiding and trading place. The honorable director of the North Borneo Company (NBC), W. Cowie, who had began his eastern career as a gun-runner, knew it well; he must have given full support to the transfer of the capital from Kudat to this more suitable spot. An NBC ▲ *298, 316* settlement was started here by William Pryer before the company received its charter. Assisted by a small staff of three, a barrel of flour, seventeen chickens and six rifles, Pryer defended the place against all comers and attracted a growing population of traders and settlers. Sandakan was declared the capital of Sabah in 1884; by the early 20th century it had a club, a newspaper, a church, a school and a race-course.

World War Two demolished Sandakan; only the walls of the Anglican church and half a cow-shed were reported as still standing after the last bombardment. Sandakan now spreads along the deep-blue harbor and creeps up the hill. The entire town was rebuilt along the waterfront; modern office and hotel blocks overlook the harbor. The water village of Sim Sim is surmounted by a futuristic mosque on dry land.

**ST MICHAEL'S CHURCH.** The church is built of stone, which may explain why it was not completed until thirteen years after its foundation in 1893. Rock from Buli Sim Sim was used, and stone and workmen were later imported from China. If the NBC government was well inclined it supplied convict labor, but this could never be relied upon. Regular prayers were held in the school, but the foundation anniversary was always celebrated with a "special service within the stone walls". The stone walls may have taken long to build, but they survived the war – unlike the rest of Sandakan.

**PUU JIH SHI TEMPLE.** Completed in 1987, this temple stands high on the hill's crest and cost more than RM3 million to build, much of the money being raised locally. The temple committee has hit upon a unique way of reminding contributors to settle dues promptly: each lamp in the temple's standing lanterns has a sponsor's name written across it in elegant calligraphy. Should the sponsor default, the light is extinguished. Visitors report that most of the lights have been shining brightly – the system works!

**THE FISH MARKET.** Travelers from other parts of Malaysia head for the colorful fish market, where the selection of marine produce is overwhelming.

## SEPILOK

Sepilok near Sandakan is where apes are taught to climb. At Malaysia's largest orang utan rehabilitaton center ▲ *308–9*, captive animals are retrained to fit them for life in the jungle. Sepilok also shelters a pair of Asian two-horned rhinos, seventy species of other mammals, over two hundred species of birds and a host of wild plants in its 14,000 acres of forest reserve.

**BATU SAPI**
The name means "cow rock". This structure (above) stands on two sandstone feet in shallow water near Sandakan. Strangely shaped by wave erosion, it is expected to collapse in the course of time.

**RANAU DEATH MARCH**
During World War Two, the Japanese maintained a large PoW camp in Sandakan. The camp was moved inland in 1944. Prison conditions were harsh, the inmates undernourished and suffering from tropical diseases. In this condition, eighteen hundred Australian and six hundred British PoWs were forced to march on jungle tracks to Ranau. Of the 2400 emaciated prisoners who started the trek, six reached Ranau almost a year later. A memorial in Kundasang commemorates this wartime tragedy.

The orang utan was once a common forest dweller in Sumatra and Borneo, but wildlife preservation authorities estimate that only a few thousand survive in the wild today. An adult orang utan requires at least 1000 acres of virgin forest to subsist; as the habitat dwindles, the orang utan population declines. Mothers teach their young ones climbing, foraging, and nest-making for the first few years of life. The orang utan is protected in Borneo, but unscrupulous hunters still kill adult females and sell the young.

**"THE ORAN-OOTAN"**

"…those they call Oran-ootans, which in their language signifies Men of the Woods: These grow up to be six foot high; they walk upright, have longer Arms than Men, tolerable good Faces (handsomer I am sure than some Hottentots that I have seen), large Teeth, no Tails nor Hair, but on those Parts where it grows on human Bodies; they are very nimble footed and mighty strong; they throw great Stones, Sticks and Billets at those Persons that offend them…."
Daniel Beeckman, *Voyage to and from the Island of Borneo*, 1718

Early depictions (such as this picture of an orang utan battling with Dyaks from Alfred Russel Wallace's *The Malay Archipelago*) tend to exaggerate the ferocity of the orang utan.

**WILDLIFE REHABILITATION CENTERS**

At the Sarawak and Sabah wildlife rehabilitation centers, wardens bottle-feed the young orang utans, wean them with vegetables and fruit, and teach them to climb small saplings and creepers. As they grow bigger, the orang utans learn to make their own leaf nests each night, but they all have food provided for them.

**Wallace's first encounter**
"Just a week after my arrival at the mines, I first saw a Mias [as the natives called it]. I was out collecting insects, when I heard a rustling in a tree near, and, looking up, saw a large red-haired animal moving slowly along, hanging from the branches by its arms. It passed on from tree to tree till it was lost in the jungle, which was so swampy that I could not follow it." Alfred Russel Wallace, *The Malay Archipelago*, 1869

**Simia satyrus**
The male orang utan (*Simia satyrus*) weighs about 140 pounds and has an arm-span of up to 6 feet. This picture was taken from an old painting by C.J. Temminck, c. 1839–47.

**From branch to branch**
The orang utan is one of the most arboreal apes. Its usual method of movement is brachiation: moving from branch to branch by its arms. It does this at a measured pace, catching the next tree or sapling with a hand or a foot.

**Food**
The orang utan is a vegetarian and likes sour, bitter, and unripe shoots, and occasionally grubs and honey. It seldom descends to the ground to drink, but quenches its thirst from rainwater trapped in tree hollows. The durian is one of its favorite fruits.

# SABAH – THE EAST COAST

**BAJAU LAUT**
The Bajau Laut are the sea gypsies of yore. Children learn to swim while they learn to walk. Much of the preserved fish of eastern Sabah is salted and sun-dried by Bajau women. The Cagayan women of Pulau Libaran, a coconut-growing coral island, make beautiful pandanus mats for sale.

**PIRATES**
Before visiting the islands, tourists should inform the local police station of their route and approximate timetable. Today's pirates do not confine themselves to gold doubloons; they are quite aware of the value of good engines, diving or filming equipment, or gold wristwatches.

The east coast of Sabah is occasionally referred to as the "Wild East", a reference to the sea rovers and lumberjacks supposedly at large there. There is probably no greater contrast between Sabah's quietly industrious west coast and misty interior plains than the sun-drenched world of islands and coral reefs that is the Far East. Here, a transient population has been at home for centuries… and not at home. Take the Bajau, now divided into the settled Bajau and the sea Bajau. According to census data, this blanket term includes Illanun (an early Illanun pirate c. 1848 is shown above), Suluk, Obian and Binadan seafarers, many of them at home on houseboats rather than in houses, others settled in flimsy huts built over the low tide. Agricultural populations the world over treat the nomad with suspicion; many of Sabah's sea rovers have no citizenship status. In the Sulu Sea, memories of piracy are still fresh. When early European traders came to this region, they found the major rivers uninhabited as far as 40 miles from the coast. Riverside farmers, tired of having each year's harvest robbed from them by force of arms, fled into the more inaccessible highlands.

## SUKAU

The township of Sukau on the lower Kinabatangan River is a case in point. A nearby village used to be the headquarters of this area, home of the birds'-nests collectors who regularly harvested the nearby Gomontong caves. When the NBC took over the area a dispute about collecting rights arose, which was settled by the murder of the village headman. There is a legend that a Chinese town once stood on the Kinabatangan, long ago, to account for the name "Chinese River". No trace of such a settlement has ever been found, but the story cannot be absolutely discounted.

**THE KINABATANGAN RIVER.** The Kinabatangan is Sabah's longest river; it drains a catchment of 6400 square miles. Rising in the mountains of central Borneo, it flows 330 miles eastwards into the Sulu Sea. The lower reaches of the Kinabatangan are sparsely inhabited, swampy forest. The farmer's despair is a nature lover's paradise, where enchanted days can be spent observing the flora and fauna of the unique ecosystem. Proboscis monkeys abound here and kingfishers and egrets, and Sabah's wild elephants may be heard crashing through the undergrowth at dusk.

**BATU TULUG CAVE.** Many east Sabahans used to dispose of their dead by placing the coffins in a designated burial cave ● *78–9.* The dry air inside the higher caves sometimes mummified

the remains. Batu Tulug contains a number of noteworthy old coffins. Unfortunately, the more accessible caves have been looted of grave-gifts which could have thrown light on the culture of past centuries.

## SEMPORNA

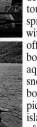

Most visitors get to Semporna by road from Tawau. What used to be a mere track is now a good motoring road, which permits rapid progress through lush oil palm and cocoa plantations, with glimpses of the sea every now and then. From not much more than a fishing village, Semporna has developed into a marine tourism center. Hotels have sprung up on the waterfront, with boating services that offer every possible water-borne activity: water-skiing, aquabike pedaling, diving, snorkeling, photography, boating, camping, and picnicking on outlying islands. The idyllic location of Semporna should not tempt adventurous tourists into attempting solo outings in small craft. Local guides know which areas are safe and which are best avoided. Pirate attacks in this area are not unheard-of, though they usually involve trading or fishing boats. Fresh seafood is one of Semporna's most famous delights. Visitors may buy their choice from fishermen as the catch is landed, and take it to their hotels to be cooked.

**PULAU BOHEY DULANG.** Pulau Bohey Dulang has a feature not present on the other islands around it: a pearl farm. A Japanese company is growing cultured pearls in the clear waters around this quiet island. Visitors who want to stop at Bohey Dulang need to make prior arrangements with the managing company.

**TINGKAYU STONE-TOOL SITE.** Stone tools recovered from Tingkayu, the dry bed of a prehistoric lake, have astonished archeologists. In quality and workmanship they pre-date similar artefacts from Southeast Asia by about ten thousand years – somebody in Sabah was chipping fine flakes c. thirty thousand years ago!

## DANUM VALLEY FIELD CENTRE

Danum Valley Field Centre is a 175-square-mile forest reserve run by the Sabah Foundation. Established in 1985, the center runs training and research programs jointly with tertiary institutions. Visitors should get permits and book accommodation at the Sabah Foundation office in Lahad Datu, once a "Wild East" town, before proceeding to the Borneo Rainforest Lodge in Danum Valley.

**MADAI CAVE**
Like Gomontong, Madai Cave is known to the local population as a birds' nests cave. Scientists know it for something else: evidence of human habitation fifteen thousand years ago has been found.

**SEMPORNA OCEAN TOURISM CENTRE**
This is a hotel built on stilts in the shallows, just like coastal village houses. It is approached by plankwalks, built of local woods to blend with its surroundings. The center offers comfortable guest rooms and a seafood restaurant.

**BIRDS' NESTS**
South of Sandakan, the Gomontong caves have yielded edible birds' nests for centuries. The caves were jealously guarded, sold or handed down from father to son; lives were lost in fights over nesting rights, or in the perilous work of collecting. A popular Chinese food tonic, birds' nests (above) gathered from the caves are today sold in various grades according to their quality. The product is retailed at local medical halls.

**TURTLE ISLANDS**
The turtle islands of Selingaan, Gulisaan, and Bakkungan Kecil are an hour's ride by speedboat from Sandakan. Marine turtles come ashore to lay here between August and December.
Their eggs are collected to hatch in enclosures so the hatchlings will be safe from marauders. Turtles are also tagged for research purposes. Since the islands were protected in 1977, egg production has increased.

**SIPADAN MARINE LIFE**
The waters around Sipadan teem with fish and a wide variety of corals. Underwater visibility is up to 100 feet at most times. Turtles lumber up the sandy beaches here, too, and lay their eggs. Sipadan is also frequented by marine birds such as frigate birds, sea eagles, terns and several species of seagull. However, human interference threatens this paradise. Sipadan should be declared a marine national park, but it is a territory disputed between Indonesia and Malaysia.

## TAWAU

In the early days of the NBC, Tawau was disputed territory. The Dutch claimed it, sort of, but nobody ever got round to surveying the boundary; even now, some islands off Tawau remain under dispute. Tawau proudly calls itself the plantation capital of Malaysia, and with reason: Tawau's rich volcanic soil is ideal for growing cocoa, making Sabah Malaysia's largest cocoa exporter. Oil palm, rubber and other crops are also grown on huge estates ■ *24–5*; Malaysia's first large-scale commercial forest plantation, run by the Sabah Foundation, lies in the fertile hinterland of Tawau. The more accessible jungle is logged. Ships of all nations call at Tawau port to carry off the precious freight. Tawau is the last port of call before Indonesia; the smaller shipping in the harbor is overwhelmingly Indonesian and Filipino. There is now also an air link to Tarakan in East Kalimantan.

**THE TAWAU HILLS PARK.** The park is about 18 miles' drive through agricultural estates from town. The Tawau River, which flows though the park, cascades over a set of cliffs near a favorite picnic and swimming spot. A trail leads to the top of Bombalai Hill. The view over Tawau, the bay, and the hinterland is rewarding; as an extra bonus for stout hill-trekkers, a hot spring bubbles out of the ground.

**THE FISH MARKET.** The market at Tawau is a hive of activity: large baskets of fish and other marine creatures are carried in on long poles; busy housewives jostle each other for first pick; a fishmonger squatting in front of a chopping block hacks an enormous fish into neat slices; Bajau women sell multi-colored mats, hats, and baskets in one corner, a short dark man spreads a tray of shell-craft in another. Salt fish is a specialty of the east coast; travelers who cannot take fresh fish back to Kuala Lumpur or Singapore like to stock up on these durable delicacies.

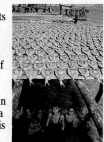

## SIPADAN

Sipadan looks like any other island dotting the surface of the deep blue Sulu Sea. From underneath, however, it's a different story: Sipadan is an oceanic island. Evidence of a long-ago volcanic explosion, it rises from the ocean floor. Visitors intending to go there need to inform the district office and Marine Police at their point of departure (usually Semporna), and are advised to go only in fair-sized groups and with a knowledgeable local guide.

# BRUNEI DARUSSALAM

Brunei and Oman are the only sultanates that are also members of the United Nations. Brunei Darussalam joined in January 1984 after achieving independence from Britain.

The Royal Family of Brunei Darussalam is among the longest-reigning of all Southeast Asian dynasties. Its first sultan, Mohammed Shah, is thought to have converted to Islam and been installed as sultan by the ruler of Temasik (Johor) in the late 14th century. Once the rulers of territory extending from Borneo to Luzon (Manila), the Brunei sultans saw their territory gradually reduced to a mere 2226 square miles by the late 19th century. The discovery of oil in Brunei in 1906 and its subsequent exploitation laid the foundations of the country's current wealth. The present sultan, Hassanal Bolkiah Mu'izzaddin Waddaulah, acceded to the throne in 1967.

**THE ISTANA NURUL IMAN**
The Istana Nural Iman in Bandar Seri Begawan was built for Brunei Darussalam's independence ceremonies in 1984.

The royal regalia form a powerful link with the country's traditional heritage. The ceremonial crown and the *kris si naga* are displayed in the Bangunan Alat Kebesaran Di Raja exhibition hall in Bandar Seri Begawan.

**Genealogy of the present Royal Family of Brunei Darussalam**

Sultan Omar Ali Saifuddin Sa'adul Khairi Waddin III (1916-86, r. 1950-67) *m* Raja Isteri Damit (1924-79)

(1) Raja Isteri Saleha (1946-) *m* Sultan Hassanal Bolkiah Mu'izzaddin Waddaulah (1946-, r. 1967-) *m* (2) Pengiran Isteri Mariam (1955-)

- (1) Pengiran Anak Putri Rashidah Sa'adatul Bolkiah (1969-)
- (1) Pengiran Anak Putri Muta-wakillah Hayatul Bolkiah (1971-)
- (1) Pengiran Muda al-Muhtadee Billah (1974-)
- (1) Pengiran Anak Putri Majeedah Nu'urul Bulqiah (1976-)
- (1) Pengiran Anak Putri Hafizah Sururul Bolkiah (1980-)
- (1) Pengiran Muda Abdul Malik (1983-)
- (2) Pengiran Muda Abdul Azim (1982-)
- (2) Pengiran Anak Putri Azemah Ni'matul Bolkiah (1984-)
- (2) Pengiran Anak Putri Fadzilah Lubabul Bulqiah (1985-)
- (2) Pengiran Muda Abdul Mateen (1991-)

**Negara Brunei Darussalam**
Brunei Darussalam occupies an area of 3580 square miles and is situated between Sarawak and the South China Sea. Its population of 250,000 includes 69 percent Malays, 19 percent Chinese and 5.5 percent Borneo natives; a sizeable expatriate community is employed in the petroleum and other industries. Nearly 70 percent of the sultanate's land surface is covered in tropical forest. Brunei remained a British protectorate until as late as the 1980's, and it was only in 1984 that it became independent. Today, it is one of the few surviving absolute monarchies, ruled by a hereditary line that stretches back unbroken for six hundred years.

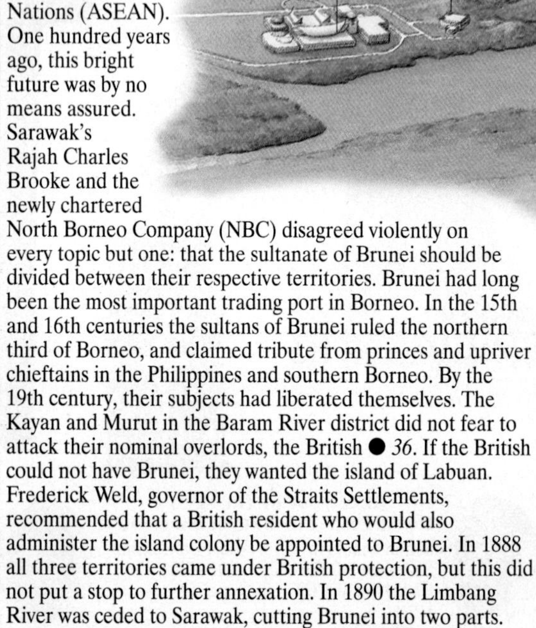


Today, Negara Brunei Darussalam is an independent state, prosperous and secure as a member of the Association of Southeast Asian Nations (ASEAN). One hundred years ago, this bright future was by no means assured. Sarawak's Rajah Charles Brooke and the newly chartered North Borneo Company (NBC) disagreed violently on every topic but one: that the sultanate of Brunei should be divided between their respective territories. Brunei had long been the most important trading port in Borneo. In the 15th and 16th centuries the sultans of Brunei ruled the northern third of Borneo, and claimed tribute from princes and upriver chieftains in the Philippines and southern Borneo. By the 19th century, their subjects had liberated themselves. The Kayan and Murut in the Baram River district did not fear to attack their nominal overlords, the British ● *36*. If the British could not have Brunei, they wanted the island of Labuan. Frederick Weld, governor of the Straits Settlements, recommended that a British resident who would also administer the island colony be appointed to Brunei. In 1888 all three territories came under British protection, but this did not put a stop to further annexation. In 1890 the Limbang River was ceded to Sarawak, cutting Brunei into two parts. The sultanate, a fraction of its former self, seemed destined to survive as a historical curiosity only. The discovery of oil changed this gloomy prospect. In 1987 the government had a revenue of B$2.7 billion, excluding investment income.

## Kampung Ayer

Kampung Ayer, or the Water Village, is the most enduring monument to Brunei's ancient glory. While none of its buildings – wooden structures built on wooden piles over the river – are themselves very old, the same village was described by Magellan's chronicler Pigafetta, and earlier Chinese sources record a similar city farther down the river near Kota

Batu. The village's trestle walks stretch over 14 miles and almost thirty thousand people live here. The village is accessible by water taxi – a light sampan with an outboard motor – for a fee of about B$2. Ancient traditions of boat building, weaving, and brassware-making are carried out in different districts within Kampung Ayer.

**THE OMAR ALI SAIFUDDIEN MOSQUE.** This mosque dominates the city of Bandar Seri Begawan and is considered one of the most magnificent in Southeast Asia. Located on the edges of the Kampung Ayer, by Kampung Sungri Kedayan, the Omar Ali Saifuddien Mosque is at its best at night, with a magical quality straight out of the Arabian Nights. One of the mosque's many unique features is a replica of a 16th-century barge or "Mahligai" set in a lagoon, where religious ceremonies such as Qu'ran reading competitions are held. Muslims believe that a person who uses his wealth for charitable causes such as the building of mosques will be rewarded tenfold in heaven – with the result that no expense was spared in the construction of the mosque. Marble from Italy, granite from Shanghai, stained glass and chandeliers from England, and carpets from Belgium and Saudi Arabia are some of the more exotic materials used.

**ARTS AND HANDICRAFT CENTRE.** At the other end of town, running along the Brunei River towards the bay, is Jalan Kota Batu. The first landmark here is an eight-story building shaped like the scabbard of a kris, the traditional Malay dagger. Built in 1984 to help revive traditional crafts that were rapidly disappearing, the center carries out its mission through courses and workshops where skills in silversmithing, brassmaking, weaving, and basketry are taught to young Bruneians. Among the many "live" exhibits on display are weavers working on *jong sarat* – traditional sarongs of gold cloth. These sarongs were worn by the nobility and aristocracy on ceremonial occasions for centuries and are still highly sought after in Brunei Darussalam.

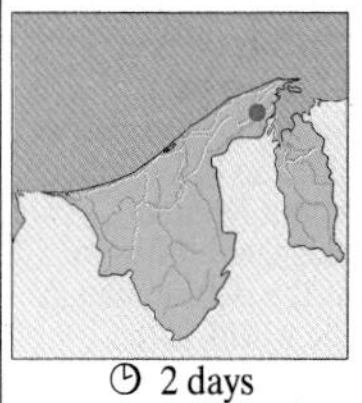

◷ 2 days

**BRUNEI 1522**
"That city is entirely built in salt water, except the houses of the King and certain chiefs. It contains twenty-five thousand fires [families]. The houses are all constructed of wood and built up from the ground on tall pillars. When the tide is high the women go in boats through the settlement selling the articles necessary to maintain life. There is a large brick wall in front of the King's house with towers like a fort, in which were mounted fifty-six bronze pieces, and six of iron. During the time of our stay there, many pieces were discharged."
A. Pigafetta, translated by D. E. Brown, *Brunei Museum Journal*

**THE RICHEST MAN IN THE WORLD**
Sultan Haji Hassanal Bolkiah of Brunei, whom *Fortune* magazine refers to as the richest man in the world, is the twenty-ninth sultan of a monarchy that has the distinction of being the oldest surviving royal line in the world. The sultan ascended the throne in 1967, when he was nineteen and barely out of the Royal Military Academy at Sandhurst. The sultan's academic background has given him a marked preference for things military, and he often appears in public in safari-suits or military garb, and is adept at handling such military hardware as British-made Scorpion tanks. A polo enthusiast and keen marksman, the sultan is also a qualified helicopter pilot who enjoys nothing more than taking to the skies in one of his gold-fitted stereo-equipped helicopters.

## BANDAR SERI BEGAWAN

**ROYAL REGALIA MUSEUM.** The Bangunan Alat Kebesaran Di Raja, to give it its official Malay name, is a remarkable institution, half museum and half national shrine. Formerly the Winston Churchill Memorial Building, and a repository for Churchill memorabilia, it has been rebuilt and extended to house the coronation regalia of His Majesty Sultan Haji Hassanal Bolkiah. In the regalia resides the right of the ruler to govern, and so the display here of the sacred kris of office, the Si-Naga, the golden cat, and other of the most important objects of the sultanate is attended with a great deal of respect. Visitors must take off their shoes when entering the building. Inside the first exhibit is the royal coronation carriage in which the sultan rode to his coronation in 1967, and again in 1992 to mark the twenty-fifth anniversary of his ascension. Also here is the Constitutional History Gallery, which details the history of the constitution and Brunei's development from 1847, along with archival documents, photographs, and films. Another gallery documents the sultan's life before his coronation.
**ISTANA NURUL IMAN.** A short distance from the central district of Bandar Seri Begawan is the sultan's palace. The Istana Nurul Iman, which means "Palace of the Light of Faith", is about 2 miles west of Jalan Tutong, on a low hill overlooking the Brunei River. Its distinctive, long tip-tilted roofs draw their inspiration from Borneo longhouses ● *76–7*. The building is a series of massive but floating horizontal forms (a trademark of Filipino architect Locsin) broken by two glittering 22-carat gold domes. The Istana boasts 1788 rooms and a throne room that seats 2000, earning it the distinction of being the largest residential palace in the world. Although the palace is officially closed to the public, it opens its doors during Hari Raya Puasa, when the sultan meets his subjects. Alternatively, a good exterior vantage point is from the Persiaran Damuan, a landscaped park set between Jalan Tutong and the Brunei River. Proboscis monkeys can often be sighted in the mangroves ■ *20–1* opposite the park.

## KOTA BATU

A few miles downstream from Bandar Seri Begawan town, or Bandar for short, is Kota Batu – literally "Stone Fort" – the site of Brunei town from very early days up to about the 15th century. Hills run right down to the river here, and the narrowness of the channel and a strategically placed island allowed medieval Bruneians to fortify the river mouth,

Cruising on a royal barge, 1845.

building a large palisade across the river just downstream from the site of the present museum. The area is a very rich archeological site, yielding many ceramics and wooden remains preserved in the anerobic mud.

**The Brunei Museum.** The museum building is styled along Islamic lines, its exterior a pastiche of Brunei Malay motifs similar to those on the sultan's tomb. An important collection of Chinese ceramics, many unearthed in Kota Batu, is the heart of the History Gallery. Brunei was for centuries famous for its bronze casting and brassware industries and the Museum's collection of bronze cannons attests to this. It is among the most impressive of the ethnographic collections housed in the Brunei Culture Gallery. Other galleries include a Natural History Section, an Oil and Gas Industry Gallery sponsored by Brunei Shell Petroleum, and a sixth section where temporary exhibitions are mounted. The sultan's personal collection of Islamic art, formed from the best available in London showrooms, is housed in a separate gallery, and guarded by Gurkhas under his direct command. Admission to the museum is free.

**Sultan Bolkiah's Tomb.** Sultan Bolkiah (1473–1521), the fifth sultan of Brunei, was known as the Singing Captain. He is buried here in a stately tomb carved from basaltic stone (right). The motifs decorating his tomb reflect the artistic development of Islam, which was growing in importance in Southeast Asia, and accommodating itself with the older religions of the region.

**Malay Technology Museum.** The red-roofed building at the edge of the Brunei River, down the hill from the Brunei Museum, is the Malay Technology Museum. Opened in 1990, its three galleries celebrate the development of industries and handicrafts of Brunei's indigenous peoples. Included here are traditional fishing, roof-building, boat-building, copper tooling, blacksmithing, weaving, and hunting exhibits. Notable among them is the loom set up for *songket* weaving. The exhibits are a series of contextual or "cameo" settings, using original materials wherever possible in order to heighten the authenticity of the museum experience.

**The Singing Captain**
Sultan Bolkiah was called "Nakhoda Ragam" (the Singing Captain) because of his talent for playing the drum and lute. Sultan Bolkiah presided over the golden age of Brunei, when its power extended over the island of Borneo and as far north as the Philippines. It is believed that in his later years he would take with him on his voyages a group of artisans, who prepared royal tombs in distant parts of the archipelago so that he could be given a decent burial in the event of his death at sea. In the end, he died while returning home from a voyage to Java.

For a negotiable rate of about B$20, you can take a water taxi on a half-hour tour of the Brunei River and Kampung Ayer. Dusk is pleasant, when the setting sun frames the wooden stilt houses within a golden penumbra and infuses the marble façade of the nearby mosque with a rosy glow.

An early engraving of Labuan.

**BLACK GOLD**
After many years of prospecting, the British Malayan Petroleum Company (Shell) finally found oil in 1929. The story goes that two oil executives, exhausted after riding bicycles down the beach that served as a road between Seria and Kuala Belait, lay down for a rest and sniffed oil. To reach Shell's operation here in the 1930's the sultan, Ahmad Tajuddin, would also have used the beach as a road – this time in a car.

**LUN DAYEH**
The Murut of early accounts may be found in western Sabah, eastern Sarawak and upriver Brunei. An active and formerly warlike people (right), they call themselves Lun Dayeh, Lun Bawang, Lun Lod, or Tagal, depending on geographical location. Their annual Pesta Lun Bawang at Lawas, a Sarawak township on the direct bus route to Kota Kinabalu, attracts large crowds from the surrounding valleys and hills as far away as Ba Kelalang.

## WEST OF BANDAR SERI BEGAWAN

**JERUDONG.** Between Bandar and Jerudong the coast is mostly hilly. Cliffs exposed at Jerudong Beach reveal coal seams, evidence of the mineral wealth hidden in the tortured sedimentary strata, which underlie much of Brunei Darussalam. Large, futuristic villas owned by the sultan's family members dot the area around Jerudong Park, a private polo and golf complex.

**TUTONG AND BELAIT DISTRICTS.** West of Jerudong the hills give way to a flat alluvial plain. The coasts here have been built up by sediment from Borneo's interior. Mangroves and nipa palms colonize the muddy shallows, especially near the mouths of the many small but sediment-heavy rivers. As more sediment is trapped by the mangrove root systems, the ground level is raised, and more vegetation becomes established as salinity levels drop. Gradually, mature brackish mangrove swamps ■ *20–1* become peat forests.

**SERIA AND KUALA BELAIT.** These are the towns that oil built, beginning with the discovery of the Seria field in 1929. "Nodding donkey" oil pumps dot the company-town landscape of trim bungalows and tidy gardens. The beach near the 1,000,000th-Barrel Monument offers a good sunset view of the offshore oil installations. A bridge across the Belait River leads to Miri, Sarawak.

## BRUNEI BAY

**BRUNEI-MUARA DISTRICT.** The Brunei River runs from Bandar to the north end of the bay, where the beaches at Selasa and near the port of Muara are popular on weekends. Up in the hills above Selasa beach are the remains of the Brooketon coal mine, which was operated by Sarawak for a time under license from the sultan.

**TEMBURONG DISTRICT.** Motor launches leave the pier in front of the food center on Jalan Kota Batu for Temburong's capital, Bungar. The boat ride is an excellent introduction to the ecosystems of the bay area. The launch winds through channels of mangroves, then emerges into the broad expanse of Brunei Bay, one of Southeast Asia's most fecund fishing grounds. After re-entering the mangroves, the boat pulls up at the riverside pier of Bangar. Temburong is home to mainly Murut people. Beyond the last longhouse ● *76–7* on the Temburong River is one of Borneo's most beautiful rainforests ■ *22–3*, a protected reserve, and home to a major forest research project undertaken by Britain's Royal Society of Geographers and the University of Brunei Darussalam.

**LABUAN.** Commanding the approaches to Brunei Bay is Labuan, a Malaysian Federal Territory and former British Crown Colony. Recent measures to establish an offshore financial center here may finally make the picturesque island a commercial success, something previous owners have failed to achieve.

# Practical information

# ◆ Getting to Singapore, Malaysia and Brunei Darussalam

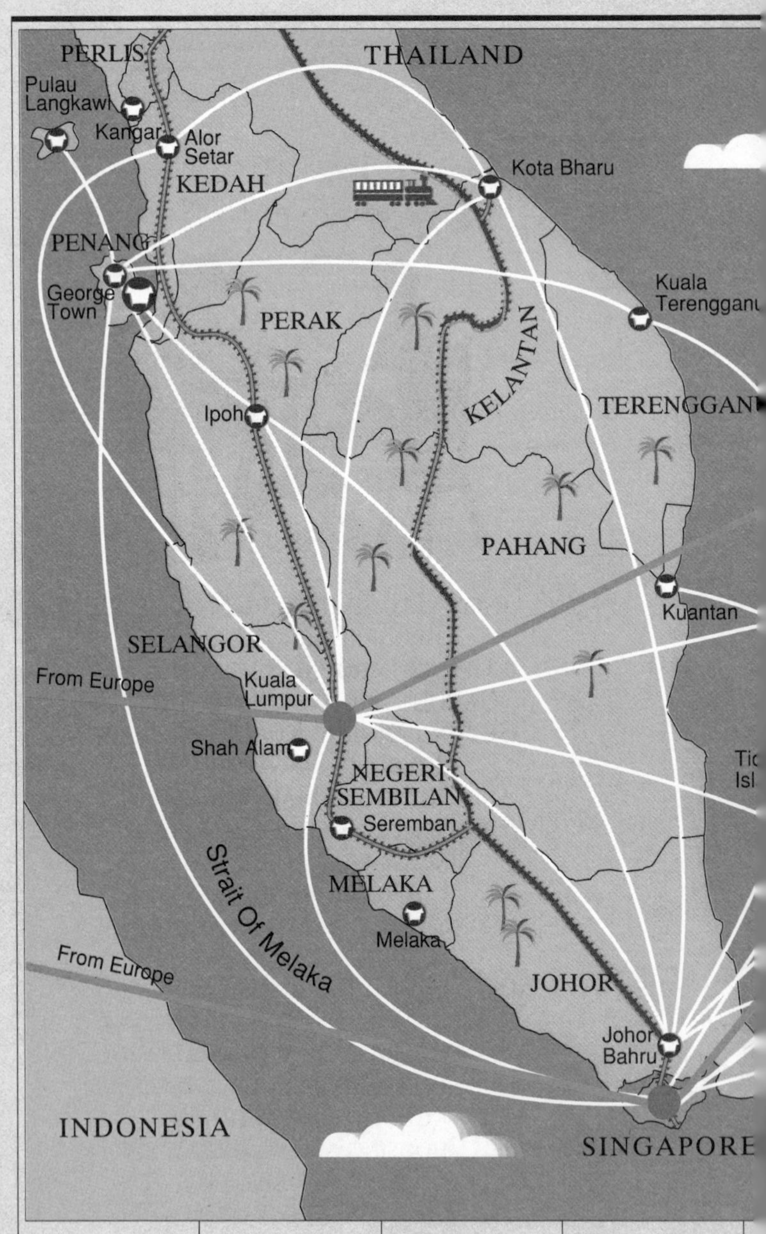


**By air**
London to Singapore: British Airways and Singapore Airlines have daily non-stop flights taking about 13 hours. Roundtrip tickets range from about £600 to £4,300, less for budget tickets. Arrival is at ultra-efficient Changi airport, where air-conditioned taxis are plentiful. The ride to the city costs about S$15 and takes about 20 minutes. Air-conditioned bus no. 390 takes a little longer, but at S$1.50.
London to Kuala Lumpur: British Airways and Malaysian Airlines have daily non-stop flights. Fares are the same those to Singapore. Subang Airport is 13 miles from the center of Kuala Lumpur. Taxi fare for the 1-hour ride costs RM22 (buy a coupon at the entrance kiosk). The airport bus to the city costs a few ringgit.

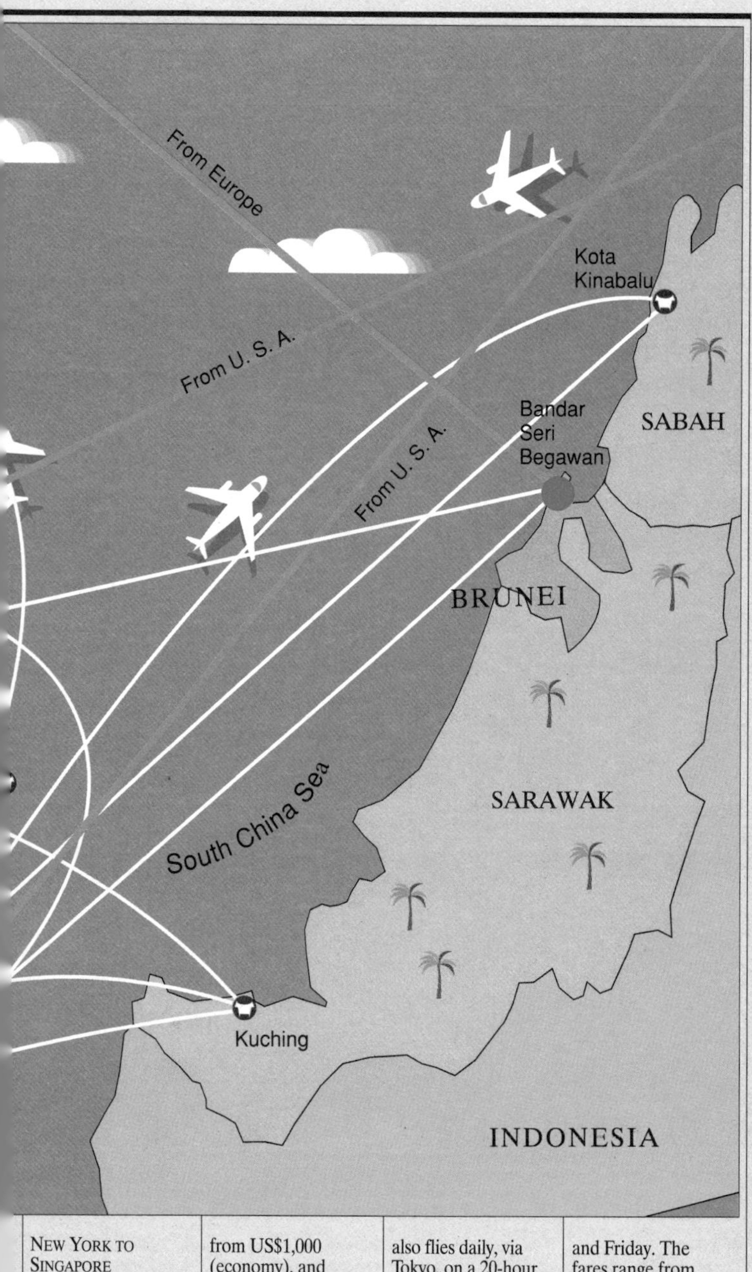


NEW YORK TO SINGAPORE (connections to Kuala Lumpur): Roundtrip tickets from US$1,225 (economy) roundtrip, US$3,980 (business). LOS ANGELES TO SINGAPORE: Roundtrip tickets from US$1,000 (economy), and US$3,150 (business). SAN FRANCISCO TO SINGAPORE: Singapore Airlines flies via Hong Kong daily, with one-way airfares between US$1282–2669. Northwest Airlines also flies daily, via Tokyo, on a 20-hour flight, with one-way fares from US$1,276–2,663. LOS ANGELES TO KUALA LUMPUR: Malaysian Airlines operates a daily flight, except Wednesday and Friday. The fares range from US$2,015–2,663. TO BANDAR SERI BEGAWAN: Frequent flights from Kuala Lumpur (RM856–1,216) and Singapore (S$754–1,120).

## ◆ Getting from Singapore to Malaysia

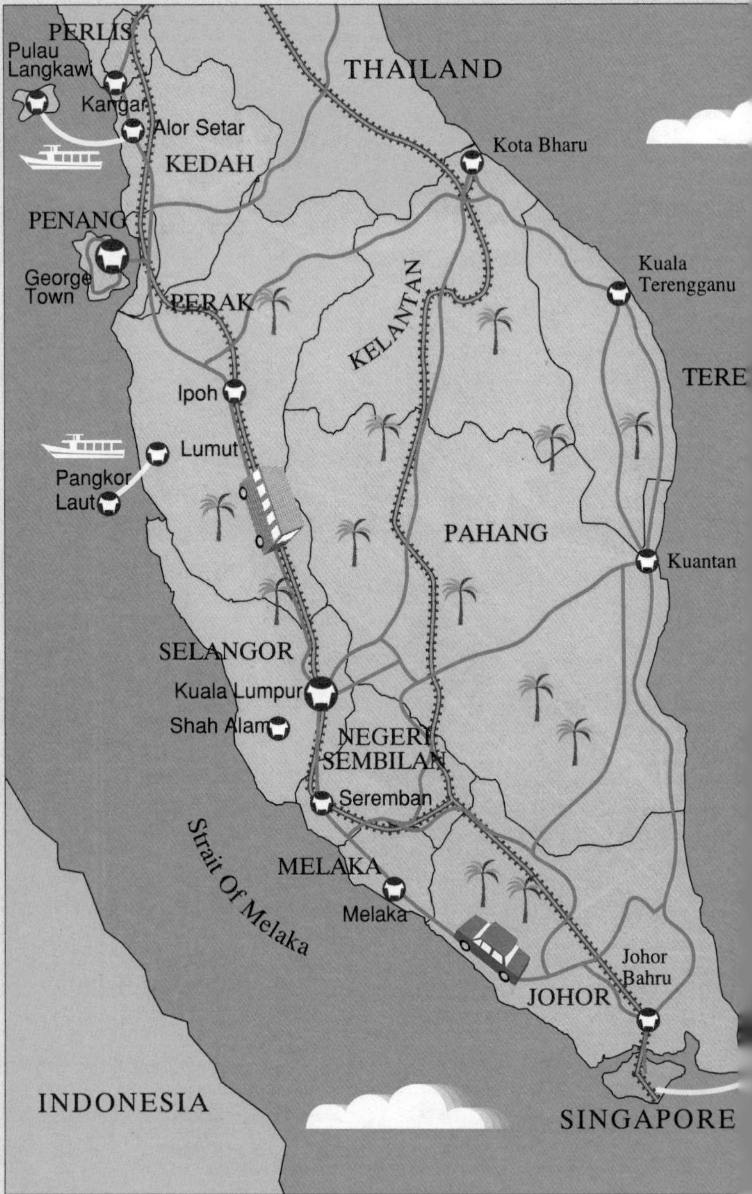

**By train**
There are six Singapore-KL train services daily.
The first train leaves Tanjong Pagar, Singapore, for Kuala Lumpur at 7.45am, arriving at the Malaysian capital at

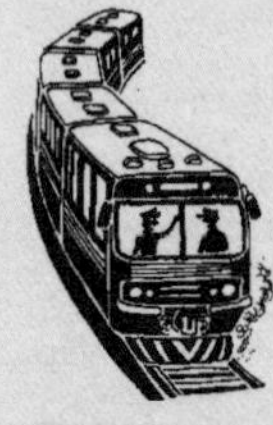

2.30pm. An express service runs at 2.45pm Fares for the 7-hour journey range between RM18 and RM60, depending on the seating class.

**By bus**
The Singapore–Kuala Lumpur 8-hour bus journey costs S$18. Tickets can be purchased from Pan Malaysia Express Pte Ltd (tel. 292 9254) at the Kallang Bahru/ Lavender Street junction, near the Lavender MRT station. There are two

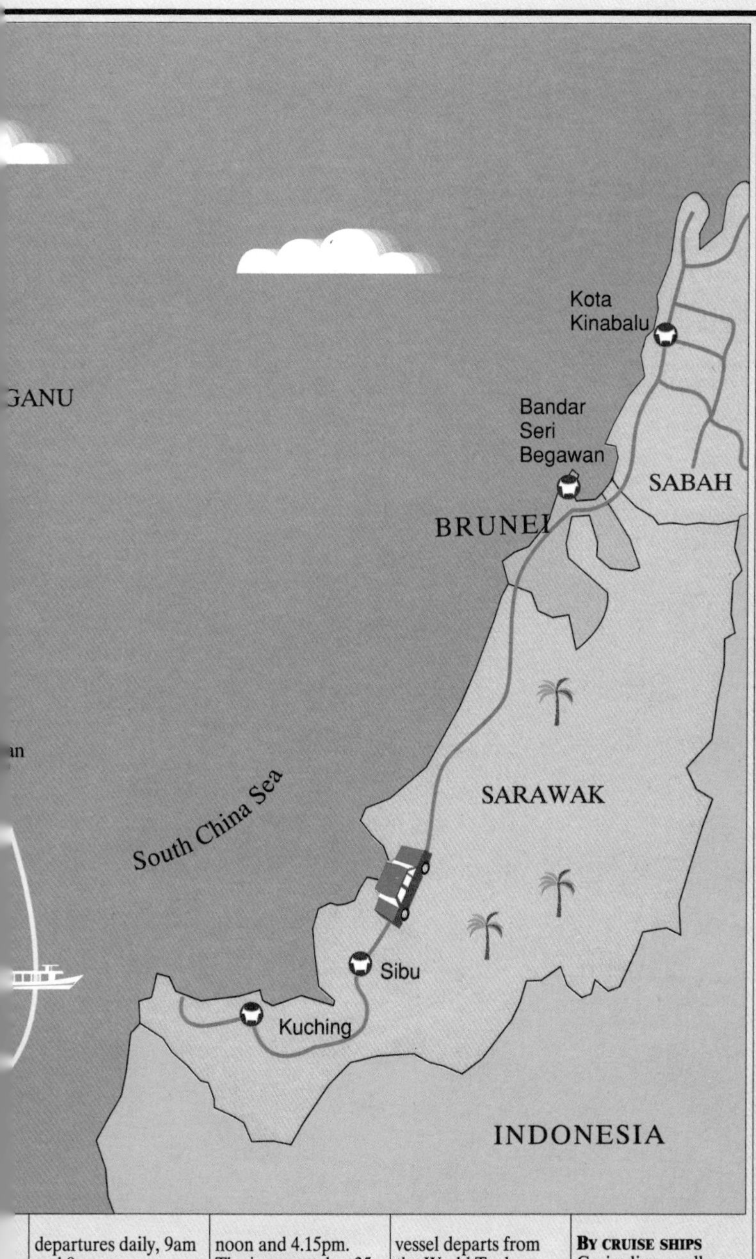


departures daily, 9am and 9pm.

**By ferry**
Ferrylink services (tel. 545 3600) operate between Singapore (near Changi airport) and Johor (Tanjung Belungkor) at 9am, noon and 4.15pm. The journey takes 35 minutes and a round-trip fare is S$24. Resort Cruises (S) Pte Ltd (tel. 278 4677) offer a daily 5-hour ferry service between Singapore and Tioman. The vessel departs from the World Trade Centre ferry terminal at 7.50am daily, except Wednesday. A round-trip fare is S$144. The ferry leaves Tioman for Singapore at about 1.30pm.

**By cruise ships**
Cruise liners call on Singapore, docking at the World Trade Centre terminal throughout the year. Peak travel periods occur during the school vacation in June and December.

The front of a bus bears its service number. At the side of the bus near the entrance is a plate which also states the destination and the route the bus takes.

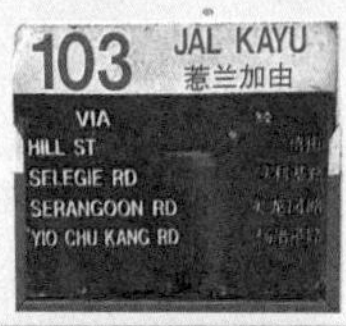

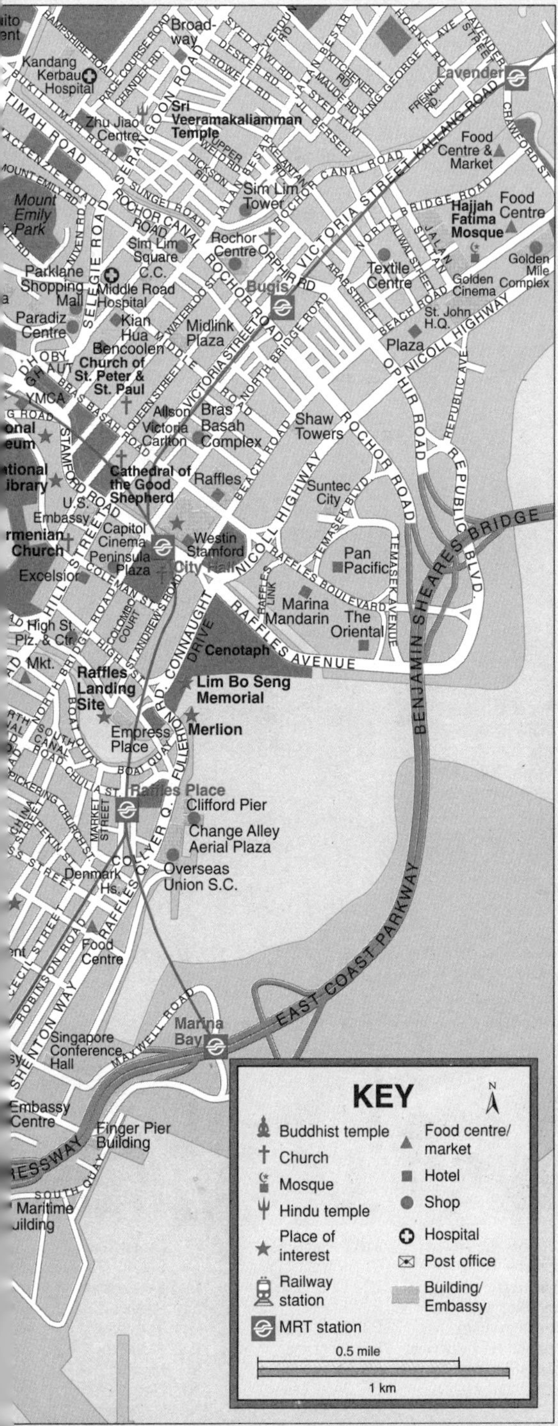

**By MRT**
One of the most advanced in the world, Singapore's MRT system is gleaming, cool, and efficient. Journeys on the two main lines – north–south and east–west – cost between 60 cents and S$1.50 with the use of a farecard.

**By bus**
Bus services are generally frequent and reliable. However, unless your destination is listed at the bus stop, it can be difficult to work out which to take. Fares range from 50 cents to S$1. Air-conditioned buses charge slightly higher. The buses are one-man operated; you slot the exact fare into a box next to the driver. A farecard may also be used.

**By taxi**
Taxis are metered and are managed by a few companies. The flagfall is S$2.40 for the first 1.5 km (one mile) and 10 cents for every additional 225 meters. Higher charges are made for journeys in the CBD (Central Business District), from Changi airportpre-booked taxis, and hire after midnight. Taxis are in short supply during the rush hour or when it rains. Hotels often have a taxi calling system at their main entrance.

N16
N17
N18
N20
N21
N22
N23
W12 W11 W10 W9
W8
W7
W6
W5
W4

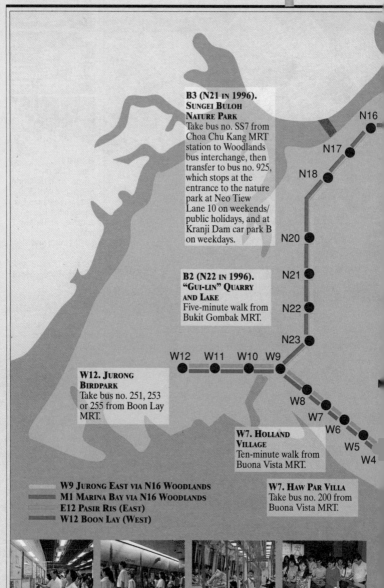

**B3 (N21 IN 1996). SUNGEI BULOH NATURE PARK**
Take bus no. SS7 from Choa Chu Kang MRT station to Woodlands bus interchange, then transfer to bus no. 925, which stops at the entrance to the nature park at Neo Tiew Lane 10 on weekends/ public holidays, and at Kranji Dam car park B on weekdays.

**B2 (N22 IN 1996). "GUI-LIN" QUARRY AND LAKE**
Five-minute walk from Bukit Gombak MRT.

**W12. JURONG BIRDPARK**
Take bus no. 251, 253 or 255 from Boon Lay MRT.

**W7. HOLLAND VILLAGE**
Ten-minute walk from Buona Vista MRT.

**W7. HAW PAR VILLA**
Take bus no. 200 from Buona Vista MRT.

**W9 JURONG EAST VIA N16 WOODLANDS**
**M1 MARINA BAY VIA N16 WOODLANDS**
**E12 PASIR RIS (EAST)**
**W12 BOON LAY (WEST)**

The Woodlands Extension to the present MRT system comprises six new stations linking Yishun (N12) with Choa Chu Kang (N21) to form a loop. The extension services the new towns in the northern part of the island, together with a new bus interchange, opened recently right below the Woodlands MRT station.

**MRT STATIONS:**
C1 RAFFLES PLACE
C2 CITY HALL
E1 BUGIS
E2 LAVENDER
E3 KALLANG
E4 ALJUNIED
E5 PAYA LEBAR
E6 EUNOS
E7 KEMBANGAN
E8 BEDOK
E9 TANAH MERAH
E10 SIMEI
E11 TAMPINES
E12 PASIR RIS
M1 MARINA BAY
N1 DHOBY GHAUT
N2 SOMERSET

Singapore's MRT operates from 6am to midnight. Fares range from 60 cents to S$1.50. Dispensing machines issue single-trip fare-cards. Window counters sell multiple-trip fare-cards of S$5 (children), S$10, S$20 and S$50, as well as souvenir fare-cards at S$6 each. Several tourist attractions can be reached by MRT and bus (see map).

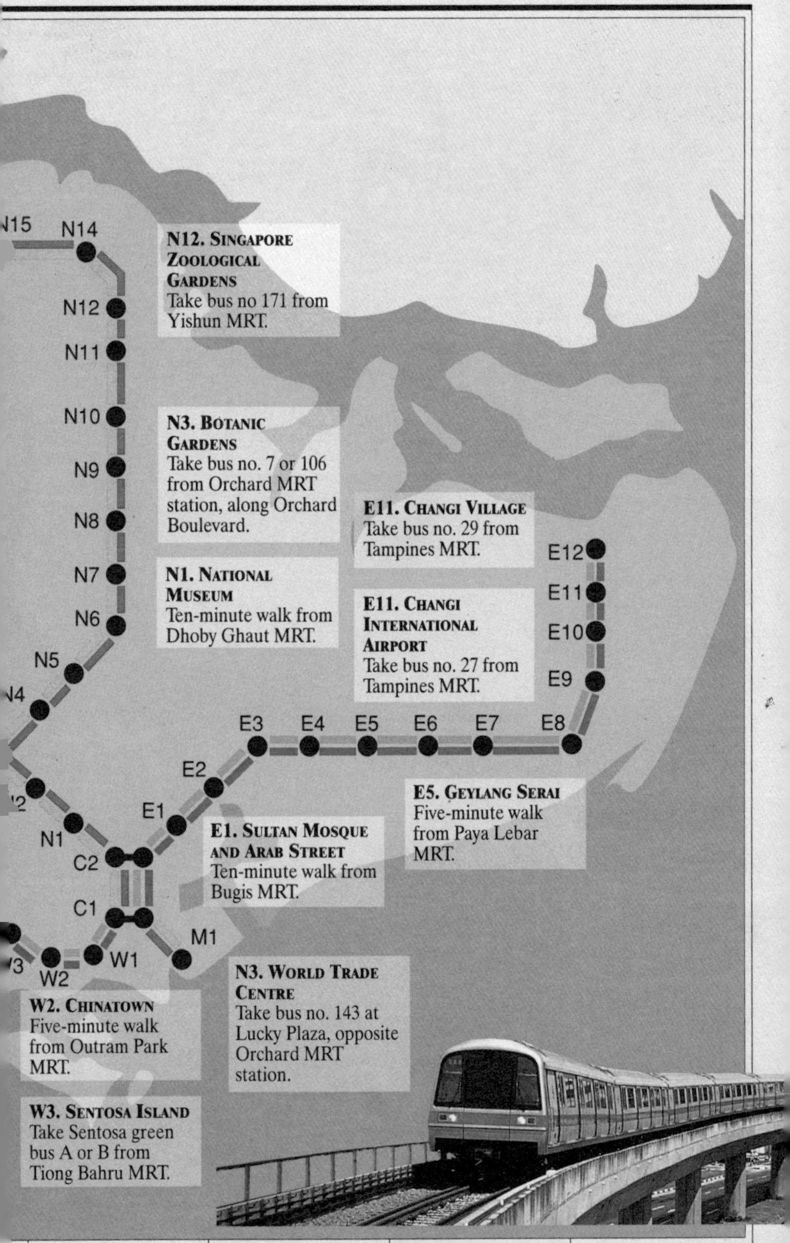

N15 N14 N12 N11 N10 N9 N8 N7 N6 N5 N4 N2 N1 C2 C1 M1 W1 W2 W3 E1 E2 E3 E4 E5 E6 E7 E8 E9 E10 E11 E12

**N12. Singapore Zoological Gardens**
Take bus no 171 from Yishun MRT.

**N3. Botanic Gardens**
Take bus no. 7 or 106 from Orchard MRT station, along Orchard Boulevard.

**N1. National Museum**
Ten-minute walk from Dhoby Ghaut MRT.

**E11. Changi Village**
Take bus no. 29 from Tampines MRT.

**E11. Changi International Airport**
Take bus no. 27 from Tampines MRT.

**E5. Geylang Serai**
Five-minute walk from Paya Lebar MRT.

**E1. Sultan Mosque and Arab Street**
Ten-minute walk from Bugis MRT.

**N3. World Trade Centre**
Take bus no. 143 at Lucky Plaza, opposite Orchard MRT station.

**W2. Chinatown**
Five-minute walk from Outram Park MRT.

**W3. Sentosa Island**
Take Sentosa green bus A or B from Tiong Bahru MRT.

| | | | |
|---|---|---|---|
| N3 Orchard | N12 Yishun | N23 Bukit Batok | W9 Jurong East |
| N4 Newton | N14 Sembawang | W1 Tanjong Pagar | W10 Chinese Garden |
| N5 Novena | N15 Admiralty | W2 Outram Park | W11 Lakeside |
| N6 Toa Payoh | N16 Woodlands | W3 Tiong Bahru | W12 Boon Lay |
| N7 Braddell | N17 Marsiling | W4 Redhill | |
| N8 Bishan | N18 Kranji | W5 Queenstown | |
| N9 Ang Mo Kio | N20 Yew Tee | W6 Commonwealth | |
| N10 Yio Chu Kang | N21 Choa Chu Kang | W7 Buona Vista | |
| N11 Khatib | N22 Bukit Gombok | W8 Clementi | |

**BY TAXI**

Taxis are numerous in Kuala Lumpur and can be hailed along the street or at the many taxi stands. Fares are metered, except on long journeys, when the taxi driver may quote a fare at the start of the ride. It costs RM1 for the first 2 kilometers (1.2 miles) and 10 sen for each subsequent 200 meters. There are also share-cabs (four passengers to a vehicle) for outbound and inter-state journeys. These taxis usually wait at pick-up points near bus terminals.

**BY BUS**

Bus journeys can be quite difficult for first-time visitors. There are many types of services and rather irregular schedules, but the fares are cheap. Destinations are shown at the front of the bus. The bus conductor might be of help too. Buses leave the Klang bus terminal for the airport, Shah Alam and Klang. Buses at the Pudu Raya terminal cover city and inter-state routes. Mini-buses charge 50 cents from all terminals.

**BY TRISHAW**

Trishaws are readily available but a price should be agreed at the start of the ride.

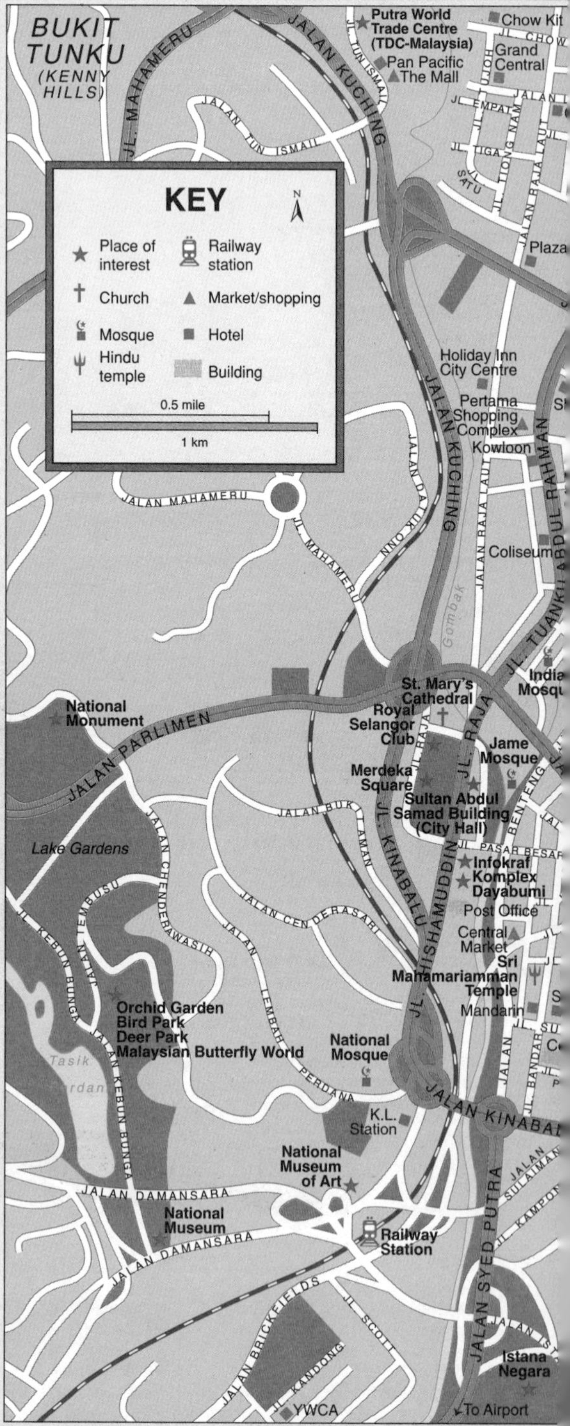

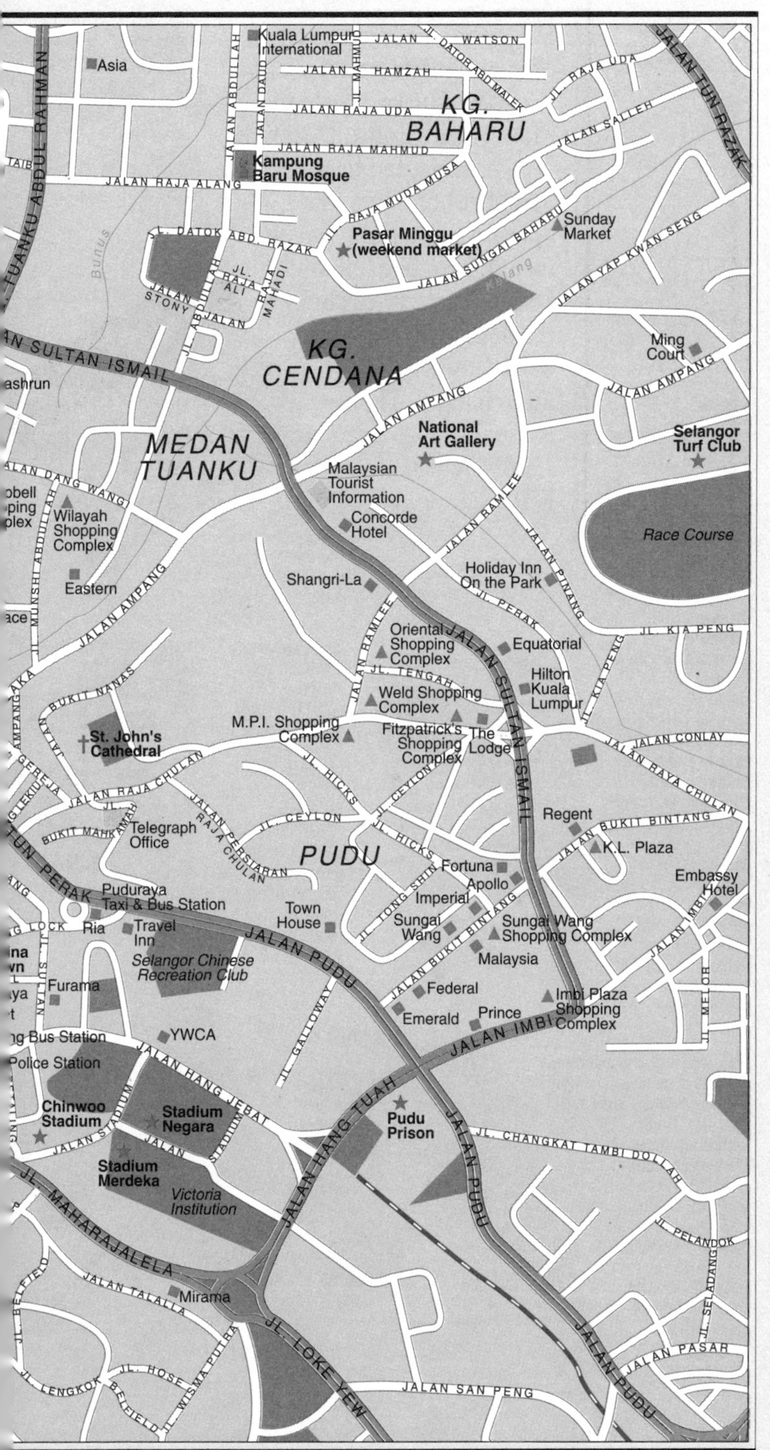

KG. BAHARU
KG. CENDANA
MEDAN TUANKU
PUDU
Kuala Lumpur International
Asia
Kampung Baru Mosque
Pasar Minggu (weekend market)
Sunday Market
Ming Court
National Art Gallery
Selangor Turf Club
Race Course
Malaysian Tourist Information
Concorde Hotel
Wilayah Shopping Complex
Eastern
Shangri-La
Holiday Inn On the Park
Oriental Shopping Complex
Equatorial
Hilton Kuala Lumpur
Weld Shopping Complex
M.P.I. Shopping Complex
Fitzpatrick's Shopping Complex
The Lodge
St. John's Cathedral
Telegraph Office
Regent
K.L. Plaza
Fortuna
Apollo
Imperial
Embassy Hotel
Puduraya Taxi & Bus Station
Ria
Travel Inn
Town House
Sungai Wang
Sungai Wang Shopping Complex
Malaysia
Selangor Chinese Recreation Club
Furama
Federal
Emerald
Prince
Imbi Plaza Shopping Complex
YWCA
Police Station
Chinwoo Stadium
Stadium Negara
Stadium Merdeka
Victoria Institution
Pudu Prison
Mirama
JALAN TUANKU ABDUL RAHMAN
JALAN SULTAN ISMAIL
JALAN TUN RAZAK
JALAN RAJA UDA
JALAN RAJA MAHMUD
JALAN RAJA ALANG
JALAN HAMZAH
JALAN WATSON
JL. DATOK ABD. RAZAK
JALAN SUNGAI BAHARU
JALAN YAP KWAN SENG
JALAN AMPANG
JALAN RAMLEE
JALAN PINANG
JL. PERAK
JL. KIA PENG
JL. TENGAH
JALAN CONLAY
JALAN RAYA CHULAN
JALAN BUKIT BINTANG
JL. HICKS
JL. CEYLON
JALAN PUDU
JALAN IMBI
JALAN HANG TUAH
JALAN HANG JEBAT
JALAN STADIUM
JL. MAHARAJALELA
JL. LOKE YEW
JALAN SAN PENG
JALAN PASAR
JL. CHANGKAT TAMBI DOLLAH
JL. PELANDOK
JALAN TUN PERAK
JALAN GALLOWAY
JALAN TALALLA
JALAN WISMA PUTRA
JL. BELFIELD

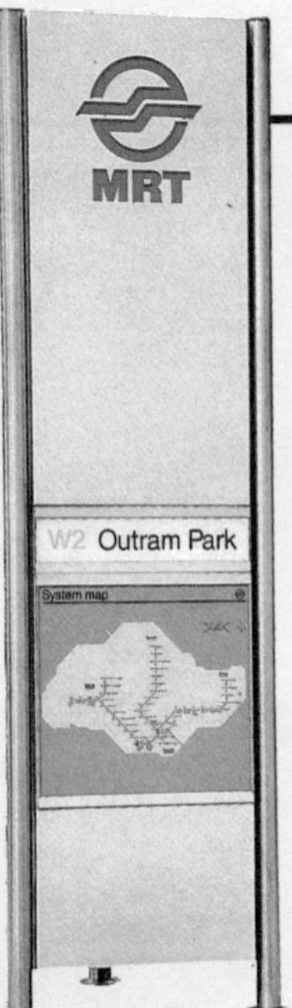


To facilitate travel on public transport, fare-cards are available for use on the MRT as well as on most public buses.

Singapore is served by an efficient public transport network. The cross-island Mass Rapid Transit (MRT) is complemented by a huge fleet of buses that operate seven days a week, including public holidays. Feeder bus services link residential estates with MRT/bus interchanges. There is usually a taxi stand at each MRT station.

**BUS SIGNBOARD**
A plate next to the entrance of the bus highlights the service number and route.

**PARKING LOT COUPONS**
Vehicles parked in public car parks should have valid coupons displayed on the dashboard. Half-hourly and hourly coupons are validated by tearing off the respective number tabs. Wardens make regular checks to ensure that the rule is adhered to. Errant vehicle owners can be fined for the offence.

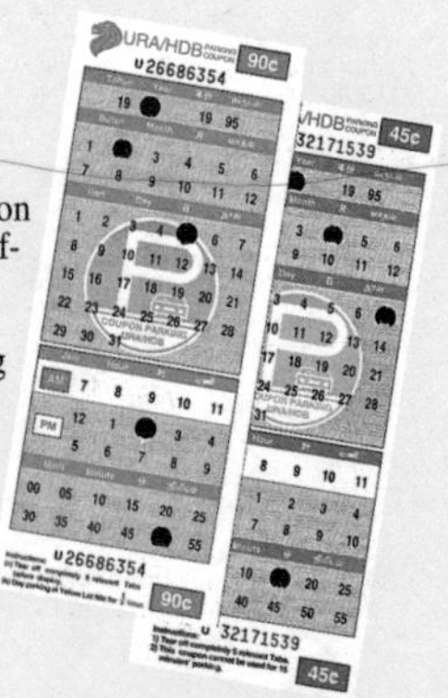


**AREA LICENSES**
The Central Business District (CBD) system was introduced to reduce traffic congestion in the city. To enter the "Restricted Zone" during the day, motorists must purchase and display an area license. Daily and monthly area licenses are sold at roadside booths, post offices and some gas stations.

**NEWSPAPERS AND JOURNALS**
The English-language dailies are *The Straits Times* and *Business Times*, complemented by an afternoon tabloid, *The New Paper*. On Sundays, the only English paper available is *The Sunday Times*. There are also dailies published in the republic's other three official languages – Chinese, Malay, and Tamil.

**TELEPHONE**
Orange coin-phones (right) are everywhere – usually outside stores. The charge for a local call is 10 cents for 3 minutes. Local and overseas calls may be made with a phone-card (above) from telephone booths in shopping centers and at MRT stations.

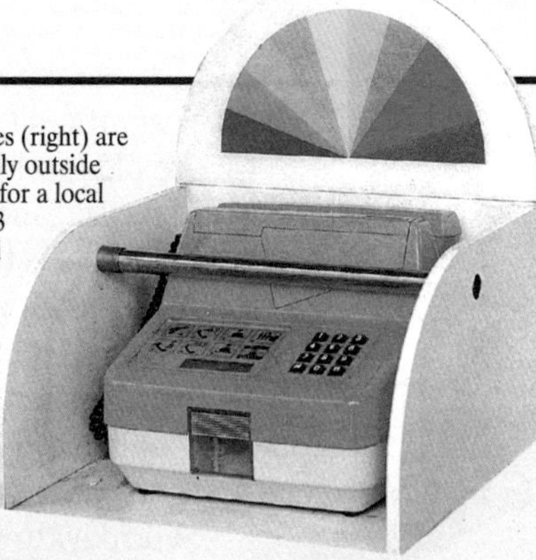

**CLEAN AND GREEN**
To encourage living in a clean and green environment, signs such as these are put up in parks. Anti-littering signs are also visible on city streets. Litterbugs caught in the act are handed Corrective Work Orders to clean up designated places for a day.

**CURRENCY**
The unit of currency is the Singapore dollar, in denominations of $1, $2, $5, $10, $20, $50, $100, $500, $1000, and $10,000. Coins are in denominations of 1, 5, 10, 20, 50, and 100 cents. The Brunei Darussalam currency is accepted (at par) in Singapore. The current rate of exchange is £1= S$2.09 and US$1=S$1.4 (August 1996).

**POSTAL SERVICES**
Local postage for letters is 22 cents. Mail boxes, bearing the words Singapore POST, are square and painted white and pastel blue. There are post offices in major shopping complexes such as Chinatown Point, Orchard Point, Plaza Singapura, and Raffles City Shopping Centre. The General Post Office at Change Alley and the branch at Comcentre, Somerset Road, open round the clock for basic postal services.

**CAPTIVATING BACK**
Creativity on the back panel of a tourist coach.

Post offices (*pejabat pos*) are plentiful throughout Malaysia, and even in small towns the staff speak and understand English. Opening hours are from 8am to 5pm Monday to Friday, and from 8am until noon on Saturday. In Kuala Lumpur, the General Post Office is housed in the Dayabumi Complex – the white, Islamic-style skyscraper – on Jalan Sultan Hishamuddin. It is connected to the Central Market by a pedestrian walkway spanning the Klang River.

**POSTAGE**
Stamps can be bought from the *setam* counter. Aerograms to all destinations cost 50 sen. Letters sent to destinations within Malaysia cost 30 sen for the first 20 gm, and 50 sen for 20–50 gm; postcards cost 20 sen.

**TELEPHONE**
A local phone call costs 10 sen for the first 3 minutes, and 10 sen for each additional 3 minutes (indicated by a beeping noise). Public telephones are found in Telekom offices, shopping centers, usually outside post offices and by the roadside. There are two kinds – those that accept coins (most) and those that accept Kadfon and Unifon plastic phone cards. Kadfons can be bought at all Telekom shops (*kedai Telekom*), while Unifons are available at gas stations and neighborhood stores. Both phone-cards are available in denominations of RM10, RM20, RM50.

Country codes, the price of a 3-minute full-rate call, and their reduced rate time (on Malaysian time) is as follows:

**TELEPHONE CALL (3-MIN) CHARGES**

| COUNTRY | CODE | PRICE (RM) | HOURS |
|---|---|---|---|
| Australia | 61 | 11.70 | 9pm to 7am |
| France | 33 | 18.00 | midnight to noon |
| Germany | 49 | 18.00 | midnight to noon |
| Japan | 81 | 16.20 | 9pm to 7am |
| UK | 44 | 22.50 | midnight to noon |
| US | 1 | 15.00 | 3am to 9am |

New Straits Times

**Time differences**
Kuala Lumpur is exactly 8 hours ahead of Greenwich Mean Time, 13 hours ahead of American Eastern Standard Time, 16 hours ahead of Pacific Standard Time, and 2 hours ahead of Australian Eastern Standard Time.

南洋商報
NANYANG SIANG PAU

Utusan
MALAYSIA

**Newspapers**
Besides international dailies, the country has local newspapers available in English, Malay, Chinese, and Tamil. The leading English dailies published in the peninsula are *The New Straits Times*, *Malay Mail*, *The Star*, and *The Sun*. The Malay paper *Berita Harian* has the largest circulation. In East Malaysia, the English newspapers in circulation are *Sarawak Tribune* and the daily *Borneo Bulletin*.

**Banks**
Banks open 10am to 3pm Monday to Friday, and 9.30am to 11.30am on Saturday. In Kedah, Kelantan, Perlis, and Terengganu, they are closed on Thursday afternoons and Fridays. Travelers' checks are accepted by all banks, which charge a small commission. Money-changers are prolific in Kuala Lumpur, Penang, and Johor Bahru. In Kuala Lumpur they center around the Jalan Tuanku Abdul Rahman/Jalan Masjid area, in the shopping malls, the railway station, and airport.

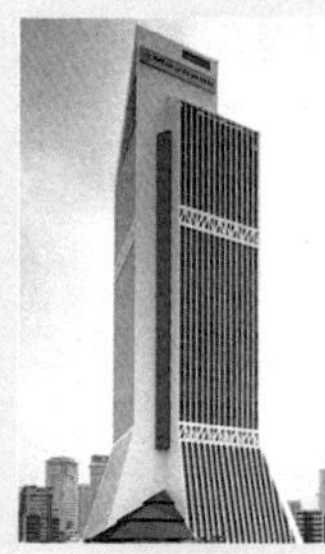

**Money**
Malaysian currency is the ringgit (dollar) of 100 sen (cents). The abbreviation used is RM. Notes are issued in denominations of RM1, RM5, RM10, RM20, RM50, RM100, RM500, RM1000; coins in circulation are 1, 5, 10, 20, 50 sen and RM1. With the introduction of the RM1 coin the RM1 dollar bill is being phased out.

National Day is celebrated with much pomp and splendor in the three countries. The ceremony begins with the traditional parade, followed by a mass display of calisthenics by students and young people from cultural associations, and climaxed by a display of fireworks. Singapore celebrates its National Day on August 9. Malaysia's National Day falls on August 31, while Brunei Darussalam's Independence Day is January 1.

**HOLIDAYS AND FESTIVALS**

| | January | February | March | April | May | June | July | August | September | October | November | December |
|---|---|---|---|---|---|---|---|---|---|---|---|---|
| Chinese New Year | • | • | | | | | | | | | | |
| Thaipusam | | • | | | | | | | | | | |
| Hari Raya Puasa | | | • | | | | | | | | | |
| Good Friday | | | | • | | | | | | | | |
| Labor Day | | | | | 1 | | | | | | | |
| Vesak Day | | | | | • | | | | | | | |
| Dumpling Festival/ Dragon Boat Race | | | | | | • | | | | | | |
| Hungry Ghosts Festival | | | | | | | | • | | | | |
| Lantern/Mooncake Festival | | | | | | | | | | • | | |
| Deepavali | | | | | | | | | | • | | |
| Christmas | | | | | | | | | | | | 25 |

**CHINESE NEW YEAR**
The young pay respects to their elders and receive *hong bao* (red gift packets with token money) for good luck. The auspicious event is celebrated over fifteen days with reunion dinners, group outings among friends, and trips to temples. A Chingay parade is held in the streets of Penang and Singapore.

**THAIPUSAM.** In an act of thanksgiving to Lord Subramaniam for answering their prayers, Hindu devotees parade the streets (late January). Several bare-bodied and entranced male participants carry *kavadi* (metal cage with spikes and peacock feathers) and walk barefoot from one Hindu temple to another. At the temple, a firewalking ceremony is conducted. The participants believe the act will cleanse them of their sins.

**HARI RAYA PUASA**
Celebrated by Muslims who fast during the month of Ramadan, Hari Raya Puasa is a major festival in the region. Streets near major mosques are abuzz with shoppers in the late afternoon, when the fast breaks. Stalls display Hari Raya delicacies, garments, carpets, and assorted decorative items for the home. Greetings are exchanged among family members on the day itself, followed by visits to the mosque and to the homes of relatives and friends.

**HUNGRY GHOSTS' FESTIVAL.** During the seventh Lunar month, many Chinese pay tribute to their deceased relatives by offering food and burning joss paper. Road shows such as *wayang* and *godai* are held in the outskirts and in residential estates. Sponsors for such shows are treated to dinner under a pitched tent. An auction serves as a side attraction for the diners.

**LANTERN/MOONCAKE FESTIVAL.** On the fifteenth day of the eighth month of the Lunar calendar, groups of children can be seen touring the neighborhood with lighted paper or plastic lanterns. The Chinese Garden in Singapore organizes the annual Lantern Festival with a host of activities, attracting both tourists and locals. Mooncakes (pastries filled with bean paste, lotus seed, and egg yolk) are sold in boxes at shops and in hotel lobbies.

**DEEPAVALI**
Celebrated by Hindus, the Festival of Lights marks the triumph of good over evil. Homes are lit up with oil lamps. Family visits are part of the celebration. Devotees offer thanksgiving prayers at the temple. Singapore's Little India district comes alive with bright lights and night bazaars for three weeks.

**CHRISTMAS**
Singapore's Orchard Road dazzles at night as hotels and shopping centers along the stretch put up colorful bunting, and lights usher in the Yuletide season. Caroling sessions are held in many hotel lobbies and homes.

Singapore, Malaysia, and Brunei Darussalam share a tropical climate that is hot and humid. The humidity discourages prolonged outdoor activity and makes air-conditioning at night almost mandatory. The region receives about 10 hours of sunshine daily. Showers are brief and intermittent. However, during year-end monsoon periods, thunderstorms wreak havoc on several low-lying rural areas of Peninsular Malaysia, and road access becomes quite impossible because of floods.

**MONTHLY AVERAGE TEMPERATURE (IN FAHRENHEIT)**

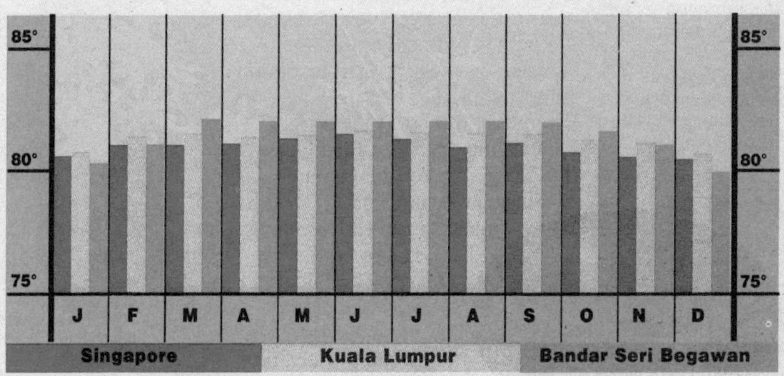


**TEMPERATURE**

Singapore, Malaysia, and Brunei Darussalam enjoy a tropical climate. Temperatures range from 85°F (30°c) in the day to 75°F (24°c) at night, with an average daily temperature of 80°F (26°c). The hill resorts in Malaysia are cooler between March and September.

**MONTHLY RAINFALL (IN INCHES)**

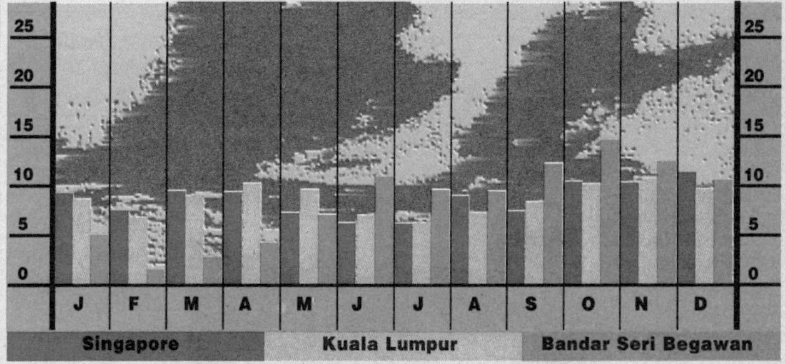


**WIND AND RAIN**

Rainfall in Singapore is usually brief and scattered, and the wettest months are November to January. Southwest monsoons blow over the west coast of Peninsular Malaysia from May to October, while the more severe northeast monsoons hit the east coast of the peninsula and the west coast of Sarawak, northeast Sabah, and Brunei Darussalam from November to February.

**TAKING IT EASY**
Dress lightly, in cotton or other natural fiber or you'll find yourself dripping from just crossing the road. Walk slowly in Singapore and leave rushing to the locals. Otherwise, the high humidity will hit you even more than the 24-hour heat (often tempered by sea breezes and afternoon rain showers). It's sensible not to venture far in the intense heat of the afternoon – most Singaporeans don't. However, to make up for any daytime torpor, night activities extend long and late in Singapore.

**DAY 1.** The cool of the morning makes a walk in Singapore's Botanic Gardens a good start to the day. Watch out for one of the first rubber trees planted in Asia, thereby launching the region's lucrative rubber trade. After lunch at the hawker center just outside the garden's main entrance, take a taxi to the 175-acre Bukit Timah Nature Reserve, which makes Singapore the only world city to boast a primary rainforest. On a short trek there, you will find over 800 species of native plants and wildlife which includes cheeky monkeys. In the evening, head for Clifford Pier to go on a cruise of Singapore's harbor or southern islands, either by basic bumboat or lavish catamaran. Short but pleasant cruises up the Singapore River leave from near the Raffles Landing Site on North Boat Quay (tel. 227 7287). You could join Singapore's hardworking wealth-makers in an early-evening beer. Happy Hours last until 8pm, and Boat Quay in the heart of the city is just the place, though the conservation zone of Tanjong Pagar is not bad either.

**NIGHT SAFARI**
Located next to the Singapore Zoological Gardens and occupying a 100-acre plot, the world's first and only Night Safari opened in June 1994. About 1,200 tropical animals of about 100 species are displayed in a wild rainforest setting. Visitors can explore the safari through the nature walk trails. Admission fees are S$15 (adult) and S$10 (child), and tram rides at S$3 (adult) and S$2 (child). No cameras or torches are allowed in. Opening hours are from 7.30pm to midnight daily. To get there, take SBS bus no. 138 from Yio Chu Kang MRT station.

**DAY 2.** Spend the morning visiting the Singapore Zoological Gardens, rated among the best zoos in the world. Return to the city for a high-tea buffet at Compass Rose near the top (sixty-nine storys up) of the world's tallest hotel, Westin Stamford, next to City Hall MRT station. Or take afternoon tea at Alkaff Mansion, a restored colonial mansion on its own little hill to the west of the city, overlooking the harbor. Later, take a trip by bus to Changi Village, which has an agreeable out-of-town atmosphere, with its small jetty (boats go from here to unspoilt Pulau Ubin), and beach perfect for a relaxing sunset stroll. Soon it's time to tackle Singapore's lively nightlife.

A popular night spot is Zouk, a fashionable complex with a half-outdoors bar, MTV bar, a huge disco dancefloor,

the more upscale Velvet Underground club, a Deli and a boutique. Fabrice's, in Marriott's basement, is noted for its world music. The authentic Hard Rock Cafe, with occasional live music, stays open till 2am. Planet Hollywood is nearby, in Liat Towers. Among the liveliest of town bars is Brannigan's in the Hyatt Regency Hotel basement. Also notable is 5 Emerald Hill (in a restored shophouse) with its neighboring Que Pasa wine bar and Ice Cold pub.

**Day 3.** The Arab Street area makes an excellent morning outing, with shops opening at 10am and many little Muslim restaurants noisily beckoning. Chinatown and Little India as a whole are better explored on foot during the early evening. Sentosa is Singapore's "fun" island but the discerning will find it too theme-park artificial. One genuine attraction is its World War Two Fort Siloso. The cable-car ride from its mid-point station at World Trade Centre across to Sentosa is definitely for those unalarmed by heights. A more authentic afternoon outing is the East Coast Park, with its beach and its many variations of Singaporeans-at-play – plus plentiful eating and drinking spots. One such spot is the East Coast Park Seafood Centre , which is also popular with locals and offers a choice of nine neighboring (and competing) restaurants. An out-of-the-sun afternoon can be spent exploring Singapore's grand old lady, the famous Raffles Hotel (below). Combine this with a visit to the nearby National Museum, a colonial building with superb regular displays plus occasional exhibitions. The nearby Singapore Art Museum is worth a visit as is Chijmes, and check out The Substation (on Armenian St.) for alternative local arts. Evening can be spent shopping along Orchard Road. Stores open till 9pm. Make it to Newton Food Centre near Newton MRT, popular with tourists and locals alike. Newton doesn't close until 4am.

**Changi Village**
Changi Village offers numerous little eating and drinking spots, including the animated Europa (live music) bar and, outdoors, Charlie's Snack Bar (attached to the main hawker center) which stocks a wide range of imported beers and solid English "nosh", such as fish and chips. Le Meridien Changi is a classy hotel if you need refreshing in a sophisticated setting. You can get there by taxi, or no. 2 bus to Changi Village.

**Cool relief**
A sensible strategy while out-and-about is to make regular "cool-off" calls in air-conditioned shopping centers and replace some of your lost fluids with an iced fruit drink. Don't forget, too, that most public toilets require a 10 cents coin – and there's a fine if you don't flush.

# ◆ Jurong Birdpark

Set in 50 acres of lush tropical vegetation, Jurong Birdpark houses over seven thousand birds representing six hundred species from Africa, South America, Asia, and Europe. An air-conditioned Panorail runs through the birdpark, which is open seven days a week. Entry to the birdpark is S$9 for adults and S$3 for children; tickets for the Panorail ride cost S$2 for adults and S$1 for children.

GRAY HERON

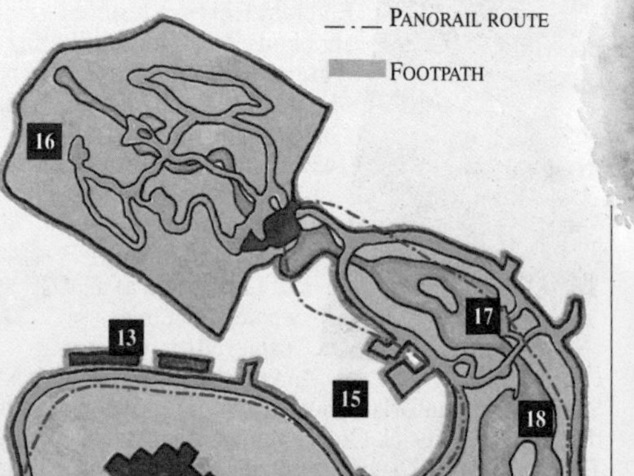

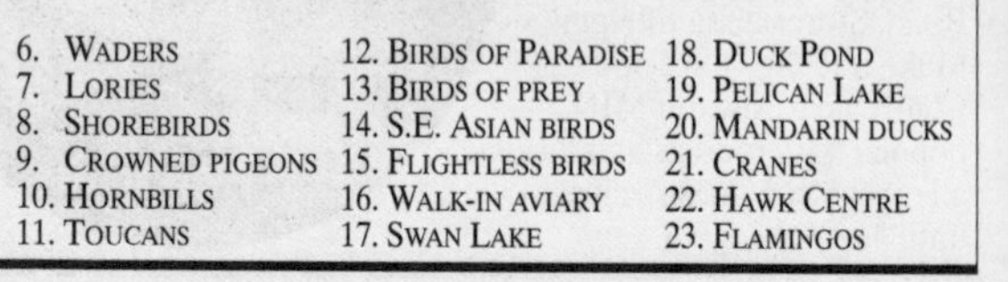

— . — PANORAIL ROUTE

FOOTPATH

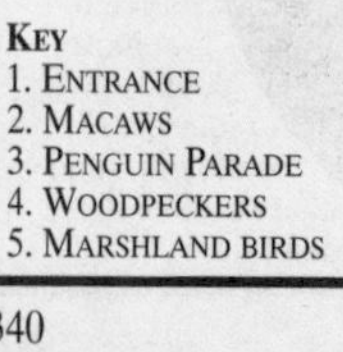

JURONG BIRDPARK

**Key**

1. Entrance
2. Macaws
3. Penguin Parade
4. Woodpeckers
5. Marshland birds
6. Waders
7. Lories
8. Shorebirds
9. Crowned pigeons
10. Hornbills
11. Toucans
12. Birds of Paradise
13. Birds of prey
14. S.E. Asian birds
15. Flightless birds
16. Walk-in aviary
17. Swan Lake
18. Duck Pond
19. Pelican Lake
20. Mandarin ducks
21. Cranes
22. Hawk Centre
23. Flamingos

The 218-acre park consists of mudflats, fresh and brackish-water ponds, mangroves, coconut groves, grassed areas, and small orchards. It is home to about 140 species of indigenous and migratory birds and a multitude of wetland flora and fauna. The park is open daily between 7.30am and 7pm. Admission charges are S$1 for adults and 50 cents for children.

BLACK-NAPED ORIOLE

BARN SWALLOW

DOLLARBIRD

WATERCOCK

WHIMBREL

BLUE-THROATED BEE-EATER

TIGER SHRIKE

LITTLE HERON

COMMON KINGFISHER

REDSHANK

**A SHOPPER'S DELIGHT**
Shopping is a major lure for the millions of visitors Singapore welcomes each year. Orchard Road favorites include Wisma Atria, Centrepoint, Ngee Ann City, Scotts, and, south of Raffles City, Marina Square. Lucky Plaza and Far East Plaza are disliked by some locals and both have attracted complaints from tourists. Orchard Road is also home to Japanese-style department stores: Sogo (with a superb food hall at Paragon), Isetan, Yaohan, and Takashimaya. Other retail giants include Robinson's, Tangs, Metro, and John Little. All are open all day on Sundays.

**QUALITY SERVICE**
The Singapore Tourist Promotion Board (STPB) and the Consumers' Association of Singapore operate a Good Retailer system to encourage high standards of service. Look for the red and white Merlion symbol. The STPB will also handle shopping complaints.

**FACTORY REJECTS.** Slightly marred rejects or perfect over-runs from some of the biggest fashion names (Gap, Ralph Lauren, Next, and other Western houses that have their clothes made in Southeast Asia) can be found at eye-popping prices (S$10–S$20) at air-conditioned specialist stores such as Factory Outlet (biggest branch at Takashimaya basement, on Orchard Road).

**CUSTOM-MADE CLOTHING.** Part of the fun of visiting Singapore is to take away perfect "copycat" suits or dresses made "in next to no time". Exercise caution and insist on two fittings and 48-hour delivery. And if the price is right, why not? Change Alley Aerial Plaza near Collyer Quay has several outlets, while more upmarket tailors can be found at the Tanglin Shopping Centre.

**ETHNIC GOODS.** The Arab Street area off Beach Road specializes in batik (sarongs, shirts, etc), but its most favored (and photographed) shops are those on Arab Street itself, offering basketware, rattan, and bamboo products spilling out over the pavement. Chinatown also promises fascinating surprises (be sure to visit a medical hall), such as Chinese character and Western name seals that you can have carved quickly to give your letters an exotic touch.

**CAMERAS.** Orchard Road is full of camera shops at duty-free prices but often, especially in centers such as Lucky Plaza, the shop assistants are just too pushy. Instead, and especially if you need qualified professional advice, take in the excellent range of cameras and accessories at Cathay Photo Store (outlets at Peninsula Plaza and Marina Square).

**COMPUTERS AND ELECTRICAL GOODS.** For computers, software and peripherals at around US prices, Funan Centre (Raffles City end of North Bridge Road) and Sim Lim Square (Rochor Canal Road) can't be beaten. Don't forget to bargain! Sim Lim Square is also the place for audio/video equipment, including CD players.

**ANTIQUES.** Tanglin Shopping Centre has a good range of carpet, map, fine art, antique, and curio dealers. For a single-store treasure-house of arts and crafts, visit Lim's at #02-01 Holland Road Shopping Centre in Holland Village.

Above all else, Singapore means food. The island groans under the weight of it. Instead of greeting you with "Hallo", Singaporeans often ask, "Have you eaten?" It's a serious matter if the answer is no! The coffee-shop/hawker-center system offers "free seating" and a wide range of food at an average S$3–S$5 per plate. Many open 24 hours a day. And the national passion for food extends all the way up the culinary ladder to the very peaks of gastronomy (usually within first-class hotels). Singapore offers the entire range of regional Southeast Asian specialties, including authentic vegetarian food. However if you really must, you can still "chill out" at those familiar fast-food joints.

**DELECTABLE DISHES.** Although there is no one clear-cut "Oscar-winning" national dish, there are several candidates. Do try at least one of these hawker-center dishes while in Singapore – your taste buds will thank you!

* Laksa (rice-flour noodles with prawns, fish-cake slices, and beansprouts in rich, spicy gravy)
* Hainanese Chicken Rice (plain, but sophisticated)
* Bak Kut Teh (rich pork bone soup with spices, soya sauce, and red chili, a hearty dish)
* Chili or Pepper Crab
* Seafood (lobster, prawn, shrimp, squid, crab, and more)
* Fish Head Curry (in a curry gravy with spices and coconut milk)
* Satay (mutton, beef, or chicken pieces grilled on a stick, dipped in hot peanut sauce, and eaten with rice cakes)
* Char Kway Teow (broad flat noodles in black soya and sweet sauces, often with clams)
* Gado Gado (vegetable salad)
* Nasi Lemak (rice boiled in coconut milk)
* Nasi Biryani (spiced saffron yellow rice served with mutton or chicken curry)
* Rojak (mixed salad of fruit, vegetables, and peanut gravy)
* Roti Prata (Indian dough pancake, eaten with curry sauce).

**NO SMOKING**
Smoking is strictly banned (stiff fines) in all air-conditioned eating places, and also in bars where food is served.

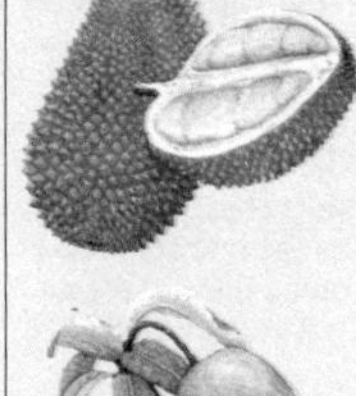

**FRUIT**
Whatever cuisine you choose, there's only one way to finish up a meal – with the tropical fruits in which Singapore abounds! There's the famous and very "in" durian, but also bananas, "jambu", jackfruit, longan, lychee, mango, mangosteen, papaya, pineapple, rambutan, starfruit, watermelon, and many more…

# ◆ West Malaysia in Ten Days

**On the road**
West Malaysia can easily be circumnavigated in a ten-day drive. Directional signboards in Malay are displayed at intervals along major routes. Roads vary from first-class freeways to winding, scenic drives snaking through jungle, traversing coconut groves and rubber estates, and skirting miles of empty beaches.
A recently opened highway runs the length of the peninsula, linking the city of Johor Bahru with Haadyai, a town in south Thailand. Traffic is always heavy around Kuala Lumpur and truck convoys often make the main roads on the west coast slow going. In the interior and along the east coast traffic is much lighter.

**Day 1.** Breakfast Malaysian-style at a roadside stall in Kuala Lumpur, then stroll around Merdeka Square, past the copper-domed Sultan Abdul Samad Building and Infokraf, a government-run crafts store. Continue down Jalan Sultan Hishamuddin to the Moorish-style Railway Station and the National Museum. Chinatown, across the river, is great for lunch. Visit the Indian and Chinese temples in the area and spend the afternoon shopping at Central Market. After dark, Jalan Petaling in Chinatown becomes a busy street bazaar.

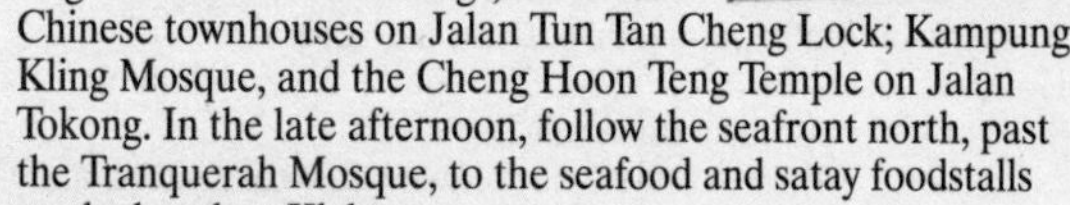

**Day 2.** Start early, taking the expressway to Melaka, passing through rubber plantations, and traversing Negeri Sembilan. Take the Ayer Keroh exit and follow the signs to Melaka town. Lunch at the Malay foodstalls opposite the Padang downtown. Musts in Melaka include St Paul's Hill; the Town Square, ringed with Dutch buildings; the Straits Chinese townhouses on Jalan Tun Tan Cheng Lock; Kampung Kling Mosque, and the Cheng Hoon Teng Temple on Jalan Tokong. In the late afternoon, follow the seafront north, past the Tranquerah Mosque, to the seafood and satay foodstalls on the beach at Klebang.

**Day 3.** Drive south to Muar past some of the prettiest traditional Malay houses on the west coast. A few miles before Muar, turn left to Tangkak, then head for Segamat, which has many good restaurants. After lunch, take the main highway north, then turn right onto the Tun Razak Highway which cuts through Pahang state to Kuantan. On arrival in Kuantan, stay in the town itself, or drive north to Teluk Chempedak and its beach resorts.

**Day 4.** An early-morning dip in the sea and then on to Kuala Terengganu. The highway parallels the sea, running past the fishing village of Beserah, then Sungai Udang and Kampung Cherating. Further north, it skirts sleepy fishing towns; then Kerteh, the high-tech center of Malaysia's petroleum industry. North of Dungun, take the turnoff to Tanjung Jara, a resort hotel overlooking a lagoon. Nine miles south of Kuala Terengganu is Marang, a fishing village. Town sights include the fort of Bukit Puteri, the French-inspired royal palace, and the lanes of old Chinatown. The best dining is to be had along Pantai Batu Buruk.

**Day 5.** Follow the signs to Kota Bharu. Take the Sultan Mahmud Bridge north out of town, then leave the main highway and head for Penarik, known for its *kolek* fishing boats. Drive back to Bandar Permaisuri on the main road north and continue along Route 3, crossing the Kelantan border north of Jertih. The main road continues through Pasir Puteh and Selinsing, past ricefields and rural villages to Kota Bharu, the hub of Malay culture. Stay at a resort along Pantai Cahaya Bulan (Moonlight Beach), which holds workshops on silk-brocade weaving, wood-carving, and kite-making. Visit the town's

**Market bustle**
The busy Central Market in Kota Bahru is a must-see, with its fruit – durians, rambutan, and duku in season – vegetables, spices, batik, *songket*, and handicrafts.

**Hair oil**
Consumer product on the shelf of a grocery store in Johor Bahru.

Central Market and the Royal Museum; watch *rebana* drumming, top-spinning, and *silat* at the Cultural Centre. Dine at the stalls opposite the Central Market, famous for their *ayam percik* – sautéed, barbecued chicken.

**Day 6.** Cross the Kelantan River and follow Route 3 through Pasir Mas to Tanah Merah. Head west on the East–West Highway which climbs the ranges in east Kelantan. Farther on at Grik, take Route 76 through Keroh and Baling in east Kedah to Sungai Petani. Head south on Highway 1 to Butterworth, then follow the signs to Penang Bridge, which links the mainland with Penang.

**Day 7.** Breakfast beside the harbor at the E & O Hotel, then wander around Georgetown. Musts include Fort Cornwallis, Kuan Yin Temple, Kapitan Kling Mosque, and the ornate Khoo Kongsi clanhouse. Penang is famous for its balmy beaches, as well as its food – try the Indian-style curries and rice. After lunch, drive along the north shore to Batu Ferringhi, where you can swim, water-ski, or para-glide. At dusk, head for the open-air food stalls at Gurney Drive.

**Day 8.** Return to the mainland and take Highway 1 south to Kuala Kangsar. From here proceed to Ipoh, renowned for its colonial architecture and Chinese food. Follow Highway 1 south to Tapah, then turn off for Tanah Rata, the main town of the Cameron Highlands. The road winds upwards through jungles and hills until it reaches the plateau, 6000 feet above sea level. Have dinner at one of the colonial hotels.

**Day 9.** Drive out to the Sungai Palas Tea Plantation and see the tea-pickers at work. Take the peninsula's highest road to cloud-wreathed Gunung Brinchang or go for a jungle walk through the moss-draped oak forests. Spend a night there in colonial nostalgia, and dine beside a roaring log fire.

**Day 10.** Head back to Kuala Lumpur with a short detour at Kuala Woh, in a forest reserve, where a trail leads to an Orang Asli village. Drive south through Bidor to buy guava – the town's specialty. Route 1 passes Slim River, then Tanjung Malim, where it joins the expressway to the capital city. At the end of the journey, celebrate with a traditional Malay meal and cultural show at the Sri Melayu Restaurant.

**Carpets**
Velvet carpets with colorful and intricate designs are a must on the shopping list for many visitors.

**Cameron Highlands**
The cool climate of the Cameron Highlands is suited to crops otherwise rare in tropical zones. Terraced market gardens produce temperate-zone varieties such as strawberries, lettuce, and tomatoes.

**BATIK.** The cheapest and best batik cloth comes from Kelantan, followed by cloth from Terengganu. Between Kota Bharu and the beach, workshops specialize in stamped batiks, others produce stamped rayon cloth, and yet others hand-painted rayon, cotton, and silk. Another source of batik is the Central Market in Kota Bharu. The complex opposite has a couple of floors devoted to Kelantanese textiles. In Terengganu, the Central Market is excellent for batik and, just out of town, at Chendering, Suterasemai manufactures hand-painted batiks on silk grown, spun, and woven in Terengganu. Kuala Lumpur is the next best location in terms of choice; but prices there are much higher. Batik Malaysia in Jalan Tun Perak, Karyaneka on Jalan Raja Chulan, and Central Market are recommended. At Plaza Yow Chuan, on the corner of Jalan Tun Razak and Jalan Ampang, several shops specialize in tailor-made outfits of original hand-painted silk batik, and Gab in adjacent City Square has collarless shirts in both rayon and silk. Some textile shops on Jalan Tun Razak sell batik by the meter, but check that it is real batik, not a screen-print. The real test is smell. If it smells like wax, it's real. The price of batik increases with the number of colors: plain blue and white Terengganu batiks are cheap as they involve only one waxing and dyeing. Multi-colored Kelantan sarongs are the top of the range. Dyes used in Malaysia are fast and batiks can safely be washed in machines.

**SILVERWARE.** Formerly, Malay silver, and goldsmiths were attached to royal courts to produce ceremonial and traditional items. When the British arrived, the craftsmen turned to cutlery, tea-sets, and trays as demand for their traditional items declined. Modern designs are contemporary, with the patterns still classically Malay, utilizing Islamic leaf and flower designs. In Kampung Sireh on the outskirts of Kota Bharu craftsmen still work on the premises of several famous silversmiths, and prices are reasonable as here you are buying from the source. Good buys include jewelry boxes and filigree jewelry. Kelantanese silversmiths'

**SONGKET (SILK BROCADE)**
The east coast is the best place to buy *songket*. You get to see all the processes involved, from spinning and setting up the warp to the final weaving. The more gold or silver threads incorporated into the design, the more expensive the finished cloth will be. Most silk-weaving workshops have a wide range of cloth from reasonably priced fabrics with scattered gold designs to full gold versions (*kain songket penuh*). At Kampung Penambang, 2 miles from Kota Bharu, several famous silk-weaving workshops are run by royal weavers. In Terengganu *songket* is available at boutiques near Central Market, Nor Atikah Songket in the MARA Building, and the Karyaneka Handicraft Centre, 8 miles away, at Rusila. Original designs and fine weaving characterize the silks at Tengku Ismail's workshop on Jalan Kenanga. Karyaneka on Jalan Raja Chulan and Central Market in Kuala Lumpur sell *songket* by the meter.

JALAN HANG JEBAT
POSKOD 75200 MELAKA
JONKER STREET

work is also available at Central Market in Kuala Lumpur, and at all Kraftangan outlets. Antique Malay silverware commands high prices, and the best pieces remain in royal collections or in museums. However, some antique shops along Jonkers Street in Melaka occasionally have silverware for sale. Apart from Malay silverware, Melaka antique dealers also have collections of Straits Chinese silver dating from the 19th and early 20th century. Good buys are bangles featuring birds and flowers.

**Pottery.** The best-known traditional work originates from a small town in Perak, and is known as Labu Sayong. It typically takes the form of a water-carrier shaped like a gourd. The ceramics come in two hues: a natural ocher and a dull black finish characteristic of classical Sayong pottery. The black color is obtained by packing rice husks around the pot when it is fired. At the village, (accessible only by car) you can see potters at work and can buy their wares direct from them. However, there is not a great choice as much of their work is usually made to order. Pottery is abundant at Kraftangan complex in Enggor, on the main Kuala Kangsar–Ipoh highway. Here, potters are trained and there is a larger variety of pots, both ocher-colored and black. The traditional water-holder is a good buy, although a little difficult to transport.

**Basketware.** These are among the most colorful of all Malaysian crafts. Materials used range from woven cane to a type of pandanus leaf. Most weavers still work on the east coast: the Kraftangan workshop at Rusila offers an excellent selection. All government-run craft shops throughout the peninsula, however, stock the same goods. Cheaper wares are to be found at Rusila, at the shops along the seafront south of the Kraftangan, and on the road to Marang. Good buys include circular cane fruit baskets and large baskets for holding dried flowers. Woven table mats of pandanus leaves make excellent gifts and are easy to pack. Large conical food-covers are colorful, attractive, and handy for keeping insects off food. Woven pandanus handbags with leather trim are also fashionable. Although government-run craft shops may be a little pricey, you can be assured that the goods available there are genuinely Malaysian-made.

**Pewter**
Malaysia's best-known pewter producer, Royal Selangor, is world-famous and was given the privilege to use "Royal" on its name by the sultan of Selangor. At its workshop on the outskirts of Kuala Lumpur, visitors can see all aspects of pewter-making. Pewter shops on Jalan Tuanku Abdul Rahman and at the Mall on Jalan Putra offer a wide range of products, as do the souvenir boutiques and handicrafts corners in major department stores that stock Royal Selangor. Pewter-wares come in two styles: the classical dull finish and a shiny finish resembling silver. Good buys include Art Nouveau picture frames, jewelry boxes, tea sets, salt and pepper shakers, and novelty figurines.

**WHAT TO BRING**
Trekking in the rainforest is hot and sweaty and trying to keep dry while on the trail can seem virtually impossible. Travel light and wash your clothes in the evening, letting them dry overnight. It is a bit uncomfortable putting on damp clothes, but they soon become wet again anyway. Always ensure you have at least one set of dry clothes (wrapped in plastic) to change into at night. Footwear should offer a good grip and stand up to mud and moisture. A sturdy pair of training shoes will suffice for most conditions – hiking boots are not essential.

**WHERE TO STAY**
The Mulu National Park contains resthouses and chalets available to the public. Many travel companies operating in the Mulu area have their own guesthouses which provide simple home-stay-type facilities.

## MULU CAVES VIA THE HEADHUNTER TRAIL

Borneo is famous for its rainforests, rivers, and the longhouse lifestyle of the indigenous people. No visit to Sarawak is complete without experiencing these. The best-preserved rainforests are in the national parks, and the Mulu National Park with its giant caves is currently one of the best known. An excellent trip to Mulu, which includes an overnight stay at an Iban longhouse, river travel by longboat, and some pleasant jungle trekking, follows a route known as the "Headhunter's Trail", a name whose origins are dubious but there is no doubt that this six-day route at a cost of US$75 gives the traveler a superb look at interior Sarawak.

**DAY 1.** The itinerary starts in the town of Miri and with a flight on an eighteen-seater Twin Otter to Limbang. From here a 1-hour car ride takes you to the Limbang River, followed by a 2-hour longboat ride upriver to the Iban Rumah Bala Lesong Longhouse. You pass the night in the longhouse as guests of the village headman, entertained Iban-style in the evening.

**DAY 2.** A day of river and rainforest, starting with 4 to 6 hours in longboats (depending on the water level), then 5 hours of jungle trekking to Camp 5 in Mulu National Park. (During periods of low water it may be necessary to pull the boat through the shallows.) The trek to Camp 5 (on the Melinau River)

takes 5 hours along a marked trail through primary lowland rainforest. The terrain is flat but demands care nonetheless. At 5pm (or later, depending on the water level), you arrive at Camp 5, a simple shelter with raised sleeping platforms. A basic toilet is provided and the river is used for washing.

**Day 3.** Camp 5 lies at the base of Mount Api, a limestone mountain, eroded through the ages to form spectacular pinnacles. The climb to view these takes 4–5 hours along a steep and demanding trail, but the reward is a sight of the 148-foot-tall "spires", as well as rhododendrons, orchids, pitcher plants, and mossy sub-montane rainforest. After lunch, begin the descent to Camp 5, where a refreshing swim awaits you in the Melinau River.

**Day 4.** After breakfast, make an adventurous 5-hour jungle trek to the Litut River junction, then proceed downriver by longboat (2 hours) to the Clearwater Cave entrance. Enjoy a prepared lunch before visiting parts of the longest cave system in Southeast Asia. After Clearwater Cave, continue downriver by boat 5 minutes to the entrance of the Wind Cave. Continue downriver 1 more hour to the Borneo Adventure Lodge (Kuching office, tel. 82-245 175 and fax 82-422 626) for the night – comfortable beds, showers, and guesthouse accommodation.

**Day 5.** Depart at 10am by boat for the Park. From here it is an easy stroll along the 2-mile plankwalk to the Deer Cave. Explore parts of the largest passage in the world and have a picnic lunch in the Garden of Eden. Spectacular Lang's Cave lies adjacent to Deer Cave. In the evening, wait for the millions of bats on their nightly feeding forays. Return to the boats along the plankwalk and to the lodge for the night.

**Day 6.** Early departure by longboat downriver to Long Terawan (2 hours), then by express boat to Marudi (3 hours). After lunch, continue by express to Kuala Baram (3 hours), then by road to Miri. Alternatively, fly to Miri from Mulu by Twin Otter.

**Longhouse etiquette**

One of the most remarkable things about visiting a longhouse is the overwhelming hospitality of your hosts. However, you should observe certain rules and local *adat* (customs). Your guide should fill you in on the details of the *adat*, but here is some basic etiquette: Remove your footwear before entering the longhouse. If you wish to decline something offered to you (e.g, cigarettes, drink, or food) do it by thanking the host and lightly touching the edge of the plate, cup, or container. When invited to sit down by your host, do so, if only for a couple of minutes. When bathing, use a bathing suit or underwear (men) and a sarong or wrap (women).

# USEFUL ADDRESSES

- VIEW
- CENTRAL
- OUTSKIRTS
- PARKING
- SUPERVISED PARKING
- TELEVISION
- CALM
- SWIMMING POOL
- CREDIT CARDS
- MUSIC

NB: Most hotels listed accept credit cards. Hotel rooms are air-conditioned. Some beach-resorts provide non air-conditioned rooms as well. Information provided is current at time of going to press.

| | Page | Swimming Pool | TV in Room | Parking | View from Room | Restaurant/s | 24-Hour Service | No. of Rooms | Class |
|---|---|---|---|---|---|---|---|---|---|
| **SINGAPORE** | | | | | | | | | |
| Allson Hotel | 359 | ● | ● | ● | ● | 3 | ● | 450 | ◆◆ |
| Boulevard Hotel | 359 | ● | ● | ● | ● | 5 | ● | 500 | ◆◆◆ |
| Cairnhill Hotel | 359 | ● | ● | ● | ● | 2 | ● | 195 | ◆◆ |
| Carlton Hotel | 359 | ● | ● | ● | ● | 4 | ● | 300 | ◆◆◆ |
| Cockpit Hotel | 359 | | ● | ● | ● | 2 | ● | 170 | ◆◆ |
| Crown Prince Hotel | 359 | ● | ● | ● | ● | 3 | ● | 303 | ◆◆◆ |
| Elizabeth Hotel | 359 | ● | ● | ● | ● | 2 | ● | 246 | ◆◆◆ |
| Hotel Equatorial | 359 | ● | ● | ● | ● | 4 | ● | 228 | ◆◆ |
| Four Seasons Hotel | 360 | ● | ● | ● | ● | 5 | ● | 257 | ◆◆◆ |
| Goodwood Park Hotel | 360 | ● | ● | ● | ● | 6 | ● | 235 | ◆◆◆ |
| Harbour View Dai-Ichi | 360 | ● | ● | ● | ● | 2 | ● | 416 | ◆◆◆ |
| Singapore Hilton | 360 | ● | ● | ● | ● | 4 | ● | 435 | ◆◆◆ |
| Holiday Inn Park View | 360 | ● | ● | ● | ● | 4 | ● | 320 | ◆◆◆ |
| Hyatt Regency | 360 | ● | ● | ● | ● | 4 | ● | 700 | ◆◆◆ |
| Majestic Hotel | 360 | | ● | | | 1 | ● | 24 | ◆ |
| Mandarin Singapore | 360 | ● | ● | ● | ● | 5 | ● | 1066 | ◆◆◆ |
| Marina Mandarin | 360 | ● | ● | ● | ● | 4 | ● | 575 | ◆◆◆ |
| New Park Hotel | 360 | ● | ● | ● | ● | 2 | ● | 531 | ◆◆◆ |
| Novotel Orchid | 360 | ● | ● | ● | ● | 3 | ● | 450 | ◆◆◆ |
| Omni Marco Polo | 360 | ● | ● | ● | ● | 2 | ● | 600 | ◆◆◆ |
| Orchard Hotel | 360 | ● | ● | ● | ● | 3 | ● | 679 | ◆◆◆ |
| Orchard Parade Hotel | 360 | ● | ● | ● | ● | 2 | ● | 306 | ◆◆◆ |
| The Oriental Singapore | 360 | ● | ● | ● | ● | 5 | ● | 516 | ◆◆◆ |
| Pan Pacific Hotel | 360 | ● | ● | ● | ● | 5 | ● | 800 | ◆◆◆ |
| Paramount Hotel | 360 | ● | ● | ● | ● | 2 | ● | 250 | ◆◆◆ |
| Hotel Phoenix | 360 | | ● | ● | ● | 2 | ● | 305 | ◆◆◆ |
| Plaza Hotel | 360 | ● | ● | ● | ● | 2 | ● | 350 | ◆◆◆ |
| Raffles Hotel | 361 | ● | ● | ● | | 6 | ● | 104 | ◆◆◆ |
| The Regent of Singapore | 361 | ● | ● | ● | ● | 3 | ● | 441 | ◆◆◆ |
| Riverview Hotel | 361 | ● | ● | ● | ● | 4 | ● | 472 | ◆◆ |
| Seaview Hotel | 361 | ● | ● | ● | ● | 1 | ● | 435 | ◆◆◆ |
| Shangri-la Hotel | 361 | ● | ● | ● | ● | 5 | ● | 826 | ◆◆◆ |
| Westin Plaza/Westin Stamford | 361 | ● | ● | ● | ● | 8 | ● | 2700 | ◆◆◆ |
| **WEST MALAYSIA – KUALA LUMPUR & SHAH ALAM** | | | | | | | | | |
| Hotel Istana | 363 | ● | ● | ● | ● | 3 | ● | 516 | ◆◆◆ |
| Kuala Lumpur Hilton | 363 | ● | ● | ● | ● | 4 | ● | 581 | ◆◆◆ |
| Pan Pacific Hotel, Kuala Lumpur | 363 | ● | ● | ● | ● | 5 | ● | 533 | ◆◆◆ |
| The Regent of Kuala Lumpur | 363 | ● | ● | ● | ● | 2 | ● | 469 | ◆◆◆ |
| Holiday Inn Shah Alam | 364 | ● | ● | ● | ● | 2 | ● | 154 | ◆◆◆ |
| Petaling Jaya Hilton, Shah Alam | 364 | ● | ● | ● | ● | 3 | ● | 500 | ◆◆◆ |
| The Shangri-la | 363 | ● | ● | ● | ● | 7 | ● | 720 | ◆◆◆ |
| **WEST MALAYSIA – MELAKA** | | | | | | | | | |
| The City Bayview | 365 | ● | ● | ● | ● | 3 | ● | 182 | ◆◆ |
| Emperor Hotel | 365 | ● | ● | ● | ● | 2 | ● | 241 | ◆ |
| Malacca Village Paradise Resort | 365 | ● | ● | ● | ● | 3 | ● | 146 | ◆ |
| Melaka Renaissance Hotel | 365 | ● | ● | ● | ● | 3 | ● | 300 | ◆◆ |
| Shah's Beach Resort | 365 | ● | ● | ● | | 1 | ● | 55 | ◆◆ |
| **WEST MALAYSIA – SEREMBAN & PORT DICKSON** | | | | | | | | | |
| Mee Lee Hotel | 365 | | | ● | | - | | 18 | ◆ |
| Ming Court Beach Hotel | 365 | ● | ● | ● | ● | 1 | ● | 165 | ◆ |
| Regency Hotel and Resort | 365 | ● | ● | ● | ● | 3 | ● | 217 | ◆◆ |
| **WEST MALAYSIA – PULAU PANGKOR & IPOH** | | | | | | | | | |
| Pan Pacific Resort | 365 | | ● | ● | | 3 | ● | 45 | ◆◆◆ |
| Pangkor Laut & Resort | 365 | ● | | | | 2 | ● | 135 | ◆◆◆ |
| Seaview Hotel | 365 | | | | | 1 | ● | 60 | ◆ |
| Hotel Excelsior, Ipoh | 366 | | ● | ● | ● | 3 | ● | 200 | ◆◆ |
| The Royal Casuarina, Ipoh | 366 | ● | ● | ● | ● | 2 | ● | 198 | ◆◆ |
| **WEST MALAYSIA – PENANG** | | | | | | | | | |
| Crown Prince Hotel | 366 | ● | ● | ● | ● | 2 | ● | 295 | ◆ |
| E & O Hotel | 366 | ● | ● | ● | ● | 2 | ● | 100 | ◆ |

♦ *Room rates S$100/RM160 and below*

♦♦ *Room rates between S$100/RM160 and S$150/RM240*

♦♦♦ *Room rates above S$150/RM240*
*Note: Brunei $ at par with Singapore $*

| | Page | Swimming Pool | TV in Room | Parking | View from Room | Restaurant/s | 24-Hour Service | No. of Rooms | Class |
|---|---|---|---|---|---|---|---|---|---|
| **Equatorial Penang** | *366* | ● | ● | ● | ● | 4 | ● | 413 | ♦♦♦ |
| **Penang Mutiara** | *366* | ● | ● | ● | ● | 5 | ● | 440 | ♦♦♦ |
| **Rasa Sayang Hotel** | *367* | ● | ● | ● | ● | 3 | ● | 300 | ♦♦♦ |
| **WEST MALAYSIA – LANGKAWI & ALOR SETAR** | | | | | | | | | |
| **Semarak Beach Resort** | *367* | | | | | 1 | ● | 26 | ♦ |
| **Langkawi Island Resort** | *367* | ● | ● | ● | ● | 2 | ● | 213 | ♦♦ |
| **Pelangi Beach Resort** | *367* | ● | ● | ● | ● | 2 | ● | 350 | ♦♦♦ |
| **Grand Continental, Alor Setar** | *367* | | ● | ● | ● | 1 | ● | 150 | ♦ |
| **WEST MALAYSIA – AROUND KUANTAN** | | | | | | | | | |
| **Hyatt Regency Kuantan** | *368* | ● | ● | ● | ● | 2 | ● | 185 | ♦♦ |
| **Merlin Inn Resort** | *368* | ● | ● | ● | ● | 1 | ● | 106 | ♦♦ |
| **WEST MALAYSIA – AROUND KOTA BHARU** | | | | | | | | | |
| **Kencana Inn** | *368* | | ● | ● | | - | ● | 53 | ♦ |
| **Hotel Perdana** | *368* | ● | ● | | ● | 2 | ● | 136 | ♦♦ |
| **Perdana Resort** | *368* | ● | ● | ● | ● | 1 | ● | 120 | ♦ |
| **WEST MALAYSIA – KUALA TERENGGANU** | | | | | | | | | |
| **Motel Desa** | *369* | ● | ● | ● | ● | 1 | ● | 20 | ♦ |
| **Primula Beach Resort** | *369* | ● | ● | ● | ● | 3 | ● | 235 | ♦ |
| **Tanjong Jara Beach Hotel** | *369* | ● | ● | ● | ● | 1 | ● | 100 | ♦♦ |
| **WEST MALAYSIA – PULAU TIOMAN** | | | | | | | | | |
| **Berjaya Imperial Beach Resort** | *369* | ● | ● | | ● | 4 | ● | 373 | ♦♦♦ |
| **Samudra Swiss Cottages** | *369* | ● | ● | ● | | 1 | ● | 20 | ♦ |
| **WEST MALAYSIA – AROUND JOHOR BAHRU** | | | | | | | | | |
| **Holiday Inn/Crowne Plaza Johor Bahru** | *369* | ● | ● | ● | ● | 4 | ● | 300 | ♦♦ |
| **Puteri Pan Pacific** | *369* | ● | ● | ● | ● | 7 | ● | 500 | ♦♦♦ |
| **EAST MALAYSIA – KUCHING & SANTUBONG** | | | | | | | | | |
| **Borneo Hotel** | *372* | ● | ● | ● | ● | 1 | ● | 65 | ♦ |
| **Holiday Inn** | *372* | ● | ● | ● | ● | 3 | ● | 200 | ♦ |
| **Kuching Hilton** | *372* | ● | ● | ● | ● | 3 | ● | 320 | ♦♦♦ |
| **Liwah Hotel** | *372* | | ● | ● | ● | 2 | ● | 100 | ♦ |
| **Holiday Inn Damai Beach Resort (Santubong)** | *372* | ● | ● | ● | ● | 2 | ● | 276 | ♦♦ |
| **EAST MALAYSIA – SIBU** | | | | | | | | | |
| **Garden Hotel** | *373* | | ● | ● | | 1 | ● | 40 | ♦ |
| **Li Hua Hotel** | *373* | | ● | ● | | 2 | ● | 77 | ♦ |
| **Premier Hotel** | *373* | | ● | ● | ● | 2 | ● | 143 | ♦ |
| **Hotel Zuhra** | *373* | | ● | ● | | 1 | ● | 33 | ♦ |
| **EAST MALAYSIA – BINTULU & MIRI** | | | | | | | | | |
| **Royal Hotel, Bintulu** | *373* | | ● | | | - | ● | 36 | ♦ |
| **Plaza Hotel, Bintulu** | *373* | ● | ● | ● | ● | 3 | ● | 161 | ♦ |
| **Park Hotel, Miri** | *373* | | ● | ● | ● | 2 | ● | 93 | ♦♦ |
| **Hotel Plaza Regency, Miri** | *373* | | ● | ● | | 2 | ● | 70 | ♦ |
| **EAST MALAYSIA – KOTA KINABALU** | | | | | | | | | |
| **Hotel Capital** | *374* | ● | ● | ● | ● | 2 | ● | 102 | ♦ |
| **Hotel Jesselton** | *374* | | ● | | | 2 | ● | 26 | ♦ |
| **Hyatt Kinabalu** | *374* | ● | ● | ● | ● | 3 | ● | 350 | ♦♦♦ |
| **Kinabalu Park (at the Park Headquarters)** | *374* | | | | ● | - | | 26* | ♦ |
| **Palace Hotel** | *375* | ● | ● | ● | ● | 1 | ● | 160 | ♦♦ |
| **Hotel Shangrila** | *375* | ● | ● | ● | ● | 3 | ● | 126 | ♦ |
| **Tanjung Aru Beach Hotel** | *375* | ● | ● | ● | ● | 2 | ● | 500 | ♦♦♦ |
| **EAST MALAYSIA – SANDAKAN** | | | | | | | | | |
| **Hotel City View** | *375* | | ● | ● | | 1 | ● | 29 | ♦ |
| **Hotel Nak** | *375* | | ● | ● | | 1 | ● | 42 | ♦ |
| **Ramada Renaissance** | *375* | ● | ● | ● | ● | 2 | ● | 96 | ♦♦♦ |
| **Hotel Siang Garden** | *375* | | ● | ● | | 1 | ● | 55 | ♦ |
| **BRUNEI DARUSSALAM – BANDAR SERI BEGAWAN** | | | | | | | | | |
| **Ang's Hotel** | *376* | ● | ● | ● | | 1 | ● | 80 | ♦♦♦ |
| **Brunei Hotel** | *376* | | ● | | | 2 | ● | 73 | ♦♦♦ |
| **Crowne Princess** | *376* | | ● | ● | ● | 1 | ● | 117 | ♦♦ |
| **Riverview Hotel** | *376* | | ● | ● | ● | 3 | ● | 126 | ♦♦ |
| **Sheraton Utama** | *376* | ● | ● | ● | ● | 2 | ● | 154 | ♦♦♦ |

***Overnight accommodation available in chalets, cabins and dormitories. Check details in listing under Kota Kinabalu.**

◆ Less than S$15/RM25
◆◆ Between S$15/RM25 and S$25/RM40
◆◆◆ Above S$25/RM40
Note: Brunei $ at par with Singapore $

| | PAGE | PRICE (PER PERSON) | CREDIT CARDS | AIR-CONDITIONED | SPECIALTIES | CLIENTELE |
|---|---|---|---|---|---|---|
| **SINGAPORE** | | | | | | |
| AZIZA'S | 358 | ◆◆ | ● | ● | M | T |
| BAN SENG RESTAURANT | 358 | ◆◆ | ● | ● | C | L |
| BANANA LEAF APOLLO | 358 | ◆◆ | ● | ● | I | T L |
| BARON'S TABLE | 359 | ◆◆ | ● | ● | E | T L |
| CHICO'S N CHARLIE'S | 359 | ◆ | ● | ● | X | T L |
| CHINA PALACE | 359 | ◆◆ | ● | ● | C | T L |
| GORDON GRILL | 359 | ◆◆ | ● | ● | E | T |
| GRAND CITY | 359 | ◆◆ | ● | ● | C | T L |
| HAEBOK'S | 359 | ◆◆ | ● | ● | K | T L |
| HAPPY REALM | 359 | ◆◆ | ● | ● | CV | L |
| KOBE | 359 | ◆ | ● | ● | J | T |
| KOMALA VILAS | 359 | ◆ | | ● | I | T L |
| NEW ORLEANS | 359 | ◆◆◆ | ● | ● | E | T L |
| PALM BEACH | 359 | ◆◆ | ● | ● | S | T L |
| PREGO | 359 | ◆◆ | ● | ● | E | T |
| RESTAURANT LATOUR | 359 | ◆◆◆ | ● | ● | E | L |
| SAIGON | 359 | ◆◆ | ● | ● | V | T |
| SANUR | 359 | ◆◆ | ● | ● | N | T |
| SWEE KEE CHICKEN RICE | 359 | ◆ | ● | ● | C | T L |
| TAI TONG HOI KEE | 359 | ◆ | | | C | T |
| THE TANDOOR | 359 | ◆◆ | ● | ● | I | T |
| TGI FRIDAY'S | 359 | ◆◆ | ● | ● | E | T Y |
| THANYING RESTAURANT | 359 | ◆◆ | ● | ● | H | T L |
| **KUALA LUMPUR (WEST MALAYSIA)** | | | | | | |
| CHILI RESTAURANT | 363 | ◆ | | | N | T L |
| HARD ROCK CAFÉ | | ◆ | ● | ● | E | T L |
| OMAR KHAYAM RESTAURANT | 363 | ◆ | ● | ● | F | T L |
| SHANG PALACE | 363 | ◆◆ | ● | ● | C | T Y |
| SRI MELAYU RESTAURANT | 363 | ◆◆◆ | | | M | T L |
| **SHAH ALAM (WEST MALAYSIA)** | | | | | | |
| EDEN SEAFOOD VILLAGE | 364 | ◆◆ | ● | ● | C, E | L |
| LAKEVIEW FLOATING RESTAURANT | 364 | ◆◆ | ● | ● | C, S | T |

SPECIALTIES
A : Asian
C : Chinese
CV : Chinese Vegetarian
E : Continental
H : Thai
I : Indian
J : Japanese
K : Korean
M : Malay
N : Indonesian
P : Peranakan
PO : Portuguese
S : Seafood
V : Vietnamese
X : Mexican

CLIENTELE
T : Tourist
L : Local
Y : Youth

| | Page | Price (per person) | Credit cards | Air-conditioned | Specialties | Clientele |
|---|---|---|---|---|---|---|
| **MELAKA (WEST MALAYSIA)** | | | | | | |
| Long Feng Restaurant | 365 | ♦♦ | ● | ● | C | L |
| Nyonya Makko | 365 | ♦♦ | ● | ● | P | T L |
| Ole Sayang Restaurant | 365 | ♦ | ● | ● | P | T L |
| Peranakan Restaurant | 365 | ♦ | ● | ● | P | T L |
| Restoran de Lisbon | 365 | ♦ | | | PO | L |
| Restoran de Portugis | 365 | ♦ | | | PO | L |
| Shang San Restaurant | 365 | ♦♦ | ● | ● | C | L |
| Sri Lakshmi Villas | 365 | ♦ | | ● | I | L |
| Summerfield's Coffee Shop | 365 | ♦♦ | ● | ● | A, E | T L |
| **PENANG (WEST MALAYSIA)** | | | | | | |
| Chuan Lock Hooi | 366 | ♦ | | ● | C | T L |
| Dragon King Restaurant | 366 | ♦ | | ● | P | T L |
| Rasa Sayang Hotel Coffee Garden | 366 | ♦♦ | ● | ● | A | T L |
| **KUCHING (EAST MALAYSIA)** | | | | | | |
| Golden Dragon | 372 | ♦♦ | ● | ● | C | T L |
| Koreana Korean Restaurant | 372 | ♦♦ | ● | ● | K | T L |
| Lok Thian | 372 | ♦ | ● | ● | H | T L |
| Meisan Restaurant | 372 | ♦ | ● | ● | C | L |
| **KOTA KINABALU (EAST MALAYSIA)** | | | | | | |
| Restaurant Bilal | 374 | ♦ | | | M | L |
| Gardenia Steak and Lobster Restaurant | 374 | ♦♦ | ● | ● | E | T L |
| Nan Xing Restaurant | 374 | ♦ | | ● | C | L |
| Port View Seafood | 374 | ♦♦ | ● | | S | T L |
| Rocky's Fun Pub/Café | 374 | ♦♦ | ● | ● | E | T Y |
| Sentosa Restaurant | 374 | ♦ | | | M | L |
| **SANDAKAN (EAST MALAYSIA)** | | | | | | |
| Ming Restaurant | 375 | ♦♦ | ● | ● | C | T L |
| XO Steak House | 375 | ♦ | ● | ● | E | T L |
| **BANDAR SERI BEGAWAN (BRUNEI DARUSSALAM)** | | | | | | |
| Pondok Sari Wangi | 376 | ♦ | ● | ● | M | L |
| Stadium Restaurant | 376 | ♦♦ | ● | ● | C | T L |

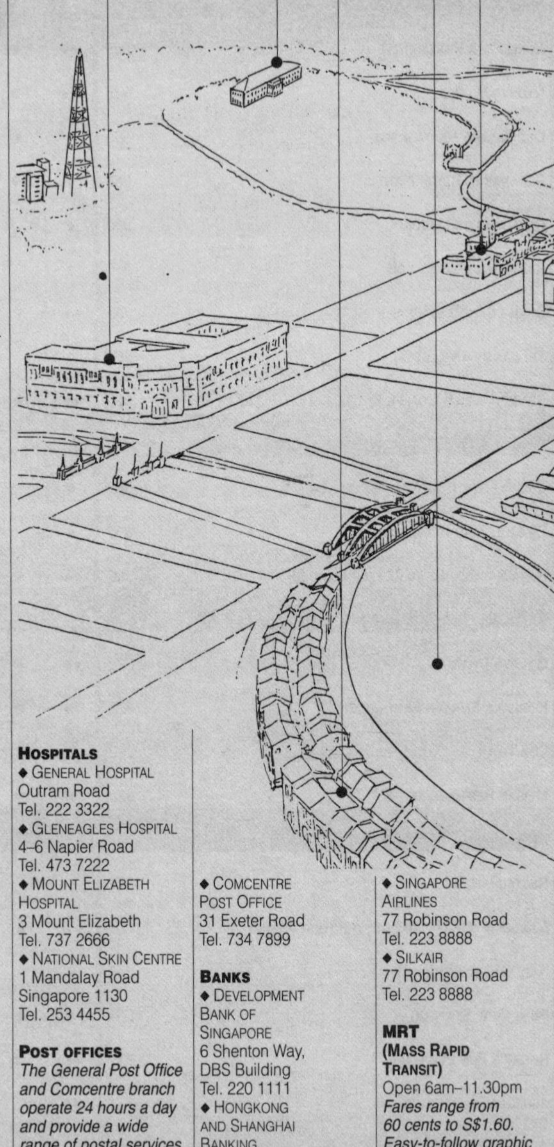


## GENERAL

*Visitors from America, Western Europe, and Commonwealth countries do not need a visa for a fourteen-day stay, provided they have proof of onward journey and adequate funds. Visas can be extended for a further fourteen-day period by applying to the Immigration Department.*

### USEFUL INFORMATION

**SINGAPORE TOURIST PROMOTION BOARDS**

◆ HEAD OFFICE, SINGAPORE
Tourism Court
1 Orchard Spring Lane
Singapore 247729
Tel. 736 6622
Fax 736 9423

◆ UK
1st Floor,
Carrington House,
126–30 Regent Street
London W1R 5FE
Tel. (0171) 437 0033
Fax (0171) 734 2191

◆ US
580 Fifth Avenue
12th Floor
New York, NY 10036
Tel. (212) 302 4861
Fax (212) 302 4801

◆ AUSTRALIA
Suite 1202, Level 12,
Westpac Plaza
60 Margaret Street
Sydney, NSW 2000
Tel. (02) 241 37712
Fax (02) 252 3586

**TELEPHONE**

*Numbers starting with 1800 are toll-free. Public telephones and pay-phones charge 10 cents for every 3 minutes. Phone cards of value S$2 upward are available at post offices and local stores. Overseas calls can be made at public phone booths in MRT stations.*

**EMERGENCY SERVICES**

◆ POLICE
Tel. 990
◆ FIRE AND AMBULANCE
Tel. 995
◆ TANGLIN POLICE STATION
Napier Road
Tel. 733 0000

**HOSPITALS**

◆ GENERAL HOSPITAL
Outram Road
Tel. 222 3322
◆ GLENEAGLES HOSPITAL
4–6 Napier Road
Tel. 473 7222
◆ MOUNT ELIZABETH HOSPITAL
3 Mount Elizabeth
Tel. 737 2666
◆ NATIONAL SKIN CENTRE
1 Mandalay Road
Singapore 1130
Tel. 253 4455

**POST OFFICES**

*The General Post Office and Comcentre branch operate 24 hours a day and provide a wide range of postal services.*

◆ ENQUIRIES
Tel. 165
◆ GENERAL POST OFFICE
Change Alley
Tel. 538 6899
◆ CHINATOWN POINT PO
133 New Bridge Road
#02–42
Tel.538 7899
◆ COLOMBO COURT POST OFFICE
Colombo Court
#01–01
Tel. 339 8899
◆ COMCENTRE POST OFFICE
31 Exeter Road
Tel. 734 7899

**BANKS**

◆ DEVELOPMENT BANK OF SINGAPORE
6 Shenton Way,
DBS Building
Tel. 220 1111
◆ HONGKONG AND SHANGHAI BANKING CORPORATION
10 Collyer Quay
Ocean Building
Tel. 530 5000
◆ STANDARD CHARTERED BANK
6 Battery Road
Tel. 225 8888

**AIR TRAVEL**

◆ FLIGHT INFORMATION
Tel. 542 4422
or 542 1234
◆ SINGAPORE AIRLINES
77 Robinson Road
Tel. 223 8888
◆ SILKAIR
77 Robinson Road
Tel. 223 8888

**MRT (MASS RAPID TRANSIT)**

Open 6am–11.30pm
*Fares range from 60 cents to S$1.60. Easy-to-follow graphic signs at MRT stations indicate the stops and their corresponding fares. Uniformed MRT officers are on hand at each station to answer queries. Visitors can buy an MRT Tourist Souvenir Ticket – valid for 120 days and worth S$5.50 of traveling fare – or a single-trip fare-card at the station.*

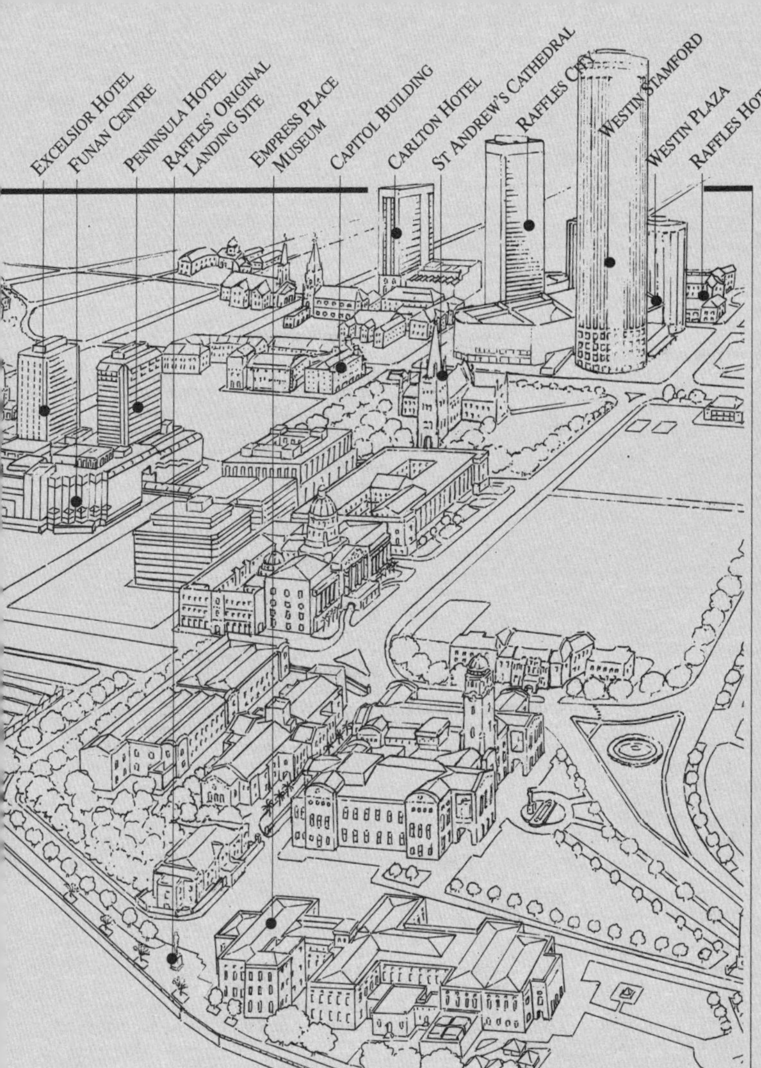


**Bus**

◆ Singapore Bus Service
Tel. 1800 287 2727.
6am–midnight
*Complementing the MRT in public transport, the SBS is the major bus operator for daily island-wide commuting. Fares on SBS buses range from 60 cents to S$1.40 (air-conditioned) and from 50 cents to S$1.10 (non-air-conditioned). Singapore Explorer bus tickets at S$5 a day or S$12 for three days are on sale at hotel reception desks.*

**Taxi** (24-hours Call-a-Cab)
NTUC Comfort
Tel. 552 1111

**TIBS Taxis**
Tel. 481 1211
*There are over 14,000 taxis operating throughout Singapore's roads. Taxi stands can be seen dotted around the city district. Taxi fares are is S$2.40 for the first kilometer (0.6 mile),then 10 cents for each additional 240 meters (275 yards) up to 10 kilometers, and 10 cents for every 225 meters (248 yards) thereafter. Extra charges apply to fares in the following cases: a S$3 surcharge for a trip from Changi Airport; a S$2.20 surcharge for telephone reservations; and a 50 percent levy on the fare for trips after midnight.*

**Car rental**

◆ Avis
200 Orchard Boulevard
Boulevard Hotel
Tel. 737 1668

◆ C & P Rent-a-Car
35 Scotts Road
Tel. 736 6666

◆ Hertz
280 Kampong Arang Road
Tel. 447 3388

## Culture

**Haw Par Villa Dragon World**
262 Pasir Panjang Road Tel. 774 0300
SBS bus nos 10, 30, 51, 143, and 200
9am–6pm daily.
Admission S$16.50 adult and S$10.50 child.
*Chinese legends and mythology depicted in colorful larger-than-life statues; side shows and thrilling boat rides.*

**Ming Village**
32 Pandan Road
Tel. 265 7711
Fax 266 2465
SBS bus no 78 from Clementi MRT station/bus interchange
*The largest pottery center in the region. In-house tours of factory and showroom.*

**NATIONAL LIBRARY, CENTRAL**
Stamford Road
Tel. 337 7355
9am–8pm Mon.–Fri.; 9am–5pm Sat., and 1pm–5pm Sun.

**NATIONAL MUSEUM**
Stamford Road
Tel. 337 7355
9am–5pm daily; closed Mon.
Admission S$3 adult, S$1.50 child. Free admission to art gallery.
*Collections include early furniture, dress accessories and Straits Chinese collection. Free guided tours in English Tue.–Fri. at 11am.*

**SINGAPORE ART MUSEUM**
71 Bras Basah Road
Tel. 332 3222
A short walk from Dhoby Ghaut MRT station
9am–5.30pm daily; closed on Mondays.
Admission S$3 adult, S$1.50 child
*The national art gallery showcases 20th-century art practices in Singapore and Southeast Asia.*

**SINGAPORE SCIENCE CENTRE**
Science Centre Road, Tel. 560 3316
Ten-minute walk from Jurong East MRT/bus interchange
Open 10am–6pm daily; closed on Mondays.
Admission S$3 adult, S$1.50 child
*About six hundred mobile and static exhibits, a planetarium and an omni-theater (admission charged).*

## PARKS AND GARDENS

**BOTANICAL GARDENS**
Napier Road
5am–midnight
Free admission.
*135 acres of flora and fauna; ponds, orchid enclosure, greenhouse.*

**BUKIT TIMAH NATURE RESERVE**
177 Hindhede Drive
Tel. 468 5736
SBS bus nos 171 or 182 from Newton MRT station
8.30am–6pm daily
*This 81-hectare reserve contains more plant species than the entire North American continent. Well-marked paths l ead through the jungle. At the heart of the reserve lies Singapore's highest point – Bukit Timah Hill.*

**CHINESE GARDEN & JAPANESE GARDEN**
Yuan Ching Road
Near Chinese Garden MRT station.
Tel. 264 3455
Fax 265 8133
9am–6pm
Admission S$4.50 adult, S$2 child.
*Two gardens linked by a bridge; lots of greenery, pagodas, and pavilions.*

**CROCODILE PARADISE**
241 Jalan Ahmad Ibrahim (next to Jurong Birdpark)Tel. 261 8866
Fax 261 7778
9am–6pm daily.
Admission S$6.00 adult, S$3.00 child
*Crocodile wrestling show, crocodile park, koi fish pond, and leather-products store.*

**FORT CANNING PARK**
Fort Canning Hill
A short walk from Dhoby Ghaut MRT station
Open daily
*A park rich in history – a sacred site where early Malay kings settled and the spot founder Sir Stamford Raffles built his own bungalow, Singapore's first Government House.*

**JURONG BIRDPARK**
Jalan Ahmad Ibrahim
Tel. 265 0022
Fax 261 1869
SBS bus nos 194 and 251 from Boon Lay MRT station/bus interchange.
9am–6pm
Admission S$9.27 adult, S$3.09 child
*Birdshows, waterfall, walk-in aviary, penguin parade, panorail rides, theatrette; over seven thousand exotic birds from six hundred species around the world.*

**SENTOSA**
Island resort opposite World Trade Centre
Tel. 743 8668
Gate admission fees S$5 adult, S$3 child.
Air-conditioned buses to and from Sentosa charge S$6 adult and S$4 child for a roundtrip, inclusive of admission fees to the island. Passengers can take this shuttle service, operating at 10-minute intervals, either from the bus-stop at Tiong Bahru MRT station or World Trade Centre. The island is also accessible by ferry, cable car or overland by the Causeway-bridge.
*Asian Village, Maritime Museum, musical fountain, Surrender Chambers, Fort Siloso, golf courses, roller-skating rink, cycling tracks, food center, beaches, nature walks, and monorail rides.*

**SINGAPORE ZOOLOGICAL GARDENS**
Mandai Lake Road
Tel. 269 3411
Fax 367 2974
8.30am–6pm
Admission S$9.27 adult, S$4.12 child. The night safari, next to the zoo, runs from 7.30pm till midnight; S$15.45 adult and S$10.30 child.
Take SBS bus 138 from Yio Chu Kang MRT station
*The zoo has more than 1,600 creatures in natural settings. The night safari is the first of its kind in the world and includes tram rides and forest walks.*

**TANG DYNASTY CITY**
2 Yuan Ching Road
Tel. 261 1116
9.30am–6.30pm daily.
Admission S$15 adult, S$10 child
*Theme park with replicas of structures from 7th century Chang-an of the Tang dynasty; ancient wedding rituals and acrobatic stunts.*

## RESTAURANTS

*Smoking is prohibited. The bill includes a 10 percent service charge and 4 percent government tax.*

**AZIZA'S**
#02–15 Albert Court
Tel. 235 1130
*Excellent and authentic Malay cuisine including Nasi Minyak, and Ikan Terutop .*

**BAN SENG RESTAURANT**
79 New Bridge Road
Tel. 533 1471
*Teochew cuisine.*

**BANANA LEAF APOLLO**
56 Race Course Road
Tel. 293 8682
*South Indian cuisine, with fish-head curry, a hot favorite.*

**◆ LAU PA SAT ◆**

Dwarfed by the surrounding skyscrapers, the Lau Pa Sat market is a fine example of a Victorian cast-iron structure. Closed to visitors, the future of this market is yet to be charted.

**BARON'S TABLE**
Royal Holiday Inn
Crowne Plaza
25 Scotts Road
Tel. 737 7966
*German smokehouse Dried Beef, Black Forest Ham.*

**CHICO'S N CHARLIE'S**
#05–01 Liat Towers
541 Orchard Road
Tel. 734 1783
*Mexican favorites: tacos, burritos, and Margarita cocktails .*

**CHINA PALACE**
20 Bideford Road
#02-00 Wellington Bldg
Tel. 235 1378
*Spicy Sichuan food.*

**GORDON GRILL**
Goodwood Park Hotel
22 Scotts Road
Tel. 737 7411
*Cozy setting; offers English and Scottish cuisine.*

**GRAND CITY**
#07-04 Cathay Building
11 Dhoby Ghaut
Tel. 338 3622
*Peking Duck, Drunken Prawns, Suckling Pig.*

**HAEBOK'S**
44 Tanjong Pagar Road
Tel. 223 9003
*Wide variety of Korean cuisine at its best; Bulgogi, Kalbi Gui (ox ribs) and others.*

**HAPPY REALM**
#03 16 Pearl Centre
Eu Tong Sen Street
Tel. 222 6141
*Chinese vegetarian.*

**KOBE**
#04–06 Tanglin
Shopping Centre
19 Tanglin Road
Tel. 734 6796
*Japanese cuisine. Sukiyaki, shabu shabu, beef and seafood barbecue-style.*

**KOMALA VILAS**
76 Serangoon Road
Tel. 293 6980
*Thosai (rice pancake) and dal; thali (set meal) on banana leaf.*

**NEW ORLEANS**
Holiday Inn Parkview
11 Cavenagh Road
Tel. 733 8333
*Creole food, Seafood Gumbo, Southern Fried Chicken, soft-shell crab.*

**PALM BEACH**
5 Stadium Walk
Kallang Park Leisure
Drome
Tel. 334 3088
*Crabs, lobsters, prawns – steamed, or with sauce, pepper, and chili.*

**PREGO**
Westin Stamford Hotel
Tel. 338 8585
*Excellent pasta, Osso Bucco and Scallopine di vitello.*

**RESTAURANT LATOUR**
Shangri-La Hotel
22 Orange Grove Road
Tel. 737 3644
*Known for its excellent service and menu amid Edwardian setting. One of the best in town.*

**SAIGON**
#04–03 Cairnhill Place
15 Cairnhill Road
Tel. 235 0626
*Vietnamese food. Chao Tom (barbecued prawns on sugar cane) and Lotus Duck are just two of the delights on offer.*

**SANUR**
#04–17 Centrepoint
176 Orchard Road
Tel. 734 2192
*Indonesian delights such as Tahu Telor (Fried bean curd and egg with spicy sauce), Ikan Pepes (spiced fish steamed in banana leaf), and others.*

**SWEE KEE CHICKEN RICE**
51 Middle Road
Tel. 338 6986
*Hainanese specialty in traditional coffee-shop setting.*

**TAI TONG HOI KEE**
3 Mosque Street
Tel. 223 3484
*Dim sum – Chinese morning snacks.*

**THE TANDOOR**
Holiday Inn Parkview
11 Cavenagh Road
Tel. 733 8333
*North Indian delights – Tandoori chicken and marinated tiger prawns.*

**TGI FRIDAY'S**
The Glass House
Park Mall Annexe
Penang Road
Tel. 334 7811
*American delights include Chicken Janga salads, broccoli soup.*

**THANYING RESTAURANT**
Amara Hotel
Tanjong Pagar Road
Tel. 222 4688
*Thai specialties such as Krathong Thong, prawns wrapped in beancurd, deep-fried pouches of minced pork, and Tom Yam soup.*

## HOTELS

*A selection of air-conditioned hotels, located within central and shopping districts. Add 10 percent service charge and 4 percent tax to the room rates.*

**ALLSON HOTEL**
101 Victoria Street
Tel. 336 0811
*On major road; near church, bookstores, and Bugis Street bazaar.*
*S$150–S$400*

**BOULEVARD HOTEL**
200 Orchard Boulevard
Tel. 737 2911
*AVIS car rental outlet; near Hard Rock Café, and shopping centers.*
*S$240–S$400*

**CAIRNHILL HOTEL**
19 Cairnhill Circle
Tel. 734 6622
*In residential district, overlooking Orchard and Emerald Hill Roads.*
*S$160–S$200*

**CARLTON HOTEL**
76 Bras Basah Road
Tel. 338 8333
*On major road; near cathedral, bookstores, and Raffles City shopping complex.*
*S$280–S$350*

**COCKPIT HOTEL**
6–7 Oxley Rise
Tel. 737 9111
*Near Killiney Road post office and Park Mall shopping complex.*
*S$170–S$200*

**CROWN PRINCE HOTEL**
270 Orchard Road
Tel. 732 1111.
*Within busy shopping district; opposite Ngee Ann City and Paragon shopping complexes.*
*S$260–S$320*

**ELIZABETH HOTEL**
24 Mount Elizabeth
Tel. 738 1188.
*Newly upgraded hotel overlooking Orchard Road; near hospital.*
*S$240–S$300*

**HOTEL EQUATORIAL**
429 Bukit Timah Road
Tel. 732 0431.
*Within residential district and near YMCA.*
*S$145–S$200*

BOULEVARD HOTEL
SINGAPORE HILTON
LANE CRAWFORD PLACE
SHAW HOUSE
SINGAPORE MARRIOT
NGEE ANN CITY

**FOUR SEASONS**
50 Cuscaden Road
Tel. 734 1110
*Off Orchard Road, behind Forum Shopping Mall.*
*S$420–4,000*

**GOODWOOD PARK HOTEL**
22 Scotts Road
Tel. 737 7411
*Near recreation clubs and shopping centers.*
*S$355–450*

**HARBOUR VIEW DAI-ICHI**
81 Anson Road
Tel. 224 1133
*In business district and near railway station.*
*S$180–240*

**SINGAPORE HILTON**
581 Orchard Road
Tel. 737 2233
*Next to Forum Shopping Mall and opposite Thai Embassy.*
*S$270–330*

**HOLIDAY INN PARK VIEW**
11 Cavenagh Road
Tel. 733 8333
*Near Centrepoint, food center, and market.*
*S$250–300*

**HYATT REGENCY**
10–12 Scotts Road
Tel. 733 1188
*Spacious hotel in busy shopping district and movie theater complex.*
*S$360–420*

**MAJESTIC HOTEL**
31–7 Bukit Pasoh Road
Tel. 222 3377
*Traditional small hotel, near Outram Park MRT station and Chinatown.*
*S$55–65*

**MANDARIN SINGAPORE**
333 Orchard Road
Tel. 737 4411
*In the heart of Orchard Road, beside Ngee Ann City shopping complex.*
*S$280–340*

**MARINA MANDARIN**
6 Raffles Boulevard, Marina Square
Tel. 338 3388
*Sweeping views of the waterfront; inside large shopping complex.*
*S$315–430*

**NEW PARK HOTEL**
181 Kitchener Road
Tel. 291 5533
*Adjoining shopping arcade; within Little India; near shophouses.*
*S$180–360*

**NOVOTEL ORCHID**
214 Dunearn Road
Tel. 250 3322
*Rooms for the handicapped; within central suburban area.*
*S$200–60*

**OMNI MARCO POLO**
247 Tanglin Road
Tel. 474 7141
*Near Botanic Gardens, next to Australian High Commission and British Council.*
*S$135–350*

**ORCHARD HOTEL**
442 Orchard Road
Tel. 734 7766
*Next to Delfi Orchard shopping center and Thai Embassy.*
*S$190–290*

**ORCHARD PARADE**
1 Tanglin Road
Tel. 737 1133
*Next to Forum Shopping Mall, near Hard Rock Café.*
*S$210–60*

**THE ORIENTAL SINGAPORE**
5 Raffles Avenue, Marina Square
Tel. 338 0066
*Continental cuisine and local food fare; inside busy shopping center.*
*S$320–400*

**PAN PACIFIC HOTEL**
7 Raffles Boulevard, Marina Square
Tel. 336 8111
*Well-equipped business service center, in busy shopping complex.*
*S$300–440*

**PARAMOUNT HOTEL**
Marine Parade Road
Tel. 344 5577
*Near shophouses and shopping centers.*
*S$160–205*

**HOTEL PHOENIX**
Orchard/Somerset Road
Tel. 737 8666
*Adjoining shopping mall; next to Somerset MRT station.*
*S$190–260*

**PLAZA HOTEL**
7500A Beach Road
Tel. 298 0011
*Near Arab Street and movie theaters, next to a department store.*
*S$180–290*

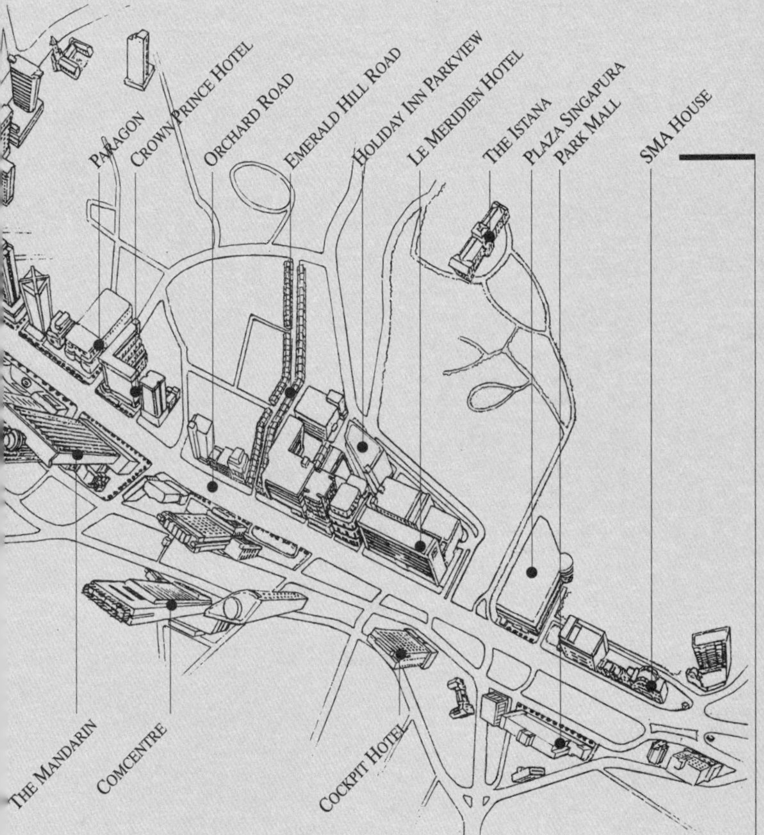

Paragon
Crown Prince Hotel
Orchard Road
Emerald Hill Road
Holiday Inn Parkview
Le Meridien Hotel
The Istana
Plaza Singapura
Park Mall
SMA House
The Mandarin
Comcentre
Cockpit Hotel

**Raffles Hotel**
1 Beach Road
Tel. 337 1886
*Classical grandeur and favorite of writers such as Somerset Maugham.*
*S$650–6,000*

**The Regent of Singapore**
1 Cuscaden Road
Tel. 733 8888
*Local and continental food fare; 5 minutes from Orchard Road.*
*S$230–300*

**Riverview Hotel**
382 Havelock Road
Tel. 732 9922
*Along the riverbank; near Clarke Quay.*
*S$160–80*

**Seaview Hotel**
26 Amber Close
Tel. 345 2222
*Cozy hotel on the east coast; near shophouses and shopping complex.*
*S$120–160*

**Shangri-la Hotel**
22 Orange Grove Road
Tel. 737 3644
*Plush and spacious hotel with fine dining and service.*
*S$300–490*

**Westin Plaza and Westin Stamford**
2 Stamford Road
Tel. 338 1866
*The world's tallest hotel (73 stories); adjoining Raffles City; linked to City Hall MRT station.*
*S$220–50*

**• Hard Rock Café •**

Memorabilia of popular musicians, singers and actors decorate the inside walls of the American food outlet at Cuscaden Road.

## Nightlife

### Pubs and Lounges

*Most nightspots offer "happy hours" (drinks at reduced rates) from 6.30–8pm.*

**Hard Rock Café**
HPL House
Cuscaden Road
(behind Forum Shopping Mall)
Tel. 235 5232
*American food served amid memorabilia of rock and roll musicians.*

**Saxophone**
23 Cuppage Terrace
(behind Centrepoint)
Tel. 235 8385
*Restaurant and pub in a restored shophouse; popular haunt for jazz lovers and night birds.*

**TGIF**
#04–44/50
Far East Plaza
Scotts Road
Tel. 235 6181
*One of the pioneer nightspots; restaurant-cum-discotheque.*

**Zouk**
17–21 Jiak Kim Street
Tel. 738 2988
*An upbeat nightspot which serves as disco, wine bar, pub, karaoke lounge and restaurant; dining by the riverside.*

DAYABUMI

## GENERAL

*Visitors must have a passport valid for at least six months. Citizens from Commonwealth countries (except India and Sri Lanka) may enter without a visa. Those from the US, Germany, France, Czechoslovakia, Italy, Norway, Denmark, Sweden, Belgium, South Korea, Austria, Japan, Finland, Iceland, Luxembourg and Tunisia, Algeria, Jordan, Bahrain, Kuwait, Lebanon, Egypt, North Yemen, Oman, Qatar, Saudi Arabia, Turkey and the United Arab Emirates do not require a visa if their stay in Malaysia does not exceed three months.*

**HEALTH**

*Visitors from yellow-fever epidemic zones and infected areas require vaccination; children below the age of one are exempted.*

**TIPPING**

*Restaurants, coffee houses and hotel food and beverage outlets add a 10 percent service charge and 5 percent government tax to the bill.*

### USEFUL INFORMATION

**MALAYSIA TOURISM PROMOTION BOARDS**

◆ HEAD OFFICE, KUALA LUMPUR
25th Floor,
Menara Dato Onn,
Putra World Trade Centre,
Jalan Tun Ismail,
50480 Kuala Lumpur,
Malaysia
Tel. 293 5188
Fax. 293 5884

◆ UK
57 Trafalgar Square
London,
WC 2N 5DU
Tel. (0171) 930 7932
Fax (0171) 930 9015

◆ US
595 Madison Ave
Suite 1800
New York, NY 10022
Tel. (212) 754 1113/4/5
Fax (212) 754 1116

◆ AUSTRALIA
65 York Street
Sydney
NSW 2000
Tel. (02) 294 441
or 294 442
or 294 443
Fax 262 2026

## KUALA LUMPUR

**DIALING CODE**

03 followed by the telephone number

### USEFUL INFORMATION

**EMBASSIES AND CONSULATES**

◆ UK
185 Jalan Ampang
Tel. 248 2122

◆ US
376 Jalan Tun Razak
Tel. 248 9011

◆ AUSTRALIA
6 Jalan Yap Kwan Seng
Tel. 242 3122

**EMERGENCY SERVICES**

Dial 999 for police, ambulance, or the fire brigade

**POLICE ASSISTANCE**

Look for police posts (*Pondok Polis*) in the city, or contact the KL Tourist Police.
Tel. 241 5522, ext 1355

**POST OFFICE**

Dayabumi Complex
Jalan Sultan Hishamuddin
Tel. 274 1122
Mon.–Thur.
8am–12.45pm,
2pm–4.15pm;
Fri. 8am–12.15pm;
2.45pm–4.15pm
Sat.8am–12.45pm

**AIRLINES**

◆ MALAYSIA AIRLINES
Bangunan MAS,
Jalan Sultan Ismail
Tel. 746 3000

◆ SINGAPORE AIRLINES
2 Jalan Dang Wangi
Tel. 292 3122

◆ UNITED AIRLINES
2–5 Bangunan MAS
Jalan Sultan Ismail
Tel. 261 1433

**AIRPORT**

Subang Jaya
Tel. 746 1014.
*A new airport is planned to open in 1997.*

**TRAIN**

KUALA LUMPUR RAILWAY STATION
Tel. 274 7435
*The railway links Kuala Lumpur with Bangkok in the north and Singapore in the south. There are several daily services and train fares vary, depending on class of accommodation and distance.*

**BUS**

INTRA-CITY SERVICES
Terminals at Pudu Raya Bus Station, Chow Kit Road and Kota Raya Shopping Complex.
*Bus fares are 20 sen for the first kilometer and 5 sen for each kilometer thereafter. Mini buses charge a flat rate of 50 sen.*

◆ OUTBOUND SERVICES
PUTRA BUS STATION
opposite Putra World Trade Centre
Tel. 442 9530
East coast-bound.

◆ PUDU RAYA BUS STATION
Tel. 230 0245
North- and south-bound.

**TAXIS**

*There are taxi stands at shopping complexes and hotels. Fares are RM1 for the first kilometer, and 10 sen for every 200 meters thereafter. There is a 50% levy between midnight and 6am. A RM1 fee is charged for taxi phone reservations.*

**CAR RENTAL**

◆ AVIS
40 Jalan Sultan Ismail
Tel. 241 7144

◆ BUDGET
29 Jalan Yap Kwan Seng
Tel. 242 5166

◆ HERTZ
Lot 214A International Complex,
Jalan Sultan Ismail
Tel. 243 3433

### TOURIST OFFICES

◆ Level 2, Putra World Trade Centre,
Jalan Tun Ismail
Tel. 441 1295

◆ KL VISITORS CENTRE
Inside Kuala Lumpur Railway Station
Tel. 274 6063

◆ MALAYSIA TOURIST INFORMATION COMPLEX (MATIC)
Lot 109, Jalan Ampang
Tel. 242 3929

CENTRAL MARKET

**◆ CENTRAL MARKET ◆**

This arts center by the Klang River, displays the works of local artists and craftspeople, including plaque engravers, woodcrafters, portrait artists, and batik painters.

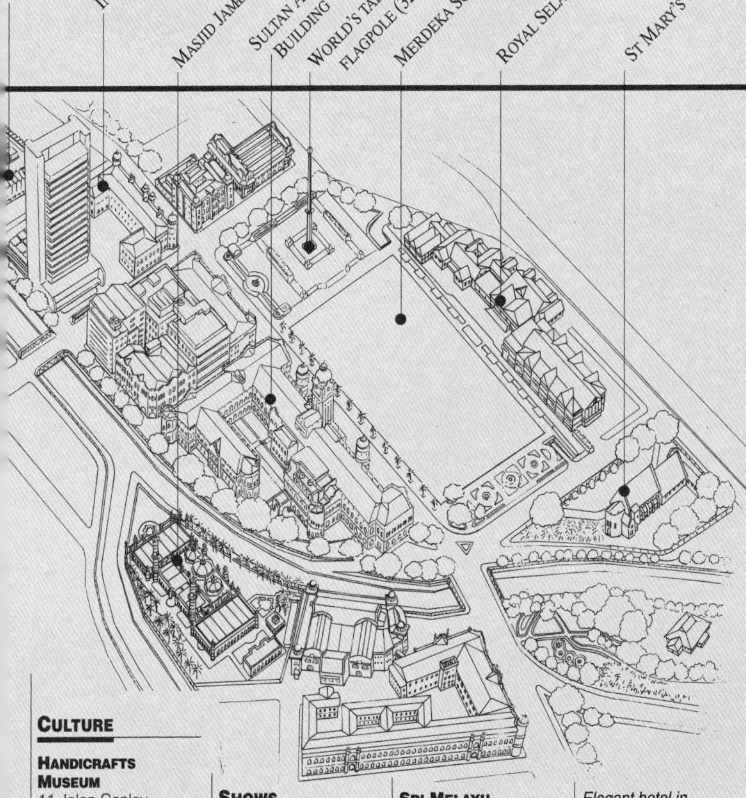


## CULTURE

**HANDICRAFTS MUSEUM**
11 Jalan Conlay
Tel. 241 3117
Open 9.30am–5pm
*Traditional handicrafts, with demonstrations. Free admission.*

**MEMORIAL TUN RAZAK**
Sri Taman Jalan Perdana
Tel. 291 2111, 291 2246
Open 9am–5pm Tue.–Sun.
*Personal and official memorabilia of the former prime minister. Free admission.*

**MUZIUM NEGARA**
Jalan Damansara
Tel. 282 6255
Open 9am–6pm daily
*Archeological artifacts, natural-history exhibits. Admission RM1. Free for children under 12.*

**NATIONAL ART GALLERY**
1 Jalan Sultan Hishamuddin
Tel. 230 0157
Open 10am–6pm daily
*Permanent collections of local and foreign works. Free admission.*

## SHOWS

*Scan the local dailies for theater, shows, and festival events.*

**AUDITORIUM DBKL**
Jalan Raja Laut
Tel. 298 7555

**PANGGUNG BANDARAYA**
Jalan Raja
Tel. 291 8381.

## RESTAURANTS

**CHILI RESTAURANT**
35 Jalan Ampang
Tel. 201 0242
*Serves Nyonya cuisine.*

**OMAR KHAYAM RESTAURANT**
5 Jalan Medan Tuanku
Tel. 291 1016
*Specialties include North Indian dishes.*

**SHANG PALACE**
Shangri-La Hotel, Jalan Sultan Ismail
Tel. 232 2388
*Dim sum (steamed buns, porridge, deep-fried rolls, dumplings; served from trolleys).*

**SRI MELAYU RESTAURANT**
Jalan Stonor
Tel. 245 1833
*Superb Malay cuisine with cultural show daily.*

## HOTELS

**HOTEL ISTANA**
73 Jalan Raja Chulan
Tel. 241 9988
Fax 244 0111
*Within business district.*
*RM390–850*

**KUALA LUMPUR HILTON**
Jalan Sultan Ismail
Tel. 242 2322
Fax 244 2157
*Near museums.*
*RM400 to RM580*

**PAN PACIFIC**
Jalan Putra
Tel. 442 5555
Fax 443 8717
*Near Putra World Trade Centre and the Mall.*
*RM340–1,200*

**THE REGENT OF KUALA LUMPUR**
160 Jalan Bukit Bintang
Tel. 241 8000
Fax 245 7732
*Elegant hotel in central shopping district.*
*RM450–520*

**THE SHANGRI-LA**
11 Jalan Sultan Ismail
Tel. 232 2388
Fax 230 1514
*Opposite Hard Rock Café and near Lot 10 shopping center.*
*RM440 –4,100*

## NIGHTLIFE

**BLUE MOON**
Equatorial Hotel
Jalan Sultan Ismail
Tel. 261 7777

**TSIM SHA TSUI**
1 Jalan Kia Peng
Tel. 241 4929

**NIGHT MARKETS (PASAR MALAM)**
Nightly at Chinatown in Petaling Street and on Saturdays at Jalan Tuanku Abdul Rahman, near Chow Kit district.
Open 6pm–11pm
*Prepared food, clothing, cosmetics, kitchenware, curios, shoes, bags, and souvenirs.*

## AROUND KUALA LUMPUR AND SHAH ALAM

**DIALING CODE**
03 followed by the telephone number.

### CULTURE

**BATU CAVES**
Located 8 miles north of Kuala Lumpur, off the main road to Ipoh.
*Limestone massif, with a century-old Hindu shrine in Temple Cave.*

**MARA MUSEUM AND ART GALLERY**
Mara Institute of Technology
Shah Alam.
Tel. 556 4502
Open 9am–4pm daily, 9am–12.30pm Sat.
Free admission.
*Collection of works of art by students and local artists.*

**MUSEUM OF ABORIGINAL AFFAIRS**
KM 24, Jalan Pahang, Gombak.
Tel. 689 2122
Open 9am–5.30pm daily, except Fri.
Free admission.
*Exhibits of history, culture, and lifestyle of the aboriginal tribes of Peninsular Malaysia.*

**NATURAL RUBBER MUSEUM**
Kampong Melayu, Sungai Buloh
Tel. 656 1121
Open 10am–4pm daily. Closed Fri. and public holidays.
Free admission.
*Exhibits on the natural rubber industry .*

**SULTAN ALAM SHAH MUSEUM**
Persiaran Perdagangan
Shah Alam
Tel. 559 0050
Open 9am–6pm. Closed Fri. 12.15–2.45pm
Free admission.
*Historical, cultural, and natural-history artifacts from Selangor state.*

### PARKS AND GARDENS

**TEMPLER PARK**
About 12 miles north of Kuala Lumpur, off the North–south Highway.
*3000 acres of flora and fauna, against a backdrop of limestone hills.*

**ZOO NEGARA**
Ulu Klang
Tel. 408 3422
9am–6pm daily.
Admission RM5 and RM1 for child under 12
*Two hundred species of animals and birds.*

### RESTAURANTS

**EDEN SEAFOOD VILLAGE**
25–32 Jalan SS22/23
Damansara Jaya
Tel. 719 3184

**LAKEVIEW FLOATING RESTAURANT**
Tasik Tengah, Taman Tasik, Shah Alam
Tel. 550 5995

### HOTELS

**HOLIDAY INN**
Plaza Perangsang
Persiaran Perbandaran
Shah Alam
Tel. 550 3696
Fax 550 3913
*From RM340*

**PETALING JAYA HILTON**
2 Jalan Barat
Petaling Jaya
Tel. 755 9122
Fax 755 3909
*RM250–320*

## MELAKA

**DIALING CODE**
06 followed by the telephone number, unless otherwise stated.

### USEFUL INFORMATION

**TOURIST POLICE**
MALACCA TOURIST POLICE STATION
Tel. 282 2222

**AIR TRAVEL**
FLIGHT INFORMATION
Tel. 222 648
*Melaka's Bukit Berendam Airport is about 6 miles from the town, and services flights from Ipoh, Singapore and Pekan Baru in Sumatra.*

**AIRLINES**
MALAYSIA AIRLINES
Tel. 235 722, 235 723
ATLAS TRAVEL
Tel. 220 777
PELANCONGAN KOTA MALACCA
Tel. 247 728

**TAXIS**
Tel. 223 630 for reservations
*Taxis operate along Melaka's busiest roads, but they do not always use the meter: strike a bargain before boarding. Share-a-cabs to common destinations are popular and economical, especially for budget travelers.*

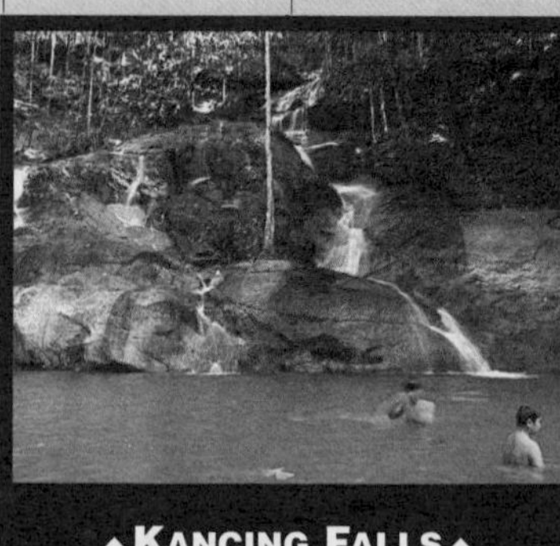

**◆ KANCING FALLS ◆**

The main attraction in Kanching Forest Reserve, next to Templer Park, is also the most popular waterfall in Selangor. It cascades down from a height of 600 feet.

**BUSES**
Malacca–Kuala Lumpur.
Tel. 222 503
Malacca–Port Dickson/Klang.
Tel. 233 642
Malacca–Ipoh, Butterworth.
Tel. 220 687
*Express bus services operate two-way routes between Melaka and major towns in the other states. Fares range from RM3 (Muar) to RM30 (Kota Bharu).*

**FERRY**
SEA SAFARI (MELAKA)
Tel. 235 882
*River cruises along the Melaka River, passing old Melaka town. Boarding point near the river bridge. Fares range between RM2 and RM4 for the hour-long cruise.*

**BANKS**
◆ HONGKONG & SHANGHAI BANKING CORPORATION
1A Jalan Kota
Tel. 222 399
◆ MALAYSIAN FRENCH BANK
Wisma TGH,
Jalan Taming Sari
Tel. 223 239

**CAR RENTAL**
◆ AVIS
124 Jalan Bendahara
Tel. 246 710, 224 991
◆ SINTAT
Ramada Renaissance Hotel
Tel. 248 888

### TOURIST OFFICES

◆ JALAN KOTA,
Town Square
Tel. 283 6538
◆ MALACCA STATE DEVELOPMENT CORPORATION
Grahamaju, Peti Surat 221, 75740 Malacca.
Tel. 220 643
Fax. 249 686
◆ AYER KEROH
Tel. 325 811

### CULTURE

**BABA NYONYA HERITAGE MUSEUM**
48 & 50 Jalan Tun Tan Cheng Lock
Tel. 231 273
10am–12.30pm; 2–4.30pm

*Examples of Peranakan houses with exhibits on the rich culture and lifestyle of the Straits-born Chinese. Admission RM7*

**PROCLAMATION OF INDEPENDENCE MEMORIAL JALAN PARAMESWARA**
75000 Melaka.
Tel. 241 231
Open 9am–6pm.
Closed Fri. noon–3pm
*Historical records of the early Malacca Sultanate and modern Malaysia. Free admission.*

## RESTAURANTS

**LONG FENG RESTAURANT**
Melaka Renaissance, Jalan Bendahara
Tel. 248 888
*Serves Chinese cuisine.*

**NYONYA MAKKO**
123 Taman Malacca
Tel. 240 737

**OLE SAYANG RESTAURANT**
198–199 Taman Malacca Jaya
Tel. 231 966
*Serves Nonya cuisine.*

**PERANAKAN RESTAURANT**
Nava Hoe Villa, 317 Klebang Besar
Tel. 354 436

**RESTORAN ANDA**
8B Jalan Hang Tuah
Tel. 231 984
*Serves Malay cuisine.*

**RESTORAN DE LISBON**
Portuguese Square
Tel. 248 067

**RESTORAN DE PORTUGIS**
Portuguese Square
Tel. 243 156

**SHANG SAN RESTAURANT**
Park Plaza, Ayer Keroh
Tel. 323 600
*Serves Chinese cuisine.*

**SRI LAKSHMI VILLAS**
2 Jalan Bendahara.
Tel. 224 926
*Serves Indian cuisine.*

**SUMMERFIELD'S COFFEE SHOP**
Melaka Renaissance
Tel. 248 888
*Serves Western cuisine.*

## HOTELS

**THE CITY BAYVIEW**
Jalan Bendahara
Tel. 283 9888
Fax 283 6699
*RM250–2,500*

**EMPEROR HOTEL**
123 Jalan Munshi Abdullah
Tel. 284 9495
Fax 283 8989
*RM140–690*

**MALACCA VILLAGE PARADISE RESORT**
Ayer Keroh
Tel. 232 3600
Fax 325 955
*RM250–360*

**MELAKA RENAISSANCE HOTEL**
Jalan Bendahara
Tel. 284 8888
Fax 283 5351
*RM300–2,800*

**SHAH'S BEACH RESORT**
6th mile, Tanjong Keling
Tel. 511 120
Fax 511 088
*RM92–150*

# SEREMBAN AND PORT DICKSON

**DIALING CODE**
06 followed by the telephone number, unless otherwise stated.

## TOURIST OFFICES

◆ c/o INVESTMENT CENTRE
State Economic Planning Unit, Office of the State Secretary, 5th Floor, Wisma Negeri
70503 Seremban
Tel. 762 2311

◆ STATE ECONOMIC DEVELOPMENT CORPORATION, NEGERI SEMBILAN
Jalan Yam Tuan
70000 Seremban
Tel. 723 251

## CULTURE

**CULTURAL HANDICRAFT COMPLEX**
Taman Seni Budaya
70200 Seremban
Tel. 763 1149
Open 9.30am–6pm, Closed Thur. from 1pm and Fri. noon–2.50pm
*Handicrafts on display and megaliths within the complex. Cultural exhibitions. Free admission.*

## HOTELS

**MEE LEE HOTEL**
47 Jalan Tuan Sheikh,
70000 Seremban
Tel. 730 162
*RM50*

**MING COURT BEACH HOTEL**
Batu 7, Jalan Pantai
71000 Port Dickson
Tel. 662 5244
Fax 662 5899
*RM210–260*

**THE REGENCY HOTEL AND RESORT**
5th mile, Jalan Pantai
71007 Port Dickson
Tel. 647 4090
Fax 647 5016
*RM210–260*

# PULAU PANGKOR

**DIALING CODE**
05 followed by the telephone number.

## USEFUL INFORMATION

*About 30 minutes by ferry (RM3 per person) from Lumut, a coastal village in Perak. There are buses and taxis, as well as motor-bikes and bicycles, for rent on Pulau Pangkor.*

## TOURIST OFFICES

◆ STATE ECONOMIC PLANNING UNIT
Jalan Dewan
30000 Ipoh, Perak
Tel. 532 800, 531 957

◆ PERAK TOURIST ASSOC.
c/o The Royal Casuarina
18 Jalan Gopeng
30250 Ipoh, Perak
Tel. 532 008

## HOTELS

**PAN PACIFIC RESORT**
Telok Belanga
323000 Pulau Pangkor
Tel. 685 1399, 685 1091
Fax 685 2390
*RM300–800*

**PANGKOR LAUT RESORT**
32300 Pulau Pangkor
Tel. 685 1375
Fax 685 1320
*RM400–1,100*

**SEAVIEW HOTEL**
Pulau Pangkor
Tel. 685 1929
Fax 685 1035
*RM115*

PANTAI KOK

## IPOH AND TAIPING

**DIALING CODE**
05 followed by the telephone number, unless otherwise stated.

### USEFUL INFORMATION

**AIR TRAVEL**
*Ipoh airport services two-way domestic flights from Kuala Lumpur, Penang, and Johor Bahru.*
◆ MALAYSIA AIRLINES:
Lot 108,
Bangunan Seri Kinta,
Jalan Sultan Idris Shah,
30000 Ipoh, Perak
Tel. 514 155

### TOURIST OFFICES

◆ IPOH TOURIST INFORMATION CENTRE
Jalan Dato Sagor
30000 Ipoh
Tel. 253 2800
◆ PERAK TOURIST ASSOCIATION
c/o The Royal Casuarina
18 Jalan Gopeng
30250 Ipoh, Perak
Tel. 253 2008

### CULTURE

**GEOLOGICAL SURVEY MUSEUM**
Jalan Sultan Azlan Shah
(3 miles from Ipoh)
Tel. 557 644
or 557 685
9am–12.30pm and 2–4pm daily, Sat 9.30am–12.30pm
Free admission.
*Over six hundred geological specimens of Malaysia: tin ore, fossils, and precious stones.*

**PERAK MUSEUM**
Jalan Taming Sari
Taiping, Perak
Tel. 822 057
Open 9.30am–5pm, Fri. 9.30am–noon, 2.30pm–5pm
Free admission.
*Ethnographical artifacts and theme exhibitions.*

### PARKS AND GARDENS

**DEPARTMENT OF WILDLIFE AND NATIONAL PARKS**
Tel. 532 411

**TAIPING LAKE GARDENS**
10am–6pm
*155-acre park with lakes; overhanging branches of trees form a natural archway.*

### HOTELS

**HOTEL EXCELSIOR**
Clarke Street
30300 Ipoh, Perak
Tel. 253 6666
Fax 253 6912
*RM188–338*

**THE ROYAL CASUARINA**
18 Jalan Gopeng
30250 Ipoh, Perak
Tel. 255 5555
Fax 255 8177
*RM220–2,200*

## PENANG

**DIALING CODE**
04 followed by the telephone number

### USEFUL INFORMATION

**POLICE AND AMBULANCE**
Tel. 999

**HOSPITALS**
◆ GENERAL HOSPITAL
Tel. 229 3333
◆ ADVENTIST HOSPITAL
Tel. 226 1133

**POSTAL SERVICES**
Lebuh Downing
Tel. 261 9222
8am–6pm

**AIRPORT**
◆ BAYAN LEPAS INTERNATIONAL AIRPORT
Tel. 643 0811

**TAXIS**
Tel. 262 5127

**CAR RENTAL**
◆ AVIS
E & O Hotel
10 Lebuh Farquhar
Tel. 263 1685

### TOURIST OFFICES

◆ MTPB OFFICE
Level 4, KOMTAR
Jalan Penang
Tel. 261 9067
9.30am–6.30pm.
◆ NORTHERN REGIONAL OFFICE
10 Jalan Tun Syed Sheh Barakbah
Tel. 261 9067
Fax 623 688
◆ PENANG TOURIST ASSOCIATION
Bangunan Penang Port Commission
Tel. 616 663

### CULTURE

**PENANG MUSEUM**
Lebuh Farquhar
Tel. 261 3144
9am–5pm.
Admission is free.
*Paintings and historical records, relics, and Peranakan exhibits.*

### RESTAURANTS

**CHUAN LOCK HOOI**
1E–F, McAlister Road
Tel. 226 1171
*Serves Chinese cuisine.*

**DRAGON KING RESTAURANT**
99 Lebuh Bishop
Tel. 261 8035
*Serves Nonya cuisine.*

**RASA SAYANG HOTEL COFFEE GARDEN**
Batu Ferringhi
Tel. 881 1811
Serves Western cuisine.

### HOTELS

**CROWN PRINCE HOTEL**
Tanjung Bungah
Tel. 890 4111
Fax 890 4777
*RM210–700*

**E & O HOTEL**
10 Lebuh Farquhar
Tel. 263 0630
Fax 263 4833
*RM158–270*

**EQUATORIAL HOTEL PENANG**
1 Jalan Bukit Jambul
Tel. 643 8000
Fax 644 8000
*RM280–1,950*

**PENANG MUTIARA BEACH RESORT**
Teluk Bahang
Tel. 881 1133
Fax 881 2233
*RM385–6000*

◆ PENANG ◆

Lebuh Campbell in Georgetown is the favorite shopping area for many local Chinese. The Merlin Penang can be seen in the distance.

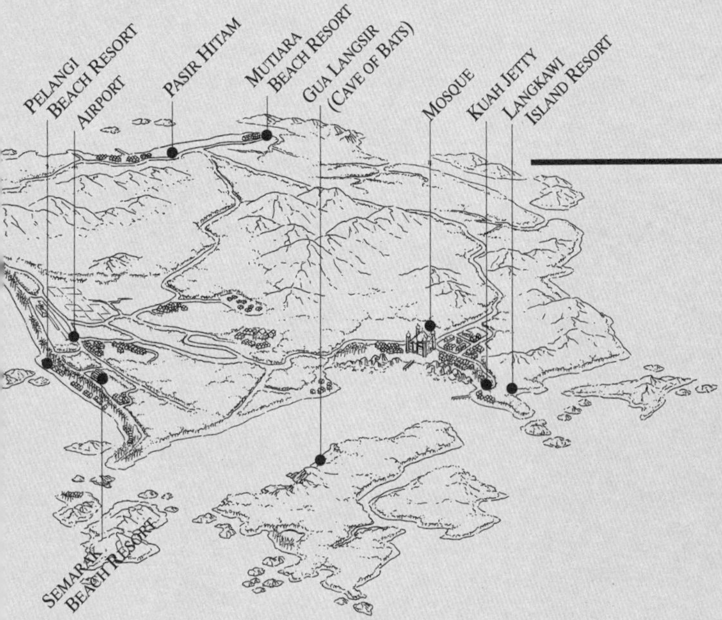

PELANGI BEACH RESORT
AIRPORT
PASIR HITAM
MUTIARA BEACH RESORT
GUA LANGSIR (CAVE OF BATS)
MOSQUE
KUAH JETTY
LANGKAWI ISLAND RESORT
SEMARAK BEACH RESORT

**SHANGRI-LA'S RASA SAYANG HOTEL**
Batu Ferringhi
Tel. 881 1811
Fax 881 1984
*RM280–3,500*

## NIGHTLIFE

**NIGHT MARKETS (PASAR MALAM)**
Nightly along Batu Ferringhi and also on some streets in Georgetown (check daily papers).6–11pm
*Costume jewelry, curios, souvenirs, watches, clothing, bags, and trinkets. Bargain before buying.*

# LANGKAWI

**DIALING CODE**
04 followed by the telephone number.

## USEFUL INFORMATION

**AIR TRAVEL**
*Daily flights by Malaysia Airlines from Penang, Kuala Lumpur and Singapore to airport at Padang Mat Sirat.*

**FERRY**
*One-hour trip (fare, RM10–12 per person) departures from Kuala Perlis and Kuala Kedah.*

## TOURIST OFFICES

◆ MTPB OFFICE
Kuah Jetty Terminal
Tel. 966 9416

◆ LANGKAWI TOURIST INFORMATION CENTRE
Tel. 966 7789
Fax 955 1159

## HOTELS

**LANGKAWI ISLAND RESORT**
Pantai Syed Omar
Tel. 916 209
Fax 916 414
*RM160 and above*

**PELANGI BEACH RESORT**
Pantai Cenang
Tel. 955 1001
Fax 955 1122
*RM286–990*

**SEMARAK BEACH RESORT**
Pantai Cenang
Tel. 955 1377
Fax 955 1159
*RM78–250*

# ALOR SETAR

**DIALING CODE**
04 followed by the telephone number

## USEFUL INFORMATION

◆ CULTURAL, ARTS AND TOURISM UNIT,
Kedah State Secretariat
Wisma Negeri
Tel. 772 2088
Fax 771 0467

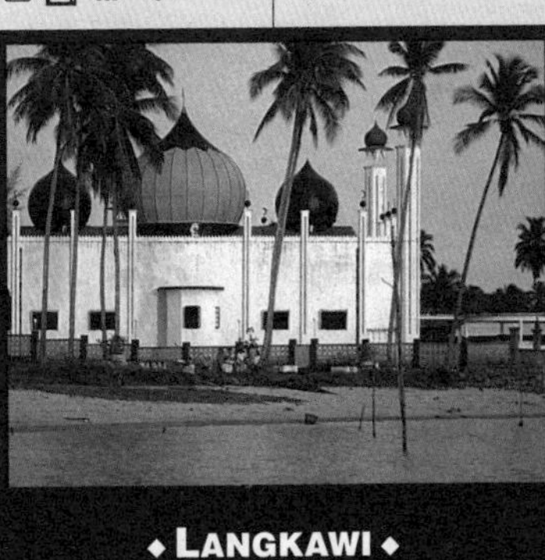

◆ **LANGKAWI** ◆

The mosque at Kuah on Langkawi.

## BANKS

◆ STANDARD CHARTERED
Jalan Raja
Tel. 772 6444

◆ SOUTHERN BANK
Jalan Kota
Tel. 772 9522

## CULTURE

**MUZIUM DI RAJA (KEDAH ROYAL MUSEUM)**
Medan Bandar,
Jalan Raja
Tel. 772 7937
10am–6pm daily;
Fridays 10am–noon;
2.30pm–6pm.
Free admission.
*Royal artifacts and photographs on the Kedah sultanate.*

**MUZIUM NEGERI (KEDAH STATE MUSEUM)**
Lebuhraya Darulaman, Bakar Bata
Tel. 773 1162
Open 10am–6pm daily;
Fri. 9.30am–noon, 2–6pm
Free admission.
*Ethnographic, archeological, and natural-history artifacts; theme exhibitions.*

## HOTELS

**GRAND CONTINENTAL**
134 Jalan Sultan Badlishah
Tel. 733 5917
Fax 733 5161
*RM150–300*

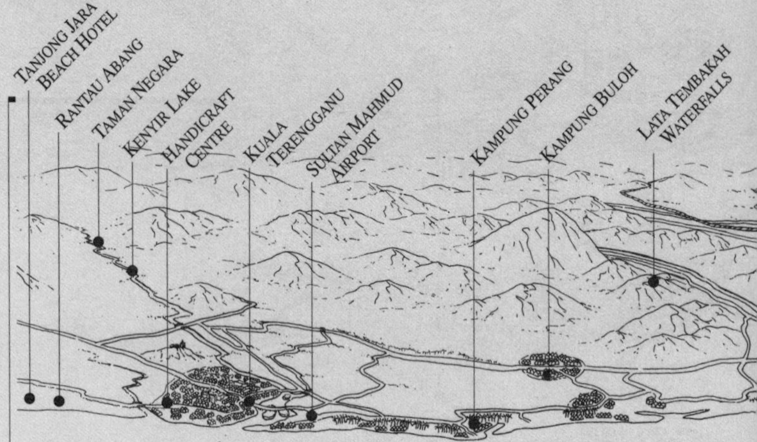


## AROUND KUANTAN

**DIALING CODE**
09 followed by the telephone number, unless otherwise stated.

### USEFUL INFORMATION

**MALAYSIA AIRLINES**
Tel. 514 1218
*Direct flights from Singapore and Kuala Lumpur to Kuantan.*

**BUS SERVICES**
Kuantan–Kuala Lumpur
Kuantan–Kuala Terengganu
Kuantan–Kota Bharu
Tel. 514 1784

**CAR RENTAL**
◆ AVIS
102 Jalan Teluk Sisek
Tel. 523 666, 523 831

**TAXI**
Tel. 504 478

### TOURIST OFFICE

◆ 15th Floor, Kompleks Teruntum, Jalan Mahkota
25000 Kuantan, Pahang
Tel. 622 1893
Fax 622 1791

### CULTURE

**MUSEUM SULTAN ABU BAKAR**
Jalan Sultan Ahmad
26600 Pekan, Pahang
Tel. 421 371.
9.30am–5pm.
Closed Fridays 12.15pm–3pm.
Free admission.
*Treasures from a wrecked Chinese junk and the Pahang royal heritage; ceramics.*

### HOTELS

**HYATT REGENCY KUANTAN**
Teluk Chempedak
Tel. 513 1234
Fax 513 7577
*RM245–880*

**MERLIN INN RESORT**
Teluk Chempedak
(next to Hyatt Regency)
Tel. 514 1388
Fax 513 3001
*RM220–300*

## AROUND KOTA BHARU

**DIALING CODE**
09 followed by the telephone number, unless otherwise stated

### USEFUL INFORMATION

**BUS**
SKMK BUS SERVICES
*Buses at the Jalan Pendek station operate within Kota Bharu. The Langgar, Jalan Pasir Puteh and Jalan Hamzah terminuses are for outbound buses.*

**CAR RENTAL**
◆ MARS KELANTAN INTERNATIONAL TRAVEL
Tel. 744 737

**TRAIN**
WAKAF BHARU STATION
Tel. 796 986
*KTM Timuran Express runs daily (except Monday) services from Singapore to Tumpat and passes through Wakaf Bharu station.*

**TAXI**
Tel. 781 076, 785 624
*Taxis stop at the Jalan Pendek taxi stand. Some taxis may be hired for sightseeing at about RM15 per hour or about RM75 for the whole day.*

### TOURIST OFFICE

◆ JALAN SULTAN IBRAHIM
15050 Kota Bharu
Tel. 748 5534
8am–12.45pm; 2pm–4.30pm.
Closed Thur. and Fri..

### HOTELS

**KENCANA INN**
Jalan Padang Garong
Tel. 744 0944
Fax 744 0181
*RM60, RM75 with TV*

**HOTEL PERDANA**
Jalan Mahmud
Tel. 748 5000
Fax 744 7621
*RM170–600*

**PERDANA RESORT**
Jalan Kuala Pa'Amat
Tel. 774 4000
Fax 774 4980
*RM120–210*

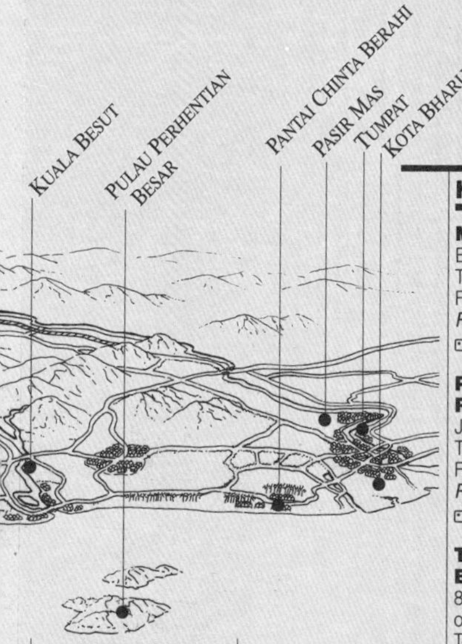


## KUALA TERENGGANU

**DIALING CODE**
09 followed by the telephone number

### USEFUL INFORMATION

**AIR TRAVEL**
◆ AIRPORT INFORMATION
Tel. 626 4500
◆ MAS OFFICE
Tel. 622 2266
*Daily flights from Kuala Lumpur, Penang.*

**TAXI**
Tel. 622 1158

### TOURIST OFFICE

◆ 2243 Ground Floor, Wisma MCIS
Jalan Sultan Zainal Abidin
Tel. 622 1433
Fax 622 1791

### CULTURE

**TERENGGANU STATE MUSEUM**
Jalan Cherong Lanjut
Tel. 622 1444
8am–4pm Sat.–Wed., 8am–12.45pm, Thursdays.
Admission free.
*Historical records, maritime collection, and royal heritage.*

**CENTRAL MARKET**
Next to Sungai Terengganu.
*Fresh produce, brassware, brocade, baskets, batik, souvenirs and trinkets.*

**GELANGGANG SENI (CULTURAL CENTRE)**
Pantai Batu Buruk, Kuala Terengganu
Performances: Thur., Fri. and Sat., 5pm–6.30pm
*Malay games and pastimes, "silat" performances.*

**PULAU DUYUNG BOAT BUILDERS**
*Boat-building based on traditional methods by skilled craftsmen.*

**TURTLE-WATCHING**
INFORMATION CENTRE
Rantau Abang, 35 miles south of Kuala Terengganu
Tel 824 4169
*Turtle egg-laying season May to September.*

### HOTELS

**MOTEL DESA**
Bukit Pak Apil
Tel. 622 3033
Fax 622 3863
*RM115–130*

**PRIMULA BEACH RESORT**
Jalan Persinggahan
Tel. 622 2100
Fax 623 3360
*RM130–1,500*

**TANJONG JARA BEACH HOTEL**
8th mile, off Jalan Dungun
Tel. 844 1801
Fax 844 2653
*RM 260–500*

## PULAU TIOMAN

### USEFUL INFORMATION

**AIR TRAVEL**
◆ PELANGI AIR SDN BHD.
MAS Complex
Subang Airport
Tel. 03-776 555
*Pelangi Air and Silkair operate several daily flights from Kuala Lumpur (1 hour) and Singapore (50 minutes) to Tioman Island.*

**BOAT TRIP**
MERSING BOAT ASSOCIATION
Tel. 07-779 2501

### TOURIST OFFICE

◆ THE TOURIST CENTRE
Mersing, Johor
Tel. 07-779 1204

### HOTELS

**BERJAYA IMPERIAL BEACH RESORT**
Tel. 09-414 5445
Fax 09-414 5718
*RM340–1,200*

**SAMUDRA SWISS COTTAGES**
Tekek Village/ Beach
Tel. 07-214 8728
Fax 07-213 2293
*RM58–78*

## AROUND JOHOR BAHRU

**DIALING CODE**
07 followed by the telephone number

### TOURIST OFFICE

◆ MTPB
#04–01 Tun Abdul Razak Complex
Jalan Wong Ah Fook
80000 Johor Bahru
Tel. 222 3591
Fax 223 5502

### CULTURE

**ROYAL ABU BAKAR MUSEUM**
Istana Besar, Johor Bahru
Tel. 222 0351
9am–5pm
Admission charged.
*Treasures from the royal collection.*

### HOTELS

**HOLIDAY INN/ CROWNE PLAZA JOHOR BAHRU**
Jalan Dato Sulaiman
Century Garden
Tel. 332 3800
Fax 331 8894
*RM 290–2,500*

**THE PUTERI PAN PACIFIC HOTEL**
Jalan Salim
Tel. 233 3333
Fax 223 6622
*RM280–1,500*

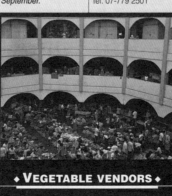

◆ **VEGETABLE VENDORS** ◆

Vegetable vendors, mostly women, form the majority of stallholders at the busy Central Market in Kota Bharu.

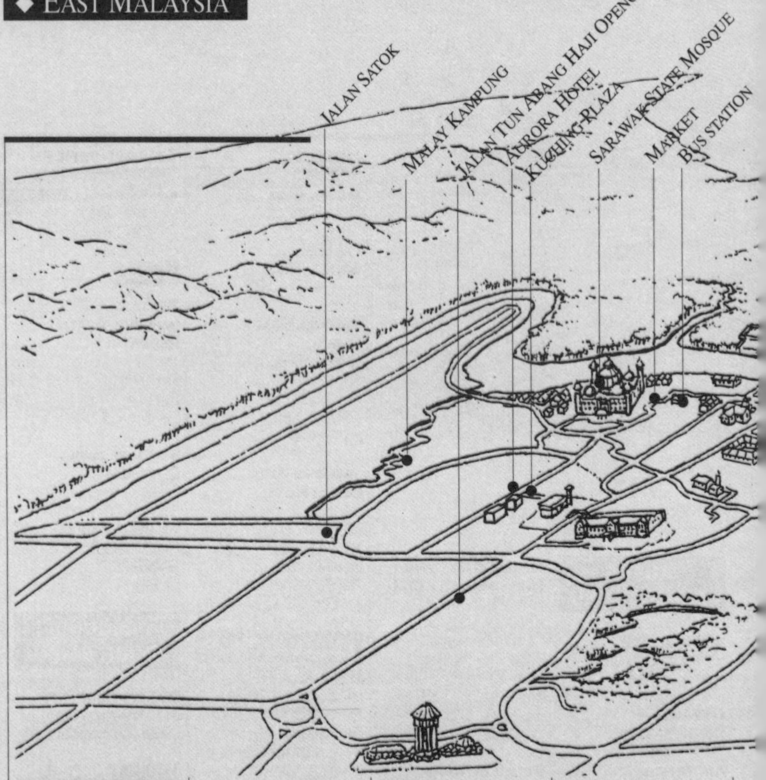

Jalan Satok
Malay Kampung
Jalan Tun Abang Haji Openg
Aurora Hotel
Kuching Plaza
Sarawak State Mosque
Market
Bus Station

## GENERAL

*Visitors to the East Malaysia states of Sarawak and Sabah have to pass through immigration, even if they have just arrived from Peninsular Malaysia. The same requirement also applies to travel between Sabah and Sarawak. A new 60-day permit is issued for Sarawak and a 30-day permit for Sabah. The same permits can be used when re-entering Peninsular Malaysia.*

**HEALTH**
*It is advisable to take precautionary measures such as vaccinations and a course of anti-malaria pills before traveling, especially if you intend to explore the wildlife areas in the two states. A well-equipped first-aid kit is also useful in case of emergency.*

**TIPPING**
*Tipping is not necessary. As is the practise in Peninsular Malaysia, hotels and restaurants automatically add a 10 percent service charge and 5 percent government tax to the bill.*

## KUCHING

**DIALING CODE**
082 followed by the telephone number, unless otherwise stated.

### ◆ FORT MARGHERITA ◆

Built in 1879, the fort served as the headquarters of the Sarawak Constabulary. Today it is a police museum with exhibits of weapons, collections of uniforms, and historical records.

## USEFUL INFORMATION

**NATIONAL PARKS AND WILDLIFE OFFICE**
Wisma Sumber Alam, 93050 Kuching
Tel. 442 180, 442 201
Open 8am–4.15pm Mon.–Fri. (closed for an hour at lunchtime) and 8am–12.45pm Sat.
*No longer issue parking permits.*

**IMMIGRATION OFFICE**
Jalan Simpang Tiga
Tel. 240 301

**HOSPITAL**
Kuching General Hospital
Jalan Tun Abang Haji Openg
Tel. 257 555

**POST OFFICE**
Jalan Tun Abang Haji Openg
Open 8am–6pm, Mon.–Sat., 8am–noon Sun.
Tel. 242 211

**AIR TRAVEL**
◆ BRITISH AIRWAYS
Tel. 242 367
◆ MALAYSIA AIRLINES
Jalan Song Thian Cheok
Tel. 244 144
◆ ROYAL BRUNEI AIRLINES
Rugayah Building
Tel. 243 344
◆ SINGAPORE AIRLINES
Wisma Bukit Mata Kuching
Tel. 240 266
*Malaysia Airlines flies daily to Kuching and Miri from Singapore, Kuala Lumpur, Johor Bahru, and Kota Kinabalu. It operates several daily domestic flights by Kokker 50 and 18-seater Twin Otter to*

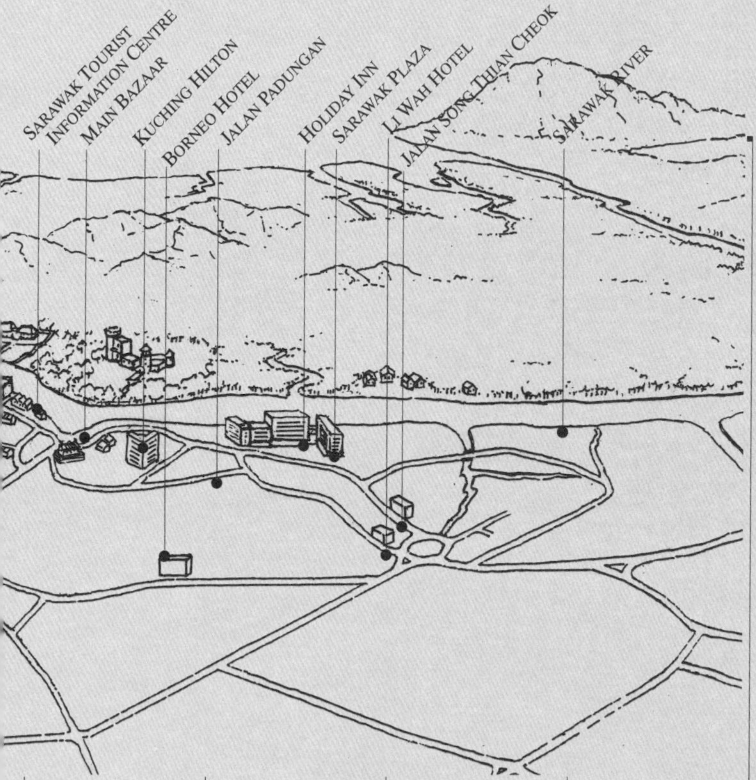

Sarawak Tourist Information Centre
Main Bazaar
Kuching Hilton
Borneo Hotel
Jalan Padungan
Holiday Inn
Sarawak Plaza
Li Wah Hotel
Jalan Song Thian Cheok
Sarawak River

*rural areas, shuttling between Kuching, Sibu, Miri, and Bintulu. There are direct flights to Pontianak, Hong Kong, Tokyo and Seoul from Kuching and Kota Kinabalu.*

**CHARTERED FLIGHTS**

◆ HORNBILL SKYWAYS
Tel. 455 737
*Helicopters and planes can be chartered to remote areas.*

**CAR RENTAL**

◆ AVIS
Holiday Inn Kuching next to Sarawak Plaza
Tel. 411 370

◆ MAHANA RENT-A-CAR
Jalan Borneo, opposite Kuching Hilton
Tel. 411 370, 488 288
*With better roads it is possible to drive yourself from Kuching to Miri.*

**EXPRESS BOATS**

◆ CONCORD MARINE
Metropole Inn Hotel
22, Jalan Green Hill
Tel. 412 551

◆ EXPRES PERTAMA
196 Padungan Road
Tel. 414 735

◆ EXPRES BAHAGIA
50 Padungan Road
Tel. 421 948

◆ FOLLOW ME
Tel. 423 507
*Trips by express boat on various time schedules for the Kuching–Sibu route, with a change-over of boat mid-way at Sarikei wharf. Board at Pending jetty. The 4-hour trip costs RM30. Bookings must be made at least one day in advance. Visitors may also contact the Sarawak Tourist Information Centre for advice.*

**CARGO BOATS**

◆ SIAM COMPANY
Tel. 242 832

◆ SOUTH EAST ASIA SHIPPING
Tel. 336 220

◆ SOUTHERN NAVIGATION
Tel. 242 613

*Regular trips by cargo vessels to Bintulu, Miri, and other Sarawak towns at around RM10.*

**TAXIS**

*Taxis operate between the airport and Kuching town, charging about RM12 for a one-way trip. As it is not the practice for taxis in Kuching to use the meter, passengers should negotiate with the driver before boarding. As a guide, a ride from the market to the wharf is about RM9.*

**BUS**

◆ CHIN LIAN LONG
Tel. 32 766

◆ SARAWAK TRANSPORT COMPANY
Tel. 242 967

*Check on bus fares and services with bus companies or the tourist information center.*

**BANKS**

◆ HONGKONG & SHANGHAI BANKING CORPORATION
Jalan Tun Abang Haji Openg
Tel. 259 111
Open 9.30am–3pm Mon.–Fri., 9.30–11.30am Sat. Closed Sun. and public holidays.

## TOURIST OFFICES

◆ MTPB
Rugayah Building
Jalan Song Thian Cheok,
93100 Kuching
Tel. 246 575, 246 775
Fax. 246 442

◆ SARAWAK TOURISM BOARD
#3, 44 Wisma Satok
Open 8am–9pm daily
Tel. 423 600
Fax 416 700

◆ SARAWAK TOURIST INFORMATION CENTRE
Mosque Road
Tel. 410 942
*Apply here for National Park permits and accommodation reservations.*

## SHOPPING

**JALAN SATOK**
*The street bazaar at Jalan Satok runs from Saturday afternoon till late evening, resuming early Sunday morning. Plants, antiques, toys, handicrafts, garments, and medicinal herbs.*

## EXCURSIONS

◆ ASIA OVERLAND
286 West Wood Park
Jalan Tabuah, Kuching
Tel. 251 162
Fax 251 178
◆ BORNEO ADVENTURE
55 Main Bazaar
Tel. 245 175
◆ CPH TRAVEL AGENCIES
70 Padungan Road
Tel. 243 708
◆ IBANIKA EXPEDITION
411A, 4th Floor,
Wisma Saberkas,
Tel. 424 022
◆ SINGAI TRAVEL SERVICE
Jalan Chan Chin Ann
Tel. 420 918
*Trips to longhouses and national parks are conducted by several tour operators. It is advisable to compare fares beforehand.*

**BOAT CRUISES**
Enquire at Holiday Inn Kuching.
Tel. 247 763
*Romantic three-hour sunset cruises down the Sarawak River to Santubong, on board MV "Equatorial", 5pm to 8.30pm.*

## CULTURE

**POLICE MUSEUM**
Fort Margherita
Open 9.15am–5pm
Closed Mon.
Admission free.
*Bring IC, it's inside the Police School.*

**SARAWAK STATE MUSEUM**
Jalan Tun Abang Haji
Open 9.15am–5pm, Sat.–Thur. Closed Fri.
Tel. 258 388, 244 232.
Admission free.
*Reputably one of the best museums in Asia. Tribal artifacts and heritage collection, whale skeletons and brassware.*

## RESTAURANTS

**GOLDEN DRAGON**
Central Road
Tel. 425 236

**KOREANA KOREAN RESTAURANT**
H5/G Jalan Borneo
Tamasri
Tel. 255 072

**LOK THIAN**
Pending Road
Tel. 331 310

**MEISAN RESTAURANT**
Holiday Inn Kuching
Tel. 423 111

## HOTELS

**BORNEO HOTEL**
30C–F Tabuan Road, near Reservoir Park
Tel. 244 121
Fax 254 848
*RM110–290*

**HOLIDAY INN**
Jalan Tunku Abdul Rahman
Tel. 423 111
Fax 428 911
*RM200–1,350*

**KUCHING HILTON**
Jalan Tunku Abdul Rahman
Tel. 248 200, 248 201
Fax. 482 984
*RM290–2,650*

**LIWAH HOTEL**
Lot 187, Section 47
Jalan Song Thian Cheok
Tel. 429 222
Fax 423 690
*RM80–100*

# AROUND KUCHING

**DIALING CODE**
082 followed by the telephone number.

## CULTURE

**SARAWAK CULTURAL VILLAGE**
Near the beach resorts of Damai
Tel. 422 411
Open 9am–5.30pm
Admission RM45 adult, RM25 child.
*Also known as the Living Museum, the village is set in a 14-acre tropical forest at the base of Mount Santubong. Highlights of exhibits include longhouse models, Chinese and Malay houses, tribal artifacts, blowpipe-making, sago processing, handicrafts demonstration; cultural shows; souvenirs.*

## PARKS

*Obtain permits from Sarawak Tourist Information Centre, Kuching Tel. 410 941.*

**CAMP PERMAI SARAWAK**
Menara SEDC, Jalan Tuanku Abdul Rahman, 83100 Kuching
Tel. 416 777, 428 602
Fax 244 585, 243 716.
*45 acres of tropical rainforest with jungle streams, beach, and a spectacular view of Mount Santubong. The site is near Sarawalk Cultural Village and about 16 miles from Kuching.*

**BAKO NATIONAL PARK**
Tel. 246 477
(bungalow/hostel accommodation)
*Take a 45-minute bus ride (RM3, round trip) from the Kuching bus station near Electra House to Bako village. Buses depart hourly. Continue the journey on a 30-minute speedboat ride (RM25) from the village to the park. Flora and fauna over 18 miles of eight well-marked trails; mangrove swamps. Wildlife includes long-tailed macaques, monitor lizards, hornbills, and proboscis monkeys.*

## HOTEL

**HOLIDAY INN DAMAI BEACH RESORT**
Santubong
Tel. 846 999
Fax. 846 049
*RM280–RM1250*

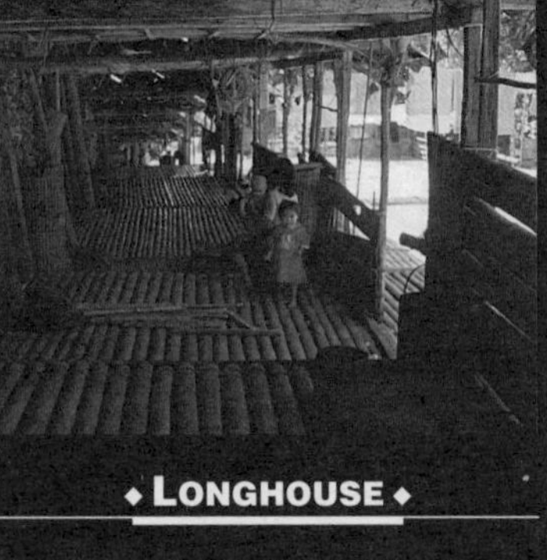

**◆ LONGHOUSE ◆**

The roomy interior of a Bidayuh longhouse located off the Kuching–Serian highway. Some longhouses provide overnight accommodation for visitors.

## SIBU, BINTULU, AND MIRI

### USEFUL INFORMATION

**AIRLINES**

◆ MALAYSIA AIRLINES SIBU OFFICE:
61 Jalan Tuanku Abdul Rahman, Sibu
Tel. 084-326 155
8am–5pm. Mon.–Fri., 8am–noon, Sat., and 9am–11am, Sun..

◆ BINTULU OFFICE:
Jalan Masjid, Bintulu
Tel. 086-331 554
8.30am–4.30pm. Mon.–Fri., 8am–3.30pm Sat., 8.30am–12.30pm Sun.

**BOAT TRIPS**

◆ EXPRES PERTAMA
14 Khoo Peng Loong Road, Sibu
Tel. 084-335 055

◆ EXPRES BAHAGIA
20A Blacksmith Road, Sibu
Tel. 084-319 228.

◆ FOLLOW ME
23 Jalan Maju, Sibu
Tel. 084-324 184.

◆ CONCORD MARINE
1 Bank Road, Sibu
Tel. 084-331 593.

**BUS TRIPS**

*A trip from Sibu to Bintulu on an air-conditioned bus takes 4 hours and costs RM18; to Miri, via Batu Niah, it takes 8 hours and the fare is RM35. The first bus leaves the station near the esplanade at Khoo Peng Loong Road in Sibu at 6am. There are also two other services later in the morning.*

### PARKS

*Contact National Parks and Wildlife (Miri office tel. 085-333 61, Kuching office, tel. 082-248 088) in advance for entry permits, tour guides, and overnight stays in the parks.*

**NIAH NATIONAL PARK AND NIAH CAVES**

*7848 acres of forest reserves and a network of limestone caves, including the Great Cave – one of the largest in the world.*

**MOUNT MULU NATIONAL PARK**

*Sarawak's largest park, covering 210 square miles of montane forests, limestone caves, and swamps. Tour guides available at RM30 per day.*

### HOTELS

**(IN SIBU) GARDEN HOTEL**
1 Hua Ping Road
Tel. 084-317 888
*RM60–80*

**LI HUA HOTEL**
Long Bridge Commercial Centre
Tel. 084-324 000
Fax 326 272
*RM80–200*

**PREMIER HOTEL**
Jalan Kampong Nyabor
Tel. 084-323 222
Fax 323 399
*RM120–160*

**HOTEL ZUHRA**
Jalan Kampung Nyabor
Tel. 084-310 711
Fax 320 712
*RM60–90*

**(IN BINTULU) ROYAL HOTEL**
Jalan Pedada/Jalan Abang Galau
Tel. 086-332 166
Fax 334 028
*RM100–120*

**PLAZA HOTEL**
116 Taman Sri Dayang
Tel. 086-335 111
Fax 086-332 742
*RM160–1,515*

**(IN MIRI) PARK HOTEL**
Jalan Raja
Tel. 085-414 555
Fax 085-414 488
*RM140–400*

**HOTEL PLAZA REGENCY**
47 Jalan Brooke
Tel. 085-413 113
Fax 085-414 458
*From RM80*

## KOTA KINABALU

**DIALING CODE**

088 followed by the telephone number.

### USEFUL INFORMATION

**AIRLINES**

◆ BRITISH AIRWAYS
19 Jalan Haji Saman
Tel. 585 11

◆ CATHAY PACIFIC
Kuwara Complex
Tel. 547 33

◆ MALAYSIA AIRLINES
Karamunsing Complex
Jalan Tunku Abdul Rahman
Tel. 514 55
*Daily flights to/from Kota Kinabalu. Some domestic flights are serviced by the airline's 12-seater Twin Otter.*

**TAXIS**

Tel. 521 13, 563 46, 521 48, 526 69
*Taxis operate around the shopping areas downtown. They charge RM1.40 for the first kilometer and RM1 for each subsequent kilometer. Enterprising taxi drivers may want to bargain with passengers before the trip.*

**BUS SERVICES**

*Minibuses service Kota Kinabalu and the towns and villages around it. Bus trips are regular and economical, and drivers willingly pick up and let off passengers along the route.*

**CAR RENTAL**

◆ E&C LIMOUSINE SERVICES
1st Floor, Lot 6, Block J, Segama Complex, Jalan Datuk Salleh Sulong
Tel. 576 79, 221 466

◆ KINABALU RENT-A-CAR
Lot 3–61, 3rd Floor, Karamunsing Complex
Jalan Tunku Abdul Rahman
Tel. 232 602, 219 888

◆ TRAVEL RENT-A-CAR
Lot G20, Ground Floor, Wisma Sabah
Jalan Haji Saman
Tel. 568 38, 222 708
Fax 221 751

### TOURIST OFFICES

◆ SABAH TOURISM PROMOTION CORPORATION
51 Jalan Gaya
Tel. 218 620, 212 121, 219 311 or 219 400
Fax 212 075

◆ TOURISM DEVELOPMENT CORPORATION, SABAH
1 Jalan Segunting
Wing On Life Building
88000 Kota Kinabalu
Tel. 248 698, 211 732
Fax 241 764
8am–12.45pm, 2pm–4.15pm Mon.–Fri., 8am–12.45pm Sat.

◆ SABAH PARKS OFFICE
Lot 3, Block K, Sinsurah Complex, Jalan Tun Faud Stephens
88806 Kota Kinabalu
Tel. 211 881, 211 652
Fax 221 001

**◆ MOUNT SANTUBONG ◆**

At 2740 feet high, Mount Santubong overlooks a neat row of kampung houses near the Sarawak River.

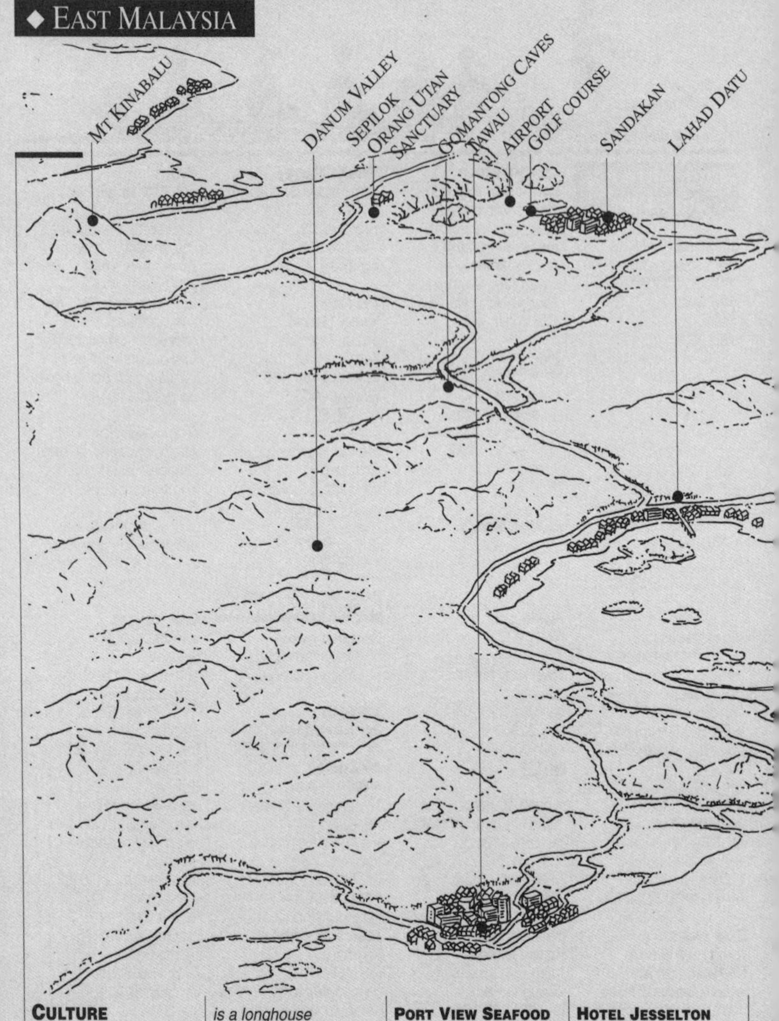


## CULTURE

**THE BRITISH COUNCIL**
Wing On Life Building
1 Jalan Segunting
Tel. 540 56
*Well-stocked library.*

**SABAH STATE MUSEUM**
Jalan Tuanku Abdul Rahman
Tel. 531 99
10am–6pm Mon.–Thur.;
9am–6pm weekends and holidays.
Admission free
*This museum, housed within an eye-catching fishbone-structure building, contains historical and tribal artifacts and a collection of old photographs. The museum also has an art gallery, a Science Centre and a Multivision theater. Next to the museum is a longhouse complex with exhibits such as household implements and traditional farm tools.*

## RESTAURANTS

**RESTAURANT BILAL**
Segama Shopping Complex, Jalan Datuk Salleh Sulong
Tel. 571 93
*South Indian roti canai and curry dishes.*

**GARDENIA STEAK AND LOBSTER RESTAURANT**
69 Jalan Gaya
Tel. 223 333.
*Western and seafood.*

**NAN XING RESTAURANT**
Jalan Pantai
Tel. 212 900.
*Cantonese specialties.*

**PORT VIEW SEAFOOD**
Jalan Haji Saman
Tel 242 875.
*Local seafood dishes.*

**ROCKY'S FUN PUB/CAFÉ**
1st Floor, Lot 52, Jalan Gaya
Tel. 221 643.
*Trendy fast-food outlet by day; discotheque by night.*

**SENTOSA RESTAURANT**
Lot 1, Block B, Sinsuran Complex.
Tel. 211 658.
*Reasonably good and economical local food.*

## HOTELS

**HOTEL CAPITAL**
23 Jalan Haji Saman
Tel. 231 999
Fax 237 222
*RM160–200*

**HOTEL JESSELTON**
69 Jalan Gaya
Tel. 223 333
Fax 240 401
*RM220–310*

**MAY PLAZA HOTEL**
Jalan Datuk Salleh Sulong
Tel. 215 418
*RM70*

**HYATT KINABALU**
Jalan Datuk Salleh Sulong
Tel. 221 234
Fax 225 972
*RM310–1,250*

**KINABALU PARK**
Sabah Parks Office, Kota Kinabalu
Tel. 211 585
Fax 221 001
*Chalets and cabins with cooking facilities. RM10–250 (student), RM3 (hostel)*

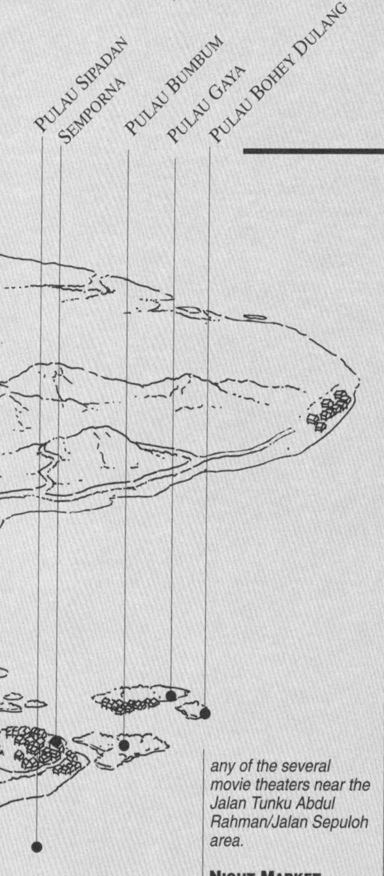


**PALACE HOTEL**
1 Jalan Tangi,
Karamunsing
Tel. 211 911
Fax 211 600.
*RM150–360*

**HOTEL SHANGRILA**
Bandaran Berjaya
Tel. 212 800
Fax 212 078.
*RM160–450*

**TANJUNG ARU BEACH HOTEL**
Jalan Ari, Tanjung Aru
Tel. 225 800
Fax 217 155.
*RM295–1,500*

## NIGHTLIFE

**CULTURAL PERFORMANCES**
MALAY KAMPUNG SHOW
Tanjung Aru Beach
Resort Hotel
Tel. 587 11

**MOVIE THEATERS**
*Movie buffs can catch the latest releases at any of the several movie theaters near the Jalan Tunku Abdul Rahman/Jalan Sepuloh area.*

**NIGHT MARKET**
*The Night Market on the waterfront is worth visiting.*

## SANDAKAN

**DIALING CODE**
089 followed by the telephone number, unless otherwise stated.

## USEFUL INFORMATION

**AIR TRAVEL**
◆ MALAYSIA AIRLINES
Sabah Building
Tel. 273 996
8am–4.30pm
Mondays–Fridays;
8am–3pm Saturdays;
8am–noon, Sundays.
*Daily domestic flights by national carrier Malaysia Airlines to and from Sandakan.*

## TOURIST OFFICE

**SABAH PARKS OFFICE**
Consult the office in
Kota Kinabalu.
Tel. 088-211 881
or 211 652
Fax 088-221 001

## EXCURSIONS

**WILDLIFE EXPEDITIONS**
Ground Floor, Ramada
Renaissance Hotel,
Jalan Utara
Tel. 273 093
Fax 214 299
*Guided tours to Sepilok Orang Utan Sanctuary, Gomantong Caves and Turtle Islands Park.*

## CULTURE

**SEPILOK ORANG UTAN SANCTUARY**
About 15 miles from Sandakan. Take the local bus to Sepilok from the bus stop near the central market
*Sprawling 14,000 acres of forest reserves; also houses the Information Nature Education Centre, mini-museum and small theater. Feeding times for the apes at 10am, 11am, and 2.30pm. Admission RM10. There is no charge for cameras but an RM10 levy for video recorders.*

◆ **SABAH STATE MUSEUM** ◆

The structural design of the museum in Kota Kinabalu easily catches the visitor's eye.

## RESTAURANTS

**MING RESTAURANT**
Ramada Renaissance
Jalan Utara
Tel. 213 299
*Dim sum and Cantonese cuisine.*

**XO STEAK HOUSE**
Hsiang Garden Estate
opposite Hsiang
Garden Hotel
Tel. 440 33
*Grill steak and seafood.*

## HOTELS

**HOTEL CITY VIEW**
Lot 1, Block 23,
Jalan Tiga
Tel. 271 122
Fax 273 115
*RM120–140*

**HOTEL NAK**
Edinburgh Street
Tel. 272 988
Fax 272 879
*RM85–115*

**RAMADA RENAISSANCE**
Jalan Utara
Tel. 213 299
Fax 271 271
*RM250–270*

**HOTEL RAMAI**
Tel. 273 222
*RM100*
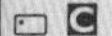

**HOTEL SIANG GARDEN**
Leila Road
Tel. 273 122
Fax 273 127
*RM80–110*

## GENERAL

*Visitors from Malaysia, Singapore, Indonesia, US and UK can stay for up to 30 days without a visa. Visitors from Belgium, Canada, Denmark, France, Germany, Japan, Lichtenstein, Luxemburg, Maldives, Netherlands, Norway, Philippines, South Korea, Sweden, Switzerland and Thailand are exempted from visas for visits of up to 14 days.*

**CURRENCY AND EXCHANGE RATES**
*Currency used is the Brunei dollar (B$), in denominations of B$1, B$5, B$10, B$50, B$100, B$500, B$1000, and B$10,000. Coins are in denominations of 1, 5, 10, 20, and 50 cents. The Brunei dollar is at par with the Singapore dollar.*

## BANDAR SERI BEGAWAN

**DIALING CODE**
02 followed by the telephone number.

### USEFUL INFORMATION

**AMBULANCE**
Tel. 222 366

**POLICE ASSISTANCE**
Tel. 222 333
or 242 334

**POSTAL SERVICES**
Jalan Elizabeth Dua
Tel. 243 101
*Post offices are open from 7.45am to 4.30pm daily. Closed on Friday and Sunday.*

**FLIGHT INFORMATION**
Tel. 331 747
*Royal Brunei Airlines flies to Bandar Seri Begawan daily from Singapore, and Monday, Tuesday, Friday and Sunday from Kuala Lumpur.*

**AIRLINES**
◆ ROYAL BRUNEI AIRLINES
RBA Plaza, Jalan Sultan
Bandar Seri Begawan
Tel. 242 222 or 225 931
Fax 244 737
◆ MALAYSIAN AIRLINES
144 Jalan Pemancha
Tel. 224 141
◆ SINGAPORE AIRLINES
Jalan Sultan
Tel. 227 253

**WATER TAXI (BOAT)**
*Water taxis ply the Brunei River between the extensive Kampong Ayer settlement and Temburong. Fares between 50 cents and B$2 per passenger.*

**TAXI**
Tel. 222 214, 226 853
*Taxis charge B$3 for the first kilometer and 20 cents for each additional 200 meters (220 yards). A levy of B$5 for a trip to/from the ariport is added to the fare. There is also a B$3 levy for telephone reservation.*

**CAR RENTAL**
◆ AVIS
Block 4, Hasbullah Building, 4 Jalan Gadong
Tel. 242 284
◆ AZIZAH CAR RENTALS
National Car Systems
1st Floor, Hasbullah Building, 4 Jalan Gadong
Tel. 224 921

**BANKS**
*Banks open from 9am to 3pm on weekdays and 9am to 11am on Saturdays.*

◆ INTERNATIONAL BANK OF BRUNEI (IBB)
Jalan Roberts
Tel. 220 286
◆ CITIBANK NA
Jalan Sultan
Tel. 243 983
◆ HONGKONG AND SHANGHAI BANKING CORPORATION
Jalan Roberts
Tel. 242 305

### TOURIST INFORMATION

**INFORMATION COUNTER**
Brunei International Airport
Tel. 317 94

**PUBLIC RELATIONS**, Information Division, Ministry of Culture, Youth and Sports, Brunei Darussalam.
Tel. 225 803

### CULTURE

**MUSEUMS**
General inquiries:
Tel. 244 545

**BANGUAN ALAT KEBESARAN DI RAJA**
(formerly WINSTON CHURCHILL MEMORIAL)
Jalan Sultan
Admission free.
*Exhibition hall displaying royal coronation carriage, the royal crown, historical documents and pictures on the proclamation of the 1959 constitution; gallery on the life of the sultan of Brunei Darussalam.*

**THE BRUNEI MUSEUM AND THE MALAY TECHONOLOGY MUSEUM**
Kota Batu, 4 miles from Bandar Seri Begawan. Taxi ride from the city costs about B$6.
10am–5pm Tue.–Sun., 10am–11.30am, 2.30pm–5pm Fri..
Admission free.
*Collection of 15th-century treasures, ceramics, oil paintings, musical instruments. Nearby is the Malay Technology Museum housing architectural models, fishing and agricultural implements.*

### RESTAURANTS

**PONDOK SARI WANGI**
Abdul Razak Complex
Jalan Gadong
Tel. 445 043
*Delectable Indonesian cuisine.*

**STADIUM RESTAURANT**
Stadium Negara
Hassanal Bolkiah
Tel. 244 858
*Dim sum.*

### HOTELS

**ANG'S HOTEL**
Jalan Tasek Lama
Tel. 243 553
Fax 227 302
*B$160–200*

**BRUNEI HOTEL**
95 Jalan Pemancha
Tel. 242 372
Fax 226 196
*B$160–400*

**THE CROWNE PRINCESS**
Jalan Tutong
Tel. 241 128
Fax 241 138
*B$110–350*

**RIVERVIEW HOTEL**
Jalan Gadong
Tel. 238 238
Fax 237 999
*B$110–550*

**SHERATON UTAMA**
Jalan Bendahara
Tel. 244 272
Fax 221 579
*B$210–1,400*

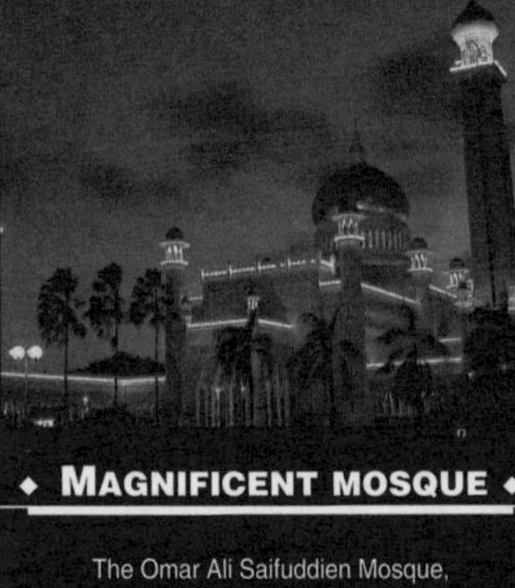

**◆ MAGNIFICENT MOSQUE ◆**

The Omar Ali Saifuddien Mosque, built in 1958, is a landmark in Bandar Seri Begawan.

**PRONUNCIATION NOTE:**
a = a, as in arm
c = ch, as in chair
e = e, as in mermaid
u = oo, as in book
g = hard g, as in get

**ESSENTIALS**
I/me : *saya*
we : *kami/kita*
you : *awak (informal)*
he/she : *dia*
they : *mereka*
what? : *apa?*
who? : *siapa?*
when? : *bila?*
where? : *di mana?*
how? : *bagaimana?*
why? : *mengapa?*
this : *ini*
that : *itu*
here : *di sini*
there : *di sana/di situ*
from : *dari*
to (a place) : *ke*

**USEFUL WORDS**
help : *tolong*
to meet : *bertemu*
to come : *mari/datang*
to go : *pergi*
to enter : *masuk*
to leave : *keluar*
to sit : *dudok*
to stand : *diri*
to rest : *rehat*
to read : *baca*
to see : *nampak*
to look : *tengok*
to change : *tukar*
to bathe : *mandi*
to wait : *tunggu/nanti*
to sleep : *tidur*
to arrive : *tiba/sampai*
early : *siang/awal*
late : *lambat*
far : *jauh*
near : *dekat*
hot : *panas*
cold : *sejuk*
sick : *sakit*
fever : *demam*
headache : *kepala pening/kepala sakit*
stomach ache : *sakit perut*
garden : *kebun*
house : *rumah*
room : *bilik*
television : *televisyen*
book : *buku*
newspaper : *surat khabar*

**GREETINGS**
How are you? : *Apa khabar?*
I'm fine, thank you : *Khabar baik, terima kasih.*
You are welcome : *Sama sama.*
Good morning : *Selamat pagi.*
Good afternoon : *Selamat tengah hari.*
Good evening : *Selamat petang.*
Good night : *Selamat malam*
Bon voyage/Goodbye: *Selamat jalan* (spoken by host) / *Selamat tinggal* (spoken by guest).

**GENERAL**
Excuse me : *Ma'afkan saya.*
Yes : *Ya.*
No : *Tidak/Bukan.*
My name is... : *Nama saya...*
I come from... : *Saya datang dari...*
May I use the phone? : *Boleh kah saya gunakan telefon?*
I want to speak to... : *Saya hendak berchakap dengan...*
I am sorry : *Saya minta ma'af.*

**DINING**
hungry : *lapar*
thirsty : *haus*
restaurant : *restoran*
coffee shop : *kedai kopi*
table : *meja*
chair : *kerusi*
menu : *menu*
food : *makanan*
drink : *minuman*
to eat : *makan*
to drink : *minum*
coffee : *kopi*
tea : *teh*
sugar : *gula*
milk : *susu*
coffee with milk : *kopi susu*
coffee with sugar : *kopi O*
tea with milk : *teh susu*
tea with sugar : *teh O*
sweet : *manis*
hot water : *air panas*
ice water : *air sejuk*
potato: *kentang*
onion : *bawang*
soup : *sup*
meat : *daging*
chicken : *ayam*
beef : *daging lembu*
mutton : *daging kambing*
pork : *daging babi*
fish : *ikan*
prawn : *udang*
crab : *kepiting*
vegetables : *sayur*
seafood : *makanan laut*
bread : *roti*
egg : *telor*
beans : *kacang*
fried noodles : *mee goreng*
fried rice : *nasi goreng*
fruits : *buah-buahan*
bill : *bil*

**SHOPPING**
shopping center : *pusat beli-belah*
shop : *kedai*
market : *pasar*
shirt : *baju*
cloth : *kain*
shoes : *kasut*
bag : *beg*
price : *harga*
money : *wang/duit*
to buy : *beli*
to sell : *jual*
to change : *tukar*
expensive : *mahal*
good : *bagus/baik*
defective : *rosak*
color : *warna*
small : *kecil*
big : *besar*
long : *panjang*
short : *pendek*
How much? : *Berapa?*
This is too costly : *Ini paling mahal.*
Have you something cheaper? : *Adakah yang lebeh murah?*
I'll come back later : *Saya akan datang kemudian.*

**GETTING AROUND**
country : *negeri*
city : *bandar*
beach : *pantai*
sea : *laut*
river : *sungai*
bridge : *jembatan*
road : *jalanraya*
building : *bangunan*
office : *pejabat*
shop : *kedai*
vehicle/car : *kereta*
telephone : *telefon*
bus stop : *perhentian bas*
taxi stand : *perhentian teksi*
railway station : *stesen kereta api*
hospital : *hospital*
toilet : *ketandas*
post office : *pejabat pos*
letter (mail) : *surat*
postage stamp : *setem*
where to? : *ke-mana?*
I want to go to... : *Saya hendak ke-...*
How far is it? : *Berapa jauh?*
How long is it? : *Berapa lama?*
Turn right : *Belok kanan.*
Turn left : *Belok kiri*
Go straight : *Jalan terus.*
Please stop here : *Tolong berhenti di sini.*
Could you please take me to...? : *Boleh kah encik bawa saya ke...?*
Where do I get off? : *Di mana kah boleh saya turun?*
North : *Utara*
South : *Selatan*
East : *Timor*
West : *Barat*

**NUMBERS**
0 : *kosong*
1 : *satu*
2 : *dua*
3 : *tiga*
4 : *empat*
5 : *lima*
6 : *enam*
7 : *tujoh*
8 : *lapan*
9 : *sembilan*
10 : *sepuloh*
11 : *sebelas*
12 : *dua belas*
13 : *tiga belas*
14 : *empat belas*
15 : *lima belas*
20 : *dua puloh*
30 : *tiga puloh*
100 : *seratus*
200 : *dua ratus*
1000 : *seribu*
5000 : *lima ribu*
10,000 : *sepuloh ribu*
100,000 : *seratus ribu*
1,000,000 : *sejuta*

**TIME**
day : *hari*
time : *waktu/masa*
hour : *jam*
minute : *minit*
second : *sa'at*
What time is it? : *Sekarang pukul berapa?*
8 o'clock : *pukul lapan*
two hours : *dua jam*

**CALENDAR**
Monday : *hari Isnin*
Tuesday : *hari Selasa*
Wednesday : *hari Rabu*
Thursday : *hari Khamis*
Friday : *hari Juma'at*
Saturday : *hari Sabtu*
Sunday : *hari Ahad*
today : *hari ini*
yesterday : *kelmarin*
tomorrow : *besok/esok*
day after tomorrow : *rusa*
week : *minggu*
month : *bulan*
year : *tahun*

**FAMILY**
family : *keluarga*
female : *perempuan*
male : *lelaki*
mother : *ibu/emak*
father : *ayah/bapa*
child : *anak*

◆ ***Adat*** : a Malay code of ethics.

◆ ***Baju*** : shirt; *baju kurung* is a long-sleeved tunic.

◆ ***Bak Kut Teh*** : pork rib herbal soup taken with rice as a meal.

◆ ***Batik*** : traditional art of fabric design using wax, either with a printing block or a wax pen.

◆ ***Bidang*** : a short tubular skirt worn by the Iban women of Sarawak.

◆ ***Bharata Natyam*** : an Indian dance form, originated in Tamil Nadu, southern India.

◆ ***Bomoh*** : a village exorcist.

◆ ***Bulan Puasa*** : see Ramadan.

◆ ***Canting*** : manuscript pen look-alike made of bamboo for dipping into wax, and applying batik designs onto cloth.

◆ ***Chakare*** : Chinese puppet show.

◆ ***Cheongsam*** : a traditional one-piece tight-fitting dress worn by Chinese women of all ages.

◆ ***Chettiar*** : Indian money-lenders.

◆ ***Curry Puff*** : deep-fried pastry with curry paste and fillings of egg, potato, and chicken; a convenient take-away snack for many.

◆ ***Destar*** : stiffened folded handkerchief worn as a headdress by Bajau horsemen.

◆ ***Dhoby*** : laundry. Indian *dhoby* men were a common sight around Singapore's Dhoby Ghaut in the 19th century. They washed linens and clothes by the river, now a canal facing the National Museum at Stamford Road.

◆ ***Durian*** : prickly tropical fruit with thick creamy flesh; favorite of many locals.

◆ ***Er-hu*** : a two-stringed violin.

◆ ***Feng Shui*** : Chinese geomancy.

◆ ***Godai*** : musical road show with skits usually held in conjunction with *wayang* performances during the Hungry Ghosts Festival around August/September.

◆ ***Gopuram*** : a distinctive feature of the Hindu temple, it is a tapering tower with many colorful carvings around its sides of Hindu gods and goddesses in various poses.

◆ ***Hasta*** : finger gestures which tell a story in an Indian dance.

◆ ***Hong Bao*** : a red packet which contains dollar notes, given away for good luck by family elders during Chinese New Year and by guests at Chinese weddings to the bridal couple.

◆ ***Ice Kachang*** : a dessert of finely crushed ice topped with red beans, sago, seaweed, maize, jelly, evaporated milk, and colored syrup.

◆ ***Ikan Bilis*** : small anchovy-like fish.

◆ ***Istana*** : palace, usually the official residence of the head of state or a sultan.

◆ ***Jamu*** : a herbal preparation from Indonesia.

◆ ***Jong Sarat*** : sarongs of gold cloth.

◆ ***Kain Songket*** : silk fabric with intricate embroidered designs, usually made into a suit worn on special occasions such as a wedding.

◆ ***Kaki Lima*** : five-foot way – a sheltered pedestrian walkway lining a row of shophouses.

◆ ***Kalimah Shahadah***: Islamic Declaration of Faith taken by Muslim as an act of affirmation.

◆ ***Kathak*** : a northern India dance form.

◆ ***Kavadi*** : a metal cage with spikes decorated with peacock plumes, carried by the Hindu devotee as an act of thanksgiving or as a plea for forgiveness before Lord Subramaniam. On Thaipusam, a procession of male *kavadi* carriers – barefooted and in a trance – parade the streets from one Hindu temple to another, accompanied by family members and friends.

◆ ***Kelinga Mee*** : noodles and fried seafood with sauce made from sweet potato and tamarind. Sold by hawkers along the Penang waterfront.

◆ ***Kepala*** : the human head. In traditional Malay attire, the word refers to an 18-inch scarf with elaborate designs, wrapped over the trousers at the waist.

◆ ***Keropok*** : fish or prawn crackers, eaten as a snack or added to some Malay dishes such as *gado gado* and *tahu goreng*.

◆ ***Ketupat*** : plain rice compacted into small dumplings and leaf-wrapped, complement to *satay* and peanut gravy.

◆ ***Kopi*** : coffee with milk.

◆ ***Kopi Kosong*** : coffee without milk or sugar.

◆ ***Kopi O*** : coffee with sugar.

◆ ***Kopi Tiam*** : Hokkien (a Chinese dialect) for coffee shop.

◆ ***Kramat*** : Malay for tomb.

◆ ***Kris*** : a dagger with a wavy blade, considered by many Malays as a sacred heirloom.

◆ ***Latex*** : thick milky liquid from the rubber tree for onward processing into rubber products, such as shoes and tires.

◆ ***Lebuhraya*** : Malay for expressway.

◆ ***Lijeng*** : a 35-foot-high and 3-foot-wide column of tribal burial structure in Sarawak. It contains the bones and remains of a tribal chief and those of his followers. Other forms of burial structure are the *Kelirieng* and the *Salong*. Made from ironwood, they have intricate carvings.

◆ ***Malai*** : perfumed garlands sold in Indian shops.

◆ ***Masjid*** : Arabic for mosque.

◆ ***Mausim*** : Arabic for season *(musim* in Malay) from which the word monsoon is derived.

◆ ***Merdeka*** : Malay for Independence.

◆ ***Moyang*** : ancestors.

◆ ***Mridanga*** : cylindrical drum with strings, a major component of the Indian orchestra.

◆ ***Mui Tsai*** : young girl sold off as a domestic slave to a wealthy family.

◆ ***Munshi*** : a language teacher during the colonial era in Malaya.

◆ ***Murtabak*** : Indian-style omelette pizza topped with hot and spicy minced mutton and onion fillings; may be eaten with curry gravy as an option.

◆ ***Nattuvanar*** : Indian lead singers.

◆ ***Nasi Kandar*** : literally yoke rice. The name was coined in the days when rice and dishes were carried in trays hung from a pole suspended on the shoulder yokes of an itinerant hawker.

◆ ***Nasi Padang*** : rice with small servings of hot and spicy dishes.

◆ ***Nobat*** : musical instruments of an orchestra performing before the royal family.

◆ ***Nyonya Kueh*** : assorted sweet starchy cakes of various flavors, shapes and colors, some coated with ground coconut. They serve as popular local snacks.

◆ ***Odissi*** : a classical dance form performed by Indian women.

◆ ***Orang Asli*** : aboriginal inhabitants of Peninsular Malaysia.

◆ ***Orang utan*** : ape-like forest inhabitant.

◆ ***Padang*** : Malay for field. The word is used to name two spacious city greens – one in Singapore and the other in Kuala Lumpur – which have been the pitch for many cricket matches as well as a venue for national day parades.

◆ ***Padi*** : pronounced "pah dee", Malay equivalent of the term "rice paddy".

◆ ***Parang*** : long knife.

◆ ***Penghulu*** : Malay village chieftain.

◆ ***Peranakan*** : a Straits-born Chinese *Baba* (male) and *Nyonya* (female); descendant of several generations of merchants from China who traded and settled in Malaya, and later married Malay women in the peninsula. Rich in cultural heritage, the Peranakan community today is concentrated mainly in Singapore, Melaka, and Penang.

◆ ***Pintu Pagar*** : half doors, in front of the main door of a Peranakan house.

◆ ***Pondok*** : a small hut.

◆ ***Popiah*** : a Chinese spring-roll delicacy with fillings of bean sprouts, turnip, shrimps, crab meat, and egg, topped by chili and sauce.

◆ ***Por Tay Hee*** : Chinese opera road show (*wayang*).

◆ ***Pua*** : a textile of the Ibans, believed to possess mystical qualities.

◆ ***Ramadan (bulan puasa)*** : annual fasting month for Muslims, climaxing on a public holiday, Hari Raya Puasa and involving family visits and feasting.

◆ ***Rojak*** : street food sold in two versions, one by Chinese and the other by Indians. The former is salad-like with slices of turnip, cuttlefish, pineapple, nutmeg, dough fritter, cucumber, and young mango, all mixed in prawn paste, sugar, and ground peanuts. The Indian *rojak* is a hodgepodge of pieces of potato, squid, hard-boiled egg, and dough filled with shrimps. They are dipped in gravy prepared from sugar, peanuts, and starch.

◆ ***Roti Mariam*** : flavored wheat pancake prepared by Indian Muslim restaurants.

◆ ***Roti Prata*** : meal of oiled wheat flour fried on a flat plate, eaten with curry gravy; the Indian equivalent of the Italian pizza.

◆ ***Rumah Tangga*** : family household.

◆ ***Salong*** : an elevated and spacious burial chamber supported by sturdy posts of ironwood to specially house the coffin of a tribal chief and those of his family members.

◆ ***Sarong*** : a two-yard-long wrap-around cloth worn by Malay men and women from the waist down. Checkered sarongs are styled for men while batik and floral sarongs are for women.

◆ ***Sarong Kebaya*** : traditional Malay outfit for a woman.

◆ ***Satay*** : barbecued pieces of meat (chicken, beef, mutton) in wooden skewers, eaten with peanut gravy. The *satay* man stokes and vigorously fans the fire to bring out the aroma, thereby attracting curious passersby to his stall.

◆ ***Shuangxi*** : the "double happiness" Chinese character associated with marriage.

◆ ***Silat*** : a form of Malay martial arts.

◆ ***Singakerti*** : a float shaped like a mythical beast at ancient royal processions.

◆ ***Sinseh*** : Chinese physician who also prescribes medicine from his shop.

◆ ***Songkok Haji*** : symbolic white cap worn by male Muslims who have completed their pilgrimage to Mecca and who are known as *hajis*.

◆ ***Sumpit*** : a finely crafted blowpipe used by the Orang Asli.

◆ ***Surau*** : a prayer room.

◆ ***Talam*** : cymbals.

◆ ***Tamu*** : a market in East Malaysia. The word also means "meeting".

◆ ***Teh*** : tea with milk.

◆ ***Teh Kosong*** : tea without milk or sugar.

◆ ***Teh O*** : tea with sugar.

◆ ***Tengkolok*** : stiffened cloth headwrapper worn at ceremonial events.

◆ ***Tika Sembayang*** : a prayer mat.

◆ ***Tongkangs*** : barges carrying cargo such as sacks of rice, sugar and potato and onion. For many decades, they were very much a part of the Singapore River scene when the island was first a vibrant center of trade and a major stop for merchant vessels plying the East–West Indies sea route.

◆ ***Tudung Saji*** : colorful, conical food covers.

◆ ***Veena*** : a wooden oversized, long-necked string instrument.

◆ ***Wau Bulan*** : a colorful and fancifully designed kite of the east coast from Peninsular Malaysia.

◆ ***Wayang*** : Malay for stage show but usually taken to mean street performances of Chinese opera.

◆ ***Wayang Kulit*** : shadow puppet theater from Kelantan, Peninsular Malaysia.

◆ ***Won Ton Mee*** : noodles and barbecued pork slices with chili or tomato sauce, accompanied by a bowl of soup containing meat balls wrapped in flour.

# APPENDICES

**1** *Jungle scene near Sungei Belawan*, 1907, Kleingrottse. © John Falconer.
**2–3** *The Prince of Wales' Theatre Group, Kuala Kangsar, Perak, 15 July 1897.* © John Falconer.
**4–5** Main picture: *Telok Ayer Bay, Singapore,* 1890's. Inset: *Boat Quay and Singapore River,* 1890's. © John Falconer.
**6–7** Main picture: *Interior of a Kayan longhouse*, Charles Hose, c. 1900. © John Falconer. Inset: Kayans, Charles Hose, c. 1900. © John Falconer.
**9** *View of cascading waterfall, Penang, 18th century*, lithograph by Robert Smith. © John Falconer.
**16** *Chinese junk*, 1826. National Archives, Singapore. Maps, Jeffery Mark Jansen. *Teak, lianas, bamboo* and *orchids*, watercolor, Jeffery Mark Jansen.
**17** *Waterfall*, Frank Yong/WWF. *Monsoon waves*, Sarala Aikanathan/WWF. *Flood*, Mikhail Kavanagh/WWF.
**18–19** All watercolor illustrations by Anuar bin Abdul Rahim.
**19** *Soft coral*, Valerie Taylor/WWF Malaysia. *Hard coral*, Valerie Taylor/WWF Malaysia.
**20–21** Main illustration, *nipa* and *crocodile*, Anuar bin Abdul Rahim. All other illustrations by Jeffery Mark Jansen.
**22** *Fungi russula*, Rodney Lai/WWF Malaysia. *Entoloma*, Rodney Lai/WWF Malaysia. *Sunburst Fungus*, Dionysius Sharma/WWF Malaysia. *Xeromphaline*, Rodney Lai/WWF Malaysia. *Rhinoceros hornbill, orang utan, Bornean gibbon, brush-tailed porcupine* and *Bulwer's pheasant*, watercolor, Jeffery Mark Jansen. *Colugo* and *binturong*, watercolor, Anuar bin Abdul Rahim.
**23** Main illustration, *Leopard and pangolin*, watercolor, Anuar bin Abdul Rahim. *White-bellied woodpecker, banteng* and *Rafflesia*, watercolor, Jeffery Mark Jansen.
**24–25** *Oil palms*, Georg Gerster. All watercolor illustrations by Anuar bin Abdul Rahim.
**26** *Starfruit*, Slim Sreedhara. *Bark jacket*, Dennis Lau.
**26–27** *Fruit bowl*, Lawrence Lim.
**27** *Old photo*, G.R. Lambert and Co. © John Falconer. *Chili and pepper*, Slim Sreedhara (2).
**29** *Rhododendrons*, Tommy Chang.
**30** *Clearing the land*, Lena Chan/WWF Malaysia. *Harvesting and winnowing*, Slim Sreedhara (2).
**31** *Chinatown, Singapore,* c.1930. © John Falconer.
**32** *Neolithic footed dish*, Muzium Negara, Kuala Lumpur, David Bowden Photo Library. *Bronze age container*, Muzium Negara, Kuala Lumpur, David Bowden Photo Library. Old map, National Museum, Singapore.
**32–33** *Kuching river scene*, old engraving. © John Falconer.
**33** *Inscribed stone tablet*, Srivijaya, c.7th–13th century, Muzium Negara, Kuala Lumpur. *Bronze statue*, Muzium Negara, Kuala Lumpur, David Bowden Photo Library.
**34** *Door den Oost – Indischen Archipel*, hand-colored print by Hugo v. Pedersen, 1906. Antiques of the Orient, Singapore. *Drawing by C.W.M. van de Velde.* Chromo-lithograph by Tresling and Co. Antiques of the Orient, Singapore.
**35** *Dutch tomb, Melaka.* © John Falconer. *Johnnie Walker advertisement*, Straits Produce, December 15, 1927. © John Falconer. *Penang waterfront*, watercolor engraving. © John Falconer.
**36** *Sir Frank Swettenham*, old print. © John Falconer. *Bornean river scene*, early engraving. © John Falconer.
**37** Cartoon, Straits Produce, December 15, 1927. © John Falconer. *Tin mining, Selangor*, old print. © John Falconer.
**38** *Currency note. Press cutting. Japanese surrender, 1945*, old print, Imperial War Museum. © John Falconer.
**39** *Demonstration in Sarawak, 1946*, old print, © John Falconer. *Malaya Independence ceremony, 1957.* © Royal Commonwealth Society.
**40** *Malaysia billboard*, © Ministry of Information and the Arts, Singapore. *Tunku Abdul Rahman*, © John Falconer.
**41** *Stamp*, Singapore. *Parliament House, Singapore*, Lawrence Lim. *Public housing, Singapore*, Guido Alberto Rossi.
**42** *Chinese book cover*, Singapore, 1954. *Tamil book cover*, Singapore, 1957. *Malay textbook cover*, Singapore, 1959. *Jawi script*, Anuar bin Abdul Rahim. *Singapore newspaper mastheads*, Lawrence Lim. *Boys' school*, National Archives, Singapore.
**43** *Penan mat design*, Dennis Lau.
**44** *Terengganu stone*, Muzium Negara, Kuala Lumpur, David Bowden Photo Library. *Muslims at prayer*, Radin bin Mohd. Nor Saleh. *Celebrating Hari Raya*, Radin bin Mohd. Nor Saleh.
**44–45** *Praying times on clock, Ubudiah Mosque*, Radin bin Mohd. Nor Saleh. *Prayer mat*, Radin bin Mohd. Nor Saleh.
**45** Photos by Radin bin Mohd. Nor Saleh. *Cleansing ritual. Songkok. Qu'ran writings. Selangor State Mosque.*
**46** *Batik designs* (2), Radin bin Mohd. Nor Saleh. *Batik printing block*, David Bowden Photo Library. *Batik painters*, Radin bin Mohd. Nor Saleh. *Canting pen*, Tara Sosrowardoyo. *Stamped batik*, Radin bin Mohd. Nor Saleh.
**47** *Songket weaver*, Halim Studio. *Silk fabrics*, Radin bin Mohd. Nor Saleh. *Kain songket*, Halim Studio. *Kepala of kain songket*, Halim Studio. *Kain lemar*, Halim Studio.
**48** *Owl spirit figure*, David Bowden Photo Library. *Melanau sickness images*, Dennis Lau. *Kenyah mask*, Dennis Lau. *Mah-meri masks* (2), David Bowden Photo Library.
**49** *Ceremonial hornbill*, Sarawak Museum. *Iban masks* (3), Dennis Lau. Moyang figures (2), David Bowden Photo Library. *Dog sculpture*, Sarawak Museum.
**50** *Utensils*, Dennis Lau. *Swords*, Dennis Lau. *Kenyah mask*, Dennis Lau.
**50–51** *Tribal vests and headgear*, print, F. Retzel, *The History of Mankind* (3 vols, London, 1898) © John Falconer.
**51** *Tattooed Dayaks*, engraving, Carl Bock. © Antiques of the Orient. *Tinjar carvings*, Dennis Lau. *Selapak grave*, Charles Hose c. 1900. © John Falconer. *Orang Ulu totem*, Dennis Lau.
**52** *Wayang performing couple*, National Archives, Singapore. *Child actor*, print, National Archives, Singapore.
**52–53** *Wayang with audience*, hand-colored wood engraving, *Illustrated London News*, 1887/Antiques of the Orient, Singapore.
**53** *Puppets*, Lawrence Lim. *Backstage musician*, National Archives, Singapore. *Swordplay on stage*, *The Graphic*/Antiques of the Orient, Singapore. *Soloist*, Lawrence Lim. *Great World*, National Archives, Singapore.
**54** *Joss paper*, Lawrence Lim. *Lion dance*, Lawrence Lim. *Lanterns and dragon*, Ministry of Information and the Arts, Singapore. *Solo wayang performer*, Ministry of Information and the Arts, Singapore.
**54–55** *Burning giant jossticks*, Dennis Lau.
**55** *Medium in ritual*, Singapore Tourist Promotion Board, Singapore. *Oranges*, Lawrence Lim. *Three candlesticks*, Lawrence Lim. *Pig offerings, Hungry Ghost Festival*, John

萬

意

*Fare-card*, Lawrence Lim.
**328–329** Map, Tan Seok Lui.
*MRT signpost*, Lawrence Lim.
All other photographs courtesy of Mass Rapid Transit Corporation, Singapore.
**330–331** Map, Periplus Editions.
**330** *Taxi*, Radin bin Mohd. Nor Saleh.
*Minibus*, Radin bin Mohd. Nor Saleh.
**332–333** All photographs by Lawrence Lim.
*MRT display board.*
*Parking coupons and area licenses.*
*Newspapers*
*Fare-card.*
*Bus number plate.*
*Cardphone and phone-cards.*
*Coin-phone.*
*Signboards* (2).
*Currency notes, coins*
*Stamps* (2).
*Postbox.*
**334–335** All photographs by Radin bin Mohd. Nor Saleh, unless otherwise stated.
*Postbox.*
*Cardphone.*
*Stamps.*
*Phone-card.*
*Rear panel of bus.*
*Newspaper mastheads.*
*Currency notes, coins.*
*Maybank building.*
**336** *Indian dancers and Malay couple*, ink drawings, Jimmy Ang.
*National Day parade, Singapore*, Ministry of Information and the Arts, Singapore.
*Dragon and lion dancers*, Jimmy Ang.
**337** *Macritchie Reservoir, Singapore*, Lawrence Lim.
Bar charts, Tan Seok Lui.
**338–339** Photographs by Lawrence Lim.
**338** *Signpost.*
*Botanic Gardens entrance.*
*Stamford Raffles statue.*
*Antelopes.*
*Alkaff Mansion.*
**339** *Changi Village.*
*Batik.*
*Cable-car tickets.*
*Raffles Hotel.*
**340** Photographs courtesy of Jurong Birdpark, Singapore.
*Parakeet.*
*White-bellied sea eagle with bird trainer.*
*Flamingos.*
*Birds and boy.*
*Gray heron.*
Location map, Tan Seok Lui.
Map, Lim Yew Cheong.
**341** *Mangroves*, Anuar bin Abdul Rahim.
Bird illusrations, Lim Yew Cheong.
*Watercock.*
*Redshank.*
*Whimbrel.*
*Common kingfisher.*
*Blue-throated bee-eater.*
*Black-naped oriole.*
*Barn swallow.*
*Dollarbird.*
*Tiger shrike.*
*Little heron.*
Location map, Tan Seok Lui.
**342** All photographs by Lawrence Lim.
*Shopping bags.*
*Logo*, courtesy of Singapore Tourist Promotion Board.
*Chinese medical hall.*
*Chinese herbal products and tonic.*
**343** All photographs by Lawrence Lim.
*Chicken rice.*
*Char kway teow.*
*Rojak.*
*Bak kut teh.*
*Fruit*, watercolor drawings, Anuar bin Abdul Rahim.
**344** *Bus silhouette*, ink drawing, Jimmy Chan.
*Photographs by* Radin bin Mohd. Nor Saleh.
*Signposts.*
*Central market.*
*Window of Peranakan house.*
**345** *Hair oil*, Radin bin Mohd. Nor Saleh.
*Carpets*, Tourism Malaysia.
*Cameron Highlands*, Radin bin Mohd. Nor Saleh.
*Kite-flying*, Tourism Malaysia.
**346** Photos by Radin bin Mohd. Nor Saleh.
*Batik.*
*Weaving* kain songket.
**346–347** *Baskets.*
**347** *Road sign*, Julia Fitzgerald.
*Pewter*, ink drawing.
*Teaset* (2), *Aw Pottery*, Radin bin Mohd. Nor Saleh.
**348–349** Photographs by Robert Basiuk, Borneo Adventure.
*Plankway to longhouse, Limbang River.*
*Limestone pinnacles, Mulu National Park.*
*Iban longhouse.*
*Tutoh river.*
*Entrance to Tiger Cave, Mulu National Park.*
**356–357** Map, Anuar bin Abdul Rahim.
**357** *Bus*, Jimmy Ang.
**358** *Lau Pa Sat*, Lawrence Lim.
**359** *Motifs and satay man*, Jimmy Ang.
**360** *Sunbather*, ink drawing, Jimmy Ang.
**350–361** *Map*, Anuar bin Abdul Rahim.
**361** *Guitar, Hard Rock Café*, Lawrence Lim.
**362** *Central Market, Kuala Lumpur*, Radin bin Mohd. Nor Saleh.
**362–363** *Map*, Anuar bin Abdul Rahim.
**364** *Kanching Falls*, Radin bin Mohd. Nor Saleh.
**365** *Motifs and Malay couple*, Jimmy Ang.
**366** *Street in Georgetown, Penang*, Radin bin Mohd. Nor Saleh.
**366–367** Map, Anuar bin Abdul Rahim.
**367** *Mosque*, Radin bin Mohd. Nor Saleh.
**368–369** Map, Anuar bin Abdul Rahim.
**368** *Malay kampung house*, ink drawing, Jimmy Ang.
**369** *Central market, Kota Bharu*, Radin bin Mohd. Nor Saleh.
**370–371** *Map*, Anuar bin Abdul Rahim.
**370** *Fort Margherita*, Dennis Lau.
**371** *Trishaw*, ink drawing, Jimmy Ang.
**372** *Mosque*, ink drawing, Jimmy Ang.
*Longhouse*, Dennis Lau.
**373** *Boat with passengers*, ink drawing, Jimmy Ang.
*Mount Santubong*, Dennis Lau.
**374–375** Map, Anuar bin Abdul Rahim.
**375** *Road sweeper*, ink drawing, Jimmy Ang.
*Sabah State Museum*, Tommy Chang.
**376** *Omar Ali Saifuddien Mosque*, Editions Didier Millet.

*We have not been able to trace the heirs or publishers of certain documents. An account is being held open for them at our offices.*

◆ ART ◆

◆ MUNAN (Heidi): *Sarawak Crafts,* Oxford University Press, 1989.

◆ ETHNOLOGY ◆

◆ BROOKE (Margaret): *My Life in Sarawak,* London, 1913.
◆ CLAVELL (James): *King Rat,* M. Joseph, London, 1963.
◆ CLIFFORD (Hugh Charles): *In Court and Kampung,* London, 1897.
◆ HARRISSON (Tom): *The Peoples of Sarawak,* Kuching, 1959.
◆ HARRISSON (Tom): *Savage Civilization,* New York, 1937.
◆ HOSE (Charles): *Natural Man, A Record from Borneo,* London, 1926.
◆ HOSE (Charles): *The Pagan Tribes of Borneo,* London, 1912.
◆ NIEUWENHUIS (Anton Willem): *Quer Durch Borneo,* Leyden, 1900.
◆ ROTH (Henry Ling): *The Natives of Sarawak and British North Borneo, vols I & II,* London, 1896.
◆ WALLACE (Alfred Russel): *The Malay Archipelago,* Singapore, 1987.

◆ HISTORY ◆

◆ FARRELL (James Gordon): *The Singapore Grip,* London, 1978.
◆ HARON (Daud): *Sejarah Melayu,* Kuala Lumpur, 1989.
◆ HARRISON (Cuthbert Woodville), editor: *An Illustrated Guide to the Federated Malay States,* London, 1910.
◆ KHOO (Gilbert) and LO (Dorothy): *Asian Transformation, A History of South-east, South and East Asia,* Singapore, 1977.
◆ PIGAFETTA (Antonio), edited by SANDERLIN (George): *A Journal of Magellan's Voyage,* New York, 1964.
◆ PIGAFETTA (Antonio): *A Narrative Account of the First Circumnavigation,* New Haven, 1969.
◆ RANSONNET (Eduard von): *Skizzen aus Djhore und Singapur,* Brunswick, 1876.
◆ SHAW (William): *Tin and Pewterware,* from *Federation Museums Journal, vol. XV, New Series 1970,* Kuala Lumpur, 1970 reprint.
◆ ST JOHN (Spenser): *Life in the Forests of the Far East,* London, 1862.
◆ ST JOHN (Spenser): *The Life of Sir James Brooke, Rajah of Sarawak,* Edinburgh, 1879
◆ ST JOHN (Spenser): *Rajah Brooke: The Englishman as Ruler of an Eastern State,* London, 1899.
◆ THOMSON (John Turnbull): *Some Glimpses of Life in the Far East* (London, 1864; reprinted as *Glimpses into Life in Malayan Lands,* Singapore, 1984.
◆ UMAR (Junus): *Sejarah Melayu,* Petaling Jaya, 1984.
◆ VAILLANT (August-NIcholas): *Voyage autour du monde exécuté pendant les années 1836 et 1837 sur la Corvette La Bonite,* Paris, 1845-52.

◆ LITERATURE ◆

◆ ABDUL KADIR (Abdullah): *Hikayat Abdullah,* Singapore, 1849.
◆ BALFOUR (Patrick): *Grand Tour: Diary of and Eastward Journey,* New York, 1935.
◆ BEECKMAN (Daniel): *A Voyage to and from the Island of Borneo,* London, 1718.
◆ TUN MAMBANG (Bandahara Sri Narawangsa): *Malay Annals,* Melaka, 1021 Hj.
◆ BIRD (Isabella): *The Golden Chersonese,* London, 1883.
◆ BRADDELL (Sir Roland St John): *The Lights of Singapore,* London, 1947.
◆ BURGESS (Anthony): *Time for a Tiger,* London, 1956.
◆ CHAU (Ju Kua): *A Record of Foreign Nations,* Fukien, c. 1225.
◆ CLIFFORD (Hugh): *Saleh, A Prince of Malaya,* New York, 1926.
◆ CRAWFURD (John): *History of the Indian Archipelago,* Edinburgh, 1820.
◆ EARL (George Windsor): *The Eastern Seas,* London, c. 1837.
◆ ENTERI ANAK GAWING and GUDOM ANAK ENTERI, recorded by Carol Rubenstein: *Sarawak Museum Journal Special Monograph No. 2, 1973,* Kuching, 1973.
◆ FAUCONNIER (Henri): *The Soul of Malaya,* London, 1931.
◆ HARRISSON (Tom): *Borneo Writings and Related Matters,* Sarawak Museum, Kuching, 1966.
◆ HARRISSON (Tom): *Explorations in Central Borneo,* London, 1949.
◆ HARRISSON (Tom): *World Within: A Borneo Story,* London, 1959.
◆ KON (Stella): *Trial,* Singapore, 1986.
◆ LIM (Janet): *A Slave Girl in Singapore,* London, 1958.
◆ MAUGHAM (William Somerset): *Maugham's Borneo Stories,* selected and with an introduction by G.V. de Freitas, Hong Kong, 1976.
◆ MAUGHAM (William Somerset): *Maugham's Malayan Stories,* selected and with an introduction by Anthony Burgess, Singapore, 1969.
◆ PIRES (Thome): *The Suma Oriental of Tome Pires,* London, 1944.
◆ PRYER (William B., Mrs): *A Decade in Borneo,* London, 1894.
◆ RANSONNET (Eduard von): *Skizzen aus Djhore und Singapur,* Brunswick, 1876.
◆ SAID (Abdul Samad): *Salina,* Kuala Lumpur, 1975.
◆ SWEETSER (Delight): *One Way Round the World,* Indianapolis, c. 1898.
◆ THEROUX (Paul): *The Great Railway Bazaar,* London, 1975.

◆ NATURE AND GEOGRAPHY ◆

◆ BRIGGS (John J.R.): *Mountains of Malaysia,* Petaling Jaya, 1985.
◆ HOLTTUM (R.E.): *Plant Life in Malaya,* Leyden, 1907.
◆ SYMTHIES (B. E.): *The Birds of Borneo,* London, 1960.

◆ NOTES

# Index

◆ **A** ◆



◆ **B** ◆



◆ **C** ◆

◆ D ◆



◆ E ◆



◆ F ◆



◆ G ◆

◆ **L** ◆



◆ **M** ◆

◆ T ◆



◆ U ◆

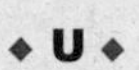



◆ V ◆

◆ RESTAURANTS ◆



◆ HOTELS ◆



◆ MOSQUES ◆



◆ MUSEUMS ◆

### ◆ SHOPPING ◆



### ◆ TEMPLES ◆



### ◆ WATERFALLS ◆

# KUALA LUMPUR

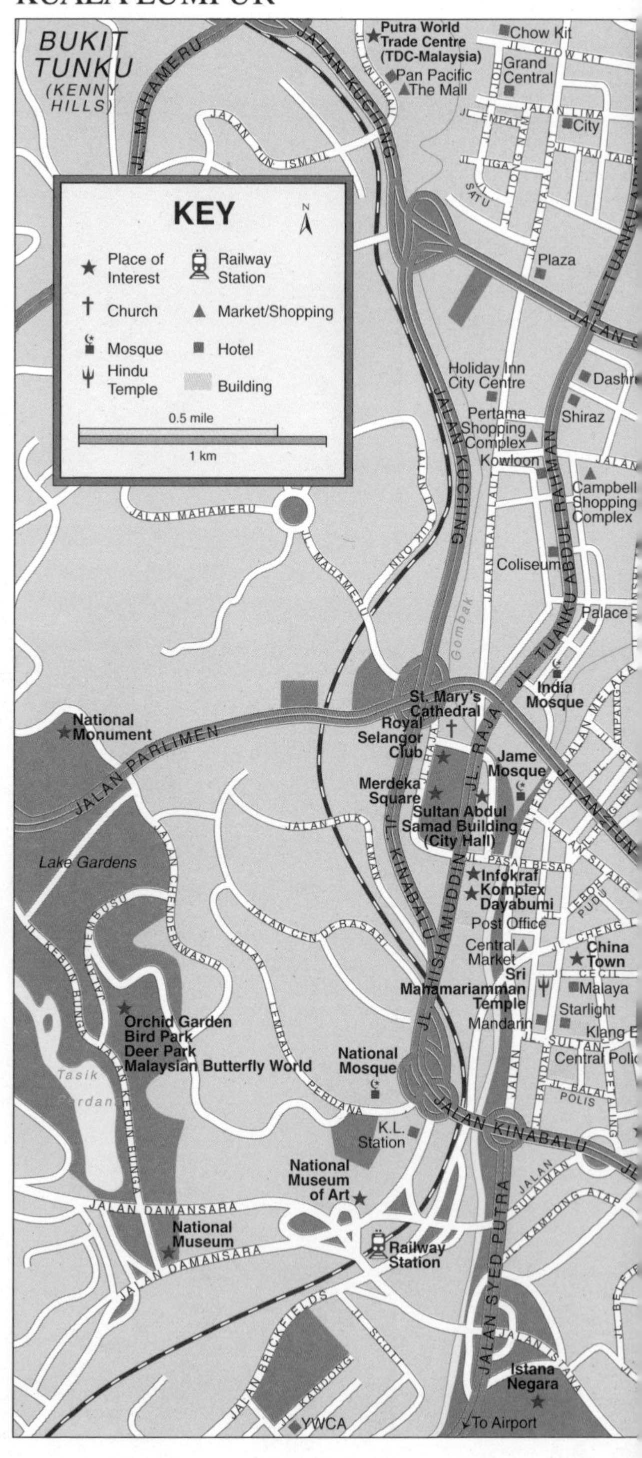

BUKIT TUNKU
(KENNY HILLS)
JL. MAHAMERU
JALAN KUCHING
JALAN TUN ISMAIL
Putra World Trade Centre (TDC-Malaysia)
Pan Pacific
The Mall
Chow Kit
JL. CHOW KIT
Grand Central
JALAN LIMA
JL. EMPAT
City
JL. HAJI TAIB
JL. TIGA
JL. SATU
Plaza
JL. TUANKU ABDUL RAHMAN
KEY
N
Place of Interest
Railway Station
Church
Market/Shopping
Mosque
Hotel
Hindu Temple
Building
0.5 mile
1 km
Holiday Inn City Centre
Dashr
Pertama Shopping Complex
Shiraz
Kowloon
Campbell Shopping Complex
JALAN MAHAMERU
JALAN DATUK ONN
JALAN RAJA LAUT
Coliseum
Gombak
Palace
India Mosque
St. Mary's Cathedral
Royal Selangor Club
National Monument
JALAN PARLIMEN
JL. RAJA
Jame Mosque
JALAN MELAKA
Merdeka Square
Sultan Abdul Samad Building (City Hall)
JALAN TUN
JALAN BUKIT AMAN
JL. KINABALU
JL. PASAR BESAR
Lake Gardens
Infokraf
Komplex Dayabumi
Post Office
JALAN CENDERASARI
JALAN CENDERAWASIH
JALAN TEMBUSU
JL. KEBUN BUNGA
Central Market
China Town
JL. HISHAMUDDIN
Sri Mahamariamman Temple
Malaya
Starlight
Mandarin
Klang
Orchid Garden
Bird Park
Deer Park
Malaysian Butterfly World
National Mosque
JL. SULTAN
Central Polic
Tasik Perdana
JALAN PERDANA
JL. BALAI POLIS
K.L. Station
JALAN KINABALU
National Museum of Art
JALAN SULAIMAN
JALAN DAMANSARA
National Museum
Railway Station
JL. KAMPONG ATAP
JALAN SYED PUTRA
JL. BRICKFIELDS
JL. SCOTT
JALAN BRICKFIELDS
JL. KANDANG
JALAN ISTANA
Istana Negara
YWCA
To Airport